Who's Who of Br...

Also by John Chilton

Sidney Bechet: The Wizard of Jazz
The Song of the Hawk: The Life and Recordings of Coleman Hawkins
Billie's Blues: A Survey of Billie Holiday's Career 1933–59
Let the Good Times Roll: The Story of Louis Jordan and his Music
Who's Who of Jazz – Storyville to Swing Street
Stomp Off, Let's Go: The Story of Bob Crosby's Bob Cats and Big Band
Teach Yourself Jazz
A Jazz Nursery: The Story of the Jenkins' Orphanage Band
McKinney's Music: A Bio-discography of McKinney's Cotton Pickers
Louis: The Louis Armstrong Story (with Max Jones)

Titles of related interest from Cassell:

Popular Music: A Select Bibliography
Edited by John Shepherd, David Horn, Paul Oliver, Dave Laing and Peter Wicke
1997
0-7201-2344-5 (hb)

Popular Music and Local Identity: Rock, Pop and Rap in Europe and Oceania
by Tony Mitchell
1996
0-7185-0019-9 (hb)
0-7185-0016-4 (pb)

I Guess I'll Get the Papers and Go Home
by Adolphus 'Doc' Cheatham, edited by Alyn Shipton
1996
0-304-33611-4 (hb)

Teddy Wilson Talks Jazz: The Autobiography of Teddy Wilson
by Teddy Wilson, edited by Humphrey van Loo and Arie Ligthart
Foreword by Benny Goodman
1996
0-304-33610-6 (hb)

Marshal Royal: Jazz Survivor
by Marshal Royal with Claire P. Gordon
1996
0-304-33836-2 (hb)

Who's Who
of British Jazz

John Chilton

CASSELL

London and Washington

Cassell
Wellington House, 125 Strand, London WC2R 0BB
PO Box 605, Herndon, VA 20172

First published in Great Britain in 1997 by Cassell
by arrangement with Bayou Press Ltd

British Library Cataloguing-in-Publication Data
A catalogue record for this book is available from the British Library.

ISBN 0-304-33909-1 (hardback)
       0-304-33910-5 (paperback)

Typeset by BookEns Ltd, Royston, Herts.
Printed and bound in Great Britain by Redwood Books, Trowbridge, Wiltshire.

Contents

Preface

The career summaries within this book detail the work of musicians from every era of British jazz, ranging from those who played in the 1920s to today's young jazz stars. The emphasis is on musicians who work professionally (or who did so in the past). All styles of jazz are represented.

This is the first published work devoted solely to the careers of British jazz musicians. I am pleased to say that I have been able to include details of hundreds of players whose working lives have been excluded from all previous reference books.

Brief histories of a number of pioneering local jazz bands are included but it is not practical to detail all of the vast number of semi-professional jazz groups that, happily, exist throughout Britain. This is not a reflection of their skills. Many contain talented musicians and bands such as Colin Kingwell's Jazz Bandits, Dave Brennan's Jubilee Jazz Band and Sonny Monk's Band have introduced hundreds of listeners to the sound of jazz during the many years they have been in existence.

Freelance recordings are not, as a rule, mentioned, and the size of any entry is not meant to be a measure of talent. The career details of musicians who remain with a particular band for many years will obviously not take up as many lines as the entries of more restless performers. Whenever feasible I have ascertained dates by referring to contemporary newspapers and magazines. This has not always been possible and even the most helpful musician cannot always provide an exact sequence of events.

Entry headings are the name by which a musician is generally known, and under which he or she worked: original or real names are given in parenthesis. Dates of birth or death are given when these can be firmly established, and places of birth or death are generally given in the form that applied at the time. Hence county towns or towns which were county boroughs are not followed by a county name, and names of counties do not necessarily correspond to today's local government boundaries. There will be differences between entries where a town or city has belonged to different counties at different times. Changes in foreign names are generally given in parenthesis.

Jazz musicians born in the USA are not given individual entries, because details of the work of American veterans in Britain were covered in my *Who's Who of Jazz – Storyville to Swing Street*. Younger American musicians will, it is hoped, be the subject of a future book.

A selected list of bandleaders mentioned in the text is included at the back of the book. Some were born outside Britain, others were non-playing conductors, several are semi-professionals. Many are instrumentalists who specialized in bandleading from early on, never becoming involved in various career moves that would justify an individual entry.

Jazz fans can never agree on the contents of any listing of musicians. I sincerely hope that I have not omitted any of your favourites.

John Chilton
London, 1996

Acknowledgements

Enormous thanks to Nick Dellow for his help and good advice. Special thanks to Alasdair Fenton, Jim Godbolt, Chris Hayes, Roger Horton, Andrew Huxtable, Tony Middleton, Brian Peerless, Howard Rye and Alyn Shipton. Also special thanks to the National Jazz Foundation Archive at Loughton Library, Essex, and to all those musicians who took the time and trouble to check their entries and to offer additional information.

Grateful thanks also to John Altman, Bob Bampton, Brian Blain, Jeff Brooks, Ron Brown, Peter Cameron, Percy Carter, Tom Chilton, Derek Coller, Bill Colyer, John Cowley, Don Cox, John Cumming (Serious Speakout), Barry Dawson, Mrs J. Deuchar, Kate Dunbar, Les Evans, Digby Fairweather, John Featherstone, Barbara Feldman, David Forbes, Barry Fox, Andrew Gardner, Ken Gilbert, David Griffiths, John Griffiths, Susan Gough (Central Library, Southend), Peter Goulding, Tony Harrison, Will Hemmings, Jack Higgins, Colin Hill, Rod Hopton, Ian Howarth, June Hyland, Terry Hyland, Charles Imeson, Stan James, Ken Jones, Pete King, John Lawrence, Phyl Lewis, Solly Lipsitz, Cyril Loney, Dennis Matthews, David Mellor, Ian Miller, Musicians' Social and Benevolent Council, Musicians' Union, Peter Newbrook, Alan Newby, Laurie Paris, Performing Right Society, Arthur Pilkington, Michael Pointon, Chris Pope, J. Lyman Potts, James Richardson, Dr Mac Robinson, Mart Rodger, Andrew Simons (National Sound Archive), Jim Simpson, Nat Slavin, Keith Smeltzer, Eric Speak, Tony Spurgeon, Alan Stevens, Dave Stevens, Mike Sutcliffe, Denny Termer, Trevor Thompson, Peter Vacher, Ken Vail, Steve Walker, Marion Wasser, Tony Williams (Spotlite Records), Val Wilmer, Charlie Wilson, Wood Green Wally and Oscar Yeo.

A

ABBOTT, Derek
trumpet/piano accordion/arranger

Born: Chorley, Lancashire, 29 December 1922
Died: Chorley, Lancashire, 10 April 1977

Summer season on piano accordion with Richard Valery's Orchestra (1939), began doubling on trumpet during 1940 season with Richard Valery. Served in the RAF and played in Ralph Green's RAF Band (1942). Invalided out of the service in 1944. Worked with Freddie Platt's Band in Rochdale (1944) then, later that year, joined Oscar Rabin in London as trumpeter and arranger. With Oscar Rabin until joining Geraldo in January 1946. Left Geraldo to work with John Dankworth from 1953. Spent several years in Jack Parnell's Associated Television Orchestra before ill health caused retirement. During the last years of his life he taught music in the Chorley area.

ABRAMS, Max (Max ABRAMOVITCH)
drums/tympani/xylophone/vibraphone

Born: Glasgow, Scotland, 11 August 1907
Died: Eastbourne, East Sussex,
5 November 1995

Played in local Boys' Brigade Band as a teenager. Worked in a juvenile group (Archie Pitt's Busby Band) in the mid-1920s. With Chalmers Wood at Glasgow Locarno in 1928. To South Africa with saxophonist Vic Davis (1930). Returned to Britain in 1931 and worked with Joe Gibson before joining saxophonist Tommy Kinsman at Ciro's Club, London, in autumn 1931. With Teddy Sinclair in 1932 then with Jack Hylton (1932–3) before joining house band at the Gargoyle Club, London, in the summer of 1933. With Sydney Lipton from 1934 until 1935, with Carroll Gibbons from 1935 until 1939. During this period established his reputation as highly successful drum teacher. He also led his own recording bands and made drum tuition records. With Geraldo from 1939 to 1940, then worked for several months with Sid Phillips before joining Ambrose in the summer of 1941. Toured variety halls with George Scott-Wood in 1942 and 1943, then, as a Sub-Lieutenant in the Royal Navy Volunteer Reserves, coached cadet bands, also led own band at Du Barry's Club, London (1943). With Jack Payne from summer of 1944 until late 1945, then worked briefly with Stephane Grappelli before rejoining Sid Phillips from December 1945 until the early 1950s, also worked with Arthur Coppersmith in 1950. Freelanced thereafter and ran own prestigious drum school in London. Continued to teach full time until 1977, then moved to Eastbourne, Sussex, where he occasionally took on new pupils until the early 1990s.

ACQUAYE, 'Speedy' Nii Moi
conga drum/percussion

Born: Accra, Gold Coast, 7 June 1931
Died: London, 15 September 1993

Served in the Gold Coast Regiment before moving to Britain during the early 1950s. Acted in pantomime, then settled in London and began sitting in with various bands. Worked in Kenny Graham's Afro-Cubists and guested with Ronnie Scott and Tubby Hayes. Regularly with Herbie Goins' Nightimers (1966). Spent six years in Georgie Fame's Blue Flames. Later worked with Dade Krama and with Adzido.

ADAMS, Bruce
trumpet/flugelhorn

Born: Birkenhead, Cheshire, 3 July 1951

Father Bob was a comedian, guitarist and vocalist, mother Helen a dancer. Parents worked on music hall circuit until settling in Glasgow in 1954. Took up trumpet at eleven, was soon gigging in Glasgow area, and taking lessons from Maurice Deans. Won *Opportunity Knocks* television talent show at fourteen. Left school at fifteen, toured in variety act with his father, then played at Montreal's *Expo '67* and did CSE tour in Aden with comedian Tony Hancock. Again toured in family act also worked on *QE2* and *Canberra*, until father died in 1973. Returned to freelance in Glasgow, co-led quintet and big band with saxophonist Bill Fanning. Won various jazz awards in the early 1980s, worked with Dick Hyman at Edinburgh Festival in 1985 and in 1995, with Benny Carter at Glasgow Festival (1986), Bob Wilber, Edinburgh (1986), also featured at festivals in Canada and USA. Worked mainly in band accompanying comedian Freddie Starr (1986–9), then moved to London to freelance. Toured Germany with American trombonist Bill Allred (1990), led own quartet, and then in 1992 formed quintet with Alan Barnes, also accompanied singer Val Wiseman (1992). Part of new Kenny Baker's Dozen (from 1993), also in Bob Wilber's Big Band. Prolific freelance work, also continued to work regularly with Alan Barnes into the mid-1990s. Guested with Peter Long's Echoes of Ellington (1996).

AIREY-SMITH, 'Bill' (James William SMITH)
drums/vocals

Born: Barnsley, Yorkshire, 3 June 1901
Died: Dartford, Kent, 12 December 1982

Father of trombonist Mike Smith. Served as a regular in the British Army in 1916–23 (in France and India), was then a trumpeter. Left the Army and specialized on drums, during the 1920s, 1930s and 1940s worked with Sydney Lipton, Debroy Somers, Howard Jacobs, Reg Batten, Freddy Bretherton, Jack Payne, Jack Hylton, Mantovani, etc. Led own bands and played in various theatre orchestras. During World War II served in the Royal Artillery as a driver (1941–2). After being invalided out, joined Ben Frankel's Orchestra (August 1942). With John Blore's Orchestra, Marcel Gardner and in Alf Lewis's Trio (1947) before playing for many years for the Crazy Gang at the Victoria Palace, London. Left music to become a publican.

ALDRICH, 'Ronnie' Ronald Frank
piano/tenor sax/violin/clarinet/arranger/composer

Born: Erith, Kent, 15 February 1916
Died: Clatterbridge, Wirral,
30 September 1993

Started on piano and violin, studied at the Guildhall School of Music, played in the Folkestone Municipal Orchestra, then began playing tenor sax and clarinet on first professional dates. With Syd Wyner's Band on clarinet, tenor sax and violin (1932). Worked on sax and clarinet in Calcutta, India (1934), returned to Britain and became part of a piano double-act with Freddie Aspinall during the 1930s, also accompanied singers Sam Browne and Elsie Carlisle. Specialized on piano from this period onwards, worked with Freddy Ballerini's Band (1938) and with Syd Harris (1939). Did film studio and theatre work, also toured with Teddy White's Orchestra in *Shoot the Works* (1939). Joined RAF in early 1940 and became founder-member of the Squadronaires (sharing piano duties with Jimmy Miller). Remained with the Squadronaires after demobilization and took over leadership (from Jimmy Miller) in 1950. The group was subsequently billed as

Ronnie Aldrich and the Squadronaires until it disbanded in 1964. Thereafter Aldrich became a musical director for television and radio orchestras. Retired to the Isle of Man in the 1970s.

ALLANDALE, Eric
trombone/vocals

Born: Dominica, West Indies, 1936

Came to Britain in 1954. Played trumpet in the Hammersmith Borough Brass Band then switched to trombone and led own local band. Own band played residency at Cellar Club, Greek Street, London (1958). Joined Teddy Layton in late 1958. With Sonny Morris from early 1959 until summer 1960. Formed own Jazz Knights in July 1960, played season in Germany, then returned to London in January 1961. Continued to lead own band for several years until joining the Foundations in the late 1960s. Subsequently moved to South Africa. Returned to London but did not resume full time playing.

ALLARD, Gray
tenor sax/clarinet

Born: Faversham, Kent, 1926
Died: Essex, 25 November 1991

From a musical family. After National Service became a Metropolitan policeman until 1950, then took up alto sax, soon changed to tenor sax and studied with Aubrey Frank. Worked with Ken Mackintosh, then played aboard the *Queen Mary* liner in Ronnie Ball's Band. Led own band for summer season at Folkestone (1951), then worked for four months with Ralph Sharon before briefly joining Basil and Ivor Kirchin's Band (March 1952). With Hal Graham at Rialto, Liverpool (1952) and with Bill Findlay for summer season on the Isle of Wight (1952). With Arthur Parkman's Orchestra in Bristol, then again did summer season with Bill Findlay (1953). With Jack Nathan (1953), then joined Carl Barriteau in early 1954. With Oscar Rabin from September 1954 until May 1956. With Jack Parnell (1956), Lou Preager (1957), Tommy Whittle (1958), then joined the Band of the Coldstream Guards. Worked in Freddy Staff's Big Band in 1966, then worked in various Peter Ind line-ups from the early 1970s. Settled in Harlow, Essex, and became a music teacher.

ALLEN, 'Pete' Peter
saxes/clarinet/vocals

Born: Newbury, Berkshire, 23 November 1953

Son of Bernie Allen (banjo/guitar/vocals). Worked in his father's band from 1971. Served in police force for three years, then moved to the West Country and worked with Rod Mason's Band from spring of 1976 until February 1978. Returned to Newbury and took over leadership of his father's band, which made its debut under Pete's name in June 1978. The band enjoyed widespread success in the 1980s and 1990s, including tours of America. During the 1990s, the band played a long residency at Pete Allen's Jazz Grill in Bath, but also appeared at various jazz festivals and took part in a show that paid tribute to the Original Dixieland Jazz Band.

ALLEN, 'Tony' Anthony
drums

Born: Stratford East, London, 6 October 1938

Played trumpet in Boys' Brigade Band then switched to drums. With Len Doughty's Band before working with Charlie Galbraith from autumn 1960 until autumn 1962. With singer Clinton Ford, Mickey Ashman and Monty Sunshine, then worked with Freddy Randall from 1964 until 1968. Worked in Dave Jones' Band (1968), then freelanced with many jazz groups and accompanied visiting American musicians (did several tours with Wild Bill Davison). Led own band during the 1970s and worked in Pat Mason's Trio and with Charlie Galbraith. Freelanced from the mid-1970s, then worked with Digby Fairweather, Keith Smith and with the Al Fairweather-Ralph Laing All Stars, before moving to Spain in 1983. Continues to play regularly in Spain, usually in bands consisting of expatriates.

AMBROSE, 'Bert' Bertram
violin

Born: East London, 15 September 1896
Died: Leeds, Yorkshire, 12 June 1971

At fifteen went to the USA with his aunt. Played violin in Emil Coleman's Band at Reisenweber's Restaurant, New York, for six weeks (1916), then worked in orchestra, backing floor shows at Palais Royal, New York. Formed own band in New York (1917) for residencies at Palais Royal and Club de Vingt. Returned to London to work at the Embassy Club in Bond Street (1920). Left in the following year, returned to New York to play residency at the Clover Gardens, then moved back to London to take own seven-piece band into the Embassy Club in late 1922 (this became a ten-piece band in 1926). Led big band at May Fair Hotel, London, from March 1927 until July 1933, then returned to the Embassy until July 1936 (during this period visited USA in 1934 and led for summer season in Biarritz in 1934). Further residency at May Fair Hotel (September 1936 to January 1937), also took band to work in Paris (July 1937) and Cannes (August 1937). Together with bandleader Jack Harris, bought Ciro's Club, London. Each took it in turn to lead their band there, usually for a six month stay. Ambrose also led at other London venues including the Café de Paris (1938) and did radio and film work, and tours. Led own Octet (late 1938–9). Broke up band but used sidemen for radio and recordings in 1939. Led briefly at the May Fair Hotel in 1940, disbanded then formed new Octette, mainly for stage shows (1940–1). Used pick-up band throughout World War II for radio and recordings but occasionally formed big band for stage shows (1942). Again led at Ciro's (1945–7), also played for summer season in Monte Carlo (1946). Led at Nightingale Club, London (1948–9). Sporadically led own bands during the 1950s, including a touring unit (with Tubby Hayes, Phil Seamen, etc.) in 1953. Played residency at Cafe de Paris (September 1955 to April 1956) then did a final widespread tour of Britain (May to September 1956). Thereafter was mainly active in personal management, his artistes included singer Kathy Kirby. Throughout his career Ambrose employed many jazz musicians including Americans such as Sylvester Ahola, Perley Breed, Henry Levine and Danny Polo. His popular vocalistes included Phyllis Robins, Helen Raymond, Elsie Carlisle, Evelyn Dall, Vera Lynn, Polly Ward, Anne Shelton, Helen McKay, Nadia Dore, etc. Male singers included Sam Browne, Donald Stewart, Donald Hill, Gerry Fitzgerald, Clive Evard, Denny Dennis, etc.

AMSTELL, 'Billy' William
clarinet/saxes/composer/arranger

Born: Stepney, London, 20 August 1911

Brother of saxophonist Micky Amstell (1901–79). Piano from age of ten, alto sax three years later. First professional work with Bertram D'Arcy's Baby Band (1925–6). With Herman

Darewski's Orchestra from late 1927, then worked with saxophonist Charles Watson's Band in London and Glasgow for fourteen months (from April 1928). Worked briefly in Grosvenor House band then worked with Roy Fox from May until August 1931 (having previously made recordings with Fox). With Ambrose from September 1931 until summer of 1940 (originally on alto sax, but specialized on tenor sax from September 1932), also worked with Jack Harris at the London Casino (April to July 1939). Joined RAF in summer of 1940, played in service bands and led own RAF Quintet until being invalided out in December 1943. With Geraldo from February 1944 until September 1945, then rejoined Ambrose from October 1945 until March 1947. Briefly with Nat Allen's Band then worked mainly in Stanley Black's Orchestra from October 1947 until April 1954, but also freelanced and led own groups. Active freelance during the 1950s, 1960s and 1970s, often with ensembles led by Geoff Love, Eric Robinson, George Chisholm, Bobby Mickleburgh, Woolf Phillips, Sid Phillips, etc. Part-owner (with Joe Crossman) of Modern Music Shop in London. Also played aboard various cruise liners. Continued to lead own small band in the 1980s and 1990s, specializing on clarinet. Autobiography *Don't Fuss Mr. Ambrose*, first published in 1986.

APPLETON, Joe
tenor sax/clarinet

Born: Jamaica, West Indies, *c.*1900
Deceased

Played in West Indies Regiment Band, left them in Cuba and subsequently made his way to Britain *c.*1924. Led own band in England during the 1920s, residencies in London, Manchester and Birmingham. Led own Hot Maniacs (1931–2), also briefly with George Clapham and Oscar Dawkins. With Leslie Thompson's Emperors of Jazz, then did stage tour with Ken Johnson (1936). Led own band at Shim Sham Club, London (1937) and at Rainbow Roof Club (1937). In Blue Caribbean Band (1937–8), with Fela Sowande (1939), Rudolph Dunbar's Harlem Knights (1940), Al Jennings, Cyril Blake, Hetty Booth (1941), Clarie Wears, Carl Barriteau, Cyril Blake (1942), briefly with Sid Phillips at Ciro's (1942). With Harry Leader on stage tour (and in London) 1943, with Max Abrams (1943). Leslie 'Jiver' Hutchinson (1944). With Lou Preager, then again with Cyril Blake (1947–8). Toured Germany with American cornetist Rex Stewart (1948). Own band at Starlight Room, London (1949), and at Panama Club, London (1950–5). Worked in Singapore, India and New Zealand with Bertie King (1956). Led own band in Geneva, Switzerland (1956).

APPLEYARD, Peter
vibes/drums

Born: Cleethorpes, Lincolnshire, 26 August 1928

Played piano at fourteen then took up drums. Played local gigs around the Cleethorpes and Grimsby area, then toured with Felix Mendelssohn's Hawaiians. Worked with Bob Walker at the Gaiety, Grimsby. Joined RAF and during stay in the services began doubling on vibes. With Jimmy Macaffer in Dundee (late 1948), with Charley Berry in Isle of Wight for summer season (1949), then worked with Harry Brooker's Band in Southend (late 1949) before leaving Britain in late December 1949 to work in Bermuda with Jack Wallace's Band. Emigrated to Canada in October 1951 (later becoming a Canadian citizen). Played in Royal Canadian Air Force Orchestra then worked with Calvin Jackson Quartet from 1953–5. Subsequently led own quartet in Canada and in the USA, during which time provided backing group for Gloria De Haven. During the 1960s settled into Toronto residencies, then ran own successful television shows. Accompanied many visiting artistes, and worked with Benny Goodman often from mid-1971. Made tours of Europe with Goodman from 1972. Represented Canada in ORTF Orchestra in Paris (1972). Continued to be featured in own television shows. Formed band of ex-Goodman sidemen for tours during the 1980s, was also part of Peanuts Hucko's All Stars. Continued to tour during the 1990s, and made many solo appearances at international jazz festivals.

APPS, 'Bill' William James
saxes/clarinet/bass clarinet/flute/piccolo

Born: Tunbridge Wells, Kent, 18 August 1908
Died: London, April 1993

Originally played the violin. Gigged in Tunbridge Wells with the Allegro Dance Band (1927-8). With Ray Starita in the early 1930s, also worked in Gerry Moore's Band (1932). Three years with Sydney Kyte (1933–6), then joined Lew Stone from 1936 until 1938. With Debroy Somers (1938–9), then again worked with Lew Stone (1940). Briefly with Peter Mendoza (1940), Sid Phillips (1940) and Carroll Gibbons (early 1941), before joining the RAF and becoming part of the Skyrockets (also gigged with Ambrose in 1942). Remained with the Skyrockets after World War II ended, then became a session musician, freelancing on radio, recordings and television. Worked with Billy Cotton during the 1960s, and also played in various theatre orchestras until 1975, thereafter coached amateur bands (and played tenor sax with them at the age of 80).

ARCHER, 'Tony' Anthony John
double bass

Born: Dulwich, London, 14 July 1938

Originally played cello, took up double bass at sixteen. Early trio work with Phil Kinorra and John Burch. Worked professionally in Scotland then toured US bases in Europe with John Burch's Trio (1959). During the early 1960s worked in Stu Hamer's Quintet, with Harold McNair, Gus Galbraith, Bobby Wellins-Ken Wray Quintet, Peter King's Quintet and deputized in the play *The Connection*. Worked often with Don Rendell during the 1960s, was in Roy Budd's Trio in the mid-1960s. With Eddie Thompson and with Dick Morrissey. Regularly in Tony Lee's Trio throughout the 1970s, also did various sessions, freelanced and worked briefly with Humphrey Lyttelton and John Dankworth. Active freelance throughout the 1980s and 1990s with Tony Lee, Dick Morrissey, Best of British Jazz, Don Rendell, Willie Garnett, Stan Robinson, the Colville Collection, etc.

ARDLEY, Neil Richard
composer/keyboards

Born: Carshalton, Surrey, 26 May 1937

Originally played piano and tenor sax. Graduated with BSc from Bristol University in 1959. Studied arranging and composing with Ray Premru during the early 1960s, also took some lessons from Bill Russo. Joined New Jazz Orchestra (formed by Clive Burrows) in 1963, and became musical director of this ensemble from 1964 until 1969 (it began recording in 1965). Led own orchestras of varying sizes from 1969. His *Symphony of Amaranths* (1971) utilized a 25-piece line-up. His interest in the music of Bali produced his *Biformal from Bali*, which was featured at the 1974 Camden Jazz Festival, and his *Kaleidoscope of Rainbows* (1975). He often wrote for television and for European radio orchestras in the 1970s and 1980s. From the 1970s through to the 1990s has enjoyed success as an author, writing books on music, computers and natural history. Settled in Derbyshire and continued composing. Formed Zyklus in 1988, which has made great use of electronic sounds. Active in the 1990s, composed *On the Four Winds* for saxophonist John Williams' New Perspectives (1994).

ARGÜELLES, Julian
saxes/flute/clarinet/recorder/percussion/composer

Born: Litchfield, Staffordshire, 28 January 1966

Brother of drummer Steve. Played in various bands around the Birmingham area. Featured with National Youth Jazz Orchestra and with the European Community Big Band. Moved to London in 1984, studied at Trinity College. Joined Loose Tubes in 1985, did widespread touring with that unit throughout its existence. In Django Bates' Delightful Precipice, and in quartet led by Steve Argüelles. With Simon Purcell in Jazz Train, and co-led Simon Purcell's Quartet from 1985 to 1990. With Chris McGregor's Brotherhood of Breath. Won Pat Smythe award in 1987. During the 1990s worked with Kenny Wheeler, Mike Gibbs, Django Bates, Tommy Smith, John Taylor, Julian Joseph, Carla Bley, etc. Co-led quintet with Steve, also leads own line-ups (trio, quartets and octet). Has worked in Portugal and in Britain with pianist Mario Leghina. Often with Stan Tracey in 1996. National tour with own quartet (Mike Walker, guitar, Steve Watts, bass, and Martin France, drums) in May 1996.

ARGÜELLES, 'Steve' Stephen
drums/composer

Born: Crowborough, Sussex, 16 November 1963

Brother of saxophonist Julian. Played drums from early teens. Raised in Birmingham area, played in Midland Youth Orchestra and did local gigs. Moved to London, studied at the Chelsea Art College and began playing gigs, some with Bobby Wellins. Joined the National Youth Jazz Orchestra. Led own quartet (1984), then became founder-member of Loose Tubes. In Human Chain (with Django Bates), Iain Ballamy's Quartet (1987), Tommy Smith's Quartet from 1987 and Sextet into the 1990s. Also worked with Gordon Beck, Geoff Castle, Chris McGregor, Dudu Pukwana's Zila, John Taylor, etc. Accompanied visiting American musicians, Lee Konitz, George Coleman, Bobby Watson, Steve Lacy, Charlie Mariano, Mose Allison, etc., also worked with harmonica player Toots Thielemans. With Kenny Wheeler's Big Band, and co-led Argüelles-Nick Purnell Big Band. Worked in France with various line-ups during the mid-1990s, also with Martin Speake group (1996), Tony Coe Quartet (1996) and freelancing extensively. Commissioned composition performed by own octet at Le Mans Festival in April 1996.

ARMATAGE, John
drums/arranger

Born: Newcastle upon Tyne, 5 August 1929

Served in the Royal Navy. After release freelanced in London, gigging with Bob Parker's Band (1957). Turned professional in 1958, working summer season in John Chilton's Band. Joined Bruce Turner early in 1959 and worked regularly in Bruce Turner's Jump Band until 1964, during this period also played in Wally Fawkes' Band. Led own Jump Band, accompanying visiting American musicians (1964), then again worked with Bruce Turner in 1965. Freelanced in the late 1960s, often working in duos with Phil Rhodes on organ, also with pianist Doug Murray's Band.

During the 1970s spent seven years in Alan Elsdon's Band (until June 1978), then worked with Peter Allen for two years. During the 1970s played in various reunions of Bruce Turner's Jump Band and also worked often in Ron Russell's Band. During the 1980s worked with Eggy Ley's Hot Shots, with Trevor Whiting's Swingtet, with Tiny Winters' Kettners Five, etc., but mainly with Terry Lightfoot into the 1990s. Successful freelancing in the mid-1990s, part of Ian Hunter-Randall's All Stars (1995).

ARMIT, Ian Born: Fife, Scotland, 11 April 1929
piano/composer Died: Zurich, Switzerland, 18 February 1992

Studied classical music from early childhood. Spent two years in the RAF (1947–9) and toured Middle East in service bands. Worked as a sales representative from 1949 until 1957, but played semi-professionally with Mike Daniels (1951), Bobby Mickleburgh (1952), the Christie Brothers, and again with Mickleburgh (1954). With Cy Laurie (1956), then spent a year with Sandy Brown from summer of 1956. Gave up job to join Humphrey Lyttelton from summer 1957 until autumn 1963. With Long John Baldry from early 1964, worked often with Baldry until the early 1970s (including tours of the USA and Canada), also toured Britain with various American jazz and blues artistes. Played long residency at the Georgian Club, London, then became musical director for Joan Littlewood's Theatre Workshop (often working at the Theatre Royal, Stratford East, London). Gigged with various jazz groups in the 1970s, including spell with Ian Bell (1975), then moved to Switzerland to work with Bob Wallis in 1976. Made his home in the Zurich area and worked with the Piccadilly Six, the Harlem Ramblers, the Old Rivertown Band, etc. In the summer of 1989 worked in Britain as part of McJazz. Joined New Riverside Band in Switzerland (1990), then formed own quartet.

ARNOLD, Reg Born: London, 25 January 1919
trumpet/piano/vocals Died: Mannheim, Germany, 15 January 1963

Piano first, then cornet in Barnet Silver Prize Band. With drummer George Bright's Band (1939), then joined house band at the Nut House, London and worked with Aubrey Frank at the Nest Club, London (1939) before joining the Army from October 1939 until January 1946, during this period worked with Sid Millward's Army Band in France (1944) and with the *Stars in Battledress* show. Toured with Vic Lewis (1946-7), then worked with Billy Munn (1947). Led own band at the Orchard Room, Purley, from autumn 1947 until January 1948. With Felix King (1948), Frank Weir (1949), Eric Winstone (1949) then joined Joe Loss (1950). Left Joe Loss in May 1955 to work in double act with vocalist Howard Jones. Enjoyed considerable international success with Jones, but occasionally fronted own band for specific engagements, and deputized for indisposed leader Johnny Wollaston at Majestic Ballroom, Leeds, in early 1961. Died of a heart attack while working in Germany.

ASH, 'Vic' Victor Born: East London, 9 March 1930
clarinet/saxes/flute

Cousin of guitarist Maurice Ash. Clarinet from age of fourteen, then saxes, alto first then tenor. Worked as a salesman but played semi-professionally including tour of Germany with Stan Tracey (and trumpeter Victor Graham). Returned to London, gigged with Paul Hyman's Band and Eddie Thompson, played for a week with Nat Gonella in Aberdeen. Became fully professional by joining Kenny Baker's Sextet from early 1951 for two years. Regularly with Vic Lewis' Orchestra from 1953. Left Lewis to lead own quartet which toured with US singer Maxine Sullivan (1954). Freelanced in jazz clubs and worked in Jazz Today Unit. Played a series with Kenny Baker's Dozen. Did one trip on liner *Queen Mary* (September 1956), also with own quartet toured Britain with Cab Calloway and with Hoagy Carmichael. With Vic Lewis again (spring 1957) then again led own quartet. Took quartet to USA (1957) and sextet to USA (1958). Again with Vic Lewis (1959) then again led own line-ups. To USA with Vic Lewis (spring 1960). Co-led Jazz Five (with Harry Klein) from 1960 until spring 1962, then worked regularly with John Dankworth (1962–5). Worked for two weeks in Ray Charles' Orchestra in France and Britain. Freelance work in studios throughout the 1960s, gigged with many bandleaders including Grischa Farfel (1965). Worked in Bermuda with Joe Wylie's Band from 1966 until March 1969. Returned to Britain and did extensive freelance work through the 1970s, 1980s and 1990s. Worked on over twenty European and Middle Eastern tours with Frank Sinatra, also accompanied Peggy Lee, Lena Horne, Tony Bennett, etc. Regularly with Harry Stoneham's Band on BBC Television, also played in many varying line-ups, in Dave Hancock's Big Band, with Cliff Hardy, in Allan Ganley's Big Band, in Spain with Ian Henry's Quartet (1981), etc. Regularly featured with BBC Big Band (including 1992 tour of North America). Has occasionally played for West End shows including: *Privates on Parade*, *42nd Street*, *Match Girls*, *City of Angels*. Continues to freelance successfully including engagements with Kenny Baker's New Dozen.

ASHMAN, 'Mickey' Michael Lewis   Born: Kingsbury, London, 12 November 1927
double bass

Worked for De Havilland Aircraft Company as an apprentice before joining the RAF. Took up double bass while in RAF and played occasional gigs. After demobilization played locally in NW London and Middlesex with Jimmy Skidmore, drummer Brian England and guitarist Tony Lofthouse, worked regularly in trio led by pianist Charlie Barber. With Mike Daniels for fourteen months from March 1949. With Humphrey Lyttelton from May 1950 until August 1955, left to work with Chris Barber from August 1955 until spring 1956. Brief stay with Eric Delaney (April 1956) then joined Lonnie Donegan's Skiffle Group from summer 1956 until May 1958, during this period worked for seven weeks with Ken Colyer (1956) while Donegan was on a solo tour of the USA. Led own band from July 1958 until 1965, freelanced with various leaders including Bob Wallis, then again worked with Chris Barber before spending three years with Terry Lightfoot. Left Lightfoot in the early 1970s, then freelanced with Tony Raine All Stars, etc., before working for seven years with Monty Sunshine into the 1980s. During the 1980s and 1990s prolific freelance work with various bands, regularly with Dick Cook's Jambalaya, and with Neville Dickie's Trio, also fifteen months in John Petters' Legends of British Trad (1992–3). Played in Canada with Neville Dickie's Rhythmakers in September 1994. Continued to play regularly through the 1990s.

ASHTON, 'Bill' William Michael Allingham   Born: Blackpool, Lancashire, 6 December 1936
saxes/clarinet/composer

Father was an amateur musician who played many instruments. Took up saxophone and clarinet at school, while serving in the RAF played in service band. After demobilization studied at St Peter's College, Oxford. Founded University Dance Band (the Ambassadors), founded OU Modern Jazz Club and Oxford University Big Band. Taught in France 1960–1, gigged with the Stardust Combo. Returned to Oxford, won award in Inter-University Jazz Band Competition (1962). Toured US bases in France, returned to England in 1963. Worked in Red Bludd's Bluesicians in London, and taught French in various London schools. Together with Pat Evans co-founded the London Schools' Jazz Orchestra, soon to be renamed London Youth Jazz Orchestra before adopting the lasting title: the National Youth Jazz Orchestra. Gave up teaching languages in 1973, to work full time with NYJO, a position he continues to occupy through the 1990s. During that time NYJO toured with Shorty Rogers, John Dankworth, John Williams and a number of singers. Ashton has written many songs (either words or music or both). He was made a Fellow of the Leeds College of Music in 1995. NYJO has successfully completed many international tours. Some of its illustrious members and ex-members include: Julian Argüelles, Steve Argüelles, Guy Barker, Pete Beachill, Chris Biscoe, Geoff Castle, Mark Chandler, Andy Cleyndert, Jay Craig, Lorraine Craig, Malcolm Creese, Andy Cuss, Chris Dagley, Scott Garland, Tim Garland, Sarah Gilbertson, Lisa Grahame, John Halton, Paul Hart, Jacqui Hicks, Clive Hitchcock, Nigel Hitchcock, James Hunt, Chris Hunter, Laurence Juber, Sandra King, Chris Laurence, Pete Long, Paul Lytton, Andy Mackintosh, Howard McGill, Steve Melling, Paul Morgan, Paul Nieman, Mark Nightingale, Dave O'Higgins, Mark Ong, Andy Pask, Dick Pearce, Gerard Presencer, Frank Ricotti, Dennis Rollins, Winston Rollins, Pete Saberton, Neil Sidwell, Steve Sidwell, Malcolm Earle Smith, Mike Smith, Michael Tarquin Smith, Stan Sulzmann, Bob Sydor, Jamie Talbot, Rick Taylor, Phil Todd, Jim Tomlinson, Andy Vinter, Ben Waghorn, Alan Wakeman, Danny Waldmann, Paul Weimar, Paul Westwood, Mark White, Patrick White, Neil Yates.

ASPLAND, Robin Michael   Born: Leeds, Yorkshire, 6 December 1961
keyboards/arranger/composer

Joined local church choir at seven. Studied music at Roundhay High School, and then gained BA in music at Colchester Institute. Also received jazz tuition from Reg Webb. Was later taught by Lionel Grigson. Did first gigs on drums with a trad jazz band (while still at school). Played piano with various groups before moving to London in 1984, played in Pasadena Roof Orchestra from 1985, subsequently featured with Don Weller, Pete King, Jim Mullen, Dick Morrissey, Kenny Wheeler, Ronnie Scott, Iain Ballamy, Gary Meek, Julian Argüelles, Matt Wates, Orphy Robinson, Fairer Sax, Desperately Seeking Fusion, etc. Accompanied various visiting musicians, including George Coleman, Arturo Sandoval, etc. and backed singers Claire Martin, Tina May, Mark Murphy, etc. In 1995 continued to work in the Dankworth Generation Band, and also with Dave O'Higgins' Quartet and the Pizza Express Modern Jazz Sextet, as well as freelancing on various recordings including a Van Morrison-Georgie Fame album.

AUGER, Brian
Born: London, 18 July 1939
piano/organ/composer

With vibes-player Dave Morse's Quintet (1960–2). Led own trio. Worked briefly in Tommy Whittle's Quartet (late 1962 to early 1963). Toured Germany in band led by trumpeter Murray Campbell (early 1963). Worked with Alexis Korner and with John McLaughlin. Began specializing on Hammond organ. Formed new trio called Brian Auger Trinity (summer 1963), was joined by singer Julie Driscoll and achieved widespread success, then augmented by singers Long John Baldry and Rod Stewart, consolidated under the name Steam Packet (1965). Big selling recordings with Julie Driscoll. After Driscoll left in the late 1960s, reverted to Trinity, then formed Oblivion Express in summer of 1970, which thrived for three years. Auger then divided his time between working in the USA and Europe, enjoying considerable success. In 1985 he joined up temporarily with a re-formed Spencer Davis group. Led own Blues Revival. Worked mainly out of Los Angeles. Returned to London in April 1996 and played dates with new version of Oblivion Express.

AVON CITIES JAZZ BAND
Began playing in the Bristol and Bath area in 1949. Two of its founder-members, trumpeter Geoff Nichols and trombonist-soprano saxophonist Mike Hitchings were still in the line-up in the mid-1990s. Pianist Dave Collett has been with the band for over 30 years and drummer Chris Pope left in 1995 after 31 years (replaced by Frank Woodford). The band's long-serving clarinet player, Ray Bush, left in 1984 and moved to the USA. Bassist Clive Morton has over twenty years' service. Other members of the 1995 band were: Andrew Barrett (guitar), Martin Genge (tenor sax) and John Barton (alto sax). Some of the band's former members include:

Banjo/guitarists: Wayne Chandler, Frank Feeney, Jay Hawkins
Bassists: Malcolm Wright, John Phipps, John Macey, Bernie Attridge, Tony Baylis
Pianists: Jan Ridd, John Critchinson
Drummer: Basil Wright

The band successfully featured a skiffle group during the 1960s comprising Ray Bush (guitar/vocals), Geoff Nichols (double bass), Wayne Chandler (guitar) and Mike Hitchings (mandolin).

B

BABBINGTON, Roy
Born: Kempston, Bedfordshire, 8 July 1940
double bass/bass guitar

Played gigs around the Bedford area then worked professionally in Scotland with Harry Bence (1962). Did club and palais work before settling in London during the late 1960s. During the 1970s played many freelance sessions and worked with Alexis Korner, Ian Carr's Nucleus, Mike Westbrook, Keith Tippett, Mike Gibbs, Barbara Thompson, Harold Beckett. Long spells in Soft

Machine from 1973. During the late 1970s began long musical association with Stan Tracey which lasted until the mid-1990s. Played at the National Theatre and accompanied visiting American musicians, also regularly in the BBC Radio Orchestra and Big Band (including trip to North America in 1992). Freelanced with various line-ups including regular work in Don Weller-Bryan Spring Quartet. Was featured on the sound track of the film *White Mischief*. Active freelance in the 1990s, with Allan Stuart's Octet, Alan Skidmore's Quartet, in trio with Sue Hawker and Bob Koral, etc., also leads own trio which regularly accompanied American singer Marlene VerPlanck on her 1990s visits to Britain.

BACON, Max
drums

Born: London, 1 March 1904
Died: London, 3 December 1969

Brother Sydney was also a drummer. Uncle of drummer Maurice Burman. Played first gigs at Finsbury Park Palais, London, then worked with the Clarions at Brett's Club before joining Leon Van Straten (1926). With Ambrose in spring 1927, then briefly with Kit-Cat Band (under direction of Al Starita) before rejoining Ambrose in autumn 1927. Recorded with Ronnie Munro and with Fred Elizalde (1927). Worked with Ambrose throughout the 1930s (also recorded with Lew Stone and Sid Phillips). Began entertaining troops with ENSA (1940) and from summer 1941 worked almost exclusively as a variety artiste, originally in a triple act with Evelyn Dall and Sam Browne then as a solo act (as a comedian-drummer). Continued in variety and clubs throughout the 1950s, combining this with work as an actor (in films and on stage). Wrote drummers' instruction book *Max on Swing*. Was related to multi-instrumentalist Victor Feldman.

BAILEY, Derek
guitar/composer

Born: Sheffield, Yorkshire, 29 January 1930

From a musical family, his uncle was a professional guitarist. Played guitar from age of eleven. Wide variety of professional work in the 1950s including palais bands, variety club groups, accompanying popular singers and playing in night club line-ups. Joined trio with Tony Oxley and Gavin Bryars then worked in Sheffield with Barry Whitworth's Quartet (1966) before moving to London. Did night club work but soon became part of John Stevens' Spontaneous Music Ensemble. Worked with Evan Parker from 1968, led own trio and played in Globe Unity Orchestra. Accompanied Steve Lacy (1973), with Eddie Prévost (1974), worked in Paul Rutherford's Iskra 1903 over a period of three years. Established Company in 1976, which, over a number of years featured many of the world's leading free improvizers. Played duos with Anthony Braxton, Steve Lacy, Tony Coe, Han Bennink, Paul Lytton, etc. Played in Kenny Wheeler's band (1978) but from this point onwards mainly active as a soloist. Toured North America in 1979. Worked in Japan, South America, Africa, etc. with Company through the 1980s and 1990s. Featured as a soloist at various international festivals and in instructional television series *On The Edge*. In various duos during the early 1990s including work with Phil Wachsmann and John Surman. With Locofoco (1993). During 1995 worked in USA with William Parker, with Tony Oxley and with Russian percussionist Robyn Schulkovsky, further international solo appearances. Co-founded Incus label in 1970. Wrote *Improvisation and its Nature and Practice in Music* (first published in 1980).

BAIN 'Jock' (John Cockburn BAIRNSFATHER)
trombone

Born: Edinburgh, Scotland, 8 June 1914
Died: April 1997

Brother of trumpeter Bruce Bain (died 1995). Violin from age of seven, played trombone at school and performed in City of Edinburgh Brass Band. Did palais work at fourteen. With Duncan Brodie in Portobello and with Danny McCormack in Dundee (1934). To London in 1935, worked with Tommy Finnigan at the Streatham Locarno. With Roy Fox for three and a half years from autumn 1935 then joined Jack Harris (1939). With Ambrose (1942), Maurice Winnick (1943), Phil Green (1944). With Geraldo from the end of 1944 until September 1947, rejoined Maurice Winnick briefly, then again worked with Geraldo. Left Geraldo to open own photographic shop in Edinburgh (1948), but soon returned to London and rejoined Maurice Winnick (1949). Again worked with Geraldo in the early 1950s, then brief stays with Ambrose (1953) and Carroll Gibbons (1953) before becoming highly successful freelance musician working in varied line-ups, with Mantovani and on tours of Europe with Benny Goodman.

BAKER, 'Ginger' Peter
drums

Born: Lewisham, London, 19 August 1939

Brief spell on trumpet then took up drums at sixteen. Worked with Hugh Rainey and Bob Wallis in the Storyville Jazzmen then joined Terry Lightfoot (1957). With Pete Deuchar, then toured Denmark with Diz Disley (early 1958). Worked in Ken Oldham's Band at Cricklewood Palais (1959), with Leslie Douglas in Europe and gigged with Brian Dee, Dudley Moore, etc. (1960). Brief stays in bands led by Danny Haggerty, Gus Galbraith, Bobby Wellins, Ken Wray, Mike Taylor, Bert Courtley (including work in Germany) and Joe Harriott. Worked in John Burch Octet and in Alexis Korner's Blues Incorporated before joining newly formed Graham Bond Organization in spring 1963. Remained with Graham Bond until summer 1966, then became founder-member of Cream (with Jack Bruce and Eric Clapton) until break-up in late 1968. Toured USA with own Blind Faith then organized Air Force (late 1969). Also guested with Phil Seamen's big band. Led various ensembles and guested with groups into the 1990s. Based in Denver, Colorado, in the 1990s.

BAKER, 'Kenny' Kenneth
trumpet/flugelhorn/vocals/arranger/composer

Born: Withernsea, Yorkshire, 1 March 1921

Father played sax and clarinet, mother played piano. Began on piano, sax, violin and piano-accordion then uncle gave him a tenor horn. Soon switched to cornet and played in local Gospel Mission Band, later led own band at Queen's Hotel, Withernsea. Moved with family to Hull, worked in music shop, played in West Hull Silver Band and played local gigs on trumpet in Manley's Orchestra. Turned professional by joining comedian Sandy Powell's touring party. Did summer season at Teignmouth with band led by Leicester drummer Les Watson (1939), returned to Hull at outbreak of World War II, then rejoined Sandy Powell and played three week season at the London Coliseum. Played for a week with Alan Green at Streatham Locarno then joined Lew Stone at the Palace Theatre, London for revue *Under Your Hat*. In Van Phillips' Orchestra for Jack Buchanan show *Top Hat and Tails* (spring 1940), worked briefly with Ambrose and Maurice Winnick. With Freddy Bretherton's Orchestra (from late 1940) in Garrison Theatre Show (played as part of Sid Millward's Band), also did freelance broadcasts including some with Ken Johnson. Worked in octet led by Canadian pianist Matt Heft in London (1941), also played gigs with Miff Ferrie and with Tito Burns (1941). Joined RAF in February 1942. Played in RAF Fighter Command Band, but also deputized in American Base Command Dance Band (1943). Spent last part of service in RAF Regiment at Grantham, Lincolnshire, guested with Ambrose, Squadronaires, Geraldo and Sidney Gross when service commitments allowed. After demobilization joined Ted Heath from 1945 until December 1948. With Ambrose from late 1948 until summer 1949, guested with Skyrockets in July 1949, accompanying Benny Goodman at London Palladium, by this time extremely active as a freelance session musician. Together with Norman Stenfalt played for *A Streetcar Named Desire* (1950), worked with Robert Farnon (December 1950 to March 1951). Led own octet from March 1951 until March 1953, again worked with Lew Stone (1952). Doubled on flugelhorn from 1952. Led own Baker's Dozen for long-running BBC radio series (from April 1952). Led own quartet on tour from August 1953 until November 1954. During the 1950s and 1960s played many theatre dates as a solo variety act (including seasons at Blackpool). Played on various film soundtracks (including *Genevieve*). Continued with prolific freelance work from the 1960s onwards, regularly with Jack Parnell's Orchestra, and subsequently in Don Lusher's 'Ted Heath' Orchestra. Accompanied many American artistes, and worked in Europe with Gerry Mulligan, Benny Goodman, etc. Guested with many small jazz groups through to the mid-1990s, and appeared regularly with *The Best of British Jazz* package (1996). Re-formed own Baker's Dozen for specific engagements in 1993, 1994 and 1995 (and recordings).

BALDOCK, 'Ken' Kenneth Ernest
double bass/piano/composer/arranger

Born: Chiswick, London, 5 April 1932

Piano from age of six. First local gigs with trumpeter Billy Talbot, saxist Gary Chevins, etc. Sat in at White Hart, Acton, before serving in Canada as an RAF navigator. Played piano in station band at Winnipeg, and began tentative efforts on double bass. After demobilization studied at Guildhall School of Music, London, on piano (with double bass as second instrument). Worked on piano with drummer Billy Long (1957), deputized in Rex Ruttley's Band. To Germany, piano and vocals with Val Merrall's Band (March 1958) then worked in France and Germany with Franz Hackert's Band and began doubling on double bass. Worked on piano in Germany with clarinettist Fritz Schpannuth's Band. Returned to London, began specializing on double bass, studied with James Merret, Sr. Worked with pianist Chuck Gates, and at Savoy Hotel, London, in Chick Lovelle's Sorentinos. With Eddie Thompson, and Ronnie Roullier then toured with Johnny Wiltshire and the Trebletones (1962). Toured Germany, France and Italy with singer Rosemary Clooney. With Miff Smith at the Celebrite Club, London (1963), then worked regularly in Roger Webb's Trio (1964–5) for television series and club work. Freelance session work from this point onwards, also with Bill Le Sage (1965), with Pat Smythe, Brian Lemon and Alan Branscombe at Annie's Room, London (1965–6). Toured with Dakota Staton. Gigs with Vic Ash, Tony Kinsey, Stan Tracey, Gordon Beck. etc. Began long musical association with John Dankworth and Cleo Laine in 1965. Toured with Ronnie Scott's Big Band and regularly accompanied visiting musicians at Ronnie Scott's Club. With Danny Moss' Quartet, Bob Burns-Kathy Stobart, Keith Tippett, Dave Shepherd, etc. With trios led by Colin Purbrook and Brian Lemon from late 1960s. Led own band from 1972, deputized in Jack Parnell's Orchestra and worked regularly with Freddy Randall-Dave Shepherd Band (1972–3), then again with Stan Tracey. Accompanied many visiting American artistes including Benny Carter, Teddy Wilson, Al Haig, Blossom Dearie, Ernestine Anderson, Helen Humes, etc. In Ronnie Scott's Quartet from February 1975 until December 1976 (during this period worked in Oscar Peterson's Trio for two television series). Again led own band from 1977, temporarily out of action through head injuries (early 1979). Again led own band, guested with Louis Hayes' Band, worked in Pat Smythe's Trio. Regularly with Bobby Wellins from 1981 until 1986. Played in ship's band aboard *Royal Viking* liner (1986), then worked regularly in John Chilton's Feetwarmers (accompanying George Melly) from 1987 through the 1990s. Continues to play freelance sessions. Taught throughout the 1970s and 1980s at the Barry Summer School. Still occasionally doubles on piano.

BALDRY, 'Long John' John
vocals/guitar

Born: England, 12 January 1941

Was a commercial artist before becoming a professional singer. Toured Denmark with Bob Cort (1959), and sang with folk group the Thameside Four and with Rambling Jack Elliott. From 1960 onwards guested with various jazz groups led by Ian Bell, Mickey Ashman, Bob Wallis, etc. Regularly with Ken Sims' Vintage Jazz Band from summer 1961. Solo work in Cologne and Frankfurt during summer of 1962. Returned to London, gigged with Alexis Korner's Blues Incorporated in early 1963, then joined Cyril Davies' All Stars in February 1963. After Davies' death became leader of the unit and with personnel changes this formed the basis of a new group, Long John Baldry and his Hoochie Coochie Men (early 1964). Disbanded in August 1965, became part of Steam Packet (with Rod Stewart and Julie Driscoll) then worked as a solo act from 1966, soon achieving world wide success with recording of 'Let the Heartaches Begin' (1967). Thereafter did international touring throughout the 1970s and 1980s before settling in Canada. Occasionally visits to Britain and on one trip did concert work with Keith Smith. Based in Vancouver, Canada, in the mid-1990s.

BALDWIN, 'Len' Leonard Sidney George
trombone

Born: Braintree, Essex, 17 October 1939

Took up trombone at sixteen. Formed own band the Dauphin Street Six in 1959, which turned professional in February 1961, and toured successfully for six years. Temporarily left full time music, then worked with Ken Colyer and with the re-formed Crane River Jazz Band during the 1970s. With Ken Sims from 1981 through the 1990s, also gigged with various other leaders in the 1980s including Monty Sunshine and Geoff Downs and played in the Crescent City Jazz Band.

BALL, 'Cliff' Clifford
double bass/bass guitar

Born: Fulham, London, 28 January 1927

Son of bassist Dick Ball. Originally taught by father, played double bass and bass trombone in the Royal Ordnance Band during Army service. After being demobilized in November 1948, led own Melody Makers and gigged with various bands around the Crystal Palace area, then joined Kenny Graham's Afro Cubists. Later worked with Johnnie Gray at Churchill's, with Oscar Rabin at the

Lyceum, and with Kenny Baker's Quartet (1953–4). Freelanced before joining Johnny Wiltshire and the Trebletones. Left full time playing to work in his father's newsagency business. Has continued to play double bass and bass guitar with various groups in the Folkestone and Dover area including work with the Invicta Jazz Band.

BALL, 'Dick' Richard Marsh
double bass/sousaphone

Born: Southwark, London, 26 December 1903
Died: Kent, 1978

Father of bassist Cliff Ball. Was originally taught music at the Greenwich Naval School from eleven to fifteen. Subsequently worked with Charlie Tucker, Marius B. Winter, Eddie Gross-Bart, Leslie 'Hutch' Hutchinson and Jack Shields before joining Howard Jacobs. Left Jacobs to work with Ambrose from autumn 1933. With Jack Harris in 1937, then again worked with Ambrose before joining Maurice Winnick (spring 1939). Ran own newsagent's business in the early 1940s then served as a reserve policeman in Liverpool (1944). After World War II resumed as a newsagent and retired from music. Throughout his career did a good deal of freelance radio and recording work.

BALL, 'Kenny' Kenneth Daniel
trumpet/vocals

Born: Ilford, Essex, 22 May 1930

Trumpet from the age of fourteen. Played in Ilford Sea Cadet Band. Did National Service in REME (1948–50). Worked for electrical goods company but played gigs with the Orchettes and Stan Fry. Depped for Freddy Randall and played regularly at British Legion Hall, Leytonstone. With Charlie Galbraith (1951–2) and gigged with Geoff Turner's Band (1953), before turning professional by joining Sid Phillips in late 1953. With Sid Phillips until August 1954, briefly with Norman Cave, then led own Chicagoans briefly before rejoining Sid Phillips in late 1954. Left Phillips to join Eric Delaney in 1956, left in late 1956 to form own band in 1957. With Terry Lightfoot from spring 1958 until September 1958, then formed own Jazzmen, which made debut in October 1958. Several hit records and many successful tours with the Jazzmen, whose busy schedule hasn't diminished through the 1990s.

BALL, 'Ronnie' Ronald
piano

Born: Birmingham, Warwickshire, 22 December 1927
Died: New York, USA, 1984

Played local gigs from age of fifteen. Did season at Newquay in Jackson Cox's Band (1947), then worked with Billy Forrest's Band in Southsea (1947–8). After playing South Coast season with Johnny Franks (1948), moved to London and worked in Reggie Goff's Sextet before briefly leading own trio at Murray's Club (December 1948 to January 1949). With Cab Kaye's Band in summer of 1949, guested with Leslie Douglas (late 1949), then joined Ken Grieff's Band on liner *Queen Mary* (late 1949). Studied with Lennie Tristano during New York stopovers. Led own band on *Queen Mary* (1950 to early 1951). Gigged with Joe Muddel's group in London (1950–1), led own Trio at 51 Club, London, and occasionally led various line-ups, including one featuring four tenor saxists. Regularly with Frank Weir (summer 1951) and Paul Adam (autumn 1951 to winter 1951). Emigrated to USA in January 1952, worked in Chuck Wayne's Trio (1952) and was then hospitalized with lung ailment for most of 1953. Joined Kai Winding in late 1953, then worked with Lee Konitz (1954). Was later featured in many famous small groups including Gene Krupa's Trio and Roy Eldridge's Quartet, also toured with Jazz At The Philharmonic and with Buddy Rich. Worked mainly in New York in the 1960s and 1970s, then left full time playing and worked doing transcriptions for a music publisher during the last part of his life.

BALLAMY, Iain
saxes/flute/piano/composer

Born: Guildford, Surrey, 20 February 1964

Son of pianist Mark Ballamy. Began on piano at six, took up alto sax at fourteen. Did City and Guilds course in repairing instruments. Sat in with Tony Lee Trio and took a few lessons from Kathy Stobart. Formed own quintet, specializing on tenor sax, in January 1983, then led quartet (with Django Bates on piano, Steve Argüelles on drums and Mick Hutton on bass) from 1983. In Clark Tracey's short-lived quartet (1983). Founder-member of Loose Tubes in 1984. Formed new quartet, Bush Sense, (with Steve Argüelles on drums, Mario Castronari on bass and Dale Barlow on sax). With Jim Mullen (late 1985–6) and from 1985 part of Billy Jenkins' Voice of God Collective. Founder-member of Bill Bruford's Earth Works, regularly with Bruford during the 1980s and 1990s, including tour of Japan. During the 1980s also worked with Gordon Beck, Stan Sulzmann, John Taylor and in Gil Evans' British Orchestra. Continued to lead own line-up through the 1990s, also worked often with Django Bates' groups, Delightful Precipice and Human Chain. Was featured at Vienna Festival (1995). Worked with singers Ian Shaw and Claire Martin, with pianist John Donaldson's Quartet, etc.

BAMPTON, Claude
piano/piano accordion/composer

Born: North London, 28 June 1908
Died: Clerkenwell, London, 20 March 1969

Worked with the Cavendish Dance Band on sax and clarinet (1930), also led own semi-professional Bandits throughout the early 1930s. Turned professional by joining band led by drummer Bill Airey-Smith (spring 1935), but soon took up post as guest conductor on Italy's Radio Turin (June to September 1935), and made various recordings in Italy. Returned to London and formed band for residency at the Prince's Theatre, which provided the music for the play *The Frog* (for which Bampton wrote the score). From the mid-1930s was coach for the National Institute for the Blind Dance Band, which included George Shearing, (Bampton himself had normal eyesight). Led own band in the late 1930s, then played in the Palladium Orchestra (under Freddy Bretherton) in the early 1940s. Spent two-and-a-half years as Director of Music at St Dunstan's (an institute for the blind) from 1944 until 1946, thereafter worked mainly as a solo pianist and music director, combining this with professional work as a photographer and as a piano teacher. Played at the Horse Shoe Inn, London, in the late 1950s and at the 142 Club in the 1960s.

BANCROFT, 'Tom' Thomas Peter
drums/composer

Born: Lambeth, London, 29 January 1967

Father a pianist, twin brother Phil plays sax and clarinet, sister Sophie is a singer. Started on drums at seven. Moved with family to Scotland at age of nine. Played in family trio with father and brother. Gigged around Edinburgh from age of sixteen. While studying medicine at Cambridge began writing for Fineline quartet, gigged with them in London and East Anglia during the mid-1980s. From September 1988 to May 1989 studied arranging and composing with trumpeter Joe Sullivan at McGill University in Montreal, Canada. Formed group Orange Ear Ensemble in Montreal, also recorded with various student bands in Montreal and visited New York. Returned to Scotland in 1989 and formed new version of Orange Ear Ensemble. Received commission to write for own big band, which began gigging in 1990. By 1996 this band was doing national tours and being featured at various festivals. First worked with Tommy Smith in 1991, toured with Smith's Quartet in 1992, and during that year became a qualified doctor of medicine. Worked in Russia with pianist Chick Lyall (1991) and returned to Rostov-on-Don a year later, did medical work there for two months and gigged with local bands. Played with Sun Ra at Edinburgh Festival (1992) and has also worked with Martin Taylor, Jason Rebello, Julian Argüelles, Stan Sulzmann, Sheila Jordan, etc. During the mid-1990s active in organizing Pandemonium at Glasgow Festival. Continues to play gigs around the Edinburgh area, with Chick Lyall's Quartet and with guitarist Kevin Mackenzie's Quartet, etc. Toured Hungary (October 1995) in the AAB Trio (alongside brother Phil). Worked in France and Scotland with Kilt Couture (1994 and 1995). Own big band did successful national tour (February 1996) which featured Bancroft's suite *Birkhedges* (commissioned by Birmingham Jazz in 1995).

BARBER, 'Chris' Donald Christopher
Born: Welwyn, Hertfordshire, 17 April 1930
trombone/double bass/cornet/baritone
horn/arranger

First instrument was small violin at age of seven, began playing full-size violin at school, while evacuated to Royston, Cambridgeshire, during World War II. Bought trombone from Harry Brown (1948), playing gigs with Beryl Bryden's Backroom Boys (1949), two weeks with Cy Laurie, occasionally sat in with Doug Whitton's Band, formed own band 1949. Together with his then clarinettist Alex Revell, played gigs with Reg Rigden's Original Dixielanders (late 1949 to early 1950), continued to lead own band from 1950, also studied trombone and double bass at the Guildhall School of Music (1951–4). In September 1952 formed quintet (with Monty Sunshine, Lonnie Donegan, Jim Bray and Ron Bowden) which began rehearsing regularly, and, with the addition of trumpeter Pat Halcox played gigs at the Club Creole, London in December 1952 to January 1953. When Pat Halcox declined the offer to turn professional, Barber wrote to Ken Colyer (then in the USA) who returned to London and joined the band in March 1953 (as its nominal leader). After a year, Colyer departed and Barber was appointed leader. Halcox reconsidered his previous decision and joined the band in place of Colyer. Shortly afterwards (in the summer of 1954) singer Ottilie Patterson first sat in with the band before joining them full time. Chris and Ottilie married in November 1959, they were divorced in 1983. For over 40 years Barber has continued to lead his own highly successful and widely travelled Jazz and Blues Band. He also organized tours for (and accompanied) numerous American jazz and blues stars, including Sister Rosetta Tharpe, Muddy Waters, Louis Jordan, Wild Bill Davis, Edmond Hall, Russell Procope, Trummy Young, John Lewis, and gospel singer Alex Bradford. His own band continues to make wide-ranging international tours and has played many times in the USA. Barber regularly assembles former sidemen for widespread reunion tours, including a 1994 package celebrating the band's 40th anniversary. Awarded the OBE in 1991. Barber was one of the first British bandleaders to organize a skiffle group (using it as a band-within-a-band). He also occasionally led his own brass band.

BARKER, Guy
trumpet/flugelhorn/composer

Born: Chiswick, London, 26 December 1957

Trumpet from an early age. Played in Harrow Youth Jazz Orchestra (directed by Ray Crane); with the National Youth Jazz Orchestra from fourteen, continued to be featured with them for over seven years. Began long musical association with John Dankworth in the late 1970s, toured Britain with own quintet. Studied at Royal College of Music, but didn't complete the course because of working trip to USA. With Chris Hunter's Quintet (1980–2), in Geoff Castle's Band (1981). From this period onwards worked often in various Stan Tracey line-ups through to the 1990s. With Mike Westbrook, Alan Skidmore, Georgie Fame, and Clark Tracey (including international touring). Toured in bands accompanying Frank Sinatra, Sammy Davis, Liza Minelli, Lena Horne, Mel Tormé, etc. and worked in Italy with Ornette Coleman. Worked in Europe with Gil Evans, and again led own group. Extensive freelance session work, for radio, television, films and recordings (many with rock groups); guested with the London Symphony Orchestra. In the late 1980s began appearing with Keith Nichols' line-ups for long-running series of tributes to jazz stars of yesteryear, notably Bix Beiderbecke. During the early 1990s worked in Jack Sharpe's Big Band, with Carla Bley (four tours) and with Stan Tracey. Visited Hong Kong with Georgie Fame, toured with Tommy Smith Sextet, played in Indonesia and Hong Kong (1995). Was Musical Director for Hermeto Pascoal's Orchestra UK tour (1994). Worked in Colin Towns' Orchestra (1995), with Julian Joseph Big Band (1995), recorded with Van Morrison. Toured with own Quartet (1994), then led own International Quintet featuring Alex Dankworth (bass), Icelandic saxophonist Sigurdur Flosason, Portuguese pianist Bernardo Sassetti and Ralph Salmins (or Connor Guilfoyle) on drums. Continues to be a featured soloist in a wide variety of line-ups. Guested with the London Sinfonietta (March 1996) and with Tommy Smith's Sextet (1996), also continues to lead own line-ups, including new quartet (1996).

BARNES, Alan
alto sax/baritone sax/clarinet

Born: Altrincham, Cheshire, 23 July 1959

Clarinet at twelve, sax at fifteen. Played in Frodsham with local traditional jazz band. Studied at Leeds College of Music from 1977 until 1980. Moved to London, played occasionally in the Midnite Follies Orchestra but regularly with the Pasadena Roof Orchestra from 1981 to 1983. With Tommy Chase's Quartet from late 1983 until 1986. Toured Japan with drummer Steve White and the Renegades, also worked often with Bob Wilber's Big Band (including Nice Jazz Festival). With Dave Lee (1988), led own quartet, then worked regularly with Humphrey Lyttelton from September 1988 until January 1993; during this period also with Pizza Express Modern Jazz Sextet (from November 1989), co-led quintet with John Barnes, worked with Mike Westbrook and toured with own quintet. Freelanced with many line-ups in the 1990s, including the BBC Radio Orchestra, Mike Westbrook's Big Band, Vile Bodies, Kenny Baker's Dozen, Ian Cruickshank's Band, duos with Gary Potter and in Potter's Quartet, Anthony Kerr's group, Don Weller's Big Band, etc. From early 1993 through the mid-1990s often worked in quintet co-led with Bruce Adams, and continued to freelance, including work in Peter Long's Echoes of Ellington, and brief tour with Freddie Hubbard (spring 1996).

BARNES, 'Bert' Albert George
piano/arranger/composer

Born: Stoke-on-Trent, 10 September 1906
Died: June 1974

Worked with Reg Batten, Percy Chandler and Maurice Winnick before joining Ambrose from March 1933 until October 1937, also worked as a publisher's staff arranger (recorded with Sid Phillips in 1936). With the Heralds of Swing from inauguration (1939), then again worked with Maurice Winnick (late 1939–40). Briefly in Sid Phillips' Trio (1940), then rejoined Ambrose in summer of 1940. Worked in Max Abrams' Septet (1943), then became freelance arranger, accompanist and musical director. Out of action through illness in the late 1950s, recovered and resumed previous schedule until emigrating to Australia, where he became a director of music for ABC Television.

BARNES, John
clarinet/saxes/flute/drums/vocals

Born: Manchester, Lancashire, 15 May 1932

Began playing clarinet at seventeen. Served in Royal Army Pay Corps, after demobilization joined Ray Leclerc's Band in 1952, which soon became the Zenith Six. Remained with this band (based in Manchester) until moving to London in November 1955 to join Mike Daniels. Left Mike Daniels to join Alan Elsdon in June 1961 (took up alto sax in 1957 and baritone sax in 1963). Left Alan Elsdon to join Alex Welsh in June 1964, regularly with Alex Welsh until September 1977 (except for three months' absence through injuries suffered in January 1967 road crash). Freelanced with various bands, but worked regularly in the Midnite Follies Orchestra from their January 1978 debut for two years. Worked with Digby Fairweather, Lennie Hastings, Alan Elsdon, co-leading with Bruce Turner and in duo with Roy Williams. With Humphrey Lyttelton from November 1979 until March 1991. During this period also co-led quintet with Alan Barnes, and played at Nice Jazz Festival with *Jazz Journal* All Stars, and with George Chisholm's Gentlemen of Jazz, as well as taking part in Mike Daniels' Reunion Band, touring with Donald Swann, and playing occasionally in Tiny Winters' Kettners Five. Continues to freelance through the 1990s, working in various Martin Litton line-ups, with Keith Smith, Bob Hunt's Ellington Orchestra and in the Great British Jazz Band (co-led by Digby Fairweather and Pete Strange). During the mid-1990s also part of the occasional Tenor Madness (with Spike Robinson and Bobby Wellins).

BARNETT, 'Pat' Charles Henry
trumpet/mellophone/vocals

Born: Cardiff, Glamorgan, 5 July 1915

Taught himself cornet as a teenager, then joined local Boys' Brigade Band. First professional work with Bernard Ash's twelve-piece band, first in South Wales then in Ireland and Scotland. Became part of breakaway quintet led by drummer Billy Peters which played residencies in Dundee and Edinburgh. Joined Billy Mason's Band in Scotland (1938) and did widespread touring with them. When the band broke up in Peterborough, he moved to London and worked with Billy Griffiths at Tottenham Palais. Joined Eddie Carroll's Band in London (1939) until the end of the year, briefly with Oscar Grasso, then joined Sid Millward's Band for ENSA tour of France during early part of World War II. Served in RAF from 1940 until 1946, played in station quintet and in big RAF band led by Cyril Stapleton. After demobilization worked mainly with Harry Parry during the years 1946 to 1950. With Cyril Grantham at Dorchester Hotel, London, then with Felix King (March 1951 to November 1952). With Ian Stewart at the Savoy Hotel and with Sidney Simone at the Dorchester. Played regularly at the Dorchester until 1958, then freelanced on sessions and in theatre orchestras until retiring in 1978.

BARNETT, Stanley
tenor sax/clarinet/violin

Born: *c.*1900

Took violin lessons from Belinfanti during early teens. First professional work in Blackpool as part of Feldman's Orchestra. Later led own band in Blackpool, Manchester, Liverpool and Leeds (began doubling on tenor sax). Led own band in Düsseldorf and remained in Germany for five years, during this period also played engagements in Denmark and Sweden. Returned to London *c.*1931, led own band at the Carlton Danse Salon then became leader of Madame Tussaud's Orchestra (1932-3). Own band at Prince's Club then led at Fischer's (early 1935) for a year. Own band in Cannes, France (1936), then led Ambrose Blue Lyres (1936). Own band at Café Anglais (1938). Led quartet for ENSA tours in World War II until being injured in 1941. Led own quartet at the Savoy Hotel (1947) and did seasons at Clacton, Margate, Isle of Man, etc., until retiring from full time playing in the mid-1950s to run own booking agency.

BARR, Keith
saxes/clarinet/oboe/arranger/composer

Born: London, 1927
Died: Sydney, Australia, 1971

Played piano during childhood, then specialized on tenor sax at fourteen. Served in the Army from 1945 to 1947 including posting in Austria. After demobilization played in Cab Kaye's Band in West Bromwich (1948). Played in Frank Abbott's Band aboard liner *Queen Mary* and did a London residency with Abbott (1949–50). With Ralph Sharon (1951), then joined Reg Wale on liner *Caronia* (summer 1952). With Ambrose (1953), Ken Moule (1955), Basil and Ivor Kirchin (1955–6), then joined Paul Adam (1956). With Jack Nathan (1957) then worked with Jack Parnell, John Dankworth, etc., before moving to Australia in 1960. Worked first in Sydney, then in Melbourne and Adelaide with Bob Bertles. Settled in Sydney and played in many line-ups including groups led by John Sangster and Jackie Dougan. His death occurred when he suffered a diabetic coma and toppled out of an apartment window.

BARRIGO, Don
tenor sax/alto sax/bass sax/clarinet/flute/
violin/vocals/arranger

Born: London, 12 June 1906
Died: South Africa, 4 May 1977

Worked in London with band led by American saxophonist Don Parker (1926). With Teddy Sinclair's Band in London (autumn 1927). Worked in Germany, with Harry and Sid Roy, with Freddy Schweitzer's Band, and again with Don Parker's Orchestra, before returning to London in late 1929. Again worked in Germany and Denmark, returned to London and played in Billy Mayerl's Orchestra before joining Percival Mackey's Band (September 1931) also deputized with Ambrose (1931). Worked in France with Serge Glykson's Band (1932), also played in band that accompanied Louis Armstrong on his 1932 visit to Europe. With Bert Bowen's Band in London (1933) with Howard Jacobs (summer 1933), with Phil Cardew, and also led own band (1934). With Maurice Winnick (November 1933 to March 1934), with violinist Lou Simmonds (1934), then joined Lew Stone (January 1935). Also featured with Nat Gonella's Georgians. Worked often with Lew Stone from 1935 until 1941, also guested with Val Rosing's Band (1936), briefly with Al Bowlly (March 1937), led own Banditos (1938), own Hawaiian style group (1939), worked as a comedian (1939). Was part of Ambrose's Blue Lyres (directed by Stanley Barnett) in 1940, also in Eddie Carroll's Band (1940), Maurice Winnick's Orchestra (1940). With Harry Roy for a month (March 1941), briefly with Sid Phillips, then served in the Army from May 1941 until June 1944. Freelanced then joined Frank Weir's Band at the Plaza, Derby. Led own band at the Potomac Club, London (1945). Again with Lew Stone from March to December 1946, left to emigrate to South Africa. Opened physiotherapy clinic and combined this with leading own band in Johannesburg (1948) and touring in Africa with Billy Farrell's Band. Later ran own night club and booking agency. After a jaw operation in 1953, he specialized on violin, subsequently fronted various bands and also worked as an actor.

BARRITEAU, Carl Aldric Stanley
clarinet/saxes/piano/arranger

Born: Trinidad, West Indies, 7 February 1914

Received first musical tuition at the Belmont Orphanage, Trinidad, subsequently played in the Trinidad Constabulary Band and remained with them for some years, also gigged in Bert McClean's Jazz Hounds and with the Williams Brothers' Blue Rhythm Band. Moved to Britain, arrived 5 May 1937 and joined Ken Johnson twelve days later. Worked with Johnson until March 1941 and suffered injuries in the air raid that killed Johnson. Own band at Cotton Club, London (June 1941), briefly with Lew Stone, then worked with Ambrose from July until September 1941. With Chappie D'Amato (October 1941), Hatchett's Swingtette (late 1941 to April 1942). Guested with Geraldo and began leading own West Indian Dance Orchestra on gigs and on radio (May 1942). Recorded with Eric Winstone. Two weeks with Joe Loss (summer 1942). Formed own band in November 1942. Guested on radio with Van Phillips, Phil Green and Tommy Bromley. Led own band through World War II, variety tours, etc. Led own band on ENSA tour of Europe (1945). Led own band at Embassy Club, London and played many one-night stands. Led own band for a two year residency at the Eldorado Ballroom, Leith, Scotland, from May 1949. With Cyril Stapleton from June 1951 until March 1952, then re-formed own band until following solo career in 1957. Worked in double act with singer Mae Cooper during the late 1950s and 1960s, occasionally forming up a band for specific engagements, including tour with the Platters, a season in Guernsey, and a tour of American bases in Germany. Emigrated to Australia and made this his base for widespread touring throughout Australasia and the Orient. Became an Australian citizen; living in Sydney during the 1990s.

BARTON, John
banjo/guitar/vocals

Born: Hanwell, London, 7 April 1939

Started on ukulele at six, later heard Les Paul and took up guitar. On banjo with Steve Lane (1957), also gigged with Colin Kingwell's Jazz Bandits. To Denmark with Graham Stewart (deputizing for Jimmy Forey) in spring 1958, worked regularly with Stewart (1959), then did two years' National Service in the Army, joining Alan Elsdon immediately upon being demobilized (June 1961). Left to lead own group the Roadrunners, rejoined Alan Elsdon, then spent six months with Kenny Ball. Again with Alan Elsdon (as part of the Voodoos). Left to play a year's residency at the Georgian Club, London with pianist Ian Armit. Three months with Chris Barber, then became cabaret ventriloquist and singer for two years; as Joe Barton worked as a puppeteer for television shows. Subsequently worked for over ten years as a BBC Special Effects Designer. Gigging regularly on guitar, banjo and vocals through the 1990s.

BASTABLE, 'Johnny' John Sidney
banjo/guitar/vocals

Born: 22 November 1929
Died: 5 December 1985

Worked with the Eagle Jazzband and with Trevor Williams in Middlesex before joining Ken Colyer in the summer of 1954. Took over leadership of the band when Colyer temporarily retired through ill health in 1971. Bastable led the group, as Johnny Bastable's Chosen Six, for two years. He subsequently taught banjo and freelanced with various bands including the Riverside Five Plus One. Bastable first led his Chosen Six for sessions recorded for Doug Dobell's 77 record label in 1957 and 1958, both of these line-ups featured Acker Bilk.

BATES, 'Barney' Colin
piano/arranger

Born: Wales, 1 April 1932

Moved to Lowestoft at fourteen, later studied at Art School and played cornet in local jazz bands. Played in London University Jazz Band, then joined Terry Lightfoot on piano in May 1957. Left after two months, gigged with Mike Peters. Rejoined Terry Lightfoot in January 1958, left in September 1958 to join Kenny Ball's newly-formed band on piano (doubling tuba). Left Kenny Ball in May 1960. Worked with Wally Fawkes (1960), then joined Al Fairweather-Sandy Brown All Stars from March until May 1961. Again with Wally Fawkes and freelancing then rejoining Terry Lightfoot from January 1962 until summer 1963. Worked for almost three years with Alan Elsdon. With Monty Sunshine (1968) and Terry Lightfoot (1968). Freelanced and played solo piano then worked with Acker Bilk for five years until autumn 1977. Led own trio from the late 1970s, worked with various visiting American musicians. Worked briefly with Keith Smith (1978), Alex Welsh (1978) and briefly with George Melly and John Chilton's Feetwarmers. During the 1980s worked with Keith Smith, Digby Fairweather, Sweet Substitute, etc. and played solo residencies. Worked often with Diz Disley in the early 1990s and again briefly with Terry Lightfoot. Joined Chez Chesterman's Hot Stuff in 1993. Continued to play regularly including solo piano work in various clubs until suffering serious injuries in a cycling accident (May 1996), then resumed freelancing.

BATES, 'Django' Leon
keyboards/tenor horn/trumpet/composer

Born: Beckenham, Kent, 2 October 1960

Father a musician, brother Roland a trombonist. Studied piano, violin and trumpet as a teenager in London, first at the Centre for Young Musicians and then at Morley College. Briefly attended the Royal College of Music. Gigged in North London and led own group from 1979. Own trio played residency at John Edge's Waterside Club in Rotherhithe. Worked in the Skank Orchestra (with Iain Ballamy), in Tim Whitehead's Borderline (1981–3), in Clark Tracey's Quartet (1983), with Dudu Pukwana's Zila. Worked again with Iain Ballamy, with Harold Beckett, and became founder-member of Loose Tubes in 1984. With saxophonist Ken Stubbs in First House (including touring Europe), and also part of Bill Bruford's Earth Works (from the 1980s through to 1994), but from early 1980s heavily involved in running own Human Chain, which provided the basis of the eighteen-piece unit Delightful Precipice in the early 1990s. Has undertaken world-wide touring and achieved considerable success with various compositions, which include film soundtracks, and music for drama and dance. Played in Piano Triad and in duo with Joanna MacGregor. Human Chain provided music for the Fifth Floor Theatre Company's production of Simon Black's *Out There* in autumn 1995. Played in Vienna (September 1995), then worked in New York (late 1995). Led Delightful Precipice at festivals (1996).

BATES, 'Phil' Philip Francis
double bass

Born: Brixton, London, 19 June 1931

Father was a bassist and guitarist. Took up double bass in late teens. After service in the Army began playing gigs, including some with pianist Jack Honeyborne. Worked in Jimmy Currie's Quartet. Regularly at the 51 Club, London with Harry Klein, Vic Ash (1956), with Tubby Hayes-Ronnie Scott Jazz Couriers (1958). Toured with Sarah Vaughan, worked in Jack Sharpe's Quintet and in Peter King's Quartet. Played on liner *Mauretania* in Lennie Metcalfe's Band, then worked briefly with John Dankworth (early 1960) before joining Ronnie Ross-Bert Courtley Jazztet from April 1960 until February 1961. Played in theatre orchestras and worked in Kenny Gordon's Trio (1961) and briefly with Sandy Brown. With Alan Clarke in Purley (summer 1962) then regularly with Dick Morrissey from October 1962 until 1968. During this period also with Tony Kinsey's Quintet (at Annie's Room, London) and in Harry South's Big Band. Played in house band at Churchill's Club. Briefly with Tubby Hayes Quartet (1968), then again worked in Pete King's Quartet (1968). Successful freelance from 1970 onwards, including work on cruise liners with Benny Perrin's Band, also accompanied visiting musicians including Sonny Stitt, Jimmy Witherspoon, Judy Collins, Tom Paxton, etc. Worked throughout Europe with Stephane Grappelli for five years during the late 1970s. Worked in Martin Blackwell's Trio and played many gigs for South London Jazz Federation. Leading own trio in 1996, and freelancing.

BATES, 'Tucker' Collin Moffat
piano/composer

Born: New South Wales, Australia, 25 February 1931
Died: New South Wales, Australia, 17 August 1991

Played boogie-woogie on radio as a schoolboy, later studied with Roy Maling. Worked with many line-ups in Sydney, often with bassist Barry Dillon, then moved to England in 1954. Gigged mainly in London but also did a season in Scunthorpe. Moved back to Australia in 1957, then returned to England in late 1958. Led own quartet, which featured saxophonist Dave Aarons (with whom he had worked in Australia). Also led own trio at the Troubadour in Old Brompton Road, London, during the late 1950s. Worked with Wally Fawkes (1959), then joined Bruce Turner's Jump Band from early 1960 until 1964. During this period also deputized in Cyril Stapleton's Orchestra (summer 1961). Again led trio at the Troubadour but also played long solo residency at Flanagan's Restaurant in Kensington. Continued to play jazz gigs and occasionally worked with

Bruce Turner in the early 1970s. From 1971 was part of the Wally Fawkes-John Chilton Feetwarmers and in January 1974 resumed full time touring by working with John Chilton's Feetwarmers accompanying George Melly. Left in October 1977 to play again at Flanagan's Restaurant, and to play gigs with Alan Elsdon, Digby Fairweather, John Barnes, Five-a-Slide, Alan Barnes, etc, and to accompany various visiting American musicians. Rejoined John Chilton's Feetwarmers and George Melly from early 1983 until March 1990. After a tour of the Far East and Australasia he remained behind to settle with his wife in Sydney. He continued to play gigs in that city until shortly before he died of cancer.

BAYLIS, 'Tony' Anthony John
Born: London, 25 May 1935
double bass/bass guitar/sousaphone

Worked with various semi-professional traditional bands in the late 1950s then joined Ian Bell (1961). Led own Jazz Confessors Quintet mainly in the London area (1962–4). Briefly with Bruce Turner, Mick Mulligan and the Fairweather-Brown All Stars. Played for three months in the Clyde Valley Stompers while Ron Mathewson recovered from a hernia operation. Varied freelance work, gigs with Lennie Felix Trio, Pat Hawes, etc., and six months with Franz Pinter's Band at the Playboy Club (late 1965–6). With Long John Baldry's Hoochie Coochie Men (1965), then brief spell in Rod Stewart's Band. On sousaphone with the Temperance Seven for a year (1967) then worked with Alex Welsh (including trip to Newport Jazz Festival) from May 1968 until January 1969. Joined Adge Cutler and the Wurzels (on sousaphone) in January 1969. Remained with the Wurzels after Adge Cutler lost his life in a car crash (1974), and finally left the group in January 1984. By this time had moved to the Bristol area. Worked there regularly with the Dukes of Swing through the late 1980s and early 1990s. Spent a year with Pete Allen (1987–8) then in 1989 began long stay in the Avon Cities Jazz Band. Continues to work mainly in the Bristol area through the 1990s.

BEAMENT, 'Ted' Edward John
Born: Basingstoke, Hampshire, 10 February 1941
piano/composer

Born in Basingstoke while mother was evacuated during World War II, but grew up in Willesden area of London. Father, Ted, played piano and brother Peter is a percussionist. Ted's daughter, Jane, is a professional pianist. Began playing piano at thirteen, did first gig two years later. Worked as a salesman until age of twenty-eight, but played many varied gigs. Turned professional and played seasons and worked on board cruise liners. Led own trio and quartet, regularly accompanied visiting Americans: Sonny Stitt, Joe Newman, Harry Edison, Allan Eager, Jon Eardley, etc. Played in Spike Robinson's Quartet. Did world cruise on liner *QE2* in band led by bass-guitarist Tommy McQuater, Jr. Has regularly accompanied various singers including Maxine Daniels, Helen Shapiro, Joia Claire, etc. Worked often with Willie Garnett, Tommy Whittle, Jimmy Skidmore, Don Weller, Don Rendell, Adrian Macintosh, etc. Joined Humphrey Lyttelton in February 1995.

BEAZLEY, Graham Ivor
double bass/trombone

Born: 10 June 1932
Died: 1979

During the 1950s worked with Eric Silk, Mike Peters and various other jazz bands. Left Dick Charlesworth in 1961 to play a summer season in the Channel Isles. With the Confederates in 1963, briefly with Freddy Randall in 1964, then joined the Bournemouth Symphony Orchestra. He combined this with freelance jazz work, playing on cruise liners and running own business repairing stringed instruments.

BECK, Gordon James
piano/composer

Born: Brixton, London, 16 September 1938

Family moved to South Harrow when Gordon was an infant. Classical piano studied from thirteen to sixteen. Worked as an aeronautical design draughtsman from sixteen until twenty-two. Lived in Canada 1957–8, sat in with local jazz groups. Returned to London, worked in Dave Morse Quintet at Octave Club, Southall (1958), then worked in Peter King's Quartet, including booking at Ronnie Scott's Club. Became full time musician, working in Monte Carlo with Tony Crombie's Band for three months during summer of 1960, and while there also doubled by working with Don Byas. Returned to work as a draughtsman for seven weeks then became a professional musician permanently. In Gus Galbraith's New Stars (autumn 1960), briefly in Bobby Wellins-Ken Wray Quintet (late 1960). With Vic Ash-Harry Klein Five (1961), with Tony Kinsey Quintet, and gigs with Bert Courtley's Sextet (1961). Again with Pete King Quartet then began long musical association with Tubby Hayes, working in Hayes's Quintet (1962). With Tony Kinsey Trio (1963–5), occasionally played in Harry South Big Band and also accompanied visiting American musicians, usually with own Trio from 1965. Worked in Ronnie Scott's Octet (1968), including tour of France. Spent three years with American saxophonist Phil Woods' European Rhythm Machine (including work in Europe and the USA) from 1969–72. Led own Gyroscope in 1972, in Britain and in Portugal. Prolific session work in television and films during the early 1970s. Accompanied various international artistes, guested with Major Surgery and with Ian Hamer's Sextet, toured briefly with Mike Gibbs (1978). Began recording for French labels A1 and JMS in 1978, and achieved considerable success with multi-track solo recordings. Active in jazz education during the 1970s and 1980s, notably at the Barry Summer School, Wales (until 1985). Toured Japan and USA with Allan Holdsworth (1985). Own Trio continued through the 1980s and 1990s, also solo dates, duos (with Brian Dee, etc.) and accompanying Helen Merrill on an occasional basis (from 1984–94) in Europe, touring with Didier Lockwood and playing in duos with Allan Holdsworth, including US recordings in 1995. Prolific work and extensive recordings in France, including engagements with organist Emmanuel Bex (1995). Duos in Britain with Phil Woods (May 1996).

BECKETT, 'Harry' Harold Winston
trumpet/flugelhorn/piano/composer

Born: St Michael Parish, Barbados,
West Indies, 30 May 1935

His son, Louis, plays guitar, keyboards and drums. First played trumpet at school in Barbados, and in local Salvation Army Band. Original inspiration was local star Michael Wyatt. Moved to Britain in 1954, worked with Leslie 'Jiver' Hutchinson (1955), freelanced (mainly in London) and often worked with Ambrose Campbell. Worked with Charles Mingus on film *All Night Long* in 1961. Regularly with Graham Collier line-ups from the early 1960s through to the 1970s. Long musical association with Ray Russell from the late 1960s. With the New Jazz Orchestra, Herbie Goins Nightimers, Mick Eve, drummer Norman Caldas' Quintet, Martin Joseph, Barbara Thompson, John Surman, Mike Westbrook, Keef Hartley, the Brotherhood of Breath, John Warren, etc. Often worked with Stan Tracey from 1974 onwards, regularly with Kathy Stobart's Band in the 1970s, also with Mike Gibbs, Alan Cohen, Ronnie Scott, John Dankworth, etc. Led own line-ups during the 1980s, including trip to Middle East in 1984, also toured India. Worked with Art Themen, Nick Weldon, Don Weller, John Surman, Charlie Watts Big Band, etc., also worked in Denmark with John Dyani and with the New Jungle Orchestra. Toured Europe with Dudu Pukwana's Zila (1985). Part of the Jazz Warriors from 1986–91, consistently active in jazz education. Continues to freelance through the 1990s, which includes international bookings. Worked in Anglo-Italian Quartet (1991), in quartet with Elton Dean, with pianist Bruce Boardman, leading own line-ups, etc.

BEECHAM, John Michael
trombone/tuba/arranger

Born: Manor Park, Ilford, Essex, 26 November 1939

Took up trombone at fifteen, then, as a teenager (along with Mike Cotton) played in George Perry's Band before joining Peter Ridge's Jazz Band. (Left studies at Queen Mary College, London to turn professional.) Remained with Mike Cotton when that trumpeter became leader of Pete Ridge's line-up early in 1961. Stayed with Mike Cotton in the early 1970s and was thus part of the Mike Cotton Sound and Satisfaction. Began doubling on tuba during the early 1970s. Worked in Johnny Johnson's Band Waggon for a year then spent seven years with the Kinks before working with Ken Colyer from 1980 until 1983. In the early 1980s played tuba in Chris Barber's Band (augmented for international tour with Doctor John). In 1983 began working with Monty Sunshine and continued to do so through the 1990s, during this period also gigged in various other ensembles including Five-A-Slide (founder-member), Excelsior Brass Band, London Ragtime Orchestra and in John Slaughter's Blues Band.

BENCE, Harry
alto sax/clarinet

Born: Wishaw, Lanarkshire, Scotland, 20 March 1928

Married to singer Elizabeth Batty. Father (Frederick J. Bence) was a multi-instrumentalist and teacher, specializing on clarinet. Harry's son Freddie is a drummer, Harry's brother Jimmy is a saxophonist. With George Elrick at thirteen, then played lead alto in Lauri Blandford's Band in Glasgow (1943–4). Worked with Carl Barriteau then joined Joe Loss in March 1946. Served in RAF 1946–8 (led No. 4 Regional Dance Band at Henlow). Featured with Ken Mackintosh while on leave from the RAF. After demobilization rejoined Joe Loss (late 1948). Left Joe Loss in April 1950 to work with Eric Winstone (1950–1). With Ted Heath and Sydney Lipton then rejoined Eric Winstone (November 1952). Left Winstone in October 1953 to form own band, disbanded in December 1954, worked with Harry Leader, then formed new band in April 1956. Led own band at Grand Hotel, Calcutta (1957–8), subsequently led own big band in Scotland (Glasgow, Dunoon, Edinburgh) and in Sunderland during the 1960s. Led band on final voyage of the liner *Queen*

Mary, and own groups on cruise ships *Adventurer*, *Princess*, *Ambassador* and *Rotterdam* from the late 1960s through the 1970s. Briefly ran own hotel in Scotland, then became Entertainments Executive for Pontin's, led own band at holiday camps and on various liners, also directed the New Geraldo Orchestra in 1976. Led own all-star band (Jimmy Deuchar, Red Price, etc.) for year's residency at Cabaret Club in Hong Kong during the late 1970s. During the 1980s and 1990s led the New Squadronaires.

BENNETT, John Edward
Born: Hackney, London, 2 January 1936
trombone/vocals

Was originally taught piano by his father, took up trombone at sixteen, played in Southgate County School Orchestra. With Trevor Williams before joining Terry Lightfoot in October 1956 (replacing John Hunt). Left Terry Lightfoot to join Kenny Ball in September 1958, continued to work with Kenny Ball through the 1990s.

BENSON, Ivy
Born: Leeds, Yorkshire, 11 November 1913
alto sax/piano/vocals
Died: Clacton, Essex, 6 May 1993

Began on piano (first broadcast at the age of nine) then specialized on alto sax. Discovered by Leeds cinema organist Henry Croudson and subsequently played in Edna Croudson's Rhythm Girls (a sextet that worked mainly in Yorkshire) from 1929 until the mid-1930s. Toured with Hylda Baker's Show and led briefly at Hylda's Club in London (early 1937), then joined Teddy Joyce's New Ladies Orchestra (February 1937), became leader of Teddy Joyce's Girl Friends, then joined Harold Ramsay's Orchestra (1938). Moved back to Leeds to recuperate from illness, worked locally with George Adamson's Band, then ran own touring *Meet the Girls* show before taking own octet into Streatham Locarno, London, for summer 1940 residency. Moved to the Ritz, Manchester (1940), then formed own touring band which did shows for ENSA (Entertainments National Service Association) throughout World War II, and played the London Palladium (1943). Continued to play for servicemen overseas during the 1950s, 1960s and 1970s, combining these tours with work in theatres, ballrooms and on radio and television. Led own band until the early 1980s, then moved to Clacton and played local gigs on piano, organ and vocals until a few days before her death.

BENSON, John Edwin
Born: North London, 20 July 1947
double bass/tuba/guitar/vocals

Introduced to jazz by his clarinet-playing brother Gerry. Started on banjo, then played guitar in skiffle groups, and with rock and roll and rhythm-and-blues bands. During the late 1960s led own band and worked in Tony Allen's Band as well as freelancing in clubs and on seasons. Later played with Brian Knight's Blues By Six and with Monty Sunshine (until summer 1977). Joined Kenny Ball in August 1977, making debut in Perth, Australia. Featured with Kenny Ball through the 1990s.

BENSTEAD, 'Bobby' Robert
trumpet

Born: Shepherd's Bush, London, 1922
Died: Winnipeg, Canada, 1960

Left Stan Atkins to join Oscar Rabin (April 1938). Played regularly with Oscar Rabin's Band before serving in the RAF during World War II. Rejoined Rabin in late 1945 and remained until the early 1950s. Played in the London Palladium Orchestra then emigrated to Canada and played for two-and-a-half years in a Canadian Army band before dying suddenly.

BENTLEY, 'Jack' John Alexander
trombone/cello/composer

Born: Salford, Lancashire, 29 April 1913
Died: Cookham, Berkshire, 22 April 1994

Father was a cellist with the Hallé Orchestra. Began on cello. Joined the Army as a musician at the age of fourteen. Studied at the Royal School of Military Music, Kneller Hall, Twickenham and began specializing on trombone. Became a sergeant and played in the band of the Second Hampshire Regiment. Bought himself out of the service in 1936 to join Mrs Jack Hylton's Band, later worked in Jack Hylton's Band until rejoining the Army in autumn 1939. Managed to combine freelance playing with service in the Irish Guards' Band, working with Raymond Doughty's Band at Cricklewood Palais, London (late 1939), in Queen's Theatre Orchestra (early 1940), with Geraldo (1940), Jack Payne (1941), Jack Jackson (1942), London Symphony Orchestra (1942) and with Harry Roy. Toured Italy and North Africa with the Band of the Irish Guards (1944), then returned to Britain. Worked with Ambrose (1945). After demobilization joined Ted Heath for five years, until September 1950. Left Heath to compose and to write scripts. Became show-business editor of the *Sunday Mirror* until retiring at 65. Continued to write scripts for television. Was married to actress Wendy Craig.

BERLY, 'Harry' Henry J.
viola/clarinet/tenor sax/ocarina

Born: 1905
Died: London, 1937

With Geoffrey Goodhart's Orchestra at the Piccadilly Hotel, London (1925), then, as part of Jean Pougnet's String Quartet was added to Jack Hylton's Kit-Cat Band (1926). Worked with Jack Hylton's Orchestra from 1926 until 1930. With Arthur Lally (April 1930 to April 1931). With Roy Fox at Monseigneur Restaurant from June 1931, remained when Lew Stone took over band in 1932. Extensive freelance recordings in the late 1920s and early 1930s. With Teddy Joyce (1935) toured with the Radio Three in 1936. Died in the path of an underground train at the Oval station, London.

BERRY, 'Steve' Stephen
double bass/bass guitar/cello/
composer/arranger

Born: Gosport, Hampshire, 24 August 1957

Moved with family to Shropshire at age of eight. Took up guitar at fifteen, became singer/ songwriter, guitarist. Moved to London in 1979, bought double bass and took lessons from Chris Laurence. In 1980 teamed up with Django Bates and drummer Dave Pattman. This trio (with Dave Trigwell sometimes taking Dave Pattman's place) played regularly at John Edge's Waterside Club in Rotherhithe. Steve Buckley (alto sax) and Chris Batchelor (trumpet) joined the trio there;

later these five all played together in the twenty-one piece Loose Tubes. Initially, in 1983, they were part of Graham Collier's Creative Music Workshop Band from which Loose Tubes later evolved (in 1984). Steve Berry, Django Bates and administrator Colin Lazzerini (who thought of the name) became the principal organizers of Loose Tubes, with Berry and Bates contributing many of the group's arrangements. Berry remained with Loose Tubes until the summer of 1989. During the 1980s he also played for various West End shows, including *Blues in the Night,* and freelanced. He gigged and recorded with Billy Jenkins, recorded with Ian Carr, etc. Led own trio from 1987 (which first recorded in 1988). During the late 1980s and early 1990s worked with visiting American musicians including Scott Hamilton, Tal Farlow, Art Farmer and pianist Ellyn Rucker. Has accompanied various singers including June Tabor, Dagmar Krause and Ute Lemper. Often with Mike Westbrook's Big Band since 1991. Leading own Foolish Hearts quartet in 1996 (with Nikki Iles, Anthony Kerr and Bosco de Oliveira) and since the late 1980s extremely active in music education: at colleges, on summer courses, workshops, etc.

BILK, 'Acker' Bernard Stanley
Born: Pensford, Somerset, 28 January 1929
clarinet/vocals

Played piano as a child but took up clarinet while serving in Egypt with the Royal Engineers (1948). After demobilization formed own band which played regularly in Bristol. Moved to London, played for seven months with Ken Colyer, then, for domestic reasons, moved back to the West Country in late 1954. Again led Paramount Jazz Band in Bristol area; the band also toured Poland in the summer of 1956. Acker deputized in Bristol's Crescent City Stompers during early 1957, then resumed leading his own band. The band, with personnel changes, played a residency in London during the summer of 1957. It became fully professional in October 1957 and soon afterwards played dates in Düsseldorf, Germany. The band's success was consolidated by Acker's 1961 recording of 'Stranger on the Shore'. Widespread international touring by the band followed, and many subsequent sessions for Acker with string accompaniment. The band's wide-ranging schedule continued through the 1990s. Acker also played a series of duo dates with Humphrey Lyttelton in 1993 and 1994.

BILLETT, 'Cuff' Keith Stewart
Born: Portsmouth, Hampshire, 30 June 1940
trumpet

Began playing trumpet at fifteen. With the Vieux Carré Band (1956–60). Left to work with Barry Martyn from 1960 until 1967, during this period also played in the New Teao Brass Band. Co-led Strong Jazz, with Bill Greenow (1967–9), also in the New Tia Juana Band (1964–9) and in Mike Casimir's Paragon Brass Band. Toured briefly in drummer Guy Fenton's Band (1974). Led own New Europa Band from 1970 through the 1990s. During the 1980s and 1990s worked with Martin Boorman's Mardi Gras Band, Colin Strickland's Hand Reared Boys, Dick Cook's Jambalaya, and with John Petters. First visited USA in 1963; guest appearance in New York and Minneapolis in 1990. Throughout his career has regularly accompanied visiting American musicians, recording with many of them. Has also been part of Butch Thompson's King Oliver Centennial Band since 1985, (playing alongside cornetist Charlie De Vore).

BIRD, Keith Charles
saxes/clarinet

Born: 9 April 1922
Died: 1983

Father was a professional saxophonist. Took up sax at fifteen, played first gigs at sixteen with semi-professional bands in NW London, then at seventeen played professionally for a summer season at Clacton, Essex. With Johnny Claes (1942), then did ENSA (Entertainments National Service Association) tours with Herman Darewski. Joined RAF. While stationed near Newcastle upon Tyne played local gigs, then after posting to RAF Uxbridge led own quintet in Ealing before serving in Italy (1944) as part of the Desert Air Force Band. After demobilization joined Geraldo for seven years from September 1946, during this period also led own sextet, which was featured in the film *Melody Club*. Active freelance during the 1960s and 1970s, playing many sessions, with Robert Farnon, Ted Heath etc., and worked in BBC Theatre Orchestra.

BISCOE, 'Chris' Christopher Dennis
saxes/clarinet/flute/piccolo/composer

Born: East Barnet, Hertfordshire,
5 February 1947

Started on alto sax at sixteen. Studied English at Sussex University, then settled in London. Played in National Youth Jazz Orchestra from 1970 until 1973. Occasionally led own groups from 1969. Led Broken Biscuits from 1974 to 1976 (Sam Fendridge on bass, Dick Pearce on trumpet), was also part of Julian Marshall's Equus (1975) and occasionally with John Walters' Landscape (1975). Regularly with Trevor Taylor's Worlds in Collision (1976), often in Red Brass (Dick Pearce on trumpet, Pete Hurt on saxophone) for several years from 1975. With Talisker in the early 1980s. In 1979 began long, continuing musical association with Mike Westbrook; widespread international touring in various Westbrook line-ups including the Trio (with Mike and Kate Westbrook). Frequently in Brotherhood of Breath through the 1980s and early 1990s. With George Russell's Anglo-American Living Time Orchestra for tours from 1986 through to the mid-1990s (including recordings). Worked in Europe with double bassist Didier Levallet. Biscoe's quartet, formed in 1979, developed into a quintet (with the addition of Italian trombonist Danilo Terenzi) and then into a sextet, which has recorded for Biscoe's own label Walking Wig. His collective free improvising quartet, Full Monte, formed in 1988 (with guitarist Brian Godding, drummer Tony Marsh and Brazilian bassist Marcio Mattos) has continued to perform in Britain and France through to 1996, recently collaborating on record with French violinist Dominique Pifarely. Biscoe continues his varied work schedule through the 1990s: with Mike Westbrook, leading own groups, working with cellist Ben Davis' group, in Hermeto Pascoal's Big Band, in the Baritone Band, in the London Jazz Orchestra, etc.

BISHOP, 'Dicky' Richard William
guitar/banjo/vocals

Born: London, 16 April 1935

In Brent Valley Jazz Band during the late 1940s. Worked with the Albemarle Jazz Band, then did two years in the RAF (played in service jazz band with Terry Lightfoot). After demobilization gigged with Alan Elsdon, then worked in Charlie Conner's Band, also worked as a solo country singer and guitarist. Joined Chris Barber in 1954 (also featured in Barber's Skiffle Group). Left Barber in late 1956 to work with Lonnie Donegan. Led own Sidekicks, then worked with Mickey Ashman from summer 1958 until spring 1959. With Kenny Ball from spring 1959 until early

1960, again led Sidekicks, then rejoined Kenny Ball from May until November 1960. With Monty Sunshine from early 1961 to spring 1964. Gave up playing temporarily, then formed own Trio (with Buck Taylor on bass). With Terry Lightfoot from 1968 to 1971. Moved to West Country, joined Roy Pellett's Band in summer 1972. Worked with Rod Mason-Ian Wheeler Band (1974–5) and with Rod Mason before rejoining Roy Pellett for work in Europe. Settled in Germany and continued to play regularly. Guested with Chris Barber for widespread touring in 1994, featured with Papa Humbser's Jazzmen in Ulm, Germany (1995).

BLACK, Stanley
piano/arranger/composer

Born: London, 14 June 1913

Originally taught by Rae Robertson, first professional work at Empress Kinema, Islington, then worked in Maurice Burman's Band (1930). Won *Melody Maker* arranging contest (1931). With Sydney Lipton (1931), accompanied Leslie 'Hutch' Hutchinson at London Palladium (late 1931) and played residency at Empress Rooms, Kensington (1932). With Howard Jacobs, Joe Orlando, Maurice Winnick, etc., before working with Lew Stone from July 1934 until November 1935, recorded with Coleman Hawkins (1934). Briefly with Teddy Joyce (1935) then worked regularly with Harry Roy from January 1936 until 1940 (including trip to South America in 1938). Briefly with Ambrose then spent a few months in the RAF (1940), before rejoining Harry Roy until September 1941. Concentrated on arranging and conducting, became leader of the BBC Dance Orchestra in 1944, later led various BBC Orchestras, then became musical director for Associated Pathé. Subsequently did a great deal of composing and conducting for films, television and recordings. Did regular international tours with own orchestra and also appeared as a guest conductor for various classical orchestras throughout the world. Awarded OBE.

BLAIR, 'Eddie' Edward Dunning
trumpet/flugelhorn

Born: Johnstone, Renfrewshire, Scotland, 25 June 1927

Father played cornet and violin. Eddie began on cornet at ten and soon joined the Johnstone Silver Band for three years. Played with other brass bands and did various jazz gigs and dance band work before joining the Royal Corps of Signals from 1945 until autumn 1948. He was not an Army musician but played regularly in various service dance bands. After demobilization studied at Glasgow College of Technology. Played in George Scott Henderson's Quintet and various other jazz groups and worked with Bert Tobias in Glasgow. With Ken Mackintosh in Glasgow (for six weeks), then took leave from college and played further two weeks with Mackintosh in London before returning to Glasgow to work regularly with Bert Tobias, from December 1950 until joining Johnny Dankworth Seven in August 1951. With Dankworth until joining Ted Heath from May 1954 until summer of 1965, thereafter became highly successful freelance through the 1990s, featured with many ensembles both as a section player and as a jazz soloist.

BLAKE, Cyril McDonald
trumpet/guitar/vocals

Born: Trinidad, West Indies, 1897
Died: London, 3 December 1951

Brother of drummer George 'Happy' Blake. Took up banjo and guitar while staying with relatives in New York City. Served in the Merchant Navy during World War I, then settled in Britain.

Worked on guitar with the Southern Syncopated Orchestra in Britain (1921). Married Olive Douglas in Manchester (November 1923). Worked in London in various West End clubs during the 1920s then moved to France and played in various cabaret clubs. Played trumpet in Thompson's Negro Band during the late 1920s, including tour of Germany, Holland, Norway, Denmark and Spain. Toured with various shows in France, and is said to have worked with Josephine Baker. Continued to double on trumpet and guitar. Joined Leon Abbey's Band in Europe and worked with them in London (March 1930). Worked in France with Moise Simon's Rhumba Band for five months. By now specializing on trumpet he worked in London with pianist Jack London, with Happy Blake and in Rudolph Dunbar's Orchestra during the years 1933-4. Again with Happy Blake (1934-5). In Leslie Thompson's Emperors of Jazz, then joined Ken Johnson (1936). Briefly with Ike Hatch (1936). With Joe Appleton's Band (1937). Led own band at Havana Club, London and worked there with Jack Davies (1938-9). With Rudolph Dunbar (1940). Formed own band (leading on trumpet) and played various residencies in London: at Jig's Club (from 1941), Bag O'Nails (1942), Havana Club (1942), West One (1942), Barbarina (1942-3), Chesterfield (1944), Panama (1946), Goose and Gander (1947), Blue Lagoon (1948), etc. Again served briefly in the Merchant Navy during World War II and worked with Don Marino Barreto (1941), also toured with Clarie Wears' Rhumba Band (1942). During the 1940s occasionally played in various calypso groups (usually on guitar). Led own Calypso Serenaders (1950), worked in drummer Freddy Newstead's Band (1951), played gigs with Charlie Galbraith and did variety act with Slim Harris. Toured Germany with calypso singer Lord Kitchener (1951).

BLANNIN, 'Pete' Peter
double bass

Born: East London, 22 May 1926

Made tentative efforts on guitar and drums, then took up bass and gigged around the West Ham area. Served in Merchant Navy then lived for two years in New Zealand (1946-8). Returned to London, worked in the Jive Bombers, and in Southsea with Johnny Franks (1948). With Revell Terry for six months at the Stork Club (1949), then to Sweden and Norway with organist Robin Richmond (July to August 1949). Gigged with Victor Feldman and with Leon Roy Big Band (late 1949). In Jock Scott's Band aboard liner *Caronia* for world cruise (late 1949-50). With Ronnie Ball on liner *Queen Mary*, studied with Arnold Fishkind in New York (1951). With Ronnie Ball in London (spring 1951), then toured with Vic Lewis before brief spell with Frank Weir at Churchill's, London. Again with Ronnie Ball trio (September 1951 to January 1952). With Johnnie Gray, then to India with Eddie Carroll for Calcutta and New Delhi residencies (July 1952 to March 1953), subsequently with Victor Feldman in Bombay until October 1953. Returned to London, worked with Harry Parry at the Washington Club, gigged with Tony Kinsey, then worked with Bill McGuffie and with Ambrose (summer 1954), deputized in Ted Heath's Band. With Tino Christidi at the Pigalle, London (1954), then joined Tubby Hayes (1955). With Tony Kinsey (1956-7), with Oscar Rabin at the Lyceum Ballroom, London (1958). With Don Rendell-Bert Courtley Jazz Committee (1959), left to work with Humphrey Lyttelton (March 1960 to late 1964), then joined Long John Baldry for several months. With Ian Armit at the Georgian Club, London in the 1960s, then left full time music to attend college for three years, subsequently became a teacher and freelance bassist. Lived and taught in Sweden (1974-6) then returned to England and taught music and general subjects until resuming full time playing in the 1990s, leading own quartet, gigging and working often in the Cambridge Riverside Band.

BLOCK, Jack (used BLAKE and MYERS as his stage names)
trumpet

Born: Hackney, London, 10 July 1898
Died: London, August 1966

Was originally taught music in an Orphanage Band, subsequently played in a Jewish Lads' Brigade Band. Worked in the Frisco Jazz Band at Hammersmith Palais (December 1920 to March 1921). With the Albany Jazz Band in Birmingham (1921) then worked in Ostend with the Six Clocks before playing residency in Norway with Laurie Huntington's Dixie Five (September 1921). With the Happy Six and with Mitchell's Syncopated Orchestra in London (October 1921 to July 1922). With the Happy Four (1922–3) and with the Happy Six in Paris (1923). With Moody's Broadway Four (1924–5) then, together with the trombonist from that band, Ellis Jackson, formed double act 'Blake and Jackson'. Left professional music in the early 1930s and became a publican.

BLUNDY, 'Gordon' Henry Gordon
trombone/piano/vocals

Born: North London, 11 May 1930

Played with the Georgia Jazz Band, Geoff Kemp's Band, Tony (Lonnie) Donegan's Band, Bill Brunskill and George Webb's Dixielanders before working regularly in Mike Daniels' Delta Jazz Band from August 1952 until October 1960. During this period also gigged with various bands including Sandy Brown's (1954). Rejoined Mike Daniels from February 1961 until July 1964. With Brian Green's New Orleans Stompers for five years from 1964. Temporarily gave up regular playing for two years before resuming full schedule and joining the Midnite Follies Orchestra from July 1978 through the 1980s, also worked with Harry Gold for two years from late 1979. Occasionally with the London Ragtime Orchestra including trip to Switzerland. Was part of the Mike Daniels Reunion Band from 1985 until December 1993. Worked with Brian Green again from 1994, but also active with other bands, including Vile Bodies, through the 1990s, and leading own Jazz Knights (1996).

BOND, Graham John Clifton
alto sax/organ/piano/vocals

Born: Romford area, Essex, 28 October 1937
Died: Finsbury Park, London, 8 May 1974

Piano from age of six, oboe and cello at school, then took up alto sax at fifteen. Played in band formed at school. Co-led the Terry Graham Trio (with drummer Terry Lovelock). Brief Army service. Played piano (and some alto sax) in Majorca during summer of 1957. Gigged around the London area, often with Terry Lovelock, occasionally with John Burch, Dick Heckstall-Smith and Dick Morrissey. With Goudie Charles Quintet (spring 1960). Worked as a salesman, joined Don Rendell Quintet in May 1961, also occasionally in New Departures Band (accompanying Pete Brown and Michael Horovitz). Left Don Rendell to join Alexis Korner's Blues Incorporated (autumn 1962), also with John Burch's Octet in the early 1960s. Left Alexis Korner in February 1963 to form own organ trio, which developed into the Graham Bond Organization. Led this group until 1968, then worked spasmodically in the USA before returning to Britain in August 1969 to form new group, Initiation. Worked in Ginger Baker's Airforce until early 1971. Worked with Jack Bruce (1971) and with Pete Brown (1972). Suffered ill health but worked briefly in Magus in late 1973. Died in the path of an underground train at Finsbury Park station. A biography by Harry Shapiro, *Graham Bond – The Mighty Shadow*, was first published in 1992.

BOURKE, 'Stan' Stanley Williams
Born: Tottenham, London, 21 October 1929
drums

Family moved to Stanmore, Middlesex when Stan was three. At eleven played in local Church Lads' Brigade Band, at sixteen joined Billy Minting's Band (directed by trumpeter Nick Nichol) for residency at Wembley Town Hall. Gigged with various line-ups before joining Freddy Randall from late 1953 until early 1957. Left to work in Betty Smith's Quintet for over four years, then joined Phil Tate in June 1961. Worked with Tate for several years on a full time basis, and later fulfilled special engagements with him, such as 25 years playing for the Miss World contest. Extensive freelance work for radio, records and television from 1970 onwards; qualified as a pilot in 1968. Played residency at Danny La Rue's Club with trumpeter Ian Hamilton, and from the 1970s through to the 1990s played various West End shows including *Chorus Line*, *42nd Street*, *City of Angels*, etc., but continued to play jazz dates with Eddie Thompson's Trio, Kenny Baker, Jack Emblow-John McLevy, Digby Fairweather, Val Wiseman, Dave Shepherd, etc., and to back many visiting Americans including Ruby Braff, Al Grey, Kenny Davern, etc.

BOWDEN, Colin Albert Edwin
Born: Hampstead, London, 29 February 1932
drums

Started playing drums after RAF service (1950–2). Sat in with Steve Lane's Band, then joined Cy Laurie. With Jeremy French's Band, with Trevor Williams and with Sonny Morris before joining Ken Colyer in September 1955. Left Colyer in June 1961 to work with Alan Elsdon for six months. With Ken Sims from early 1962 until joining Doug Richford from August 1962 until 1963 (including tour of Denmark). Temporarily left full time music but gigged with many bands. Led own trio in Seven Kings, Essex and played in Mike Daniels' Band (1966). Moved out of London and worked with Barry Palser from 1967. With the New Crane River Jazz Band intermittently from 1972 through the 1980s (including tour of Germany). Occasionally with Ken Colyer in the 1970s and played gigs with Sammy Rimington (1977) and with Lord Arsenal (Allan Bradley). During the 1980s and 1990s freelanced with many musicians including Cy Laurie, Eggy Ley, Sonny Morris, Phil Mason, etc. Extensive international touring with Chris Barber in 1994. Many freelance sessions throughout his career, including recordings with Humphrey Lyttelton and Alex Welsh.

BOWDEN, 'Ron' Ronald Arthur
Born: Fulham, London, 22 February 1928
drums

Gigged around West London with pianist Ralph Dollimore and tenor saxist Pete Hawker, then joined the Crane River Jazz Band in March 1949. With Ken Colyer in 1953, then worked with Chris Barber from May 1954 until November 1957. Ran own restaurant in Brighton for a year (from early 1958), and played local gigs with pianist Terry Whitney and trumpeter Les Jowett. Returned to London, toured with singer Wee Willie Harris before joining Kenny Ball in July 1959, replacing Tony Budd (1931–76). With Kenny Ball through the 1990s, but also played various reunion tours with Chris Barber (25th anniversary, 40th anniversary, etc.).

BOWLLY, 'Al' Albert
vocals/guitar/banjo/piano

Born: Delagoa Bay, Lourenco Marques, Mozambique, 7 January 1899
Died: London, 17 April 1941

Mother from Lebanon, father from Greece. Brother, Misch a pianist, cousin of bandleader Bill Gerhardi. Spent early life in Durban and Johannesburg, South Africa, gigged with local bands on banjo and guitar. Joined Edgar Adeler's Syncopators and left home to tour India, then moved on to work at the Grand Hotel, Calcutta. Joined Jimmy Lequime's Band in Calcutta (on banjo and vocals), then worked with Lequime (and with Monia Liter) in Singapore until 1927, then rejoined Edgar Adeler. Travelled to Germany in 1927, worked first with violinist Robert Gaden, later with Arthur Briggs, George Carhart, Fred Bird and John Abriani. Brief stay in Paris, then returned to Germany. Moved to London to join Fred Elizalde in October 1928, left a year later, toured briefly with the Blue Boys. Began recording regularly with Ray Noble in 1930. Joined Roy Fox in 1931. With Lew Stone from 1932 until 1934 (except for season in Holland with Ray Noble, August 1933, and solo variety dates). Prolific freelance recordings throughout 1930s. Sailed to USA with Ray Noble in September 1934, and worked in the USA with Noble before returning to Britain in late 1936. Formed own short-lived band for March 1937 debut, throat trouble caused the group to disband and eventually led to surgery in the USA in autumn 1937. Returned to London in December 1937. Rejoined Lew Stone in 1938. Freelance recordings, and guest appearances on radio shows. Further throat problems curtailed activities in 1939. Then formed duo with singer-guitarist Jimmy Messini (1940), also did solo variety tours and further freelance recordings in 1940 and 1941. He was killed in a World War II air raid; a landmine dropped close to his flat in Jermyn Street, London. *Al Bowlly*, by Sid Colin and Tony Staveacre, was first published in 1979.

BOYLE, Gary
guitar/composer

Born: Patna, Bihar, India, 24 November 1941

Moved to London with his family in the late 1940s. Took up guitar in his early teens and played local gigs before working with pianist-organist Brian Auger and singer Julie Driscoll in 1966. Studied at Leeds College of Music for two years, then rejoined Brian Auger. During the early 1970s worked with Mike Westbrook, Keith Tippett, Mike Gibbs, Alan Jackson's Kinkade, John Dankworth, etc. Taught at summer schools. Led own Isotope from 1972 until 1975, then settled in Colne, Lancashire, and used this as a base for widespread touring, gigging and appearing at various international festivals. Mainly occupied with leading own successful trio, Triple Echo, during the 1990s, but also worked in duo with John Etheridge, with Nancy Hunter's Band, etc., also toured Britain with Eberhard Weber in 1992. Moved to South West France in 1995 but continued to fulfil international touring schedule.

BRAMWELL, 'Bill' William
guitar/bass/vocals

Born: 1919
Died: 13 September 1968

Started on guitar but played double bass (and guitar) during service in RAF. Mainly on guitar while stationed in Malta. After demobilization worked with Freddy Randall (1947–8), briefly with Carlo Krahmer, then went to South Africa with Reg Wale's Band to play a residency in Cape Town (early 1948). Returned to Britain in May 1950, did solo guitar and vocal act in clubs, then joined Jack La Roc's Quartet (1950). With Rex Denby (late 1950), then worked aboard *Caronia* liner in Reg Wale's Band (1950–1). With Gerry Moore (on bass) during the early 1950s, and with Leslie 'Jiver' Hutchinson, Harry Gold (1954–5) and Laurie Gold (1956). With Dill Jones (bass and guitar) late 1956 to summer 1957. With Chas McDevitt Skiffle Group (1957), then joined Mick Mulligan (on guitar) in 1958. Active freelance during the 1960s (mainly on guitar) with Dave Lee, Fairweather-Brown All Stars, Steve Benbow, Tony Coe, etc., also composed for television, including *Candid Camera* theme.

BRANSCOMBE, Alan
multi-instrumentalist

Born: Wallasey, Cheshire, 4 June 1936
Died: London, 27 October 1986

His grandfather was a professional musician, his father was a semi-professional drummer. Began playing drums at four, alto sax at twelve. Did ENSA (Entertainments National Service Organization) tours as a child. Played gigs on piano and alto sax as a schoolboy. Left Wallasey Grammar School at sixteen, did a summer season in Guernsey, then returned home and worked in Ellesmere Port in band led by Artie Williams, also worked in Liverpool with Paul Vaughan's Band, and led own group. Became an Army musician (1954–6) and served in Germany with the Third Hussars, mainly playing clarinet. After demobilization again worked in Liverpool, with Red Carter, etc., also led own band at the Cavern (1957), then joined Lennie Metcalfe's Band on the liner *Mauretania* (playing alto sax) on cruises to the West Indies and USA (late 1957). Settled in London and joined Vic Ash's Sextet (summer 1958) playing piano, vibes, alto and tenor saxes. Left Ash in autumn 1959 to work for nine months in Tony Kinsey's Quartet (mainly on alto sax) then joined John Dankworth in summer of 1960 (on piano and vibes). Spent almost five years with Dankworth. During this period also accompanied visiting American musicians, and worked occasionally with Tony Crombie and in Downbeat Big Band, etc. Toured Japan with Stanley Black (1965). With Harry South Big Band (late 1965), then concentrated on freelance work and played many recording and television sessions, often working as a house-musician at Ronnie Scott's Club. Recorded with Stan Tracey, Tubby Hayes. Was out of action for several months through pneumonia (spring 1969), then played in Tubby Hayes' Big Band (July 1969). Toured Europe with Stan Getz in 1970, then returned to active freelance schedule, played in Bobby Lamb-Ray Premru Big Band, and often worked in Ian Hamer's Sextet, in Stan Tracey's Orchestra, and in Tony Kinsey's Band. Despite persistent ill health, and suffering injuries in a fall, continued to freelance, and occasionally co-led a quintet with Jack Sharpe. Much of the final year of his life was spent in hospital.

BRAY, 'Jim' James Michael
double bass/sousaphone

Born: Richmond, Surrey, 24 April 1927

Educated in Texas during World War II, then served in the Fleet Air Arm as a pilot. Took up tuba in 1948, double bass two years later. With Lonnie Donegan's Band, Bill Brunskill and Ray Orpwood's Phoenix Jazz Band before joining Ken Colyer in March 1953, remaining when Chris

Barber became leader in 1954. Left Barber to join Humphrey Lyttelton in August 1955. Left Lyttelton in June 1957, worked with Laurie Gold, Mick Mulligan, Johnny Parker and Diz Disley before joining Graham Stewart for a year in June 1958. Further work with Diz Disley, then temporary return to Chris Barber in February 1960. With Bruce Turner's Jump Band from spring 1960 until 1964. Spent several years teaching in India, then returned to London and did prolific freelance work with many jazz groups, including long spell with Bill Brunskill. During the 1980s often played in Bahrain with band organized by drummer David Mills. Toured Germany with Lonnie Donegan (1981), and did several reunion tours with Chris Barber (covering the years 1975 to 1994). Spent long periods in India during the mid-1990s, but continued to freelance mainly with bands in and around London.

BREEN, Bobby (Victor GARRICK)
vocals/conga drum

Born: Kingston, Jamaica, West Indies, 9 April 1927
Died: Sutton, Surrey, 18 December 1972

Served in the Merchant Navy before settling in Britain. Worked with Tommy Smith's Band in Liverpool, then moved to London in the 1950s. With Tony Crombie before joining Tubby Hayes. Worked for several years with John Dankworth during the 1960s, also with quintet led by guitarist Wes Minster (1962). During the late 1960s and early 1970s appeared mainly in cabaret but also guested with various small groups including Jack Duff's Quartet, Tony Lee's Trio, Eddie Thompson's Trio, etc., until hospitalized with cancer.

BREEZE, Eric
trombone/trumpet

Born: Manchester, Lancashire, 27 December 1912
Deceased

Brother Wilf was a bandleader. Left school to work in house band at the Palais Royale in Manchester then completed long stay in Phil Richardson's Band at the Oxford Galleries, Newcastle upon Tyne before settling in London. With Jack Hylton from 1932, until joining Ambrose from early 1936 until early 1938 (during this period also did extensive freelance work, including both radio and recordings). With Geraldo before working with Jack Harris, then rejoined Ambrose briefly. With Billy Ternent then again worked with Jack Harris. With John Borelli's Orchestra, then worked (on trombone and trumpet) with Geraldo in 1940, prior to joining the RAF where he became a member of the Squadronaires. Left the Squadronaires in late 1948 and joined Maurice Winnick before rejoining Ambrose (1949). Did prolific session work in the 1950s, including regular work in George Melachrino's Orchestra, then moved back to Manchester.

BRESLAW, 'Lennie' Leonard Benjamin
drums

Born: Whitechapel, London, 6 August 1930

Family name originally Breslau. Began playing drums while evacuated to Berkshire, played local gigs, then moved back to London. Did a succession of club dates then worked with Harry Parry and Ralph Sharon (1951) and in Jimmy Currie's Quartet. With Ken Moule (1954-5), then joined Tubby Hayes from February to July 1955. With Jack Sharpe's Quintet, then worked in Portugal with Harry Robbins (1956). Subsequently toured Germany with Swedish pianist Lars Werner and played Swiss residency on Lake Lugano with Freddy Ballerini. With Lennie Metcalfe's Band on liner *Mauretania* (late 1957 to 1958) and on the *Caronia* with tenorist Johnny Evans. Went to India for nine month season with Ashley Kozack, Harry South and Dick Morrissey (1961). During the 1960s and 1970s worked in many line-ups. Led own Trio at Venus Room, London, for four years, worked with Vic Ash-Harry Klein Jazz Five, with Jimmy Currie's Band (accompanying Val Doonican), Ian and Stu Hamer, the Herman Wilson-Pete Myers Quintet, John Burch's Octet, Les Condon's Quintet, and with Bobby Wellins and Annie Ross. Played in National Theatre Orchestra for two years. Freelanced in London from 1976 through the 1990s, occasionally doubling on piano.

BRETHERTON, Freddy
piano/arranger

Born: Ramsbottom, Lancashire, 1908
Died: London, 15 March 1954

Piano from age of nine, worked as a printer in calico mill, then joined Florida Dance Band in 1929, with them won *Melody Maker* contest individual award. Moved to London and joined band organized by Edgar Jackson. Worked with Jack Hylton and Ray Starita. Did freelance arranging including work for Ambrose. With Mickey Lewis at the Gargoyle Club, London, then led own band at Spider's Web (1933) before joining Sydney Lipton in September 1934. Left Lipton in spring 1936 and again led at Spider's Web (1936) before taking own band to Sweden in autumn of 1937. Disbanded in Sweden and joined Arne Hülphershas' Band (spring 1938). Returned to Britain in summer of 1938 and joined Jack Hylton as staff arranger and second pianist. Conducted London Palladium Orchestra during the early 1940s and thereafter worked as musical director and conductor at various London theatres, including long stay at the Victoria Palace.

BRIDGE, Paul Robert
double bass

Born: Bury, Lancashire, 24 May 1940

Trumpet from fourteen, played in school band with Rod Hamer and Doug Whaley. Did gigs around the Manchester area (including some with pianist Brian Priestley). Led Durham University Jazz Band on trumpet, took up double bass in 1962. Played in the Manchester area with Art Taylor's All Stars (with Rod Hamer, Chris Holmes, etc.), gigged with Roy Bower, Alan Hare, Gordon Robinson, Frank Toms, Barry Whitworth, Quinny Lawrence, Eric Ferguson and Stockport tenor saxophonist Brian Smith. Moved to London in 1971. Gigged with Mike Cotton and Lennie Hastings before beginning long musical association with Don Rendell. During the 1970s and early 1980s also with John Picard, Dave Defries' Big Band, Bob Downes, Graham Collier, Trevor Tomkins, Don Weller, Bryan Spring, Triton (with Alan Wakeman and Nigel Morris) and the London Jazz Big Band. Regularly with Humphrey Lyttelton from August 1983 through the 1990s, during this period also freelanced with Brian Leake's Sweet and Sour, with Brian Priestley's Sextet, with Graham Collier, etc.

BRIGHT, Sidney
piano/arranger

Born: London, 10 August 1903
Died: London, 1976

Twin brother of Gerald Bright (Geraldo). Studied at Royal Academy of Music then worked with Jack Hylton's Kit-Cat Band (1925–8). Accompanied violinist Albert Sandler, then worked in Al

Starita's Piccadilly Players (from April 1928), eventually becoming leader of that group (from December 1929 until May 1931). Led own recording band (1930). With Joe Kaye at Berkeley Hotel, London (1931), then played second piano for Carroll Gibbons in Savoy Hotel Orpheans (1932–3). Extensive freelance work during the 1930s, often working in ensembles led by Geraldo. Again with Carroll Gibbons (early 1939), then again worked with Geraldo in the 1940s. Later appeared regularly in the London Studio Players during the 1950s and 1960s, then worked as a solo pianist at the Café Royal, London.

BROCKLEHURST, Brian F.
double bass/guitar

Born: Buxton, Derbyshire, 16 August 1930

Father was a musician. Guitar from the age of twelve, took up double bass as a teenager. First professional work on drums and guitar at the Spa Hotel, Buxton, then worked on double bass with pianist Reg Farrell. Played double bass, guitar and drums in Dennis Ashworth's Orchestra for summer season in Llandudno (1949). Thereafter specialized on double bass. Worked with Rae Allen before joining Phil Moss in Manchester (late 1951). With Morris Mack, then worked with Ivor Raymonde in Bournemouth (late 1952 to October 1953). Moved to London, worked often with pianist Eddie Thompson then played brief season in India with Joe Crossman (spring 1954). Returned to London, worked with Norman Burns, Bert Courtley, then joined Ken Mackintosh (1955). With Jack Parnell from January 1956 until March 1957. Briefly with Don Rendell, then toured the USA with Tommy Whittle. With Humphrey Lyttelton from June 1957 until March 1960. With Eddie Thompson Quintet (spring 1960) then worked with Tony Kinsey (1960–1), and with Ted Heath. Successful freelance from the beginning of the 1960s through the 1990s, often worked with Harry Smith, Eddie Thompson, Cedric West, etc. Appeared with Terry Lightfoot's Band in film *It's Trad Dad* (1962), also toured Japan with Stanley Black. Played on countless radio shows and led own various groups, including Brocade, also accompanied many visiting American musicians.

BROMLEY, 'Tommy' Thomas Priestley
double bass

Born: Wandsworth, London, 1 August 1913
Died: France, 23 May 1947

Began on cello. Worked with Tommy Kinsman (1936), then freelanced on commercial radio. With Harold Beren's Band (1939), Syd Dean, Peter Mendoza and Sid Phillips (1940). With Ken Johnson (1941), sustained leg injuries in the air raid in which Johnson died (March 1941). In Chappie D'Amato's Band (1941). With Harry Parry (late 1941 and early 1942), Ambrose (summer 1942). Led own band at American service clubs in London, and at Feldman Club. Also worked in the 1940s with Lew Stone, Frank Weir, Ted Heath, Al Collins, Eric Winstone, Stephane Grappelli, George Shearing, etc. With Harry Hayes (1945) and Ambrose (1946). Ill health caused premature retirement, moved to France, died in a car crash.

BROOKS, Elkie (Elaine BOOKBINDER)
vocals

Born: Salford, Lancashire, 25 February 1945

Niece of bandleader Nat Bookbinder; her brother, Tony Bookbinder, is a drummer. Originally worked under stage name of Elaine Mansfield. With Eric Delaney and in the Kevin Kent Four before playing cabaret dates in France and Spain, often worked with Humphrey Lyttelton in 1967. Sang in jazz-rock Dada and Vinegar Joe, then temporarily moved to USA to work in Wet Willie. Continued to guest with jazz groups, including engagements with Humphrey Lyttelton in 1974, but then concentrated on highly successful solo career, undertaking international concert tours.

BROWN, Georgia (Lillie KLOT)
vocals

Born: Whitechapel, London, 21 October 1933
Died: London, 5 July 1992

Family name was originally Kleotz. In 1950 did first professional singing at the Stork Room, London, subsequently worked at the Embassy Club (1951), then toured US bases in Germany before working in cabaret with Bernard Hilda's Orchestra in Spain, France and Italy. Concentrated on working as a singer-actress and was featured (as Lucy) in *The Threepenny Opera* in London (1954) and later in New York. After a brief stay in California moved back to Britain and sang with Tony Crombie's Band. Resumed acting and appeared in *The Lily White Boys* (1960), later that year starred in *Oliver*, first in London then in New York. Moved back to London and appeared in *Maggie May*, in various television shows and later at the Royal Court Theatre, London, in *Man in Man* (1971). Moved to the USA in 1976 and worked there on stage, in films and on television. Regularly returned to London, appeared in own one-woman show and in *42nd Street*. Made latterday appearances in the television show *Cheers* (1991) and in the film *Victim of Love* (1991). Returned to London to take part in a tribute to Sammy Davis Jr.

BROWN, 'Gerry' Gerald Marwood
trumpet/harmonica

Born: Poole, Dorset, 18 July 1931

Played harmonica as a child then took up violin at fourteen. Began playing trumpet during Army service in Egypt. After demobilization gigged around the South Coast area, then formed own band which became Southsea contest winners in 1956. Remained Bournemouth-based until turning professional in 1960. Subsequently Gerry Brown's Jazzmen did widespread touring (including dates with Louis Armstrong's All Stars in 1962). Eventually Gerry quit touring and settled again on the South Coast and freelanced. Later worked in Pedro Harris' Mission Hall Jazz Band. At the onset of Harris's fatal illness, Brown was elected leader. Continued to work with this group through the 1990s and led own line-ups as well as guesting with various groups.

BROWN, Harry
trombone/guitar

Born: London, *c.*1925

With George Webb's Dixielanders (1946–7). Led own Inebriated Seven. With Humphrey Lyttelton from February 1948 until January 1949. With Carlo Krahmer, including trip to Paris (1949). With Reg Rigden's Original Dixielanders (1949–50). With Joe Daniels (1951), Freddy Randall (1951), Mike Daniels (late 1951 to spring 1952). Summer season with Ralph Sharon in Weymouth (1952). With Francisco Condé (late 1952), Peter Leigh (1953), Joe Daniels (1953), Johnnie Gray (1953), Norman Long (1953), Peter Vaughan (1954), the Tomasso Brothers (1955). With Laurie Gold from autumn 1956 to spring 1957. Freelanced, then worked on trombone and guitar in bassist Danny Haggerty's Band (1960), before working as a professional music copyist in the 1960s. Ill health prevented him from playing regularly thereafter.

BROWN, 'Sandy' Alexander
clarinet/piano/organ/vocals/composer

Born: Izatnagar, India, 25 February 1929
Died: London, 15 March 1975

Father was a Scottish railway engineer working in India. Family moved to Scotland during the early 1930s, settling in Edinburgh. Sandy took up clarinet at twelve and two years later formed band at the Royal High School. After leaving school served in the Royal Army Ordnance Corps until 1949, then formed own band (and studied architecture and acoustic engineering). Brown's band played various Edinburgh residencies, including the West End Café (1953) and occasionally moved South to play various engagements in England. In the autumn of 1954 Brown moved permanently to London and soon afterwards formed his own band, which included his long-time musical colleague trumpeter-arranger Al Fairweather. In late 1957 Brown handed over the band to Fairweather, to concentrate on his architectural business, but continued to play gigs. Then, in autumn of 1958, he resumed working regularly with Fairweather in the co-led Fairweather-Brown All Stars. This partnership continued until Fairweather joined Acker Bilk in autumn 1966. Brown then led his own band, and guested with various groups. He also recorded in New York with Earle Warren in 1974 (during one of his many business trips to the USA). In early 1975 he played dates with the Fairweather-Brown Reunion Band. *The McJazz Manuscripts*, a collection of Brown's writings, was first published in 1979.

BROWN, 'Terry' Terence David
trumpet

Born: Islington, London, 20 August 1928
Died: Surrey, 4 May 1996

Piano at eight, trumpet at thirteen. At fourteen played in Mickey Bryan's Rugcutters and did local gigs before working with Johnny Claes from March to September 1945. With Johnny Brown's Band in London, gigs with Harry Roy, then worked with Ken Turner's Band in Derby. To Eire with Tony Crombie's Band (1947). Worked in London with Les Simon's Band and with Tubby Hayes. With Dennis Hale's Band for summer season in Brighton (1948), then gigged with Sid Millward's Band. Member of original Johnny Dankworth Seven (spring 1950) then worked with Russ Allen at the Stork Club, London (September 1950). Joined Ralph Sharon (early 1951), gigs with Teddy Foster, with Kenny Graham (August 1951). Led own band from October 1951 until spring 1952, again with Ralph Sharon (June 1952), then briefly rejoined Kenny Graham (October 1952). With Harry Hayes (late 1952 to April 1953), Harry Klein Quintet (1953) and prolific freelance work at various London jazz clubs. Briefly in bassist Cliff Ball's Band (late 1956). Stint with Don Rendell interrupted by appendicitis (February 1957). With Bruce Turner's Jump Band from May 1957 until October 1958, then left full time playing to become a successful recording manager for various companies into the mid-1990s.

BRUCE, 'Jack' John Symon Asher
bass/keyboards/harmonica/vocals/composer

Born: Bishopbriggs, Lanarkshire, Scotland, 14 May 1943

School in Glasgow, then scholarship to study cello and composition at Royal Scottish Academy of Music (1960). Gigged in Glasgow on double bass, briefly with Scotsville Jazzmen (1962) and played in Italy before moving to London where he worked with Alexis Korner (late 1962 to early 1963). With the Graham Bond Organization from early 1963 until 1965. With John Mayall, Mike Taylor, Manfred Mann, Dick Heckstall-Smith, John Burch, etc., before becoming part of Cream

(1966–8). After that group broke up, played with the New Jazz Orchestra, with Mike Gibbs and toured the USA with own Friends (1970). In Europe with own quartet (1971), with Leslie West and Corky Laing (1972). With Tony Williams' Lifetime, then led own groups and freelanced internationally during the 1980s, also worked with Rocket 88, Charlie Watts' Big Band, Soft Machine, Carla Bley, Joachim Kühn, Mose Allison, etc. Toured in 1995 (doubling keyboards and vocals) with keyboardist Bernie Worrell.

BRUCE, Ralph Sinclair
clarinet/alto sax/arranger

Born: Manchester, Lancashire, 6 November 1908
Died: London, 1975

With drummer Alan Holmes' Swing Sextet in the Midlands (1938). In Henry Reed's Rag Pickers (1939). With Harry Gold from late 1945 until May 1948. With Felix King (1948), Miff Ferrie (1949) and Joe Daniels, before working successfully as a cartoonist and painter. Continued to play gigs into the 1970s.

BRUN, Philippe
trumpet/violin/arranger/composer

Born: Paris, France, 29 April 1908
Died: Paris, France, 14 January 1994

Formed the Collegians with school friends. Studied violin at Paris Conservatoire of Music, took up cornet in 1926. Played in band led by pianist Doctor Larrazet before joining the Grégoriens' Stage Band, led by 'Grégor' (Krikor Kelekian 1898-1971) in 1928. Also worked with visiting Americans Danny Polo and Bud Freeman. Briefly with Ray Ventura, then moved to England and joined Jack Hylton in late 1929. Left Hylton in 1936 to lead own band in France and to be featured with Bob Huber. Led own recording bands in the late 1930s and did freelance sessions but worked regularly in Ray Ventura's Band from September 1936 until 1940. Moved to Switzerland in 1940, and played there with local musicians through most of World War II then returned to France and formed own small band. Later guested with various bands and played in jam sessions before retiring from playing in the early 1960s.

BRUNSKILL, 'Bill' William
trumpet

Born: East London, 2 February 1920

Father of banjoist Bill (who emigrated to Australia in 1971). Originally played guitar in the Jacobson Brothers' Band, then took up trumpet. Served in the Army during World War II. Gigged around East London, led own band, then played in Cy Laurie's Band, in Lonnie Donegan's Band and in Bob Dawbarn's Barnstormers (1954–5). This last-named unit formed the basis of the band Bill formed in 1955. That same year, Bill's band began a sixteen-year residency at the Fighting Cocks in Kingston, Surrey. Bill's Band also played for many years at the Lord Napier in Thornton Heath, and were televised there in 1984 as part of the television documentary *Whatever Happened to Bill Brunskill?* The band also played engagements in Holland and Belgium. Bill guested with various bands during a playing visit to Australia in the 1980s. Continued to play regularly through the 1990s.

BRYANT, 'Richie' Richard John   Born: Chew Magna, Somerset, 24 March 1941
drums

Began playing drums at thirteen. During the late 1950s played around Bristol and Cheltenham with Tim Newman's Celebration Jazz Band, then joined Eric Allandale's New Orleans Knights in 1960. Moved back to Bristol area in early 1960s, played for almost a year in small group led by pianist-vibraphonist Jan Ridd, then joined Terry Lightfoot for four years. Gigged with Bob Wallis, Alan Elsdon, etc., then spent further three years with Terry Lightfoot. Freelanced from 1970 to 1972, playing wide variety of line-ups including work with Dave Shepherd, Brian Lemon, Stan Greig, Johnny Hawksworth, Fred Hunt, etc. Joined Acker Bilk in May 1972 and remained through the 1990s, also featured with the 100 Club All Stars. Played at several Edinburgh Jazz Festivals during the early 1990s, and often led own band.

BRYCE, Owen   Born: Woolwich, London, 8 August 1920
trumpet/piano/composer

His son Jan is a trombonist. Led own band during the early 1940s then became founder-member of George Webb's Dixielanders in summer of 1943. When George Webb joined Humphrey Lyttelton's Band, Bryce became (with Reg Rigden) part of the newly-formed Original Dixielanders (early 1949). Subsequently led own band from 1956, which played a long residency at Maidstone Jazz Club in the 1950s and early 1960s. Disbanded in 1961, but re-formed the following year and continued to play regularly, making many visits to Europe. Took part in reunion of Original Dixielanders in 1986. Made many playing visits to New Orleans. Has for many years organized jazz tuition courses (in company with his wife Iris) and has written instruction books, *How to Play Jazz I, II, III* and *IV*. His quartet enjoys widespread success throughout the Midlands (1995) and he continues to run a six-piece band.

BRYDEN, Beryl Audrey   Born: Norwich, Norfolk, 11 May 1920
vocals/washboard

Organized the Norwich Rhythm Club in 1939. Moved to Cambridge in 1942 and sang with local bands. Settled in London. Occasionally guested with George Webb's Dixielanders from summer of 1945, briefly with John Haim's Jelly Roll Kings (1948), subsequently led own Washboard Wonders and Backroom Boys during the late 1940s. Made many appearances with Freddy Randall's Band from January 1948 through the 1950s. Gigs with Mike Daniels, Cy Laurie, Charlie Galbraith during the 1950s. Professional debut in Paris (July 1953) with Maxime Saury's Band. Later that year again worked in Paris, with Mickey Larche's Band. Frequently with the Dutch Swing College from 1954 through to the late 1960s. Guested with Fatty George's Band in Austria (1954) and in Europe with the Dixieland Pipers and the Downtown Jazz Band. Guested with Alex Welsh from the late 1950s, and also with Eggy Ley in Germany (1959). Long solo tour of Europe (1960), then worked regularly with Monty Sunshine from 1961. Also undertook tour of the Far East with Johnny Parker and Diz Disley in 1963. Solo tours of Africa (1966) and Australia (1971). Widespread international bookings through the 1970s and 1980s, and guesting with Alex Welsh, Kenny Ball, Roy Pellett, Colin Symons, Rod Mason, Pete Allen, etc. Active throughout the mid-1990s, in *Salute to Satchmo* show with Digby Fairweather, in *I've Got What it Takes* with Keith

Nichols and guesting with both Laurie Chescoe's Band and Cy Laurie. Appeared at 50th Australian Jazz Convention (1995).

BUDD, Roy Frederick
piano/composer

Born: Mitcham, Surrey, 14 March 1947
Died: England, 7 August 1993

Cousin of drummer Trevor Tomkins. Self-taught infant prodigy. Featured on stage, television and radio as a twelve year old. At seventeen led own trio for residencies at the Lilliput Hall, Bermondsey, the Hooter Club, Croydon and the Bull's Head, Barnes. Appeared at the London Palladium in the 1960s and appeared on popular television shows before being commissioned to write film music. Moved to Hollywood and enjoyed success as a composer and musical director but continued to work occasionally in a trio format. Returned to Britain, again led trio in the 1990s, combining this with writing commitments. Died from a brain haemorrhage.

BURBERRY, 'Mickey' Michael
alto sax/reeds

Born: London, 1900

Played clarinet and violin at school, took up alto sax *c.*1919. Played gigs in London, then worked with Johnny Stein and his London Celebrity Five in Liverpool and New Brighton during the early 1920s, also played with this band on transatlantic liners. Moved with Stein to Edinburgh and there took over leadership, playing in Scotland for four years before returning to London to work in Dave Frost's Band. Played in Switzerland with Leslie Jeffries during winter of 1927–8. Returned to England and worked at 43 Club and with Alan Selby, before joining Billy Cotton in August 1928. Remained with Cotton until 1942. Moved to Edinburgh and worked with Joe Orlando's Band during World War II. Led own band at Gleneagles during the 1950s and 1960s, doubling on electric organ, then retired.

BURBRIDGE, Graham Alfred
drums

Born: Bow, London, 1 October 1933

Began playing drums shortly before National Service in the RAF. Played in station trio with Maurice Hynson (piano) and Pete Elderfield (double bass). After demobilization played various London gigs with this group. Joined Sandy Brown in 1955 (replacing Ian Bell) and remained until joining Chris Barber in November 1957. Worked with Chris Barber until June 1976, then gave up playing.

BURCH, John (John Alexander BURCHELL)
piano/composer

Born: London, 6 January 1932

Played boogie-woogie as a child, studied piano from twelve. With the Army in Germany, played in service bands. After demobilization gigged around the London area, with Graham Bond, Terry Lovelock, etc., then in the late 1950s worked with own Trio on US bases in Europe. To France with Jeff Clyne and Bobby Wellins (May 1959). With Allan Ganley-Keith Christie Jazzmakers from summer 1960. Joined Don Rendell Quartet in early 1961. With Rendell until late 1962, then began leading own octet, which continued to flourish intermittently through the 1970s and 1980s.

Accompanied many visiting American musicians at Ronnie Scott's Club. Often worked in Tommy Whittle's Quartet during the 1960s, also in Lennie Breslaw's Trio and freelanced with many groups. Taught regularly at jazz summer schools. During the 1970s often worked with Ray Warleigh, Kathy Stobart and Georgie Fame. Played in Yugoslavia with Ron Russell Quintet (1974). With the Tony Mann Trio and with Lennie Best Quartet in the early 1980s, then regularly in Dick Morrissey's Quartet from the mid-1980s through to the 1990s. Continues with successful freelance playing and composing, reunion dates with Don Rendell in the Roaring Band (1996). Leading own line-ups.

BURCHELL, 'Chas' Charles
tenor sax/baritone sax/flute

Born: London, 30 October 1925
Died: Middlesex, 3 June 1986

Originally played ukulele and guitar, took up alto sax and played local gigs in 1943. Switched to tenor sax and played in both RAF and Army bands from late 1943, including serving with the 4th British Divisional Band in Greece. Formed own quintet after demobilization (1947) and freelanced. Played season on the Isle of Wight (1949), returned to London and quit professional music to work as a factory administrations manager, but continued to play many jazz gigs, mainly in the West London (occasionally playing baritone sax). Played for several years in various bands led by Toni Anton, regularly with bassist Ken Hogston's Quintet in the mid-1950s. For a period of over twenty years (beginning in the late 1950s) played regularly in a quintet (together with Mike Hennessey, piano, Brian Hennessey, drums and Brian Wood, trumpet). Regularly worked with Peter Ind groups during the late 1960s and 1970s, and accompanied various visiting American musicians. Guested with Lennie Best's Quintet in the late 1970s, co-led band with Geoff Simkins (1985). The Chastet continued to perpetuate Burchell's memory during the 1990s.

BURMAN, Maurice
drums/piano/vocals

Born: London, 14 June 1908
Died: London, 11 May 1961

Pupil (and nephew) of drummer Max Bacon. With Sam Costa's Band (1929), then led own band at Windsor and Margate (1930). With Edgar Jackson's Band (led by Harry Gold) at the Spider's Web Club (1932), then worked mainly with Roy Fox from 1932 until 1938. Briefly with Denis Van Thal's Orchestra (summer 1938), then worked with Billy Bissett from autumn 1938 until summer 1939. With Jack Nathan (late 1939 to early 1940), Sid Phillips (spring 1940). Briefly with Ambrose and with George Scott-Wood Big Band (spring 1941). Long spell with Geraldo until spring 1946, then spent two years in Switzerland recuperating from tuberculosis. Returned to London and became columnist for the *Melody Maker* and also ran own school of singing. Not to be confused with drummer-vocalist Len Bermon (born London, 1912), who worked with Henry Hall, Spike Hughes, Billy Mason, etc. In early years occasionally played trumpet with his own band. During his stay with Geraldo, he sometimes played trumpet at jam sessions.

BURNAP, Campbell
trombone/vocals

Born: Derby, 10 September 1939

Of Scottish ancestry. Spent early years in Scotland, but returned to England aged seven. Played washboard in band led by school friend, clarinettist Chris Blount. Emigrated to Wellington, New

Zealand, in 1959. Worked as a civil servant, took up trombone. Played in the Omega Jazz Band (led by pianist Derek Green) for three years. Moved on to Australia, worked with various bands in Sydney and Melbourne for a further three years. Returned to Britain (via USA and Mexico) and joined Terry Lightfoot in autumn of 1965 for nine months, then worked with Monty Sunshine for six months before returning to Australia in December 1966. Worked with various bands in Australia, then returned to London in summer of 1969. Guested with Arthur Coyne's Band in Derby. With Ian Armit's Band at Georgian Club, London (late 1969 to March 1970). With Alan Elsdon (replacing Mike Nash) from late 1970 until late 1975. During this period did teacher training and gained Teacher's Certificate. From 1974 did occasional work as an extra in films and television. From 1976 until 1980 played regular seasons in Switzerland, with Dick Charlesworth, Geoff Simkins, pianist Alan Rogers, etc. Original member of the Midnite Follies Orchestra from January until June 1978, also worked in Pat Halcox's All Stars, with Pete Allen, Bob Bryan, Keith Smith and led own quintet. Flew to Australia to join Acker Bilk in September 1980, left Bilk in July 1987. In Five-a-Slide. Occasionally in Alex Welsh's Band in 1980. From the late 1980s was featured regularly at Finland's annual Kaamos Jazz Festival. Was featured with John Petters' Legends of British Jazz, occasionally co-led quintet with Geoff Simkins. Featured with the 100 Club All Stars throughout the 1990s. Prolific work as a radio presenter from 1988, with own shows on BBC and on commercial stations. Gave live county cricket commentaries for British Telecom's ball-by-ball service (1990). Freelances with various line-ups through the 1990s and guests at various festivals and in jazz clubs. Guested with Ed Polcer's Band in New York (1994). Lectured on 'The Swing Era' in Beijing, China (April 1996). Regularly writes articles on jazz and liner-notes.

BURNS, 'Bob' Robert
tenor sax/reeds/violin

Born: Toronto, Canada, 16 May 1923

Played alto sax and violin in his father's band as a teenager. To Britain with the Canadian Central Air Force Band during World War II. Studied at Royal College of Music and gained ARCM. Gigged with various bands in London and worked briefly in Denis Rose's Orchestra (1945). Returned to Canada, worked in Mart Kenny's Western Gentlemen, then returned to Britain in 1948 for further studies. With Duncan Whyte (June 1948) and Ronnie Pleydell, before joining Ted Heath (on baritone sax) from September 1948 until January 1949. Worked with Ambrose, Geraldo and George Melachrino. With Jack Parnell from spring 1951 until spring 1952. Freelanced, then rejoined Parnell in early 1953 and remained to work in Jack Parnell's ATV Orchestra for many years. Also did extensive work in classical ensembles, working with London Symphony Orchestra and Royal Philharmonic Orchestra, and did many jazz club gigs. During the early 1970s worked on several occasions in Europe with Benny Goodman. Continued to play regularly in jazz clubs, sometimes leading own small group, also co-led quintet with Kathy Stobart. Was featured in Great Jazz Solos Revisited in 1978. Extensive freelance sessions in the 1980s, also led own quintet for West End show *Three Men on a Horse* (1988). Moved back to Canada. Recovered from cardiac attack and resumed regular playing in the 1990s.

BURNS, Norman
drums

Born: London, 11 March 1920
Died: Australia, June 1994

Played drums from early teens. First professional work on P&O liners. Worked with Ken Kind and with Billy Smith at Cricklewood Palais before joining Teddy Foster in June 1943. With Lew Stone (1943–4) then joined Frank Weir in October 1944. With George Shearing's Quartet (January 1945), occasionally with Ted Heath and Geraldo, then rejoined Frank Weir (October 1945). Left Weir to join Ambrose's Ciro Club Band (November 1945), then again rejoined Weir (May 1946). In Ronnie Selby's Trio (early 1947), briefly with Harry Hayes and Tito Burns. Again with Frank Weir (summer 1947). With Ronnie Pleydell (1948), then again with Ambrose (late 1948–9). With Lew Stone (1951). Then led own successful quintet from 1951. Subsequently left full time music and moved to Australia.

BURNS, 'Tito' Nathan
piano accordion

Born: North London, 7 February 1921

Married to vocalist Terry Devon. Was not related to drummer Norman Burns, but worked with him in a North London semi-pro band in the 1930s. First gig with Felix Mendelssohn, subsequently worked with Gerry Fitzgerald's Trio, with Don Marino Barreto and Lou Preager. With Carl Barriteau at the Cotton Club, Dean Street, London (1941), then led own band at the Panama Club, London (1941). With Don Marino Barreto (1942), then took own Swing Band into the Nut House, London (1942). Served in the RAF from 1942, was part of the RAF Regiment Sextet (1943), then after aircrew training was on active service in the Far East. When World War II ended formed own Radio SEAC Sextet. After demobilization joined pianist Clarrie Wears' Sextet (1946), then led own highly successful sextet from January 1947 until August 1955, also hosted the long-running BBC radio series *Accordion Club*. Quit full time playing to become an agent and impresario, who brought many top-line American artistes to Britain. Later became Head of Variety Programming at London Weekend Television.

BURTON, 'Tommy' Thomas William
piano/saxes/clarinet/guitar/vocals

Born: Bilston, nr Wolverhampton, Warwickshire, 10 January 1935

Piano lessons from age of eight, clarinet at fifteen, alto sax at sixteen. First gig on clarinet and alto sax with Pete Young and his Chitterling Twisters (1950) (the band later became Pete Young's Imperial New Orleans Jazz Band). Subsequently played piano with Johnny Fenton and the Fentones until being called up for service in the RAF (1953). During five years in the RAF organized various service dance bands, and did first broadcast on a Forces Show. During latter stage of RAF service led Thunderfoot Burton's Celestial Three in Walsall. After demobilization in 1958 led own Ravemen on guitar and vocals, then fronted own Combo on tenor sax and vocals during the 1960s. Formed own Sporting House Quartet in the late 1960s and continued to lead the group through the 1990s. From 1972 to 1978 ran own public house (the Lord Raglan in Wolverhampton). In 1989 began a series of regular visits to New Orleans, where he guested with various bands on piano and also played in marching bands on alto sax. Often in duo with guitarist-banjoist Tom 'Spats' Langham (1995–6).

BUSBY, 'Laddy' Alan Haydn
trombone

Born: Maidenhead, Berkshire, 1 July 1920
Died: Isle of Man, 27 August 1985

Son of pianist-composer Bob Busby (1901–52). Toured with Teddy Joyce's Juveniles (1935). With Sonny Farrar (1937), then toured with Billy Williams' Youth on Parade Orchestra (1938). With Bob Busby's Orchestra (1939) then joined Jack Harris (1939). With Eddie Carroll (1940) and freelanced with Ambrose, Ken Johnson and Lou Levy. Played in East Surrey Regimental Band during World War II, and gigged when circumstances permitted. After demobilization worked with Harry Hayes (1945), then joined Ted Heath from September 1945 until January 1947. Again worked with Eddie Carroll (1947), then joined Geraldo in 1947. During the early 1950s worked with Stanley Black, Jack Parnell and Cyril Stapleton's BBC Show Band, then became hugely successful freelance session man through the 1970s and 1980s before retiring to the Isle of Man.

BUSH, 'Lennie' Leonard Walter
double bass

Born: Shepherd's Bush, London, 6 June 1927

Father of trumpeter Andy Bush. Played violin as a child. Took up double bass at sixteen. A year later was part of a variety act (The Rolling Stones and Dawn). Played at the Fullado Club, London in 1946. With Jerry Hoey, Carl Barriteau and Johnny Brown (in Southampton), then worked in Billy Kaye's Band (in Cambridge and in Chelmsford). Also worked at the Rex Ballroom, Cambridge with Arthur Gibson's Band. Worked often with Nat Gonella from early 1948. Worked at Sherry's in Brighton with tenor saxist Harry Java (summer 1948) then joined Duncan Whyte. Founder-member of Club Eleven (December 1948). From 1950 onwards did an enormous amount of freelance work, playing sessions, concerts, jazz clubs, etc. With Roy Fox (1951), with tenor saxist Pat Bateson at Ritz Ballroom, Manchester (1952). Joined Ronnie Scott in October 1952, and worked with Scott until 1956. During this period also worked in Tony Crombie's Band (including bookings in Israel). Accompanied Louis Armstrong at Royal Festival Hall, London (December 1956). In spring 1957 began long musical association with Jack Parnell's ATV Orchestra. Continued to play jazz gigs, worked in Jazz Today Unit, with Dizzy Reece, with Tony Kinsey's groups, often in duo with Alan Clare, etc., and played on innumerable recordings. Toured Europe four times with Benny Goodman and accompanied many visiting American musicians including Zoot Sims, Roy Eldridge, Joe Pass, Clark Terry, etc. Worked often with Stephane Grappelli during the early 1970s (including touring) and continued to be part of duos with Alan Clare (through to the 1980s). Work and recordings with Stan Tracey. Worked in various theatrical shows including an eight year run of *Me and My Girl*, also *Bubbling Brown Sugar*, *City of Angels*, *Guys and Dolls* (at the National Theatre), etc. Often in Don Lusher's Ted Heath Band during the 1990s. Regularly featured with The Best of British Jazz (Kenny Baker, Don Lusher, etc.) through to the 1990s. Early in his career Lennie studied at the Guildhall School of Music under James Merret, Snr.

BUSIAKIEWICZ, Richard Stephen Peter
piano

Born: Amersham, Buckinghamshire,
14 January 1963

Both parents from Poland. Began playing piano at age of six. Played solo gigs in restaurants as a teenager and at seventeen took brother Henry's place as pianist in Caravelle, an Anglo-Polish quintet which played commercial engagements around the London area. Studied at Amersham College and subsequently worked for the National Economic Development Office, but continued to play regularly and often sat in at Merlin's Cave, Chalfont St Giles. Played residency at the Archduke Wine Bar, London, in duo with bassist Martin Klute and did solo hotel residencies. Changed day job and began working for the Fyffe Banana Company. From the mid-1980s often played in trio with Leon Clayton (bass) and his father, Eddie Clayton (drums). Left Fyffe's in early 1987 and became fully professional. Joined Tommy Chase in October 1987 and stayed for eighteen months. Formed own quartet, with Gerard Presencer (trumpet), Steve Taylor (drums), Leon Clayton (bass), which became a quintet with the addition of tenor saxist Kevin Flanagan. (Quintet made television debut in May 1991.) Worked for a year in Dave Jean-Baptiste's Quintet and began playing gigs at the Bull's Head, Barnes, with Dick Morrissey, Don Weller, etc. Began working with American tenor saxist Spike Robinson at the Bull's Head in 1992 and subsequently became permanent member of Robinson's Quartet (February 1993). Accompanied many other American musicians during the 1990s, including Scott Hamilton, Bill Berry, Ken Peplowski, Warren Vaché, Urbie Green, Bob Wilber, Ed Polcer, Bobby Shew, Herb Geller, George Masso, Teddy Edwards, Harry Allen, Rick Margitza, etc. Worked often with Claire Martin (1993–4). In January 1994 became regular member of Ray Gelato's Giants, doing widespread international touring, but continues to play many freelance engagements and to work with Spike Robinson and other American musicians.

BUTCHER, 'Stan' Stanley Robert
piano/arranger

Born: London, 26 January 1920

Died: 1987

Was in the Army Infantry Division during World War II and led the Polar Bears service band. After demobilization co-led band with Don Lusher in Pembroke Bay, then worked with Joe Daniels (1947–8). Led own band in Dundee and worked in Scotland with Bertie King before joining Freddy Randall (1951). With Bernie Stanton's Sextet then again worked with Freddy Randall (late 1951). Led own band at Slough Palais (1952), then worked with Geoff Sowden (1953) and Jack Newman (1954). Subsequently led own bands and freelanced (as pianist and arranger), often worked with Stan Reynolds during the 1970s.

BUTTS, John
drums

Born: Slough, Buckinghamshire, 1941

Died: Bermuda, West Indies, 30 December 1966

With Derek Sinclair's Band in Blackburn then worked in Newcastle with the Don Smith Band and in the Emcee Five before joining Ronnie Ross Quartet and Tentet in late 1962. With John Dankworth (1963–4). With Humphrey Lyttelton, Tubby Hayes, Gordon Beck and the Tony Coe-John Picard Quintet (1965). With Dick Morrissey (1966), then went to Bermuda in June 1966 to work in Joe Wylie's Band. Suffered fatal injuries in a motorized cycling accident.

C

CAIRNS, 'Forrie' Forrest
clarinet/saxes

Born: Glasgow, Scotland, 23 June 1936

Brother of pianist John Cairns (born 1933). Played mandolin from age of eight until eleven, appearing with Maisie Johnson's Ragtime Mandoliniers. At eighteen played clarinet in Glasgow University Jazz Band, which became known as the Vernon Jazz Band. With Jim McHarg's Band. Gave up teaching to become professional musician. Led own band which became the Scottish All Stars (1958). Joined Clyde Valley Stompers in early 1959, left in early 1961 to remain in Scotland. Formed own Clansmen in spring 1961, extensive touring until early 1963, then returned to Scotland and formed new band. Moved south and freelanced in the London area during the 1960s and 1970s, working with Alexander's Jazzmen, Ron Russell, Ian Bell, Ian Armit, Fionna Duncan, etc. Began long musical association with Bob Wallis in the late 1960s. With Wallis through to the 1980s, working mainly in Switzerland. Subsequently made his home in Switzerland and from the late 1980s through the 1990s worked in the Piccadilly Six (led by trumpeter Dave Stewart), also intermittently with Idiomox. During the 1980s took part in Clyde Valley Stompers Reunion Tours, and appeared in the McJazz All Stars.

CALVERT, Leon
trumpet/flugelhorn

Born: Westcliff-on-Sea, Essex, 26 June 1927

Family moved to Manchester when Leon was an infant. He began playing trumpet during childhood and turned professional as a teenager with Jack Nieman's Band at the Plaza, Manchester. Moved with this band to London and worked with them at the Royal, Tottenham. Subsequently played with Harold Gale's Band at the same venue (1945). With Jack Amlot and Frank Weir (1946), then brief spells with Woolf Phillips, Billy Munn, Nat Allen and Jack Jackson, before joining Paul Lombard's Band aboard liner *Mauretania* (late 1947 to spring 1948). With Oscar Rabin (spring 1948 to summer 1949), also original member of Club Eleven (December 1948) and thus became part of John Dankworth's Quintet. With Frank Weir (1949–50) and Ambrose (1949). Extensive freelance session work, also with Bill Collins and leading own band (1950). With Tito Burns (November 1950 to May 1951), then long stay of almost four years with Carroll Gibbons. During 1955–6 worked with Jack Newman, Ambrose, Ken Moule, Arthur Coppersmith, Buddy Featherstonhaugh and the London Jazz Orchestra. With Denny Boyce (summer 1958 to summer 1961), also with Tony Crombie in the late 1950s. With Vic Lewis (including tour of USA in 1960), then again with John Dankworth from summer 1961 until 1963, also gigs with Alan Clarke's Band. Thereafter concentrated on successful freelance work in radio, films, television and recordings (was lead trumpet on *Top of the Pops* television show for eight years). Continued to play jazz gigs. Playing regularly through the 1990s, with the Sounds of Seventeen, Jazz Spell, George Thorby's Band, etc.

CAMPBELL, Duncan
trumpet/flugelhorn/vocals

Born: Glasgow, Scotland, 31 May 1926

Father, Archibald Campbell, was a trumpeter who later became a drummer. Duncan's wife, June Pressley, was a professional saxophonist who now teaches piano. Worked at Green's Playhouse in Glasgow at fourteen years old. With Matt Moore's Band in Glasgow and Manchester (1946), with Dick Denny and with Charlie Young's Band in Inverness, before working with Tommy Sampson from early 1947 until early 1948. With Lou Preager, then joined Tito Burns (spring 1948). Briefly with Teddy Foster and with Dennis Hale in Brighton then rejoined Lou Preager (September 1948). With Cyril Stapleton (1949–50) then joined Ted Heath from October 1950. Remained with Ted Heath for eighteen years and subsequently worked briefly with Ralph Dollimore's Ted Heath Band. Prolific session work from the 1970s through the 1990s, also worked in George Chisholm's Gentlemen of Jazz, in Don Lusher's Ted Heath Band, with Harry Gold (including tour of Germany), in Bob Wilber's Big Band, in Vile Bodies, etc., as well as leading own group.

CARDEW, 'Phil' Philip
saxes/clarinet/arranger

Born: London, July 1903
Died: Sussex, October 1960

Gained LRAM then gigged in London, before working in the Kit-Cat Club Band (directed by Al Starita) in 1926. With Jack Hylton's Piccadilly Revels (directed by Ray Starita), late 1926–8. With Fred Elizalde (April to December 1929), then joined Jack Hylton until January 1931. Worked briefly with Billy Mason, before specializing as an arranger, writing for Jack Hylton, Jack Payne, Henry Hall, Lew Stone, Roy Fox, etc., and for films, radio and television.

CAREW, Les (Leslie PRIESTLEY)
trombone/vocals

Born: Lincoln, 15 August 1908
Died: St Albans, Hertfordshire, 16 March 1994

Raised in Shipley, Yorkshire. Worked as an apprentice in local mill, took up trombone at seventeen. Played in local bands, then moved to London and worked with Billy Cotton and Ray Starita, before joining Jack Hylton in autumn 1930. With Jack Harris in 1937, then worked mainly with Ambrose from 1937 until serving briefly in the Armed Forces. Then rejoined Ambrose (at one stage leading Ambrose's Octet). Briefly with Chappie D'Amato in 1943, then again with Ambrose until 1947. With Geraldo from September 1948, then again with Ambrose during the early 1950s. From this period onwards mainly active as a freelance, working with Mantovani, Eric Robinson, George Melachrino, etc. His widow is the musical educator Avril Dankworth (sister of John Dankworth).

CAREY, 'Dave' David Arthur
drums/vibes/washboard

Born: Coulsdon, Surrey, 8 November 1914

Father was a pianist. Drums from an early age, led own band (mostly around the Croydon area) during the 1930s. Opened own instrument shop in Streatham during spring of 1939 (the forerunner of his Swing Shop record business which flourished for many years). Freelanced during the 1940s, including gigs with pianist Gerry Moore. Worked briefly in Britain with visiting Australian band led by pianist Graeme Bell (May to July 1948), then joined Humphrey Lyttelton from September 1948 to September 1949 (replaced by Bernard Saward). Recorded in London with Rex Stewart (September 1949). Led own band during the 1950s and 1960s, but also guested with Freddy Clayton, Allan Leat, the Fourteen Foot Band, John Chilton, Roy Vaughan, etc.

CARMELLO, Janusz
Born: Warsaw, Poland, 1 January 1944
pocket trumpet/trumpet/flugelhorn

Began playing trumpet while studying engineering at college. Played at student clubs, then joined the Six Dixielanders. Moved to Italy in 1966, lived briefly in Tuscany, then settled in Milan. Played local gigs, then joined the Milan College Jazz Society. Worked as a design engineer until moving to London in 1973. Sat in (and gigged with) various bands, and played in Pete Allen's Band (1979). Was also featured in Peter Ind's Great Jazz Solos Revisited. Two year lay-off, then resumed regular playing and built considerable reputation as a soloist, guesting at many international festivals during the 1980s and 1990s, sometimes as a guest star, sometimes with own band. Temporarily indisposed through ill health late 1995 to early 1996, then resumed regular playing.

CARR, Ian
Born: Dumfries, Scotland, 21 April 1933
trumpet/flugelhorn/composer/arranger

Brother of Mike Carr. Their mother played ukulele and piano. Was raised in the North-East of England (South Shields, Seaburn, Barnard Castle, Gainford); took piano lessons from age of twelve. Began playing trumpet at school (1950) and soon won Carroll Levis talent show (in duo with brother Mike) which resulted in doing first broadcast at the age of seventeen. Played trumpet while at King's College, Newcastle (studying English Literature). Served in Army from 1956–8, gained commission in infantry regiment and 'guested' on trumpet-cornet with service bands and local groups in Britain and Germany. After demobilization, travelled in Europe (Nice, Corsica, Monte Carlo), playing occasional gigs, then returned to the North-east and joined brother Mike in recently formed Emcee Five replacing trumpeter Dougie Smith, early in 1960. Left Emcee Five in August 1962, moved to London and worked with Harold McNair until joining Don Rendell in November. After a brief period of inaction through appendicitis, rejoined Rendell in February 1963 and became co-leader of quintet (with Rendell) until July 1969. During this period also worked in Europe with Don Byas (1968) and with the New Jazz Orchestra, with Joe Harriott, Harry South's Big Band, John Stevens, Trevor Watts, gigged with Mike Westbrook and Colin Peters and co-led quartet with John McLaughlin. Formed own Nucleus in September 1969 which achieved widespread international success, including engagements in the USA (appeared at Newport Jazz Festival 1970, etc.), in South America, India, and throughout Europe until the late 1980s. Also worked with Michael Garrick's Sextet until 1970, with Keith Tippett's Centipede in France, and in 1975 began a twenty year occasional participation in the United Jazz and Rock Ensemble. From 1982 Associate Professor at Guildhall School of Music; also directed the Interchange performance and composition workshop in London. Led own Orchestra UK in 1989, played in George Russell's Living Time Orchestra (1989–93) and worked in the London Jazz Orchestra in the 1990s. Has written various books including works on *Miles Davis* (1982), *Keith Jarrett* (1990), *Music Outside: Contemporary Jazz in Britain* (1973) and (with Digby Fairweather and Brian Priestley) *Jazz, The Essential Companion* (1987) and *Jazz, The Rough Guide* (1995).

CARR, 'Mike' Michael Anthony
Born: South Shields, Co. Durham, 7 December 1937
organ/piano/vibes/marimba/composer

Brother of trumpeter Ian Carr. They did their first broadcast together when Mike was thirteen. Self-taught musician. Served in RAF from 1956 to 1958, played gigs while serving in Cyprus. Returned to Newcastle area, worked as a salesman but was active in formation of the Emcee Five, which soon achieved recording successes (1960–3). Played some gigs with Harold McNair, then turned professional and worked for two years in South Africa (from December 1963) on piano and vibes with Nolan Ranger Orchestra in Cape Town, then moved to Salisbury (in what was then Rhodesia) and played vibes for two months with pianist Jeremy Lubbock (1965). Settled in London, freelance work included brief spell accompanying Lita Roza. Began specializing on organ from March 1966, also worked with Herbie Goins and the Nightimers (1966). Formed own trio, worked in Europe. Regularly accompanied visiting American musicians: toured with Coleman Hawkins in Britain (1967) and worked with Don Byas in Portugal (1968). Played in Pendulum duo with Tony Crombie. Worked in Portugal with Academic Quintet Plus Two (1968), then spent five months working in Mozambique with this group (1969). Led trio in Portugal (Ronnie Scott and Tony Crombie) in 1970 and then became part of Ronnie Scott's Trio; originally with Tony Crombie on drums, later with the South African drummer Bobby Gien (who died in 1983 aged 44). Carr remained with Ronnie Scott until mid-1975, then again led own group. Also toured Europe with drummer Sonny Payne (1976) and toured Britain with drummer Kenny Clarke (1978). Throughout the 1980s and 1990s has continued to lead own line-ups (on piano and organ) including own trio, quartet and group Cargo. Has also accompanied many American stars, notably the tenor saxists Arnett Cobb, Johnny Griffin, Illinois Jacquet, Buddy Tate, Plas Johnson, etc. Runs own highly successful recording labels: Cargo and Birdland. Leads own groups (1996) and continues to accompany visiting musicians including Art Farmer, Buddy De Franco, Terry Gibbs. etc.

CARR, 'Tony' Antonio
Born: Malta, 24 October 1930
drums

Moved to London in 1952, worked with Roy Fox and Frank King (1953), then (in 1954) did the first of several annual European tours with Billy Eckstine. Worked with guitarist Chick Lovelle at the Savoy Hotel, London, then, in the 1960s, played with many jazz groups: Ronnie Ross's Quintet (including trip to Czechoslovakia), with Humphrey Lyttelton (1964–5), with Danny Moss's Quartet, in Spike Heatley's Trio, in Bill Le Sage's Trio, etc. Subsequently did international touring with Alan Price and with Donovan. From the 1970s through the 1990s active as a freelance, specializing in Latin-American percussion.

CARROLL, 'Eddie'
Born: 1907
piano/accordion/composer/arranger
Died: Somerset, December 1969

Piano from early childhood, did professional work at New Cross Palais before working in Glasgow at the age of seventeen. Led own band, then joined Al Starita (1929), and remained when this band was taken over by Sidney Bright (1930). Briefly in Ernest Ritte's Band (summer 1930), then worked in London and in Belgium playing second piano in Hal Kemp's Band (September 1930).

In Joe Kaye's Band (late 1930), then played second piano (and piano accordion) with Ambrose (1931). Occasional gigs with the Night Watchmen and in Rex Owen's Nephews (late 1931). With Maurice Winnick, Reg Purslove (1932), then became second pianist with Lew Stone (late 1932 to 1934). With Henry Hall from January to April 1934. Five months as accompanist for Elsie Carlisle and Sam Browne (1934). Freelance recordings with Nat Gonella, Spike Hughes, Ray Noble, etc., during the 1930s. Organized own band to play at Empress Rooms, London from October 1934. Musical director for the liner *Queen Mary* (1936). Led own bands 1937-40. Served as an officer in Royal Army Ordnance Corps (1941–5) continued to broadcast occasionally. Led own band at Imperial Hotel, Torquay (1946), then played residency at Quaglino's, London, from late 1946 until spring 1950. Led own band in England and Italy (1951–2), then took band to New Delhi, India, in spring 1952 for sixteen month booking, again worked in Italy (late 1953). Own band at Hammersmith Palais. Played in piano duo (with Norman Percival) for Agatha Christie play *Spider's Web* (1955). Moved to Burnham-on-Sea, Somerset, and played summer seasons there until the last two years of his life when ill health forced his retirement.

CARTER, 'Nigel' Eric Nigel Born: Salford, Manchester, Lancashire, 27 August 1938
trumpet

Played cornet in Peakdale Brass Band from the age of seven. Trumpet in and around Buxton area with band led by his sax-playing brother Roy Carter. Sat in with Graeme Bell's Australian Jazz Band at twelve and with Humphrey Lyttelton and Freddy Randall during early teens. Joined Ferodo Works Brass Band and played local dance gigs prior to playing in the Royal Signals Band from 1957 to 1959. After demobilization worked with Syd Dean, Harry Leader, Derek Sinclair (in Blackburn) and Ken Turner at Ritz Ballroom, Manchester. With singer Johnny Kildare's Band in Scotland (1963), also with Eddie Jackman in Bristol. Moved to London in 1965, worked with Wally Johnstone in Stevenage, then temporarily left music for eighteen months before joining Ronnie Smith's Band at Top Rank Ballroom in Watford. With Ken Mackintosh for two years, and with Tony Evans, Geoff Walker, etc., then joined BBC Radio Orchestra in 1972 and continues to play for them through the 1990s.

CARTER, 'Viv' Vivian James Born: Springvale, Victoria, Australia, 2 May 1935
drums/washboard

Played drums from the age of fourteen. Did local gigs, then moved to Britain in the mid-1950s. Worked with trumpeter Trevor Williams, then joined Mike Peters. Left Peters in late 1956 and joined Cy Laurie. Briefly with Acker Bilk, and occasionally in Ken Colyer's Omega Brass Band, also worked in Bob Cort's Skiffle Group (autumn 1957). Worked in Germany with Pete Deuchar, then joined Dick Charlesworth until October 1961. Briefly with Ken Sims (early 1962), with Mickey Ashman, with Australian trombonist Llew Hird, and again with Pete Deuchar (1963). Returned to Australia in 1964, worked around Melbourne, then moved to Sydney a year later, returned briefly to Europe with Geoff Bull in 1972. Continues to play into the 1990s, with Eclipse Alley Five, San Francisco Jazz Band, Geoff Bull's Band, etc.

CARTWRIGHT, Deirdre
guitar/composer

Born: London, 27 July 1956

Played piano as a child. Took up guitar at fifteen, self-taught. Gave up social science degree studies to become a professional musician. Recorded with Ivy Benson and played in all sorts of line-ups, large and small, during the 1970s. Part of Jam Today from the mid-1970s. With the Guest Stars from 1981 until 1987 during which time they played all over the world. Deirdre was a feature presenter for the BBC Television series *Rockschool*. Together with bassist Alison Rayner formed Blow the Fuse in the late 1980s, which has continued to flourish through the 1990s, touring and making many appearances at North London's Vortex Jazz Bar, also played the Purcell Room, London, in April 1996. Deirdre's own group has done widespread touring throughout Britain, and played in Germany and Greece. She has also worked with Pete King, Annie Whitehead, Steve Lodder, Ian Shaw and Carol Grimes and toured with Jamaican pianist Marjorie Whylie.

CASH, Bernie
double bass/trumpet/saxes/flute/
piccolo/arranger/composer

Born: Scarborough, Yorkshire, 18 January 1935
Died: Germany, 7 October 1988

Brother of reed-player Tony Cash, who worked with Ian Bell, Eric Silk, Bob Wallis, Pat Hawes, Joe Daniels, etc., before becoming a television producer and author. Bernie took up trumpet at fifteen. Was an RAF navigator (serving part of his three years in Canada). Moved to London in 1955, gigged with Bobby Mickleburgh and Bruce Turner, then worked in Germany with Eggy Ley. Moved back to Scarborough and took up double bass. Did summer season with Harry Gold, then studied for two years at St John's College, York, and Trinity College, Cambridge. Worked with Diz Disley's Soho String Quintet (1961) and Dave Shepherd (1961), Oscar Rabin and Johnny Duncan. Did summer season in Torquay with Charles Ernescoe, then moved back to Yorkshire and worked with Leeds-based Bryan Layton Trio (1966–7). Was inspirational in the founding of the Leeds School of Music jazz courses (1967). Continued to play double bass as main instrument but also played saxes and flute by this time. Taught woodwinds and brass. Led own band in Bridlington area in the late 1960s. From the 1960s studied and worked with Peter Ind. Organized the ten-piece Great Jazz Solos Revisited in 1977. Completed MPhil in 1982 with a thesis on Lester Young, which eventually led to a collaboration with playwright Alan Plater that resulted in the televised opera *Prez* (1986). Bernie Cash worked occasionally on double bass in the BBC Northern Symphony Orchestra and with the York Opera Company. He died suddenly while on tour with Royal Philharmonic Orchestra, suffering a heart attack while jogging near Düsseldorf, Germany.

CASTLE, 'Dave' David Richard
saxes/clarinet/flute/composer/arranger

Born: Trinidad, West Indies, 7 April 1939

Moved to Sheffield, England, in 1947, then lived in Berkhamsted, Hertfordshire, from 1951. Clarinet from fourteen, alto and baritone saxes from seventeen. Played in Lol Coxhill's Just Jazz Unit (1960). Moved into London in 1961, led own quartet and worked briefly in John Picard's Band. Spent three months with Humphrey Lyttelton (late 1961). With Fat John Cox (1962), with Alexis Korner (1963–4) and with Mac Macalister (1963). With Eric Delaney (1964), then again with Alexis Korner (1964). Joined Ronnie Dunne Quartet (1964), worked with this group (renamed RDQ) in the Canary Islands and Majorca (the band specialized in close harmony vocals). With RDQ in Sweden (1966) and Israel (1967), moved to Sweden. Freelanced in radio, television and films, backed visiting stars such as Sammy Davis Jr, Lena Horne, Buddy De Franco, etc. Own Sax Avenue in late 1970s, later with Mikael Raberg's Big Band and with the Stockholm Jazz Orchestra (led by Frederik Noren). Occasionally with Gugge Hedrenius, Ann Marie Hennings and Lars Sjösten's Octet. Regular playing (and teaching) through the 1990s.

CASTLE, 'Geoff' Geoffrey Charles
piano/synthesizer/composer/arranger

Born: London, 8 June 1949

Piano from childhood, played in NYJO from 1967 until 1970, then worked with Graham Collier from 1970 until 1974. During this period also worked on organ at the Latin Quarter Club, London. With Ian Carr's Nucleus from 1974 until 1982, during this time also participated in travelling Musicians' Union Rock Workshop. Own Strange Fruit from 1977 into the early 1980s, occasionally with Derek Wadsworth's Blind Alley throughout the 1980s. Presented own suite *Impressions of New York* at Camden Festival (1980). Toured with Jimmy Giuffre (1982). Lived in New Zealand, 1983-4, composed film music and recorded *Southern Excursion* with tenorist Brian Smith; played at Auckland Jazz Festival with Chuck Finlay. Returned to Britain at the end of 1984, accompanied George Coleman (1985 and 1986). Led own groups during the 1980s and 1990s. Worked in Paz, and with the Blue Angels in the 1990s, also revisited New Zealand in early 1993 and worked there with American flautist Phil Horn. Toured Britain with own ten-piece and did variety of jazz work, including duos with harmonica player Brendon Pawer. Formed own record label, Turret, in 1994. Active for many years in jazz education, was part of Eddie Harvey's Jazz Education Society, taught on Hull Jazz Course and at Wavendon Summer School, etc., also ran workshops at the Guildhall School of Music.

CATON, Lauderic
guitar/double bass/arranger

Born: Pala Seco, Trinidad, West Indies, August 1910

Studied violin and flute during childhood, specialized on guitar from age of sixteen. Led own band in Trinidad, then worked in Martinique (1937) before sailing to Europe to work in France and Belgium. Moved to London in 1940. Played residency with Cyril Blake Band (1941), with Harry Parry's Sextet from late 1941 until joining Johnny Claes in June 1942. With Bertie King's Quintet (1943), then began leading trio at Caribbean Club, London until 1946. In Ray Ellington's Quartet from late 1947 until recurrent ill health caused him to leave in April 1949. Worked with Errol Barrow's Trio in London (1950), sang in vocal trio (1951). Played at Casanova Club, London (1952), did some acting, and toured Europe with Coleridge Goode (July–September 1954). Then retired from regular playing and lived in the Bloomsbury district of London into the 1990s.

CAVE, Norman
trombone/piano

Born: Liverpool, Lancashire, 2 June 1925

Played piano from childhood, took up trombone and became part of the Salvation Army Band in Liverpool. Played trombone in the 7th Hussars Band during Army service. After demobilization in

November 1949 joined Freddy Randall on piano, but switched to trombone with Randall from May 1950. Worked in Liverpool with Mrs Wilf Hamer's Band in late 1950 and 1951, then rejoined Freddy Randall in July 1951. With Harry Gold for a year from autumn 1952, then two months with Freddy Randall in late 1953. Led own band in 1953 and 1954, then worked with Sid Phillips from October 1954 until July 1957. During the late 1950s, 1960s and 1970s worked with Betty Smith, Bernie Stanton, Bruce Turner, Danny Moss, Bobby Mickleburgh, Kenny Baker, Chick Mayes, Cyril Stapleton, etc., but in the late 1970s worked mainly as a solo pianist or as an accompanist for singers. Moved to California in July 1981. Continues to play on keyboards and on trombone (1995).

CECIL, Malcolm
double bass/synthesizer

Born: London, 9 January 1937

Piano from the age of four; studied physics but took up double bass at sixteen and became a professional musician within a year. Played in Portugal and Sweden with Harry Robbins and Dizzy Reece (1956), returned to England and worked with Ronnie Scott. With Scott and Tubby Hayes for debut of the Jazz Couriers (April 1957). Joined Dill Jones Trio in June 1957. Served in RAF from 1958, while stationed in the North East became co-founder of the Emcee Five (spring 1959), played gigs in the Newcastle area. After demobilization became an electronics consultant but continued with widespread musical activity. With Pete King Quartet (early 1960), then joined Harry Klein-Vic Ash Jazz Five in spring 1960 and worked with them for over a year. During this period also appeared in the play *The Connection* (early 1961) and worked with pianist Art Fairbanks (late 1960). With Dick Morrissey Quartet (1961), Bobby Wellins Quartet (1961) and briefly with Chris Barber for tour of Scandinavia (September 1961). Worked with Brian Dee Trio (late 1962), then joined Stan Tracey Trio (1963-4), accompanying many visiting American musicians, also with Ronnie Scott (1963-4) and with BBC Radio Orchestra. With John Fourie Quartet (1965) then, through ill health, played less and spent more time developing synthesizers. Moved to South Africa in December 1967, but soon settled in the USA, and became a successful producer and synthesizer programmer, who was also part of an orchestra for synthesizers.

CHAMBERLAIN, 'Ron' Ronald H.
alto sax/soprano sax/clarinet/flute/piccolo

Born: London, 12 May 1924

Violin at eight, piano accordion at fourteen, then alto, clarinet and soprano sax at fifteen. Began gigging as a teenager, then became founder-member of the Jive Bombers. Joined Army at eighteen, played in various service bands including the Blue Rockets, was then medically discharged after nine months. With Carlo Krahmer's Band at the Gremlin Club, and at the Nut House (1943-4). In the Vic Lewis-Jack Parnell Jazzmen (1945-6), then worked with Vic Lewis from 1946, and remained to be featured with Lewis' Big Band into the early 1950s. Freelanced and worked regularly with Norrie Paramor during the early 1950s, then worked for over ten years with Ted Heath from 1956. Extensive freelance session work through the 1970s, 1980s and 1990s, backing many visiting American stars, including Frank Sinatra. Played in various big bands including the Bobby Lamb-Ray Premru Orchestra, the Million Airs, Don Lusher's Ted Heath Orchestra (1990s) and spent six months with Syd Lawrence.

CHAMBERS, George
trumpet
Born: Belfast, Northern Ireland, 18 January 1939

Began on trumpet-cornet in 1955 and played in the Crescendo Jazzmen during the late 1950s and early 1960s. Formed Apex Jazz Band in 1966 and set up the Belfast Jazz Society during the same year. The Apex Jazz Band continues to flourish through the 1990s, having accompanied many visiting musicians including Sammy Price, Alton Purnell, Dick Wellstood, George Masso, Ken Colyer, Roy Williams, etc. Played various overseas tours including USA, Holland, Germany, etc., and appeared at various festivals in England and Scotland.

CHANDLER, Wayne
banjo/guitar
Born: Pontypridd, Glamorgan, Wales, 31 May 1935

Raised in Bristol. Took up guitar, then banjo. National Service in RAF from 1953-5. After demobilization trained as a teacher. Joined the Avon Cities Jazz Band in 1955 (was also featured in Ray Bush's Skiffle Group). Joined Terry Lightfoot in autumn 1957. Joined Cy Laurie in late 1957 (replacing Pat Wade), toured Germany with Cy Laurie, returned to London, then moved out to Germany in September 1958 to work in Eggy Ley's Band. Left Eggy Ley to join the Ken Sims-Ian Wheeler Vintage Jazz Band in September 1960, left in February 1961 to rejoin Terry Lightfoot. Moved back to the West Country in spring of 1965 and freelanced with various bands in the Bristol area, including the Blue Note Jazzband (led by soprano saxist Roger Bennett), also played in the Al Fairweather-Ralph Laing All Stars and with Ralph Laing's Groove Juice. Continues to play regularly (1996).

CHAPMAN, 'Pete' Peter Leslie
double bass
Born: Chingford, Essex, 27 December 1937

Played drums then took up double bass in 1960. Gigged with local bands before working with Dave Shepherd in 1968, and with the Alan Littlejohns-Tony Milliner Sextet. During the 1970s worked in Olav Vass's Quintet at Tiberio's, London, and co-led quintet with Gene Cottrell. Played for numerous West End shows during the 1970s and 1980s including *Ain't Misbehavin'*, *Billy*, *Mame*, *Show Boat*, *Grease*, *Barnum*, etc. Deputized in the London Jazz Big Band and worked with Tony Lee, Ted Beament, etc. Accompanied many visiting American musicians including Mose Allison, Wild Bill Davison, Peanuts Hucko, Barney Kessel, Teddy Wilson, etc. Worked regularly for Royal Shakespeare Company from 1985, but continues to play many freelance jazz dates through the 1990s.

CHARLESWORTH, 'Dick' Richard Anthony
clarinet/saxes
Born: Sheffield, Yorkshire, 8 January 1932

Took up clarinet at seventeen, moved to Hull. Worked for Ministry of Labour from 1948, posted to London 1952. Gigged in South London with the Parkside Rhythm Band then joined Jim Waller's Jazzmen (1954). Formed own band in July 1956 which turned professional in January 1959. Continued to lead City Gents until 1964, then led band aboard the P&O liner *Orsova* in 1964. Led on liners *Canberra* and *Himalaya* in the 1960s, then settled in Spain and ran own bar from 1969 until 1977. Occasionally played local gigs with visiting musicians (Diz Disley, etc.). On return visits to Britain guested with various bands. Moved back to England in 1977, began freelancing, then worked regularly with Keith Smith from spring 1979 until early 1980, before joining Rod Mason. Regularly with Alan Littlejohns during the 1980s, also led own band (which played in the Middle East and in Munich, Germany). With John Petters' Legends of British Trad during the 1990s, also with Hot Stuff. Continues to lead own quartet through the 1990s and guests with various bands.

CHASE, 'Tommy' Thomas
drums
Born: Manchester, Lancashire, 22 March 1947

Played on summer season, in night clubs and on cruise liners before settling in London. Led own quartet at the Little Theatre Club in early 1973. Briefly inactive through hand operation in 1973, then resumed leading own group which achieved considerable success through the 1980s and 1990s. Over a twenty year span, the group has featured many jazz musicians, including guitarist Dave Cliff, Chris Watson, Adrian Huxley; saxophonists Alan Barnes, Paul Zec, Dave Lewis, Kevin Flanagan; bassists Andy Cleyndert, Martin Klute, Steve Rose, Danny Padmore; pianists Richard Bush, Nick Weldon, etc. Chase has also accompanied various visiting American jazz musicians including Al Haig, Joe Albany and Jon Eardley.

CHESCOE, 'Laurie' Lawrence Charles George
drums
Born: Clapham, London, 18 April 1933

Played in Guy's Hospital Jazz Band while working at the hospital as a laboratory technician. With Stan Sowden's Jazz Aces (1954–5), played in Poland with Dave Burman's Band (summer 1956). In Colin Smith's Band (1957), with Teddy Layton (1957 to early 1959), Sonny Morris (spring 1959). Left Morris to join newly formed Eric Allandale Band (July 1960), left in autumn 1962 to join Monty Sunshine until 1964. With Dick Charlesworth (late 1964) then joined Bruce Turner (1965). Often with Bob Wallis from 1966 until 1973) (including a residency in Switzerland). Worked for a year with George Webb's Dixielanders, did three months in the Black Bottom Stompers, then began long musical association with Keith Nichols, working in various of Nichols' line-ups. With Midnite Follies Orchestra from its debut in January 1978. Also accompanied various American musicians, including Yank Lawson, Billy Butterfield, etc., and toured with Wild Bill Davison in the Anglo American All Stars. Regularly with Alan Elsdon from June 1978 until 1990, during this period also worked with Alex Welsh (1981–3) and with Alan Littlejohns' Jazzers. Made three trips to Vancouver, Canada, with Hugh Rainey and played on various Mediterranean cruises. Formed own Good Time Jazz in August 1990, which has continued to flourish through the 1990s.

CHESTERMAN, 'Chez' Graham Robertson
trumpet
Born: Putney, London, 24 February 1940

Raised in Yorkshire. Began on trumpet, played banjo for a while in the Bay City Band, then specialized on trumpet and worked in Hull with the 2.19 Band and with the Unity Jazz Band (1958). Left the 2.19 Band and moved to London (spring 1959). Led own Scintilla Jassband

(1960), then joined Pete Deuchar's Professors of Ragtime (1960). With Alex Revell and with Neil Millett during the early 1960s; began ten year occasional musical association with Eric Lister. In the Riverside Jazz Band (1963), with London City Stompers (1965), remained when Max Collie became leader (early 1966). In Johnny Parker's Band (1966–9), during this period also worked in Phil Franklin's Swing Sextet and with Bill Greenow's Strong Jazz. Led own band for three years then temporarily ceased gigging. Lived in Chesterfield, then moved to Billericay and worked for six months in the Black Bottom Stompers (1975). Worked in the Midlands with the Zenith Hot Stompers for two years from the late 1970s. Moved back to the London area in 1982, period of musical inactivity, then played for six months in the Northside Stompers (1988), before joining Pete Allen for nine months in 1989. With John Petters in the early 1990s until forming own Hot Stuff in June 1992. Continues to lead own group through the 1990s, also gigs with John Petters, and with pianist Barney Bates.

CHILTON, John James
trumpet/composer/arranger

Born: London, 16 July 1932

Took up cornet at twelve while evacuated to Yardley Gobion (a Northamptonshire village). Switched to trumpet at seventeen and played local gigs around the Kenton area in Middlesex. National Service in RAF (1950–2) then formed own band. Turned professional and played residency with own band at Butlin's, Skegness, in summer of 1958. Briefly in Bob Parker's Band, then worked in Bruce Turner's Jump Band from December 1958 until January 1963 (leaves of absence to play 1959 summer season with Ronnie Smith's Band and to play a world cruise in Don Shearman's Band on the liner *Iberia*, December 1959 to April 1960). Played in and arranged for Alex Welsh Big Band (1963–4), deputized for ailing Bob Wallis (1963) and played gigs with Alexander's Jazzmen. Played piano on a few 'pop' recordings (1963–5). Formed own quartet which played residency at the 100 Club, London from 1964 to 1966. Regularly in Mike Daniels Big Band from spring 1964 until early 1967. Formed own Swing Kings (John Lee, reeds, Frank Brooker, reeds, Roy Vaughan, piano, John 'Chuck' Smith, drums, Peter Hughes, Keith Howard, Keith 'Spike' Holmes, double bass) which backed various visiting American musicians including Buck Clayton, Ben Webster, Bill Coleman and Charlie Shavers. Began working with Wally Fawkes in March 1968, also played gigs with Bill Greenow, Doug Murray, Colin Bowden, etc. Disbanded Swing Kings and co-led Feetwarmers with Wally Fawkes from 1969 to 1973, also played London residencies with Bruce Turner (1972–4). From summer of 1970 George Melly occasionally guested with The Feetwarmers. When the partnership became a full time enterprise in January 1974, Wally Fawkes and Bruce Turner left and the group operated as a quartet accompanying George Melly. Together they did widespread international touring from 1974 through the 1990s, playing in the USA, Canada, Australia, New Zealand, Asia, and throughout Europe. During this time the group utilized the services of Tucker Bates, Stan Greig, Barney Bates, Bruce Boardman, Martin Litton, Ron Rubin and Jonathan Vinten (pianists), Steve Fagg, Barry Dillon, Ron Rubin, Ken Baldock (double bassists) and John 'Chuck' Smith, Eddie Taylor (drummers). Chilton has written various books including biographies of Sidney Bechet, Coleman Hawkins, Billie Holiday and Louis Jordan.

CHILTON, Johnny
drums

Born: Ilford, Essex, 1912
Deceased

Piano as a child, then gigged on drums around the Southend area. First professional work with Al Lever's Band in Brighton (for a year), then worked with Archie Alexander's Band in Aberdeen (1934). With Jack Padbury's Band in Nottingham (spring 1934), then again worked with Archie Alexander. To Amsterdam, Holland, with Neville Bishop's Band (1936), then long stay in Freddy Bretherton's Band (1937–8) including tour of Sweden. To South Africa with Laurie Page (1938), returned to England and joined Stan Atkins (summer 1939). With Jack Doyle (late 1939), Teddy Joyce (late 1939 to early 1940), Eddie Carroll (early 1940) then joined RAF. Played in service bands with Cyril Stapleton, and with Steve Race, also part of Leslie Douglas' Bomber Command Band. After demobilization worked briefly as a band manager then left full time music to become the Swedish representative of a British industrial company (1946). Remained in Sweden for many years, then moved back to England and retired to the South Coast.

CHILVER, 'Pete' Peter William
guitar

Born: Windsor, Berkshire, 19 October 1924

Played piano during childhood, took up guitar at thirteen. Played guitar in own band, the Silver Sovereigns (Slough, 1940), then together with Ralph Sharon worked in the Embassy Aces (Slough, 1942). Released from essential war work (as a draughtsman) to broadcast with Johnny Claes, Teddy Foster, Jimmy Messini, etc. Joined Ray Ellington's Band in summer of 1946, worked with him at Bag O'Nails Club, etc., until late 1946, then joined Tito Burns. During 1947 worked with Jack Jackson, George Shearing, Stephane Grappelli, etc. With Ted Heath from March 1948 until October 1948. With Ambrose late 1948 to autumn 1949. During this period guested with the Skyrockets to accompany Benny Goodman at the London Palladium (July 1949). Freelanced with various bands on sessions, etc., joined Ralph Sharon's Sextet in late 1949. Moved to Scotland in April 1950 and began managing a hotel in North Berwick. Subsequently ran West End Cafe in Edinburgh during the 1950s. Continued to work successfully in management and never resumed professional playing.

CHISHOLM, George
trombone/piano/arranger/euphonium/
baritone horn

Born: Glasgow, Scotland, 29 March 1915
Died: 6 December 1997

Father a drummer, mother a pianist, and two brothers (Ron and Bert) also proficient musicians on piano and trumpet. Played first engagements on piano at Delmarnock Road Cinema in Glasgow. Joined children's concert party the Merry Magnets; spell on trumpet, then took up trombone (lessons from Jimmy Chalmers). Played piano at Tower Ballroom, then worked on trombone with Louis Freeman at the Glasgow Playhouse (spring 1934). With violinist Jack Ansell's Band at Glasgow Playhouse (September 1934), then on piano doubling trombone (and arranging) with Louis Freeman at the same venue (1935). Moved to London to work in Teddy Joyce's Band (June 1935), returned to Glasgow the following year and played piano and trombone in Duncan Whyte's Band at the Playhouse. From this period onwards specialized on trombone, moved to London, gigged with various bands then joined resident band at Nest Club, Kingley

Street. Worked in Holland with Benny Carter (summer 1937). Freelanced in London, then worked briefly with Eddie Carroll (late 1937). Brief return to Teddy Joyce (early 1938) before long period of on-and-off employment with Ambrose (from 1938 until early 1940). During this period also freelanced with George Elrick, Joe Crossman and Ken Johnson, also recorded with Fats Waller in London (1938). Founder-member of short-lived Heralds of Swing from their February 1939 debut. Joined RAF in March 1940, and soon became founder-member of the Squadronaires. Remained with this band throughout World War II and after demobilization. Left Squadronaires in May 1950, freelanced (mainly in the studios), also played residency with Alan Kane's Band from May 1951 until joining BBC Show Band (then led by Cyril Stapleton) from 1952 until 1957. Regular member of Kenny Baker's Dozen during the 1950s, also freelanced with various leaders including Lew Stone, Bill Munn, and Harry Roy in the 1940s and 1950s. Worked with Jack Parnell's ATV Orchestra, then, in early 1961, joined the *Black and White Minstrel Show*. Made many guest appearances with Alex Welsh's Band in the 1960s and 1970s, including widespread touring with *Salute to Satchmo* show (1978). Overcame coronary problems (1978). Mainly freelancing from 1965, was featured on many shows, on stage, radio (*The Goon Show*, etc.) and television, often doing own comedy routine. Led own Gentlemen of Jazz for many years (including appearing at Nice Jazz Festival), also featured at Dick Gibson's Jazz Party in Denver, Colorado, USA in 1980. Awarded OBE in 1984. Persistent ill health forced his retirement in the early 1990s.

CHISHOLM, George
trumpet/flugelhorn

Born: Newcastle upon Tyne, 10 January 1947

Piano lessons from age of nine, played in school band; to London in 1963 to record on piano for musical director Johnny Gregory. Returned home and began specializing on trumpet, played many gigs in the North East, including own quintet in Whitley Bay (1967). Did summer season in Val Merral's Band (1967). Moved to London in 1969 to work with Val Merral at Douglas House Club, also played in various rehearsal big bands. In 1970 began working with John Williams' Octet and with Alan Stuart's Octet. Led own quintet (with tenorist Gerry Gibbs), then joined Tony Milliner's Sextet in 1971. During the early 1970s played in big bands led by: Tony Faulkner, Stan Tracey, Mike Gibbs, John Dankworth, Mike Westbrook, Alan Cohen and Keith Tippett. With Maynard Ferguson's Big Band (1972). In 1973 to Norway to represent Britain in European Broadcasting Union Big Band. Played on many freelance sessions in the 1970s, accompanying Frank Sinatra, Nancy Wilson, Joe Williams, etc. Led own Funk Band on an occasional basis from 1973 until 1980. With BBC Radio Big Band (1974–5) also worked with John Warren, Brian Miller, Ronnie Ross, Ken Baldock, Ray Wordsworth, Duncan Lamont, Herman Wilson, Tony Kinsey, John Dankworth, Dave Hancock, Bobby Lamb-Ray Premru, etc., during the late 1970s and early 1980s. Led own quintet and eleven piece band. Studied trumpet with Tommy McQuater from 1970 until 1983. Emigrated to New Zealand in February 1983 and works there in radio and television studio orchestra, and with the New Zealand Symphony Orchestra and the Auckland Philharmonia, as well as appearing as a jazz soloist at various international festivals through the 1990s. Brief return to Britain in spring 1994 to work with Elaine Delmar. Further solo dates in Britain (1996).

CHRISTIE, 'Keith' Ronald Keith
trombone

Born: Blackpool, Lancashire, 6 January 1931
Died: London, 16 December 1980

Brother of clarinettist Ian Christie (born 24 June 1927). Took up trombone at thirteen, lessons from Ernie Houghton in Blackpool; later studied at the Guildhall School of Music, London. Co-led the Christie Brothers' Stompers, then worked with Joe Kirkham in the Isle of Man and with Les Sherry at the Fleetwood Marine Hall, before joining Humphrey Lyttelton in January 1949. Served in the RAF but often managed to play weekend gigs with Lyttelton, and rejoined the band full time after demobilization. Left Lyttelton in July 1951 to re-form Christie Brothers' Stompers. Disbanded in July 1953 and joined John Dankworth, left to work with Tommy Whittle from September 1955 until late 1956, also played in Jazz Today Unit and often with Kenny Baker's Dozen. Joined Ted Heath from January 1957 until October 1959 then (with Allan Ganley) co-led the Jazzmakers. To USA for tour with Vic Lewis (spring 1960), then again worked with the Jazzmakers until they disbanded in early 1962. Rejoined Ted Heath and often worked with Heath during the 1960s, but also prolific freelance playing, which continued throughout the 1970s. Co-led quintet (with Jimmy Deuchar) in 1964, played in Harry South's Big Band (1965). Played on several of Benny Goodman's European tours during the early 1970s, also in Tubby Hayes' Big Band, the Bobby Lamb-Ray Premru Band, with Kenny Wheeler, Ronnie Ross, Ian Hamer's Sextet, Gene Cottrell's Band, Brian Cooper, Tony Kinsey's Big Band, Paul Fenoulhet, occasionally in the London Jazz Big Band. Played for London production of *Bubbling Brown Sugar*. Was injured in an accident, resumed playing briefly, including concert work with the Best of British Jazz.

CHRISTMAS, 'Art' Arthur
saxes/trombone/piano/
multi-instrumentalist

Born: Kingston, Ontario, Canada, 22 December 1905
Died: Ontario, Canada, 23 September 1961

His younger brother Bill was a trumpeter. To Britain in 1925 as first trumpeter with Paul Specht's Canadians (led by Orville Johnson), subsequently worked in the New Prince's Toronto Band (led by Alfie Noakes) 1926. Worked extensively in Europe during the late 1920s and led own band in Budapest and Berlin. Briefly with the Savoy Orpheans in London, then joined Billy Mason in late 1930. With Dave Frost (1931), Percival Mackey (September 1931 to 1933) then long stay with Roy Fox, playing saxes/trumpet/trombone/xylophone/drums/piano and bagpipes (from March 1933 until late 1938). With Arthur Roseberry (1938–9), Sid Millward's Nitwits (1939), Joe Ferrie (1939), then several months with Jack Jackson, before working mainly with Jack Payne from 1940 until late 1946. Played a show *For the Fun of It* in 1946 and 1947, then led own Foulharmonic Band for radio and stage show *Ignorance is Bliss* (1947–50). During the 1950s became a publican in Hackney, London, then moved back to Canada and taught music in Ontario.

CLAES, Johnny
trumpet

Born: London, 1916
Died: Brussels, Belgium, 3 February 1956

Father Belgian, mother Scottish. Schools in Belgium, France and Italy, then further education in England. Bought first trumpet while at grammar school in Oxford (1934). Moved to London, studied Economics at Regent Street Polytechnic, and gigged in band which included writer Max Jones on tenor sax. While playing at Tufnell Park Palais was signed by Billy Mason. Briefly with

Mason, then began work at Nest Club, London, worked with Fred Stanley's Band. Accompanied American Valaida Snow in Europe as part of Johnny Pillitz's Band. Recorded with Gerry Moore (1937). Worked briefly with Coleman Hawkins in Holland (1937), then joined Eddie Meenk's Band in The Hague. Freelanced in Switzerland, Italy and France then joined tenor saxist Johnny Fresco's band in Holland (1938–9), also worked as a crane-driver in father's business and gigged in Belgium with Jack Kluger's Band (1939–40). Two brief visits to London in 1939, then moved back to England in March 1940. Joined house band at the Boogie Woogie Club, London, in March 1940, later that year toured in Teddy Joyce's Band. Led own Clae Pigeons from 1941 for various London club residencies, also guested with Harry Parry's Band (1942). Led own band during World War II then opened own club in Blankenberge, Belgium, in 1946. During following year started own import and export company in Belgium, gave up playing trumpet professionally and became increasingly active as a racing car driver (he competed at Goodwood, Silverstone and Le Mans during the 1950s). After being seriously ill for two months he died while awaiting an operation. *Johnny Claes, A Bio-discography*, by Tony Middleton, was first published in 1994.

CLARE, Alan George (Alan George JAYCOCK)
piano/piano accordion/composer

Born: Walthamstow, London,
31 May 1921
Died: West London, 29 November 1993

Began playing piano during early childhood. Left school at fourteen and began playing in London night clubs, often worked with drummer Carlo Krahmer. With Stephen Miller's Quartet (1940) and with Roy Marsh's Trio, then worked with Stephane Grappelli at Le Suivi Club, London (1941). Played residency at the Cocoanut Grove and for a short while played duets with George Shearing at the Starlight Club. Briefly with Sid Phillips before joining the Army. Served in a Scottish regiment initially then played in a *Stars in Battledress* production. After being demobilized in summer of 1946, played club dates, then worked regularly in Sid Millward's Nitwits from late summer of 1946 until summer of 1948. Again worked with Stephane Grappelli (1948–50), also did brief tour with Jack Jackson (1949). Guested with Maurice Winnick and with Ted Heath. Played long residency at the Studio Club, London (1950–6), during this period also worked with Grischa Farfel (September 1950 to February 1951), Kenny Baker (March to April 1951) and with Harry Parry (1951). With Harry Hayes for three months in spring of 1955, then resumed at the Studio Club. During the late 1950s worked at various London clubs including The Star, Kool Kanary, Rake and Downbeat. During the 1960s continued to work mainly as a night club pianist, often with own trio, but also appeared in (and toured with) *The Bed Sitting Room*, and took part in various *Goon Show* productions, often appearing with Spike Milligan on television in the 1960s and 1970s. Occasionally accompanied Adelaide Hall, and also worked again with Stephane Grappelli in the early 1970s. Continued to play night club residencies in the 1980s and early 1990s but ill health often interrupted his work schedule.

CLARE, 'Kenny' Kenneth
drums

Born: Leytonstone, London, 8 June 1929
Died: London, 11 January 1985

Father a drummer, mother played piano. Drums from age thirteen. Worked in Will de Barr's Royal Forest Band (1946) then joined RAF in 1947 and played in various service bands. With

Dennis Hale in Brighton before working with Oscar Rabin from October 1949 until joining Jack Parnell in September 1954. Left Parnell to join John Dankworth from September 1955 until September 1960. With Dudley Moore Trio (1960–1), also did prolific freelance work, often accompanying visiting American stars. During the 1960s and 1970s was featured with Nelson Riddle, with Ted Heath (1962–5), with Tony Bennett (including world tours), with Tom Jones (tours of US), Johnny Spence, the Bobby Lamb-Ray Premru Orchestra, Henry Mancini, Stanley Black (including tour of Japan 1967), etc. With Kenny Clarke-Francy Boland Big Band (1967–72), subsequently with Francy Boland Orchestra, and with Peter Herbolzheimer. Continued to freelance successfully through the 1980s, also worked with John Dankworth and Cleo Laine (including tour of Australia), with Pizza Express All Stars (from May 1980), and deputizing for the injured Ronnie Verrall in Syd Lawrence's Band (1984).

CLARKE, 'Bob'
violin

Born: Scotland, c.1930

Shipwright by trade. Played in resident trio at London's Cottage Club during the mid-1950s, was also part of Diz Disley's Soho String Quintet. Worked in duo with guitarist Danny Pursford, then played in Switzerland, Russia and Iceland, before fulfilling long residency at the Lido in Paris, which led to work in Las Vegas, USA. Returned to Britain, then again did international bookings before playing long residency at the Crazy Horse in Paris from 1965 until 1973. Settled in Sussex, continued to play regularly, guested with Dave Holt's Quartet (1980), later moved back to Scotland and ran own hotel.

CLARVIS, Paul
drums/percussion

Born: Enfield, Middlesex, 9 April 1963

Began playing drums at twelve. Part of dixieland band at school in Edmonton, London, then played in local rock groups. Drum tuition from Jimmy Benson, later studied in Manchester with Dave Hassell and in Toronto with Jim Blackley. Tabla tuition from Yousuf Ali Khan. Won scholarship to the Royal College of Music and studied there from 1981–3. Did various West End shows including *West Side Story*, began doing prolific session work as percussionist with the principal orchestras. Worked under Leonard Bernstein. Increasingly active in jazz circles during the 1990s. Leads own Orquestra Mahatma (working and recording) also with Gordon Beck, Nick Weldon, etc. During 1996 freelanced in many varied line-ups including Stan Sulzmann's Quartet, Martin Speake's Fever Pitch, Steve Waterman's Quartet, with singer Christine Tobin, Alec Dankworth's Trio, as well as backing visiting American musicians.

CLAYTON, 'Freddie' Frederick G.
trumpet

Born: Edinburgh, Scotland, 13 March 1927
Died: London, 18 October 1989

Brother Stanley was a musician. Played piano at ten, trumpet from age of twelve. Teenage member of Grassmarket Mission Band in Edinburgh. Played in various bands from fourteen (mainly in Edinburgh and Dundee), including Dick Denny, George Adams, Benny Loban, Jack Watmore and Bertini. Moved to London as a member of George Elrick's Band (February 1943). Briefly with Lew Stone (1944), then long spell with Geraldo from late 1944 until May 1948. With

Don Carlos and Maurice Winnick (1948), then joined Ambrose (December 1948). With Sydney Lipton from 1949 until 1952, also led own small group for jazz concerts. Regular member of Kenny Baker's Dozen from the 1950s. With the Black and White Minstrel Show Orchestra, also guested with local jazz groups and freelanced until ill health ended his playing career, thereafter he worked as a script-writer and journalist.

CLEGG, Carole Anne
Born: Stanley, Co. Durham, 19 May 1946
vocals

Various music teachers including Sam West. Sang with local bands: the Phoenix Jazzband, the House Party Quartet and the Savoy Jazzmen (which featured her husband, saxophonist and clarinettist Eric Clegg). Guested with Humphrey Lyttelton, Roy Williams, John Barnes, Pat Halcox, etc., and toured Eastern Europe. Together with Eric Clegg formed Speakeasy (co-leader bassist Ian Heslop), which toured Britain through the 1990s and appeared at many festivals. Their Gospel Concert programme has also been performed at many festivals.

CLEYNDERT, 'Andy' Nicholas Andrew De Jong
Born: Birmingham, Warwickshire, 8 January 1963
double bass

Family moved to Bishop's Stortford in the late 1960s. Two sisters became professional musicians. Piano, bassoon, violin and vocal tuition during schooldays in Newport, Essex. First played double bass at eleven, brief lessons, thereafter self-taught. Left school at eighteen, gigged with traditional bands in London, worked briefly with Julian Stringle and John Petters. Worked for six months at Les Ambassadeurs Club, London, also played briefly in the National Youth Jazz Orchestra. At nineteen joined Tony Mann Trio for two month residency at a Manchester club. Returned to London. Weekly gigs with John Altman's Band, then worked with Bobby Wellins and in Don Weller-Bryan Spring Quartet, also part of Clark Tracey's Quartet (1983). Recorded with Tommy Chase. During the mid-1980s resumed non-musical studies and subsequently gained degree in maths and psychology. Resumed full musical activities and toured with various American musicians including Ted Curson, Bobby Watson, Slim Gaillard, Red Rodney, etc. Played in annual formation of Kenny Wheeler's Big Band. During the late 1980s and early 1990s worked with Kathy Stobart, Bryan Spring Trio, Louis Stewart, Don Weller, etc. Joined Ronnie Scott's Band in March 1992, continued to play freelance dates. During Ronnie Scott's indisposition (1995–6) played regularly in John Critchinson's Trio and Quartet, in line-ups led by Stan Tracey, Martin Drew and in Colin Purbrook's Trio. Toured with American pianist Gene Harris (May–June 1996).

CLIFF, 'Dave' David John
Born: Hexham, Northumberland, 25 June 1944
guitar/bass guitar

Took up guitar at fourteen but didn't work at it seriously until five years later. Raised in Newcastle upon Tyne. Played local gigs with various bands including quintet led by trumpeter George Chisholm. Studied at Leeds College of Music (1967–70) then moved to London in 1971. Began working with Peter Ind in various line-ups (which during the 1970s included touring with Warne Marsh, Lee Konitz, etc.) also worked with Chas Burchell. With Tommy Chase (1972–5) and played gigs with Tony Lee. During the mid-1970s co-led quartet with trumpeter Ray

Manderson. Worked in the USA with Bob Wilber (1977) and played briefly in Israel (including television dates) then returned to Britain and played in Great Jazz Solos Revisited (1978). Co-led quintet with alto saxophonist Jim Livesey (1979). With Alex Welsh (1981), working increasingly as a freelance from the early 1980s, also active as a guitar teacher. Often in Bob Wilber line-ups during the 1980s and 1990s, also in Bruce Turner's Quartet in the 1980s. With Alan Barnes, Georgie Fame, Mike Carr Trio, etc., also worked with visiting Americans: Warren Vaché, Harry Allen, Kenny Davern, etc. Toured with Humphrey Lyttelton-Acker Bilk (1993–4), and worked often in quintet co-led with Geoff Simkins. Widespread freelance playing through the 1990s, and teaching at Trinity College, Wavendon, etc.

CLIFFORD, Winston
drums/vocals

Born: Islington, London, 19 September 1965

Began playing drums at fourteen. Took lessons at school from Bill Eyden (1979), later studied with Trevor Tomkins at the Guildhall School of Music (1985). First gigs with Lionel Grigson at Zigi's Club, London. Played in various line-ups, working with Courtney Pine, Steve Williamson, Julian Joseph, Jason Rebello, Pete King, Will Gaines, Bheki Mseleku, etc. Began long musical association with Jonathan Gee in the mid-1980s which has continued into 1996, also worked regularly with Orphy Robinson from the 1980s until 1995. With Tim Garland's Quartet from 1996. Part of flautist Rowland Sutherland's Mistura through the 1990s, also Mario Castronari's Roadside Picnic, with Dylan Fowler's Frevo, in Eddie Jones' quartet and quintet, with Ciyo Brown, Juwon Agungbe and in Mo Nazam's group. Occasionally leads own bands. Has recorded with Jean Toussaint, Andy Hamilton, Brian Dee's Trio, Harry Beckett's Quintet and sang on record with Jan Ponsford's Vocal Chords. Has worked with various visiting Americans including Art Farmer, Eddie Harris, Monty Alexander (1991 tour), Larry Coryell, Archie Shepp, Dave Valentin and with singer Carmen Lundy on several of her visits to Britain. Worked in New York with Carmen Lundy (May 1996).

CLYNE, 'Jeff' Jeffrey Ovid
double bass/bass guitar/composer

Born: London, 29 January 1937

Briefly played tenor saxophone at seventeen, then switched to double bass. During Army service played for two years in Third Hussars' Band (mainly in Germany) alongside Alan Branscombe (1955–7). After demobilization worked briefly with tenorist Gerry Skelton (autumn 1957). With Tony Crombie, Stan Tracey and Paul Adam before working for three months on the liner *Mauretania* in Lennie Metcalfe's Band. With Ronnie Scott-Tubby Hayes Jazz Couriers (late 1958 to May 1959) then worked in US air bases in France with Bobby Wellins. Returned to Britain and worked with Vic Ash (September to October 1959) then joined Tubby Hayes Quartet (1959–61). Thereafter often worked with Hayes throughout the 1960s. Occasionally with New Departures Jazz and Poetry (with Michael Horovitz and Pete Brown) from 1961. With Terry Shannon Trio (1962), Tony Kinsey Trio (1963), and (from 1965) Gordon Beck's Trio. Worked as house musician at Ronnie Scott's Club from early 1966, often as part of Stan Tracey's group, also worked with Spontaneous Music Ensemble from 1966. To USA for further studies (October 1966 to February 1967), then again worked with Gordon Beck and with Roy Budd Trio (1968). During the late 1960s worked with Dudley Moore's Trio, with Tony Oxley, with Don Rendell-Ian Carr Quintet (1968), Keith Tippett (1969), on bass guitar with Ian Carr's Nucleus (1969–71), including engagements in the USA, and with Trevor Watts in Amalgam. With Alan Skidmore's Quintet in the early 1970s, also with many groups including Bob Downes' Open Music (1974) and in London Jazz Composers' Orchestra. With Gary Boyle's Isotope, Bob Barter's Trio, Phil Lee's Gilgamesh and co-leading own Turning Point (with Pepi Lemer). Extensive freelance work continued into the 1980s and 1990s, worked with many singers including Blossom Dearie, Annie Ross, Marion Montgomery, Norma Winstone, etc., occasionally in Jimmy Hastings-John Horler Quintet, in Gorden Beck's Trio, duos with Phil Lee, and accompanying many visiting American musicians. A key figure in British jazz education he is co-director (with Trevor Tomkins) of the Wavendon summer jazz course, also teaches at Guildhall and Royal Academy.

COE, Peter
Born: Cambridge, 1930
tenor sax/soprano sax

Turned professional to work with the Jimmy Simmonds Big Band (1961). Joined Georgie Fame in 1963, was featured on various hit records. Toured with Diana Ross, Stevie Wonder, Martha and the Vandellas, etc. Led own band and played many gigs with Tony Lee's Trio. Formed own big band in 1975 (the Ceeporte Big Band) which twice won the BBC Big Band Championships (in 1976 and 1978). Worked regularly in Don Lang's Band from the late 1970s. Moved to Spain in 1987, continues to play jazz, mainly in Fuengirola.

COE, 'Tony' Anthony George
Born: Canterbury, Kent, 29 November 1934
saxes/B flat and C clarinets/bass
clarinet/piano/composer

Father George also a reed player. Tony first played clarinet in the Simon Langton School Orchestra in Canterbury. Played local gigs with the Stour River Jazz Band and with Johnny Kelk's Eagle Jazz Band, then joined Joe Daniels for summer season at Ayr, Scotland (1952). Toured with Joe Daniels until March 1953, then joined East Kent Regiment for three years' Army service, playing clarinet and alto sax (serving in Kenya and in Germany). After demobilization, played at American air bases in France with Mickey Bryant's Band (1956), then rejoined Joe Daniels in October 1956. Left in May 1957 to work with Humphrey Lyttelton until October 1961. Briefly in Canadian pianist Galt McDermott's Quartet, then led own quartet and quintet (1961–2), also toured briefly with Kenny Baker (March 1962) and led quartet for Mediterranean and Black Sea cruises (summer 1962). With Al Fairweather-Sandy Brown All Stars (1962–3). Often with Humphrey Lyttelton (including big band) from late 1963 until 1968, also with John Dankworth (1967–8). Co-led quintet with John Picard in the 1960s and the 1970s. With Kenny Clarke-Francy Boland Big Band (1968–72), also began long musical association with Stan Tracey. Co-led with Kenny Wheeler (from April 1970), worked in Matrix (with clarinettist Alan Hacker) and freelanced extensively through the 1970s, 1980s and 1990s. During the 1970s and 1980s worked with Bob Cornford on several musical projects including Three. Was occasionally part of Derek Bailey's Company. With Mike Gibbs Anglo-American Band (1983) and in subsequent Gibbs' line-ups. Played for Dee Dee Bridgewater's *Lady Day* show (1987). Success as a composer and as a featured soloist on film soundtracks. Prolific freelance work as a player and writer through the 1990s, was awarded the Danish Jazzpar prize in March 1995. Touring with own quartet in 1995 and 1996.

COFFEY, 'Denny' Dennis
double bass/vocals

Born: Liverpool, Lancashire, 2 January 1927

Brother of singer Joy Coffey. Raised in London, began playing double bass at National Association of Boys' Clubs in Islington. Later played in orchestra led by Ernie Cookson and took music lessons from Claude Bampton, Served in Army (REME) (in 1944–8) and played in various service bands. Joined Doug Whitton's Band in the late 1940s, then worked with Mike Daniels (1950) and with the Galleon Jazz Band, before joining Dick Hawdon's Band. Regularly with the Christie Brothers' Stompers (1951–2), led own Red Hot Beans (1952), then worked with Cab Kaye for two months (1953) and did one trip playing on transatlantic liner. Led own quartet in Birmingham and worked with Bobby Mickleburgh, Alex Welsh, George Webb and Ken Colyer. Did stints with Chris Barber during the 1950s and worked occasionally with Mick Mulligan. Led own trio in Jersey for seasons during the 1950s, also worked in Berne, Switzerland, for two months in band led by saxophonist George Smith (late 1956). Led own trio at Les Ambassadeurs, London during the late 1950s, then retired from playing in 1960 but continued to work occasionally as a vocalist, singing on commercials and appearing on television.

COHEN, Alan Bernard
saxes/clarinet/arranger/composer

Born: London, 25 November 1934

Studied composition at the Royal Academy of Music, subsequently taught at Junior Department of Royal College of Music. Formed own big band, which played at Ronnie Scott's 'Old Place', Gerrard Street, London, in August 1967. Arranged for various jazz ensembles, for singers (including Bing Crosby) and for European radio bands. Led own Ellington tribute band in the early 1970s and taught and directed at the City Literary Institute, London. Fronted the new Paul Whiteman Orchestra (1975). Co-led (with Keith Nichols) the Midnite Follies Orchestra from January 1978 through to the mid-1980s. Musical director and arranger for Charlie Watts' Big Band (1985). Organized (and arranged for) band that backed Cab Calloway on British television (1988), subsequently formed own small group but also active as arranger and composer as well as teaching sax and clarinet at Westminster School. Recent projects for the Guildhall School of Music and the Royal Academy of Music include complete performances of Duke Ellington's *Black, Brown and Beige* (1996).

COHEN, 'Ben' Benjamin
cornet

Born: Forest Gate, London, 15 February 1929

Raised in the Ilford area. Learnt cornet while serving in the RAF. With Chris Barber from 1948 until 1951. Worked with various jazz bands in the 1950s including Cy Laurie's. With Ian Bell from late 1956 until joining Alex Revell in 1962 (occasionally deputized in the Temperance Seven during the early 1960s), also played in the Monks Jazz Band (alongside trombonist Sandy Axon). Recorded with Brian White (1961). With Mike Daniels' Big Band in 1964 then ceased playing regularly for eight years. With George Webb from the early 1970s, gigged with Chris Watford's Elite Syncopators (1976) and again worked with the Temperance Seven. During the 1980s and 1990s worked with Ray Foxley, Sonny Dee, Rusty Taylor, etc., regularly with Brian White. Formed own Hot Five in September 1993, also leads own Hot Seven.

COLE, Geoff
trombone

Born: Pinner, Middlesex, 23 May 1934

Family moved to Exeter in 1946. Started on guitar in 1951, switched to banjo in 1952 and joined local Crescent City Stompers a year later. Took up trombone in late 1953. Led own Saratoga Jazzmen (1954–6). With Crescent City Stompers on trombone (1957) then co-led band with clarinettist Mike Mayer from early 1958. Sat in with Ken Colyer in 1958. Moved to London in September 1960. With Kenny Robinson's Jazz Band for three months then joined San Jacinto Jazzmen (led by clarinettist Norrie Cox) in January 1961. Deputized for Graham Stewart in Ken Colyer's Band, subsequently joined Colyer full time in June 1961. With Colyer until 1971 (including accompanying visiting American musicians, George Lewis, etc.), then worked under Johnny Bastable's leadership until early 1973. During 1972 took leave of absence to tour USA with Barry Martyn. Again toured USA with Barry Martyn in 1973, returned to England and joined Andy Ford's Georgia Jazz Band, became leader of this band in 1975. Played in Denmark with Brian White's Magna Jazz Band in 1979 and joined them permanently in 1981. Widespread touring with Brian White, playing with him in the Magna Jazz Band in Muggsy Remembered, and in the Bob Crosby and Kid Ory tribute bands through the 1990s. Has also recorded under his own name.

COLEMAN, Fitzroy
guitar/composer

Born: Toco, Trinidad, West Indies, c.1922

Played with local bands before moving to Britain to join the All Star Caribbean Orchestra organised by Al Jennings in late 1945. Worked with Jennings in Britain and in France (1946). Played gigs in Paris, then again worked with Al Jennings' Quintet in London (late 1946). With Carl Barriteau (1947), freelanced in various night club bands, then worked with Cyril Blake (1949–50). With trumpeter Dennis Walton's Band (late 1950), Alberto (Albert Smith) in early 1951, and Errol Barrow. Toured and recorded with Freddy Grant-Humphrey Lyttelton Paseo Jazz Band (1952). With Cy Grant (1953–4), Johnny Kerrison (1954), Arthur Coppersmith (1954), Noel Brown (1955). Freelanced with many calypso and rhumba bands during the 1950s and 1960s, also active on the folk music club circuit in the 1960s. Moved back to Trinidad.

COLIN, 'Sid' Sidney
guitar/vocals/composer/lyricist

Born: 31 August 1915
Died: 12 December 1989

Worked as a commercial artist but broadcast with the Radio Four and the Four Aces (1935), also featured in Al Berlin's Juveniles. Joined Sid Millward's Band (1936). Worked with Jack Jackson. With Don Barrigo's Banditos (early 1938), with Lew Stone (1938) and again with Sid Millward (1938). With the Heralds of Swing (1939), briefly with Ambrose (1939), then again worked with Lew Stone (late 1939). Joined RAF in early 1940 and became part of the Squadronaires (1940).

Freelanced with Geraldo (1940–1). After demobilization freelanced in London and began writing comedy scripts for BBC radio. Later wrote for television (including *The Army Game*), then, during the 1970s, became Head of Light Entertainment at Yorkshire Television, also wrote for the theatre. Author of *And the Bands Played On* (1977), *Ella (The Life and Times of Ella Fitzgerald)* (1986) and *Al Bowlly* (with Tony Staveacre) (1979).

COLLIE, 'Max' John Maxwell　　　　Born: Melbourne, Australia, 21 February 1931
trombone

Played in and around Melbourne with the Malvern Municipal Band before forming own Jazz Bandits in 1948. Later, led own Jazz Kings in Melbourne from 1950 through to 1962. Flew from Australia to join the Melbourne New Orleans Jazz Band in Europe (April 1962). After that tour ended in April 1963, he remained in Britain and joined the London City Stompers, the personnel of which provided the nucleus of Max Collie's Rhythm Aces, formed in February 1966. The Rhythm Aces toured Europe extensively and made four playing visits to the USA (during their 1975 tour they won a World Championship in Indianapolis). The band's successes continued through the 1990s, being featured as the main component in various touring shows devised by Max Collie. Widespread touring, including visits to Germany and Japan took place in the mid-1990s and in Britain they continued to play clubs, festivals and concerts.

COLLIER, Graham James　　　　Born: Tynemouth, Northumberland, 21 February 1937
double bass/composer/arranger

Father played drums. Raised in Luton, began playing trumpet at eleven. Served as an Army musician in the band of the Green Howards from age of sixteen until twenty-three (including three years' posting in Hong Kong). Originally he played trumpet but later on in Army Service began specializing on double bass. Won composing competition organized by *Down Beat* magazine and as a result gained opportunity to attend Berklee School of Music in Boston USA, from 1961 until graduating in September 1963 (the first British musician to do so). While a student in the USA played with various bands including Jimmy Dorsey's, also played and arranged for Herb Pomeroy's Band. Moved back to Britain and formed own septet in April 1964, which played a long residence at the north London pub, the Camden Head. The line-up gradually changed size and instrumentation and the ensemble became known as Graham Collier's Music. By the 1970s Collier was established as an important contemporary composer but he continued to lead his own groups and to play at various international festivals (and toured India in 1979). He formed his own Mosaic record label in 1976. He consolidated his reputation in the 1980s and 1990s but rarely played double bass. He worked mainly as a conductor, keyboard player and teacher. Internationally active as a jazz educator (in Europe and in the USA) and, since 1987, artistic director of the jazz degree course at the Royal Academy of Music. Has composed for films, television, radio orchestras and the stage. His books include *Inside Jazz*, *John and Cleo*, *Jazz and Compositional Devices* and *Interaction – Opening up the Jazz Ensemble*. He was awarded the OBE in 1987. Besides his many other activities he is also co-editor of *Jazz Changes*, the journal of the International Association of Schools of Jazz.

COLLINS, Derek B.
tenor sax/clarinet/flute

Born: Blackpool, Lancashire, 21 January 1925

His late wife was the singer Bebe Moran. Played harmonica as a child with local group then took up clarinet and sax. Led own band (as Butch Collins) while still in his teens. Worked with Les Ernest's Band in Minehead, with Jack Watmore's Band in Dundee (1944–5), and with Melville Christie's Band in Amesbury, before touring with Jack Jackson. With bassist Johnny Skilton's Band in Southampton and London, then worked with Roy Fox on tour and in the Isle of Man (1947). Began working often with Bill Saville's Orchestra in the late 1940s. With Howard Lucraft's Septet (1950). From the 1950s through to the 1980s mainly active as a session musician, featured with Peter Knight, Geoff Love, Jack Emblow, Steve Race, Ken Beaumont, Brian Fahey, Johnny Pearson, Dennis Wilson, Norman Percival, Bobby Lamb-Ray Premru, etc. Toured with various singers including Judy Garland and Shirley Bassey. Worked on the liner *Queen Mary* and played on radio and recordings with Kenny Baker.

COLVILLE, 'Randy' Randolph
clarinet/saxes/arranger

Born: Glasgow, Scotland, 23 May 1942

Moved with family to Whitehaven area of Cumbria at the age of four. Took up clarinet at fourteen and played with the Carlisle Symphony Orchestra a year later. Moved to Aberdeen in 1958, studied at Gordons College and sat in with local jazz groups. Further studies at King Edward VII School in Morpeth, Northumberland, played in school jazz band. Moved to Manchester to attend the Northern School of Music. Played in Rod Hamer's Band, led own quartet (1966) and worked in trombonist Mike Knowles' Band (1967–8). Led own quintet (1969) and own Swingtet (1970), gigged with the Old Fashioned Love Band in Stoke, then, when they disbanded, adopted the name for brief while during the early 1970s. Played in the Jazz Aces, then joined the Saints Jazz Band, replacing Alan Radcliffe (early 1974). Again led own quartet (1975), which toured with Teddy Wilson. Moved to Gillingham in late summer of 1975 to teach at Kent Music School (an occupation that has continued into the mid-1990s). Worked with Rod Hamer's Dixieland Six from 1976 through to the 1980s, also with Benny Simkins' Band, and with Harry Walton (1977). With Digby Fairweather Friends from 1978, also became part of the Midnite Follies Orchestra from 1979. In 1981 began long musical association with Alan Elsdon's Band, freelanced with various other bands, often with Harry Gold in the late 1980s and 1990s, and worked briefly with Humphrey Lyttelton in Duke Ellington tribute concerts. Worked briefly in the USA with Muggsy Remembered Band in late summer of 1993. In 1989 began leading own successful Colville Collection, an enterprise that continues to flourish through the 1990s, also guests with various other bands and often works in line-ups organized by Keith Nichols.

COLYER, 'Ken' Kenneth
trumpet/vocals/guitar

Born: Great Yarmouth, Norfolk, 18 April 1928
Died: near Nice, France, 8 March 1988

Brother of washboard player William John 'Bill' Colyer (born 1922). Raised in Cranford, Middlesex. Did various day jobs, then served in the Merchant Navy until late 1948, taught himself to play trumpet. Worked as a cleaner on the London Underground, rehearsed with Mick Mulligan's Band, then formed Crane River Jazz Band in early 1949. Led this band until joining the

73

Christie Brothers' Stompers from July until November 1951, served again in Merchant Navy (a move that eventually took him to New Orleans, Louisiana, where he played with various celebrated musicians). Moved back to London and became leader of a band that had been assembled by Chris Barber (March 1953). Left just over a year later and formed own new band (in May 1954) which played residencies in Germany and gradually built up reputation throughout Europe. Ken also led the Omega Brass Band for outdoor engagements and was one of the pioneers of skiffle music. His band backed various visiting American musicians, and Ken himself worked with George Lewis in the USA (1958). During the 1950s and 1960s, Colyer's band often appeared at the club bearing his name, on the site of Studio 51, Great Newport Street, London WC2. He continued to lead throughout the 1960s; various absences through ill health, including hospitalization in 1962. Featured at the Australian Jazz Convention in January 1963. Ill health caused him to disband in the spring of 1971 (the band was taken over by John Bastable). In late 1971 he had recovered sufficiently to guest with Barry Martyn. He again led a band and from 1972 until 1978 regularly took part in recreations of the Crane River Jazz Band (including tours of Europe). Ken also guested with various bands including Chris Blount's and the Phoenix Jazz Band. Also played solo dates in Germany, Holland, Canada, etc. He led his own All Star Jazzmen in the 1980s and was featured in Max Collie's *New Orleans Mardi Gras* show from 1984. Poor health eventually forced him to retire from regular playing. He moved to France and sat in with a local band shortly before his death. His autobiography *When Dreams Are in the Dust* was published posthumously in 1989. The Ken Colyer Trust Band has continued through the 1990s to venerate the trumpeter's work. Many ex-Ken Colyer musicians are given individual entries: Mickey Ashman, Len Baldwin, Chris Barber, John Bastable, John Beecham, Acker Bilk, Colin Bowden, Ron Bowden, Jim Bray, Geoff Cole, Peter Deuchar, Diz Disley, Lonnie Donegan, Mac Duncan, Pete Dyer, Ray Foxley, Jack Gilbert, Stan Greig, Pat Hawes, Annie Hawkins, Dave Kier, Alexis Korner, Sonny Morris, Malcolm Murphy, Ed O'Donnell, Johnny Parker, Mike Pointon, Pete Ridge, Sammy Rimington, Paul Sealey, Ray Smith, Graham Stewart, Monty Sunshine, Gerry Turnham, Ian Wheeler. Those who played only in the Omega Band are not listed. Others who played in Ken Colyer's Bands include:

Clarinet:	Tony Pyke, Keith Box, John Wurr, George Berry, Ian Turner, Dave Baily and Bruce Bakewell.
Trombone:	Les Handscombe, Mike Sherbourne, Mick Clift, Kenny Blakemore, John Finch and Barry Palser.
Drums:	Bryan Hetherington, Mike McCombe, Paul Rosenberg, Brian Chadwick, Gordon Pettit, Eric Skinner, Pete Lay, Tony Scriven, Neil Millett, Gerry Card and Will Wilkinson.
Double bass:	Dick Smith, Ron Ward, Julian Davies, Ken Ames, Ray Holland, Arthur Bird, Derek Jones, Keith Donald, Bill Cole, Alyn Shipton, Robin Tankard, Allan 'Jinx' Johns and Tony Taylor.
Banjo:	Ben Marshall, Bill Stotesbury, Tim Phillips, Jim McIntosh, John Griffiths, Brian Mitchell, Dave Brennan, Derek Roberts, Louis Lince, Stu Morrison and Pete Morecombe.
Piano:	Bob Kelly, Richard Simmons.

CONDON, 'Les' Leslie Richard
trumpet/arranger/composer

Born: Kennington, London, 23 February 1930

Cousin of trumpeter Jeff Condon. Took up trumpet at seventeen, played in local (Stockwell) band with saxophonist Lennie Dawes. Did National Service in the RAF (1948–50), played regularly in the Eager Beavers at RAF Wroughton, etc. Worked with saxist Miles Mitchell's Band in Wembley (1951) and did gigs with Kenny Graham. Turned professional in 1952 and played on Cunard transatlantic liners, also worked with Les Simons (1952). With Harry Hayes (spring 1953), brief season in Isle of Man with Stanley Barnett (summer 1953). With Roy Fox, Johnny Rogers, Kathy Stobart, and Harry Bence (1953). With Ronnie Scott, Tony Crombie and Denny Boyce during the mid-1950s but mainly with Tubby Hayes from February 1955 until September 1956. With tenorist Jackie Fisher (late 1956), then briefly with Roy Kenton at Wimbledon Palais before beginning long musical association with Tony Kinsey in summer 1957. With Woody Herman for British tour (April 1959), often in Downbeat Big Band from 1959 onwards with Harry South's Big Band, Stan Tracey's Big Band, etc. Occasionally in Humphrey Lyttelton's Big Band. Prolific freelance session work from early 1960s onwards, also with Tony Crombie (1959), Eddie Thompson's Quintet (1960) and in Joe Harriott's Quintet (1961). Worked in clarinettist Donald Purchese's Theatre Orchestra, and for a month in Michel Legrand's Orchestra at the Royalty Theatre, London (1960). With Alan Clarke's Band at Orchid Ballroom, Purley (1962) and with Bobby Wellins in the New Departures Quintet (1963). Often worked with Tony Kinsey in the 1960s and 1970s. With John Dankworth line-ups (1967), with Kenny Graham (1967) and often with Ronnie Ross in Sextet and Tentet from 1968 onwards, also with Art Ellefsen's Band (1968). Worked for two weeks with Ray Charles Big Band during their European tour. Arranged for many line-ups throughout his career, also worked with Philly Joe Jones, Benny Golson, Lalo Schifrin, etc. but also continued to freelance on sessions for Tubby Hayes, Ronnie Scott, Joe Harriott, Georgie Fame, Paul Gonsalves, Ray Nance, etc., and with various bands. Played for show *Bubbling Brown Sugar* for two years, also worked in Sun City, South Africa, in 1981, accompanying singers Jack Jones and Helen Reddy. Continued to play regularly until 1990 when dental problems curtailed professional schedule. Continues to sit-in with various jazz groups (1996) but increasingly devoting time to playing the piano.

COOK, 'Dick' Richard Francis
B flat, A and E flat clarinets/bass clarinet/saxes

Born: Keythorpe Hall, Tugby, Leicestershire,
19 May 1936

Began on guitar and banjo in 1956, switched to clarinet in 1960. Played for two years in Nottingham with Les Devotees before living in New Orleans from 1966 to 1968 (during this period played E flat clarinet in the Olympia Brass Band and worked in quartet with trumpeter Clive Wilson and drummer Trevor Richards). Moved back to England, then worked (and recorded) with Harold Dejan's Olympia Brass Band in Berlin (summer 1968). Settled in London and worked in Mike Casimir's New Iberia Stompers from 1968, and in the Paragon Brass Band. Began leading own Jambalaya which continues to flourish through the 1990s. Accompanied visiting American musicians including Alvin Alcorn and Albert Nicholas and played at the Nice Festival with the New Iberia in 1974 and 1975. Made regular return trips to the USA and played in Belgium and Holland (often with the Belgian Cotton City Jazz Band). Co-led the Inter Cities

Jazz Band (with trumpeter Teddy Fullick) from 1976, toured Europe with this band and played at Lugano Festival, accompanied American musicians, Al Casey, Teddy Johnson, and Snub Mosley. Toured and recorded with drummer Freddy Kohlman. In 1978, with pianist Ray Smith, helped instigate the London Ragtime Orchestra. Is Assistant Leader (Leader: Mike Brown) of the Excelsior New Orleans Brass Band and Vintage Jazzband which, like the London Ragtime Orchestra, continues to operate through the 1990s. Toured with Chris Barber (including the USA) in the Dr John package (1980). Freelance dates in Switzerland (early 1996). Continues to lead Jambalaya and own trio through the 1990s.

COOKE, 'Micky' Michael Edward
Born: Hyde, Cheshire, 6 August 1945
trombone/vocals

Took up trombone at fifteen, a year later began gigging with the Blue Lotus Jazzmen in and around Manchester. Worked with Johnny Tippett, and in Smokey City Six (with Sheila Collier) before joining Red River Jazzmen (late 1966). Left Red River Jazzmen to join Terry Lightfoot in spring of 1968, remained with Lightfoot for seven years. Joined Alan Elsdon in late 1975. Freelanced with Dave Shepherd, Lennie Hastings, Digby Fairweather, etc., then joined Alex Welsh in 1978, Pete Allen in 1979, also played occasionally in Al Fairweather-Ralph Laing All Stars. With Keith Smith from 1980 until 1987, then worked for two months in Switzerland with the Piccadilly Six before joining Acker Bilk in the summer of 1987. Continues with Bilk through the 1990s.

COOPER, Alan Swainston
Born: Leeds, Yorkshire, 15 February 1931
clarinet/bass clarinet/soprano sax/arranger

Played in Vernon Street Ramblers while studying at Leeds College of Art. Joined Yorkshire Jazz Band in January 1949. After finishing studies moved to London to teach art. From the mid-1950s worked with Lennie Hastings, in quartet with Bernie Cash, with Johnny Parker (1957), etc. From early 1957 often played in the Temperance Seven (originally on bass clarinet). With Graham Stewart's Band (1958–9), then worked regularly on clarinet with the Temperance Seven until January 1962. Freelanced with various bands and deputized in Alex Welsh's Band on several occasions during the 1960s, also with Freddy Randall occasionally (1966–8). With Alexander's Jazzmen (1968) and in Colin Bowden's Trio in the late 1960s. With the New Temperance Seven from 1969 until 1973, during this period also played in Dick Powell's Long Swing Quintet (1971). Guested with Bob Kerr. Often in various Keith Nichols' line-ups from 1975, occasional gigs with the Temperance Seven in the late 1970s. Was often part of the British All Stars which drummer David Mills organized for work in the Middle East during the 1980s. Again worked with the Temperance Seven in 1981 and 1982. Led own band and own trio in the 1990s, often gigged in Dick Laurie's Elastic Band and freelanced in London before moving to Hay-on-Wye, where he often works with Martin Litton and cellist Stanley Adler (1996).

COOPER, 'Andy' Ian Francis Andrew
Born: Elgin, Scotland, 23 February 1942
clarinet/sax/vocals

Born during father's RAF service in Scotland, spent infancy and childhood in Liverpool. Began playing music at thirteen while at St Elysian College and went on to Cambridge to study art. Played gigs with the University Jazz Band and with the Riverside Seven during the late 1950s. Turned professional in 1962, joined the London City Stompers in Germany (1962). Left London City Stompers to work with Charlie Galbraith (1964), then with Alan Elsdon from autumn 1966 until joining Kenny Ball in November 1967. Continued to work with Kenny Ball through the 1990s.

COOPER, 'Dougie' Douglas
drums

Born: Weymouth, Dorset, 3 September 1929

Father played alto sax. Began on drums at age of six. Played gigs in early teens; moved with parents to London. Left school and joined George Evans, then worked with Ronnie Munroe before joining Tommy Sampson (1947–8). With Paul Fenoulhet, Joe Loss and Dennis Hale, then temporarily left the music profession to help his father run a hotel in Weymouth. Resumed full time playing and worked with Harry Roy at Pwllheli holiday camp (1952) then joined Tito Burns in late 1952. During the late 1940s and early 1950s also worked with Nat Temple, Nat Allen, Eric Winstone and Edmundo Ros. Rejoined Tito Burns until autumn 1954 band break-up then worked with Geraldo (1954–5). With Bert Courtley-Jack Seymour Band (1956), then joined Oscar Rabin. Managed hotel in Weymouth, then played in South Africa accompanying various artistes including Eve Boswell (1965–6). Returned to hotel management in Weymouth, then moved to Grand Rapids, Michigan, USA, in 1977. Played with various ensembles including big band led by Bruce Early and with Jimmy Forrest-Al Grey group, deputized briefly in Count Basie's Band. Moved back to Weymouth in 1979, gigged with local bands and led own trio and quartet through the 1990s.

COTTON, 'Billy' William
drums

Born: Westminster, London, 6 May 1899
Died: Wembley, Middlesex, 25 March 1969

Served in the Royal Fusiliers as a drummer boy (at fifteen), was later commissioned in the Royal Flying Corps. After demobilization gigged with Gilbert Coombes and his Fifth Avenue Orchestra (based in Kilburn, London). Worked in band co-led by his nephew (violinist Laurie Johnson) and pianist Arthur Rosebery at Ealing Palais (September 1923 to February 1924). With Johnson and Rosebery (who soon left) co-led band billed as Al Johnson and the San Prado Band at Wembley Exhibition (from April 1924). Subsequently worked with Jack Howard's Band at the Olympia Ballroom. Led own London Savannah Band at Regent Ballroom, Brighton, then played residency in Southport and at London's Astoria Ballroom prior to residency at Streatham Locarno in summer of 1930. Appeared at Ciro's Club in London, and Ciro's in Paris (from late 1930). Played stage shows at the Alhambra Theatre, London, then enjoyed long tours of the British music halls. Subsequently enjoyed enormous popular success on radio and television. Died while attending a boxing match. His autobiography *I Did It My Way* was first published in 1970.

COTTON, 'Mike' Michael Edward
trumpet/harmonica/vocals

Born: Tottenham, London, 12 August 1939

Began playing trumpet in 1957. First gigs with George Perry's Jazz Band then spent three months in Ian Bell's Band. Deputized for Mike Daniels (1959), then joined Pete Ridge's Band in December 1959. Took over leadership of Peter Ridge's Band in early 1961 and after residencies in Germany (1961), continued to lead successfully through the 1960s (adopting the name Mike Cotton Sound in early 1964). Briefly led new band Satisfaction (1970-1), then accompanied the Kinks (1971–3). With Acker Bilk from April 1973 until June 1991, during this period guested with various bands and accompanied visiting American musicians. During the 1990s worked with Harry Strutters Hot Rhythm Orchestra, with Bob Hunt's Ellington Orchestra, Stan Greig's Boogie Band, the 100 Club All Stars, in quintet co-led with John Barnes, with Campbell Burnap (including dates in Finland, 1995) and with the Great British Jazz Band.

COUGHLAN, 'Frank' Francis James
trombone/trumpet/tenor sax/
arranger/vocals

Born: New South Wales, Australia, 10 September 1904
Died: New South Wales, Australia, April 1979

From a musical family. Worked with many bands in Sydney and Melbourne before moving to Britain in December 1928. Joined Arthur Rosebery (December 1928), then worked with Fred Elizalde from early 1929. Worked with Jack Hylton, Al Starita and Al Collins before returning to Australia in December 1929. With Harry White, Ern Pettifer, Don Rankin, etc., and led own band. From April 1936 until its closure in December 1970, his band played many residencies at The Trocadero, Sydney. (Coughlan also led an Army band during World War II.)

COURTLEY, 'Bert' Herbert
trumpet

Born: Moston, Lancashire, 11 September 1929
Died: Croydon, Surrey, 13 September 1969

Toured Scandinavia with the Royal Kiltie Juniors (1947). Returned to Manchester and worked in Bill Edge's Band before joining Tommy Sampson (late 1947). With Teddy Foster (1948). With Kathy Stobart's Band in early 1950 then (with Kathy Stobart) joined Vic Lewis (spring 1951). Married Kathy Stobart in October 1951. With Geraldo (April to May 1952) then joined Ken Mackintosh from spring 1952. With Eric Delaney for a year from summer 1954. Co-led band with bassist Jack Seymour (1956). With Tubby Hayes (early 1957), in Jazz Today Unit (spring 1957), then worked with Jack Parnell before joining Don Rendell in 1957. Worked with John Dankworth (1958) and played gigs in Humphrey Lyttelton's Big Band, then joined Cyril Stapleton in late 1958. Toured with Woody Herman's Anglo-American Alliance (April 1959). Co-led band with Ronnie Ross from May 1960 until February 1961. Freelance session work during the 1960s. Co-led band with Kathy Stobart during the early 1960s. Took own band to Germany, then spent three years with Ted Heath. Suffered ill health during the last three years of his life but continued to freelance and worked in quintet with Kathy Stobart as well as playing in Harry South's Big Band.

COX, 'Gary' Francis Gary
saxes/woodwind

Born: Aberdeen, Scotland, 16 September 1934

Served as an Army bandsman, left after four years' service (1955). Moved to London, played various gigs with Ronnie Stephenson, Ronnie Scott and Tubby Hayes, etc., then returned to Scotland. Freelanced, then joined Don Smith's Band in Luton (mainly on tenor sax). Remained with Smith when the band moved to Newcastle upon Tyne. During the three years spent with Don Smith's Band, became founder-member of EmCee Five in Newcastle (1962). Worked with Colin Hulme's Band, then joined the BBC Northern Dance Orchestra from 1963 to 1974. During this period also played lead alto sax in Maynard Ferguson's Band (1968). Became part of the Millionaires Big Band from 1974–6. During the years 1975 to 1993 did four long stints in Syd Lawrence's Orchestra, including one stay that lasted from 1985 to 1993. During the 1980s and 1990s played many jazz gigs, led own quintet and did regular small band work with drummer Tony Richards.

COX, John Ambrose
drums

Born: Bristol, 20 June 1933

His son Ullrich is a drummer. Led own trio (which accompanied many visiting jazz musicians) at Bristol Jazz Club (1955). Moved to London, played various gigs including spell in Harry Beckett's Latin American Band, then went to Germany with Dave Keir's Band (summer 1956). Returned to London, worked with Teddy Layton and did trio work before returning to Germany with Eggy Ley. With Graham Stewart in England (1959) and in duo with pianist Norman Long, then rejoined Eggy Ley (April 1960). With Diz Disley (1961) and Johnny Parker's Band, then joined Mick Mulligan in April 1961 (also gigged with Wally Fawkes in 1961). Formed own band (as Fat John Cox) for January 1962 debut. Disbanded in 1965 to play on P&O liners. Organized new line-up in 1966, later led band specializing in Latin American music during the late 1960s and early 1970s. Freelanced through the 1970s, regularly with Dick Sudhalter in 1973. During the 1980s worked regularly with Eric Lister's group at Langan's Brasserie in London. After Lister's death in 1988 remained at this residency working in quartet led by tenor Roland Lacey through the 1990s. From the late 1980s was also featured in Ralph Laing's group Groove Juice Special.

COX, 'Terry' Terrence William Harvey
drums

Born: High Wycombe, Buckinghamshire, 13 March 1937

Sat in regularly at the Cadena Club, High Wycombe. Lessons from Jack Peach. First professional work with Michael Garrick (1960–1). In Lennie Felix Trio (1961–2). Joined Al Fairweather-Sandy Brown in late 1962, also played in Alan Littlejohns-Tony Milliner Band (1963). With Sandy Brown's Band and with Denny Wright before joining Alexis Korner. Left to take part in the formation of Pentangle. With Pentangle from 1968 until 1973. During this period also freelanced with many groups, and worked in the Roger Webb Trio (1970), with Bobby Lamb-Ray Premru Orchestra (1971), etc. Accompanied various visiting American musicians including Benny Carter, Jon Hendricks, etc. Worked with Cleo Laine and John Dankworth, and with Ronnie Scott. Toured with Roy Orbison, Gilbert O'Sullivan, etc., and worked with David Bowie, Elton John, etc. Moved to Minorca in the late 1960s. Regularly with Charles Aznavour for six years. Took part in Pentangle reunion. Recovered from injuries sustained when knocked down by vehicle in Guildford, Surrey (1982) and resumed playing. Is based in Minorca, where he and his wife run the Pan Y Vino restaurant in Torret, but continues to play drums, working winter seasons with American keyboard player/singer Deborah Carter and playing each summer in a quartet with trumpeter Ronnie Hughes.

COXHILL, 'Lol' Lowen
saxes
Born: Portsmouth, Hampshire, 19 September 1932

Raised in Aylesbury, Buckinghamshire. Worked for seven years as a bookbinder then served in the RAF. Led own groups on tenor sax (including the Just Jazz Unit) at various venues in and around Aylesbury (1958–61). First professional playing with Tony Knight's Chessmen (touring with Rufus Thomas, 1964). With Bruno's Blues Band, the Gass, Steve Miller's Delivery, etc. in the late 1960s, toured Germany with Alexis Korner (1969) and worked as a successful busker. With Kevin Ayer's Whole World Band (1970–2). Specializing on soprano and sopranino saxes he worked with many bands in the 1970s, guested with Harry Miller, the Damned, and the Brotherhood of Breath, did duos with David Bedford, Steve Miller and Jerry Fitzgerald, worked in Paz, with Mike Westbrook, Stan Tracey, did solo tour of USA and Canada (1978). Worked briefly with Bobby Wellins (1979), led own quintet, and toured with drummer Pierre Courbois and keyboard player Jasper Van't'Hoff. In the 1980s played solo and with Kenny Shaw's Band, Mike Horovitz's New Departures, Dave Green's Fingers, Trevor Watts Moire Band, the Recedents, The Melody Four, Standard Conversions, etc. Toured Japan in 1983. During the 1970s and 1980s was a central figure in the Bracknell Jazz Festival, also worked as a television actor. Own line-ups including the seven piece Promenaders. Active through the mid-1990s, continues to be featured at many international festivals. A biography, *The Bald Soprano* by Jeff Nuttall, was first published in 1989.

CRAIG, 'Al' Alfie
drums
Born: England, July 1907
Died: Nice, France, 25 October 1981

Father was American boxer Frank Craig. Was originally a vocalist. Took up drums and worked in Europe with the visiting American show *Blackbirds* (1935). Led own band at the Shim Sham Club, London (1935–6). Recorded with Benny Carter in London (1937) and accompanied pianist Garland Wilson. With Jack Davis (1938), led own Rhythm Swingers, then joined Gerry Moore's Band at the New Florida Club, London (1939–40). Briefly with Lew Stone before serving in the RAF during World War II. After demobilization moved to Paris where he worked with Django Reinhardt, subsequently led own band in Nice (1947). Continued to lead own band in France, played seasons at the Plantation Club, Nice, in the mid-1950s before moving to Düsseldorf, Germany.

CRAIG, Archie
trumpet
Born: Glasgow, Scotland, 10 December 1914
Died: Surrey, October 1988

Lessons from his brother John. First professional work with Louis Freeman, then toured with Bobby Hinds before moving to London to work in Jack Hamilton's Band (1933). With Buddy Featherstonhaugh. Joined Sydney Lipton in February 1934, left in September 1936 to join Claude Bampton. Left Bampton in spring 1937, worked with Oscar Grasso. With Bill Woodward and George Elrick (1937) before joining Ambrose in spring 1938. Worked in Heralds of Swing (1939), then rejoined Ambrose in autumn 1939. With Ambrose's Octet in early 1940, then worked with Jack Harris before joining RAF in spring 1940. Became part of the Squadronaires and continued working with them after World War II. Active freelance in the 1960s, also worked with Joe Daniels at Butlin's, Clacton, in 1967. Took part in Squadronaires re-union in 1978.

CRAIG, 'Danny' (Daniel Burns CRAIGIE)
drums

Born: Dundee, Scotland, c.1924

Played drums from age of twelve. Led own quartet in Dumfries (1944), then moved to London, worked with Jack Lennox, Martin Hayes (1944), Felix Mendelssohn, Jack Jackson (1945), then spells with Oscar Rabin, Nat Allen and Duncan Whyte. With Harry Roy, then led own band in Devon (1948) before working with Harry Parry from late 1948 until late 1951. To Nairobi, Kenya, with Bob Navarro's Sextet (December 1951). Subsequently worked in Kenya with Bobby Leitch and led own band before returning to Britain in December 1952. Joined Harry Gold from December 1952 until May 1955, then worked with Harry Hayes, Leslie 'Jiver' Hutchinson and Ambrose (1955). Toured with Billy Daniels (1956) and worked briefly in Dave Shepherd's Band (1956). Worked with Sandy Brown, Johnny Hawkesworth, and led own group. Regularly with Dill Jones' Trio from 1957 until early 1960. Ill in hospital for several months (1961), then again worked with Dave Shepherd (late 1961). Toured briefly with Kenny Baker's Octet (spring 1962), deputized in Alex Welsh's Band (late 1962). With Judd Solo (1963), led own band and freelanced then spent twenty months in hospital (1966–7) before returning to freelance work.

CRANE, 'Ray' Raymond
trumpet

Born: Skegness, Lincolnshire, 31 October 1930
Died: Surrey, 29 June 1994

Raised in Nottingham, played there with the Mercia Jazz Band from the mid-1950s. Moved to London in February 1963 to join Bruce Turner's Jump Band, worked with Turner until 1966, and played various guest engagements with him through the 1980s. Briefly in Acker Bilk's Band (early 1967), then freelanced with various groups including Alexander's Jazzmen, Mike Daniels Big Band, Johnny Toogood's All Stars, worked with Maurice Jennings and Sid Phillips, also active as a teacher and band coach. During the early 1970s with Stan Grieg's Boogie Woogie Band, Sandy Brown, Colin Symons, Doug Murray, Sonny Dee, again with Bruce Turner and regularly in house band at the Georgian Club, London. Founder member of Stan Greig's London Jazz Big Band (February 1975), continued to work with Greig through the 1970s, also with Trevor Whiting's Swingtet, with Brian Lemon, Mike Daniels Big Band, Alvin Roy, John Petters, etc. through the 1980s. With Colin Purbrook's group in Alan Plater's *Rent Party* show (1989), also worked in Middle East with Alan Cooper and David Mills. During the early 1990s guested regularly with Dick Laurie's Elastic Band, and freelanced with Bruce Turner, Pete Strange and in Trevor Swales' Band. Ray was also a noted teacher who directed various student bands including the Harrow Youth Jazz Orchestra.

CREESE, Malcolm
double bass

Born: Bristol, 24 August 1959

Father a violinist in the London Symphony Orchestra, mother an accomplished pianist. Was a chorister for five years at St John's College, Cambridge, gained scholarship to Radley College, then studied cello for a year at the Guildhall School of Music. On cello worked in orchestras and chamber music ensembles in Britain and overseas but switched to double bass in 1984, did gigs with pianist Frank Toms and began freelancing with jazz groups. Worked with Tony Coe, John Horler, Allan Ganley, Don Weller, Alan Skidmore, Barbara Cook, Kenny Wheeler, Vic Ash, Art

Themen, Elaine Delmar, etc. and accompanied visiting musicians such as Art Farmer, Barney Kessel, George Benson, Mose Allison, Warren Vaché, Herb Ellis, etc., also worked with the Jiving Lindy Hoppers. Freelanced in diverse musical surroundings, with Sting, Diana Ross, Mel Tormé, Frank Sinatra, Rod Stewart, and with the London Symphony Orchestra, The Hallé Orchestra, etc. Has also undertaken acting roles on stage and on television. Continues with busy freelance schedule through the mid-1990s, featured regularly with Stan Tracey's various line-ups (until late 1995) and with Cleo Laine and Johnny Dankworth, also works with Tony Coe Quartet, Randy Colville, Keith Smith, Digby Fairweather, etc, and runs own recording label ABCDs.

CRIMMINS, Roy
trombone/vocals

Born: Britain, 2 August 1929

Worked in London with the Galleon Jazz Band (1950–1). With Mick Mulligan in 1952, and briefly in Dick Hawdon's Band before working with Freddy Randall from January 1953 until September 1953. Rejoined Mick Mulligan from autumn 1953 until spring 1954. Briefly with Dave Keir's Band (spring 1954) then became founder-member of Alex Welsh's Band from 1954 until 1965. Led own group in Germany (1965). Worked with various bands in Europe, and played residencies in Switzerland and Austria, some with own Roy King Dixielanders. Returned to Britain and freelanced from January 1979, then again worked with Alex Welsh until that leader's death in 1982. Often worked with Harry Gold during the 1980s, also led own quintet, played in Five-a-Slide and with various Bob Wilber line-ups. Settled in Israel in 1987 where he continued to play (and teach music).

CRITCHINSON, John William Frank
keyboards

Born: East London, 24 December 1934

Family moved to the West Country in 1939. Gigged around the Chippenham and Bath area during the 1950s, then did first professional work with tenor saxophonist Ted Carter at the Regency Ballroom, Bath, in 1957. Also helped organize the Icebox Club in Chippenham. Worked in London with Rex Ruttley's Band (1958–9). Musically inactive 1959 to 1961, then joined the Avon Cities Jazz Band early in 1961, left in early 1963 to lead own trio in Bath. Led own trio throughout the 1960s, also again played residency at the Icebox, Chippenham, backing various visiting jazz musicians into the 1970s. Own trio resident in Bristol during the early 1970s, also accompanied singer Sammi Brown and played in CDM Trio (with Martin Drew and Ron Mathewson). Worked in Bridport (1975), moved to Torquay in May 1977, led own trio at the Imperial Hotel until moving to London in October 1978. Gigged with Kathy Stobart, then joined Ronnie Scott in May 1979. Remained with Ronnie Scott through the 1990s. During Scott's indisposition, led own trio and own quartet at Ronnie Scott's Club (1995–6) and worked in Martin Drew's Quartet. Has also accompanied many visiting American jazz musicians and worked in the Morrissey-Mullen Band in the early 1980s. Often in duos with saxophonist Ned Bray (1996).

CROCKER, John Reginald
clarinet/saxes/flute

Born: Nottingham, 19 October 1937

Began playing clarinet at sixteen. During RAF service (1956–8) played in the Eagle Jazz Band while stationed in Cyprus. After demobilization gigged around the Nottingham area, then joined Trevor Jones' Jazzmen in 1959. Left Jones in early 1961 to join the Dauphin Street Six (led by Len Baldwin). Worked with Mike Cotton from 1963 until joining Chris Barber in July 1968, has remained with Barber through the 1990s. During this period also worked in the summer months with Pat Halcox's Band and led own quartet which toured Holland and Germany in the summer of 1994.

CROKER, 'Denny' Denis Frederick Edwin
trombone

Born: Bow, London, 10 March 1925

Played trombone from age of thirteen. First gigs with Will De Barr's Band in Essex (alongside Freddy Randall), again worked with Randall in drummer Freddy Mirfield's Garbage Men from 1944, (won *Melody Maker* Individual Prize with Mirfield at 1944 contest). Left Mirfield in late 1946 to work in Freddy Randall's Band. Long stay in Sid Millward's Nitwits from 1947 until 1958 (briefly rejoined Freddy Randall in 1955). After extensive touring with Millward left full time music and gigged with various bands in East London. During the 1980s and 1990s led own line-ups and worked with Digby Fairweather, Brian White, Dennis Field, Alan Littlejohns, etc.

CROMBIE, 'Tony' Anthony John
drums/piano/composer/arranger

Born: Bishopsgate, London, 27 August 1925

Mother played piano for silent films, father was a furrier. Began work in the fur trade, took up drums, played local gigs with tenor saxist Harry Robbins. Worked in band at the Mazurka Club, Denman Street, London (1941), then joined Clarie Wears. Played at the Number One Rhythm Club (spring 1942), then joined Carlo Krahmer's Band (1943) on drums with Krahmer on vibes. Briefly with Johnny Claes. To Germany with Barrie Wicks (1946), then spent a month in Jack Jackson's Band (spring 1947). Took own band to Ireland (June 1947). Worked with Woolf Phillips and Tito Burns (1947). Left Tito Burns in July 1948 to tour with Duke Ellington (as part of Jack Fallon's Trio). Returned to Tito Burns, became founder-member of Club Eleven (December 1948). During the 1950s accompanied various visiting Americans including Ella Fitzgerald, Tony Bennett and Lena Horne. In duo with Tommy Pollard (1951), then briefly with Roy Fox (August to September 1951). With Ronnie Scott 1952–4. Led own band in 1954. Worked in Victor Feldman's Trio (1954–5). Rejoined Ronnie Scott in 1956, then led own Rockets which made debut in August 1956, disbanded and led own band until late 1959. Rejoined Ronnie Scott in early 1960. Took own quartet to Monte Carlo (summer 1960). Worked as house drummer at Ronnie Scott's Club, accompanied many visiting American musicians, also active as composer, wrote incidental music (and led quartet) for the show *Why the Chicken?* (1961), wrote for films and television (sometimes co-composing with Alan Clare). Led own group for eight months in Israel (1963). Worked with organist Alan Haven from 1964 until 1967 (including bookings in Las Vegas). Toured Britain with Coleman Hawkins (late 1967). In duo with organist Mike Carr (early 1968). Worked in Ronnie Scott's Big Band (1967), including tour with the Walker Brothers, also in Ronnie Scott's Octet (from 1968). Pendulum Duo with Mike Carr (1970–1), then with Carr made up Ronnie Scott Trio from 1970–3. Worked often in Alan Clare's Trio in the 1970s and 1980s, including many engagements with Stephane Grappelli. With Stan Tracey (1974), often with Georgie Fame throughout the 1970s. Enjoyed continual success with compositions, many artistes recording his work, including Miles Davis, Stephane Grappelli, Paul Gonsalves, Tubby Hayes, Joe Henderson, Victor Feldman, Ronnie Scott, Blossom Dearie, Annie Ross, etc. Led own groups in the 1980s and 1990s, continues to freelance successfully (1996).

CROSSMAN, 'Joe' Joseph
saxes/clarinet/violin/vocals

Born: London, 20 March 1905
Died: London, 4 October 1989

Brother of trumpeter Bram Crossman (born 1915) and cousin of accordionist Gerald Crossman. Raised in St Albans. Studied violin at Guildhall School of Music, played early gigs in the Chequers Dance Band and with Maurice Bowman's Orchestra. Played a season at Plymouth with Teddy Baker's Quartet, then concentrated on alto sax and clarinet. Worked with Lorna Lareine's Rhythm Kings for five weeks, then joined Bert Zeumer's Band (also featured on violin). Worked with Ed Lee's Band in London. Joined Ambrose in 1925, moved to May Fair Hotel with that leader (March 1927), left in January 1930 and worked with Jack Hylton until rejoining Ambrose in July 1930. Left Ambrose to work with Lew Stone from November 1932 until March 1938, briefly rejoined Ambrose, returned to Lew Stone within weeks but left in September 1938 again to rejoin Ambrose. Led own band for one week in December 1938. With Jack Hylton (1939), then joined Maurice Winnick (February 1940) before again working with Ambrose (May 1940). Joined Harry Roy in November 1940. Entered RAF in September 1941. Played with various service units including the RAF Fighter Command Band, occasionally 'guesting' with civilian bands. After demobilization worked again with Lew Stone (spring 1946), then played in Monte Carlo with Ambrose's Band (summer 1946). Active freelance, also worked regularly in Ronnie Selby's Trio (1947), with Maurice Winnick (1949), Don Carlos (1950), and Lew Stone (1950). Regularly with Lew Stone from spring 1951 until spring 1953. Led own band (1953), then toured with Bobby Howell's Theatre Orchestra (1953) before taking own octet to India for season at the Taj Mahal Hotel, Bombay (from October 1953). Returned to Britain, did wide variety of work including summer season at Ramsgate with Jack Newman's Band (1956) and season with own band at Bournemouth through the 1960s, also led band on the liner *Caronia*. Continued to freelance through the 1970s, often playing on cruise liners. Retired from full time playing in 1983.

CRUMLY, 'Pat' Patrick John
saxes/flute/arranger

Born: Oxford, 9 February 1942

Clarinet from fourteen, alto sax at sixteen. Led own University Quartet at Oxford during the mid-1960s. Backed various visiting guest musicians, later led own semi-professional band around the Oxford area and gigged extensively on tenor and soprano saxes. Toured briefly with John Dankworth in 1973, began teaching at Wavendon Summer School, had own programme on

Radio Oxford (1971–5). Turned professional in 1978, toured with Jack Jones, Cleo Laine, John Dankworth Sextet, etc. Moved to London in 1979, played for West End show *Tommy*. Did tour of Middle East with Trini Lopez, freelanced with many line-ups, played for three months in Sun City, South Africa (1981). Worked with Zoot Money, Alan Price, Helen Reddy, etc., world tours with The Animals (1983), with Eric Burdon (1984). Led own Strata nine piece line-up and organized own big band, but from the late 1980s mainly led own quartet. Recording own Third World compositions. After tour of Scotland, linked up with Tam White for successful but short-lived band in the early 1990s. From 1990 work and recordings with singer Chris Farlowe. Continues to teach at Wavendon. Regularly leading own line-ups through the 1990s.

CUMMINGS, 'Jock' (William CUMMING)
drums

Born: Aberdeen, Scotland, January 1913
Died: Ruislip, Middlesex, November 1988

Father, Bill Cumming, was a professional drummer and noted teacher. 'Jock' worked regularly in Scotland before moving to London. Worked with Freddy Bretherton's Band in early 1935. Briefly with Stanley Barnett. With Sydney Lipton from April 1935 until joining Jack Hylton in January 1937. With Jack Harris (1938–9), briefly with Billy Ternent, then joined Ambrose in late 1939. Joined RAF early in 1940 and became founder-member of the Squadronaires from 1940, remained with them after service commitments ended, but left them in May 1950 to join Geraldo. Worked again with Ambrose and played in pit orchestra for *Call Me Madam* (autumn 1952) then joined BBC Show Band (directed by Cyril Stapleton) until 1957. Thereafter worked successfully as a freelance session musician in radio, recordings, television and theatre.

D

DALGLEISH, Alex
trumpet/composer/arranger

Born: Glasgow, Scotland, 18 September 1934
Died: Glasgow, 1996

Gigged with the Rhythmaires before doing National Service in the RAF. After demobilization played in Stateside Jazz Band and in the Vernon Jazz Band, both winners of Scottish National Jazz Band Championships (1956 and 1958). Led own band from 1960, disbanded in spring 1961 to join Forrie Cairns' Clansmen. Left Cairns to join the Clyde Valley Stompers in early 1963, then joined Terry Lightfoot in 1964 (including tour of the USA). Moved to Devon and played with various local groups, then returned to Glasgow in 1965. Worked in Scotland with Billy MacGregor's Band for four years, then played in Switzerland with the Piccadilly Six until 1971 (replaced by Dave Stewart). Returned to Glasgow, worked with Jimmy Philips, Johnny McVey and Tommy Sampson and played for fifteen consecutive years with the Glasgow Circus Orchestra, also did ten seasons at Butlin's holiday camps and led own band at Gleneagles Hotel for four years. Toured with Forrie

Cairns and Fiona Duncan in McJazz (1989). Led own band through the 1980s and 1990s, played gigs with George Penman and worked as an instrumental instructor in Glasgow schools.

D'AMATO, 'Chappie' Noel Albert Gennaro
saxes/clarinet/piano/guitar

Born: Fulham, London, 1897
Died: London, 13 March 1976

His sister Aida sang with Stanley Barnett's Band. Noel played banjo in Louis Mitchell's Syncopating Sextette, then worked with Jack Hylton throughout the 1920s, first on banjo and guitar then alto sax, then piano. Left Hylton in early 1933 to play guitar in Jack Jackson's Orchestra until early 1935. Led own band and worked with Billy Ternent, freelanced, then formed new band for residency at the Piccadilly Hotel, London. With Arthur Young's Band (on guitar) in late 1939. With Denis Moonan's Band (1941) then led theatre orchestra (1941), before beginning long residency at Hatchett's Club in 1942, which terminated in 1950. Subsequently became radio disc jockey and musical director. Noel's father, Carlo (born in Naples), also worked with Louis Mitchell, as did Aida.

DANIELS 'Joe' Joseph
drums

Born: Zeerut, Transvaal, South Africa, 9 March 1909
Died: Northwood, Middlesex, 2 July 1993

Brother of saxophonist-accordionist Len Daniels (1903–68). Family moved to England during Joe's childhood. He took up drums at eleven and played gigs at thirteen at Frascati's Restaurant in London. At fourteen he worked with Harry and Burton Lester's Cowboy Syncopators. Played on Cunard liners for fourteen transatlantic crossings. Worked in Max Goldberg's Criterion Dance Band (1926) in August 1926 becoming leader of that band. Took own Harvard Band to Belfast for residency (1927), later that year joined Al Tabor's Band in Birmingham. With Tabor for twelve months then brief stint with Pete Mandell (1929) and work with Jim Kelleher and his band in 1929. Six months with Billy Mason, then joined Harry Roy for almost seven years. During this period also led own Hot Shots on recordings and on radio (from mid-1935). Left Harry Roy in January 1937 to concentrate solely on leading his Hot Shots; toured Scandinavia with them in 1938. Served in the RAF during World War II, led own service band and produced shows. After demobilization, re-formed Hot Shots early in 1946, entertained troops in Italy and Austria. Solo act in Middle East (1947) and on British variety halls, then re-formed Hot Shots in summer of 1948. Active as a leader of small groups in the 1950s, 1960s and 1970s, but regularly led big bands for summer seasons at various Butlin's and Pontin's holiday camps (until 1974). Suffered a stroke in the late 1980s and ceased playing. *Joe Daniels: A Discography* by Tony Middleton, was first published in 1982.

DANIELS, Maxine (Gladys LYNCH)
vocals

Born: Stepney, London, 2 November 1930

Sister of singer Kenny Lynch. Was evacuated to Carmarthenshire, Wales, during World War II and sang at a local Eisteddfod. Returned to London, sang with Johnny Dalton's Band in Canning Town, then worked with Reg Cavell in Romford. Two years with Denny Boyce (1954–6), then made variety hall debut at Chiswick Empire in August 1956. Was featured at the London Palladium, Prince of Wales Theatre, etc., and also worked in cabaret at the Stork Club, Astor's and Churchill's. Retired from singing from 1958 until 1966. Moved to Southend and worked with Kenny Baxter's Band and with Ron Spack. Recovered from heart surgery (1988) and worked with the Pizza Express All Stars, Best of British Jazz, Harry Gold, etc. Worked with reed-player John Wurr in the late 1980s and 1990s, also toured with John Petters. Featured in the touring show *A Tribute to Ella Fitzgerald* during the 1990s and in the *Ladies of Jazz* (with Barbara Jay and Tina May) in 1996.

DANIELS, 'Mike' Michael John Brett
trumpet/alto sax/baritone sax/clarinet/arranger

Born: Norbiton, nr Kingston upon Thames, Surrey, 13 April 1928

Grandfather was a professional musician. Became interested in jazz while a pupil at Aldenham School (1941–5). Took up trumpet at sixteen. Moved with family to Stanmore, Middlesex in 1946 and in 1947 organized the Stanmore Stompers, a get-together band of varying size. In late 1947, this group stabilized as a seven-piece band which soon became known as Mike Daniels and his Delta Jazzmen. They began playing in and around the London area in early 1948, and went on to build a national reputation through widespread playing in the 1950s and 1960s. Mike Daniels formed a big band in 1964, which continued to function for over twenty years (latterly organized by saxophonist Trevor Swale). Mike himself retired temporarily from regular playing in 1974. He moved to Majorca in 1977 and did part-time playing there with the Felanitx Town Band (a reeds and brass military band). Beginning in 1985, Mike made a series of trips to Britain to lead reunion bands. He moved back to England in 1992 and reformed his own band on a permanent basis, it continues to flourish through the 1990s. Mike also guests with various bands, including Brian White's Magna Jazz Band and Trevor Swale's Sextet, he is also featured with Bob Dwyer's Hot Six. Many musicians who worked in Mike Daniels' Delta Jazzmen are given individual entries in this book, others who have played in it during its long history include: Trevor Adams (trombone), Des Bacon (piano/alto sax/clarinet), Boots Baker (trombone), Doreen Beatty (vocals), Stan Bellwood (drums), Frank Brooker (reeds), Jeff Cobb (string bass), Charlie Conner (clarinet), Bill Cotton (banjo), Pat Deeble (banjo/guitar), Eric Edwards (drums), Arthur Fryatt (drums), Gary Garratt (trombone), Trevor Glenroy (drums), Roy Hardy (drums), Ken Hogston (double bass), Mike Jefferson (piano), Alan Johnston (piano), Phyllis Keyes (vocals), John Lee (reeds), Keith Lightbody (banjo), June Mackie (vocals), Owen Maddock (sousaphone), Tony Matthews (banjo), Pat McCormick (drums), Doug Murray (piano/trombone), Bernie Newland (trombone), Geoff Over (banjo/trombone), John Poulter (reeds), Ted Prior (banjo), Bob Rogers (guitar), Reg Sims (piano), John 'Chuck' Smith (drums), Don Smith (double bass/sousaphone), Terry Thompson (reeds), Red Townsend (drums), Geoff Walker (banjo), David Webb (clarinet), Jeff Williams (trombone), John Wurr (reeds). A detailed history of the band, *Mike Daniels and the Delta Jazzmen* by Michael Bowen, was first published in 1982. It also lists those who played in Mike Daniels' Big Band.

DANKWORTH, 'Alec' Alexander William
double bass

Born: London, 14 May 1960

Son of John Dankworth and Cleo Laine, brother of singer Jacqueline (Jacqui). Played clarinet before taking up double bass. At seventeen studied at the Berklee School of Music in the USA. Worked often with his parents for ten years from 1981 (including international tours), but also with Tommy Chase, Dave O'Higgins, Tommy Smith, Jean Toussaint, Buddy De Franco, Stephane Grappelli, Michael Garrick, etc. In September 1986 began long musical association with Clark Tracey line-ups, and in the late 1980s commenced another durable connection with the Pizza Express Modern Jazz Sextet. Accompanied many visiting American musicians in the 1980s and 1990s, and played in the London Symphony Orchestra. Toured Europe and South Africa with pianist Abdullah Ibrahim (1993). During the 1990s played in the Dankworth Generation Band, in the London Jazz Orchestra, with Julian Joseph, Martin Taylor, Peter King, Pat Crumly, Dave Newton, Guy Barker, etc., and did prolific freelance work, including a brief stint with Freddie Hubbard (April 1996). Led own quintet and own trio (with drummer Paul Clarvis and guitarist John Parricelli). Freelance work included gigs with pianist Marian McPartland (May 1996).

DANKWORTH, John Philip William
alto sax/clarinet/arranger/composer

Born: Woodford, Essex, 20 September 1927

Married Cleo Laine on 18 March 1958, their children are bassist Alec (born 1960) and singer-actress Jacqueline (born 1963). John's sister Avril is a musical educator. Violin first, attended Monoux Grammar School, then studied clarinet at Royal Academy of Music (became LRAM at nineteen). At seventeen led own Quartette which won North West London *Melody Maker* contest in May 1945. By then he was also gigging (and recording) with Freddy Mirfield's Garbage Men. Continued to work with Mirfield until serving in the Army from July 1946 until June 1947. Worked in Bobby Kevin's Band aboard liner *Queen Mary* (from July 1947). Worked in London with Les Ayling (late 1947), then joined Tito Burns from March until May 1948. Further voyages on *Queen Mary* and work with Paul Fenoulhet, then joined Ambrose in late 1948. Became founder-member of Club Eleven in December 1948. Led own quartet and worked with Ambrose until July 1949, then accompanied Benny Goodman as temporary member of the Skyrockets (July 1949). Extensive freelance work included sessions with Steve Race, Joe Daniels, Mickie Binelli, Stanley Black, Frank Weir, etc. Formed own Seven in December 1949 and continued to lead them until July 1953. Led own big band from summer 1953 until spring 1960 (featured at Newport Jazz Festival, USA in 1959). Briefly led own quintet then re-formed big band (May 1960), thereafter regularly and successfully re-formed own big band through into the 1990s. Also led smaller line-ups and was part of the Dankworth Generation Band through the 1990s. Also active as Cleo Laine's musical director from 1971 onwards, touring the world leading the accompanying group. With Cleo established the Wavendon All Music Plan (near Milton Keynes) during the late 1960s which thrives into the 1990s. Throughout his career Dankworth has enjoyed widespread success with his compositions, he has written a number of extended works and many film scores. He became a Fellow of the Royal Academy in 1973 and was awarded the CBE in 1974. A biography of the Dankworths, *Cleo and John* by Graham Collier, was published in 1976.

DARE, 'Reggie' Reginald
tenor sax/clarinet/vocals/composer

Born: Dover, Kent, 1914

Died: 1963

First professional work in ship's band aboard the *SS Lancastria*. Accompanied American singer and trumpet player Valaida Snow (as part of Johnny Pillitz's Band) in Holland and Switzerland (1937). Worked in Austria with saxist Teddy White's Band (summer 1937 to spring 1938), then returned to London and played in house band at the Bag O'Nails club. With Billy Mason, then worked with drummer George Bright's Band (summer 1939). With Teddy Joyce, Russ Allen (1940), Johnny Claes (1941, 1942 and 1943). With Harry Parry (1942), Chick Mayes (1943), and in Duncan Whyte's Sextet (1943). During World War II also worked as a hospital orderly. Led own band 1944–5. Worked with Sid Gross's Band (1946), then several months of musical inactivity through a broken arm (1946). Worked with Ray Ellington and with Duncan Whyte (late 1946), then led own band at the Potomac Club, London (summer 1947). Again with Duncan Whyte (1947–8), summer season at Cliftonville with Tony Wayne (1949). Often with Winston Lee's Band from 1949 until 1955, including playing aboard the liner *Queen Mary* (1951). Freelance small band recordings with various leaders throughout his career. In the latter part of his life again worked as a hospital orderly.

DAVANI, 'Dave' David
organ/piano

Born: Cinderford, Gloucestershire, 27 December 1934

In London since infancy, piano from age of five. Specialized on piano accordion after leaving school and won Rank Cinema contest. Started leading own band. Worked with Harry Parry (1952), with Norman Burns from early 1954 until late 1955. With Tony Laurence Band at Club Tahiti, London, later led own band there. Played on gigs with Ronnie Scott, Tubby Hayes, etc., and played series of concerts with Jimmy Skidmore. With Basil Kirchin (1958) also briefly with Frank King, then again led own band. Began specializing on organ in the late 1960s. Mainly active with own various groups including an eleven-piece line-up (featuring vocalist David Essex). Toured Germany and also played organ duos with Billy Preston. Continues to lead own small group through the 1990s, mainly in the London area.

DAVIES, 'John R.T.' John Ross Twiston
multi-instrumentalist/arranger

Born: Wivelsfield, Sussex, 20 March 1927

Brother of bass player Julian. Their father was a dermatologist who played piano. Short-lived efforts on piano at age of four; played drums in school band (1940–1). Took up guitar during Army service in Austria (1945–8). After demobilization played banjo on Eel Pie Island in group with pianist Norman Day, cornetist John Postgate and singer George Melly. Together with Day and Melly, joined Mick Mulligan in October 1948. Took up trombone in 1949 and a month later played it in the Crane River Jazz Band. Left that band in spring 1951. Worked with Steve Lane (1952). In late 1954 joined Cy Laurie on trombone, playing weekday engagements (at weekends John Picard, then in the RAF played in the band). With Sandy Brown for twenty months (1955 to summer 1956), during this period took up alto sax. Played alto sax and guitar with Acker Bilk for three months in autumn 1957, then briefly led own band at Wood Green Jazz Club before freelancing. Played one gig on drums with The Barnstormers (deputizing for Brian Rust). Joined

Temperance Seven as trombonist (and arranger) from spring 1959 until 1968 (sometimes doubling on sax and trumpet) but played occasionally with the band for many years after. Worked in the Anglo-American Alliance (with Dick Sudhalter and Henry Francis) for four years from 1967. With the new Paul Whiteman Orchestra from 1972 until 1975, also with the Crane River Reunion Band from May 1972 until 1978 and again in the 1980s. After Ken Colyer's death the band played a few engagements then disbanded. Led own group Gentle Jazz through the 1990s, and freelanced. Is a noted discographer, who started his own Ristic label in 1949, he is also a leading specialist in the art of remastering recordings.

DAVIS, Beryl
vocals

Born: Plymouth, Devon, March 1923

Sister of actress Lisa Davies, their father was guitarist Harry Davis (1901–97). Tap dancing champion as a child, then sang with the Romany Band in London at fourteen. Worked in Paris and Copenhagen with the Quintet of the Hot Club of France (early 1939), then joined Oscar Rabin's Band in London (spring 1939). Again worked with the QHCF this time in London (summer 1939), then joined Arthur Young's Band (1939–40) and doubled in the show *Black Velvet*. Rejoined Oscar Rabin, then worked with Geraldo (June 1942 to April 1943). Toured theatres with Stephane Grappelli's Swingtette (spring 1943), then again worked with Oscar Rabin. Emigrated to the USA in January 1947 and enjoyed successful career there. Living in California during the 1990s.

DAVIS, Lew
trombone

Born: London, 4 August 1903
Died: London, 24 November 1986

Brother of saxophonist Ben Davis. Played in the Darnswells (directed by Syd Roy, and including Harry Roy) in 1920. With the Happy Six (with Jack Block) and in Mitchell's Syncopated Band at Rector's Club, London (1921). Worked in Dixie Five for residencies in Norway (September and October 1921), then to Ostend as part of Laurie Huntington's Dixie Five. Returned to London, worked in the Frolic Club's Five Blues (with brother Ben) and with Harry and Syd Roy in the Original Lyrical Five. With Mitchell's Syncopated Number One Orchestra at Hammersmith Palais. To Paris in guitarist Tommy Venn's Band, then toured British music halls in band led by pianist Billy Jones. Joined Jack Hylton in February 1923, remained with Hylton until autumn 1930, but did freelance work during this period. With Ray Starita in late 1930, remained for a further month when George Hurley took over leadership in January 1931. With Billy Mason (1931–3, including tour with Louis Armstrong). With Carroll Gibbons from August to October 1932, then joined Lew Stone. Remained with Lew Stone until November 1934 (but also did summer season with Ray Noble in Holland, August 1933). Left Lew Stone to join Ambrose in November 1934. Worked regularly with Ambrose during the following three years but also freelanced with Jack Harris during this period. Rejoined Lew Stone in April 1938. Extensive freelance work during the 1930s, including leading own Trombone Trio on record. Regularly with Geraldo in 1940, but increasingly active in managing own music business, which included designing mutes and mouthpieces. He combined this for a while with freelance music making, then ceased playing to concentrate on highly successful business enterprise.

DEAN, Elton
alto sax/saxello

Born: Nottingham, 28 October 1945

Raised in London. Played piano and violin as a child, then took up clarinet. Gigged with traditional bands before specializing on tenor sax. Worked in Germany with a soul band, Lester Square and the GT's. When this band broke up he remained in Germany to work with an Irish Show Band, The Crickets. Worked in Britain with the Crickets, then joined another soul band. He temporarily quit music after his saxophone was stolen. Resumed playing and worked with Long John Baldry (1967) then switched to alto sax while backing The Paper Dolls. Joined Soft Machine in late 1969, by this time had begun long musical association with Keith Tippett. Remained with Soft Machine until 1972. During the 1970s and 1980s worked with the London Composers' Orchestra, with Centipede, own Just Us Quartet, own Ninesense, in El Skid (with Alan Skidmore), Chris McGregor's Brotherhood of Breath, Ark, Georgie Fame, the Dutch band Supersister and with Carla Bley. Toured Europe and South America. During the 1990s, has led own line-ups for widespread touring, working with Harold Beckett, co-leading quartet with Howard Riley, with John Etheridge, own trio (with Paul Rogers and Mark Sanders), duos with drummer Steve Noble and with guitarist Phil Miller, also in British Saxophone Quartet.

DEANS, Danny
trumpet

Born: Glasgow, Scotland, 1920

Brother of saxophonist Mickey and trumpeter Maurice. Was taught by brass-playing father. Worked with Jack Chapman in Glasgow, before moving to London to join Eddie Carroll (1940). During the 1940s worked with Harry Roy, Jay Wilbur, Harry Parry, the Skyrockets, Eric Winstone and the Sommerfield King Band. Temporarily moved back to Scotland in 1947 and joined George Colborn at the Glasgow Palais. Left and worked with Frank Weir before touring with Carl Barriteau. Later played on the liner *Queen Mary* with Ivor Noone's Band (1949). During the 1950s worked with Bobby Leitch, again with Harry Parry, with Eric Galloway, Jimmy Cummins, Ronnie Odell (in Spain), Frank King, Dave Shand and Chico Arnez. Mainly active as a freelance from the 1960s until ill health caused retirement from full time playing.

DEANS, 'Mickey' Michael
saxes/clarinet

Born: Glasgow, Scotland, 4 August 1914
Died: Glasgow, Scotland, 6 May 1994

Father of saxophonists Michael and Bobby; brother of trumpeters Danny and Maurice. Originally learned music from his brass-playing father. Worked with Louis Freeman's Band, then moved to London and played in various night club bands. With Len Hayes (summer 1937). With Billy Mason's Band (1939), with Joe Loss, George Elrick, Ronnie Munro (1941), then returned briefly to Scotland and worked with Lauri Blandford's Band at Dennistoun Palais (early 1942). Rejoined Joe Loss (February 1942), later with Jay Wilbur, Johnny Claes, Ned Whitebread and Freddy Ballerini. With Van Phillips, Harry Parry, John McMeighan (1944), then worked with Woolf Phillips, Frank Weir, Ambrose, the Squadronaires, Carl Barriteau and Duncan Whyte, before moving back to Scotland in late 1947. He made Glasgow his base and continued to play regularly until the early 1980s.

DEE, Brian
piano/organ/composer

Born: London, 21 March 1936

Father Eddie Dee was a saxophonist and arranger. Briefly on piano at ten years of age, but didn't practice seriously until after RAF service (1954–6). Gigged mainly around the West London area, then worked with Lennie Best, Dave Morse and Vic Ash in the late 1950s. Joined Harry Klein-Vic Ash Jazz Five from March 1960 until May 1961. With Bobby Wellins before joining Tommy Whittle in September 1961. Led own trio at the Establishment Club, London (1961–3). Accompanied various singers including Lita Roza, Danny Street, etc.; worked with Frank Weir, Eric Winstone, Ken Mackintosh, etc. Toured with Tubby Hayes (1965). Solo residency at Downbeat Club, London, and at various hotels, then played in pit orchestra for *Sweet Charity* show. Many studio sessions including recordings with Bing Crosby, also toured with Peggy Lee. Own trio through the 1980s and 1990s, also often with Bob Wilber in the late 1980s and 1990s. Regularly accompanied Elaine Delmar through the 1980s and 1990s, and worked with Kenny Baker, with Bruce Adams-Alan Barnes Quintet, as well as accompanying visiting American musicians and freelancing.

DEE, Sonny (Stanley DALY)
drums

Born: King's Cross, London, 27 November 1929
Died: 1997

After serving in the RAF worked with Lou Preager, Jack Nathan and Harry Parry, then led own band. With Al Wynette's Band (1975), then worked with Harry Gold from 1975 until 1990. Formed own All Stars in 1990, a band that was featured at various festivals, concerts and club dates in Britain and abroad.

DEFFERARY, John
clarinet/alto sax/tenor sax

Born: London, 27 March 1941

Played in New Teao Brass Band and with 'Uncle' John Renshaw's Band before joining Keith Smith's Climax Jazz Band from 1962 to 1965. Led own Creole Jazz Band (1966–7). With John Keen's New Orleans Band (1968) and often (on tenor sax) with Mike Casimir's Paragon Brass Band in the late 1960s and early 1970s. Occasionally depped with Ken Colyer and gigged with Pat Hawes, John Chilton, etc. Joined Trevor Richards New Orleans Trio in March 1973 and did widespread international touring, playing for long periods in the USA (where John took lessons from Barney Bigard, having previously been coached by Albert Nicholas in Europe). In January 1977 the Trio was involved in a car smash while touring Poland. Its three members, Trevor Richards, John Defferary and pianist Bob Barton, recovered from serious injuries and resumed working together almost a year later. They played a full schedule for a further four years after which Barton and Defferary co-led Super Jazz for three years. Did various tours accompanying visiting American musicians including Louis Nelson, Alton Purnell and Freddy Kohlman, then settled in Denmark and joined Papa Bue's Viking Jazz Band in the mid-1980s. Worked with Papa Bue through the 1990s, but makes regular visits to Paris to work in various gipsy bands.

DEFRIES, 'Dave' David Colin Walter
Born: London, 24 May 1952
trumpet/flugelhorn/tenor horn/composer/arranger

Began playing trumpet as a teenager, later attended Leeds College of Music. During the late 1970s worked with Jabula, with Dudu Pukwana and with Don Weller's Major Surgery. With Chris McGregor's Brotherhood of Breath, occasionally led own big band. Together with guitarist Mark Wood formed Sunwind in 1981. Part of Loose Tubes during the 1980s, also worked with Rip, Rig and Panic and the Breakfast Band. With Charlie Watts' Big Band (1986). Toured with own quartet in the late 1980s prior to moving to France.

DELANEY, Eric
Born: Acton, London, 22 May 1924
drums/tympani/percussion

Piano from early childhood, drums from the age of ten. Played in family trio (mother on piano, father on banjo). Studied with Max Abrams. Worked in Harry Roy's Juveniles (spring 1938), was later featured in two Hughie Green shows (1938) before leading own juvenile band (1939). Worked in Pietro Diego's Argentine Orchestra (1940), did summer season with Norman Robinson's Band (1941), then worked with Ambrose (late 1941 to summer 1942). Briefly with Harry Roy's Lyricals, then joined RAF in late 1942. Featured in the RAF *Gang Show* including tours of India and Burma. Was part of the RAF revue, *The Flags Are Flying*, prior to demobilization in 1946. With Cyril Stapleton, Stephane Grappelli and Hamish Menzies (1946), then joined Geraldo from December 1946 until May 1950. Spent several months in the Squadronaires before rejoining Geraldo from January 1951 until April 1954 (also played on many freelance sessions including regular work in Kenny Baker's Dozen). Formed own band in April 1954, led until April 1965, then worked in cabaret, including bookings in Las Vegas, USA, and the Bahamas (1971–2). Reorganized own band in 1975. Continued to lead own line-ups (large and small) through the 1980s and 1990s. Played regular seasons at the Tower Ballroom, Blackpool, from 1981 to 1989. Featured at various festivals throughout the 1990s, also guested on many concerts including some with the Kenny Baker-Don Lusher All Stars.

DELMAR, Elaine
Born: Harpenden, Hertfordshire, 13 September 1939
vocals/piano

Daughter of Leslie 'Jiver' Hutchinson. Did first broadcast on piano at fourteen. Sang regularly on radio from March 1959. Occasionally sang with her father's band during the 1950s, then worked in stage musicals and cabaret. Joined the Dominoes. Featured at the Beaulieu Jazz Festival in 1959, then worked throughout Europe as a solo singer and cabaret artiste, also worked as an actress in stage and television productions (at the National Theatre, in *Finian's Rainbow*, etc). During the 1970s and 1980s was featured in various musicals, including starring role in *Bubbling Brown Sugar*. Combined cabaret appearances with work on cruise liners and jazz club bookings in the 1980s and 1990s, often appearing at Ronnie Scott's Clubs in London and Birmingham and being featured at international festivals. During the 1990s also featured in *The Ella Fitzgerald Song Book* (with Barbara Jay and Rosemary Squires) and in Keith Smith shows *Let's Do It* and *Thank You, Mr Gershwin*.

DENIZ, 'Frank' Francisco Antonio
guitar

Born: Cardiff, Glamorgan, Wales, 31 July 1912

His father (from the Portugese Cape Verde Isles) played violin and mandolin. Frank's wife, Clare plays piano, and his daughter, also Clare, is a cellist. Frank's brothers, Joe and Laurie, were both professional guitarists. Took up guitar during childhood, but served in the Merchant Navy before playing gigs around Cardiff with Ray Clements. Moved to London. Freelanced and toured with Ken Johnson before joining Jack Davies' Band briefly in 1938. Later that year worked with pianist-organist Fela Sowande at Adelaide Hall's Florida Club, London. With Al Jennings at the Kit-Cat Club (1939–40), then began long musical association with Eric Winstone, working originally in Winstone's Quartet, also briefly with Edmundo Ros in 1941. In late 1942 was recalled to the Merchant Navy. During periods of leave again worked with Eric Winstone. Worked with Stephane Grappelli and gigged with Johnny Claes, also deputized for brother Joe in Harry Parry's Sextet. In 1944, while on Merchant Navy service, was torpedoed on way to the Anzio beach-head; returned to Britain via Algiers. Extensive freelance work after World War II, radio engagements with many bands, including the Radio Rhythm Club Sextet. Formed short-lived Hawaiian group for Cocoanut Grove residency. This soon disbanded and gave way to the Hermanos Deniz Cuban Rhythm Band which enjoyed many years of success. Frank continued to play freelance gigs, guesting with the Skyrockets, doing radio work with Nat Temple and touring Britain with Hoagy Carmichael, etc. Continued to lead own band through the 1960s and 1970s, including long residency at the Talk of the Town, London. Subsequently played entr'acte music (with Joe) for the musical *Ipi Tombi* for five years during the 1970s. Played freelance dates until retiring to Spain in 1980. Makes regular return visits to Britain.

DENIZ, 'Joe' José William
guitar

Born: Cardiff, Glamorgan, Wales, 10 September 1913
Died: London, 24 April 1994

Brother of guitarists Frank and Laurie, their father played mandolin and violin. Played ukulele before taking up guitar. Served as a Merchant Seaman, then worked in Blue Hawaiians in Cardiff before moving to London in 1935. Played at the Nest Club (temporarily doubling on drums), then worked in Rudolph Dunbar's Quintet (early 1936). Joined Leslie Thompson's Emperors of Jazz which was the forerunner of Ken Johnson's Band (1936). Remained with Ken Johnson until March 1941, and was injured by the bomb that killed Johnson. Worked with Harry Parry (late 1941 to early 1942). Occasionally with Eric Winstone, also with Jack Hamilton (autumn 1942). Toured with Stephane Grappelli (1943), briefly with Geraldo, then worked in Leslie 'Jiver' Hutchinson's Band (1944). With Harry Hayes (1945), Dick Katz Trio (1946), Eddie Carroll (1947), then co-led Hermanos Deniz Cuban Rhythm Band, which played club residencies in the 1950s and 1960s. Joe also played on many sessions and worked briefly with Ambrose and with Cab Kaye's Quintet in 1958. Together with Frank played the entr'acte music for the musical *Ipi Tombi* for five years during the 1970s. Joe retired from regular playing during the 1980s and worked for several years for a photographic company.

DENIZ, 'Laurie' Laurence Richard   Born: Cardiff, Glamorgan, Wales, 17 August 1924
guitar

Brother of Frank and Joe Deniz. Worked with Buddy Featherstonhaugh, Eric Winstone and Victor Feldman, then served in the Army from 1944. After demobilization worked with Dick Katz, then joined Ray Ellington in spring of 1949, also did extensive freelance radio work. Left Ray Ellington in summer of 1953. Worked in Johnny Franks' Quartet (1953–5), with Vic Ash (1957), Cab Kaye (1958). Thereafter played many club residencies and freelance sessions (including duo work with trombonist Jim Shepherd). His son Howard is a musician.

DEPPA, Claude   Born: Cape Town, South Africa, 10 May 1958
trumpet

Moved to Britain in the mid-1970s. Was taught and inspired by Bob Bell, Harry Beckett, Kathy Stobart, Olaf Vass, Brian Booth and Dave Holdsworth. Did first gigs with Dave Holdsworth, Harry Miller and Geoff Castle. Worked with Louis Moholo, Julian Bahula's Jazz Africa, Brian Booth's Jazz Orchestra, Iggy Quail, the Jazz Warriors, Brian Abrahams, Clifford Jarvis, Prophets of Light, etc. During the 1990s was with Carla Bley's Very Big Band, Louis Moholo's Viva le Black, Tony Haynes' Grand Union Orchestra, with Elton Dean, Andy Sheppard's Co-Motion and Big Commotion Bands, and Tom Bancroft's Orchestra, as well as leading own line-ups including the Spontaneous Urban Ensemble and Frontline.

DE SOUZA, Yorke   Born: Jamaica, West Indies, 19 March 1913
piano/arranger   Died: Enfield, London, 4 October 1986

Worked with Bertie King in Jamaica, then travelled to London with King in November 1935. With Happy Blake's Band in early 1936, then worked with Leslie Thompson's Band, which formed the basis of Ken Johnson's 1936 Band. Worked with Benny Carter in Europe, then toured Britain and Australia with American singer Nina Mae McKinney (1937–8). Again worked with Ken Johnson and was injured in the London bomb blast that killed Johnson (March 1941). With George Evans (summer 1941), then joined Harry Parry (summer 1942). With Leslie 'Jiver' Hutchinson's Band (1944–7). Took a year's vacation in Jamaica, then rejoined Leslie Hutchinson in summer of 1948. Led own group in India (1949), then worked with Stephane Grappelli (1951–2). Often worked with Leslie Hutchinson in the 1950s and was injured in the automobile crash that killed that leader in November 1959. Active freelance during the 1960s, 1970s and 1980s. Worked mainly as a solo pianist in hotels and clubs, was often featured on radio. Was assistant musical director for the long-running London show *Ain't Misbehavin'*.

DEUCHAR, 'Jimmy' James   Born: Dundee, Scotland, 26 June 1930
trumpet/mellophone/flugelhorn/   Died: Dundee, Scotland, 9 September 1993
composer/arranger

His father, Jimmy Sr (a saxophonist and violinist) led a band in Scotland. Jimmy Jr was the nephew of trumpeters Chick and Billy Smith, his sons are musicians: Steve plays the drums and Simon the electric bass. Trumpet at twelve, family moved to New Malden, Surrey, in 1945. Jimmy attended Tiffins Boys' School in Kingston upon Thames and played in local Boys' Band. Family moved back to Arbroath, Scotland, where Jimmy became a professional musician at the age of fifteen, playing in Ron Webster's Band. Later worked in Dundee with Ron Webster and with Jimmy Deuchar Sr's Band. National Service in the RAF from 1948, was stationed at RAF Uxbridge, sat in at the Club Eleven and successfully auditioned for John Dankworth, joining the band after he was demobilized in May 1950. Left Dankworth in August 1951, worked with Paul Adams from August to October 1951, then brief spells with Oscar Rabin and Geraldo (and working visit to Paris with Ronnie Scott) before joining Jack Parnell from April 1952 until January 1953. With Ronnie Scott from January 1953 until August 1954. Four months in Cyril Stapleton's BBC Show Band, then formed own band. With Tony Crombie (1955), then rejoined Ronnie Scott in January 1956. With Oscar Rabin from May to October 1956, during which time played two week season in Paris with Tommy Whittle's Band (September 1956). Toured Europe with Lionel Hampton (November 1956), then worked briefly in USA with Ronnie Scott. Moved to Germany to work with Kurt Edelhagen from April 1957 to late 1959. Returned to Britain to work in Quintet with Ronnie Scott 1960–2, brief tour of USA with Vic Lewis Orchestra (spring 1960). With Tubby Hayes Quintet from February 1962. Played in film *Doctor Terror's House of Horror*. Occasionally gigged in New Departures Big Band (1962), played booking in USA with Ronnie Scott, then returned to Germany. Worked with Kenny Clarke-Francy Boland Big Band on many occasions from 1963. Regularly with Tubby Hayes until late 1964, then briefly co-led quintet with Keith Christie before moving back to Germany. Further work with Kurt Edelhagen and extensive arranging and composing including string sessions for Heinz Hötter. Moved to Ealing, London, in 1971, did freelance session work, then moved to Dundee. Mainly active as an arranger, writing for Brian Fahey and the Scottish Radio Orchestra, but resumed regular playing in 1974 and combined this with writing for various ensembles, including Paul Kühn's German Radio Band and for Gerry Van Rooyen in Holland. Led own quintet in Scotland (1976). Played on liner cruising from USA to Caribbean Islands for six months, and worked in Hong Kong for Kowloon hotel residency with Harry Bence's Band (1979). Returned to Dundee and continued playing and arranging, guested with Bobby Wishart's Band in Scotland and occasionally travelled to London to play in various big bands including the Sounds of Seventeen and Jack Sharpe's Big Band (up to 1990). Was also featured in Charlie Watts' Big Band (1985 and 1986), including trip to USA. Made several recordings in Scotland during last part of his life, and wrote string arrangements for Spike Robinson recordings. Led own quartet in the last years of his life but full scale activities were curtailed by illness and surgery.

DEUCHAR, Pete
banjo/guitar

Born: Newcastle upon Tyne, c.1930
Deceased

Gigged with local bands, then briefly joined Ken Colyer in Germany (spring 1955). Led own Vieux Carré Band in Newcastle and London from 1956. Visited New Orleans, then re-formed band for German residency (late 1957). Subsequently led own Professors of Ragtime (1959–60). Disbanded to join Dick Charlesworth in late 1960. Left Charlesworth in summer 1961 to work with Doug Richford until late 1962. Led own Country and Blues Band (1963–5), then left full time music in 1966 and as Pete Duker became a sponsored cyclist until suffering serious injuries in 1969. Recovered and (still as Pete Duker) cycled around the world (1971–2) before returning to

Britain. Played gigs with Guy Fenton's Band in Brighton in 1972 and resumed freelance musical activities temporarily. He was found dead on a railway line in Nottinghamshire.

DE VERE, Dickie (Paul RAINBIRD)
drums

Born: 1928
Deceased

Drums from the age of ten, own band at sixteen. Toured Europe with Combined Services Entertainments, returned to Britain and worked with Eddie Thompson and Stan Tracey (1949). Did summer season on the Isle of Wight before spending almost two years with Kenny Graham. Briefly with Tito Burns (September 1951), then rejoined Kenny Graham before working in India with Revell Terry (from November 1951 until April 1952). Returned to London, briefly with Benny Baker's Rumba Band in summer of 1952, then again worked with Kenny Graham. With Johnny Rogers-Lennie Metcalfe Jazz Inc (1953), then brief spells with Lew Stone, Harry Roy, Tommy Pollard, Kathy Stobart, Ronnie Scott and Eddie Thompson, before health problems caused him to quit playing. Worked as a clerk in the late 1950s then made brief comeback with Alan Clare at the Downbeat Club (autumn 1959) and with Pete King (December 1959).

DICKIE, 'Neville' George Neville
piano/vocals

Born: Brandon, Co. Durham, 1 January 1937

Piano at eleven, gigs at sixteen, at seventeen featured in Carroll Levis Talent Shows. Did two years' National Service in the RAF, then played many clubs in the North of England. Led quartet with Alan Harrison. Moved to London in 1958. Worked with the Cannonball Jazz Band and in Brian Green's Band during the 1960s. Played solo and trio dates; had chart success with 'The Robin's Return' (1968). Worked with Spencer's Washboard Kings for Blackpool season (1969), then freelanced with many bands including The Laughing Gravy Orchestra, also played duos with Keith Nichols. Since 1976 has undertaken many tours of North America, playing residencies and festivals in various American and Canadian cities, through the 1990s. During the late 1970s and 1980s played in Gene Allan's Jazzmen and in Alan Littlejohns' Band. Worked with John Petters during the early 1990s in various shows, also ran own Fats Waller tribute presentation through the 1990s. Guested with Alan Elsdon's Band and played duets with French pianist Louise Mazetier (1995). Led own Rhythmakers through the 1990s, playing successful tours, including annual shows featuring the American singer Carol Leigh.

DISLEY, 'Diz' William Charles
guitar/banjo/vocals

Born: Winnipeg, Canada, 27 May 1931

Father from Wales, mother from Derbyshire. Parents moved to Wales when Diz was four, then on to Yorkshire five years later. Played banjo in local bands including the Rotherham Jazz Hounds, also with Vernon Street Ramblers, while studying at the Leeds College of Art. Joined Yorkshire Jazz Band in 1949. Left in 1950 to join the Army (including service in Trieste). After demobilization continued studies, then worked with the Godfrey Brothers on Morecambe Pier (1953). Moved to London, worked with Jeremy French (late 1953), began specializing on guitar, worked with Mick Mulligan (January 1954), then stint with Ken Colyer's Band until rejoining Mulligan in April 1955. With Cy Laurie (April to June 1956), then joined Bob Clarke's Trio

(1956). Also worked with Sandy Brown (1956) and led own String Quintet. Worked in variety with Nancy Whiskey and with Bob Cort (1957), then spell in Germany with Lennie Hastings' Band (June to August 1957). Led own band in Denmark (February to April 1958). Regularly with own Soho String Quintet (1958–60). With Kenny Ball (February to May 1960), Alex Welsh (June 1960 to January 1961), then again led own Quintet. Also enjoyed success as a cartoonist and radio compere. Deputized with Dick Charlesworth (summer 1961), with Chris Barber (April 1962) and Acker Bilk (July 1962). Toured Far East with Beryl Bryden and Johnny Parker (late 1963). Worked mainly as a soloist on folk club circuit (1964–7). Engagements in Canada and USA (early 1968). Played folk and jazz gigs in the late 1960s and early 1970s, led own quintet and band, also worked with Johnny Van Derrick before beginning long working association with Stephane Grappelli in 1973 (interrupted by Diz breaking his wrist in 1979). Again worked on folk circuit (summer 1980). Played in Bahrain with Alan Cooper (early 1981), then resumed with Grappelli from spring 1981 until late 1982. Re-formed Soho String Quintet in 1983, again played in Middle East with Alan Cooper and David Mills. Lived in Spain for part of the 1970s and 1980s, opened jazz club (with clarinettist Bernie Holden) in Almeria in 1988. Worked mainly in Britain during the early 1990s. Led own String Quintet and regularly guested with Dick Laurie's Elastic Band (including bookings in Hong Kong). Freelanced in Europe and in the USA during the mid-1990s.

DODD, 'Pat' Walter Patrick
piano/arranger

Born: Plaistow, London, 17 March 1909
Died: Leatherhead, Surrey, 9 August 1991

Piano from the age of six. Accompanied silent movies at the age of fourteen, then joined Vic Sullivan's Band at Leyton Picture Palace for three-and-a-half years. With Victor Vorzanger at East Ham Palais, then spent fifteen months in Arnold 'Ernie' Mason's Band at Piccadilly Club, Glasgow. Co-led band with Laurie Johnson at Astoria Ballroom, London (1928). With Sydney Kyte's Berkeley Band (1929), then joined Howard Jacobs (early 1930). With Percival Mackey (late 1930), Arthur Lally (1931). Regularly with Al Collins at the Savoy Hotel, London from 1931–40. Was employed by the Savoy Group and so also played with Jack Jackson, Percival Mackey, etc. Also did prolific freelance recordings with Benny Carter, Ray Noble, Joe Daniels, etc., and film studio work. Briefly with Sid Phillips' Trio (spring 1940), then joined the RAF and became part of the Dance Orchestra of the Number One Balloon Centre which formed the basis of the Skyrockets. Played in the Skyrockets throughout World War II, and stayed with them after demobilization (1946). Toured with them and remained when they took up their long-time residency at the London Palladium in 1947; with them until August 1955. During his stay with the Skyrockets occasionally took leaves of absence, including tour with American singer Tony Martin (summer 1948), and to work in Las Vegas with Pat Kirkwood (1954), etc. Continued to work at the London Palladium but was increasingly in television, and became a musical associate for ATV at Elstree Studios until retiring in 1975.

DOLLIMORE, Ralph
piano/arranger/composer

Born: Ealing, London, 20 December 1930
Died: London, 25 August 1988

Piano from the age of five, broadcast Chopin as a schoolboy of thirteen. Army service in Royal Tank Regiment, played in service bands. Joined Kenny Graham (1951), with Terry Brown's

Sextet (1952) and then formed own trio, before working briefly in Jimmy Walker's Quintet (1952). With Ted Heath from summer of 1952 until early 1953, then worked with Eric Winstone until autumn 1953. Briefly with Harry Bence, toured with Vic Ash, then spent five years with Geraldo from spring 1954. Became musical director for various successful artistes and toured USA with singer Matt Monro (1961). Played for various theatre productions and worked as musical director for the London Palladium. Led own trio and fronted Ted Heath Band during the mid-1960s, also extensive radio and television work, playing and arranging. Played for most of 1970s and part of the 1980s as a hotel pianist in Monte Carlo, then returned to Britain and formed own small group.

DONEGAN, 'Lonnie' Anthony James
Born: Glasgow, Scotland, 29 April 1931
vocals/guitar/banjo/composer

Became interested in music while evacuated to Altrincham, Cheshire, during World War II. Served in the Army (in Britain and Austria) and then formed own band (1952), also briefly in the Phoenix Jazz Band and with Bill Brunskill. With Chris Barber Quintet prior to becoming part of newly-formed Ken Colyer Band (March 1953), played in skiffle group within Colyer's Band. Became part of Chris Barber's Band in May 1954, and was again featured within the skiffle group that produced the hit record 'Rock Island Line'. The world-wide success of that record led to Donegan forming his own group for August 1956 debut, and international touring. Over subsequent decades Donegan played bookings through Britain, in the USA, Australia, Germany, Bermuda, etc, as well as work in stage shows and pantomimes. Illness and heart surgery temporarily interrupted this schedule, but Donegan continues to work through the 1990s, and has taken part in several reunion tours organized by Chris Barber, including tour of Europe in 1994. Makes his home in Spain for part of each year.

DONNISON, Frank
Born: Plumstead, London, 22 October 1921
double bass
Died: Southend, Essex, 28 January 1994

His son Malcolm is a drummer. Played violin at school. Did National Service in Army (posted to Egypt) and during this period lost a finger on the left hand in an accident, but went on to become a first class double bassist. First professional work with Ronnie Pleydell in Bournemouth (early 1947). Worked with Oscar Rabin, then rejoined Pleydell in March 1948. With Tito Burns (1948–9). To Switzerland with Eddie Carroll (autumn 1951) also worked in Monte Carlo. Played on *Queen Mary* liner for transatlantic trip, worked in Ronnie Ball Trio before joining Geraldo in 1953. Left Geraldo in January 1956 to work with Ambrose. With Dizzy Reece Quintet (1957), Don Rendell (1957), then became increasingly involved in freelance session work with Bill McGuffie, Peter Knight, television, radio and recordings. Played in Herb Miller's Band, and worked often in the Ray Ward Trio during the late years of his life.

DONOHOE, Dave
Born: Ashton-under-Lyne, Lancashire, 22 May 1940
trombone

Took up trumpet in 1957, and formed own band two years later, then switched to trombone in 1960 and joined Ged Hone's Ragtime Band. Specialized on trombone thereafter and formed own band in 1962, also led own New Orleans marching band from 1962. Worked with George 'Kid Sheik' Cola in 1963, and later worked in Manchester with George Lewis (1966). First visited New Orleans in 1971, played at Heritage Jazz Festival in band led by Woody Allen. Again visited New Orleans in 1972 and 1973 (played with the Olympia Brass Band). Formed new band in 1974, which subsequently did many tours of Europe (including ten bookings at Ascona Festival in Switzerland). Accompanied many visiting American musicians including Alton Purnell, Louis Nelson, Wingy Manone, Thomas Jefferson, etc. In 1977 Dave toured USA with the International Band and in 1982 he guested with the Apothecaries of Jazz in Hawaii. Formed Hi Life Brass Band in 1988 which regularly plays international festivals, but also continues to lead own New Orleans Jazz Band which works throughout Europe, playing Edinburgh Festival (1995) and touring Switzerland (1995): 1996 personnel includes Teddy Fullick (trumpet), Frank Brooker (reeds) and Paul Russell (drums).

DOUGAN, 'Jackie'
drums

Born: Greenock, Scotland, 1930
Died: New South Wales, Australia, 27 January 1973

With Duncan Lamont's Band in Greenock, then worked with Bert Tobias in Glasgow and Ardrossan (1952). Did summer season in Jersey (1953). Moved to London and worked with Malcolm Mitchell's Big Band and Trio (1956). Joined Buddy Featherstonhaugh in late 1956, toured Middle East with that quintet (January to March 1957). With Tommy Whittle (including tour of USA) in 1957. With Cyril Stapleton's BBC Show Band from autumn 1957 to spring 1959. With the Jazz Committee (Bert Courtley-Don Rendell) from spring 1959 until spring 1960, with Ronnie Ross-Bert Courtley Jazztet from April 1960 until February 1961. With Ronnie Scott's Quintet (1961) and with Harry South (1961) as well as appearing (with Charles Mingus) in film *All Night Long*. Accompanied many visiting American musicians. With Stan Tracey's Trio from 1962, also gigged with Al Fairweather-Sandy Brown (1962), Brian Dee (1962), and Dick Morrissey (1962–3), then did widespread freelance work. Indisposed for part of 1964, then again worked in Stan Tracey's Trio and in Tommy Watt's New Radio Orchestra (1965). With Stan Tracey's Quartet (1966). Briefly with Joe Harriott-John Mayer Indo-Jazz Fusion, then played in new version of Kenny Graham's Afro-Cubists (1967), worked regularly in BBC Radio Orchestra. Emigrated to Australia in June 1968. Prolific freelance work, also with Lew Campbell, Don Burrows, etc., organized regular drum clinics. Died in a car accident.

DOUGHTY, 'Len' Leonard Ernest
valve trombone/cornet

Born: Beckenham, Kent, 29 July 1928
Died: 1972

After serving in the RAF, played in Doug Whitton's Band (1948-9). Was in the Galleon Jazz Band then worked regularly with Alan Littlejohns during the 1950s and 1960s, guested with Alex Welsh's Band and occasionally deputized for Alex Welsh. Played in Norman Day's Band in 1959 and occasionally led his own band from the late 1940s onwards.

DOUGLAS, 'Jim' James
guitar/banjo

Born: Gifford, nr Edinburgh, Scotland, 13 May 1942

Originally played drums in school pipe band, then took up guitar and played in a teenage band with clarinettist Pete Kerr. Turned professional to join the Hidden Town Dixielanders for tour of Germany (late 1960). Worked with Pete Kerr's Band, left to work with the Clyde Valley Stompers from spring 1961 until March 1963. Again worked with Pete Kerr from March 1963, then joined Alex Welsh from April 1964 until November 1981. Also played gigs with Lennie Hastings' Band (1970). With Keith Smith during the early 1980s and with Alan Elsdon through the 1980s, also in Eggy Ley's Hotshots and the Eastern All Stars. From July 1987 was featured in Val Wiseman's *Lady Sings the Blues* show. With the Alex Welsh Reunion Band in the 1990s, and again with Keith Smith. Toured with American cornetist Ed Polcer (1993). Worked in Europe with many American musicians, also part of the Great British Jazz Band (co-led by Digby Fairweather and Pete Strange).

DOWNEY, Alan
trumpet/flugelhorn/composer/arranger

Born: Liverpool, Lancashire, 11 February 1944

Began playing trumpet in early teens. Travelled to London each week to play in Ivor Mairants' Student Band (1959). Played at the Iron Door Club in Liverpool (1960) and worked with Ivor Kirchin's Band in Sale, Cheshire. During the 1960s worked with the BBC Midland Light Orchestra, Johnny Patrick's Big Band, Maynard Ferguson's Orchestra, etc. From the 1970s, with Bobby Lamb-Ray Premru Band, the BBC Radio Orchestra and Big Band, John Dankworth, the Norwegian Radio Orchestra, Finnish Radio Orchestra, various Symphony Orchestras, James Last, Peter Herbolzheimer, Kenny Wheeler's Big Band, etc. Prolific arranging.

DOWNS, Geoff
drums

Born: Blackheath, Kent, 21 April 1938

Played in the Royal Artillery Band during National Service. After demobilization worked with Norman Day's Chicagoans (1960), with Dave Keir's Band and in Ken Sims' Vintage Band (1961). Joined Dick Charlesworth from October 1961 until November 1964. Began long musical association with Monty Sunshine in early 1965. Left Sunshine in late 1968 and worked with Bill Nile's Delta Jazz Band and with Eggy Ley, then rejoined Sunshine and worked with him through the late 1970s, 1980s and early 1990s. During this period also with Lonnie Donegan, Cy Laurie, George Webb, Charlie Galbraith, etc., and deputized in bands led by Alex Welsh, Bob Wallis, Terry Lightfoot, Acker Bilk and Kenny Ball. Worked with various singers including Long John Baldry, Chas McDevitt, Beryl Bryden, etc. During the early 1990s worked with Max Collie, with Tommy Burton, with the Muggsy Remembered Band (led by Brian White and Alan Gresty) and own Crescent City Jazz Band until suffering a stroke in May 1993. Gradually resumed working schedule in the 1990s.

DOYLE, 'Trumps' Jack (Jack CONN)
trumpet/vocals

Born: Newcastle upon Tyne c.1908
Died: 18 May 1985

With Maurice Winnick, Neville Bishop and Alan Green before joining Billy Cotton in February 1936. Left Billy Cotton in late 1939 and briefly toured in musical act with Joe Ferrie and guitarist-singer Jimmy Messini. Led own Aces of Rhythm (1939–40) before serving in RAF, played and sang in various service groups. After demobilization did double act with trombonist George

Hackford for fifteen years then joined Sid Millward's Nitwits in 1959. Later worked in variety with his wife, Julie, who was a singer and dancer.

DRAKE, 'Ron' Ronald Stewart
clarinet/saxes

Born: Leeds, Yorkshire, 31 December 1947

Father, Ted Drake, plays banjo and guitar. Clarinet from the age of eleven, took up sax six years later. Spent nearly three years in the Yorkshire Jazz Band before joining Alan Elsdon from December 1967 until spring 1978. With Rod Mason for a year from June 1978. Regularly with Keith Smith from 1979 until the end of 1987, during this period also freelanced with various bands and frequently deputized in Alex Welsh's Band during the early 1980s. Freelanced from the late 1980s through the 1990s, guests with various jazz groups, often with Campbell Burnap (including trip to Finland, 1995), and often in band led by tuba player Bob Bates.

DREW, Martin
drums

Born: Northampton, 11 February 1944

Born while family were evacuated during World War II, returned to London in early childhood. Drum lessons from George Fierstone at age of twelve. Played gigs with local groups (including work with pianist Roy Petersen) and also featured with George Fierstone's Band. Worked professionally at seventeen in pianist Jack Gordon's Band at La Paloma Club, London, stayed for two years then reverted to semi-professional work, playing with many line-ups including Pat Evans' Big Band, Alan Stuart Octet, and Eddie Thompson's Trio. Resumed professional schedule and joined Bill Le Sage Trio, gained experience of playing with American visitors, including Frank Rosolino (1973). In 1974 began long musical association with Oscar Peterson, and did many international tours with Peterson's Trio through the 1990s. From autumn 1972 also worked regularly in Bebop Preservation Society for over three years. Worked with John Critchinson's Trio (1974) and with Tony Lee's Trio. Joined Ronnie Scott's Quartet in June 1975 and continued to work mainly with Scott through the 1990s but also accompanied many visiting American stars including Gil Evans, Ella Fitzgerald, Freddie Hubbard. Milt Jackson, Red Rodney, Zoot Sims, Nina Simone, etc. Occasionally with Morrissey-Mullen Band in the early 1980s. When not working with Ronnie Scott often leads own groups, also plays regularly in John Critchinson line-ups and accompanies visiting Americans: Gene Harris, Scott Hamilton, etc. (1996).

DRYDEN, 'Bob'
drums

Born: Leeds, Yorkshire, 1902
Died: at sea, 1950

Joined RAF as a boy entrant, began playing drums. Left the service in 1926 and formed own band which played residencies at Dreamland, Margate, the Plaza, Belfast, the Ritz, Manchester, and at the Majestic Hotel in Bombay, India. With Dave Crook's Band in London, then worked with Lew Stone (1935), being specially added for the Nat Gonella features (Gonella had worked in Bob Dryden's Band in 1928 and 1929). With Nat Gonella's Georgians from 1935 to 1939. Rejoined RAF in spring 1940, played in service bands. After demobilization again worked with Dave Crook, then gigged in Margate with Frederick Hargreaves before emigrating to Vancouver, Canada in spring 1948. Later worked with Raymond Lyall on liners sailing to and from Australia, he died on one of these voyages.

DUBBER, 'Goff' Godfrey John
clarinet/tenor sax/soprano sax

Born: Croydon, Surrey, 23 September 1934

Played clarinet in Whitgift School Orchestra. Joined Graham Stewart's Jazzmen in the early 1950s, then became part of Bob Dawbarn's Barnstormers in early 1954. Spent two years in Ian Bell's Band then served in RAF from December 1955 until December 1957. During RAF service led band at RAF Melksham, and while stationed in Lincolnshire played in local band the Pilgrim Stompers. After demobilization rejoined Ian Bell in December 1957. Left Bell in 1960. Played gigs with trumpeter Vic Roberts (1961), then often worked with the Chertsey-based Monk's Jazz Band (Sandy Axon on trombone, Ian Axon on trumpet and Rod Axon on banjo) through the 1960s. Occasionally deputized for Alan Cooper in the Temperance Seven and played many gigs with George Webb's Dixielanders (in the 1970s and 1980s), also co-led (with pianist Alan Root) the Alan Godfrey Quartet. Led own quintet (featuring trumpeter Ken Reece) in the 1980s and early 1990s, later added trombonist John Mortimer. During the mid-1980s began long musical association with Neville Dickie, worked with his Rhythmakers through the 1990s. Together with Dickie toured with John Petters. From the late 1980s through to the 1990s has played alongside Brian White in the Bechet-Mezzrow tribute band King Jazz. Deputized for Olav Vass in the Ray Terry Band during the early 1990s, then joined that band regularly in 1994.

DUFF, 'Jack' John Black Wallace
saxes/clarinet/piano

Born: Scotland, 13 August 1940

First gigs with Charlie McNair's Band and with the Royal Mile Jazzmen (1956–8). Worked professionally with the Cam Robbie Orchestra and with Geraldo (1959). Toured Germany with Ken Ramage's Dixielanders (1962), later became leader of this group. Moved to Jersey in 1964 and led own successful band there, which backed many eminent visiting musicians including Johnny Griffin, Sonny Stitt, Harry Edison, Joe Newman, Kenny Davern, Joe Harriott, Ronnie Ross, etc. Played in Jersey during the summers, then worked on board cruise liners each winter (visiting the Caribbean, USA, Australia, etc.). Continued this routine until moving back to Scotland in 1990. During the early 1990s worked with Al Fairweather, Jimmy Deuchar, Fionna Duncan, Mike Hart, etc. Often with Fat Sam's Band (including trips to Canada and the USA,) also plays in the Edinburgh Jazz Orchestra and on television in Craig McMordo's *That Swing Thang* show. Active in jazz education through the 1990s.

DUNBAR, Rudolph
clarinet/sax/composer

Born: British Guiana (now Guyana), 5 April 1899
Died: Paddington, London, 10 June 1988

Child pianist, then played clarinet in British Guiana Military Band for five years. Moved to New York in 1919, studied at Institute of Musical Art (forerunner of the Juilliard School of Music), majored in composition, piano and clarinet. Worked with violinist Jessie Smith and with the Harlem Orchestra (1923). Graduated in 1924. Often worked in Will Vodery's Plantation Orchestra accompanying the *Dixie to Broadway* show (summer 1924 to early 1925). Moved to France in 1925, played in Leon Crutcher and George Evans' Palm Beach Six (1925), combining this with music studies. Worked in Italy with Benny Peyton's Jazz Kings (summer 1926), then again worked with Palm Beach Six in France (summer 1926), then in Rome with Benny Peyton's Jazz

Kings (December 1926), then joined band led by Dan Parrish (February 1927). Moved to London, and again worked for Will Vodery in the Plantation Orchestra, touring Britain with *The Blackbirds of 1927*. Moved back to Paris for further studies, until joining Thompson's Negro Band in La Baule (summer 1928). Worked in Germany, Holland, Norway, Denmark and Spain with this band (1928–9). To London to open with Leon Abbey's Band at Deauville Restaurant (March 1930), left later that month, returned to Paris and gave recitals (1930). Studied in Leipzig and Vienna, then moved to London in summer 1931 and ran the Rudolph Dunbar School of Clarinet Playing (1931–2). During the 1930s led own bands at various London venues, including the Hyde Park Hotel, the Cossack Restaurant, Prince's Restaurant, etc., in Cambridge and on tour. Revisited the USA (1938–9). Led own twelve-piece band in London in 1940 but was by then increasingly active as a teacher, composer and conductor (conducted the Royal Philharmonic in April 1942). During (and after) World War II served in Europe as a correspondent for the Associated Negro Press. Conducted in France and in Germany during the 1940s. Settled in London from summer of 1950. Active as a composer and teacher but continued to conduct orchestras all over the world: Cuba, Russia, Egypt, Poland, etc. Wrote *A Treatise on the Clarinet*, which was first published in 1939.

DUNCAN, Fionna
vocals

Born: Garelochhead, Dunbartonshire, Scotland, 5 November 1939

Sister of pianist Ian Duncan. Joined Ballad and Blues Club while at school in Rutherglen, Glasgow. Began appearing on television and radio with Joe Gordon's Folk Four. At seventeen sang with brother's modern jazz quartet at the Glasgow University Union. Sang with the Steadfast Jazz Band in Glasgow, then won talent contest and joined Forrie Cairns' All Stars. Worked with the Clyde Valley Stompers from 1959 until spring 1961, then joined Forrie Cairns' Clansmen until 1964 before touring Germany as a solo artiste. Resident at the Georgian Club, London, from 1966 until 1971, then returned to Scotland in 1972. With George Penman's Band from 1977 until 1981, then took part in reunion of the Clyde Valley Stompers touring Britain and Canada. Appeared at Sacramento Festival, USA, with Mike Hart's Scottish Jazz Advocates (1981). Guested with Eggy Ley's Band (1984–6), then formed own successful trio (with bassist Ronnie Rae) which played many international festivals and toured Canada and Switzerland. Widespread work with own trio and as a solo singer through the 1990s.

DUNCAN, 'Mac' Malcolm Lawrence
trombone

Born: Leeds, Yorkshire, 9 February 1930
Died: London, 27 October 1981

Played for various bands around the Leeds area before serving in the Guards. While stationed at Bovington, played in Bournemouth with Ron Weldon's Band. With the White Eagle Jazz Band before working for five years with Ken Colyer (and with Colyer in the Omega Brass Band). Left Colyer early in 1960 and joined newly formed Ken Sims-Ian Wheeler Vintage Jazz Band in spring 1960. Left in early 1961 to form own short-lived band. With Micky Ashman in the early 1960s, then played for Pat Hawes (1966), Keith Smith (1968) and Rod Mason (1968–9). Accompanied Henry 'Red' Allen for London concert in 1964, and worked with various other American musicians including George Lewis. Led own band again, and guested with various bands, including Monty Sunshine's, and Guy Fenton's, again led own band (1978). Took his own life.

DUNMALL, Paul Norman
saxes/clarinet/bagpipes
Born: Welling, Kent, 6 May 1953

Studied clarinet at Blackheath Conservatoire for five years, self-taught on saxophone. Joined Marsupilami in 1969 and toured extensively in Europe. Worked in the USA from 1973 until 1976, with Johnny 'Guitar' Watson for a year, with Alice Coltrane, etc. Returned to England in 1976, played with folk musicians Kevin Dempsey, Martin Jenkins and Polly Bolton. Founder-member of Spirit Level (with pianist Tim Richards) from 1979, worked in Tenor Tonic (with Alan Skidmore) from 1985. Joined London Jazz Composers' Orchestra in 1987, also began working in Danny Thompson's Whatever. Co-founder of Mujician (1988). Continues to work with these three groups through the 1990s. Also part of the British Saxophone Quartet (with Simon Picard, Elton Dean and George Haslam) and plays in duo with Paul Rogers.

DYER, 'Pete' Peter Gordon
trombone
Born: Enfield, Middlesex,
18 September 1932

Played with Fron-Zi-Me and in New Teao before working with Mike Peters in Germany and London (1957). Joined Sonny Morris (September 1957), briefly with Bob Wallis, then joined Barry Martyn in late 1959. Toured with many visiting American musicians including George Lewis, Kid Thomas, Captain John Handy, Alton Purnell, Louis Nelson, etc. Worked mainly with the Kid Martyn Ragtime Band for ten years, including New Orleans Jazz Festival in 1968, but also briefly led own band in late 1966. With Sammy Rimington, then with Keith Smith until that leader left to work in Denmark, whereupon his place was taken by Cuff Billett. Later toured Europe with Sammy Rimington-Soren Houlind All Stars, including dates on which they accompanied visiting musicians. Toured Denmark with Alton Purnell and worked with Australian trumpeter Geoff Bull in Europe. Often worked with Ken Colyer during the 1970s, also with Keith Smith and in the Eagle Band organised by Chris Barber and Barry Martyn. During the 1980s did three tours with the Barry Martyn Re-Union Band, worked in Sammy Rimington's International Band and guested with various bands in Europe. During the 1990s with the Louisiana Joymakers, with Butch Thompson's King Oliver Centennial Band, the Ginger Pig New Orleans Band and also guested with the Ken Colyer Trust Band, Jim Holmes, John Keen, Dave Brennan, etc.

E

EAST, Roy
alto sax/baritone sax/clarinet/flute
Born: Northampton, 30 May 1930
Died: Exeter, Devon, 13 December 1995

Worked with Oscar Rabin before touring with Vic Lewis (1955–6). With Dizzy Reece (1957), Vic Ash (1958–9) and summer season with Alan Kane's Band (1958). Again with Vic Lewis (including tour of USA). Joined John Dankworth in spring of 1961. In latter years lived in Devon, led own quartet which played throughout the South West, and also worked with Billy Munn at the Imperial Hotel, Torquay.

EDWARDS, 'Ben' Benedict Henry Ashton
drums/piano

Born: Cambridge, 19 November 1908
Died: London, 18 September 1979

Pianist with the Cambridge University Ramblers. Left Cambridge in 1928, gigged in London clubs on piano then switched to drums in 1934. Played for many years in various Victor Sylvester line-ups but also did many jazz gigs and recordings, including work in Reginald Foresythe's Band (1937), Gerry Moore (1937–8), Miff Ferrie (1939), Harry Parry (1940), Jack Jackson (1941), Harry Parry (1941–2). Led own quintet at Lansdowne House (1945–6). With Reg Purslove (1950), Laurie Payne Quartet (1953), continued to work regularly with Victor Sylvester. Again led own band and freelanced during the 1950s and 1960s.

EFFORD, 'Bob' Robert
saxes/clarinet/bass clarinet/flute/
piccolo/oboe/bassoon

Born: Elephant and Castle, London, 6 April 1928

Piano during early childhood, briefly played trumpet, then took up clarinet as a teenager. Virtually self-taught on sax. Joined Les Court's Band in Nottingham briefly, then worked with Les Ayling in Dundee and London (1947 to January 1948). With Ronnie Pleydell (early 1948), then with Teddy Foster for a year before joining Frank Weir (spring 1949). With Paul Fenoulhet (1949), also toured with Vic Lewis. With Phil Tate (1950), Jack Nathan (1951), own band (1952). With Felix King (February to October 1953), then joined Geraldo (October 1953). Extensive freelancing in studios during the late 1950s, but worked regularly with Tony Kinsey Quintet from early 1957 until joining Ted Heath from September 1958 for ten years, also worked with Allan Ganley. Studio and session work in the late 1960s and 1970s, but also toured Europe with Benny Goodman (1970 and 1971). Emigrated to California, USA, in 1978, and became sought-after studio musician, playing every woodwind instrument (including bassoon, oboe and cor anglais). During the 1990s worked with many line-ups including orchestras directed by Bill Holman, Bob Florence, Les Brown, Ray Anthony, etc. Bob's wife (the former singer Joan Brooke) died in 1990.

ELIZALDE, 'Fred' Federico
piano/composer/arranger

Born: Manila, Philippines, 12 December 1907
Died: Manila, Philippines, 16 January 1979

Brother of saxophonist Manuel L. 'Lizz' Elizalde. Of Spanish parentage. Began playing piano as an infant and composed a minuet at the age of four. Studied music at the Madrid Conservatoire under Perez Casas, then, at fourteen, undertook further general studies at St Joseph's College, London, for two years before attending Stanford University, California, from 1925. Left in the summer of 1926 and subsequently led Stanford University Band for a summer 1926 engagement at the Cinderella Roof of the Biltmore Hotel in Los Angeles. Continued his music studies (with Ernest Bloch). To Cambridge, England, in September 1926 where his brother, 'Lizz', was a student. Took over the existing Quinquaginta Band (which had been formed in May 1926) and renamed them the Quinquaginta Ramblers. Began arranging and composing for the band, as well as playing piano with them. The Quinquaginta Ramblers gave their first public performance in October 1926 and made their London debut in December 1926. Elizalde left the QR in June 1927 and worked as a freelance arranger (writing for Ambrose and the Savoy Orpheans, etc.). Formed new band for residency at the Savoy Hotel, London, from 1 January 1928. Worked at the Savoy until 31 July 1929, but during this period took leave to play brief residencies in France and Belgium in 1928, and also played a season at the London Palladium. The band, which featured various imported American stars such as Adrian and Arthur Rollini, Fud Livingston, Max Farley, Bobbie Davis, Jack Rusin and Chelsea Quealey, was at one stage enlarged to a twenty-one piece ensemble. After the Savoy residency ended, the band recorded two of Elizalde's film scores, then toured the North of England (September 1929) and Scotland (December 1929). Elizalde wrote the music, and provided the band for, the short-lived *Intimate Revue* in March 1930, then disbanded and moved to Biarritz, where he studied, and composed classical music. Did world concert tour (1931) then moved to Paris. Visited London in 1932 for recordings, then moved to Spain and wrote the opera *Le Pajara Pinta*. Studies with Manuel de Falla. Conducted various orchestras in Spain, brief return to London in late 1933 for recordings, then moved back to Biarritz in May 1934. His Sinfonie Concertante was premiered in Spain in April 1935. Composing and conducting 1935-6, then served as an officer in General Franco's Army (as part of a Basque regiment) during the Spanish Civil War. Wounded at Oviedo and invalided out of the army. Moved to the Philippines in late 1937, returned to Paris in the late 1930s and remained confined to his chateau at Bayonne during the German occupation. He continued to compose. Moved to Santa Monica, California (1946), performed own Piano Concerto in London (1948). His Violin Concerto was recorded by the London Symphony Orchestra in 1950. During the 1950s directed the Manila Symphony Orchestra and was President of the Manila Broadcasting Corporation. In the 1960s he briefly directed the Orchestra of the Japanese Broadcasting Commission, but returned to Manila, where he conducted his last concert in 1974. He was an avid sportsman and led the Philippines' shooting team in the 1954 Asiad, where they gained four gold medals.

ELLEFSON, 'Art' Arthur
saxes/clarinet

Born: Moose Jaw, Canada, 17 April 1932

His son Lee is a guitarist. Played trumpet and euphonium before taking up tenor sax at sixteen. Played in Toronto in band led by trumpeter Bobby Jimby before moving to England in 1952. With Carl Barriteau from summer 1953 until spring 1955 (except for brief return to Canada in late 1954). With Harry Hayes, Roy Fox, and Frank Weir. With Vic Lewis from late 1955 until 1957 (also worked for a month in Paris with Freddie Bell and the Bellboys during summer 1957). In Allan Ganley's Quartet (spring 1958), then worked with Ronnie Ross-Allan Ganley Jazz Makers from autumn 1958 (including work in the USA). Toured Britain with Woody Herman's Anglo-American Herd (April 1959), again with Vic Lewis including tour of USA (spring 1960). Co-led group with Johnny Scott then joined John Dankworth from spring 1960. Often in quintet and sextet led by Ronnie Ross from 1966, also worked with Maynard Ferguson (1967–8). Prolific freelance work before moving back to Canada. Thereafter worked often in the USA and paid playing visits to Britain.

ELLINGTON, Ray
drums/vocals/composer

Born: Kennington, London, 17 March 1916
Died: London, 27 February 1985

Father was the black American comedian Harry Brown (from St Louis, Missouri); his mother was born in Russia. Ray's son Lance is a trombonist and vocalist. Appeared in musical comedy while still at school. Left school at fourteen and became a cabinet maker, then took up drums. Worked at various London night clubs and at the Park Lane Hotel with Rudolph Dunbar (1933), then joined guitarist John Hendricks' Hot Chocolates (1934). With Rudolph Dunbar's Quintet (1936), Gerry Moore's Quartet (1936). Joined Harry Roy in early 1937 and remained until joining the RAF in May 1940 (toured South America with Harry Roy in 1938). Played occasional dates with Lew Stone, Benny Carter, Garland Wilson and Van Phillips in the 1930s. Served in the RAF as a physical training instructor but also played in various service bands including RAF Blue Eagles (1945). Played on Sid Gross' Swing Shop concerts (1945–6). After demobilization (1946) played residencies at the Milroy and at the Bag O'Nails. Did film extra work, then worked again with Harry Roy (late 1946 to early 1947). With Stephane Grappelli and with Tito Burns in 1947, then formed own highly successful Quartet in 1947 which continued to operate into the 1980s, playing many television and radio shows (including feature spots in the BBC's *Goon Show*). Occasionally led own big band for specific engagements.

ELLIOTT, George
guitar/vocals

Born: South London, 26 June 1912

Did first gigs with Troise and his Mandoliers, thus worked with Phil Green who introduced him to freelance session work. Became house musician at HMV and freelanced for various labels including Decca, Regal, etc. Recorded with Lew Davis, Benny Carter, Freddy Gardner, etc. Other than a spell with Bert Firman at Coventry Street Club spent entire career working in studios, for recordings, radio and film soundtrack work. Pioneered multi-guitar recordings in Britain. Also worked in the early 1950s as Johnny Paradise. Led vocal group The Mermaids and own Brass Choir. Played on countless film sound tracks, including many of the *Carry On* films, and on the *Goon Show* radio programmes. Featured with Edmundo Ros, Max Jaffa, Robert Farnon, Jack Emblow, Mantovani, etc., and also on banjo with Norrie Paramor.

ELLIS, Cyril E.
trumpet/vocals

Born: Glasgow, Scotland, 23 February 1923
Died: England, November 1976

Began playing trumpet at twelve, tuition from his father, James Ellis, who was Principal Trumpet with the Scottish Orchestra for over thirty years. Played local gigs while an apprentice engineer, with George Scott Henderson (1940) and Jack Chapman (1942). Served in the Royal Navy from 1944 until 1946; while stationed at Chatham worked in band led by Claude Giddins (1946). Immediately after demobilization joined Harry Gold (from May 1946 until January 1949). With Sid Phillips from January 1949 until 1954, but played Paris Jazz Festival with Carlo Krahmer in May 1949 and appeared with Jazz Today Unit (1953). With Cyril Ornadel's Theatre Orchestra, Billy Amstell, and the Skyrockets (1954). With Bob Rowe at the London Coliseum (1955). Left full time playing to work for instrument manufacturers, Boosey and Hawkes, but gigged with various leaders including Harry Gold, Roy Vaughan etc., and with leaders around the Kent area during the 1960s.

ELRICK, George
drums/vibes/percussion/vocals

Born: Aberdeen, Scotland, 29 December 1903

Studied at Gordon's College, Aberdeen, and briefly at Aberdeen University. Worked in a chemical laboratory, but played drums in the evenings with various local bands including the Lucinians and the Rialto Band. Won prize in Rhythm contest in November 1928. Led own Embassy Band at the New Beach Ballroom, Aberdeen (1930), then moved to London in January 1931 as a fully-fledged professional musician. Played club gigs with Cyril Harling's Band before joining Nat Allen (May 1932). With Austin-Coxen piano duo (1932), with Richard Dickman Orchestra (1933). Led own band at the Gargoyle Club, and at Chez Henri (1933). With Billy Mason (autumn 1934), but soon joined Reginald Foresythe's New Music (gigged with Jack Harris and Howard Jacobs while Foresythe was in America). With Buddy Featherstonhaugh, and Ambrose (1935), then regularly with Henry Hall from late 1935 until June 1937. Freelance recordings with Joe Venuti, Valaida Snow, etc. during the 1930s. Own Show Band made debut in summer 1937, and subsequently did many successful and wide-ranging tours (including shows for ENSA in World War II). Continued to lead own band for many years, but also enjoyed success as a radio disc jockey, and as an actor and compere. His autobiography *Housewives' Choice* was published in 1991.

ELSDON, Alan R.
trumpet/flugelhorn/vocals

Born: Chiswick, London, 15 October 1934

Took up trumpet at sixteen. During the early 1950s led own Riverside Jazz Band and sat in with various bands, including Steve Lane's Southern Stompers. Joined Cy Laurie in December 1954. Left Cy Laurie to join RAF in spring 1956. Played in Fighter Command Military Band and also with Graham Stewart's Seven from about September 1957. After demobilization (February 1958), continued to work with Stewart until joining Terry Lightfoot in April 1959. While with Lightfoot was on tour with Kid Ory and Henry 'Red' Allen. Left Terry Lightfoot in May 1961. Led own band from June 1961, which accompanied various American stars in the 1960s including Edmond Hall, Wingy Manone, Albert Nicholas, Howling Wolf, Willie 'The Lion' Smith, etc., and singers Dionne Warwick, Cilla Black and the Isley Brothers. The band did widespread touring, and did many BBC radio shows, throughout the 1970s, 1980s and 1990s. During this period Elsdon has guested with many bands and was featured with the Midnite Follies Orchestra from its inception in January 1978 through to the late 1980s. He is regularly with various Keith Nichols' line-ups, and also with Neville Dickie's Rhythmakers (including work in Canada, 1994). Alan has also played on Mediterranean cruises, been featured with John Petters' Legends of Jazz and guested with various bands throughout Britain. He continues to lead own band, but also worked with Marty Grosz in Germany (1996).

EMBERSON, Norman David
drums

Born: Chingford, East London, 11 July 1945

Father played violin. Guitar as a teenager, then was given drum kit for his 21st birthday. Made debut in Ian Grant's Jazzmen (1966) then joined John Simmons' Louisiana Joymakers (1968) before working with Mike Casimir's New Iberia Stompers, which also included Dick Cook, until 1976. During the 1970s continued long musical association with Dick Cook, playing together in the London Ragtime Orchestra, and in the Inter Cities Jazz Band (which Emberson co-founded), alongside trumpeter Teddy Fullick and pianist-vocalist Maggie Kinson. Backed various American musicians with Casimir, the Inter Cities band and as a freelance, including Alvin Alcorn, Sam Lee, Louis Nelson, Alton Purnell, Emanuel Sayles, Kid Sheik and Kid Thomas. Spent almost four years with Sammy Rimington in the latter 1970s then worked with Chris Barber from March 1979 until spring 1989. During the 1990s continued to work with Dick Cook, and with Neville Dickie, also toured Europe on several occasions with American singer Lillian Boutté.

ETHERIDGE, John Michael Glyn Born: Lambeth, London, 12 January 1948
guitar/composer

Father played piano. Took up guitar at thirteen. After studying History of Art at Essex University settled in London and gigged with various progressive rock groups from 1971, working often with violinist Darrell Way. Worked with Soft Machine from 1975 until c.1980, during this time also toured regularly with Stephane Grappelli from 1976 until 1981, and gigged with various groups including Dave Chambers' Quintet (1979), and co-led quartet with violinist Ric Sanders. Did solo tour of Australia in 1982, also toured with John Stevens Freebop (1982). Taught guitar from 1982. Co-led quartet with Gary Boyle throughout the mid-1980s, toured with bassist Brian Torff. With Michael Garrick's String Trio and Sextet from the early 1980s. Led own band (1987–8) and own quartet (1988–9). Toured extensively with Birelli Lagrene (1989), worked often in Danny Thompson's Whatever, and did regular tours with Bertice Reading (including Australia in 1985). During the 1990s played in duos with guitarist Andy Summers and with Jim Mullen (including tour of Italy). Often with Paul Rogers and Nigel Morris, and with violinist Nigel Kennedy. Worked with Barney Kessel in 1990, and with Herb Ellis and Mundell Lowe (as part of the Great Guitars) in Vienna. With Dick Heckstall-Smith in Germany. Continues to lead own line-ups and also continues to teach regularly (at Jazz Academy, etc.).

EVANS, 'Dave' David Born: Perivale, Middlesex, 8 February 1942
drums

Did first gigs with Mitz Mittens in 1956. Later worked with Mike Pointon, the Salutation Brass Band, the New Teao and Ches Chesterman, before joining Pete Deuchar's Professors of Ragtime (1960). With Keith Smith from late 1960, then worked in Germany with Mac Duncan from March 1961. Returned to Britain and joined Bobby Mickleburgh's Confederates (1961). With Keith Smith again briefly in early 1962, then worked with Preston Scott's Band in Germany before rejoining Keith Smith from 1963–5. Car crash injuries (1965) necessitated temporary lay-off from playing. Worked in Switzerland with Barry Johnson's Green Leaf Band (1966) then worked with Bill Greenow's Quintet (1967–8). Played in the Gothic Jazz Band during the 1970s, and with Keith Smith, guested with Ken Colyer (1974). Worked in Germany with Chris Deutcher's Band. Accompanied many visiting Americans including Alton Purnell, Champion Jack Dupree, Sammy Price, Joe Darensbourg, Thomas Jefferson and Al Casey. Continued to work often in Gothic Jazz Band (1980s) and with Dick Cook, also with the Inter Cities Band from 1979 (with Teddy Fullick, Richard Simmons, etc.), and freelancing with various bands. Regularly with the Excelsior Jazz Band and in the London Ragtime Orchestra through to the middle 1990s, and also part of the annual re-formation of Butch Thompson's King Oliver Centennial Band.

EVANS, George
tenor sax/clarinet/composer/vocals

Born: Wood Green, London, 7 August 1915
Died: Newcastle upon Tyne, 16 February 1993

His brother Les (born 1919) became a celebrated saxophone teacher. Played banjo locally in Yale Five (with Norrie Paramor) then concentrated on tenor sax and worked briefly in the Southend area. First professional work with Al Lever's Band in Brighton (1932). Worked with Freddy Bretherton's Spider's Web Orchestra (1933–4), then spent six weeks with Lou Preager before working regularly with Sydney Lipton's Orchestra from November 1934 until January 1939. During this period also played on various freelance sessions (including recordings with Ronnie Munro) and accompanied Benny Carter in London in January 1937. With Geraldo from January 1939 until 1941, also began the first of his experimental multi-saxophone bands by leading a seven sax line-up at the Embassy Club, London, in the summer of 1941. Recorded with Lew Stone in 1940–1. Served in the Welsh Guards during World War II, and guested with Geraldo. The George Evans Orchestra began recording in 1944 but because of George's service commitments it was labelled as being directed by Les Evans. After demobilization formed band with ten saxes (and five trumpets) in February 1946 and began touring. Was taken ill in summer of 1946; his brother Les ran the band. This group disbanded in February 1947, but after recovering from illness, George started a student band in late 1948. Formed orthodox big band in summer of 1949. Played residency at Hammersmith Palais, then led twenty-piece line-up for season in Grimsby. Most often using a six-sax and five brass combination, he led at the Oxford Galleries in Newcastle upon Tyne from early 1951 until spring 1958. Then, after recording in Newcastle and London (1958–9), he retired from the music profession. Following celebrations at Newcastle's Mayfair Ballroom to honour his 70th birthday (in August 1985) he occasionally led a big band on a part-time basis in the Newcastle area.

EVANS, 'Nick' Nicholas Kenneth Dacre
trombone

Born: Newport, Monmouthshire (now Gwent),
9 January 1947

Trombone from age of eleven. Co-led Phoenix Jazz Band in Newport. Played in New Welsh Jazz Orchestra and in Welsh Jazz Sextet. Left Cardiff College with BSc in July 1969. Worked with Graham Collier after meeting him at the Barry Summer School, and soon afterwards began a long musical association with Keith Tippett. In 1972 worked for six months (with Charlie Mariano, Barre Phillips, and Stu Martin) in Ambush for engagements in Belgium and France. From 1974 often worked in Elton Dean line-ups, including Just Us. Toured Italy with Dean. Frequently worked with Dudu Pukwana's Zila, and was part of drummer Keith Bailey's short-lived group Prana. A central figure in Dreamtime from 1984 through the 1990s. Worked as a teacher of maths from 1972 through the 1990s, but continued to play music regularly, leading and freelancing.

EVERSON, Malcolm
clarinet/alto sax/baritone sax/flute

Born: Oxfordshire, 26 February 1942
Died: Twickenham, Middlesex,
24 December 1991

Played clarinet at school, then took up guitar before specializing on saxophone. Played in Colin Kingwell's Jazz Bandits during the early 1960s, then freelanced with various bands while qualifying as an architect. With Carl Spencer's Washboard Kings in the late 1960s, then worked in

Lennie Hastings' Band and with Mike Peters. With the Temperance Seven from 1969 until 1972. With Humphrey Lyttelton from 1976 until 1979. During this period also played in Stan Greig's London Jazz Big Band. Gigged with Ian Stewart's Rocket 88 in the 1980s and again worked regularly in the Temperance Seven. During the last part of his life worked in the Limousines and (in London and Wales) with the House Band.

EYDEN, 'Bill' William James
drums

Born: Hounslow, Middlesex, 4 May 1930

Played in Hounslow Army Cadet Corps Band at age of thirteen. After National Service in RAF (1948–50), took lessons from Max Abrams. Did local gigs, then worked with Basil and Ivor Kirchin's Band (sharing drumming with Basil) in summer 1952. With Ray Kirkwood (1952–5), Johnny Rogers (summer 1953). Television work with Steve Race (October to December 1953). In house band at Studio 51, London with Terry Brown, Jimmy Skidmore, Joe Muddel and Lennie Metcalfe (late 1953 to summer 1954). With Roy Fox and again with Johnny Rogers. With Harry Roy (late 1954), Malcolm Mitchell's Big Band (April to June 1955), Tubby Hayes (July 1955 to September 1956). With Jazz Couriers (Tubby Hayes-Ronnie Scott) from April 1957 debut until July 1959, also worked in Jack Sharpe's Quintet during this period. With Pat Smythe, Vic Ash-Karry Klein (1960) and again with Tubby Hayes (late 1960–1). In Terry Shannon's Trio (1962) and with pianist Maurice Allen's Trio at the Eve Club, London. With Tubby Hayes-Bobby Breen Octet, Long John Baldry and Alexis Korner in the early 1960s. Three month tour of South America with Wee Willie Harris from late 1963. Returned to Britain, worked with Georgie Fame from autumn 1964 until late 1965, then joined Stan Tracey's Trio, accompanying many visiting Americans, also worked with Dick Morrissey (summer 1966). Rejoined Tubby Hayes (autumn 1968). From the 1970s onwards freelanced successfully in many varied line-ups. Played for various West End shows including *Bubbling Brown Sugar, The Mitford Girls, Promises Promises*, etc. Regularly with the Bebop Preservation Society through the 1980s, also worked in Spain in pianist Ian Henry's Quartet. In Charlie Watts' Big Band (1985–6). Continues to play regularly in the 1990s, working with Bill Le Sage, Bobby Wellins, etc. Since the late 1970s has also taught percussion in various schools in the London area.

F

FAIRWEATHER, 'Al' Alastair
trumpet/arranger/composer

Born: Edinburgh, Scotland, 12 June 1927
Died: Edinburgh, Scotland, 21 June 1993

Raised in Portobello, attended Royal High School and joined up with fellow pupil Sandy Brown in school jazz band. Originally played trombone, then switched to trumpet. After Army service he graduated from Edinburgh Art College and played regularly in band with Sandy Brown. Travelled to London with Brown for various engagements in 1953. Sandy Brown returned to Scotland but Al stayed behind to work with Cy Laurie from January 1954 (took time off to work briefly in

Denmark with Albert Nicholas). Left Cy Laurie in late 1954 to rejoin Sandy who had moved down to London to live. In January 1958 Brown left the band and the leadership passed to Fairweather. By September 1958 Brown returned and became co-leader of the Fairweather-Brown All Stars which continued to function until Al joined Acker Bilk in June 1966. During the 1960s Fairweather freelanced occasionally and played in the Alex Welsh Big Band in 1963 and 1964. Left Acker Bilk in May 1968 and gigged with Alexander's Jazzmen (1968), then ran own café before taking teacher training course. Taught in Harrow area and resumed painting (and cartooning). During the 1970s and 1980s played and arranged for Stan Greig's London Jazz Big Band (from February 1975), worked with Sonny Dee's Band and guested in various Alan Littlejohns line-ups. Also took part in reunion of the Fairweather-Brown All Stars (February 1975). Co-led All Stars with pianist Ralph Laing and played in Laing's Groove Juice Special. Suffered a heart attack in 1983, but recovered and resumed regular playing and arranging. Moved back to Edinburgh in late 1987, played local gigs and continued to work with Groove Juice Special and to arrange for various groups including big band led by Nottingham trombonist Bob Wilson. Suffered fatal heart attack while painting a portrait.

FAIRWEATHER, 'Digby' Richard John Charles   Born: Rochford, Essex, 25 April 1946
trumpet/flugelhorn/vocals/composer

His father, a local conductor, choirmaster and senior teacher at Southend Metropolitan School of Music, played and taught piano and cello (until 1939); later he ran a photographic salon. Digby originally played drums, E-flat alto horn, violin and clarinet, then took up trumpet in 1960. Lessons from E.M. 'Bert' Collier (1965-6). Gigged around the Southend area during the early 1960s with various groups including pianist Derek Wood's Quartet, then played alto sax in trumpeter Geoff Pilgrim's Six (1961-2), clarinet in drummer Dave Mills' Jazz Band (1963-4), before reverting full time to trumpet in 1965. Worked as a librarian but gigged throughout the Essex area with saxophonist Ken Baxter (1963-8), drummer Trevor Taylor and pianist Pat Mason (1969). Led own Half Dozen (1971), joined Dave Claridge's New Orleans Jazzmen (featuring Len Page on banjo) in 1972. Subsequently with Eggy Ley, Hugh Rainey, Eric Silk, George Webb and Colin Symons (played in Dresden with Symons in 1973). Regularly with Gene Allen's Jazzmen from 1973, also often in Ron Russell's Band in the 1970s (including Prague Festival, 1974). Intermittently with Lennie Hastings' Band from 1974 to 1978, gigs with Johnny Barnes, Roy Williams, Dave Shepherd, Alvin Roy, etc., and deputizing for Alex Welsh. Turned professional in January 1977, worked with own *Songs for Sandy* presentation (1977-8), played in Keith Nichols' line-ups and worked in Velvet (with Ike Isaacs, Denny Wright and Len Skeat) from 1977. Played in Great Jazz Solos Revisited (1978), gigged with Big Bob Bryan (1976-8) and guested with many bands. With the Midnite Follies Orchestra from its beginning in January 1978 until spring of 1979. Led own Fairweather Friends from summer of 1979, and own quartet (1979). Solo tour of Scotland (October 1979). From 1979 co-directed educational charity Jazz College with pianist Stan Barker; duo with Barker from 1980. Occasional duos with Denny Wright and with Fred Hunt (1981). With Pizza Express All Stars from May 1980 until summer 1982. Played at Nice Jazz Festival with Jazz Journal All Stars, led by George Chisholm (1981). Own quartet (1982). Toured Australia alongside Danny Moss (early 1983). Led own New Georgians (playing tribute to Nat Gonella) from 1982. Again deputized for Alex Welsh (1982). Co-led Tiny

Winters' Kettners Five (1984). With Brian Priestley's Special Sextet from 1984. Worked with Donald Swann, including tour (1986), also with Alex Welsh Reunion Band from 1983. Featured with Eastern All Stars (1986), with Tony Milliner's Mingus Music (1987). With Val Wiseman's *Lady Sings the Blues* show from 1987 through the 1990s. With Martin Litton's All Star Band (1989). Led Jazz Superkings from 1988 onwards, co-led the Great British Jazz Band (with Pete Strange) from 1994, led own new Half Dozen from 1995. Featured in *Salute to Satchmo* show, from 1994. Wrote *How to Play Trumpet* (1985), co-authored *Jazz: The Essential Companion* (1987) and *Jazz: The Rough Guide* (1995). Main force behind establishment of National Jazz Foundation Archive, housed at Loughton Library, Essex. Active in Association of British Jazz Musicians and Musicians' Union Jazz section. Has regularly compered BBC radio shows through the 1990s while maintaining full playing schedule.

FALLON, 'Jack' Patrick
Born: London, Ontario, Canada, 13 October 1915
double bass/bass guitar/violin

Played violin in family band, took up double bass in 1935. Played both in Civic Symphony Orchestra and with Frank Crowley's Band. On trumpet and bass in Canadian Air Force Band, the Streamliners, who moved to Europe as part of the RCAF. Stayed in Britain after World War II, freelanced with various bands and worked with Ted Heath during summer of 1946. With Hamish Menzies at Churchill's (autumn 1946) Jack Jackson's Quintet (1947), Tito Burns (1947), vacation in Canada, then worked with Reggie Dare at the Potomac, London. Worked with Norman Burns, Alan Dean, George Shearing and Victor Feldman. With Maurice Smart Quartet (early 1948), then toured Europe with Duke Ellington (summer 1948). Accompanied Django Reinhardt and Maxine Sullivan in Britain (1948). With Eddie Carroll at Quaglino's (1949), left Carroll to work with Ralph Sharon (January 1950). With Ian Stewart, Harry Parry, Harry Hayes, Stephane Grappelli, etc. From 1950 freelanced successfully, playing on innumerable sessions, and working as a house musician at Lansdowne Studios (for Denis Preston). Also active, from 1952, as a successful agent (Cana Variety Agency). Worked in Jazz Today Unit (1953) and in Bix Curtis's In Town Jazz group, led own In Town Tonight Sextet (1954–5). Toured with Mary Lou Williams and Sarah Vaughan (1953), with Don Rendell (1954), with Lena Horne (1955), etc. With Tommy Whittle (1956), Tony Kinsey (1959), many tours with Josh White, also regularly with Johnny Duncan's Blue Grass Boys until January 1958. Regularly in Lennie Felix's Trio in the 1970s. Freelanced successfully from the 1960s through the 1990s, accompanying many visiting American jazz musicians, also playing in country and western groups, with light orchestras and in various jazz groups. Featured on countless recordings, television and radio shows.

FAME, Georgie (Clive POWELL)
Born: Leigh, Lancashire, 26 June 1943
piano/organ/vocals/composer

Father gigged in local dance bands. Georgie's sons, Tristram (born 1971) plays guitar, and James (born 1975) plays drums. Piano from age of seven, gigged with local group the Dominoes from 1957. Did season at Butlin's, Pwllheli, Wales with Rory Blackwell. To London with Blackwell in early 1959. Signed by agent Larry Parnes, played various gigs, then became accompanist for Billy Fury (1960–1). Worked briefly with Earl Watson then formed own Blue Flames (July 1962), began specializing on Hammond organ in December 1962. Played residency at Flamingo Club, London. Hit records from mid-1960s. Temporarily disbanded Blue Flames in 1966 to work with Harry South's Big Band. Played solo cabaret dates (1967–8), was also featured with Count Basie's Band (1967 and 1968). Led own band again then worked in duo with singer-keyboard player Alan Price (1971–3). Featured with own band through the 1980s and 1990s, toured Australia, guested in Scandinavia, also toured in shows devised by Keith Smith, including *Stardust Road*, a tribute to Hoagy Carmichael.

FARRELL, 'Billy' William
trumpet/piano accordion/violin/vibes

Born: South Shields, Co. Durham, *c.*1910

Father of pianist Tony Farrell. Worked with Josephine Bradley's Orchestra, with Howard Jacobs, Stanley Barnett, Buddy Featherstonhaugh, Maurice Winnick, Reg Batten, Harry Leader, Ambrose, etc. during the 1930s, and also played on a large number of freelance recordings including sides with George Scott-Wood. Worked with George Melachrino before joining the Royal Navy in World War II. Was transferred to the Royal Marines and formed service band the Blue Mariners. After demobilization worked with Sid Phillips (1945–6) then, in late 1946, moved to South Africa where he led his own band.

FAWKES, 'Wally' Walter Ernest
clarinet/soprano sax/tenor sax

Born: Vancouver, Canada, 21 June 1924

Moved to Britain in 1931. Studied at Sidcup Art School, took up clarinet at sixteen. Played (alongside Eddie Harvey) in local band then joined George Webb's Dixielanders. Studied at Camberwell School of Art (as a prelude to becoming world famous cartoonist 'Trog'), joined Humphrey Lyttelton for debut of his new band in February 1948. Remained with Lyttelton until summer of 1956, during this period worked in Switzerland (as part of Claude Aubert's Band) accompanying Sidney Bechet (1954). Formed own Troglodytes in 1957 who played long residency at the Six Bells public house, Chelsea, from March 1959. Disbanded in the mid-1960s and worked with Johnny Parker's Band and with Chez Chesterman (1965–8). Led Albion Four (with John Chilton, trumpet, Ray Smith, drums and Geoff Kemp double bass) from summer of 1968, then co-led Feetwarmers with John Chilton from 1970 until 1974 (playing a long residency at New Merlin's Cave, London). Left when the Feetwarmers began touring with George Melly (1974) and joined the Crouch End All Stars (led by pianist Graham Tayar), also took part in several Humphrey Lyttelton reunion engagements. With the Crouch End All Stars into the mid-1980s, also guested with pianist Doug Murray and made various freelance recordings. Led own small groups in London through the 1990s, often with Stan Greig (1996).

FEATHERSTONHAUGH, 'Buddy' Rupert Edward Lee
(FEATHERSTONEHAUGH)
saxes/composer

Born: Paris, France, 4 October 1909
Died: London, 12 July 1976

Began on alto sax, but specialized on tenor sax for most of his career, then changed to baritone sax in the mid-1950s. Raised in England, played in Eastbourne College Band (1927 to early 1928). Worked professionally with J. Pat O'Malley's Band at the Brent Bridge Hotel, London, then joined violinist Jean Pougnet (late 1928 to 1929). With Ambrose (1929), briefly with Ernest Ritte (1930), then worked with Rex Owen, and at the Café de Paris, London, with Spike Hughes' Nightwatchmen (also recorded extensively with Hughes). Played in France with the Cambridge Nightwatchmen. With Leslie 'Hutch' Hutchinson (1931) and Billy Mason (1931). Toured Britain with Louis Armstrong in 1932 (as part of Billy Mason's Band). Joined Bert Firman (late 1932), to Monte Carlo with Firman (spring 1933). Led own band in London (from May 1933), then joined Max Abrams' Band (January 1934). With Billy Mason again (autumn 1934), then led own band at Carlton Hotel, London (late 1934), and at Cocoanut Grove, London (1935). Prolific freelance recordings. In Reg Leopold's Orchestra (1936); worked with Benny Carter in London (January 1937). Combined freelance work with being a successful motor racing driver. With Bert Firman (November 1937–8). With Hugo Rignold's Orchestra (1939) Gerry Moore's Band (late 1939). Joined RAF, led Forces Stage Band (1941), then organized embryo version of the Skyrockets for RAF show *Contact*. Led own RAF Sextet (1943) which became resident band on BBC *Radio Rhythm Club*. Left RAF in 1946, took sextet to Iceland (October 1946). Led own quintet at the Gargoyle Club, London (1947), then spent long period mainly occupied with motor racing. Gradually drifted back into music, led own band in Staines and in Twickenham (1951–2), then played lead alto with Rae Allen's Band in Birmingham and Manchester (late 1952), also worked with Sonny Swann in Manchester. Briefly with Harry Pook's Band (January 1953), then led own band at Apollo Ballroom, Manchester, for three months before joining Pierson Webber's Quintet in London (May to October 1953). With Basil Kirchin on baritone sax (February to April 1954). Worked in Edinburgh with Vic Abbott and Johnny Black (1954). Led own octet in Edinburgh (December 1954 to April 1955) and at Eldorado Ballroom, Leith (1955), then moved back to London and formed own quintet in which he played baritone sax. The group did widespread touring and played in the Middle East. Period of musical inactivity, then played once a week with Eric Ferguson's Trio in the late 1950s. Led band on liner *Orsova* for Australian trip (playing alto sax), then retired from music and worked for a time in Earls Court, London, motor showrooms. *Buddy Featherstonhaugh*, a bio-discography by Tony Middleton, was published in 1995.

FELDMAN, Victor Stanley
piano/vibes/drums/conga drums/
composer

Born: Edgware, Middlesex, 7 April 1934
Died: Los Angeles, California, USA,
12 May 1987

His elder brothers were Robert (clarinet/alto sax; died 1992), Monty (piano/piano accordion; died 1979) and Arnold (trumpet; died 1977). Victor's sons are Trevor (drums/alto sax) and Jake (bass). Victor's mother Kitty played cello. Victor began on drums and did his first gigs at seven (he played at the No 1 Rhythm Club in London in 1941). He recorded at eight and guested with Glenn Miller's American Band of the AEF Band at ten. He worked regularly in a family trio (with Robert and Monty) at what became known as the Feldman Club, at 100 Oxford Street, London (from October 1942). Victor guested with various bands (including one led by Carlo Krahmer) and was featured in the London musical *Piccadilly Hayride* (from 1946 to early 1948) and in films. Victor began playing piano at nine, vibes at fourteen. Led own quartet (1948), own sextet (on vibes) from 1949. With Ralph Sharon from late 1949 until February 1951. With Norman Burns' Sextet and with Roy Fox (1951). Worked briefly in Paris with Ronnie Scott, then formed own band in February 1952. Worked in India with Eddie Carroll (1952), also worked with Harry Parry in India, then returned to Britain in October 1953. Worked in London with Harry Parry until January 1954, also with Jazz Today Unit (late 1953), then joined Ronnie Scott in early 1954 (on piano, vibes and conga drums). Emigrated to USA in September 1955. Achieved enormous success in America working with Woody Herman, Buddy De Franco, Cannonball Adderley, Miles Davis, Peggy Lee, etc., and playing innumerable freelance sessions. Beginning in 1956, Victor made many tours of Europe (in latter years with a group that featured his sons). He toured Russia with Benny Goodman in 1962. Victor's wife, Marilyn, who was the daughter of American pianist Fulton McGrath, died in 1984. The Feldmans were related to drummer Max Bacon.

FELIX, Lennie (Leonard JACOBUS)
piano

Born: Stamford Hill, London, 16 August 1920
Died: London, 29 December 1980

Piano from the age of five, lessons from Jules Ruben. Worked with Tito Burns, Frankie Morgan's Band, Len Newbury's Trio and Johnny Claes before serving in the RAF from late 1941 until 1945. While in RAF joined Buddy Featherstonhaugh's service band briefly before being posted to India and Ceylon. Played in RAF dance bands and did local radio work. After demobilization played on transatlantic liners. With Reg Wale before working with Freddy Randall in 1947. To South Africa with Reg Wale's Sextet (early 1948), subsequently toured Africa with Billy Farrell's Band. Worked on *Mauretania* liner with George Kennett's Band (1950). Rejoined Freddy Randall from summer 1951 until early 1952. Did solo work then worked with Frank King 1952), toured with Joe Daniels (autumn 1953), then did widespread tour of Asia entertaining troops. With Harry Gold, March to July 1954, again worked with Freddy Randall, then toured US bases in Europe with drummer Harry Lewis's Band (late 1955), subsequently played solo dates in Paris before returning to London in summer 1956. Worked in Wally Fawkes' Troglodytes in 1957 and 1958, and played summer season with Bobby Mickleburgh (1958), briefly with Sid Phillips. Played solo residencies, toured with Harry Gold, then played three month residency in Vienna until December 1959. With Nat Gonella from February to May 1960, briefly with Bernie Stanton's Band (1960), then led own trio for London residencies (1961–4). Worked with Johnny Hawksworth's Sextet (1964). Led own trio again and also did occasional dates with Freddy Randall (1966), played on various cruise liners, visiting Mediterannean ports, Australia, South Africa and Bermuda (1968). Again led own trio throughout the 1970s, accompanied visiting American musicians and played solo dates throughout Europe, and in Hong Kong (1971). Suffered fatal injuries after being knocked down by a motor car near the 606 Club, London SW10 (on 6 December 1980).

FENNER, John Michael
guitar/banjo/bass guitar

Born: Felsted, Essex, 19 May 1948

Raised in London. Early tuition from his uncle, guitarist Eric Taylor, later studied with Michael Ward. At fifteen played in local jazz club in trio with clarinettist Pete Robinson and bassist Barry Guy. Gigged with various bands, including regular work with Ron Russell. Turned professional in 1967, playing bass guitar on various liners including work with pianist Denis Latimer, while working on the *Canberra* played with Count Basie sidemen (1972). Did West End club work at Quaglino's, Café de Paris, Showboat, etc., then worked for three years with pedal steel guitarist

Gordon Huntley. Toured Germany with Phil Franklin and Geoff Simkins. Worked with Colin Symon's Jazz Band (1976) and with Cambridge City Jass Band (1978). Recorded with Bud Freeman and Wild Bill Davison. Joined Kenny Ball from September 1979 until October 1984. Worked in Europe with Eggy Ley, in Munich with Ray Crane and Eddie Taylor, with Pete Allen's Jazz Band and with Fionna Duncan. Rejoined Kenny Ball in September 1988, continued into the mid-1990s.

FENOULHET, Paul   Born: London, 20 March 1905
trombone/trumpet/French horn/arranger   Died: Ipswich, Essex, 29 December 1979

Brother of trumpeter-trombonist and bassist Arthur Fenoulhet (1910–47). Spent formative years in Torquay, Devon. First professional playing in Cornwall, then worked in Bedford with the Metro Five (autumn 1927), before settling in London to work with Arthur Rosebery and Percival Mackey. With Jack Hylton from early 1930 until December 1931, then worked mainly with Carroll Gibbons during the 1930s (from January 1932), but also played many freelance dates. Joined RAF in 1940 and became conductor of the Number One Balloon Barrage Centre Band which soon developed into the Skyrockets. After World War II ended, he continued to lead the Skyrockets until late 1947, then freelanced as a conductor and arranger. Led BBC Variety Orchestra and later became co-director of the BBC Radio Orchestra. Retired in 1970.

FENTON, 'Bernie' Bernard Shaw   Born: Doncaster, Yorkshire, 17 November 1921
piano/organ/arranger

First regular band was Bert Clegg and his Ambassadors in Mexborough, Yorkshire. Then worked with Reub Sunshine in Nottingham before moving to London. Played at Number One Rhythm Club, worked with Bram Martin (March 1941) and with Bill Smith's Band in Cricklewood, also with drummer Johnny Marks' Band. With Johnny Claes (1942), left Claes to join Oscar Rabin from late 1942 until October 1945, then joined Sid Millward (1945). With Tito Burns Sextet (1947–8), and with Norman Burns. Became founder-member of Club Eleven in December 1948. Played in quartet with John Dankworth, Laurie Morgan and Joe Muddel. With Paul Adams (1948–51), then worked with Harry Parry. Worked for many years as staff arranger for music publishers. Later specialized in 'jingles'. Active freelance throughout the 1980s and 1990s, regularly featured in the Glenn Miller tribute band led originally by Herb Miller and latterly by John Miller (1995).

FERGUSON, Alan   Born: Scotland, 1905
guitar   Died: Ayrshire, Scotland, 23 April 1959

Played semi-professionally in Kilmarnock, then joined Chalmers Wood Orchestra in Glasgow (1928). Moved to London and joined Bill Mason's Band (1930–2). Thus toured with Louis Armstrong in 1932. With Bert Firman (1933). Buddy Featherstonhaugh (1935), Duncan Whyte (1937), Reg Leopold (1937) and freelance recordings included sides with Fats Waller in London (1938). Worked with Teddy Foster and with Sydney Lipton before serving in Royal Artillery for five years. Left professional music soon after the end of World War II and did various day jobs in the small Scottish town of Hurlford.

FERGUSON, Eric
piano

Born: 1933
Died: June 1974

Worked with Barry Whitworth's Quintet in Lancashire during the early 1960s, then became house pianist at Club 43, Manchester, backing many visiting musicians. Formed jazz-rock group Monad in 1972, but continued to freelance with various jazz units. Died of a heart attack while playing at the Bridge Inn in Whitefield.

FERRIE, 'Joe' (Joseph W. FERREY)
trombone

Born: Edinburgh, Scotland, 4 February 1900
Died: 1953

Served in Army during World War I, then worked in shipyards before playing professionally with Frank Davidson and Billy Cotton in the late 1920s. With Roy Fox (1931–2), remained when Lew Stone became leader. Left Lew Stone in spring 1946. Worked in Bill Woodward's Orchestra (1936), with Jack Jackson (1936–9). Left Jackson to work briefly with Jack Doyle, then joined Eddie Carroll (1940) before spending over ten years with Geraldo (1940–51). Joe's brother, George, 'Miff' Ferrie, was also a successful trombonist, who worked with Edward Stanelli's Orchestra (1932), Roy Fox (1933), Ambrose (1935) etc., before becoming an artistes' manager (among his clients was the comedian Tommy Cooper).

FEZA, Mongezi Rawlinson
trumpet/Indian flute

Born: Queenstown, South Africa, 1945
Died: Epsom, Surrey, 14 December 1975

Trumpet from age of eight, at sixteen worked with Ronnie Beer. With the Blue Notes in the early 1960s, linked up with Chris McGregor and moved to Europe. Played dates in France and Switzerland, then travelled on to London (1965), as part of Brotherhood of Breath, played dates in Switzerland (1967). Worked in Dudu Pukwana's Band, and spent a year in Sweden (1972–3) with Johnny Dyani and Okay Temiz. Led own Music For Xaba Trio and worked with Elton Dean, in Keith Tippett's Centipede, in Harry Miller's Isipingo, etc. Died of pneumonia while a patient at a mental hospital.

FFRENCH, 'Froggy' Clinton
trumpet

Born: c.1908
Deceased

Learnt trumpet while serving in the RAF. Was subsequently part of the Cavendish Dance Band when they won three All-England contests organized by *Rhythm* magazine in 1931, 1932 and 1933. Turned professional to join Percival Mackey in late 1933. Briefly with Lew Stone in summer of 1934, then joined Howard Jacobs. With Eddie Carroll from late 1934 until late 1935 (also briefly with Sydney Kyte in this period). With Ambrose from late 1935 until September 1936, then worked mainly with Geraldo (1936–40) before rejoining the RAF and eventually became a member of the Squadronaires for several years. Regularly with George Melachrino's Orchestra in the late 1940s, also active in the studios and in many theatre orchestras including long stay in the *Black and White Minstrel Show* during the 1960s.

FIELD, Dennis
trumpet/trombone

Born: Stepney, London, 7 January 1932

Evacuated to Somerset during World War II. During Army service (1950–2) was stationed in Germany and played in the Barnstormers (with clarinettist Harry Lock). After demobilization joined Cy Laurie for nine months, then worked regularly with Eric Silk from 1953 until 1967. Brief spells with Ian Bell, Dave Keir, Jeff Downes and Patti Clarke, then again worked with Cy Laurie (1968). With Max Collie for nine months during the early 1970s, then joined George Webb for two years. During this period occasionally led own band. With Judith Durham 1974–5, including tour of Australia. Occasionally with Chris Watford and Lord Arsenal (Allan Bradley) in the 1970s; often with the Black Bottom Stompers during the late 1970s (and continued to work with them into the 1990s). Began doubling on trombone during the 1980s. Five visits to Vancouver, Canada, with Hugh Rainey, also worked with Cy Laurie again, and again with Allan Bradley's Band. Throughout the 1980s did many gigs with Pete Corrigan's Band, also worked with John Petters. Took early retirement in 1988 and became full time musician, often leading own band, working with pianist Don Nevard, with Allan Bradley, Cy Laurie, etc., through the 1990s.

FIERSTONE, George
drums/vocals

Born: London, 5 November 1917
Died: London, 13 March 1984

Brother of drummer Leslie Fierstone, father of Ray Fierstone. Joined Al Berlin's Band at thirteen, remained with Al Berlin until joining Sid Millward's Nitwits briefly in August 1938. Joined Alan Atkins in October 1938, then again worked with Sid Millward (November 1938). Founder-member of Heralds of Swing (February 1939), left at disbandment and rejoined Sid Millward. Joined Jack Harris in autumn 1939. With Harry Roy from June 1940 until May 1942. With Ambrose for a year from June 1942, with Eric Winstone (1944) then long association with the Skyrockets until December 1952 (including long residency at the London Palladium). Led own band from the 1950s, for seasons in Jersey, etc., and for regular work, mostly in London. active as a successful teacher from the 1950s onwards, also organized bands for shipping lines and worked as a booking agent.

FILLIS, 'Len' Leonard Milford
banjo/guitar/composer

Born: South Africa, 1903
Died: South Africa, 1953

Worked in Edwin Adelier's Band in South Africa, then moved to London and joined Jack Hylton's Kit-Cat Band. Left to join Fred Elizalde at the Savoy Hotel, London, in January 1928 for a year, then followed solo freelance career. With Al Starita's Blue Boys (1930), many freelance recordings with the Four Bright Sparks, the Gilt Edged Four, etc., and recorded under the name Phil Lenard. Guested with Ambrose (1933) and played in theatre orchestras. Radio work with pianist Austen Croom-Johnson (1934) and Harry Perritt's Orchestra (1934). Toured with singer Jack Buchanan (early 1935). Worked with Radio Rhythm Rascals and with Val Rosing (1935). Recorded on electric guitar in 1936. Moved back to South Africa in spring 1937, later played in Australia. Return visit to Britain in 1946, then back to South Africa.

FILMER, 'Vic' Victor Alan
piano/composer

Born: London, April 1894
Died: Manchester, 29 October 1973

Sons: Vic Jr (double bass), and Maurice (drums). Worked as a song demonstrator with a London publisher in 1910 and played ragtime in London clubs before taking engagements in Paris in 1913. Served in British Army during World War I; invalided out in April 1918. Recommenced club work, then joined Luigi Fortoni's Italian Orchestra from 1920 until 1926. Formed own band in 1929 (also acted as musical director for Pathétone film company from 1928 until 1938). Led own band in London: at Murray's (1930–1), the Ace of Spades roadhouse (1932), Hatchett's (1933) and at the Castle Restaurant, Richmond (1936). Lived in the Channel Islands in the late 1930s. Led own band through to the 1940s, including tours for ENSA in World War II. Own band in Blackpool during early 1940s, and in Penzance (1944). Left England after World War II and moved to South America (via New York) where he worked for a while in Gordon Stretton's Band. Moved to Africa in 1950. Did radio work in Durban, South Africa and in Lourenço Marques, Mozambique. Returned to England in 1960 and played occasional club dates during the 1960s, mostly in the Manchester area.

FINLAYSON, 'Tucker' Thomas Culbert
double bass

Born: Bearsden, Glasgow, Scotland, 5 May 1938

Guitar at sixteen, joined Glasgow's Delta Skiffle Group, then took up double bass and joined the Spiders' Skiffle Group. Gigged with various bands, worked with Jim Galloway, then joined Alex Dalgleish's All Stars. Two years in RAF (July 1959 to July 1961), led own service band at RAF Cranwell. On demobilization immediately joined Forrie Cairns' Clansmen and moved to London with the band. Widespread touring with Cairns in 1962 and early 1963, then settled in London and played club residencies and worked with trombonist Mick Whitehead's Band. Worked with Terry Lightfoot for eight months from August 1963, left to join Acker Bilk in June 1964, has continued to work with Bilk through the 1990s.

FIRMAN, 'Bert' (Herbert FEUERMANN)
violin/arranger

Born: London, 3 February 1903

Youngest of four brothers, all musicians (their father was a flautist and violinist). John played piano, Sam played violin, as did Sidney. Bert took violin lessons at five. Appeared and played in musical *Sally*, for two years. Joined Midnight Follies Orchestra in 1922, and soon became its leader. Became musical director for Gordon Hotels and for Zonophone Records (from 1925), led various pseudonymous bands for this label including many sides as The Rhythmic Eight, also led on Homochord label. Left Metropole Hotel residency in late 1925, led at Carlton Hotel and at Devonshire Restaurant (1927). Relinquished musical directorship at Zonophone in August 1928, and was replaced by his brother John. Moved to the USA in 1929, worked as guest conductor at NBC and worked in Hollywood, before returning to London to lead at Ciro's, and at the Ambassador's Club in Paris (1932). Led own band in Paris, Ostend, and Monte Carlo before returning to London in summer of 1937. Led fifteen-piece band at London Casino from November 1937 until January 1939. Led at Café de Paris from October 1939, then joined Army in 1940 for duration of World War II. Appeared in *Stars in Battledress* and gave solo violin recitals. Soon after the end of the war led own twelve-piece band at the Bagatelle in Paris (which for a time featured Stephane Grappelli and Django Reinhardt). When that club was sold, Firman returned to London and left the music business to work in the metals trading market until his retirement in 1976.

FISHER, 'Tony' Anthony Joseph
trumpet

Born: Levenshulme, Manchester,
27 February 1936

His father played the Double B flat brass bass, his son Mark is a keyboard player. Played cornet from age of five and was featured with various brass bands in and around Manchester during childhood. Played trumpet in local dance band, the Silver Rockets, at thirteen, then won talent contest and was featured with Carroll Levis' Discoveries for four years until serving in RAF from 1954 until 1956. While stationed at Naphill, Buckinghamshire, played regularly at the Cadena Club, High Wycombe, and led own service quintet. After demobilization worked with Ken Mackintosh from 1956 until 1959, then joined Eric Delaney's Band from 1959 until 1964. Worked often with Ted Heath from 1963 onwards, by this time increasingly busy with freelance session work, but continued to be part of various big band jazz ensembles including regular stays in Kenny Clarke-Francy Boland Big Band, in Tubby Hayes' Big Band, with Bill Russo's Orchestra, with John Dankworth, etc. Throughout the 1970s played lead trumpet with Bert Kaempfert's Orchestra, and did many other sessions in Germany, including work with Radio Orchestras in Cologne, Frankfurt, etc. Many recordings including album with Jiggs Whigham and brass contingent of the Frankfurt Symphony Orchestra, with Slide Hampton, Sacha Distel, etc. Prolific session work through the 1980s and 1990s, also playing often in Jack Sharpe's Big Band, in Don Lusher's Ted Heath Reunion Band, with Cliff Hardy, Bob Wilber's Big Band (including Nice Jazz Festival), etc. With John Dankworth, Stan Tracey Big Band, BBC Radio Big Band, etc. (1995) and (together with Marion Kaempfert) directing the Bert Kaempfert Orchestra (Bert Kaempfert having died in June 1980).

FORD, Brylo
double bass/guitar

Born: Trinidad, West Indies, c.1890
Deceased

Moved to Britain during World War I. Worked with Don Marino Barreto (1941), Cyril Blake (1941–2), Jimmy Cummins' Rhumba Band (1942). In Patrick Gibbs' Rhumba Band (1945), with Cyril Blake's Knights of Rhythm (1945) and again with Don Marino Barreto before returning to Trinidad in 1946. Moved back to Britain and worked with Francisco Condé at the Milroy Club, London (1949). With Chris Barber (early 1950), gigged with Charlie Galbraith. Featured on many calypso recordings (with Lord Beginner, etc.), also recorded as The Iron Duke. With drummer Freddy Newstead in London (1951), also worked with blues singer Big Bill Broonzy in London (1951). With Cab Kaye (1952–3) including appearance in the film *Blood Orange*.

FORD, Clinton (Ian George Stopford HARRISON)
vocals

Born: Salford, Lancashire,
4 November 1931

Became interested in jazz while working as a research laboratory assistant. Began sitting in with local bands, then joined the Merseysippi Band in 1957, first at the Cavern Club, Liverpool, later at the Mardi Gras Club. Regularly with this band for three years each winter. During the summers he worked at Butlin's holiday camp in Pwllheli, Wales, also did summer season at the Central Pier, Blackpool (1960). Joined Kenny Ball on 31 December 1960, left in spring 1961 and began highly successful solo career, making hit record 'Fanlight Fanny'. With Charlie Galbraith's Band, then guested with Dick Charlesworth, George Chisholm, Bob Wallis, Chris Barber, etc. Great deal of radio and television work through the 1960s and 1970s (toured briefly with Keith Smith in 1980). During the 1980s and 1990s worked successfully as a cabaret artiste, also did theatre work, including pantomime, combining this with many jazz dates including four visits to appear at the Sacramento Festival in California (with the Merseysippi Jazz Band).

FORESYTHE, Reginald Charles
piano/composer/arranger

Born: London, 28 May 1907
Died: London, 23 December 1958

Father was a West African barrister, his mother was English (his great-grandfather was German). Piano from the age of eight, first gigs at Reading Town Hall in 1923. Freelanced in London, then to Paris to accompany singer Zaidee Jackson (1927). Worked in Australia accompanying singer Walter Richardson (1928), then moved on to Honolulu before journeying to California where he wrote film scores for United Artistes and MGM and recorded with Paul Howard (1929). Moved to Chicago (December 1930), co-wrote with Andy Razaf, and arranged for Earl Hines, Duke Ellington, etc. To New York, broadcast with Paul Whiteman (January 1933), then returned to London (1933). Accompanied Ada Ward, then worked in band led by West Indian trumpeter Joe Smith. Accompanied Elisabeth Welch, then formed own band (1933). Led own New Music for work in clubs (Café de la Paix, Datchet Pavilion, etc.) and in film studios. Revisited USA in December 1934, again guested with Paul Whiteman and led all-star recording band in New York (which included Benny Goodman) in January 1935. Returned to Britain in February 1935. Again led New Music, recorded film sound-tracks and occasionally appeared in British films. Semi-regular piano duets with Arthur Young, radio and recordings and solo work at Datchet Club. Further trip to USA in January–March 1937, returned to Britain, freelanced, then worked briefly in Scandinavia before again duetting with Arthur Young. Led own eight-piece band at Embassy Club, London (1939), and small group at the 400 Club, and Hatchett's (1940). Joined RAF in spring 1941, subsequently gained commission and served as an officer in North Africa. After demobilization again accompanied Elisabeth Welch (1946) and played duets with Ronnie Selby. Worked in Italy (early 1948), then led band at Palace Hotel, Paignton, Devon (1948). Temporarily out of action through arthritis (spring 1949),then further seasons in Paignton. During the 1950s worked mainly as a freelance solo pianist, playing in London pubs and clubs (in Soho and Kensington).

FOSTER, Rodney
trombone/piano/vocals

Born: Belfast, Northern Ireland, 24 May 1939

Brother of reed-player Trevor Foster. Worked in White Eagles Band before joining Bryan McCluney's Ulster Rhythm Kings from summer of 1957 until forming own Jazzmen in early 1959. The Jazzmen made their television debut in October 1959 and went on to do widespread touring and recordings. Foster worked with Monty Sunshine from 1970 until 1972, then returned to Belfast and again led own band and freelanced. Active through the 1990s, playing trombone in

Leslie Brookes' Guinness All Stars, and piano in various hotels, also singing with the Belfast Jazz Orchestra (directed by Arthur Acheson).

FOSTER, 'Teddy' M.E.
trumpet/trombone/vocals

Born: London, 1 January 1908
Died: Nottingham, 5 January 1984

Younger brother Lew was a trumpeter and vocalist. Briefly played piano and drums, then took up trombone. Played local gigs, then joined Percival Mackey's Band for *Glad News* revue (1927). Later, worked with Eddie Phil Gordon (1928) and with Noni's Golden Serenaders. Switched to trumpet and worked for a year in Belgium and Switzerland, then joined Ernst van't Hoff's Band in Holland (studied with van't Hoff's father). Played with van't Hoff's Band in Birmingham, then joined Syd Seymour (1930). With Phil Richardson in Newcastle (early 1931) and with Ivor Kirchin, then led own Collegians in Birmingham (1931). With Eddie Gross-Bart's Band (1933), then joined Billy Cotton from autumn 1933 until early 1936. With Ambrose from early 1936 until August 1936, led own band briefly from August 1936, but mainly active as featured solo act, worked thus with Lou Preager's Band (1937), with Jack Payne (1938) and Joe Daniels (1939), before rejoining Billy Cotton in autumn 1939. Began leading own big band in December 1939. After a brief spell fronting the late Teddy Joyce's Band (early 1941), worked with Ambrose's Octet from September 1941 until May 1942, then worked for the rest of that year in a double act with Bart Norman (Norman Bartlett) before again forming own band (1943). Continued to lead big bands throughout the 1940s and 1950s (playing many summer seasons). Led small line-ups in the 1960s, but was mainly active in artistes' management.

FOXLEY, 'Ray' Raymond Geoffrey
piano/composer

Born: Birmingham, Warwickshire,
28 December 1928

Formed the Gutbucket Six in 1946. Played concerts at Birmingham Town Hall with own band, own trio and with the Gully Low Stompers (1947). Led own Levee Ramblers, broadcasting and playing dates in Birmingham, London, etc. Played in Paris (1952), then settled in London and worked with Bobby Mickleburgh, Mick Mulligan, Chris Barber and Mike Daniels. Also played dates in the Midlands with the Second City Jazzmen. With Ken Colyer from late 1957 until September 1960 (toured with various visiting American jazzmen including George Lewis). Moved to Bromsgrove and gigged extensively throughout the Midlands. With Ken Ingram's Band in the early 1960s, then long spell in Eddie Matthews' Jump Band, also played solo gigs and accompanied Americans in Europe. During the 1970s led own quintet and freelanced with the Jubilee Jazzmen, Henry Gardiner's Southside Jazzmen, the Paragon Jazz Band, etc., before joining Rod Mason in 1978. Worked in Europe with Mason and played residencies with various other bands in Holland, Austria, Switzerland, etc. Briefly in Chez Chesterman's Scintilla Band (1983) and did solo work. After working with Rod Mason in Düsseldorf, returned to London and rejoined Ken Colyer in 1986. After Colyer's death, Ray played in the Ken Colyer Trust Band until 1994. Own small band, solo work and freelancing through the 1990s.

FRANCE, Martin Born: Rainham, Kent, 29 February 1964
drums

Both parents were amateur musicians, mother played the piano, father the violin. Moved to Manchester in 1974, took up drums in 1975. Did first gigs in local clubs, in organ trios, etc., also worked at The Band on the Wall club, in Manchester. Moved to London in 1982. Met up with Django Bates, Mick Hutton and saxophonist Ken Stubbs and worked with them in First House. Later was part of various Django Bates' line-ups. With Loose Tubes (1988–90). Has worked with a wide variety of musicians including Kenny Wheeler, Dave Holland, Lee Konitz, Ralph Towner, Steve Swallow, Bheki Mseleku, John Taylor, Sidsel Endresen, Jason Rebello, Mario Laginha, Julian Argüelles, Eddie Parker, Norma Winstone, Henry Lowther, Stan Sulzmann, etc. During the 1990s also regularly with Iain Ballamy, with saxophonist Mark Lockheart (Perfect Houseplants), with Billy Jenkins' Voice of God Collective and continues to do widespread international touring with Django Bates' Human Chain and Delightful Precipice. Has also conducted drum clinics in Britain and abroad.

FRANK, Aubrey Born: East London, 3 June 1921
tenor sax/clarinet Died: London, 3 June 1993

Played violin at seven, took up alto sax at fourteen. Specialized on tenor sax from age of fifteen and did first professional work that year in the Savoy Junior Band. Worked with Stan Atkins, and with Reg Arnold at the Nest Club, London (late 1939). Briefly with pianist Hetty Booth's Band (early 1940), then joined Jack Harris; occasional dates with Ken Johnson's Band. With Eddie Carroll (summer 1940), then worked with Ambrose, Johnny Claes, Geraldo and George Evans before joining the RAF in late 1941. Often managed to combine service duties with musical commitments and during the period 1942–5 played dates with Johnny Claes, Ambrose, Lew Stone and Ted Heath; was also a regular member of RAF Fighter Command Band. Left RAF in December 1945, joined Ambrose from January 1946 until 1947, then worked for Frank Weir for several months in 1947. Deputized in the Skyrockets and Squadronaires, and played in Harry Hayes' Band, brief return to Frank Weir in summer of 1948. Mainly with Jack Nathan from 1949 until 1954, but also continued to undertake freelance work. From this period onwards, concentrated on studio and session work, but also with Sid Phillips, the BBC Review Orchestra, BBC Concert Orchestra and Big Band, and with the London Symphony Orchestra. Mainly active as a teacher during the last fifteen years of his life but continued to play sessions, gigs and studio dates.

FRANKLIN, 'Phil' Philip Edward Born: London, 1 July 1937
drums

Played drums and piano during childhood before specializing on drums. Joined Pete Ashton's Jazz Band at Goldsmiths Art College (1955). Led own band during Army service, then joined Cliff Harris' Blue Five (1959–60). Briefly with Ken Robinson (Ken Hine) and Sonny Morris before joining Eric Silk (1960–1). With Mike Daniels from August 1961 until January 1966 then led own Swing Sextet (1966). With Max Collie (1967–8), Alexander's Jazzmen and Cy Laurie (1968–9), also with Eggy Ley and Steve Lane during the late 1960s. During the late 1960s also worked as Promotions Manager for Premier Drum Company, then became Tour Manager for Harold

Davison's Agency (organizing tours for Duke Ellington, Harry James, Count Basie, etc.). During the early 1970s worked with Monty Sunshine, George Webb, Ron Russell and Bob Wallis, and with visiting Americans including Wild Bill Davison, Champion Jack Dupree, etc. Worked for musical instrument company, also co-led bands with Bob Taylor and Cliff Wren. Toured Australia and USA with singer Judith Durham (1973–5). Worked with the Piccadilly Six (mainly in Switzerland) from March 1978 until January 1981, then worked for six months with Hazy Osterwald in Bobby Michaels' Quartet (1981). Worked with various Swiss and German bands in the 1980s, also accompanied visiting American musicians. Led own band from 1981 through the 1990s (based in Switzerland), also Musical Director for the Casa Bar Club in Zurich.

FRANKS, Alan Martin
trumpet/flugelhorn

Born: 18 December 1924
Died: 1992

Brother Gordon Franks a pianist. With Teddy Foster (1943), George Shearing's Quartet (late 1944–5), Ted Heath (late 1945–7) and often with Frank Weir during the 1940s. With Eddie Carroll (early 1947), then rejoined Frank Weir (spring 1947). With Geraldo from 1948 until spring 1954 (again worked with Frank Weir in summer 1948). Briefly with Cyril Stapleton (spring 1952). Worked with Dave Shand (1954). Prolific session work from the 1950s to the 1980s, played for many West End Shows, but also did freelance band work with Sid Phillips, etc.

FREE, 'Jack' John
trombone

Born: Leytonstone, London, 28 March 1932

Played in Johnny Rowden's Band at Leyton High Road Youth Club in the late 1940s. Regularly with Harry Walton from 1954 until 1960 (in 1956 the band made a private recording with Louis Armstrong). With Dave Shepherd, then worked with Freddy Randall before rejoining Dave Shepherd. With Pat Mason's Band in the 1970s and with Tom Collins' Band in Colchester. Subsequently freelanced and accompanied visiting American jazz musicians. Played regularly in Joe Loss' Ambassadors from the 1970s through to the 1990s. While working with John Petters recorded with Yank Lawson and Wild Bill Davison. With the Herts and Essex All Stars in the 1990s and freelancing extensively.

FRENCH, Jeremy
trombone/trumpet

Born: Sutton Coldfield, Warwickshire, 4 July 1931
Died: London, 11 November 1989

Began playing trumpet in brass band at Tiffin School, Kingston upon Thames, Surrey in 1945. Left school in 1949, began playing dance gigs before doing National Service in the Army (1949–51). After demobilization worked with Len Beadle (1951), with Chris Barber and Cy Laurie before forming his own band (1953). Switched to trombone and worked with Trevor Williams, Alex Revell and Mick Mulligan, before joining Sandy Brown for a year from summer 1956. With Wally Fawkes from October 1957 until August 1959, briefly in Dave Keir's Band then rejoined Wally Fawkes from 1960 until January 1962. Studied at the Royal College of Music from 1960 until 1962, then for period of almost twenty years concentrated on orchestral work, but then returned to playing jazz and worked regularly in Richard Williams' Dix Six during the 1980s and also composed for Williams' films. Jeremy took part in Chris Barber's 40th Anniversary concerts shortly before succumbing to cancer.

G

GALBRAITH, 'Charlie' Charles Alfred
trombone/vocals

Born: Lambeth, London, 13 August 1920
Died: London, 16 January 1997

Played violin during childhood, but took up trombone during RAF service (1940–6). During the late 1940s worked briefly with John Haim's Jelly Roll Kings, with Cy Laurie, Reg Rigden and Mike Daniels. Led own Jazzmen from 1949 to 1954, then brief spell with Eric Silk (late 1954). With Bobby Mickleburgh (1955), George Webb, Joe Daniels and Kenny Ball (1957–8). Led own All Star Jazz Band from 1960, which toured Britain and played in Belgium (1962), Turkey (1963), France and Holland. Co-led with trumpeter Brian Jones (1963–4), then worked regularly with Monty Sunshine from 1965 to 1968. With Joe Daniels (1969). Led own band again during the 1970s and 1980s for long residencies in Bedford and Northampton. Worked occasionally with American drummer Sam Woodyard. From 1978 to 1983 played regularly in Paris (with Alan Wickham) at the Caveau de l'Huchette and at the Rue de Rivoli Slow Club, in drummer George Collier's London All Stars. Continued to freelance (1996) until shortly before dying of cancer.

GALBRAITH, 'Gus'
trumpet

Born: Derby, 18 April 1939

Played in the Original Climax Jazz Band, which formed the basis of Gus Galbraith's Sextet, who were runners-up in the All England Jazz Band Contest in 1958. The band subsequently played many clubs in London and toured Denmark (1958). The band played a residency at the Tropicana Club in 1959. Gus also played in Ivor Mairants' National Youth Orchestra (1959–60), and in Bob Barter's Band before joining John Dankworth in May 1960. With Dankworth during the early 1960s, also did freelance session work. With Johnny Fourie's group (1965). Emigrated to South Africa in 1967.

GALLOWAY, 'Jim' James Braidie
saxes/clarinet/composer

Born: Kilwinning, Ayrshire, Scotland, 28 July 1936

Raised in Dalry, a town 25 miles from Glasgow. Played clarinet, alto sax and baritone sax in local bands. Worked in Alex Dalgleish's All Stars and with own Jazz Makers before emigrating to Canada in July 1964. Took up soprano sax, joined the Metro Stompers and took over leadership in 1968, also led own big band in Toronto. Has made many return visits to Britain, making extensive tours of Europe and playing at many international festivals. Remains based in Canada, but often works in the USA alongside eminent musicians. Leads own small groups and big band through the 1990s.

GANLEY, Allan Anthony
drums/composer/arranger

Born: Tolworth, Surrey, 11 March 1931

Began playing drums during his early teens, did gigs with local bands including one led by tenor saxophonist Norman George. After serving in the RAF turned professional and joined Jimmy Walker's Quintet in summer of 1952. Left Walker in early 1953 to join Jack Parnell. Left Parnell, worked briefly with Ambrose (summer 1953), then joined John Dankworth (in Dankworth's first big band) for two years from October 1953. (Also recorded with Mary Lou Williams in January 1953.) Co-led New Jazz Group (with pianist Derek Smith) from late 1955, also featured with Kenny Baker's Dozen (1955–6) and with the Jazz Today Unit (1955–7). Visited New York and Los Angeles (1955). Worked on the *Queen Mary* liner (late 1956). Flew to USA to play dates with Ronnie Scott's Sextet (early 1957). Co-led (with Ronnie Ross) the Jazzmakers (1958–60) – appeared at Newport Jazz Festival, 1959 – and (with Keith Christie) from summer 1960. In spring of 1960 the Jazzmakers played in the USA as part of a Vic Lewis package. With Tubby Hayes Quintet from January 1962 until 1964. During the early 1960s became increasingly busy as a session musician, also appeared in the film *All Night Long*. House drummer at Ronnie Scott's Club from 1964 until 1967, accompanied many visiting American musicians, including Freddie Hubbard, Roland Kirk, Jim Hall, Art Farmer, Stan Getz, etc. Also played at Annie's Room (1965), worked with John Dankworth and Cleo Laine, and played many freelance sessions. Left Britain in February 1967 to work in Bermuda with Joe Wylie's Band. Studied arranging and composing at Berklee School of Music in Boston, USA, for four months in 1970, then returned to Bermuda. Recorded with Jim Hall and Art Farmer in New York (1976). Moved back to Britain in summer of 1976 and resumed session playing (with Henry Mancini, Nelson Riddle, Robert Farnon, Stephane Grappelli-Yehudi Menuhin, etc.) and working with various jazz groups. Over the coming years accompanied many visiting musicians including Dizzy Gillespie, Al Haig, Blossom Dearie, Peggy Lee, etc. Formed own big band which continued to assemble occasionally through the 1990s. Prolific arranging and composing for many line-ups including BBC Radio Big Band, Dankworth Generation Band, BBC Radio Orchestra and for various singers including Elaine Delmar, Marion Montgomery, Carol Kidd, Georgie Fame. Regularly with the Pizza Express All Stars, the Great British Jazz Band, Cleo Laine, John Dankworth, Dave Shepherd, Martin Taylor, etc. Accompanies many visiting musicians, plays on numerous freelance sessions, broadcasts and recordings. With Stan Tracey, Annie Ross, Tony Coe, etc. (1995), briefly out of action through broken ankle (1996), then resumed full schedule, working with Tony Coe, Scott Hamilton, etc.

GARDNER, 'Freddy' Frederick
all saxes/clarinet

Born: Kilburn, London, 23 December 1910
Died: London, 26 July 1950

His son Robin plays trombone as a hobby; his other son, Freddy Jr, is not a musician. Freddy's uncle, Charles Bryant, was a professor of trombone at Kneller Hall, and at the Royal College of Music. Freddy was a self-taught saxophonist but took advice from his uncle. He gigged on sax and clarinet from the age of sixteen. His own New Colorado Band won a *Melody Maker* award in October 1929. He won an Individual Award at the same contest. First professional work with Eddie Gross-Bart at the Ambassadors Club, London, in the late 1930. Later worked with Gross-Bart at the Café de Paris (November 1931), then joined pianist Dave Frost at Café Anglais

(August 1932). With Sydney Lipton in 1933 (took leave to play August 1933 season in Holland with Ray Noble and also played on Ray Noble's New Mayfair Orchestra recordings). With Maurice Winnick from late 1933 until spring 1934. With Howard Jacobs at Savoy Hotel (June to July 1934), then led own band at Grand Hotel, Broadstairs, for summer season. Very briefly with Ambrose (temporarily replacing Danny Polo), then freelanced before joining Lou Preager in November 1934. With Lou Preager for part of 1935, but increasingly active as a freelance, playing on many sessions throughout the 1930s. Played in Embassy Club house band and briefly deputized in Henry Hall's Band (June 1936). Toured Scotland and England with George Scott-Wood's Six Swingers (January 1937), also worked (and recorded) with Bert Firman (late 1937-8). Prolific freelance work with visiting Americans, and leading own recording band, as well as playing for radio and on film sound tracks. With Billy Bissett at Café de Paris (1939), again with Bert Firman from September 1939, remained briefly when George Melachrino became leader in late 1939. Joined Royal Navy in 1940 as an engineer, was transferred to Royal Naval Patrol Service in Lowestoft and played in RNPS Dance Band, led by pianist George Crow. Visited London on leave and made various recordings, some with own Messmates (1943-4), but continued with active service on patrol boats. Demobilized in November 1945, briefly with Ted Heath (late 1945). With Billy Munn from late 1945 through to 1946 (including summer season on the Isle of Wight). Prolific freelance work during period 1945-50, often in Nat Allen's Orchestra. Regularly featured in Mark White's BBC Jazz Club groups. Concert appearances and broadcasts in Peter York's Orchestra with whom he recorded as a featured soloist) through to 1950. He died of a brain haemorrhage.

GARFORTH, 'Jimmy'   Born: Manchester, Lancashire, 1941
drums

Worked with Dave Nelson, Mike Peters, Dave Reynolds, Mickey Ashman and Kenny Ball before joining Terry Lightfoot in late 1958. Left Lightfoot in summer of 1960. With Sims-Wheeler Vintage Band, then long spell with Mike Cotton from early 1961. With Rod Mason's Band in Plymouth during the late 1960s, then became part of the Rod Mason-Ian Wheeler Band in the 1970s (also worked in Europe with Keith Smith, 1975). Again, worked with Rod Mason in the early 1980s, then joined the Piccadilly Six (led by trumpeter Dave Stewart) based in Switzerland, and remained with them through the 1990s. Played in Pat Halcox's Summer Band (1979) during a temporary return to Britain.

GARLAND, 'Tim' (Timothy Garland WAGGETT)   Born: Ilford, Essex, 19 October 1966
tenor sax/soprano sax/composer/arranger

Father is a cellist. Raised in Canterbury. Got to Grade Eight on clarinet and piano then played alto sax from fifteen. Gave up after two years and became student of composition at the Guildhall School of Music. At twenty bought tenor sax and began specializing on this, later doubling on soprano sax. Gigged with various bands then joined Ronnie Scott's Quintet (replacing the injured Dick Pearce). Toured Europe with Ronnie Scott (1990). Led own recording quintet Points On The Curve for two years, then formed award-winning group Lammas in 1989, which continues to flourish through the 1990s. During the 1980s and 1990s also worked with Anthony Kerr, Slim

Gaillard, Jason Rebello, Norma Winstone, Kenny Wheeler, Gerard Presencer, John Taylor, the London Jazz Orchestra, Itchy Fingers (including European tour), Duncan Lamont's Big Band, etc. Continues to lead Lammas and to work in the Dankworth Generation Band, with Jim Mullen, Pete King, Anthony Kerr, Milan Lad, Geoff Castle and own quintet. Won MCPS award for *Dance for Human Folk* (1995). Teaches at Wavendon Summer School, at the Guildhall, at Leeds College and at Royal Academy of Music. Duos with American guitarist Ralph Towner (April 1996).

GARNETT, 'Willie' William Born: Haifa, Palestine (now Israel), 25 August 1936
saxes/clarinet

Father of saxophonist Alex Garnett. Born in the Middle East where his father, a regular in the British Army, was serving. The family returned to Britain in 1944. First played sax in 1950, lessons from Harry Hayes. After gigging as a semi-pro, did summer seasons and worked on various liners including one sailing from Marseilles. Worked with Jack Nathan and Jack White and did wide variety of playing including UK tours with Little Richard and gigs with Alexis Korner. Ran own rehearsal big band from the 1950s. During the 1960s travelled extensively throughout the Middle East and Europe playing with many varied ensembles. During the 1970s worked with Richard Sudhalter, Gerry Salisbury, Jimmy Skidmore, the Tally Ho Big Band, etc. Began long musical association with Alan Stuart's Octet in 1972. Founder-member of the London Jazz Big Band from February 1975, also original member of Brian Leake's Sweet and Sour. Again with Alexis Korner, and regularly with Ted Beament's Quartet (through to the 1990s). During the 1980s worked in Charlie Watts' Big Band, in Ian Stewart's Rocket 88, in Stan Greig's Boogie Band, in Tony Milliner's Mingus Music, and co-leading with trombonist Mike Hogh. Continued to play with a wide variety of jazz groups through the 1990s, including work in the Roaring Band (with Don Rendell) and on duo gigs with son Alex.

GARRICK, Michael Born: Enfield, Middlesex, 30 May 1933
piano/organ/composer/arranger

Father of Gabriel (trumpet) and Chris (violin). First became interested in jazz while a student at Enfield Grammar School. Earliest influences were Lionel Hampton, Pinetop Smith and Meade Lux Lewis. Piano lessons from George Rattee. Two years service in the RAF. Attended Ivor Mairants' School of Dance Music, London. Studied literature at Regent Street Polytechnic and at London University. Led quartet (with Pete Shade) which appeared at Beaulieu Jazz Festival (summer 1958) and played year's residency at London's Marquee Club. Ran 'Jazz Goes to College' series at Ronnie Scott's Club (1960). Led own groups during the early 1960s and provided music for long series of Jazz and Poetry concerts with Joe Harriott and Shake Keane. Studied briefly with Bill Evans. With Neil Ardley's New Jazz Orchestra from summer 1965, regularly with Don Rendell-Ian Carr Quintet from 1965 until 1969. Ran Highwayman Jazz Club, Camberley (1965–9). From the late 1960s onwards composed many choral works, including *Jazz Praises* (which was recorded in St Paul's Cathedral). Wrote many pieces for singer Norma Winstone (who was part of Garrick's Sextet from 1968). Led own groups throughout the 1970s (recording a dozen albums). In 1976 founded Wavendon Jazz Course at the request of John Dankworth. From 1977 was part of Threesome (with Norma Winstone and guitarist Phil Lee). As a mature student attended Berklee School of Music, USA, and gained an Open Fellowship there. During the 1980s worked with saxophonist Chris Hunter's Quintet, with Lol Coxhill, Adelaide Hall, Sonny Stitt, Nigel Kennedy, etc., and in Dave Green's Fingers, and the Joe Harriott Memorial Quintet. His *A Zodiac of Angels* (a 70 minute work combining jazz soloists, symphony orchestra, chorus and choreography) was performed at the Opera House, Manchester, in 1988. Active as a teacher throughout his career and Director of Jazz Academy since 1989, organizing vacation courses at the Royal Academy of Music and Regent's College. From 1981 has played a series of duos with pianists Eddie Thompson, Gordon Beck, Brian Dee and John Taylor. Formed String Trio (with John Etheridge and Dave Green) in 1983, and own big band in 1985, both of these projects continuing through the 1990s. Continues to play regularly, and is enjoying continued success as a composer. Formed own record label in 1994.

GAY, 'Al' Albert
Born: London, 25 February 1928

tenor sax/soprano sax/clarinet

Clarinet from age of thirteen, studied at Guildhall School of Music, gigged in trio led by brother Joshua Gay, then led own band around the Ilford area and worked in the Jive Bombers (1946). Did National Service, worked on Cunard liners. With Freddy Randall from 1953 until 1956. Joined Bobby Mickleburgh (October 1956), then rejoined Randall in February 1957. Joined Laurie Gold's Pieces of Eight in February 1958, remained until 1960, worked with Joe Daniels. With Bob Wallis from May 1961 until April 1963. With Alex Welsh from April 1963 until summer 1964, then worked in Long John Baldry's Hoochie Coochie Men from August 1964 until November 1964. Briefly in Original All Stars then again worked with Freddy Randall, occasionally with Alex Welsh in the late 1960s. During the early 1970s again worked with Freddy Randall, and with Stan Greig's Quintet, and with Ron Russell-Alan Wickham Band. Lived in Nottingham (1973). Played locally, then moved back to London area in late 1973. Played in Prague with Ron Russell's Band (1974). With Freddy Randall and Lennie Hastings (1975), regularly with Stan Greig's London Jazz Big Band from February 1975 until 1983, also with Alex Welsh again, from 1977 until 1981. Played in Sweden with the World's Greatest Jazz Band (1978), toured with Harry Edison (1980) and worked in Denmark and Germany with the Harlem Blues and Jazz Band. During the 1980s worked often in Stan Greig's Boogie Band, occasionally in Pizza Express All Stars, and with Dave Shepherd. Was also part of the Alex Welsh Reunion Band. Active into the 1990s, freelancing with Val Wiseman's *Lady Sings the Blues*, with Keith Smith, in Digby Fairweather's Jazz Superkings, as well as leading own group.

GAYNAIR, 'Bogey' Wilton
Born: Jamaica, West Indies, 11 January 1927
Died: Germany, 13 February 1995

tenor sax/clarinet

Older brother of saxophonist Bobby Gaynair. Studied at the Alpha Cottage School then played in the Jamaican All Stars (1948), in drummer Redver Cooke's Band and in own group before moving to Europe. Studied music in Germany but played and recorded in London during 1959. Returned to Germany and worked for some years in band led by pianist George Maycock. Played in London in May 1961, then settled in Germany. Worked for many years with Kurt Edelhagen (also featured in Third Eye). Joined Peter Herbolzheimer, but suffered a debilitating stroke in the 1980s. Was forced to abandon playing and lived near Düsseldorf during the 1990s.

GEE, Jonathan
piano/composer

Born: Jaffa, Israel, 6 March 1959

Piano from the age of six. Became a rock singer-guitarist, then reverted to piano. Attended Sheffield University, moved to London and began gigging. Freelanced in various groups, then worked with Bobby Wellins, Steve Williamson and led own trio. Accompanied Teddy Edwards, Art Farmer, David Murray and Sonny Fortune, Claire Martin, Mornington Lockett, Iain Ballamy, Courtney Pine, Tim Whitehead, Andy Sheppard, Dick Heckstall-Smith, Joan Viskant, etc. Toured Spain with Mark Murphy, worked in Israel with Steve Williamson, with Orphy Robinson in Greece, David Jean Baptiste in Holland and Ed Jones in Italy and Germany. Musical director for television and radio shows. Toured again with saxophonist Ed Jones' Quintet (1996). Continues to lead own band and trio through the 1990s.

GELATO, Ray (Ray Keith IRWIN)
tenor sax/vocals

Born: West London, 25 October 1961

Played violin at school, took up tenor sax at eighteen. Played in the Dynamite Band and began singing regularly. Formed the Chevalier Brothers in the early 1980s and did widespread touring in USA, Japan and Europe. Later formed own seven piece Giants of Jive in 1988 and toured Belgium, Italy, Finland, Holland, Norway, etc. and made two appearances at the Nice Jazz Festival. In 1995 this group was superseded by a new ensemble called Ray Gelato's Giants, whose 1996 personnel comprised Ray Gelato, Al Nicholls (tenor sax), Enrico Tomasso (trumpet), Dave Keech (trombone), Richard Busiakiewicz (piano), Clark Kent (double bass) and Alan Cox (drums). Ray Gelato occasionally guests with Peter Long's Echoes of Ellington and also works with Alex Garnett in Tough Tenors (1996).

GELLY, 'Dave' David
tenor sax/clarinet/bass clarinet

Born: Bexleyheath, Kent, 28 January 1938

Played clarinet at school then took up alto sax. Led the Cambridge University Jazz Band (on alto sax) which won the Inter-University contest in early 1961. While at University switched to tenor sax and led own quintet at Daddy's Club, Cambridge (1960–2). Returned to London after graduating and played in Blues By Six and in Neil Ardley's New Jazz Orchestra from 1964, also taught at William Penn School in Dulwich. Co-led quintet with Art Themen in the mid-1960s (a continuance of their days together at Cambridge), also co-led quintet with Barbara Thompson. During the late 1960s played in Frank Powell's Quintet and co-led quartet with Frank Ricotti. During the 1970s with John Burch, Alan Cohen, in quintet co-led with Jeff Scott, in Stylus (with Brian Priestley) and occasionally in Mike Daniels' Big Band. Continued to work with Jeff Scott into the 1980s. Also led own quartet and septet, by this time was a regular columnist on jazz in *The Observer* and frequently presented programmes on BBC radio. Continues regular writing, broadcasting and playing through the 1990s (in duo with guitarist Nigel Bennett, with the Swingbeans and freelancing in various jazz groups). *The Giants of Jazz* by Dave Gelly was first published in 1986. His *Lester Young* (in the *Jazz Masters Series*) was first published in 1984.

GERALDO (Gerald W. BRIGHT)
piano

Born: North London, 10 August 1903
Died: Switzerland, 4 May 1974

Twin brother of pianist Sidney Bright. Piano from early childhood, studied at Royal Academy of Music. Played in London cinemas on piano and organ from age of fifteen. Led own band at Lyons' Corner House, Strand, London, then joined orchestra on *SS Cameronia* for a few months. Played piano for silent films at Futurist Cinema, Liverpool, then joined band directed by Arthur Davis at the Blackpool Tower. Led own five-piece band at Hotel Metropole, Blackpool (1923–5), then formed big band for five year residency at Majestic Hotel, St Anne's, near Blackpool (from 1925). Visited South America in late 1920s, returned to London and (adopting the name Geraldo) led own Gaucho Tango Orchestra from 1930. Led this ensemble at the Savoy Hotel, London, from summer of 1930. In September 1933 he broadened his musical policy and began leading a big band (Geraldo and his Sweet Music and Orchestra). He left the Savoy in August 1940 and enjoyed widespread success through touring, radio and recording throughout the 1940s, 1950s and 1960s. During World War II, Geraldo was Head of Light Music for ENSA (Entertainments National Service Association). His band did widespread overseas touring (Middle East, Italy, etc.) in 1944. In addition to his bandleading activities, Geraldo operated a successful theatrical agency from the 1940s, which (amongst other activities) supplied musicians for many passenger liners, and those thus employed were said to be in 'Geraldo's Navy'. He died while on vacation in Switzerland.

GIBBS, George
double bass/sousaphone

Born: Kingston Hill, Surrey, 1897
Died: London, 13 April 1983

With Emil Colombo (1922–6), Teddy Sinclair (1927), Jay Whidden, and Kel Keech. During the 1930s worked with Percival Mackey, Roy Fox, Lew Stone, Jack Payne, Carroll Gibbins, Maurice Winnick, Bert Firman, Jack Harris, etc. With Arthur Young at Hatchett's Restaurant (with Stephane Grappelli and George Shearing) in 1939–40, then toured in Ambrose's Octette. Was part of BBC's resident jazz club band in the 1940s. Did radio, film and television work with Victor Sylvester, Eric Robinson, Sydney Jerome, Louis Levy, Ken Beaumont, Phyl Mastell, Peter Yorke, etc. Active freelance during the 1960s.

GIBBS, 'Mike' Michael Clement Irving
trombone/piano/composer/arranger

Born: Salisbury, Rhodesia (now Harare, Zimbabwe),
25 September 1937

Piano from age of seven, trombone from seventeen. Studied science at Pietermaritzburg University in South Africa, also took lessons in arranging in Salisbury (now Harare) with pianist Dave Simpson. At twenty-one began music studies in the USA, first at the Berklee School of Music, then (from 1961) at the Lenox School of Music and at the Boston Conservatory where he gained a Bachelor of Music degree (1963). He subsequently won a scholarship to the Tanglewood Summer School and studied composition with Aaron Copland, Gunther Schuller and others. While in America he worked with various groups, often with Gary Burton. He returned to Africa and toured for five months with a visiting English ice-show. Moved to Britain in 1965. Joined Graham Collier in spring of 1966, then worked with John Dankworth (1967–8), gigged with Humphrey Lyttelton, Tubby Hayes, Stan Tracey, etc. Led own big band from 1969, began writing for television and films. Worked often with John Dankworth in the early 1970s, occasionally with John Warren. Moved to USA in 1974 to be Composer in Residence at Berklee School of Music, but returned to Europe for specific tours, festivals and to conduct and write for various European radio orchestras. Resigned Berklee post in 1983 and freelanced in New York, composing, arranging and acting as musical director for a number of performers. Since 1985 he has made regular return trips to Britain, leading own Anglo-American Band in the 1980s and directing the Creative Jazz Orchestra for 1990s tours. He also toured with guitarist John Schofield. During the 1990s has continued to enjoy widespread success as a composer of extended works, as an orchestrator and as a writer and arranger of music for films and stage.

GILBERT, 'Jumping Jack' Jack Peter
clarinet

Born: Greenwich, London, 18 October 1938

Nephew of clarinettist Frank Noble. Began on recorder then took up clarinet. Received classical tuition but sat in with Bill Brunskill and played regularly in the Dartford area with the North Down Stompers. Spent three years in an RAF band, also played regular jazz gigs. After demobilization spent almost ten years with Eric Silk. Left Eric Silk in May 1969 and spent thirteen years with Max Collie. Began leading own band in 1982 and freelancing. During the 1990s continues to lead own Panama Jazz Band and also the Scat Cats. Teaches in schools around the Brighton area and coaches junior jazz groups.

GILBERT, 'Les' Leslie Eric
saxes/clarinet/violin

Born: Sheffield, Yorkshire, 29 March 1915
Died: Canterbury, Kent, 8 December 1979

Father (Sid) was a pianist, brother Ken a trumpeter. Les's son, Tony, is a trombonist, working in Australia. Les began on violin at the age of eight, took up tenor sax at fifteen, then specialized on alto sax from age of seventeen. Played professionally at Nottingham Palais, then moved to London and worked with Bill Airey-Smith's Spider's Web Orchestra (1935) and with the Piccadilly Hotel Orchestra (1935). With Sydney Kyte (1936–7), briefly with Orde Hamilton, then joined Eddie Carroll (featured on clarinet) in late 1937. With Lou Preager, Jack Harris and Jack Hylton (including visit to Berlin) before World War II. Briefly with George Evans. Worked with Henry Hall, then joined Ted Heath in 1945 and remained into the 1960s before becoming highly successful session musician.

GLEAVES, 'Ronnie' (Ronald STANTON-GLEAVES)
piano/vibes

Born: Bermondsey, London,
17 June 1923

Played drums in US Red Cross Band on USO tours during World War II. Later played vibes semi-professionally with trumpeter Fred Romaine's band in South London. Coached on piano by Jack Saville. Led own band at Toby's in Bermondsey for eight years (on piano and vibes). Worked with Dave Shepherd before joining Freddy Randall (1964–5). Left Randall to join Bruce Turner in spring 1965. After a year with Turner (on piano and vibes) again worked with Dave Shepherd. While with Turner and Shepherd accompanied many visiting American musicians including Teddy Wilson, Ruby Braff, Pee Wee Russell, Wild Bill Davison, Ben Webster, etc. Often worked with Dave Shepherd into the late 1980s, thereafter specialized on piano and played various club residencies through the 1990s.

GOFF, 'Reggie' Reginald
tenor sax/clarinet/vocals

Born: Gosport, Hampshire, 19 September 1915
Died: Middlesex, 16 September 1956

Led own professional band in Luton at the age of fifteen. Continued to lead own bands through the 1930s then joined Billy Ternent's BBC Dance Orchestra, later worked with Stanley Black (1944). With George Crow (1945–6) then again led own band (from wheelchair) 1947 to 1955.

GOLD, Harry
bass sax/tenor sax/clarinet/oboe/
arranger/composer/vocals

Born: Dublin, Ireland, 26 February 1907

His son David is a musical director and composer. His brother Laurie is a saxophonist and arranger. Family moved to Leytonstone, London, when Harry was four. Left school at fourteen to help his father (a tailor). With his wages he bought an alto sax. Studied at London College of Music. First paid musical work was with the Magnetic Dance Band led by Joe Loss. Subsequently gigged around east London with the Florentine Band prior to playing professionally for two weeks with a band at the Palais de Dance, Rochester, Kent (1923). Spent almost three years with the Metronomes (1926–8). Worked with Vic Filmer and Marius B. Winter (1931), then led co-operative band with Ivor Mairants at the Spider's Web roadhouse near Watford (spring 1932). With Jack Padbury at Princes Restaurant, London, sang in vocal trio later to be named the Cubs (1932). With Roy Fox from late 1932 until August 1937, sang regularly in the Cubs. With Bert Firman (1937–8), Philip Martell's Orchestra, Harold Collins and Mantovani (early 1939), then joined Oscar Rabin for four years from spring of 1939 (during this period began leading a band within a band, the Pieces of Eight). With Geraldo for eight months from June 1943. Worked as musical director for Radio Luxembourg then began leading own eight piece band at Astoria Ballroom, London (summer 1944), also freelanced, including tour of France with Eric Winstone (spring 1945) and appearances with the Liverpool Philharmonic Orchestra under the baton of André Kostelanetz (June 1946). Led own Pieces of Eight through to January 1956, then temporarily handed over leadership to brother Laurie. Did freelance sessions and arranging before forming New Beat Band for two summer seasons at Scarborough (1958–9), also toured Ireland (1958). Reunited with Laurie for year at Hammersmith Palais, London, from April 1960. Thereafter continued to lead own band for specific engagements, then worked (mainly on tenor sax) with Al Wynette's Band at Café de Paris, London (1977). Soon re-formed Pieces of Eight, which continued successfully through the 1980s, and 1990s. Harry was also part of the new Paul Whiteman Orchestra (1974–5) and worked in Dick Sudhalter's Band (1975). He has made several playing visits to the USA in the 1980s and 1990s. Awarded British Academy of Songwriters, Composers and Authors' Gold Badge of Merit (1976).

GOLD, Laurie
tenor sax/clarinet/arranger

Born: London, 28 December 1918

Went to school with Woolf Phillips and Aubrey Frank. Began on alto sax at sixteen. Lessons from his brother, Harry Gold. With Stan Atkins' Ambassadors (1937), Lew Foster's Ambassadors (1938), Johnny Claes (1939). Worked with pianist Hetty Booth's Band at the Palm Beach Club, Frith Street, London, in the spring of 1940. With Tony Carr's Mellow Music (led by Tony

Karmeli) during the summer of 1940, left to join the Army (1940). Originally in the Pioneer Corps Band then became part of George Melachrino's AEF Band, and in Blue Rockets. After demobilization joined Eric Robinson's Blue Rockets (late 1945), then worked at the Piccadilly Hotel with George Clouston before joining Harry Gold's Pieces of Eight (in early 1946). Also appeared with André Kostelanetz in Britain (1946). Remained with Harry Gold until late 1952. Left to work in band management, then rejoined Harry Gold. Took over leadership of the Pieces of Eight from January 1956 until late 1959, then again worked with Harry Gold for season at Hammersmith Palais (1960). Again led Pieces of Eight in the early 1960s, then left full time playing to work as a recording manager, and session organizer. Worked at EMI from 1966 until retiring in 1983. Moved to Clacton, Essex, where he occasionally sat in with visiting bands through the 1990s.

GOLDBERG, 'Dave' David
guitar/trombone/composer

Born: Merseyside, 22 July 1922
Died: London, 21 August 1969

Family settled in Glasgow. Took up guitar at fourteen, played gigs from age of sixteen. First professional work with Jack Chapman in Glasgow on guitar and trombone (1940). With Ronnie Munro (1941), then joined RAF and served in Canada as a pilot instructor. After demobilization specialized on guitar, joined Ted Heath and remained until moving to USA in March 1948. Played gigs in Los Angeles and worked with tenor saxophonist Corky Corcoran, then returned to Britain and rejoined Ted Heath from October 1948 until March 1949. Freelanced, then again moved to the USA (early 1950). Freelanced in Los Angeles (as Dave Gilbert) and worked as Dave Goldberg in Freddy Slack's Trio (1952). Worked in film studios, then joined dancer Katherine Dunham's show (1953). Film work (playing on soundtracks and writing) in Italy (spring 1954), before returning to Britain in April 1954. Worked in Dizzy Reece's Sextet (1954), with Harry Roy's Quintet (1954), then joined Geraldo (February 1955). In Phil Seamen's Quintet (1956) and freelanced before becoming long-time member of Jack Parnell's ATV Orchestra.

GOLDBERG, Max (Max GORGINSKI)
trumpet/mellophone

Born: East London, 19 March 1905
Died: Melbourne, Australia, 11 February 1990

Family (who were originally from Russia) emigrated to Toronto, Canada, when Max was nine months old. Played mellophone then took up cornet at nine. Played in Jewish Boys' Band and toured Canada and USA as part of the Russian Juvenile Band. First professional work was with the Novelty Sextet at Moshers Arcade in Toronto (1919). Returned to England as part of Bill Shenkman's Buffalo Orchestra in 1923, played long residency at Birmingham Palais (1924). Led own band at Moody's Club, London (late 1925). Worked with Kal Keech and his Band (1926) and in the Criterion Dance Band (1926), also at the Kit-Cat Club with Al Payne. With Savoy Havana Band for a year from October 1926, transferred to Savoy Orpheans in October 1927, toured Germany with them (late 1927 to spring 1928). Extensive freelance work from 1928 onwards, making innumerable recordings, but continued to work regularly with various line-ups including the Blue Lyres (1929), Al Collins (1929), Arthur Lally (1930), Billy Mason (1931), Melville Gideon, (1931). Featured with Ambrose from September 1931 until late 1935. With Sydney Lipton from January 1936, then rejoined Ambrose in September 1937. With Jack Harris from

November 1938. Joined Geraldo in March 1939. With Sid Phillips, then joined RAF in summer of 1941, played in service bands until released in 1944. Worked with Frank Weir (September 1944) and with Ted Heath (1945), before rejoining Ambrose (September 1945). With Maurice Winnick and Sydney Lipton, then concentrated on freelance session work, but was also featured regularly in Louis Levy's Orchestra until emigrating to Australia in 1957. Worked in the Royal Theatre Orchestra in Brisbane, then moved to Melbourne, where he became part of Channel Nine's Television Orchestra until his retirement in the 1970s. During the 1960s and 1970s also taught music for the Australian Department of Education until a stroke ended this activity in 1981.

GONELLA, 'Bruts' Adolphus James
Born: London, 31 January 1911
trumpet/mellophone

Brother of Nat Gonella. Worked with saxist Al Levitt's Band (1931), then joined house band at Bag O'Nails club (1932); toured briefly with Louis Armstrong (1932). With Billy Cotton (1933–4), then worked with pianist Ronnie Odell's Band in Liverpool (1934 to January 1935). Toured with Eddie Mans' Hollywood Serenaders (spring 1935), then joined Tommy Finnegan's Band in Manchester from May 1935 until February 1936. Briefly with Ambrose, then joined Gerry Moore's Quintet (July 1936). With Frank Fletcher's Shepherd's Bush Empire Band (March 1937), doubling this engagement with work at the Shim Sham Club in Joe Appleton's Quintet. Joined Lou Preager (September 1937). With brother Nat for radio work and tour of Scandinavia (1938). Worked in Dutch band led by tenorist Johnny Fresco (early 1939). Again worked with brother Nat in Scandinavia (summer 1939) and in Holland (late 1939). Returned to England in February 1940. Worked in London with pianist Hetty Booth's Band (April 1940). With Harry Leader and Tommy Kinsman (1940) before serving in the Royal Marines from 1940 until 1945 (visited USA with the Royal Marines in 1942). Rejoined Harry Leader (1946). Own quintet (1947), again worked with brother Nat (1949). With Freddy Bretherton, then rejoined Harry Leader (June 1949). Briefly with Sid Millward's Nitwits, then worked with Harry Gold from November 1952 until spring 1954. Joined Sid Willmot's Band in Manchester (May 1954). Settled in Manchester, worked as a painter and decorator, gigged with local bands including the East Side Jazzmen, then moved to Brighton, Sussex. Formed own band and gigged locally, then emigrated to Australia in February 1964. Settled in New South Wales. Serious illness in the 1980s ended his playing career.

GONELLA, 'Nat' Nathaniel Charles
Born: King's Cross, London, 7 March 1908
trumpet/mellophone/vocals

Brother of trumpeter Bruts Gonella. First played cornet while at St Mary's Guardian School in London, was taught by William Clarke of Kneller Hall. Worked briefly as a furrier's apprentice, then joined Archie Pitt's Busby Boys' Band. Remained with Pitt for four years, then worked with Bob Dryden's Louisville Band playing trumpet, clarinet and violin in Margate, Manchester and Belfast (1928–9). With pianist Archie Alexander in Brighton for almost a year, then joined Billy Cotton at the Streatham Locarno (late 1929), worked in Britain and France with Cotton, then joined Roy Fox (1931). With Lew Stone (1932–5), during this period also did a summer season in Holland with Ray Noble (August 1933) and did variety work in theatres, accompanied by Brian Lawrance's Quaglino Quartette (1934). While with Lew Stone began to lead small band-within-a-band the Georgians. Left Stone to lead the Georgians full time from April 1935, toured Britain, Holland, Scandinavia, etc., in period 1935–9, also recorded in USA with a pick-up band during 1938 visit. Was playing in Sweden at the outbreak of World War II, moved into Holland and France, and from there returned to Britain in summer of 1940. Formed own band again in summer 1940, then joined the Army in August 1941, played in service bands for tours of North Africa, Italy, etc., also did variety theatre work in London (spring 1945) while awaiting medical discharge from Army (summer 1945). Led own band again from 1945, did variety tours, summer seasons, ballroom dates and night club residencies into the 1950s, then worked mainly as a solo act in various touring shows (during the late 1940s worked in duo with bassist Roy Dexter and in trio with Dexter and drummer Les Jessop). Guested with various bands in the 1950s and worked as solo act in various shows, including tours with comedian Max Miller (1959). Formed own Georgian Jazz Band for February 1960 debut, then worked as featured guest star with Doug Richford's Band (1961–2). Moved to Lancashire in 1962, and used this as a base for touring northern clubs, also toured nationally with various shows including *Old Time Music Hall* (in the 1970s), continued to lead own band occasionally and to guest with jazz groups in Britain and in Holland. Moved to Gosport, Hampshire, in 1977 and occasionally guested with local bands through to the 1980s, latterly as a vocalist. Authored *Modern Style Trumpet Playing (1935);* a biography *Georgia on My Mind* by Ron Brown and Cyril Brown was first published in 1985. In September 1994 a square was named after Gonella in Gosport. Occasionally sang with bands (1996).

GOODE, Coleridge George Emmerson
double bass/violin

Born: St Andrews, Jamaica, West Indies, 29 November 1914

Father was a choirmaster and organist. Sang in choir then took up violin at twelve and studied at Royal School of Music. Moved to Scotland in 1934 to study electrical engineering at Glasgow University; continued to play violin but took up double bass in 1939. Gigged at Queen Mary Club, then worked at Locarno Ballroom, Glasgow, with Bob Smith's Band, then moved to London and began playing at Number One Rhythm Club (1942), subsequently worked in Johnny Claes' Clae Pigeons. Often with Eric Winstone during the 1940s but also worked with Bertie King (1943), Leslie 'Jiver' Hutchinson (1944), Lauderic Caton's Trio (1945) and with Caton in Dick Katz's Caribbean Trio (1945–7). During this period did recordings with Django Reinhardt and freelance work (including radio dates and films) with Stephane Grappelli and George Shearing. The Caribbean Trio (including Goode) were incorporated into Ray Ellington's Quartet in late 1947. Goode remained with Ellington until spring 1951. With Tito Burns from spring 1951 until summer 1953, then worked in the Costa Rico Trio, led own quartet, freelanced and toured Germany and North Africa with own band from July to September 1954. With Harry Hayes (1955), then joined Reg Wale's Sextet (1955). Often with Alan Clare at the Studio Club, London, from the mid-1950s, but by then was doing prolific freelance work. Regularly with Joe Harriott from spring 1958, including participating in Indo-Jazz Fusion performances in the 1960s. Often worked in Michael Garrick's Sextet and played in Georgian Club resident band during the 1960s and early 1970s. Worked mainly as a freelance from 1974, but regularly with pianist Iggy Quayle and drummer Laurie Morgan (1990s). Was also part of the Joe Harriott Memorial Quintet from 1989.

GOODMAN, 'Benny' David
drums

Born: c.1927
Died: c.1974

Worked in Sammy Herman's Windjammers (1948). Briefly with Freddy Randall (1950). With Geoff Sowden (1952 to early 1953), Ronnie Caryl (1953), then joined Paul Vaughan's Band in Liverpool (1954). Toured with Ambrose (1954), then worked with Vic Ash before spending two months with Don Rendell (November 1954 to January 1955). With Ken Moule, Vic Ash (1955) and on tour with Cab Calloway. Summer season with Harry Parry at Butlin's holiday camp (1956). With Dill Jones' Trio (late 1956), Dizzy Reece (1957), Joe Harriott (1958), then joined Lennie Metcalfe's Band on *Mauretania* liner (late 1958 to February 1959). To Germany with Bunny Gould's Rockets (1959). In Gracie Cole's Band then worked in Fairweather-Brown All Stars (1961–2), during this period also with Stan Tracey for *A Thurber Carnival* (March to June 1962). With Ronnie Scott (late 1962). Accompanied Blossom Dearie. In Keith Christie-Jimmy Deuchar Quintet (1964), then in Pete King's Quartet at Annie's Room, London (late 1965). In Pat Smythe's Trio at Annie's Room (1966). Led own trio and freelanced in the late 1960s.

GRAHAM, 'Kenny' (Kenneth Thomas SKINGLE)
saxes/clarinet/flute/arranger/composer

Born: London, 19 July 1924
Died: London, 17 February 1997

Played banjo, 'C' melody saxophone, and alto sax before specializing on tenor sax. Studied to be a civil engineer, then joined Reub Sunshine's Band on tenor sax. Worked in Billy Smith's Band at Cricklewood Palais (1942), then as 'Tex Kershaw' was in Johnny Claes' Band from summer 1942 until 1943. With Leslie 'Jiver' Hutchinson and Ken Turner's Band in Aberdeen (summer 1946). With Nat Temple (1947), with Roy Dexter's Band in Swindon (1947) and in Feldman Club Band (1947). With Fred Stanley (early 1948), then worked for several months with Nat Gonella (1948) before rejoining 'Jiver' Hutchinson (summer 1948). With Ronnie Pleydell (early 1949), Russ Allen's Band and in Victor Feldman's Sextet (1949). With Roy Bradley's Big Band and in Harry Klein's Quintet (early 1950). Formed own Afro-Cubists for April 1950 debut, the band played residencies, toured and recorded. Graham also worked with Eric Winstone (March to July 1952), with Dave Shand for radio work, and with Jack Parnell (on baritone sax) from October 1952 until February 1953. Briefly with Carl Barriteau, then again led the Afro-Cubists. Prolific arranging for Ted Heath, and Humphrey Lyttelton from 1955 onwards. Hospitalized with illness (1958), then resumed leading Afro-Cubists and arranging and composing. Visited Poland in 1959. Continued to arrange and compose through the 1960s, including writing film music. Briefly re-formed Afro-Cubists in summer of 1967, led own octet later that year. Arranging and copying in the late 1960s and 1970s then retired from full time music and worked on the London Transport system, but later began playing keyboards and alto sax (again) in the 1980s.

GRANT, Freddy
saxes/clarinet

Born: British Guiana (now Guyana), West Indies, 1905
Died: Westchester, New York, 1986

During the early 1930s toured South America in band led by Vincent Gomez. Moved to Trinidad in January 1933. Played in the Jazz Hounds, joined Trinidad Constabulary Band in February 1933, remained until July 1937, then moved to England. Worked in London with Joe Appleton's Band

(1937), with Fela Sowande (1938), Rudolph Dunbar (1940), Al Jennings (1940), Johnny Claes (1941), Cyril Blake (1941), then served in the RAF during 1942 and 1943. With Carlo Krahmer (late 1943), Leslie 'Jiver' Hutchinson (1944), again with Carlo Krahmer (1945). Also played in various night club bands. In Don Marino Barretto's Rhumba Band (1947), then worked with Cyril Blake's Calypso Serenaders. Briefly with Kenny Graham's Afro-Cubists (spring 1950), with Denis Walton (1950), Joe Appleton (1951), then led own Frederico and the Calypsonians (1951). Collaborated with Humphrey Lyttelton for Paseo Jazz Band during the early 1950s, also led own Caribbean Rhythm for concerts (1952). Joined Roberto Inglez in late 1952, then again worked with Joe Appleton (1954). Freelanced in various night club bands before moving to the USA where he led his own calypso group (as Sir Freddy Grant).

GRAPPELLI, Stephane
violin/piano

Born: Paris, France, 26 January 1908
Died: Paris, France, 1 December 1997

First played violin at twelve, piano from early teens (made several recordings on piano in the 1930s). Worked in cinemas and cafés, then gigged with Grégor and his Grégoriens, Glickman's Orchestra, etc. Led own band and gradually developed musical partnership with guitarist Django Reinhardt, resulting in the formation of the Quintet of the Hot Club of France (which enjoyed enormous popularity during the 1930s). Grappelli first visited London on vacation in September 1935 but returned with the QHCF in January 1938. He eventually settled in Britain in late 1939 and worked with Arthur Young (1939–40) before becoming featured soloist with Barney Gilbraith at Lansdowne House (1940). Overcame serious illness (1941), then worked regularly at Hatchett's, London (1942). Toured variety halls with own Swingtette and led in London for several years. Took part in reformed QHCF and again played in Britain (1945). Worked mainly in France (1947–8) including engagements with Bert Firman. Again worked in England, including residency at the Milroy Club, London (1949). Residency in Rome, Italy (early 1951), recovered from illness and toured Britain (1953). Again incapacitated by illness (early 1954), then led at the Bagatelle Club, London (1954). Further seasons in Rome, St Tropez, Paris, etc. (1955–7), briefly revisited London, then played residency at Club St Germain, Paris (1958). Featured at festivals (including Newport, USA, in 1969) during the 1960s, and extensively on recordings, consolidating his position as an international musical celebrity, playing the world's leading concert halls from the 1970s through the 1990s. Biographies include works by Raymond Horricks (1983) and Geoffrey Smith (1987) and an autobiography *Mon Violon Pour Tout Bagage* (1992). Until the 1970s it was customary to spell Grappelli's surname as Grappelly.

GRAY, Johnnie
tenor sax/clarinet

Born: Coventry, Warwickshire, 15 May 1920

Brother Brian also a tenor saxist. Played piano from age of seven, sax from fourteen. Qualified as an automobile engineer. Played in trumpeter Arthur How's Band (1941), in Billy Monk's Band (1942). Served in RAFVR. Joined Harry Parry briefly in early 1943, then worked with Johnny Claes before joining Lou Preager from May 1943 until January 1945. Left Preager to work in George Shearing's Quartet (January 1945), then worked with Harry Hayes before joining Ted Heath from September 1945 until October 1949 (during this period also worked with Ambrose at

Ciro's, London). With Robert Farnon and Lou Preager (1949), Frank Weir (1949–50), then spent a year with Sydney Lipton until September 1951. Again worked with Ambrose and freelanced before leading own band at Churchill's, London, from early 1952. Continued to lead own band through the 1960s, 1970s and 1980s, playing club residencies, working aboard the *Queen Mary* liner, and in the USA. Many overseas tours entertaining troops, also occasionally worked as a solo act before retiring to Sussex.

GREEN, 'Buzz' Alan
drums

Born: 1937
Deceased

Worked in Ted Ramm's Band (1955), then joined Dave Keir (1956). In the Celtic City Dixielanders (1957), then worked briefly in Colin Smith's Band before joining Freddy Randall (1956). After Army service worked with Ronnie Ross Quartet (1961–2) and with Harold McNair (1962), then freelanced with various groups before working in Johnny Fourie's Quartet (1965).

GREEN, 'Dave' David John
double bass

Born: Edgware, Middlesex, 5 March 1942

Sang in local church choir at thirteen. Played tea-chest bass in local skiffle group, the Zodiacs. Bought first double bass at fifteen (from Harvey Weston). Local gigs including work with trumpeter Brian 'Jo' Jones and drummer Charlie Watts in the late 1950s, then played long residency in Ilford with pianist Kenny Wallbank and drummer Peter Prince. Turned professional in August 1963, played in France with multi-instrumentalist Pete Shade. Briefly with Dave Morse group, then joined Don Rendell Quintet in December 1963, remained with this group (later billed as the Don Rendell-Ian Carr Quintet) until 1969. Worked on British television with Benny Goodman (September 1964). In 1965 also began long musical association with Humphrey Lyttelton, combining these commitments with regular work with Stan Tracey; accompanied many visiting American jazzmen. Remained with Lyttelton until 1985, continued to work with Stan Tracey through to the 1990s, often worked in Michael Garrick line-ups. With Henry Lowther's Quarternity in the mid-1970s. With Charlie Watts' Big Band in the 1980s, and also toured Europe with Gordon Beck, violinist Didier Lockwood's Quartet, as well as working with Carol Kidd, Dave Newton's Trio, Martin Taylor, Pete King's Quartet, etc. Own group Fingers active from 1979 through the 1990s. Widespread touring (including USA, Brazil and Japan) with Charlie Watts' Quintet during the early 1990s. Extensive freelance work through the 1990s, featured at many international festivals. Continues to accompany many visiting American musicians, also runs own record label.

GREENOW, 'Bill' William Rawdon
saxes/clarinet

Born: Isleworth, Middlesex, 21 July 1940

Played clarinet from sixteen, was part of school band. Played local jazz gigs, then joined the Brent River Jazz Band playing regularly on Eel Pie Island. With Bill Brunskill (1958) and with Mike Pointon (1959) while studying at art college. Left college in 1961, worked for six years with Barry Martyn, accompanied many visiting American jazzmen. During this period also occasionally with the New Teao Brass Band, and played in Belgium with the Cotton City Jazz Band. Formed own

Strong Jazz (with Cuff Billett) in late 1967 and worked in Johnny Parker's Band. Toured France with Strong Jazz, which led to him joining Les Haricots Rouges for over a year. Returned to Britain in early 1970, spent a few months in Bill Niles' Delta Jazz Band. After a period of illness gigged with Stan Greig, then spent three months with Bob Wallis before working in the Temperance Seven (on baritone sax) from early 1972 until 1974. Moved to Sweden in 1974, worked with Bent Persson, the Harlem Jazz Camels, Lars 'Sumpen' Sundgren, etc. Made return visits to Britain and guested with various bands, including Harry Strutters Hot Rhythm Orchestra, but remained based in Sweden until 1988, toured with Al Casey, Wild Bill Davison, Johnny Letman, Kenny Davern, Carrie Smith, Duke Burrell, etc. Played in Sweden and in Britain with trumpeter Willie Cook (1981) and toured throughout Europe with Waso from 1984 to 1988. Led own trio in Europe (Stan Greig, Trevor Richards) and from 1988 to 1993 often worked in Lars Edegran's Orchestra, and with the New Orleans Jazz Ladies (including recordings in New Orleans). Worked in Paris with own band (1992–3), then moved back to England freelancing successfully through the 1990s.

GREEVE, Micky
drums/percussion

Born: Manchester, Lancashire, 12 June 1914

Took up drums in late teens. Played in Scotland and on transatlantic liners, then worked with Art Thompson's Band (1942–3). With Frank King (1943), then again with Art Thompson before joining Johnny McMeighan (1944). Worked in the Skyrockets (1945–6). Briefly with Frank King, then joined Ambrose (1946). During the late 1940s worked with Geraldo, Stephane Grappelli, Eric Winstone, Harry Gold, George Melachrino, Frank Weir, etc. Left Paul Adam in 1950 and became highly successful freelance, playing in many theatre orchestras. Again with Skyrockets (1954–5). Regular teaching through to the 1990s, also continued to play small band gigs, including dates with Cab Kaye in the 1970s and Billy Amstell in the late 1980s and 1990s.

GREIG, 'Stan' Stanley Mackay
piano/drums/arranger

Born: Joppa, nr Edinburgh, Scotland, 12 August 1930

Father was a drummer and piano-tuner. Played in band with Sandy Brown and Al Fairweather while still at school. With Dougie Campbell's Band and in Archie Semple's Jazzmen before again playing in Sandy Brown's Band. Served in Royal Engineers. Moved to London in late summer of 1954 to join Ken Colyer, worked in Germany with Colyer. Joined Humphrey Lyttelton (spring 1955), until being called up for service in Suez with Royal Engineers (summer 1956). Returned to rejoin Lyttelton (late 1956) sharing drum duties with Eddie Taylor. Left Lyttelton in spring 1957 to play piano on tour with singer Brother John Sellers. Worked with Bruce Turner (on piano and drums), then rejoined Sandy Brown on drums in summer 1956. Worked with Al Fairweather-Sandy Brown Band (1958–9). During this period also worked with Geoff Sowden and with Bruce Turner (on piano). Left Fairweather-Brown to work on piano with Acker Bilk from July 1960 until July 1968. Absent through injury in autumn 1962. (Tony Raine and Fred Hunt deputized.) From this point onwards worked mainly on piano, but occasionally played drums. Worked with own quartet, with Dave Shepherd and in Johnny Hawksworth's Trio during the late 1960s and early 1970s. Formed and led London Jazz Big Band from February 1975 until 1985. With John

Chilton's Feetwarmers (accompanying singer George Melly) from autumn 1977 until spring 1980. Led own Boogie Woogie Band, also toured Europe with the Harlem Blues and Jazz Band and played many freelance dates. Rejoined Humphrey Lyttelton from Summer 1985 until early 1995, subsequently freelanced in many line-ups, including engagements in Finland with Campbell Burnap (June 1995). Visited Australia (late 1995), returned to London and continued to freelance and to work regularly with Wally Fawkes as well as leading own group.

GRESHAM, 'Pete' Peter Brian
piano

Born: East Ham, London, 21 May 1938

Piano lessons from age of eleven. Joined Steve Lane at sixteen. Left Lane to join the Storyville Jazzmen (formed by Hugh Rainey and John Mortimer) in 1955. Remained when Bob Wallis was appointed leader in 1956. National Service in the Army (1957–9), then rejoined Bob Wallis through to 1962. Joined the Civil Service in 1963 but continued to play gigs with Bob Wallis and worked in Norway and Denmark with Monty Sunshine's Band (1965). Worked for Foreign Office in Africa and played in local quartet in Khartoum (1968–9). Returned to Britain and during the 1970s resumed playing gigs with various bands, worked with Bob Wallis again and with Pete Strange, Digby Fairweather, etc. Regularly with Keith Smith (including tours of Denmark and Holland) in 1978. During the 1980s continued to play gigs, worked often with John Petters, then took own band to Zurich, Switzerland. Subsequently worked there in trumpeter Denny Ilett's Band. Often with Brian White and Alan Gresty in Muggsy Remembered during the 1990s, including festival dates in California.

GRIFFITHS, Malcolm Jesse
trombone

Born: Barnet, Hertfordshire, 29 September 1941

Played piano during childhood, trombone from age of seventeen. Gained degree in Economics, studied trombone at the London College of Music. Regularly with Mike Westbrook during the 1960s (continued to work with Westbrook into the 1980s). With John Surman (1968–9), Ray Russell (1969) and leading own quartet. With Buddy Rich Orchestra in Britain (late 1969) and in the USA (early 1970). With Chris McGregor's Brotherhood of Breath from June 1970, also with John Warren's Big Band through the 1970s, and with Alan Skidmore. With John Dankworth from 1972, Alan Cohen (1973), Harry Miller (1976), Brian Cooper's Orchestra and Georgie Fame. Began long musical association with Stan Tracey in the 1970s, continued to work with John Surman and with Mike Gibbs during the 1970s and 1980s. Organized band to work with Gil Evans for British tour. With Stan Tracey (Octet, Big Band, etc.) during the 1980s and 1990s. During winter 1984–5 played in the Welsh National Opera Orchestra. Many freelance sessions in various line-ups: with John Altman, Alan Cohen, George Fenton, Ray Russell, Gil Askey, etc. Toured with Diana Ross, Gladys Knight, the Three Degrees, etc., also regularly part of the Dedication Orchestra.

GRIMES, Carol
vocals/composer/percussion

Born: South East London, 7 April 1944

Sang on the streets of London during the 1960s, then gigged with various guitarists and harmonica players before forming own band the Race which worked in London and on the

Continent, and toured as support for various blues artistes. With Delivery (1969–71), recorded own first album, then (in 1972) formed Uncle Dog (with Dave Skinner). With London Boogie Band in the mid-1970s, recorded in the USA. Briefly in Sweet FA in the late 1970s. Formed the Crocodiles in 1982, then formed Eyes Wide Open in 1984. From 1986 featured successfully in various theatrical shows, own production company from 1987. Often worked with Ian Shaw in the early 1990s. Regular concert and festival appearances and work at Ronnie Scott's Club, working with keyboard player Janette Mason. Tour with Indian singer Najma Achtar (1995).

GUBERTINI, Ronnie
drums

Born: 1899
Deceased

His father, Leonardo Gubertini, was a drummer and tympanist who had served in the Italian Army. Ronnie's elder brother, Ted, was also a drummer who worked with the Broadway Sextette and the Selma Four in the 1920s. Ronnie began gigging in Corelli Windeatt's Band, then worked in the Albany Five before spending two years with Jack Hylton in the Queen's Hall Roof Orchestra. Became a house musician at the Savoy Hotel, London, in 1923, and subsequently worked with the Savoy Orpheans (directed by Debroy Somers) from 1923 until 1927. Briefly in the Savoy Havana Band and with the Sylvians and New Sylvians (1927). With Fred Elizalde (1928–9), Arthur Lally (1930) and with Howard Jacobs (1930–1). With Al Collins at the Savoy Hotel throughout the 1930s and early 1940s, then worked for several years with Carroll Gibbons from 1942. Extensive freelance recordings throughout his career. Left full time music and, during the 1960s, ran his own television repair service in South London.

GUY, Barry
double bass/composer/arranger

Born: London, 22 April 1947

Played trumpet, valve trombone and euphonium in local brass band, also played valve trombone in own trad band. Took up double bass and gigged around the Charlton area with clarinettist Pete Robinson's Hot Flour. Studied bass with Joe Muddel and Graham Collier. Quit job in architect's office to study at the Guildhall School of Music. Did local gigs and played in Dave Holdsworth's Sextet, also occasionally in Eddie Bayfield's Soups by Nine (1966). Joined Spontaneous Music Ensemble (with John Stevens and Trevor Watts), subsequently in Amalgam (with Trevor Watts and Paul Rutherford) during the late 1960s. Worked in house bands at Ronnie Scott's Club. During this period began working occasionally with Howard Riley's Trio (from 1967). Was regularly with Riley during the 1970s, also founded the London Jazz Composers' Orchestra in 1970 (which continued to assemble into the 1990s). Was part of Paul Rutherford's Iskra 1903 from 1970. Since that date has also worked with Derek Bailey, Bob Downes, Michael Nyman, Tony Oxley, Mike Westbrook, John Harle, Mats Gustafsson, Peter Kowald, etc. Long musical association with Evan Parker through to the mid-1990s. Has given many solo performances, and enjoys considerable success as a composer. He has played with various orchestras including the City of London Sinfonia and the BBC Symphony Orchestra. On 1996 gigs with Evan Parker and percussionist Paul Lytton he doubled on piccolo bass.

H

HAIM, John
cornet

Born: London, 1928
Died: Golders Green, London, 22 January 1949

Took up cornet at fifteen and formed own Jazz Band a year later. He later led his Jazzin' Babies before forming his Jelly Roll Kings which he continued to lead up to the time of his death. This band entered several District Dance Band Championships organised by the *Melody Maker*, and John received honourable mentions for their part in the 1947 Buckinghamshire contest. He worked as a clerk for a company in the City of London and played semi-professionally. Although it was not obvious to his audiences, John suffered from a chronic illness. Two days after he telephoned the *Melody Maker* asking them to deny rumours of his death, he died in his sleep. His brother Gerald played tuba and piano.

HALCOX, 'Pat' Patrick John
trumpet/flugelhorn/vocals/piano

Born: Chelsea, London, 18 March 1930

Began playing piano at the age of four, then took up trombone. Played trombone during RAF service (1948–50). After demobilization switched to trumpet. Studied for degree in chemistry but played semi-professionally with Colin Kingwell, and with the Brent Valley Stompers before joining the Albermarle Jazz Band in April 1952. Worked briefly with Chris Barber in late 1952 at the Club Creole, London, but continued to be part of the Albermarle Jazz Band until joining Chris Barber permanently in May 1954. Has remained with Barber through the 1990s, but during this period also played on film soundtracks (*Look Back in Anger* and *The Loneliness of the Long Distance Runner*) and from 1977 led own All Star Band during Chris Barber's summer break (during the early 1980s co-led this group with drummer Pete York). Guested with various bands during the 1970s, 1980s and 1990s, also played on several Mediterranean summer cruises. Various freelance recordings: with Art Hodes, Don Ewell, Elton John, etc. Briefly out of action through illness from July until October 1992, then resumed full schedule.

HALL, 'Albert' Alwyn
trumpet

Born: South Wales, 21 September 1929
Died: Greenford, Middlesex, 3 January 1980

Played in West London Silver Band from age six. Worked in Maurice Little's Band in Tottenham (1944) and with Johnny Brown's Band at Astoria Ballroom, London (1946). Briefly with Johnny Claes, then worked with Teddy Foster (1947) prior to brief period in the Armed Forces. Again with Teddy Foster (spring 1948). Also worked with Les Ayling, Jack Jackson and Billy Ternent before joining Tito Burns from May 1948 until November 1950. With Cyril Stapelton (November 1950 to March 1951), then rejoined Tito Burns from April 1951 to September 1952. Radio work with Steve Race, then briefly with Jack Parnell (September 1952 to November 1952). With Geraldo from November 1952 to August 1954 (also worked with Dave Shand in May 1954). With Eric Delaney from September 1954 until March 1957. Briefly with Buddy Featherstonhaugh (spring 1957), and Kenny Baker, then freelance session work for television, radio and recordings. Often with Joe Loss in the 1960s and 1970s, and occasionally with Frank Weir, and Don Lusher's Big Band. Albert's brother Cliff is a professional pianist and organist.

HALL, Henry
piano/trumpet/composer

Born: Peckham, London, 2 May 1898
Died: Eastbourne, Sussex, 28 October 1989

Originally played trumpet and piano, studied at Guildhall School of Music, and at Trinity College of Music. During World War I played in the Royal Artillery Band, then played piano in London cinemas before forming own touring trio. Played piano at Midland Hotel, Manchester (1922), and then became Musical Director of 32 bands playing at various London Midland and Scottish hotels. Led own band at Gleneagles Hotel, Perthshire, from June 1924, began recording and broadcasting with his own band that year. Moved to London to become leader of the BBC Dance Orchestra (replacing Jack Payne) in March 1932; in March 1936 Hall brought American Benny Carter into England to be staff arranger for the orchestra. Hall left the BBC in September 1937, although his *Guest Night* show ran for 25 years from 1934. He continued to lead his orchestra (mainly for stage shows and broadcasts) until 1949. Thereafter he became a successful theatrical agent, but occasionally conducted various ensembles until 1969. He was awarded the CBE in 1970. His autobiography *Here's to the Next Time* was first published in 1955.

HAMER, Ian
trumpet/flugelhorn/composer/arranger

Born: Merseyside, 11 September 1932

Brother of trumpeter-drummer Stuart and of reed player George (Wilfred George Hamer). After their bandleading father, Wilf Hamer, died in 1936, their mother Mary Daly Hamer ran the band, in which all of the three boys played during their teens. Served in RAF from summer of 1951. After release worked with Carl Barriteau, then joined Oscar Rabin (May 1954). With Vic Lewis and the Kirchin Band until working with Tubby Hayes (1955–6). With Jack Parnell, then worked in London area with Roy Kenton and with Vic Ash (1958–9). From the 1960s onwards worked with Eric Delaney, Gracie Cole, David Ede, Tubby Hayes Big Band, Harry South, Ted Heath, Kenny Wheeler, Joe Harriott, Woody Herman's Anglo-American Herd, Thad Jones-Mel Lewis, Mike Gibbs, Barbara Thompson, etc. Led own successful sextet from the early 1970s. Settled in Brighton, continued to freelance in a wide variety of groups and also active as a trumpet teacher.

HAMILTON, Andy
tenor sax

Born: Port Maria, Jamaica, West Indies,
26 March 1918

Father of trumpeter Graham and saxophonist Mark. Took up sax in early teens, led own Silvershine Band at age of eighteen. While doing non-musical work in the USA played gigs in Buffalo and Syracuse. Moved back to Jamaica and again led own band until moving to Britain in 1949. Settled in Handsworth area of Birmingham, worked in local factories but regularly played gigs throughout the Midlands. Led own Caribbean Combo, later formed own Blue Notes. Played in Milan, Italy, in 1990, debut album issued in 1991. Played solo dates and led own successful band at many widespread jazz festivals throughout the 1990s but continued to work mainly in the Midlands, playing often at the Bear in Bearwood, Birmingham.

HAMILTON, 'Steve' Stephen Kilgour
keyboards

Born: Aberdeen, Scotland, 14 August 1973

Father is bass guitarist Laurie Hamilton, who has been Steve's main teacher. He also received advice and help from pianist Peter John Vittese and guitarist Keith More. At fourteen played professionally as a solo pianist in an Aberdeen restaurant. Studied with Tommy Smith, then attended Berklee School of Music in the USA and was tutored by pianist Ray Santisi, vibes-player Gary Burton and trumpeter Herb Pomeroy. Played concerts with Gary Burton, Lew Soloff, Joe Locke, Marvin 'Smitty' Smith, etc. Returned to Scotland and worked often with Tommy Smith, also accompanied various visiting musicians including Alvin Batiste, Randy Weston, Bill Berry, Mike Gibbs, Mat Garrison, etc. Toured with Tommy Smith in summer of 1995 and with Rob Hall (1996).

HARE, Alan, E.
trombone/piano/arranger

Born: Warrington, Lancashire, 22 July 1928

Spent childhood in Chingford, Essex, then moved to Cheadle Hulme (near Manchester) at fifteen. Played trombone with the Smoky City Stompers and with the Saints Jazz Band (1951). Led own Bluenote Jazzmen from 1952 until 1958. Own big band in Manchester (1958–9). Was a civil servant by day and in this capacity worked in Hong Kong from 1959. Continued to play gigs there and worked alongside American clarinettist Tony Scott. Returned to Manchester in 1962, played piano in Southside Band (1962), was pianist and arranger in Gordon Robinson's Septet (1963–4), which won two European contests in Zurich. Formed own big band in 1964 (which accompanied Earl Hines in 1965), also briefly played trombone in Art Taylor's Group (1965). Own big band played eight year residency in Didsbury (1968–76) and played concerts at Free Trade Hall, Manchester. Alan gave up leading the big band in 1977, but re-formed an octet in the 1980s. Continues to arrange for various line-ups including the National Youth Jazz Orchestra and occasionally guests with bands in and around Manchester.

HARLE, John
alto sax/soprano sax/composer

Born: Newcastle upon Tyne, 20 September 1956

Studied at Royal College of Music from 1978 until 1981 and soon afterwards began contributing music to various film soundtracks (both as a player and as a composer), including *Betrayal* (1982), for which he played solo saxophone. Later successes included the television programme *One Man and His Sax* and his score for the film *Prick Up Your Ears*. He has continued to write and play for television and films through to his 1996 success in composing for *Deep Secrets*. These activities exist alongside his world-wide public performances on the concert platform (in New York, Japan, and throughout Europe). He has had works written for him by various contemporary composers including Sir Harrison Birtwistle. Featured (alongside Andy Sheppard) in 20th Century Saxophones. Throughout he has continued to play jazz with his own group (featuring Steve Lodder on piano), and also doing duo work with pianist John Lenehan and with pianist-composer Richard Rodney Bennett (1996).

HARPER, Don
violin/viola/composer

Born: Seddon, Victoria, Australia, c.1925

Played professionally in Australia and led own big band there, including long residency at the St Kilda Town Hall, before moving to Britain in 1955. Soon began broadcasting with own small group and guested with Billy Cotton at the London Palladium, then became musical director at the Talk of the Town cabaret in 1959. Led at the Dorchester Hotel and at Quaglino's (1959), then returned to Australia. Successfully led own small band there, which toured as support for Dave Brubeck (1963). Returned to Britain in mid-1960s, freelanced successfully and led own groups for residencies and summer seasons, then did further tours in Australia before returning to Britain in 1981. Became part of Jazz Australia UK Incorporated, co-led quintet with Denny Wright, then returned to Australia and became a university teacher.

HARRIOTT, 'Joe' Joseph Arthurlin
alto sax/baritone sax/piano/composer

Born: Jamaica, West Indies, 15 July 1928
Died: Southampton, Hampshire, 2 January 1973

Raised in a Catholic Orphanage. Played clarinet in school band. As a teenager played tenor and baritone saxes in local dance bands, then began specializing on alto sax, worked with Jamaican All Stars (1948). To Britain in 1951 with Ozzie Da Costa's Band, decided to stay, and introduced himself to London's jazz musicians by sitting in at the Feldman Club on 26 August 1951. Joined Joe Muddel's Sextet a week later. Worked regularly with Muddel until late 1952, also gigged with Pete Pitterson's Band and with Mike McKenzie's Harlem All Stars. Began long musical association with Tony Kinsey. Worked in Jazz Today Unit in spring 1955, also played in Ronnie Scott's Big Band (1955). Illness caused him to leave Tony Kinsey's Quartet, a lung infection was diagnosed and he spent several months in Pinewood Sanitarium. Worked in Tony Crombie's Quintet (summer 1956) and with Phil Seamen's Quintet, then again worked with Tony Kinsey (1957) and with Allan Ganley (1957). Formed own quartet (summer 1957), own quintet (1958), again entered Pinewood Sanitarium from autumn 1958 until December 1958. Played interval piano at Marquee Club, London (January 1959), then resumed leading own quintet (on alto sax) in February 1959. Guested with Modern Jazz Quartet for British tour (November to December 1959). Continued to lead own quintet into the mid-1960s, during this period occasionally guested with Chris Barber's Band. During the 1960s did a long series of Jazz and Poetry concerts with Michael Garrick and Shake Keane, and was subsequently featured as a member of Michael Garrick's Sextet. From 1966 through to 1970 worked regularly with violinist John Mayer in Indo-Jazz Fusions, also worked with Goanese guitarist Amancio D'Silva (1969). During the early 1970s suffered ill health but played some dates with singer Bobby Breen, did brief solo tour (early 1971), thereafter freelanced whenever possible appearing mainly in local jazz clubs until collapsing in Southampton in August 1972. He died of cancer in the Wessex Radiotherapy Unit.

HARRIS, Albert
guitar/piano/piano accordion/arranger/composer

Born: London, 13 February 1916

Piano from the age of six. Self-taught guitarist. Left school to work with Maurice Burman in Brighton and Margate on accordion. With Tony Vivian's Orchestra at the Ritz, London (autumn 1931), Al Saxon's Band at Murray's (early 1932), with Al Berlin, then joined Stanley Barnett's

Band, by this time specializing on guitar. With Jack Padbury (late 1932), left to work with Howard Jacobs (summer 1933). With Maurice Winnick (autumn 1933). Joined Lew Stone in summer 1934, left to join Teddy Joyce (late 1935). Freelance recordings included duets with Ivor Mairants (1935). Accompanied Benny Carter in London (January 1937), worked with Ambrose until emigrating to USA in spring 1938. Worked with Ray Noble in America (1938), Joe Marsala (1940), Horace Heidt (1941), etc. then concentrated on composing and arranging. Won the Ernest Bloch award. Wrote for films and taught orchestration from his home in Los Angeles. Moved to New Zealand in the 1990s.

HARRIS, 'Kenny' Kenneth Philip
drums

Born: Stamford Hill, London, 21 May 1927

Played drums occasionally during RAF service (1945–8), then gigged regularly with Jimmy Skidmore at the Music Maker's Club, London, from 1949. Freelanced, then worked with Dill Jones, Bruce Turner, etc. on the *Queen Mary* liner (1950). With Ronnie Ball (1951), then worked with Raymonde (Manuel Raymond) at Selby's, London (late 1951 to early 1952). With Ralph Sharon, Vic Ash, Jerry Allen, Jimmy Walker, Joe Saye and briefly with Nat Gonella before working on *Mauretania* (1953). With Jimmy Skidmore, Terry Brown and Eddie Thompson before emigrating to the USA in 1955. Worked in America with Ralph Sharon's Trio, in the British Jazz Trio (with pianist Derek Smith and Liverpudlian bassist John Drew, who died 1961). Played gigs with Gene Harris, Sonny Stitt, Paul Bley, Joe Saye, etc. Worked in Bermuda for three years, mainly with Hugo Pedell, also ran own Radio 2 BN jazz show. Moved to Vancouver, Canada, played regularly and produced radio shows and television commercials. Moved briefly to the USA, produced records and played for various shows, then returned to Britain in October 1990. Further radio work in Bermuda, then settled in Britain in 1992 and freelanced with Dave Shepherd, Gerry Salisbury, tenor saxophonist Jack Hunt and re-formed The British Jazz Trio (with Ray Mitchell on piano and Mike Harris on bass).

HARRIS, Max
piano/piano accordion/arranger/composer

Born: Bournemouth, Hampshire,
15 September 1918

Semi-professional work in trumpeter Lew Foster's Band, then became full time musician with Stan Atkins in 1937. Remained with Atkins until 1939, during this period also did radio work and recordings with Teddy Foster and worked briefly with Lou Hill. Was a captain in the RASC during World War II (including service in the Middle East). After demobilization joined Ronnie Munro (1946). With Carl Barriteau, then did six cruises with saxist Paul Lombard's Band aboard the *Mauretania* (1947). With Frank Gregory for ten months, then joined George Colborn (late 1948). With Don Carlos (summer 1950), before joining Jack Parnell from spring 1951. Left Parnell in the mid-1950s and arranged for BBC Show Band, and played piano on many freelance sessions. After the demise of the BBC Show Band arranged and conducted for BBC and ITV, and composed various theme songs (one of which, *The Strange World of Gurney Slade*, was a Hit Parade success). Led own orchestra on (and arranged for) many radio shows, and wrote for Ella Fitzgerald, Ted Heath, Dick Haymes, Yehudi Menuhin-Stephane Grappelli duets, etc., and composed for numerous films. Continued to play on various jazz sessions and recordings, organized tribute album to Jelly Roll Morton and took part in Australian trumpeter Bob Barnard's recordings in London. Maintains busy working schedule into the 1990s.

HARRISON, Len
double bass

Born: *c.*1912
Died: 1977

In Ken Johnson's Monarchs of Rhythm (early 1937) prior to playing a summer season in Holland with Benny Carter (1937). Returned to London, freelanced with Buddy Featherstonhaugh and Reggie Dare. Recorded with Fats Waller in London (August 1938). With Harry Roy from October 1938 until joining RAF in 1940. Did part of his service stationed in the Orkney Islands but played regularly with service bands. With Ray Ellington from 1946. During the late 1940s worked in Laurie Morgan's Elevated Music and with Tony Crombie. With Kathy Stobart (1950–1), then joined Vic Lewis briefly in spring of 1951. Again worked with Ray Ellington from April until October 1951. With Ralph Sharon (1952), then joined trumpeter Dennis Walton. Worked with pianist Chuck Gates during the late 1950s and early 1960s, then freelanced.

HART, 'Mike' Michael Warner
banjo/guitar/drums

Born: Inverness, Scotland, 23 March 1934

First gigs were on drums with Gavin's Gloryland Band (1949). On drums with Sandy Brown's Jazz Band from 1950 until 1952 (in Scotland and in England). Started own Blue Blowers in 1954, playing banjo and jug. Worked in Edinburgh with Charlie McNair's Jazz Band with Sandy Brown. Was a co-founder of the Climax Jazz Band (1956) and co-led the Society Syncopators (1957) before forming Old Bailey's Jazz Advocates in 1959. Re-formed the Society Syncopators in 1975. Led Mike Hart's Scottish Society Syncopators for ten annual visits to perform at the Sacramento Dixieland Jubilee in the USA, also played at other American festivals and toured throughout Europe, Canada and Barbados. In 1992 toured Australia with the original Climax Reunion Band, continues to play regularly through the 1990s. Founded the Edinburgh International Jazz Festival in 1979, and continues to be its director. Awarded the MBE in 1995.

HART, Paul
piano/bass/violin/composer/arranger

Born: London, March 1954

Spent formative years in Seven Kings, Ilford. Piano from age of six, violin at eleven, viola at thirteen. Joined National Youth Jazz Orchestra at sixteen, playing bass guitar. Studied at Royal College of Music. Joined John Dankworth on bass at eighteen, was also featured on violin, and accompanied Cleo Laine on piano during the early 1980s (including American tour). Became highly successful arranger and composer whose extended works include a Concerto for Organ and Jazz Orchestra. Prolific writing for television and films.

HARTY, 'Bill' William John
drums

Born: Waterford, Ireland, 1899
Died: Los Angeles, USA, 1959

Took up drums while working as a draughtsman at the Dunlop Tyre Company. Moved to Birmingham after World War I and gigged with local bands (1919–20) and deputized in the

American Crescent City Band. Moved to London and played residency at the Lugano Club. Extensive travels in Europe during the 1920s, played for four months in Oslo, Norway and for two-and-a-half years in Germany. Returned to Britain and worked with Harry Shalson's Band, and with Al Starita (1928–9) and Jean Pougnet (1930), before joining Bill Gerhardi's Grosvenor House Band in spring of 1930. With Percival Mackey (autumn 1930), then joined Arthur Lally (January 1931). Joined Roy Fox in summer of 1931 and stayed when Lew Stone took over the band in 1932. Remained with Lew Stone until September 1934, then became Ray Noble's manager (having previously played on many Ray Noble recordings and worked in Holland with Noble in August 1933). Sailed to USA with Noble in 1934, and played in (and managed) the various bands that Noble led in the USA during his early years there. He returned to Britain as drummer (and manager) of Ray Noble's Canadian Orchestra (summer 1938), after that tour he returned to the USA and continued to work as Noble's manager (forsaking the drums) through to the 1950s. He also ran his own booking agency in Hollywood.

HARVEY, 'Eddie' Edward Thomas   Born: Blackpool, Lancashire, 15 November 1925
trombone/piano/arranger

Piano from the age of seven. Family lived in Gosport, Hampshire from 1933 until 1939, then moved to Sidcup, Kent. Played trombone with an accordion band in Kent (alongside clarinettist Wally Fawkes), then, while working as a student engineer at the Vickers Armstrong factory, joined George Webb's Dixielanders (on trombone) in 1943. Remained with Webb until 1946, then served in the RAF until joining Freddy Randall from June 1948 until October 1949. With Graeme Bell, and with Carlo Krahmer in 1948, and with Joe Daniels in 1949. With Vic Lewis prior to becoming a founder-member of John Dankworth's Seven in March 1950. Studied at Guildhall School of Music (1950–2). Left Dankworth in January 1955. Active as freelance arranger, trombonist and pianist. With Bert Courtley-Jack Seymour Band (1956). With Don Rendell Sextet from June 1957 until disbandment in July 1958, also worked in Jazz Today Unit in 1957. Toured as part of Woody Herman's Anglo-American Herd in April 1959. With Don Rendell-Bert Courtley Jazz Committee from spring 1959 until spring 1960. Began leading own occasional big band in 1960. Freelanced in various line-ups and worked in big bands led by Maynard Ferguson, John Dankworth, Ronnie Scott, etc. Wrote for television. Mainly on piano with Humphrey Lyttelton from autumn 1963 until 1972 (arranged extensively for Lyttelton and for Jack Parnell's ATV Orchestra). Later combined arranging and freelance playing (Picard-Coe Quintet, Tony Milliner's band, own groups, etc.) with duties as Assistant Music Master at Haileybury College in Hertfordshire (from the early 1970s until 1985). At the forefront of jazz education in Britain for over twenty years. Taught at the City Literary Institute in London, and at various summer schools. Studied jazz education at Berklee School of Music, USA. Served on many Arts Council panels. Continues to play regularly through the 1990s (mainly on piano). Teaching at Guildhall School of Music (1995–6), also active on summer schools and various weekend jazz courses. Wrote *Teach Yourself Jazz Piano* (1974).

HASTIE, 'Will' William   Born: Auchengray, Lanarkshire, Scotland, 1926
clarinet/alto sax/penny whistle

Played cornet in the Forth Brass Band, did casual gigs with the Rhythm Rascals, then switched to clarinet. Worked for GEC in Dundee during the early 1950s, sat in with Duncan Whyte's Band, was transferred to Carlisle and Birmingham, played with local groups including the Albany Quintet. Brief spell with Freddy Randall, then back to Carlisle, played with local dance bands, then moved south again and joined Lennie Hastings' band for season in Germany (1957). Briefly with Mickey Ashman's Band (summer 1958), then joined Mike Peters (1958). With Pete Ridge's Band (1959–60), then worked with Eric Allandale (1960–1), including two seasons in Germany. Freelanced in London with pianist Tony Wainwright, Ian Bell, Pete Deuchar, etc., and deputized in Alex Welsh's Band. Joined the Temperance Seven in late 1963, and has continued to work with them through the mid-1990s. During this period has also worked in many line-ups including Keith Nichols' Ragtime Orchestra, with Lord Arsenal (Allan Bradley) and with drummer David Mills. Was briefly in the original line-up of the Midnite Follies Orchestra (1978).

HASTINGS, 'Jimmie' James Brian Gordon
Born: Aberdeen, Scotland, 12 May 1938
saxes/clarinet/flute

Father was an accomplished pianist; piano from age of three. Spent early childhood in India, returned to Scotland at age of eight, settled in Banffshire, and played many dance gigs on piano. Then took up alto sax at sixteen, clarinet at eighteen and tenor sax at twenty-one. Played local gigs on alto sax, clarinet and piano accordion, before moving South in 1959. Spent fifteen months in Canterbury, then became based in London. Did seven world cruises aboard the *Southern Cross* liner in the early 1960s, then worked in France, Jersey and London with band led by trumpeter Ronnie Caryl (1963–4). Worked on the *Orcades* in Jack Honeyborn's Band and played at Top Rank Ballroom, Croydon, with Reg Brooks. Freelanced in London, spent two years in Ken Mackintosh's Orchestra, then worked in BBC Radio Orchestra from summer 1969 until October 1973. During the 1970s played in occasional big bands led by Dave Hancock, Les Simons and Tony Kinsey (also did quartet work with Kinsey). Worked in band accompanying Frank Sinatra. In the 1970s began long musical association with John Dankworth which continued through the 1990s (in the Dankworth Generation Band). Played in various West End shows, also part of National Health group and accompanying various visiting American musicians such as Red Rodney, Billy Mitchell, Art Farmer, Kenny Davern, etc. Worked in Michael Garrick's Sextet, and through the 1990s in quintet co-led with John Horler. Taught at the Royal Academy and at London College of Music. Joined Humphrey Lyttelton in January 1993.

HASTINGS, 'Lennie' Leonard
drums/vocals
Born: Carshalton, Surrey, 5 January 1925
Died: Isleworth, Middlesex, 14 July 1978

First gigs with Surrey band, Mickey Bryant's Rugcutters (1942). First professional work with female group Myra Morrison and her Juvenile Rhythm Queens. Joined Army, subsequently worked in *Stars in Battledress* productions. With altoist Les Simons's Quintet (1949), worked with various small bands, and gigged with Nevil Skrimshire (1950). Joined Freddy Randall on last day of 1950, left in November 1953. With Norman Cave's Band, Jazz Today Unit and Eddie Thompson Trio before rejoining Freddy Randall from June to August 1954. Again with Norman Cave from August 1954. In October 1954 Cave left and handed over leadership to Hastings who disbanded two months later to join Alex Welsh from December 1954 until January 1957 (except for period in spring 1956 when he worked with Mickey Bryant at USAF bases in France). With

Johnny Duncan's Blue Grass Boys from February 1957 until October 1959 (also led own band in Düsseldorf, Germany, June to August 1957). Again led band for residency in Düsseldorf, Germany (November 1959 to January 1960), then joined Nat Gonella from February until May 1960. Briefly in Ken Sims-Ian Wheeler Vintage Jazz Band, then rejoined Alex Welsh from June 1960 until suffering illness in early 1972. Recovered and formed own band in autumn 1972, subsequently played in Brian Lemon Trio, in various Stan Grieg line-ups including the London Jazz Big Band) and in Dave Shepherd's Quintet. Worked regularly in Fred Hunt's Trio until suffering a stroke in February 1978.

HAVEN, Alan
Born: Manchester, Lancashire, 1 April 1935
organ/piano/synthesizer/vocals

Piano from age of eight. Worked with Hector Gedell Trio during the early 1950s, then led own trio at Bolton Palais for several years (began doubling organ there). Toured as part of *Swing with the Stars*, met Ronnie Scott, moved to London and played residency at Ronnie Scott's Club with organ group from 1962. Developed an international reputation and played the first of several seasons in Las Vegas in early 1966 (with Tony Crombie on drums). Played throughout Europe in the 1980s and 1990s, including residencies in Spain.

HAWDON, 'Dick' Richard
Born: Leeds, Yorkshire, 27 August 1927
trumpet/flugelhorn/double bass/arranger

Originally played cello, then took up trumpet. First gigs with the Royal Garden Quartet, service in the Army, then joined the Twin City Washboard Beaters, which was the forerunner of the Yorkshire Jazz Band. Combined playing in the Yorkshire Jazz Band with college studies. Moved to London in 1951. Led own band (1951), then worked for several months with Chris Barber (July to November 1951), before spending two years in the Christie Brothers' Stompers. Briefly with Norman Cave's Band (December 1953 to January 1954), then worked in Don Rendell's Sextet from May 1954 until joining Tubby Hayes in February 1955. With Basil and Ivor Kirchin from September 1966 until March 1957. With John Dankworth from March 1957 until April 1960, briefly with Harry Gold, then rejoined new Dankworth Band from May 1960. With Terry Lightfoot from May 1961 until November 1962. With Sid Phillips and with Oscar Rabin until rejoining Dankworth in January 1963. Again briefly with Terry Lightfoot in May 1963, then played in various night clubs, including three years' work with Sidney Simone and Burt Rhodes at the Talk of the Town, London, and a year at the Prince of Wales Theatre. Moved back to Yorkshire, worked at the Majestic Ballroom, Leeds, then led house band at Batley Variety Club for a year from 1967. Took up teaching post at the City of Leeds College of Music in 1968, and became Head of Light Music in 1974. Continued to play regularly (mainly on double bass) with various line-ups and regularly accompanied visiting American musicians. Led own quintet and worked on bass and trumpet throughout the 1980s. Retired from full time college duties in 1993.

HAWES, 'Pat' Patrick Vernon
Born: Stanmore, Middlesex, 29 July 1928
piano

Won talent contest in 1943 playing boogie-woogie. Worked around the Pinner area with George

Hall's Dance Band, then joined John Haim's Jelly Roll Kings. Left Haim to join Humphrey Lyttelton until September 1948, then served in the RAF until late 1950. During this period became part of the Crane River Jazz Band (in 1949), occasionally playing trombone with them during the band's early days. Left the Crane River Jazz Band (with Ken Colyer) to join the Christie Brothers' Stompers from July 1951 until late 1952. Led own trio in 1953, then joined short-lived band led by singer Neva Raphaello (the nucleus of this group became the Dave Carey Band). With Dave Carey from autumn 1954 until April 1957 (replaced by Roy Vaughan). Led own band 1957–9. Freelanced, then worked with Alex Revell (1962). From 1963 played a series of gigs with Ken Colyer. Led own quintet through the 1960s. Occasionally with John Chilton-Bruce Turner Quintet in the early 1970s. From 1972 took part in many reunions of the Crane River Jazz Band (including tours of Europe). During the 1970s and 1980s did a great deal of solo work, also regularly with tenorist Ivor Elliott. Again with Ken Colyer during the early 1980s, and with Ken Colyer Trust Band (1988–9). Prolific freelance work in the 1990s, with Rod Chambers' Band, Mike Pointon, Chez Chesterman, etc. Joined Brian White's Magna Jazz Band in 1993, also worked with White in King Jazz. Has been a regular contributor to *Jazz Journal* since January 1993.

HAWKINS, 'Annie' Allison Anne Geddes   Born: Melbourne, Australia, 1 September 1942
double bass

Father a multi-instrumentalist. Played tea-chest bass while a student at Melbourne University. Took up double bass and sat in with local bands, then moved to Britain in 1962 to join up with Max Collie. Worked in London City Stompers (with Collie) from 1964 and became part of the original Max Collie Rhythm Aces (1966). Gigged with Chez Chesterman and with Bill Brunskill, then temporarily left full time playing to raise family. Moved to Loughborough in 1972 and gigged with various bands, playing regularly in Jazz Spectrum in Nottingham, and in Johnny Hobbs' Trio and Stompers. Worked occasionally with Ken Colyer during the 1970s and regularly with Sammy Rimington from 1978 (initially alternating with Alyn Shipton) but full time from 1980, through the early 1980s (including tours of Europe). During the 1980s worked with many different line-ups: toured with Malc Murphy, worked with Allan Bradley, Joy Coffey, Les Moore, etc. Moved to Leeds in May 1992 and began working regularly with French Quarter band, also guested with Dennis Armstrong's Spartan Jazzband through the 1990s. Temporary returns to Australia in 1992, 1994, and 1995.

HAWKINS, Derek   Born: Shepherd's Bush, London, 25 September 1918
saxes/clarinet

Took up clarinet at fifteen, alto sax a year later. Played local gigs, then spent several years with Fred Hedley's Band and won individual awards working with this band at various contests. Played in Vic Lewis-Jack Parnell Jazzmen (1944–5), then did an ENSA (Entertainments National Service Organization) tour with Eric Winstone. Briefly featured with Ted Heath. With Frank Weir for a year from summer of 1945, brief spell with Ambrose, then rejoined Frank Weir until late 1946. With Roy Fox from late 1946 until September 1947. Moved to Glasgow in 1950 and became successful music teacher from 1950 until 1978, then gradually devoted more time to instrument repairing and achieved a formidable reputation in that profession during the 1990s.

HAWKSWORTH, 'Johnny' John
double bass/piano/composer

Born: London, 20 January 1924

Piano lessons at school, then served in the RAF as a navigator (stationed in South Africa). Returned to Britain, played double bass with Buddy Featherstonhaugh's Band at RAF Eastchurch, then, after demobilization, with Featherstonhaugh at the Gargoyle Club, London (1947). With Tommy Sampson's Band (1948) then joined Joe Saye's Trio (1949). Briefly with Ronnie Pleydell (early 1950), with Tito Burns from March 1950 until May 1951, then joined Ted Heath until early 1965 (occasionally freelanced with other groups during Heath band holidays, including brief season with Basil Kirchin in spring 1953; also led own sextet at River Club in Chelsea in 1964 and worked in Lennie Felix's Trio in the early 1960s). Became musical director for Thames Television, and enjoyed success as a composer. Continued to freelance on bass, and briefly on sitar. Led own Trio through to the early 1970s, and worked with Stephane Grappelli, then moved to Singapore before settling in Sydney, Australia, where he freelanced (mainly on piano) during the 1990s.

HAYES, 'Harry' Henry Richard
alto sax/soprano sax/clarinet/arranger/composer

Born: Marylebone, London, 23 March 1909

Began playing soprano saxophone at eleven, some lessons from Jack Miranda. First paid work was a two week spell at Gloucester Palais with Harry Westfield's Band. First regular professional engagements with Alan Selby in Brighton (1925–6). With Al Payne's Kittens (1926), Julian Vedey (1926), the Empress Rooms Orchestra and again in Brighton prior to joining Fred Elizalde in December 1927. Left to work with Sydney Kyte (late 1929), then joined Billy Mason at the Café de Paris, London (1930). With Sydney Lipton (summer 1931), then rejoined Billy Mason (and thus toured with Louis Armstrong in 1932). With Bert Firman (late 1932), Ambrose's Blue Lyres (late 1932 to spring 1933). With Harry Perritt, then joined Maurice Winnick. With Ord Hamilton's Band (autumn 1934), then rejoined Maurice Winnick, also briefly with Buddy Featherstonhaugh at the Cocoanut Grove (April 1935) and with Billy Mason at the Florida Club. With Maurice Winnick (1935), Harry Roy (1936), then worked mainly with Sydney Lipton from summer 1936 until early 1939 (played many freelance recording dates and accompanied Benny Carter in London, January 1937). With Geraldo from January 1939 until 1942, combining this work whenever possible with Army duties (served in the Regimental Band of the Welsh Guards from 1940 until 1944). During this period also guested with various bandleaders: George Evans, Johnny Claes, etc. Released from Army in October 1944, played in EMI house band and led own recording band from November 1944. Led own band from late 1945 (played long residency at Churchill's until May 1947). With Ambrose (late 1948–9) then again with Sydney Lipton (1949–50). Led own bands during the 1950s and 1960s, at Winston's Club from 1958–65, and quintet for West End show *The Tunnel of Love*. Also active as a teacher and as the owner of a London music shop (from 1947). Widespread freelance work, including regular broadcasts with Kenny Baker's Dozen from 1952–8, briefly with Ambrose again in spring 1953. Retired from regular playing in the mid-1960s, but continued to run own record and musical instrument shops into the 1980s. Played during guest appearance at Birmingham Jazz Festival in 1992. In 1992 celebrated 50 years of marriage to singer Primrose Orrock (who was featured with Roy Fox, Jack Hylton, Harry Parry, Sydney Lipton, etc).

HAYES, 'Tubby' Edward Brian
tenor sax/saxes/vibes/flute/
composer/arranger

Born: Raynes Park, London, 30 January 1935
Died: Hammersmith, London, 8 June 1973

Father, Teddy Hayes, was a violinist with the BBC Revue Orchestra. Began on violin at the age of eight, then piano from ten and tenor sax from December 1946. Attended Rutlish Grammar School. Gigged with semi-professional bands in the late 1940s. With Martin Feldman's Band (early 1951), then joined Kenny Baker's Sextet in February 1951. Later that year worked with Roy Fox and in Terry Brown's Band. With Tito Burns (1952), Ambrose (1953), Vic Lewis (1953) and freelanced in various jazz clubs. With Jack Parnell (1954), then led own band from April 1955 until October 1956. Widespread freelance work (took up vibes in December 1956), played in Downbeat Big Band and then co-led Jazz Couriers (with Ronnie Scott) from April 1957 until August 1959. Led own quartet from August 1959, became musical director of the Downbeat Big Band in 1959. During the 1960s led own quartet, quintet, octet and big band, also played solo dates in the USA (1961, 1962, 1964, 1965) and deputized (in London) for Paul Gonsalves in the Duke Ellington Orchestra (February 1964). Worked briefly on various occasions in Ronnie Scott's Big Band, temporarily out of action through serious illnesses in 1966, 1967 and 1969, then underwent heart surgery in 1969. Again in hospital in summer of 1970, but resumed leading own big band in November 1970, played freelance dates (including work with John Stevens) then further heart surgery in June 1971. Concentrated on composing and arranging for a while, then resumed playing in December 1971, subsequently worked in Sweden and Norway (February 1972), also played in Bebop Preservation Society (1972). Led own quartet and deputized in the Bobby Lamb-Ray Premru Orchestra (late summer 1972). Worked in Ian Hamer's Sextet (1973) and continued gigging until being taken ill at Brighton in May 1973. Was subsequently admitted to Hammersmith Hospital.

HEASMAN, 'Ronnie' Ronald A.
trumpet

Born: 1928
Died: 1963

With Billy Forrest's Band (1945). Worked with organist Robin Richmond's Band (including tour of Scandinavia), then joined Oscar Rabin in September 1949. Left Rabin after fifteen months to join Geraldo, then worked for several years with Eric Winstone from May 1951. With Sid Wright's Band in London (1957), then briefly with Eric Delaney (summer 1957). With Cyril Stapleton, Jack Parnell, Ted Heath and the BBC Revue Orchestra, besides freelancing on various sessions. Toured Europe with Rosemary Clooney and worked in tenorist Derek Butterworth's band (late 1962).

HEATH, 'Ted' George Edward
trombone/composer

Born: London, 30 March 1900
Died: Virginia Water, Surrey, 18 November 1969

Was younger brother of trumpeter Harold 'Bert' Heath. Father led Wandsworth Borough Prize Band, in which Ted played as a teenager. He began on tenor horn at six and took up trombone at fourteen. Was a coach-building apprentice, but left to become a professional musician, playing in an organized busking band on the streets of London (1919–21). With the Broadway Five (1922), worked briefly in the Queen's Hall Roof Garden Orchestra then joined the Southern Syncopated Orchestra (from the USA) for engagements in Austria. Returned to London and played in Jack

Hylton's Kit-Cat Band (directed by Al Starita) 1925–7, then toured with Jack Hylton's Metrognomes. Extensive freelance recordings throughout the 1920s (Bert Firman, Harry Bidgood, etc.). Joined Ambrose in October 1928 and worked mainly with that leader for eight years, also did freelance work in film studios and for radio and recordings. With Sydney Lipton from January 1936 until January 1940. Briefly with pianist Tim Clayton at Lansdowne House, then joined Maurice Winnick at the Dorchester Hotel, London. Brief return to Sydney Lipton (late 1940), then joined Geraldo (1941). With Geraldo during World War II, including tour of the Middle East 1944), but also freelanced and led own broadcasting band from 29 August 1942. Left Geraldo in May 1945 to lead own big band (Ted Heath and his Music) which achieved international success over the following two decades, touring the USA, Australia, etc. The band played a long series of Swing Sessions at the London Palladium from December 1945. Ted Heath's autobiography, *Listen to My Music*, was first published in 1957. He achieved success with songs co-composed with his second wife Moira. A Ted Heath Tribute Band (led by Don Lusher) has continued to flourish throughout the 1990s.

HEATLEY, 'Spike' Brian John
double bass/cello

Born: London, 17 February 1933

Played clarinet from age of thirteen, then gigged on drums with own local band before specializing on double bass. With Harry Bence (spring 1956), then played a season with Alan Ross at the Palace Hotel, Karachi. With Bernie Stanton (early 1958), Duncan Lamont (spring 1958), Vic Ash (summer 1958–9), also worked in Dill Jones' Trio and accompanied various singers including Georgia Brown, Helen Merrill, etc. Briefly in Ronnie Scott-Tubby Hayes Jazz Couriers, then worked in Tubby Hayes' Quartet until joining Eddie Thompson Trio (October 1959). Rejoined Vic Ash (late 1959), then again worked with Eddie Thompson and with Ronnie Scott (1960). With John Dankworth from spring 1960 until February 1962. Toured with Kenny Baker (March 1962) and worked with Alexis Korner before playing on cruises (Black Sea and Mediterranean) with Tony Coe's Quartet (summer 1962). With Tony Coe Quintet (1963), often with Danny Moss from 1964 onwards, also regularly in various Ronnie Ross line-ups throughout the 1960s and 1970s. Worked with Maynard Ferguson in 1967. With Bill Le Sage from the late 1960s and thus worked often in the Bebop Preservation Society in the 1970s, combined this with freelancing and leading own line-ups and accompanying many visiting musicians and singers throughout Europe in the 1980s. Toured Britain with Canadian pianist Oliver Jones (1990) then moved to France and made this his base for freelance playing.

HECKSTALL-SMITH, 'Dick' Richard Malden
saxes

Born: Ludlow, Shropshire,
26 September 1934

Five years at Gordonstoun School, Scotland. Early efforts on the piano, lessons on clarinet. Attended Foxhole School, Dartington (1949–52). Alto sax briefly at fifteen, soprano sax soon afterwards. To Sidney Sussex College in Cambridge in 1953, led University Jazz Band on soprano sax. Worked as a hospital orderly for eight months before becoming professional musician in 1957. Joined Sandy Brown in December 1957, played tenor sax from 1958. Gigged with Bob Parker's band. Left Sandy Brown to play summer season with Ronnie Smith's band at Butlin's

Filey camp in 1958. On baritone sax with Basil Kirchin's band (late 1958 to early 1959), then worked with Jimmy Gridley's Band before doing international touring for five months with Jerome Robbins' *Ballet USA* (1959). Led own group and gigged with various leaders including Dick Williams, then did residency at the Blue Lagoon Club before working in Bert Courtley's Band (including month in Germany, 1961). During the early 1960s, played occasionally in John Burch's Octet, with Ginger Baker and gigged with Michael Horovitz and Pete Brown. Worked regularly in Alexis Korner's Blues Incorporated from spring 1962 until August 1963. With Graham Bond Organization from August 1963 until July 1967. With John Mayall's Blues Breakers for a year from August 1967, then joined John Hiseman's Colosseum from September 1968 until October 1971. Led own group Manchild briefly until temporarily incapacitated by back trouble; studied for BSc degree in London and was musically inactive for almost three years. Resumed regular playing, led own Quintet, then joined Big Chief in the late 1970s. During the 1980s also worked in own Tough Tenors, in Main Squeeze, Electric Dream, DHSS, with John Stevens, etc. Played many dates in Germany with the Hamburg Blues Band from 1984 through the 1990s, also continued to lead DHSS Sextet. Guested with various groups, and played reunion dates with Colosseum in Europe (1994–5). His autobiography, *The Safest Place in the World*, was first published in 1989.

HENDERSON, 'Russ' Russell
piano/steel drum

Born: Trinidad, West Indies, 1 January 1924

Two sisters studied piano. Began on piano at an early age and did solo work as a teenager before forming own trio. Moved to England in 1951, ostensibly to study piano tuning but soon became a professional musician. Freelanced with many groups and played regularly in band led by saxist Wally Stewart and band led by trumpeter Tommy Spring. Led own band for long residency at La Ronde Club, London, from the late 1950s, by this time was also playing steel drum with various groups before forming own highly successful Steel Band which has continued through the 1990s. Recorded with John Surman in 1968. Continues to freelance extensively on piano through the 1990s, leads own trio and quartet, and often works in duo with singer Barry Stevenson.

HENRY, Doreen
vocals

Born: Leeds, Yorkshire, 9 January 1906
Died: Leeds, Yorkshire, 9 June 1990

Moved to the USA in 1926 and was soon featured on own radio programme on station WPCH (New York), singing and playing piano. Moved back to England in 1939 and married ex-rugby international Richard Auty (1910–95). Sang with Billy Ternent and Henry Hall during World War II, often guested with Billy Munn, recorded with Stephane Grappelli in 1945, and later with Ralph Sharon. During visits to the USA sang with Jack Teagarden's Band and guested with Henry Levine's Band. Relinquished vocal career in the early 1950s in order to raise family, but continued to sing into the 1980s.

HEWETT, 'Dave' Dave Philip
trombone/cornet/baritone horn

Born: Caterham, Surrey, 30 July 1942

Father played euphonium. Began on cornet at ten, played in Salvation Army for several years, then took up trombone. Played trombone in Alexander's Jazzmen (led by Len Barton) through the

1960s, also on cornet in Mike Daniels' Big Band (1964–5). On trombone with Freddy Randall-Dave Shepherd Band from 1972–6 (including Montreux Jazz Festival), freelanced on trombone with various bands and also played cornet with the Seven Aces (in Kent) during the early 1980s. Temporary absence from playing through dental problems, then guested with Bill Brunskill before working regularly (on trombone) with Alan Elsdon (1986–9). Gigged with Laurie Chescoe in the late 1980s, then became founder-member of Laurie Chescoe's Good Time Jazz in August 1990 and has worked with this group through the 1990s.

HIGGINS, Malcolm
trumpet

Born: Wishaw, Lanarkshire, Scotland, 4 April 1932

Played in the Canal Street Jazzmen and worked with Jim McHarg and Forrie Cairns (1958), then, together with Cairns, joined Ian Menzies' Clyde Valley Stompers from early 1959 until autumn 1961. Again with Jim McHarg (1961–2), then toured briefly with the Clyde Valley Stompers until returning to Scotland in early 1963. Played with various bands, worked with Pete Kerr (1967), then emigrated to Canada and played regularly with various jazz groups, many of them containing expatriate musicians from Scotland. Made return visits to Britain to play in Clyde Valley Stompers reunion tours and to be featured as a soloist at Scottish festivals during the 1990s.

HINES, Harry
saxes/clarinet

Born: Nuneaton, Warwickshire, 17 January 1898
Died: 1971

Learnt music while a Naval Cadet. Served in the Merchant Navy, then became a professional musician. Worked with Archie Alexander (1927), with Billy Mason in Scotland and with Teddy Brown's Ciro Orchestra in London. With Leslie Jeffries' Rialto Orchestra before joining Jay Whidden briefly in spring of 1928, then worked with Jean Pougnet in early 1930 before joining Joe Kaye (1930–1). With Ambrose before playing regularly with Al Collins from late 1932, also played on many freelance recordings, including some with Spike Hughes. With Maurice Winnick from 1940 until 1947, including wartime overseas tours entertaining troops, then formed own highly successful comedy band Doctor Crock and his Crackpots.

HISEMAN, 'Jon' Philip John
drums/composer

Born: London, 21 June 1944

Married to Barbara Thompson. Played violin and piano as a child, drums at high school, first gigs with Ian Bird (1961). During the following four years worked with Mike Taylor's Trio and Quartet, in Neil Ardley's New Jazz Orchestra, in Group Sounds Five. With Howard Riley's Trio intermittently from autumn 1965 until summer 1968, regularly with Graham Bond Organization from summer 1966 to summer 1967, then joined Georgie Fame. With John Mayall (late 1967–8), with Alan Haven, John Surman, Don Rendell, etc. Formed own Colosseum summer 1968, disbanded in late 1971. With Barbara Thompson's Jubiaba and leading own Tempest group (1973–4). Re-formed Colosseum in summer 1975, then worked in United Jazz and Rock Ensemble from the mid-1970s through to the 1980s. During the 1980s and 1990s regularly in Barbara Thompson groups and with her in Sans Frontier (1992), and managing own recording studio. Did series of reunion dates in Europe with Colosseum (1994 and 1995).

HITCHCOCK, Nigel Glen
saxes

Born: Bognor Regis, Sussex, 4 January 1971

Brother of saxophonist Clive (born 7 January 1966). Began playing alto sax at the age of eight, and played first gigs with a local band a month later. Was featured with the National Youth Jazz Orchestra at eleven, and remained with them for six years. Also played in Tim Colwell's South Coast Jazz Friends. With Itchy Fingers from September 1988. During the following year co-led Self Portrait (with Phil Mulford). Won Pat Smythe Award in 1989. Worked in big bands led by Jack Sharpe, John Altman, Stan Tracey, etc., also did innumerable 'pop' sessions. With Clark Tracey, Barbara Thompson, and Laurence Cottle's Band and Quintet. Highly successful freelance throughout the 1990s.

HODGE, 'Pete' Peter John
trombone/euphonium

Born: Euston, London, 30 January 1930

Began playing trombone at St Marylebone Grammar School. Joined RAF Central Band in 1948 and served until 1953 (including overseas tours). During this period also played regularly in Mike Daniels' Delta Jazzmen (1951–2), and in Bobby Mickleburgh's Bobcats (summer 1952–3). After leaving the RAF, worked with Harry Gold (1953–5), Laurie Gold (1956) and Freddy Randall (from autumn 1956). Spent eight years with Sid Phillips (during this time also played briefly, in 1961, in the Clyde Valley Stompers). With Jack Nathan at the Pigalle, then played in many West End theatre orchestras during the late 1960s, 1970s and 1980s for shows: *Hello Dolly*, *Ain't Misbehavin'*, *Chorus Line*, *42nd Street*, etc. Worked in Bob Wilber's Big Band at Nice Festival (1987). From 1989 onwards resumed regular small band jazz work. Regularly with Sonny Dee All Stars through the 1990s and freelancing with various bands including the Black Cat Rhythm Rag.

HODGKISS, Allan
guitar

Born: c.1917
Died: 1986

Self-taught guitarist. Did night club work in the late 1930s, playing residencies at various London venues, the Panama, the Palm Beach, etc. Was invalided out of the Royal Berkshire Regiment in World War II and joined Frank Weir's Band. Worked (and recorded with) Carlo Krahmer, George Shearing, etc. Toured with Stephane Grappelli (1945) and recorded in London with Django Reinhardt (1946). With Sid Millward's Quintet (1945), then joined Billy Munn (1945). Played at Paris Jazz Festival in 1949, also worked with Miff Ferrie, Jack Payne, Henry Hall, Nat Temple, etc., and did freelance session work.

HOGG, Derek
drums

Born: Oldham, Lancashire, 8 April 1928

Worked with dance bands and show orchestras before joining Freddy Randall from late 1953 until June 1954. With Don Rendell from June 1954 until summer 1957, but also worked with Joe Saye Quartet (late 1954), Ken Moule Seven (March to April 1955) and Buddy Featherstonhaugh (1956). Again with Buddy Featherstonhaugh in 1958, also with Kenny Baker. With Sandy Brown's Band and then with Fairweather-Brown Band (from September 1958). With Tommy Whittle at the

Dorchester Hotel, then worked with Vic Lewis (1959–60), including 1960 tour of USA. With Squadronaires then toured with Donald Purchese in *Here Is the News* show (August 1960). With Pat Smythe Trio, Dudley Moore Trio (1961). Regularly in Danny Moss' Quartet from 1962 through to 1987. During this period also worked in Tony Coe's Quintet, with Colin Purbrook's Trio, toured Europe with Rosemary Clooney, and did extensive freelance work which continued into the 1980s. Often part of Digby Fairweather's Friends during the early 1980s. Retired from regular playing in 1987.

HOLDER, Frank Claude
Born: Georgetown, British Guiana (now Guyana), 2 April 1925
vocals/conga drum/bongoes

Joined RAF in 1944, served in Britain from March 1945 until 1948, sang with various service groups including band at RAF Cranwell led by Geoff Head. After demobilization, began doubling on conga drums and sang and played in Leslie 'Jiver' Hutchinson's band (1948). Worked in André Messeder's band (1949–50), also played and sang in John Carioca's band at Churchill's Club, London. Featured with John Dankworth for several years until summer of 1956. Played and sang in many Latin-American groups, including one led by the Deniz Brothers, also worked in Joe Harriott's band (1960). From 1958 onwards developed a career as a freelance entertainer and cabaret artiste, touring regularly on the variety halls and club circuit, also enjoyed success as an actor. Appeared with the Scottish National Orchestra in 1973 in work written by Wilfred Mellors. Continued to freelance through the 1990s, singing, playing and acting.

HOLDSWORTH, Allan
Born: Leeds, Yorkshire, 6 August 1946
guitar/violin/composer

Originally played sax and clarinet. Took up guitar at seventeen. Gigged in and around Leeds before moving to London in the late 1960s. Worked in Ian Carr's Nucleus and (on violin) with John Hiseman during the early 1970s. With Soft Machine from late 1973 until spring 1975 then worked in the USA in Tony Williams' Lifetime. Returned to Britain and worked with Bill Bruford in UK (1976) and later in Bruford's own band. Also worked with French violinist Jean-Luc Ponty and with John Stevens before rejoining Soft Machine. Moved to the USA in the late 1970s originally to rejoin Tony Williams, then settled in America and led own groups. Toured Japan in 1985 (with Gordon Beck on piano) also in duo with Beck (1988). Continues to play and record regularly (1996).

HOLDSWORTH, 'Dave' David Allan
Born: Morley, West Yorkshire, 7 March 1942
trumpet/valve trombone/tuba/
composer/arranger

Began on cornet at seven, played in various Yorkshire brass bands. Gigged with local dance bands from sixteen, then became interested in jazz while studying at Keele University. Left University in 1964, moved to London and gigged with various jazz groups and led own band. Subsequently worked with Mike Westbrook, Graham Collier, Chris MacGregor, Mike Osborne Quartet and Septet, London Jazz Composers' Orchestra, Spirit Level, Tony Oxley Septet. Moved to South Coast, with bands in and around Brighton area, and with French musicians in Bordeaux. Gave up day work in education to devote more time to playing, arranging and composing. In autumn of 1994 formed own nine piece Rhythm-a-Ning (featuring the compositions of Thelonious Monk).

HOLLAND, 'Dave' David
double bass/cello/piano/composer

Born: Wolverhampton, Warwickshire, 1 October 1946

Played ukulele during early childhood, switched to guitar then to bass guitar. Bass guitar with local band, Steve Brett and the Mavericks, then played summer season in Scarborough (1964) with Midland tenor saxophonist Trevor Orton. Switched to double bass, accompanied American singer Johnny Ray on three week tour, then settled temporarily in London for nine months' residency at the Chanticleer Club, Victoria. Did second summer season in Scarborough with Trevor Orton (1965), then, in autumn 1965, began three years' studies at Guildhall School of Music (under James Merret, Jr). Gigged with various bands during period 1966–8, including Alan Littlejohns-Tony Milliner Sextet, Roy Budd Trio, Alan Cohen Big Band, John Stevens, Kenny Wheeler, John Surman, Mike Westbrook, Humphrey Lyttelton, Ronnie Scott, Evan Parker, Chris McGregor, Tubby Hayes, etc. While working with Elaine Delmar at Ronnie Scott's Club, London (July to August 1968) was heard by Miles Davis, who invited him to record in the USA. This marked the beginning of a renowned international career which continued through the 1990s. Has made many recordings and widespread tours with a vast assortment of top jazz musicians, and has also enjoyed considerable success as a teacher in Canada and the USA.

HOLLOWAY, 'Laurie' Laurence
piano/composer/arranger

Born: Oldham, Lancashire, 31 March 1938

Piano lessons during early childhood, at thirteen was organist in local church. Played local dance gigs in Oldham. Turned professional in 1954 and worked with Sid Willmot in Weymouth, the Isle of Bute and Leeds. With Arthur Plant in Dundee (1956) and then worked on liners with Arthur Plant. Summer season in Isle of Man with Vic Davies (1957). With Joe Daniels, then worked with Alan Kane at the Gargoyle Club, doubled by playing with Ronnie Rand at the Astoria Ballroom, also gigged at Manor House with Mike Senn and Jack Sharpe. With Cyril Stapleton (summer 1960), then regular work on Radio Luxembourg with Stephane Grappelli. Briefly in Derek Butterworth's Quintet (1961), to USA with Johnnie Gray's Band (early 1962) for work in the Catskills. Returned to London, played in duo with bassist Joe Muddel at the Vaudeville Club and played for show *Blitz*. Wrote musical *Instant Marriage* (with Bob Grant), which ran for a year at Piccadilly Theatre, London (1964). Accompanied Bob Brookmeyer and Clark Terry on *Jazz 625* television show, also played residency at Annie's Room (1965) and worked with various visiting American musicians. Married American singer Marion Montgomery (Marian Maud Runnels, born Natchez, Mississippi, 17 November 1934) in 1965 and worked in the USA with her. With John Dankworth and Cleo Laine (1966–7). Musical director for Englebert Humperdinck from 1969 to 1975, also worked with Judy Garland, Liza Minelli, again with Stephane Grappelli, etc. From the 1970s through the 1990s active as musical director for many television shows, composer of many theme songs. Works regularly with wife, Marion Montgomery, through the 1990s, also leads own groups and continues to arrange and compose.

HOLMES, 'Chris' Christoper   Born: Manchester, Lancashire, 1943
piano

Gained BMus and GRSM through studies at Royal Northern College of Music and Manchester University. While at University played local gigs with various Dixieland bands and worked with Randolph Colville. Turned professional after graduation and moved to London to join band being organized by drummer Lennie Hastings, but Hastings abandoned the plan and stayed with Alex Welsh. Remained in London and gigged with various bands, worked regularly with Bob Wallis. Played solo piano engagement, then worked at Forty Thieves' Club in Bermuda for a year, accompanying many visiting artistes including singer Joe Williams. Returned to Britain, freelanced and ran own band, then taught music in schools before moving back to Manchester. Formed own highly successful trio (Pete Taylor on bass and Pete Staples on drums), did radio and club work and backed many visiting American musicians. Became Head of Music at a Manchester school in the 1990s, but continues to lead own trio.

HOOPER, Lew   Born: Plymouth, Devon, 22 April 1925
tenor sax/clarinet/flute

Started playing double bass at fifteen, sat in with local bands then began doubling on tenor sax from age sixteen. Played regularly at the Plymouth Rhythm Club in the late 1940s (having given up double bass), formed own Boptet, also co-led Plymouth Swing Club Big Band. Toured with George Evans in 1950, then played seven year residency at Oxford Galleries, Newcastle upon Tyne, with George Evans. Did summer seasons and played American bases in France and Spain (1958–60). Two years with pianist Gerry Moore on liner *Caronia* (1961–2). Worked regularly at the Tally Ho, London from 1963, with Denny Ogden's Quintet and Octet, and with Alan Littlejohns. From 1966 until 1969 with Alan Littlejohns-Tony Milliner Sextet, accompanying visiting American jazzmen: Bill Coleman, Peanuts Hucko, Earle Warren, etc. With Freddy Randall in the early 1970s, then worked in Sonny Dee's Band. Worked in France with Bill Coleman (1977), then freelanced, mainly around the London area. During the 1980s did three year residency at Langan's Brasserie, London (on alto sax), with tenor saxophonist Roland Lacey, pianist Dave Curtis, bassist Russ Allen and drummer John Cox. Indisposed through illness in early 1990s, then resumed regular playing.

HOPKINSON, 'Hoppy' George Ernest   Born: Elston, Nottingham, 2 September 1922
drums/washboard

Began playing drums as a teenager. Served in North Africa and Italy with the Royal Signals during World War II, played gigs with Army dance bands. After demobilization played in Eric Lovell's Jazz Revivalists which formed the basis of Mick Gill's Imperial Dixielanders, also led own New Orleans Band (1949). Left Mick Gill and joined Humphrey Lyttelton from December 1949 until May 1955. Briefly led own band (October 1955). Worked with Graham Stewart (late 1956 to May 1957) and with Alex Revell. With Eric Silk from 1958 until spring 1961, then gave up playing for over thirty years but began gigging again in 1994 with Freddy Legon, Mickey Ashman, etc.

HORLER, John Douglas
piano/arranger/composer

Born: Lymington, Hampshire, 26 February 1947

Son of trumpeter Ronnie Horler (born 1922) and brother of trombonist Dave (born 1943). Began on piano at six, later briefly played trombone. Played gigs with father's band, then studied piano and clarinet at the Royal Academy of Music from 1963–7. Led own trio for four months on cruise liner (1967), returned to Lymington for a while, then began freelancing in London during the late 1960s and early 1970s. Did a year in Bob Layzell's Band and gigged with the Bobby Lamb-Ray Premru Orchestra and with Alan Littlejohns-Tony Milliner band, Tony Faulkner's Big Band, etc. Worked briefly in Germany with Elaine Delmar, played in BBC Radio Big Band (1972) and with Dave Hancock's Quintet and Big Band, regularly in Maynard Ferguson's Big Band. With Tony Coe's Quartet and Ronnie Ross's Quartet through the 1980s, and (during 1980s and 1990s) in quintet co-led with Jimmie Hastings, often worked in Pete King's Quintet over a period of many years. With Kenny Baldock's Trio at Ronnie Scott's Club, with Dave Green and with Kenny Wheeler. Has accompanied many visiting musicians including: Chet Baker, Zoot Sims, Pepper Adams, Art Farmer, Clark Terry, Herb Geller, etc. Regularly with John Dankworth from 1984. Led own trio through the 1990s, worked occasionally with Elaine Delmar, and freelanced with many varied line-ups, including Tony Coe's Quartet (1996).

HORROX, Frank (Frank HORROCKS)
piano/arranger/composer

Born: Bolton, Lancashire, 15 February 1924
Died: Bavaria, 21 February 1972

Married to trombonist Ruth Harrison. Piano lessons from age of five, later studied at Trinity College. Professional at seventeen with Bertini's Band, worked with Dick Denny at Edinburgh Palais and toured as accompanist for comedian Arthur Askey (1942). Served in Army from late 1942 until May 1947 and was featured in *Stars in Battledress* shows. After demobilization worked as a staff arranger for publishers Campbell Connelly. Also worked with Reggie Goff (1947) before joining Vic Lewis. With Basil Kirchin from November 1948 to January 1949, then again briefly with Vic Lewis before joining Paul Fenoulhet (1949). Joined Ted Heath (replacing Dave Simpson) from October 1949 until July 1952. With Lew Stone at the Pigalle, London (from July 1952), also extensive freelance arranging and work on film *The Blue Lamp* (with Jack Parnell). Rejoined Ted Heath from February 1953 until September 1957, but also toured USA with Heath in 1958. In Raymond Gordon's Orchestra at the London Hippodrome (September to November 1958). Thereafter mainly active as a freelance pianist and arranger for many musical directors including Alyn Ainsworth, Frank Chacksfield, Ken Thorne, etc., but also played jazz gigs, with own small band (occasionally on organ). Succumbed to cancer at a clinic in Bavaria.

HOWARD, Bert
double bass/composer

Born: Walthamstow, London, 10 August 1915
Died: 1994

Piano from age of nine, at sixteen took lessons from Gerry Moore. Did semi-professional gigs with various bands, including Freddy Mirfield's, then joined RAF in 1940 and took up double bass. Invalided out of the RAF in 1942, worked with Cyril Blake's Band, Howard Baker, Hal Tauber, Carlo Krahmer, Edmundo Ros and Johnny Claes. With Vic Lewis-Jack Parnell Jazzmen (1944). With Stephane Grappelli, Don Marino Barreto, Harry Hayes, and Frank Weir, then led own band in Cornwall before joining Jack Nathan (1948). Again with Carlo Krahmer (1948). Played Cambridge residency with Hughie Radcliffe (1950), then joined Ralph Sharon's Sextet (early 1951). With Harry Gold (1953), Frank King (1954), then left full time music to work as a chiropodist.

HOWARTH, Ian
drums

Born: Wigan, Lancashire, 21 August 1948

Played washboard in junior school skiffle group, trombone in Aspull School Orchestra (1962–4) before taking up drums. Was original member of Vintage Syncopators in 1965 and worked regularly with them until 1980 (gigged with them into the 1990s). Was also part of Red Hayes' Jazz Wizards (1970–1) and worked regularly in the Temperance Seven in 1973, 1975 and 1977. Led Temperance Seven from 1979 until 1985. Worked with pianist Bert Murray from the early 1970s, and later with Martin Litton and with Keith Nichols. Regularly with Alan Cooper's Trio into the mid-1990s, also active in duos with various pianists including Colin Good, Peter Muir, Richard Simmons and Jack Honeyborne.

HUGHES, Glynn
baritone sax

Born: 1942
Died: London, 1966

Baritone sax from 1960. Worked in Rick Laird's Trio, with Brian Auger, Jet Harris-Tony Meehan group, and Georgie Fame's Blue Flames before joining Herbie Goins' Nightimers. Died in a fire at his home in Shepherd's Bush, London.

HUGHES, 'Ronnie' Ronald
trumpet/flugelhorn

Born: Aberystwyth, Wales, 27 June 1925

Trumpet from age of eleven, semi-pro gigs with Everard Davies' Band at twelve, then played in local Municipal Orchestra. In RAF from late 1943 until April 1947 (including service in India). Returned to Wales to study photography, then moved to London to join Carl Barriteau (late 1947). Gigs with Nat Allen, then played in Germany with Leslie Holmes' Londonairs (spring 1948), subsequently worked in Gillingham, Kent, with Leslie Holmes. Gigged with Harry Parry, then worked for a year with Teddy Foster from late 1948. With Ted Heath from September 1949 until May 1954 (was for a time married to Heath vocalist Lita Roza). Returned to Wales, then worked with Jack Parnell from August 1954 until February 1955. Two years with Geraldo, then worked again with Jack Parnell (at ATV) and with Cyril Stapleton (1957). Led own quintet (1958), then did world cruise on liner *Caronia* with Johnny Evans (1959). Briefly at Savoy Hotel with Francisco Cavez, then long spell in BBC Radio Orchestra, also played many West End shows including *Music Man, No Strings*, etc. Toured Japan with Frank Chacksfield (1972). Worked with singer Frankie Vaughan's V. Men. With Mike Westbrook, Bobby Lamb-Ray Premru, Paul Fenoulhet, Malcolm Lockyer, Bill McGuffie, etc. Active freelance through the 1990s, often with Bob Wilber's Big Band, with Don Lusher's Ted Heath Band and guesting at various jazz clubs, etc.

HUGHES, 'Spike' Patrick Cairns
double bass/composer/arranger

Born: London, 19 October 1908
Died: England, 2 February 1987

Son of Irish composer and music critic Herbert Hughes. Originally played cello. Studied composition and orchestration in Vienna (1923–4). While in Vienna wrote arrangements for Arthur Briggs and his band (1924). Lived in Cambridge from autumn of 1925 but was only briefly a student there, in 1927. Studied conducting in Berlin (1927) and became self-taught bass player. Back in Britain he arranged for Al Starita's Band (and for Ray Starita and Jack Hylton), also played bass in the Night Watchmen (1929–30) in London and in France. Led own successful recording bands in the early 1930s, also worked briefly with Jack Hylton. Led own band for occasional gigs, including trip to Holland, freelanced on bass and played in Percival Mackey's Orchestra for C.B. Cochran's *The 1931 Revue*, later worked in Cochran's *Words and Music* touring show. Compositions featured in *High Yellow* (modern ballet devised in 1932 by American dancer, Buddy Bradley). Visited USA in 1933 to organize, and arrange for, recordings by his All American Orchestra. Played bass on a few recordings in New York, then gave up playing bass (and conducting) to concentrate on composing and journalism. Hughes had written music reviews since 1924. He later wrote regularly for the *Melody Maker*, under his own name, and using the pseudonym 'Mike'. Briefly resumed conducting for radio shows (1937) and directed own opera *Cinderella* in 1938, then resumed work as journalist, author and regular broadcaster. He wrote many books, on various subjects, including two volumes of autobiography, *Opening Bars* (first published in 1946) and *Second Chorus* (first published in 1951).

HUMBLE, Derek
alto sax/clarinet

Born: Livingston, Co. Durham, March 1930
Died: Easington, Co. Durham, 22 February 1971

Played alto sax and clarinet from early teens. Won individual awards at *Melody Maker* contests in West Hartlepool (1946) and Newcastle (1947). With Benny Nelson's Band in West Hartlepool before joining Teddy Foster in late 1948. Left Foster in spring of 1950, worked with Kathy Stobart's Band for a year, then joined Vic Lewis (March 1951). Briefly with Raymonde's Orchestra at Selby's Club, then joined Jack Parnell from April 1952 until becoming part of newly formed Ronnie Scott Band in January 1953. Briefly with Tony Crombie, then rejoined Ronnie Scott in January 1956. With Oscar Rabin in summer of 1956, then again worked with Ronnie Scott (including trip to USA) until moving to Germany to join Kurt Edelhagen (April 1957). Worked regularly with Edelhagen over a period of ten years, subsequently worked in Kenny Clarke-Francy Boland Big Band. Played engagements in Britain during occasional vacation trips, and also worked in big band led by Ronnie Scott for Scott Walker tour in 1967. Was seriously injured when mugged in Cologne, Germany (1968), but was able to play gigs with Clarke-Boland Big Band until 1970, and played in London with Gordon Beck's Trio (August 1969). However his health was badly affected and he moved back to Britain in the summer of 1970. His last regular jobs were in a quartet co-led with Phil Seamen. He died in Easington while visiting his mother.

HUNT, 'Bob' Robert Allen
trombone/cornet/saxes/clarinet/piano/tuba

Born: Kettering, Northamptonshire,
21 October 1959

Piano from the age of six, cornet at nine, trombone at eleven and saxes from thirteen. Gigged around the Kettering area as a teenager and played in local brass band. At Guildhall School of Music from sixteen, then studied for Masters degree at Leicester University. Played in Radio Leicester Big Band (led by Roger Eames). Led own Blue Rhythm Band in the Midlands from the mid-1970s. During the 1980s worked with Sid Lawrence and played for *Black and White Minstrel Show* (and in other pit orchestras). With Steve Lane, the Pasadena Roof Orchestra, Midnite Follies, Alyn Ainsworth, Kenny Baker, John McLevy, etc. Began long musical association with Harry Strutters Hot Rhythm Orchestra in the 1980s, and worked occasionally in Five-a-Slide. Regularly in Martin Litton's Red Hot Peppers during the 1990s and from 1991 leading own successful Ellington Orchestra.

HUNT, 'Fred' Frederick Herbert
piano

Born: London, 21 September 1923
Died: Weybridge, Surrey, 25 April 1986

Piano from age of thirteen, played local gigs before joining RAF in World War II (served in the Far East). After demobilization played semi-professionally with Eric Conroy's Band, then worked in Cy Laurie Four (1951) and with the Galleon Jazz Band, Beryl Bryden's Back Room Boys, and briefly with Mick Mulligan, before joining Mike Daniels in late 1952. Turned professional to work with Alex Welsh from 1954. Left Welsh in November 1962, briefly with Clinton Ford, then did club work including residency in Bournemouth (summer 1963), then rejoined Alex Welsh in April 1964. Worked mainly with Welsh until 1974, but played various freelance dates (deputized briefly in Acker Bilk's Band). Led own Trio from late 1974, guested in Copenhagen with the Kansas City Band. Moved to South Africa in September 1975, worked for Broadcasting Company and played residency in Durban, then returned to Britain in spring 1976. Again worked in Denmark, returned to Britain, worked with Dave Shepherd, and with Keith Smith, but mainly active leading own Trio from early 1978, playing residency at Pizza Express, London. Also accompanied various visiting American jazzmen, and toured with Wild Bill Davison. Guested with Keith Smith again in 1979, then played semi-regularly with Alex Welsh again during the early 1980s, but concentrated on leading own Trio until incapacitated by an illness that confined him to a wheelchair.

HUNTER, Chris
saxes/flute

Born: London, 21 February 1957

Played saxophone from age of twelve. During his teens took lessons from Les Evans and participated in jazz workshops. Joined NYJO in 1976, overseas tours included a visit to Russia. Toured with Mike Westbrook (1978–9), before doing wide variety of studio work in Britain and Europe. His work in Gil Evans' British Orchestra in 1983 marked the start of a four year musical association during which Hunter twice toured Japan with Evans and worked in the USA with him. Also worked in the USA with Mike Westbrook (1983), later that year moved to New York and joined Michel Camilo's Sextet. Began working with Mike Gibbs in 1984 and continued to do so on various tours and festivals throughout the 1980s.

HUNTER, 'Jo' Jolyon
trumpet

Born: Ealing, London, 1 December 1926

Father was actor Ian Hunter, mother actress Kathleen Pringle. Moved with Family to USA in 1935, studied at American schools and attended two military academies. Played French horn in school orchestra then began playing trumpet. Returned to Britain in 1943 and attended Royal College of Music. Army service (mainly in Germany). Played with local service bands. After demobilization joined Kenny Graham's Afro-Cubists (spring 1950). Left Graham to join Roy Fox (summer 1951). Left Fox in January 1952 to work with Jack Parnell for seven years in the 1950s. Extensive freelance session work, also worked again with Roy Fox and Kenny Graham and with Oscar Rabin from October 1956 until 1959. Moved to Brighton and worked with local bands. Active freelance on trumpet and piano, including work on cruise liner, also played harmonica in later years.

HUNTER-RANDALL, Ian
trumpet

Born: Clapham, London, 3 January 1938

With Ken Barton's Oriole Jazz Band from 1959. Also worked with Preston Scott's Jazz Band in the late 1950s. Left Ken Barton in summer of 1962 to join Len Barton's Alexander's Jazzmen, then worked with the Clyde Valley Stompers from April 1963 until 31 December 1963. With the London City Stompers (1964), then gigged with Charlie Galbraith prior to joining Monty Sunshine (1964). Left to work briefly with Acker Bilk (May to June 1966), then rejoined Monty Sunshine. Long stint with Terry Lightfoot from 1967 until late summer of 1994. Often worked with Pete Allen's Band during the years 1978 to 1981. Formed own All Star Band in 1994. Worked regularly with Laurie Chescoe's Good Time Jazz from late 1995.

HURLEY, George Joseph
violin

Born: East London, 5 August 1907
Died: London, 1997

Violin lessons from the age of six (later made brief, tentative efforts on tenor sax). Played in youth band with saxophonist Laurie Payne, then on the recommendation of pianist Arthur Leftridge (who gained fame as Ivor Kaye). George joined the Oak Club Band in the West End of London. Played in house band at the Cosmo Club in Wardour Street (with Harry Hayes), then led own band at the Florida Club (1927). Recorded with Fred Elizalde in 1927. Worked in Germany with the Original Orpheans (January to March 1928), then joined Fred Elizalde from April 1928 until spring 1930 (also recorded with Spike Hughes 1930–1). Joined Billy Mason (1930), then worked with Ray Starita (late 1930), before rejoining Billy Mason (early 1931). Again with Ray Starita from spring 1931 until summer 1932, during this period also directed band at the Kit-Cat Club. With saxophonist Charlie Spinelli (1932), then worked in band led by Mrs Ennis Hylton for almost five years. With Miff Ferrie's Band (1939), then joined Barney Gilbraith (1940). While serving as a driver in the London Fire Brigade (during World War II), played in the London Fire Brigade Orchestra. Later worked with Alfie Gray, Harry Roy, Phil Cardew, Mantovani, etc., before concentrating on freelance work. Took part in New Paul Whiteman Orchestra in 1974. Continued to freelance successfully until retiring in 1985.

HURT, 'Pete' Peter Stuart
saxes/clarinet/arranger/composer

Born: Nottingham, 5 January 1950

Studied clarinet and piano at Northern School of Music in Manchester (1968–71). Self-taught saxophonist and arranger. Played gigs with local bands in the Nottingham area. Moved to London in 1971 and shortly afterwards did first professional work with Graham Collier on alto sax. Took up tenor sax in 1974. Formed own Lighthouse Quartet (1975), which thrived throughout the 1970s. Wrote for own larger line-up and also wrote arrangements regularly for the BBC Radio Big Band. Reactivated own quartet in 1983, subsequently began regular musical association with George Russell and began long series of annual tours in Europe with Russell's Orchestra. Also toured Europe and recorded with Carla Bley. Worked often with Loose Tubes during the 1980s. With Andy Sheppard's Big Band, touring and recording, from 1989 through to the mid-1990s, also part of the London Jazz Orchestra, and leading own successful quartet.

HUTCHINSON, 'Jiver' Leslie George
trumpet/vocals

Born: Kingston, Jamaica, West Indies, 16 March 1906
Died: East Anglia, 22 November 1959

Father of singer Elaine Delmar. Played in West Indies Regiment Band and with Bertie King before moving to Britain in November 1935. Worked with Happy Blake at the Cuba Club, the Cabin Club and on stage tour (early 1936), before working briefly in Leslie Thompson's Emperors of Jazz, the forerunner of Ken Johnson's Band. With Johnson from April 1936 debut. With Jack Davies (early 1938), Al Craig (1938), Fela Sowande (late 1938 to October 1939). Played occasional dates with Ken Johnson in 1938, then rejoined Johnson in summer of 1939, also led own band at Florida Club, London (late 1939). With Sid Phillips (1941–2), also worked with Ambrose (1941) and with Maurice Burman (1942). With Geraldo (1943–4), including tour of the Middle East, also worked with Lew Stone. Formed own band in March 1944, led this until late 1949, including tours of India, Scandinavia, Holland, Czechoslovakia, Belgium, etc. Rejoined Geraldo in January 1950 and worked mainly with him until 1954, also with Geoff Love (1951). Led own group, accompanied Mary Lou Williams (late 1952), worked with George Fierstone (1953). Toured with *New York to New Orleans* show (1954), then rejoined Geraldo from May 1954 to October 1956. Led own Ebony Knights (1955), then formed new band (1956). Continued to lead own band, also acted as musical director for *Simply Heavenly* show (1958). Suffered fatal injuries in a band bus crash in Norfolk.

HUTTON, 'Mick' Michael
double bass/piano

Born: Chester, Cheshire, 5 June 1956

Played piano during schooldays, self-taught on bass. Did various work (including being road-manager for Pacific Eardrum), then worked as a train driver before turning professional in spring of 1981. Gigged with Alvin Roy and various bands, also with Martin Speake and Simon Purcell. During the 1980s worked with Django Bates, in Tim Whitehead's Borderline, with Gordon Beck, Stan Sulzmann, Alan Skidmore, Kenny Wheeler, Tommy Smith, John Taylor, Ian Ballamy. During the 1980s began long musical associations with Chris Biscoe, with Steve and Julian Argüelles, and regularly deputized in Humphrey Lyttelton's Band over a ten year period. Led own Straight Face in the early 1990s, subsequently formed own Madhouse quartet (1995), but continues to freelance with various line-ups, including work with Dave Cliff-Geoff Simkins group (1996).

HUXLEY, George Born: Portsmouth, Hampshire, 17 June 1935
clarinet/soprano and alto saxes

Family moved to the Midlands when George was an infant. Took a few clarinet lessons at school, but then gave up until hearing Humphrey Lyttelton's Band. Sat in at the Midland Jazz Club, then joined Pete Rollason's New Orleans Jazzmen. Gigged with many bands in the Midlands then regularly led own band. Over forty years later his All Star Jazz Band continues to play club gigs, concerts and festival dates. He also leads a Hot Five. Has accompanied various American visiting jazzmen and recorded for American label.

HYLTON, 'Jack' Jackson Born: Great Lever, nr Bolton, Lancashire, 2 July 1892
piano Died: London, 29 January 1965

His wife Ennis, née Parkes (1895–1957), led her own band during the 1930s. His sister was vocaliste Dolly Elsie. Billed as the Singing Millboy, he sang and danced in public from the age of seven, appearing in pierrot shows, pantomimes, etc. Learned piano and moved to London in 1913, played piano and organ in a Stoke Newington cinema. Served in Army during World War I. After demobilization formed concert part for season at Bognor Regis (1919). Was second pianist and arranger for septet at Queen's Roof Gardens. Took over leadership of Queen's Dance Orchestra in 1921, which, from December 1922, was billed as Jack Hylton and his Orchestra. The band soon commenced widespread touring and also played at the Grafton Galleries, the Piccadilly Hotel, etc., and began broadcasting in 1926. Made the first of several tours of Europe in 1927. Continued to lead with great success (including film and stage appearances) throughout the 1930s, then from 1940 active as a theatrical agent and impresario. In 1935 and 1936 he fronted a band in the USA, working with a nucleus of performers that he took with him from Britain (pianist Alec Templeton, arranger Billy Ternent, singer Pat O'Malley), together with various American musicians. The Jack Hylton Archive is housed in the University of Lancaster.

I

ILES, Nikki Anne (née BURNHAM) Born: Dunstable, Bedfordshire,
piano/clarinet/accordion/arranger/composer 16 September 1963

Married to trumpeter Richard Iles. Studied piano and clarinet at Royal Academy of Music, Junior Exhibitioner (1974–81). Jazz studies with Brian Layton at City of Leeds College of Music and with Bob Cornford. First professional gig with Bobby Wellins, subsequently accompanied Steve Argüelles, Iain Ballamy, Guy Barker, Alan Barnes, Claire Martin, Dick Pearce, Stan Sulzmann, Ricky Woodyard, etc., and toured with Don Weller, Dick Morrissey, Jim Mullen, Pete King, Gerard Presencer, etc. During the 1990s was regularly with the Sylvan Richardson Group, Mick

Hutton's Straight Face, the Creative Jazz Orchestra, Bobby Wellins Quintet, Phil Bancroft's Octet, Mike Walker's Quartet, Emanon and own band (the Architects). Continues to work as freelance accompanist. Teaches regularly at Leeds College of Music, Leeds University and at Glamorgan Summer School. Increasingly active as a composer, whose commissions include a work to celebrate a century of women in jazz, entitled *The Printmakers*, which was performed by the Creative Jazz Orchestra on tour (1995).

IMPEY, Norman
tenor sax/clarinet/flute/bass clarinet/arranger

Born: Ilford, Essex, 29 July 1911
Died: Surrey, 30 March 1977

Formed own band while still at school, subsequently joined the Astor Five which won a *Rhythm* magazine contest in 1928. First professional work with drummer Reg Spinelli (1929). With Tommy Kinsman (1931), Leslie 'Hutch' Hutchinson (spring 1932), saxophonist Jack Shields (autumn 1932). With violinist Joe Burns (1933), Billy Mason (1934), led own band (1934), then worked with Eddie Carroll (1934–5). During the 1930s also worked with Jack Harris, Debroy Somers, Hugo Rignold, Sydney Lipton, etc. With Lew Stone (1940), then worked with Joe Loss (1940–1) prior to joining RAF and playing in RAF Central Band from 1942. After demobilization worked with Chappie D'Amato's Band and with Ted Heath before becoming a long-time member of the Skyrockets from 1946. After the Skyrockets disbanded, worked with the BBC Light Orchestra and with Billy Cotton. During the 1970s taught flute and clarinet in the Merton Borough Schools and coached Youth Orchestras.

IND, Peter Vincent
double bass/composer

Born: Middlesex, 20 July 1928

Violin from age of eight, then took up piano and played local gigs. Studied at Trinity College, Cambridge, continued to play gigs on piano then began doubling on piano and double bass. From 1947 specialized on bass and studied with James Merret Sr. Gigged in Windsor area, then played Mecca Dance Hall residency before joining Joe Saye Trio (spring to summer 1949). With Freddie Barratt's Band. Briefly with Tommy Sampson before joining Frank Abbot's Band on liner *Queen Mary* (1949). Played on many transatlantic voyages (1949–51), then worked in Britain with Kenny Baker (spring 1951) before emigrating to the USA in April 1951. During the 1950s worked with many American jazz stars including Lennie Tristano and Lee Konitz, Roy Eldridge and Coleman Hawkins. From 1957 ran own recording studio (and record label Wave). Returned to Britain in late 1961, worked with John Dankworth and Ronnie Scott, then freelanced before returning to New York in January 1963. Worked mainly in California (1963–6), often played unaccompanied concerts, also toured with Lee Konitz, Warne Marsh, etc. Returned to Britain in 1966. In Phil Seamen's Quartet (late 1966), then active as freelance and teacher. Worked with Lee Konitz, Warne Marsh and Lennie Tristano in Britain. Lived mainly in Wales during the early 1970s, then moved back to London. Led own sextet, freelanced and organized own recording studio. Played series of duos with guitarist Louis Stewart (1975–8), also took part in Great Jazz Solos Revisited (1978). Active freelance through to the 1990s, ran own jazz club the Bass Clef in London from September 1984 through to early 1990s. Has written a book on cosmology.

INGHAM, Keith Christopher
piano/arranger

Born: London, 5 February 1938

Father was a church organist. Played piano from age of ten, but did not treat the enterprise seriously until ten years later. Oxford graduate in languages, played in Oxford with fellow students, but also journeyed to London to gig with Dick Williams' band. Army service included posting to Hong Kong. In Alan Littlejohns' band from 1960, worked with Littlejohns and with Dick Williams throughout the 1960s, also gigged with Wally Fawkes, Bruce Turner and Sandy Brown. Professional night club residency in 1964, then chose to play semi-professionally while working for an airline company in London. Featured with visiting American musicians at London's Jazz Expo 1969. Accompanied various visiting Americans during the 1970s. Formed duo with singer Susannah McCorkle in 1973 and worked with her in London and New York. Played regularly in Ron Russell's Band during the 1970s (including dates in Prague, 1974). Occasionally with Lennie Hastings, Dick Sudhalter and George Melly in the 1970s. Moved to the USA in November 1977, played long hotel residency, also worked with many famous jazz musicians including Benny Goodman. Toured Europe with the World's Greatest Jazz Band, and with Ed Polcer's Band. Worked with various singers including Susannah McCorkle, Maxine Sullivan, Peggy Lee, etc. and recorded with own bands. Leading own New York Nine (1996).

ISAACS, 'Ike' Isaac
guitar

Born: Rangoon, Burma, 1 December 1919
Died: Sydney, Australia, 11 January 1996

Brother Maurice played violin, brother Saul the guitar. Ike's nephew Mark is a pianist and composer. Ike played piano before taking up guitar. Gained degree in chemistry before becoming a professional musician. Played in the Jive Boys in Burma, then moved to India during World War II. Worked in a munitions factory but did SEAC radio work and led own nine-piece band at Green's Hotel in Deradun, before moving to Britain in late 1946. Worked with Leslie Douglas (late 1946), did freelance radio work including sessions with Billy Munn and Ted Heath. Briefly with Victor Feldman (June 1948), then freelanced with many line-ups. Worked with Eddie Carroll's Band in Lugano, Switzerland (September 1951). Joined Cyril Stapleton's newly formed BBC Show Band in autumn 1952. With Reg Wale's Sextet (1955). Also played regularly on BBC Radio's *Guitar Club* from 1955 until 1958. Led own groups, which later achieved big selling records. Often worked with Diz Disley and through Disley joined Stephane Grappelli for several years from the mid-1970s (including tours of Australia and the USA). With violinist Johnny Franks (1977), in duos with Martin Taylor, and with Digby Fairweather in Velvet during the 1970s. Moved to Australia in 1981, taught at the Sydney School of Guitar (later the Australian Institute of Music) until 1992. Visited Britain in the 1990s. Wrote many articles and various instruction books on the guitar.

J

JACKSON, Alan Richard Born: Mottingham, South London, 5 January 1940
drums

Worked as a graphic designer before taking up drums at 21. Played in Sounds Five, led by tenor saxophonist Milton James, then began long musical association with Mike Westbrook during the early 1960s. During the 1960s also worked in John Surman's Trio, with Keith Tippett, the New Jazz Orchestra and Howard Riley. Backed various visiting American musicians at Ronnie Scott's Club, London, during the 1970s, including Ben Webster, Eddie Harris, etc. During the early 1970s worked with the John Warren Big Band, John Surman-Mike Osborne Workshop, Alan Cohen and led own Kincade. During the latter part of the 1970s with Dick Morrissey-Terry Smith, the Bob Barter Trio, Marion Montgomery and Humphrey Lyttelton. During the 1980s and 1990s did extensive freelancing in various line-ups, regularly in Dave Green's Fingers (doubling alto sax), with the Pasadena Roof Orchestra and in Michael Garrick's Trio. From 1983 also worked in re-formed version of Kincade. Is active as a peripatetic teacher, was previously a tutor at Wavendon Summer School but now teaches at the Royal Academy of Music as part of the Jazz Academy course (1996).

JACKSON, Jack Born: Barnsley, Yorkshire, 20 February 1906
trumpet Died: Hertfordshire, 14 January 1978

Father was a conductor of brass bands. The family moved to Kent during Jack's childhood where his father led the Callender's Cable Works Band. Began on cornet at eight, school in Gravesend, played in brass bands from eleven. Studied with John Solomon at the Royal Academy of Music (with violin as second instrument). First professional work (doubling violin and cello) on Cunard liner *Samaria* (transatlantic and Mediterranean voyages). Returned to Britain, worked with Guy's Mexican Band, toured with John Grey and in show *Stage Struck*. In Bill Shenkman's Buffalo Band in Birmingham and London, then (still doubling violin and cello) led Metropole Dance Band in Ashford, Kent. To South Africa with Bert Ralton in September 1926. Worked with Bill Barton's Band after Ralton's death (January 1927), then returned to England in June 1927. Freelanced in London (gigged with Ambrose), then joined Jack Hylton from August 1927 until November 1929, by this time specializing on trumpet. Briefly with Howard Jacobs, then year with Percival Mackey from January 1930. With Arthur Lally (January to April 1931), Jack Payne (April 1931 to February 1933). Formed own band, which opened at the Dorchester Hotel, London, in August 1933. Played residencies there until April 1939 (the band featured American singer Alberta Hunter in 1934–5). Toured with own band in summer of 1939, then led at the May Fair Hotel, London, from 1940 until 1944. Toured with own show *Mayfair Merry Go Round* (1946), then concentrated on working as an agent (with Foster's Agency). Resumed leading at Churchill's and at the Potomac until becoming compere of BBC Radio's *Band Parade* in 1947. Subsequently became successful disc jockey on *Record Round Up* and on *Housewives' Choice*, but continued to play trumpet on jazz programmes and recording sessions. Solo variety act in the 1950s, continued to compere radio and television shows. Moved to Tenerife in 1962, producing his radio shows from there, also sat in with bands in Puerto Della Cruz. Returned to England in 1973, did final radio series in 1975.

JACOBSEN, 'Jock'　　　　　　　　　　　　　　　Born: London, January 1905
drums　　　　　　　　　　　　　　　　　　　　　　　　　Deceased

His brother Sidney was a guitarist who worked with Teddy Joyce, Lew Stone, the RAF Fighter Command Band, the Skyrockets, etc. Jock began drumming in his early teens and played in the Alabama Band in London during the early 1920s. He then spent several years in a band led by Archie Alexander. With Jay Whidden (1929–31), Sydney Lipton (1932–4). With Lew Stone from September 1934 until joining Teddy Joyce in November 1935. Many freelance recordings. In Reg Leopold's Orchestra (spring 1936), then rejoined Lew Stone from 1937 until joining the RAF in late 1941 (briefly with Maurice Winnick in 1940). Played in RAF Fighter Command Band before being invalided out of the service in early 1943. With Chappie D'Amato (1943), Harry Lewis (1943), then freelanced for several years before becoming a successful agent in partnership with trumpeter Norman Payne (J.P. Productions). He later managed various artistes including Max Bygraves.

JACOBSEN, 'Pete' Peter Paul George　　　　Born: Newcastle upon Tyne, 16 May 1950
piano

Began learning piano at six, studied at Worcester School for the Blind for seven years. Worked in Newcastle and Gateshead with own trio, then moved to London in 1969, studied at the Royal Academy of Music until 1972, played gigs and freelanced. During the 1970s worked with Barbara Thompson, Don Weller's Major Surgery, Gary Boyle, Chris Biscoe, etc. Freelanced extensively and began musical association with Bobby Wellins in the late 1970s, which continues through the 1990s. Worked in Dick Morrissey-Jim Mullen group during the 1980s, and toured with Robin Kenyatta, Alan Skidmore, Gary Boyle, Eberhard Weber, etc. Accompanied various American musicians, including recordings with Jimmy Knepper. In the 1990s worked with Chris Biscoe, with reed-player Charlie Hearnshaw, in Tim Whitehead's Quartet and with own trio.

JAMES, Roy (Roy James UNDERWOOD)　　　Born: Enfield, Middlesex, 15 August 1939
guitar/banjo

Ukulele at nine, guitar at fifteen. Played in local skiffle group, then began doubling on banjo and played in Bourbon Street Ramblers. Gigged with various bands, then joined Acker Bilk from 1958 until spring 1964. Did agency work and gigged with Charlie Galbraith (1964) and occasionally deputized in Terry Lightfoot's Band before spending eight years mainly with Bob Wallis. Regularly with Gene Allen Band and with Alan Littlejohns for thirteen year residency at the 100 Club, London, also often with George Webb's Band. Extensive freelancing in the 1980s, which included regular work in Geoff Downs' Crescent City Band. Long spell with Ken Sims from the late 1980s into the mid-1990s.

JAZZ WARRIORS

In 1985 the London-based Abibi Jazz Arts encouraged the idea of giving young black musicians the chance to blow jazz collectively. The result was the gathering together of the Jazz Warriors. The group, which made its debut at the Fridge in Brixton, South London, in January 1986, proved to be the launching pad for the stellar talents of a number of important jazz musicians including Courtney Pine, Orphy Robinson, Tony Remy, Philip Bent and Steve Williamson. Participation and advice came from Gary Crosby, Ray Carless, Julian Joseph, Gail Thompson and Harold Beckett (who was for a time the group's principal arranger). Among those who shared in this important experience were Cheryl Alleyne, Claude Deppa (trumpet), Brian Edwards (alto sax), Andy Grappy (trumpet and tuba), Ike Leo (bass), Kevin Robinson (trumpet), Roland Sutherland (flute), Fayyaz Virti (trombone), Cleveland Watkiss (vocals), Trevor Watkiss (keyboards) and Jason Yarde (alto sax). The enterprise continued into the early 1990s but by then most of the original members had moved on to further successes. In 1996, bassist Gary Crosby, leader of Nu Troop, was encouraging plans for a Young Jazz Warriors group to develop in the Bristol area.

JENKINS, 'Billy' Charles William
guitar/composer
Born: Bromley, Kent, 5 July 1956

Violin and piano from the age of seven, guitar at twelve. Chorister in the Bromley Parish Church Choir. Became a professional musician at fourteen. Played with various groups including Porkie, and That's My Boy. Worked and toured with Burlesque from 1972 until 1977. Year's sabbatical, spent motor cycling (1978). Co-led Trimmer and Jenkins from 1979 to 1982, during this period often worked alongside the *Comic Strip* (Rik Mayall, Alexei Sayle, etc.). Toured Europe with Ginger Baker in 1981. Formed the Voice of God Collective in 1981, which has continued into 1996 (currently featuring Iain Ballamy on saxophone, Martin France on drums, Steve Watts on bass, Dave Ramm on keyboards, and often Huw Warren on piano). Widespread international concert and festival work with this group and regular collaborations with the four piece Fun Horns of Berlin from 1993 into 1996. Since 1981, Jenkins has produced a succession of albums featuring his work on various labels (Plymouth Sounds, VOTP, Babel, etc.). From 1983 until 1993 ran the Woodwharf Studios in Greenwich. He is also a member of the Shakedown Club (with Steven Noble on percussion and Roberto Bellatella on double bass) and part of Blue Moon in a Function Room, a quartet led by Steve Argüelles.

JENKINS, Karl (William PAMP)
oboe/saxes/keyboards/composer/arranger
Born: Swansea, Glamorgan, 17 February 1944

Piano at six, oboe at thirteen. Played in National Youth Orchestra of Wales. Studied music at University College, Cardiff, and co-led (with Roger Parker) the Cardiff University Jazz Quintet (1965). Became LRAM after studies at the Royal Academy of Music. Worked with Graham Collier (1967–9), in Ronnie Scott's Big Band (summer 1969), in Ian Carr's Nucleus (1969–72). Led own band in 1972. Mainly with Soft Machine from 1972 until 1981, but also worked with Keith Tippett's Centipede, the London Composers' Jazz Orchestra and the Spontaneous Music Ensemble during the 1970s. Part of Soft Machine reunions in the 1980s but mainly active during the 1990s as a composer and arranger for films, television, etc.

JENNINGS, 'Al' Gerald
double bass/guitar

Born: Trinidad, West Indies, c.1896
Died: 1980

Served in Royal Navy during World War I, then settled in Britain. During the 1920s and 1930s led own bands throughout Europe and North Africa. Co-led band with pianist George Clapham in London during the late 1920s, later led own band at Brighton and at the Hammersmith Palais, London. Worked with Joe Appleton (1937) then played in house band at the Kit Cat Club, London (1940). Volunteered for Royal Navy early in World War II and served in the Air-Sea Rescue Unit, then led own Naval Band before joining the Blue Mariners from 1942–5 (including tour of France in late 1944). Returned to Trinidad after World War II and formed own All Star Caribbean Orchestra which arrived in England in late 1945, and worked in England and France in 1946. Continued to lead and act as master-of-ceremonies in Europe then retired from full time music.

JOHNSON 'Snake Hips' Ken
(Kenrick Reginald HUYMANS)
dancer/singer

Born: Georgetown,
British Guiana (now Guyana), 1914
Died: London, 8 March 1941

After attending Queen's College in Georgetown, he studied in England at Sir William Borlase School in Marlow, Buckinghamshire, from 1929 until 1931 (where he occasionally played the violin). He toyed with the idea of becoming a doctor of medicine but instead took up tap-dancing (coached by American, Clarence 'Buddy' Bradley). He worked briefly as a dancer (appearing in the 1934 film *Oh Daddy*). He visited the USA in 1935 and toured the West Indies before returning to Britain where he was featured with Leslie Thompson's Jamaica Emperors (1936). He soon took over the leadership of the band, which toured the variety halls and fulfilled night club residencies including a long stay at the Florida Club, London. After appearing at Willerby's Club, London, the band began a residency at the Café de Paris, London, in late 1939 and remained there until Johnson was killed by a bomb during a World War II air raid.

JONES, 'Billy' William
piano

Born: London, 1892
Died: Romford, Essex, 5 March 1972

Worked in Murray Pilcher's Ragtime Sextette and in Conrad's Novelty Minstrels before leading own quartet at Martan's Club, London. Joined the Original Dixieland Jazz Band (October 1919) for the American band's engagement at the Hammersmith Palais, London. Subsequently worked at Hammersmith Palais with Mitchell's Syncopated Orchestra, which later toured as the Happy Six (led by violinist Teddy Sinclair). Worked at Birmingham Palais with the Albany Five (1921). Played club dates at Kate Meyrick's '43' Club, London, and at the Clover and Manhattan clubs, before leading own band in Brighton (at the Metropole Hotel and at the Astor Club). Retired from music and temporarily became a bookmaker. Led own dixieland-style band in 1936. Played occasional engagements in the late 1930s and performed at own public house, Jacob's Well, in Shoreditch, London. After this hostelry was bombed in 1942, he became the landlord of the Cross Keys in Chelsea and began playing regularly again. He was featured in *The Cavalcade of Jazz* in 1946 and made guest appearances at jazz concerts and clubs. He ran his own club in Maidenhead during the early 1950s, then retired to Romford, Essex.

JONES, 'Dave'
clarinet/baritone sax

Born: Ilminster, Somerset, 22 February 1932

Family moved to Leyton, London, during the early 1940s. Began on trumpet at fourteen then switched to clarinet. First paid gig with Kenny Wallbank's Dixielanders (1948). With Johnny Rowden's Band and Len Beadle's Imperial Jazz Band, then worked with Charlie Galbraith during the early 1950s. With Bobby Mickleburgh (1954–5), also briefly in Norman Cave's Band. With Kenny Ball (1956–7) and became part of new band organized by Kenny Ball in September 1958. Remained with Kenny Ball until March 1967 (but was absent for a month's booking in Germany when his place was taken by Alan Cater). After leaving Kenny Ball, freelanced with various jazz groups and worked with Freddy Randall. Spent almost three years on baritone sax with the Kinks (alongside Mike Cotton and John Beecham) including tour of USA. Led own quartet during the 1970s, also did Mediterranean cruises with Bill Niles and co-led a band with Colin Smith that accompanied various visiting Americans, including Wild Bill Davison, Peanuts Hucko, etc. Subsequently worked with Gerry Salisbury, George Webb, Charlie Galbraith, Pat Mason, Tony Raine, Bill Niles, Alan Littlejohns, etc., and often with Ron Russell's Band and with the Gene Allen Jazzmen through the 1970s and 1980s (also made two trips to Vancouver, Canada with Hugh Rainey). With Laurie Chescoe's Good Time Jazz from August 1990 through the 1990s.

JONES, 'Dill' Dillwyn Owen
piano

Born: Newcastle Emlyn, South Wales, 19 August 1923
Died: New York, 22 June 1984

Mother was a pianist. Began playing piano at seven. Studied at Llandovery College, then became a bank clerk. Served in Royal Navy from April 1942 until April 1946 (including duties in the Far East), while stationed at Portsmouth became inspired by local pianist Bill Cole. After demobilization again worked in bank before moving to London where he enrolled at Trinity College of Music and began playing London gigs, occasionally in the Russell-Wickham Six (1946). Turned professional in 1947, worked with Duncan Whyte (1947). To Nice Festival with Derek Neville's Band (February 1948). Joined Vic Lewis in October 1948. With Harry Parry from October 1949 until May 1950, with Kathy Stobart from May to August 1950. Worked on liner *Queen Mary* 1950–1, also briefly with Kenny Graham, Dick Denny, Geoff Love's Eight, Frank Weir and violinist Raymonde's Orchestra. With Paul Adam from January 1952, joined Harry Hayes in October 1952. With Tony Kinsey's Trio (1953), also worked in Jazz Today Unit. Left Kinsey to work in Tommy Whittle's Quintet from April 1954 until September 1956. Led own Trio for *Jazz Cavalcade* tour (November 1956). Part of all-star band accompanying Louis Armstrong in London (December 1956). Own trio played various clubs, then gained residency at London's Marquee Club in January 1958. Led own Trio 1959–61 and played freelance dates. With Bert Courtley's Sextet (1961), and again led own Trio, then emigrated to the USA in October 1961. Worked in America with the Dukes of Dixieland, with Jimmy McPartland, Gene Krupa, Bob Wilber, etc. During the years 1969 until 1973 was part of the JPJ Quartet (with Budd Johnson, Bill Pemberton and Oliver Jackson), then freelanced successfully, often working in the Harlem Blues and Jazz Band. Made several playing visits to Britain, the first of which was in 1963, the last in 1983. During return trips to Wales he guested with a long-time musical colleague Wynn Lodwich.

JOSEPH, Julian
piano/clarinet/drums/composer/arranger/vocals

Born: Hammersmith,
London, 11 May 1966

His brother John plays trumpet, his brother James (who is Julian's lawyer and manager) occasionally plays drums. Their father sang with a blue beat band. Private piano lessons from age of five, also studied at Spencer Park Comprehensive School, Trinity Road, Wandsworth, where he took drum lessons from Trevor Tomkins. Took part in Ian Carr's Jazz Workshops and thus became part of the London Fusion Orchestra. Organized own rehearsal group, which included Courtney Pine, Paul Hunt, Philip Bent and James Joseph (drums) whose place was taken by Mark Mondesir. Studied music at Richmond-upon-Thames College and at the suggestion of American tutor, Tom Hartman, successfully applied for scholarship (1985) to Berklee College, USA (having been enthusiastically recommended by Ian Carr and pianist Mulgrew Miller). After a year at Berklee, he began working with saxist Branford Marsalis and made his debut at a televised concert in Jacksonville, Florida, in front of 30,000 people. Later toured USA and Canada with Branford Marsalis. Formed Berklee Jazz Ensemble which later adopted the name No Corporate Rubbish featuring Delfeayo Marsalas on trombone, Roy Hartford (trumpet), Tim Owens (vocals), (and won many inter-collegiate prizes). During his period of study at Berklee, Julian usually made five trips a year back to Britain, where he worked with Courtney Pine, with Steve Williamson, etc. He toured Japan and Australia with Courtney Pine. At Berklee he gained a Double Major, in composition and musical synthesis, and minored in performance. He moved back to London in 1990 and led own quartet (which featured saxophonist Jean Toussaint). Composed film score for *A Tale of a Vampire* (1992). Undertook classical concerts. Featured with BBC Scottish Symphony Orchestra (1993), and with the Royal Philharmonic Concert Orchestra (1994). Worked with George Coleman, and with Eddie Daniels and Johnny Griffin at the Wigmore Hall, London, toured with Chico and Von Freeman. Toured Europe, USA, Australia, India and the Caribbean with own group. In 1996, he divided his time between playing solo piano, leading own trio, and quartet (featuring saxist Peter King), leading his Forum (eight piece group), his Big Band of eighteen pieces and his Orchestra of twenty-two pieces and successfully composing for all his various line-ups and for special commissions.

JOWETT, Les
trumpet

Born: Bradford, Yorkshire, 1925
Died: Brighton, Sussex, 1960

Played cornet in a Bradford brass band, then served in the Royal Navy. After demobilization took Economics degree at Cambridge and played in University band the Woodchoppers. Moved to London to study at the London School of Economics and gigged with Ken Sykora and with Fred Perry, then worked in the Cy Laurie Four (1951–2). Joined George Webb briefly in spring of 1952, then moved to Brighton, led own band there and gigged with piano-accordionist Don Sollash. Handed over leadership of his own band to clarinettist Stuart Emsley but remained to work with this line-up, the newly-named Vanguard Jazzmen, until late 1957. Again led own band, then moved to Hatfield in early 1960. Returned to Brighton to spend the final months of his life there. Died of cancer.

JOYCE, Teddy (Edmund John CUTHBERTSON)
violin/cello/saxes

Born: Toronto, Canada, 1907
Died: Glasgow, Scotland, 10 February 1941

Father was Scottish. Born in Canada but often billed as being from the USA. His brother Taylor Joyce played guitar. Studied music in Toronto and in Detroit, USA. First professional work with Frank Silver's Band, then became a master of ceremonies in St Louis, Pittsburgh and Hollywood, before moving to London in 1934. Formed own band, disbanded and formed an all-girl band, Teddy Joyce's Girl Friends, and a young musicians' band, Teddy Joyce's Juveniles. Overcame bankruptcy and formed successful big band in the late 1930s which was playing at the Playhouse in Glasgow at the time of his fatal illness.

K

KAHN, Alfie
saxes/clarinet/flute/piano/harmonica

Born: 18 February 1914
Died: Skegness, Lincolnshire, 16 February 1996

His brother Harry played piano with Harry Roy for some years, another brother, Dave, played trumpet. Alfie toured Russia soon after leaving school. He returned to London and later worked with Lou Preager (1935). With Carl Tauber, Syd Roy's Lyricals, Val Rosing (1936). With Gerry Moore at the Palm Beach Club, London (1937). With Teddy Foster (1937), Harry Roy's Lyricals (1937), with Harry Roy's Band in Madeira (1938). Recorded with Fats Waller in London (August 1938). With Sid Millward (1938–9 and again in 1940). Recorded on harmonica with George Shearing (January 1939). Broadcast with Ken Johnson (1939), worked with Jack Harris from October 1939. Served as an air-gunner in the RAF during World War II, also led own service sextet. After demobilization again worked with Harry Roy, also with 'Jiver' Hutchinson. With Harold Collins' Theatre Orchestra (1947–8), also worked on liner *Queen Mary* in Bobby Kevin's Band (November 1947 to January 1948). Again with Harry Roy (1949–51). With Geoff Love, Harry Gold and Stanley Barnett (1951). With the Chelsea Palace Orchestra (1952). Worked for four months in brother Dave's band on liner *Caronia* (1952). Spent several years working mainly with George Fierstone's Band from 1954 (including summer seasons). Regularly taught sax and woodwinds. Extensive freelance work, increasingly on harmonica, which he played on film soundtracks and in television dramas, etc. He retired to Skegness in the mid-1980s.

KARAN, Chris
drums

Born: Melbourne, Australia, 14 October 1939

Played in night clubs in Melbourne from age of sixteen. Worked with alto saxophonist Frank Smith and with Frank Thornton, then settled in Sydney (1959), worked at the Rex Hotel with bassist Barry Dillon. Became part of the Three Out Trio (with bassist Freddy Logan and pianist Mike Knock), which left Australia to play dates in England in June 1961. Karan remained in London and joined the Dudley Moore Trio in 1962. It was the beginning of a long musical association with Dudley Moore, one that has continued into the 1990s. When Moore originally went to the USA, Karan worked with the Brian Lemon Trio (1963). Accompanied numerous visiting American musicians at Ronnie Scott's Club and at the Bull's Head, Barnes. Regularly with Roy Budd's Trio from the mid-1960s through to the late 1980s. During this period also spent eight years with Harry Stoneham's Band on BBC television. Worked with Stephane Grappelli briefly in 1972, also did widespread international touring with Caterina Valente. Subsequently did prolific freelance work with Oscar Peterson, George Shearing, Alan Haven, Billy Eckstine, Laurie Holloway, etc. Toured with Cleo Laine, the Swingle Singers, Dusty Springfield, etc. Continued with extensive freelance schedule through the 1990s, also part of Spectrum and leading own group. Has studied tabla with Alla Rakha and continues to be involved in Latin-American and Brazilian music, regularly contributing to various film scores.

KATZ, Dick
piano

Born: Hanover, Germany, 19 July 1916
Died: London, 30 March 1981

Piano from the age of five. Lived in Germany until 1933, then moved with his family to Holland. Worked as a technician with a recording company but also played piano regularly and worked with various bands including the Moochers and with Willie Lewis. Moved to England and joined Carlo Krahmer, then worked with Cyril Blake (early 1942), before deputizing (for Tommy Pollard) in Harry Parry's Sextet (summer 1942). Did war work in London, also worked with Cab Kaye (1944). Service in RAF. Played in Vic Lewis-Jack Parnell Jazzmen. Worked with Lauderic Caton's Trio at the Caribbean Club, London, also led own trio at the same venue (1946). Left Caton in September 1947 to work briefly with Buddy Featherstonhaugh, then rejoined Caribbean Trio which formed the basis of Ray Ellington's Quartet (December 1947). Remained with Ray Ellington until spring of 1959, then worked in a theatrical agency, later becoming personal manager for various artistes. Occasionally played gigs in the 1960s, and recorded with Bud Freeman in London (November 1966). Was married to singer Valerie Masters.

KAYE, 'Cab' (Augustus Kwamlah Quaye)
vocals/piano/drums/guitar

Born: London, 3 September 1921

Cab's father, Caleb Jonas Quaye (born in Africa) was a professional drummer who worked under the name of Mope Desmond; he died in a railway accident at Blisworth, Northamptonshire, in January 1922. Cab's children Caleb Jr (guitar) and Teresa 'Terri' (conga drums and vocals) both became professional musicians. Cab worked with Billy Cotton's band as a vocalist and speciality act in 1936 and 1937, then joined Doug Swallow's band in April 1937. Toured with Hal Swain's band in summer of 1937, with Alan Green's band in Hastings (September 1937), then worked for a long spell in Ivor Kirchin's band until late 1940. Briefly with Ken Johnson, then joined the Merchant Navy, sailed to South America in 1941. During leave in London worked with Don Marino Barretto then resumed Merchant Navy career until being invalided out in 1942. Worked briefly with Harry Parry (January 1943), with Princes of Rhythm (February to April 1943). Own band at the Orchard Club, London, from April 1943 until October 1944. Worked in India with Leslie 'Jiver' Hutchinson's band, then played solo residencies in Belgium (1946–7). Moved back to Britain in late 1947, sang with Tito Burns in 1948, then formed own Ministers of Swing for residency in West Bromwich (October to November). Briefly with Paul Fenoulhet's Orchestra in

1949, then worked mainly in Holland, France and Germany during years 1950 to 1956, occasionally returning to Britain to lead own band for various residencies, also did solo work in shows including a tour of Scotland in *Memories of Jolson* (November 1953). Moved back to Britain and worked with Eric Delaney for five months in 1957. Played solo residencies, then worked often with Humphrey Lyttelton (1959–60), also led own band. In August 1961 took up post in Ghana as a Government Entertainments Director, remained in Africa (mainly Ghana and Nigeria) for much of 1960s, but also played residencies in Long Island, USA, during the mid-1960s. Moved back to Britain in late 1970, played various club residencies in London and led own quartet, but worked often in various European countries, playing residencies in Switzerland, Holland, etc. through the 1970s. Subsequently featured at Amsterdam piano bar for long residency during the 1980s, returned to London occasionally and played gigs there in the early 1980s, but mainly active on the Continent through to the 1990s.

KEANE, 'Shake' Ellsworth McGranahan
trumpet/flugelhorn

Born: St Vincent, West Indies, 30 May 1927
Died: Oslo, Norway, 10 November 1997

One of a family of seven, all of whom were taught music by their father. Became a teacher in St Vincent, then moved to London in 1952 to study literature at London University. Gigged with night club bands and worked with Fitzroy Coleman, then, in the late 1950s worked in Harry White's Jazz-Latin group and toured in Mike McKenzie's Harlem All Stars. Recorded with calypso artist Lord Kitchener. With Jack Sharpe's Sextet (1960), then joined Joe Harriott's Quintet in 1960. Took year's leave from Harriott to complete studies at London School of Economics, then rejoined in 1962 for a further three years, also worked with Michael Garrick (1963–5). Worked in Germany from the mid-1960s, mainly with Kurt Edelhagen, but also with Kenny Clarke-Francy Boland Big Band and with Peter Trunk. Returned to St Vincent in the 1970s and took up government post, then moved to New York in 1980. Returned to Britain to fulfil autumn 1989 engagements with the Joe Harriott Memorial Quintet (with Martin Hathaway on alto sax).

KEIR, 'Dave' David
multi-instrumentalist

Born: Dunfermline, Fife, Scotland, 9 April 1928

Began on cornet at ten, trumpet and trombone from fourteen. Led own band, then played in Jock Turner's Jazz Band. With Archie Semple's band, took over this group when Semple joined Mick Mulligan in 1952, thus led Nova Scotia Jazz Band until moving to London in January 1953 to join Mick Mulligan (first on trombone) then on clarinet from October 1953 until early 1954. Led own band on alto sax and clarinet, also worked with Sid Phillips, Bobby Mickleburgh, Alex Welsh and Lennie Hastings before joining Freddy Randall from November 1954 until summer of 1955. Again worked with Mick Mulligan from summer of 1955 until January 1956. Led own band which toured Scotland, England and Germany (1956). To Moscow with Bruce Turner during summer of 1957, also worked in Johnny Parker's band and played alto sax in Ken Colyer's Omega Brass Band (1957). Led own Elizabethan Jazz Band (1958–9). Played violin with the Alberts, then worked with Dick Charlesworth from March 1961 until February 1962. Formed new band in May 1962. Freelanced in the South then moved back to Scotland in 1964. Temporarily left music and qualified as a teacher of Maths and Physics, but resumed regular playing in 1988 with Charlie McNair and with Frank Birnies' East Coast Jazz Band. Re-formed own band in 1993, which continues through the 1990s, also playing trombone with Mike Hart's Edinburgh Ragtimers and trumpet with the Capital Jazz Band.

KELLOCK, Brian Robert
piano
Born: Edinburgh, Scotland, 28 December 1962

Gained Bachelor of Music degree at Edinburgh University after studying there from 1982 until 1986. During this period formed own trio (with Brian Shiels, double bass, and Joe Rae on drums), also worked regularly in R and B band Tam White and the Dexters, and occasionally with Bobby Wishart in the 1980s. Subsequently worked in Tom Bancroft's Orchestra and in the John Rae Collective. Accompanied many visiting musicians (recording with Janusz Carmello, Spike Robinson, etc.) and backed singers, Fionna Duncan, Carol Kidd, etc. During the 1990s worked in Nigel Clark's Quintet and in Phil Bancroft's Big Shebang, etc. Also did two European tours with the Australian trumpeter (and multi-instrumentalist) James Morrison.

KERR, Anthony
vibes/composer
Born: Belfast, Northern Ireland, 16 October 1965

Did first gigs in Belfast with Dermod Harland, Norman Watson, etc. Studied percussion at City of Belfast School of Music (1981–4). Percussionist with RTE Symphony Orchestra (1985–8). Studied in New York with David Friedman, and with Kenny Werner (1986–8); gained scholarship to the New School of Jazz and Contemporary Music, New York (1987). Since 1988 has worked in Europe with Louis Stewart, Honor Hefferman, Homecoming, Mike Westbrook, John Taylor, Georgie Fame, London Jazz Orchestra, Frevo, Jacqui Dankworth, Charlie Watts, Norma Winstone, Tim Garland, Alan Skidmore, Peter King, Jim Mullen, etc. Teaches percussion at City of Belfast School of Music, and at Harrow School. Also teaches improvisation at various universities, at the Guildhall School, London, and at the Royal Academy of Music. During the 1990s worked successfully as a freelance with Mike Westbrook, AK Quartet, Georgie Fame, Tim Garland's Quartet, Norma Winstone, etc. Also leads own quartet.

KIDD, Carol (née DELANEY)
vocals
Born: Glasgow, Scotland, 19 October 1948

Raised in Shettleston district of Glasgow. Sang with the West Coast Jazz Band for five years from the age of fifteen. Married trombonist George Kidd, had first of her three children at seventeen. Left music to raise the family, did occasional cabaret spots and club work, then resumed singing schedule with Jimmy Feighan's band. Worked regularly with pianist Sandy Taylor, drummer Murray Smith and guitarist Alex Moore from the 1970s, also guested with guitarist Martin Taylor (1983). Featured at Ronnie Scott's Clubs (in London and Birmingham) during the 1980s and 1990s, also guested with Humprey Lyttelton's band. Was invited by Frank Sinatra to sing at his Glasgow concert (1990). Worked regularly with pianist Dave Newton. Moved south to Cambridgeshire in 1990. Featured at various festivals through the 1990s (appeared with George Shearing in 1992), played many concerts and club dates with own trio (usually Dave Newton,

Allan Ganley and Dave Green). Toured Far East in 1995. Festival, club and concert appearances in 1996.

KING, 'Bertie' Albert
alto sax/tenor sax/clarinet/flute

Born: Colón, Panama, 19 June 1912
Died: Redwood City, California, USA, 2 September 1981

Raised in Jamaica, studied music at the Alpha Cottage School, Kingston. Led own band in Jamaica before moving to Britain in November 1935. Worked with Happy Blake at the Cuba Club, London (1936), then joined Leslie Thompson's Emperors of Jazz which formed the basis of Ken Johnson's Band (1936). Worked in Holland and France with Benny Carter (1937), also played engagements with Coleman Hawkins and Eddie South. With Fela Sowande in London (late 1938) and again with Ken Johnson (1939). With Teddy Joyce (late 1939–40) and Eddie Carroll (summer 1940). Served as a stoker in Royal Navy (1941–3), while on leave worked with Neil McMormack's Band at Glasgow Locarno (early 1942). Invalided out of Navy in early 1943, joined Joe Loss in March 1943. Worked with Geraldo, Eric Winstone and Cyril Blake, then formed own band (1943). With Leslie 'Jiver' Hutchinson from 1944 to 1946. With Woolf Phillips, then joined Blue Rockets (February 1947). With Dick Katz's Caribbean Quartet (May 1947), then worked with Nat Temple (April to May 1948). Led own band at Empress Ballroom, Dundee (June 1948 to October 1950). Moved back to London, freelanced, then worked in Bournemouth with Bobby Leitch (December 1950). With Harry Parry February to August 1951. Returned to Jamaica, led own band at Hotel Casablanca, Montego Bay (autumn 1951 to spring 1952). Returned to Britain, worked with Freddy Grant and with Humphrey Lyttelton's Paseo Jazz Band, before leading again at Hotel Casablanca, Montego Bay, from September 1952. Back to Britain in spring 1954, with Cecil Black's Band at Butlin's, Skegness (summer 1954), with Vic Abbott at Edinburgh Palais until October 1954. Returned to London, recorded with Chris Barber (October 1954), worked with Mike McKenzie at Hungaria Restaurant from April to June 1955. Freelance dates with Kenny Baker, Jazz Today Unit, etc., then took own band to tour Singapore, India and New Zealand (April to July 1956). Back to Britain, with Dill Jones' Trio for *Jazz Cavalcade* tour (late 1956), and freelanced in Britain before working mainly in Jamaica from 1958 to 1963. Returned to London in 1964, played freelance dates and did residency with Frank Deniz's band at the Talk of the Town club (1965). Moved to USA. While managing a condominium in California he was the victim of a violent, fatal assault.

KING, 'Pete' Peter Stephen George
tenor sax/clarinet

Born: Bow, London, 23 August 1929

Evacuated to Budleigh Salterton during World War II. Returned to London, took tenor sax lessons from Les Evans and clarinet tuition from Jack Lewis. Worked as a semi-professional with saxophonist Jack Oliver's Band in East London. First professional work with Leslie 'Jiver' Hutchinson (1947), also worked with Kenny Graham, Teddy Foster, Leon Roy and Paul Fenoulhet. With Oscar Rabin from 1948 until joining Kathy Stobart's Band in May 1950. Left Stobart to join Jack Parnell (1952), then became founder-member of Ronnie Scott's band in January 1953. Remained with Ronnie Scott's band for four years, then became manager of the Jazz Couriers (featuring Ronnie Scott and Tubby Hayes). Retired from playing and became

Ronnie Scott's business partner, successfully running Ronnie Scott's Club in London, first in Gerrard Street and then in Frith Street.

KING, Peter John
alto and tenor saxes/composer

Born: Kingston upon Thames, Surrey, 11 August 1940

Spent early years in Tolworth, Surrey. Briefly played violin and piano, then took up clarinet at fifteen but soon began specializing on alto sax. Played in Gus Galbraith's Sextet (1958) and in Ivor Mairants' Youth Orchestra (1959). Led own quartet in 1959, then joined John Dankworth from 1960 to spring 1961. Left Dankworth and visited Paris where he sat in with Bud Powell, worked for five days with Ray Charles. Regularly with Tony Kinsey's Quintet (1961–3). Worked in quartet at Annie's Room 1963–5, also freelanced and played gigs with John Burch's Octet (1964). Again with Tony Kinsey (1965). During the second half of the 1960s worked in Tubby Hayes' Big Band, with Stan Tracey, with Philly Joe Jones, and toured Europe with Maynard Ferguson, also in Phil Seamen's Quartet (1968). Founder-member of Bebop Preservation Society in 1971, and worked with them for their occasional bookings through the 1970s and 1980s. Worked with many visiting American musicians and with John Stevens, Stan Tracey, Colin Purbrook's Quintet, Dave Hancock's Big Band, Mike Carr (including European tour 1977). Often with Georgie Fame during the 1970s and 1980s (featured on alto and tenor saxes). Was part of Great Jazz Solos Revisited (1978). Led own quintet in the 1980s. With John Stevens in the early 1980s, and with Charlie Watts' Big Band, later did widespread touring in Charlie Watts' Quintet during the 1990s. Played in various theatre orchestras for shows: *Bubbling Brown Sugar*, *The Mitford Girls*, etc., also did several tours with Sacha Distel. Featured at Berlin Festival with Phil Woods and Jackie McLean. Often with Stan Tracey during the 1990s, and freelancing with many groups. Own recording career continues to thrive including sessions with strings. Again worked alongside Phil Woods (1994), co-led quintet with Gerald Presencer (1994). With Colin Towns' Orchestra (1995), Don Weller's Big Band (1995), Julian Joseph's band (1995) and leading own small line-ups, also in Julian Joseph's Quartet (1996). Wrote extended piece for Jazz Quartet and String Quartet (1996).

KINSEY, 'Tony' Cyril Anthony
drums/piano/composer/arranger

Born: Sutton Coldfield, Warwickshire, 11 October 1927

Mother a pianist, father a violinist. Drums and piano from the age of seven (later received drum tuition from Tommy Webster). Did local gigs with pianist Ronnie Ball, then both worked professionally in Jackson Cox's Band for a summer season in Newquay (1947), later that year both played in Billy Forrest's Band in Southsea and at Wigan Palais. Moved to London in 1948, worked with Art Thompson's Band, played freelance gigs, then joined pianist Ivor Noone's Band on the liner *Queen Mary*. Did seventeen trips to the USA on the *Queen Mary*, drum tuition in New York from Bill West and from Cozy Cole. During late 1949 also worked with Revell Terry's Quintet, Leon Roy's Band and in Victor Feldman's Sextet. Briefly with Paul Adam in January 1950, then became founder-member of the Johnny Dankworth Seven (March 1950). Left after sixteen months and joined Jack Nathan from July 1951 until June 1952. During this period also worked in various clubs with Ronnie Ball's Trio. Formed own trio in 1952 (after Ronnie Ball had emigrated to the USA). Mainly active as leader of small groups during the 1950s, but also accompanied Lena Horne at the London Palladium (1952) and played briefly in Cyril Stapleton's BBC Show Band (October 1952). During the 1960s, 1970s and 1980s regularly led own quintet, occasionally guesting with other bands and active as composer, arranger and musical director. Accompanied innumerable visiting American stars, including Ella Fitzgerald, Sarah Vaughan, Billie Holiday, Oscar Peterson, Ben Webster, Harry Edison, etc. Led own big band from 1974. Continues to lead own quartet, quintet and big band through the 1990s, and to compose and arrange for various line-ups.

KIRCHIN, Basil
drums/composer

Born: Blackpool, Lancashire, 8 August 1927

Son of drummer-leader Ivor Kirchin. Did first regular playing in his father's band, then joined Harry Roy (spring 1946). Left later that year to work with father's band at the Lyceum Ballroom, London. Left Ivor's band in late 1948 to lead sextet at Paramount, Tottenham Court Road, London, until early 1949. With Teddy Foster (1949–50), Jack Nathan (1950–1), then spent three months with Ted Heath (1951). Rejoined Teddy Foster (September 1951) but left to front Ivor's band while Ivor recovered from car crash injuries (December 1951). Led own band at Ritz, Manchester (1952), then did 21 month residency at Edinburgh Palais. Co-led Kirchin Band (with Ivor) from 1954 until Ivor dropped out in June 1957. Accompanied various visiting American stars including Billy Eckstine and Sarah Vaughan. Led band for summer season in Isle of Man (1958). Travelled to India. Briefly toured USA and worked in Australia for eighteen months (mainly as musical director at the Pigalle in Sydney, also toured for promoter Lee Gordon). Returned to Britain, led octet for residency at the Samson and Hercules Ballroom, Norwich (1961). Wrote scores for films and television. Lived for a while in the USA before settling in Switzerland. Moved back to Britain in October 1978, then returned to Switzerland before settling in East Yorkshire where he was mainly active as a composer during the 1990s. *The Kirchin Band 1952–7*, a discography by Tony Middleton, was published in 1996.

KIRCHIN, Ivor
drums

Born: London, 21 January 1905

Brother Sid played saxophone and violin. Ivor's son is drummer-leader Basil Kirchin. Originally Ivor doubled on drums and sax but then specialized on drums and led own quintet in London, before playing a season at the Metropole, Blackpool. He subsequently made his home in Manchester and led own Rivoli Orchestra (1927). From 1930 began a long series of bookings on the Mecca ballroom circuit, leading his own band at the Regent and Ritz in Manchester, at Cricklewood Palais and at Sherry's, Brighton, before playing for a long residency at the Paramount, Tottenham Court Road, London (for almost eight years). Later led at the Lyceum, London (1946), and then returned to the Paramount (1950). Injuries sustained in a car crash prevented Ivor from working for several months (December 1951 to March 1952). During this period Ivor's son Basil led the band, later father and son co-led the Kirchins (until 1957). Ivor then resumed leading at various palais venues starting at the Locarno, Sale, in the summer of 1957. Played many residencies including Manchester, Liverpool (1960), Hull (1962–6), then disbanded in 1967. Settled in Hull during the early 1980s.

KLEIN, 'Harry' Harold
baritone sax/alto sax/clarinet

Born: London, 25 December 1928

Took up alto sax at fourteen, and was soon playing local gigs. Won individual award in *Melody Maker* contest with Ken Goodyear's band. Did first professional work with Ivor Kirchin's band at Paramount, Tottenham Court Road, London, then worked with Ronnie Munro and with Les Ayling (1946) before joining band led by Canadian pianist Art Thompson (July 1946). With Woolf Phillips and Duncan Whyte, then played in Pete Huggett's Band (with Bill Le Sage, Johnny Wiltshire and Johnny Flanagan) for Great Yarmouth summer season (1949). Gigged with Tommy Sampson, and worked in Victor Feldman's Sextet (late 1949). With Jack Nathan (1950 to early 1951), during this period began doubling on baritone sax. Worked in Ivor and Basil Kirchin band, and played in Geoff Love's Octet (1951). With Kenny Baker from September 1951 until early 1953. During this period also worked with Roy Fox (on tenor sax) in 1952, with Ronnie Scott and regularly with Jack Parnell's Big Band in two separate stays. Played on the radio with Kenny Baker's Dozen through the 1950s. Led own quintet (1953), then joined Tommy Whittle (1954). Left New Jazz Quartet to do two trips on the liner *Mauretania* (late 1955) also worked in the Jazz Today Unit (1955–6). Toured Europe with Stan Kenton (April 1956), again worked with Tommy Whittle (1957–8). With Tony Crombie in late 1959, then co-led Jazz Five (with Vic Ash) from early 1960 until forming own quartet in February 1962. From the early 1960s onwards worked regularly as a freelance session musician, playing on many recordings, radio and television shows, etc. He also accompanied many noted singers including Ella Fitzgerald, Tony Bennett, Tom Jones, etc., and was frequently in Johnny Spence's Big Band. He continued to play jazz dates, and also did further playing on cruises, including work on the *Queen Mary*. He also worked successfully as an actor on television. Continues to play regularly in the 1990s, in small and large line-ups, mainly on alto sax.

KORNER, Alexis
guitar/piano/vocals/mandolin

Born: Paris, France, 19 April 1928
Died: London, 1 January 1984

Piano during a childhood spent in London; self-taught guitarist. Led own band in the late 1940s, own blues quartet (1949) which often worked alongside Chris Barber's Band. With Dick Hawdon's Band (1951). Founder-member of Ken Colyer's Skiffle Group (1953), also with Chris Barber's Skiffle Group in the 1950s. Worked with singer-harmonica player Cyril Davis at the Nucleus Coffee House in London (1957). With Davis led the pioneering British R and B unit Blues Incorporated for residency at the Marquee Club, London, from 3 May 1962. Davis left in late 1962 but Korner continued leading the group until 1968. European tours with Danish singer Peter Thorup from 1969 into the 1970s. Prolific work as a journalist and radio compere but led own various bands, the last of which was with bassist Colin Hodgkinson from 1973 until 1982. Korner guested with various groups including Ian Stewart's Rocket 88 during the early 1980s.

KOZAK, Ashley
double bass

Born: Merseyside, *c.*1930

Worked in Joe Burns' Trio in Liverpool (1950). With Tommy Sampson before working in Edinburgh with Terry Brown's Band (December 1951 to January 1952). With pianist Denny

Termer at the Stork Club, London (March to September 1952). Worked in India with Harry Parry from October 1952 until September 1953. With Vic Ash (1954) and with Des Williams in Brighton (spring 1954), then briefly with Don Rendell, Dizzy Reece and Damian Robinson before joining Tony Crombie in late 1954. Again with Dizzy Reece (1955), briefly with Larry Cadidy in Leeds then joined Basil and Ivor Kirchin's Band from August 1955 to September 1956. With Tony Crombie again (1956–7). In Cab Kaye's Quintet before working again with Basil Kirchin (1958–9). With Dick Morrissey's Quartet (1960), then took own quartet (including Morrissey) for season in India (September 1961 to November 1962). From this point on became increasingly involved in personal management and agency work involving many artistes including the singer Donovan. Ashley is a cousin of the vocalist Frankie Vaughan.

KRAHMER, 'Carlo' (William Max GESERICK)   Born: Shoreditch, London, 11 March 1914
drums/vibes/marimba   Died: London, 20 April 1976

Studied with George Balderson and Max Abrams. Started gigging at thirteen and at fifteen worked in and around North London with Eddie Chick's Broadway Imperials. Suffered defective vision. Joined Claude Bampton's Orchestra sponsored by the National Institute for the Blind (which also featured George Shearing). Co-led the Lewis-Krahmer Chicagoans (with guitarist Vic Lewis). Worked in pianist Bert Messender's Band (1940), led quartet at Cotton Club, London. With Johnny Claes' Clae Pigeons during the early 1940s. Briefly with Derek Neville's Quartet and with Lew Stone (1941). Led own band at Jamboree Club, Wardour Street, London (spring 1943), and at Gremlin Club, London (on vibes), in summer 1943. Led house band for Sunday sessions at the Feldman Club, London, from 1943 until 1950. Led own band at Hatchett's and at Frascati's. Worked briefly in variety with Nat Gonella (March 1945). With Derek Neville's Band to Nice Jazz Festival (1948). A year later took own band to Paris Jazz Festival (May 1949), thereafter retired from playing to concentrate on running Esquire Records (independent jazz record company) with partner Peter Newbrook. Krahmer and Newbrook founded the company in 1947. From the late 1940s Carlo also gave drum tuition, Victor Feldman was among his pupils.

KYLE, 'Bill' William T.   Born: Dunfermline, Fife, Scotland, 1946
drums

Played early gigs with a wide variety of bands playing pop, rock, traditional and modern jazz. Professional from 1967, worked with various bands in and around Glasgow, regularly with Head from 1970 until 1981. During this period with various other line-ups including pianist Dave Saul's Quintet, co-leading with trombonist Brian Keddle, etc. Studied with Tony Williams in New York (1981–2). Active in organizing the jazz promotion body Platform (1973–87), Scottish Jazz Network (1989–91), Jazz at the Tron from 1992. Did various tours including one with own New York Pals. Featured at various festivals through the 1990s, plays regularly in the Edinburgh area; organizes and plays on tours with various visiting musicians.

L

LAINE, Cleo (Clementina Dinah CAMPBELL)　　Born: Southall, Middlesex, 28 October 1927
vocals/lyricist

Married to John Dankworth, their children are Alex and Jacqueline. Sang with local bands, mainly around West London, before joining John Dankworth's Seven in spring 1951, was then Clementina Langridge by virtue of marriage to George Langridge (1947–57). Married John Dankworth on 18 March 1958, soon afterwards combined singing successes with a distinguished career as an actress, appearing in *Flesh to the Tiger* (1958), *Valmouth* (1959), *Here Is the News* (1960), etc. Made cabaret debut in June 1961. Together with John Dankworth founded the Wavendon All Music plan in Buckinghamshire in 1969. After starring in a revival of *Showboat*, in 1971 and 1973, resumed working regularly with John Dankworth and soon developed a formidable international reputation, fortified by regular tours of the USA and Australia. Continued to work occasionally as an actress, giving acclaimed performances in *Hedda Gabler* (1980), *Into the Woods* (1989), etc. Undiminished popularity of her singing and acting has continued through the 1990s. Awarded OBE in 1979. Autobiography, *Cleo*, was first published in 1994.

LAING, Ralph　　Born: Sanquhar, Dumfries, Scotland, 26 April 1936
piano/arranger

Played trumpet with the Ayrshire Jazz Band and in Glasgow's Eagle Jazzmen (1953–6). Gained visiting fellowship to New York (October 1957), gigged with Bobby Henderson and Mickey Foulis, moved briefly to California, then returned to Britain in February 1959. Did National Service in Germany (1959–61). After demobilization played piano with Arthur Coyne's band in the Midlands during the late 1960s, by this time specializing on piano. In Nottingham-based band Jazz Spectrum throughout the early 1970s, then moved to Bristol in 1973 and played in various bands there including Roger Bennett's Blue Note Jazz Band. Occasionally in Keith Smith's Hefty Jazz, accompanying various guests including Billy Butterfield, George Chisholm, etc. Co-led All Stars (with Al Fairweather); accompanied vocal trio Sweet Substitute. Led own Groove Juice Special from 1982, including radio work and recordings. Moved back to Scotland in 1991, continues to play regularly.

LAIRD, 'Rick' Richard Quentin　　Born: Dublin, Ireland, 5 February 1941
double bass

Played piano during childhood. Moved to New Zealand at sixteen, took up guitar for two years then switched to double bass in 1959. Gigged in Auckland area then moved to Sydney, Australia. Worked with Erroll Buddle, Don Burrows, etc. Moved to Britain in mid-1962, studied at Guildhall School of Music, London. Worked with Ronnie Ross, Stan Tracey, John Dankworth, Ronnie Scott, Tubby Hayes, Tony Kinsey, Brian Auger, etc. and accompanied many visiting American musicians. Won scholarship to Berklee School of Music in Boston, USA. Moved to USA, in January 1966. Studied in Massachusetts and played gigs around the Boston area with Jimmy Mosher-Paul Fontaine Big Band, with Herb Pomeroy, Phil Woods, Charlie Mariano, etc. Doubled on bass guitar from 1968, then joined Buddy Rich. Moved back to London in late 1970, freelanced, then returned to the USA in summer of 1971, initially to work with John McLaughlin. Subsequently played with many varied line-ups before combining playing, teaching music, and photography. Based in New York. Author of instruction book *Improvising Jazz Bass* (published in 1980).

LALLY, Arthur
sax/clarinet/arranger

Born: Seaforth, Liverpool, Lancashire, 1901
Died: London, May 1940

Brother of arranger Jimmy Lally. Early musical training from his father, who was an Army bandmaster. Played cornet and trombone before taking up alto sax. First professional work at Hammersmith Palais (1922), then played at Ciro's, London, prior to joining the Savoy Orpheans from December 1925 until late 1926. With Bert Firman (1927) and at the 43 Club, London (1927). With Ambrose (1928-9), then led Ambrose's Blue Lyres from May 1929 to March 1930. Led own band 1930-1, revived Blue Lyres in April 1931 but ill health caused him to hand over leadership to Peter Rush in October 1932. His solos on alto sax and bass sax featured on many freelance recordings, notably with the Rhythmic Eight. He was also a musical director at the Decca recording company. Concentrated on arranging from 1933. During the latter part of the 1930s he suffered severe depression and he took his own life in May 1940.

LAMB, 'Bobby' Robert
trombone/composer/arranger

Born: Cork City, Ireland, 11 February 1931

His two brothers, Chris and John, were both eminent professional brass players. Began on euphonium with the Barrack Street Silver and Reed Band, playing in Cork. Gigged on trombone, then did first professional tour with Duffy's Circus Band before moving to Dublin in 1951. Worked with pianist Neil Kearn's band for six months and with Johnny Devlin's Downbeaters, then moved to London and joined Teddy Foster (1952). Left Foster and worked with Jack Parnell from late 1953 until August 1955, then emigrated to the USA. Worked with Charlie Barnet, with Stan Kenton and with Woody Herman for three years (including a tour sharing billing with Louis Armstrong's All Stars). Returned to Ireland, then moved back to London to join Cyril Stapleton's BBC Show Band. Spent a year with Geraldo's Orchestra at the London Hippodrome (1958-9). Played in various theatre orchestras then spent eight years in the BBC Variety Orchestra until 1968. Recorded with Jack Parnell, John Barry, Ted Heath, Robert Farnon, etc. From the late 1960s into the 1970s co-led big band with trombonist Ray Premru, which made various recordings, including one featuring drummers Buddy Rich, Louis Bellson and Kenny Clare. Active freelancing in television, films, radio and recordings, accompanied Frank Sinatra, Sammy Davis Jr, Bing Crosby, Lena Horne, etc. then increasingly successful as a composer. Recorded own extended work *The Children of Lir*, and in 1970 won the Ivor Novello award for composition. Was appointed Director of Jazz Studies at Trinity College of Music. Subsequently conducted, coached and wrote for the European Community Jazz Orchestra from late 1981, is also Professor of

Contemporary Music Studies at Detmold University in Germany. Directs Trinity College Big Band. During the mid-1990s various of his works (including his First Symphony) were performed throughout the world; his double concerto for trombone and violin was premiered in Edmonton, Canada. His Second Symphony was first performed in Dublin in 1994. Also active as a conductor of the Irish National Symphony Orchestra, with the NDR Orchestra in Germany and with radio orchestras in Denmark, Norway, etc.

LAMBE, Jeanie
vocals
Born: Glasgow, Scotland, 23 December 1940

Married to tenor saxophonist Danny Moss. Mother a singer, father a musician and entertainer. First stage appearances in early teens with parents, then, while living in Inverness, joined the Clyde Valley Stompers, making her Glasgow debut with them in February 1958. Left several months later to join Alex Sutherland's band in Elgin. Moved to London in 1960, sang with Kenny Ball, Alex Welsh and Charlie Galbraith before working regularly with Mike Cotton from July 1961 until April 1962. Guested with various bands including Bruce Turner's Jump Band, Chris Barber, Acker Bilk, George Chisholm, the Dutch Swing College etc., and worked in cabaret. Married Danny Moss on 6 January 1964 and thereafter worked in successful duo with him through the 1990s, including many international tours and being featured with Bobby Rosengarden's Orchestra in New York (1984). Moved with Danny Moss to Perth, Australia in 1989. They continue to make this their base for widespread international touring through the 1990s.

LAMBERT, 'Les' Leslie
trumpet/piano/vibes/vocals
Born: London, 1908
Died: 1968

Trumpet and piano from age of twelve, led own band while still at school. Worked with Alfredo and Marius Winter, then joined house-band at Murray's Club, London. Worked at Spider's Web Club (1932) and with Jack Padbury (1932), then joined Roy Fox from March 1933 until August 1938 (was part of the Cubs vocal trio). Briefly with Dennis Val Thal's Orchestra then joined Billy Bissett (September 1938, for a year). With Paul Freedman's Band at the Nut House, London (late 1939), then again worked with Dennis Van Thal (1940). Led own band at the Nut House (1940) and worked with Ben Frankel, then joined Stan Atkins (1941). Became long-time member of the Skyrockets, thereafter successfully freelanced in studios and theatre orchestras.

LAMONT, Duncan
tenor sax/clarinet/flute/trumpet/
arranger/composer
Born: Greenock, Scotland, 4 July 1931

His son Duncan Jr is a professional saxophonist. Led own band (on trumpet) in Scotland, which won awards in a 1951 *Melody Maker* contest. Moved to London, spent several months playing trumpet with Kenny Graham, then returned to Scotland. On trumpet with Bert Tobias and Harry Margolis, then switched to tenor sax and worked (on tenor sax) with Basil and Ivor Kirchin in Edinburgh and Belfast (May 1953 to May 1954). Worked with Ken Mackintosh and Eric Law (1954–5), Malcolm Mitchell (February 1955 to March 1956). With Jack Parnell, Geraldo and Eric Delaney. With Vic Lewis (including tour of USA) in early 1958, then formed own quartet, also worked in Ray Premru Sextet. Freelancing, mainly in studios, from the late 1950s, but also played in many varied line-ups including work with Pat Smythe at the Establishment Club, London (1961), with Kenny Baker (1960 and 1962), in Johnny Scott's Quintet (1963–4), with Freddy Staff's Big Band (1964), etc. Did occasional widespread touring including tours of Europe with Rosemary Clooney, Benny Goodman, etc. Played in various big bands: with Bobby Lamb-Ray Premru, with Don Lusher, etc. and in Ian Hamer's Sextet, etc. Composed and arranged for television. Led own big band from the 1970s through to the 1990s and also played in Kenny Wheeler's Big Band (1990). Highly successful freelance work temporarily interrupted by illness in the mid-1990s, then resumed regular playing.

LAMPRECHT, 'Con' Johann Conrad
saxes/guitar/composer/arranger

Born: South Africa, 17 October 1908

Led own band in Port Elizabeth, then worked in orchestra directed by comedian Charles Heslop and thus came to Britain in 1931. Worked in Edgar Jackson's Quintet, then joined Debroy Somers for two years. With Jack Payne from late 1933 until spring 1935 (during this time also did occasional dates with Sydney Lipton). With Jack Jackson (1935), then rejoined Jack Payne from early 1936 until spring 1939. With Henry Hall (1939) prior to war service, then rejoined Henry Hall from late 1945 until late 1947. Moved back to South Africa and in the early 1950s became Head of Light Music at the South African Broadcasting Company.

LANE, Steve
cornet/guitar/composer/arranger

Born: London, 7 November 1921

Father was a concertina player who recorded with the Rio Grande Tango Orchestra in the 1920s. Began on guitar at school. Wartime service included a posting to India. Played guitar in the Ragtime Trio, then switched to cornet and formed own Southern Stompers which made debut in November 1950. Continued to lead own bands through the 1990s (billed as the Red Hot Peppers from the mid-1980s) playing dates throughout Europe, included several visits to Czechoslovakia, and work in Holland, Denmark, Poland, Belgium, etc. Steve also led and recorded with the VJM Washboard Band. He has also been actively involved in running record labels and producing magazines on jazz for many years.

LANG, Don (Gordon LANGHORN)
trombone/vocals

Born: Halifax, Yorkshire, 18 January 1925
Died: Surrey, August 1992

Self-taught bassist, switched to trombone and as a member of Johnny Oldfield's Jive Five gained individual award at *Melody Maker* contest (September 1945). Worked with Peter Rose's Orchestra in Blackpool, then joined Teddy Foster (1948). With Vic Lewis for almost two years from summer of 1948, then spent over four years with Ken Mackintosh. Left Mackintosh in May 1955 and adopted the name Don Lang to front own Frantic Five. Later he led own sextette at the Empire Ballroom, London, during the 1960s, occasionally re-forming the Frantic Five for specific engagements. During the 1970s and 1980s did cabaret work as a solo artiste, also guested with various bands including Dave Marrion's and Johnny Howard's and played regularly in the Sounds of Seventeen.

LAURENCE, 'Chris' Christopher
double bass/bass guitar

Born: London, 6 January 1949

Son of pianist Tony Laurence, four brothers are musicians; grandmother was harpiste Marie Goossens (died 1992). Played piano from the age of seven, later studied at Royal Junior College of Music. Took up double bass as a teenager and studied for three years at the Guildhall School of Music, under James Merret, Jr. Played in National Youth Jazz Orchestra at sixteen. During the late 1960s was in Frank Ricotti's Quartet. From the 1970s onwards, worked with Harold Beckett, Tony Coe, Alan Cohen, Bob Cornford, Henry Lowther, John Marshall, Tony Oxley, Mick Pyne, Alan Skidmore, John Surman, John Taylor, Mike Westbrook, Kenny Wheeler, etc. Played in the BBC Symphony Orchestra and taught regularly at summer schools. During the 1980s and 1990s continued to divide his time between classical music and jazz: as Principal Bass with the London Bach Orchestra, etc., and with Ian Carr, Michael Garrick, John Surman, Tommy Smith, etc.

LAURIE, 'Cy' Cyril
clarinet

Born: London, 20 April 1926

Self-taught. Led own band in and around London in the late 1940s, then worked with Mike Daniels from summer 1949 until summer 1950. Gigged with Owen Bryce. Led own Cy Laurie Four, then formed seven-piece band in 1951 which he led with considerable success until December 1960, when ill health caused a temporary retirement (the band subsequently worked under the leadership of trombonist Terry Pitts). Cy Laurie travelled abroad, then returned to his home in Essex in 1963, but didn't resume regular playing until early 1968. Sat in with various bands, then began leading again in summer 1968. During the early 1970s guested with Max Collie, the Savoy Jazzmen, Mac Duncan, Chris Watford, etc., and played semi-regularly in the Black Bottom Stompers (1973–4). Again led own band (and quartet) from the late 1970s and regularly co-led quintet with Eggy Ley in the early 1980s, also worked with Chez Chesterman and toured with Max Collie's *Mardi Gras* show. Continued to play regularly through the 1990s, with own band, alongside Beryl Bryden, etc. He led a Reunion Band consisting of his former sideman for his 70th birthday celebrations at the 100 Club, London, in April 1996.

LAW, 'Billy' William Alexander
drums

Born: Edinburgh, Scotland, 1 August 1940

Began on drums with local Boys' Brigade at age of twelve. Played gigs around Edinburgh, then turned professional in 1960 by joining a Danish band, the Jazz Cardinals (then working in Germany). Returned to Scotland and joined the Clyde Valley Stompers, continued to work with this ensemble when it was billed as Pete Kerr's All Stars, then joined Terry Lightfoot (March 1964). Later that year worked with Long John Baldry and very briefly co-led a band with singer Rod Stewart, then joined Alex Harvey's Soul Band (early 1965). Gigged with Colin Smith's Sextet, with Lennie Felix's Trio and Alex Welsh's Band before joining Alan Elsdon. Left Elsdon in summer of 1969 and moved back to Edinburgh. Played in King's Theatre Orchestra and freelanced with Ralph Laing, Al Fairweather, etc., and took part in Clyde Valley Stompers' Reunion Tour (1982). Continues to play regularly through the 1990s.

LAWRANCE, Brian
violin/vocals

Born: Adelaide, Australia, 10 August 1907
Died: Australia, 11 September 1983

Both parents were English. Sang in stage productions as a child (in Melbourne and Sydney). Played violin at St Peter's Hall, Adelaide, then sang and played violin in *The Famous Diggers* touring show before moving to Britain in 1926. Toured variety halls for several years and worked as Eddie in double act 'Eddie and Rex' in the early 1930s. Appeared in White Brothers' show and sang with Carroll Gibbons. Led small band at various London night clubs including residency at Quaglino's. Freelance broadcasting included work with Fred Hartley's Quintet (1934), also sang with Debroy Somers as 'Larry O'Brian'. Briefly partnered Nat Gonella for stage work (1934), then again led own band which played a four year residency at Lansdowne House Hotel. Moved back to Australia in early 1940. Led own band at Romano's, Sydney, for seven years.

LAWRENCE, Syd
trumpet/arranger

Born: Shotton, nr Chester, Cheshire, 26 June 1923

Father (a drummer) ran a semi-pro band in Chester. Played violin as a child, cornet from twelve. Joined Wilf Murphy's band then did ENSA tours for eighteen months. Worked in Art Gregory's band before serving in RAF from September 1942. Featured in RAF Middle East Command Dance Orchestra (led by clarinettist Ronnie Austin). After demobilization worked with Al Powell's band in Chester (1946), won *Melody Maker* contest award. Joined Teddy Foster (autumn 1946). With Nat Temple (1947), then worked in Paul Lombard's band on liner *Mauretania* (late 1947). Again with Al Powell in Chester (early 1948), then joined Ken Mackintosh (1948). With Cyril Stapleton (1949), left to lead own band in Chester (late 1949). Rejoined Cyril Stapleton (July 1950). With Geraldo (1951), Sydney Lipton (1952–3). Moved back to Cheshire in May 1953, worked temporarily as a salesman and gigged with Dennis Williams' Quintet, then resumed full musical schedule and joined BBC Northern Variety Orchestra in March 1954 (which became Alyn Ainsworth's BBC Northern Dance Orchestra). Remained with this ensemble, but also formed own Glenn Miller-inspired band for debut gig in November 1967. This move proved to be so successful he left the BBC in late 1969 to concentrate on running the new band which has continued into the 1990s, directed by trombonist Chris Dean (1996).

LAWSON, 'Don' Michael
percussion/composer

Born: Ladbroke Grove, London, 7 July 1930

First professional work with Kenny Graham's Afro-Cubists (September 1951). Resident drummer at Studio 51, London, in 1952, working with Dizzy Reece, Bob Burns, Terry Brown and Eddie Thompson (later worked often in Thompson's Trio). Began long musical association with Ralph Dollimore. Worked with Dave Davani, Roy Fox and Ambrose before joining Kenny Baker's Quartet from summer of 1953 until late 1954, then joined Don Rendell in December 1954. With Don Rendell, Freddy Randall and Bob Burns in 1955 and played on Tony Bennett's first British tour (MD was Chuck Wayne). With Keith Bird's Quintet (1956) and in *Jazz from London* package (sharing drumming with Phil Seamen). Worked in variety with pianist Winifred Atwell; again with Don Rendell (1956). With Ken Moule, Dill Jones, Dave Shepherd, Buddy Featherstonhaugh (1957). Toured with Kenny Baker's Half Dozen (1958). With Don Harper's Quartet (1959) and

Frank Horrox (1959–61), also with Harry Roy at May Fair Hotel (1960–1). With Harry Roy at Colony Club, London, and toured Europe with the Hi Los (1962). Composed score for BBC television's *The Bacchae*, later wrote scores for *Moving On, Explorations*, etc. During the 1960s with Frank Horrox, Joe Harriott, Roger Webb's Trio, Alyn Ainsworth's Orchestra, Eric Robinson, Bob Sharples, etc. Session work and playing in West End shows including *Hello Dolly* (with Mary Martin) and *Funny Girl* (with Barbra Streisand). With Ian McPherson's Orchestra (1969–70), Marcus Dodds (1971), then in *Godspell* show (1971–5), also with Eartha Kitt, and Ken Moule's Band. On Russell Harty's television shows (1976–7). Composed *L* score for Houston Ballet Company and performed it with them in Houston (1978 and 1979). Played for *Ain't Misbehavin'* show in London, then became MD and first percussionist for Wayne Sleep's Dance Company (1980–3). Directed for Houston Ballet Company in London (1983). Freelance from 1986, gigging with Bob Burns, Mike McKenzie, Matt Ross, etc. Played for reunion of *The Boy Friend*'s original cast. Composed for BBC radio dramas including score for *Pocahontas*. Directed and played *L* for English National Ballet. Continued to play jazz gigs through the 1990s.

LAYTON, 'Teddy' Edward
clarinet/saxes/piano

Born: Lewisham, London, 19 April 1928

At fifteen played guitar in the Roy-Leon Swingtette (co-led with cousin, drummer Roy Pearce). Began specializing on clarinet and played in the Washington and Lee Band and in Kenny Wallbank's Jazz Band (1944). Served in Merchant Navy from 1944 until 1948. Worked with Mike Daniels (1952 and again 1954–5) and with Eric Silk (1952 and 1956), before forming own band in late 1956. Led this until joining Sonny Morris in late 1958. With Nat Gonella from February 1960 until summer 1961, then joined Mickey Ashman until 1963 (also recorded with Bobby Mickleburgh in 1961). Worked in Midland All Stars (1963–4) and with Bob Wallis, then played sax and clarinet in the New Tia Juana Jazzband and with the Number 18 Jazzband (1965–9). Based in Southampton, worked with various local bands and accompanied visiting American jazz musicians (1970–7), also worked with Wild Bill Davison in the 1980s. Played in Mission Hall Jazzband (1977–85). From 1981 through the 1990s led own quartet on saxes and clarinet for residency at the Concorde Club, Eastleigh, also with Stane Street Jazzband (1985–90), with Butch Thompson's King Oliver Centennial Jazz Band and with Andy Dickens' band in the 1990s. Continues to lead own quartet.

LAYZELL, 'Bob' Robert Martin
saxes/clarinet/piano/flute/violin/vocals

Born: Westminster, London, 22 June 1915

Brother of drummer Tony Layzell, uncle of drummer Martin Layzell. Played in Number One Rhythm Club Band in the 1930s, then worked with Henry Nichols, Roberto Inglez, Arthur Rosebery before joining Phil Watts. Left Watts in 1939 to work briefly with Nat Gonella, then joined RAF as part of Frank Cordell's band (which remained together and became the RAF Middle East Command Band). After demobilization joined Joe Loss from spring 1946 until November 1948. With Harry Roy from early 1949 until March 1953. With Lew Stone (1953–4), then worked on *Caronia* liner with tenor saxophonist Len Royal. With Jock Scott's band at Hatchett's, London, then joined Eddie Lambert's Quintet on *Queen Mary* liner (1959). Led own band aboard *Queen Mary* for five years in the 1960s, then led at Playboy Club for three years, later at various London clubs. Many gigs with George Fierstone and with organist Kenny Barker's Trio (1974), and with Al Wynnette's Band from late 1975. With Harry Gold from the late 1970s through to the 1980s. Continues to freelance through the 1990s.

LEAKE, Brian
piano/alto sax/clarinet/arranger/composer

Born: South Wales, 9 November 1934
Died: Middlesex, 10 November 1992

Self-taught pianist, studied architecture in Cardiff, taught himself to play clarinet and soon joined Mike Harris' Jazz Band. Did National Service in RAF. While stationed on the South Coast played clarinet in Southampton with the Climax Jazz Band (1956). Moved to London, did various day jobs, then played clarinet in Owen Bryce's Band. Began playing alto sax, took lessons from Bruce Turner. Formed own Kaycee Jazz Band in 1961. With Dave Keir's Band (1962), Mick Whitemead (1963). Freelanced on piano and reeds in the 1960s, thereafter specialized on piano, worked on P&O liners with Dick Charlesworth. Joined Alan Elsdon in May 1969. Worked regularly with Alan Elsdon through to the early 1990s, but also led own group Sweet and Sour, and continued to play engagements with Dick Charlesworth. Briefly with Digby Fairweather in early 1980s. Served on committee of the Central London branch of the Musicians' Union for several years, and often led the Al Fresco Marching Band at rallies (playing alto sax).

LEDIGO, Hugh Charles
piano/arranger/composer

Born: Bromley, Kent, 26 September 1934

Piano lessons from age of eight, later played trumpet for a while. Led own trio during Army service. After demobilization in December 1954, sat in with Dave Carey's Band and then began to play regular gigs with various jazz groups. With Dave Shepherd's Sextet and Trio in the late 1950s. Led own quintet in the early 1960s, then played residency in the Regency Club, Hackney, before West End residencies at Café de Paris, May Fair Hotel, Dorchester Hotel, etc., working with Jimmy Silver, Arthur Dimery, Ron Wilkins, George De Souza, etc. Was musical director for Showboat Club in the Strand, London, for two years. Toured with the Pasadena Roof Orchestra, then freelanced with Alan Littlejohns, Dick Charlesworth, etc. Began deputizing in Kenny Ball's Band in the 1980s and joined permanently in November 1987. With Kenny Ball through the 1990s, also occasionally deputizes in the Pasadena Roof Orchestra. Increasingly active as a composer; his choral and instrumental work was premiered in October 1995.

LEE, 'Crissie' (Christine LEEWORTHY)
drums

Born: Colchester, Essex, 17 June 1943

Began playing drums during infancy, by the age of five was in the Colchester Salvation Army Band, subsequently joined the Essex and Suffolk Massed Bands. Made first appearance on television at thirteen. Toured Europe with the Lena Kidd Seven, then joined Ivy Benson's Band for five years in the early 1960s. Formed own group, the Beat Chics, which did international touring with various stars, including the Beatles. During the late 1960s worked in the Mike Holly Big Band then formed own seven-piece band which played residencies in Europe, the Middle East and South Africa. Augmented this line-up to twelve pieces and played Mecca ballrooms and backed various guest stars on television. Led smaller line-ups again, then formed own successful big band which has flourished through the 1990s, featuring an array of soloists including Meredith White (piano), Annette Brown (trumpet), Kaye Henderson (trombone), Sarah Kelly (alto sax), Tina Hathaway and Suzanne Higgins (tenor saxes), Ali Brown (baritone sax) and Paula Gardiner (double bass).

LEE, 'Dave' David
piano/composer/arranger

Born: London, 12 August 1930

Piano from five, moved to the North-east with his family as a teenager, gigged with local bands, later won an individual award in a *Melody Maker* contest. Served in the Army. After demobilization joined a touring troupe which visited South Africa. Remained there, studied at Johannesburg Conservatory of Music. Accompanied John Dankworth in South Africa (1954). Returned to Britain in summer of 1955, worked at the Café de Paris, London (September 1955 to April 1956), and was briefly accompanist for comedian Norman Wisdom. Regularly with John Dankworth for almost four years, left in summer of 1959 to form own successful trio, which achieved considerable success on record. During the 1960s and 1970 achieved success as a composer, writing scores for films and shows: *Cranks, Our Man Crichton, The Solid Gold Cadillac*, etc. Led own trio for various television and radio shows, was musical director for television's *That Was the Week That Was*, and for various singers including Judy Garland. Lived in Ireland in the late 1970s, then moved to Los Angeles, before returning to London where he resumed regular playing in the 1980s, also composing, arranging and conducting. Obtained franchise for London-based radio station Jazz FM, which began broadcasting on Sunday 4 March 1990. Lee later relinquished his interest in the station.

LEE, 'Phil' Philip Robert
guitar/composer

Born: Maida Vale, London, 8 April 1943

Played guitar from age of thirteen, at sixteen joined Ivor Mairants' National Youth Orchestra. First professional work playing for a pantomime, then did a season with Joe 'Piano' Henderson before working in John Williams' Big Band (1963). Worked with Graham Collier for two years (1965–6), then spent two years in organist Bob Stuckey's Quartet, also worked with Mike Gibbs. From the early 1970s regularly with Henry Lowther's Quarternity, and co-led Axel with Tony Coe. Also worked with Brian Miller's Impulse, Dick Crouch's Paz, John Stevens' Quintet, in Gilgamesh and Ken Baldock's Band. Toured with Michael Legrand, Michael Garrick's Sextet, and in Threesome (with Michael Garrick and Norma Winstone). Regular radio work with Pat Smythe and from the mid-1970s teaching at annual summer schools. During the 1980s continued with similar extensive freelance schedule which included work with various big bands led by: Allan Ganley, Tony Faulkner and Michael Garrick. Many recording sessions, and various tours with Gordon Beck (1983) and a visit to Yugoslavia with Kincade (1983). Accompanied many visiting American musicians during the 1980s and 1990s, including Benny Goodman, Lee Konitz, Ken Peplowski, Kenny Davern, Eddie Daniels. Worked with Dardanelle in Europe and the USA. Varied working schedule continues through the 1990s, duos with Jeff Clyne, working with Jimmy Hastings-John Horler group, with clarinettist Julian Stringle, in Ron Mathewson's Sextet, London Jazz Orchestra, etc.

LEE, Tony
piano

Born: Whitechapel, London, 23 July 1934

Brother Arthur a pianist. Spent part of childhood evacuated to Bletchley in World War II. Self-taught. Served for five years in the RAF (mainly as a driver), then became professional musician. Gigged with many bands before forming own trio in 1961 (with Brian Jones, double bass, and Dave Pearson, drums). Later the trio included bassist Tony Archer, and various drummers including Tony Mann, Martin Drew, Terry Jenkins, etc. The trio has continued to work successfully through the 1990s, playing residencies at the Bull's Head in Barnes and accompanying many visiting American musicians at Ronnie Scott's Club and on tour. Lee also worked with Phil Seamen in the early 1970s, later with Lennie Best's Quartet and with Tommy Whittle, Pete King, George Chisholm, Don Lusher, Kenny Baker, etc.

LEGON, 'Freddy' Vincent Frederick
guitar/banjo/vocals

Born: Bermondsey, South London, 30 August 1925

Was given ukulele at fourteen but did first gigs on clarinet (and vocals) with the Blue Rhythm Boys, together with cousin Bill Bailey, who played guitar and sang. Appeared on a Carroll Levis talent show. Later played comb-and-paper (and sang) in Original London Blue Blowers with Bill Bailey. Played drums in Catford Rhythm Club Group, then took up banjo (and guitar) and joined Mike Daniels' Delta Jazzmen from March 1948 until August 1951. With Humphrey Lyttelton from August 1951 until December 1956. With Reg Rigden (1957), then long stay in Owen Bryce's band during the 1960s, also did radio work with Bill Bailey's Skiffle Group. Began working regularly with George Webb in the 1970s, and continued to do so occasionally through the 1990s. During this period also played around the Kent area in John Mason's band and freelanced with various groups including the Fidgety Feet Jazz Band.

LEMON, Brian
piano/arranger

Born: Nottingham, 11 February 1937

Father was a semi-pro violinist. Piano from childhood, tuition from Reg Conroy as a teenager. First professional work with Wylie Price at Nottingham Palais, also worked with Peter Fielding in Nottingham. Summer season at Newquay with bassist Bob Snowden, worked briefly in Birmingham with Jimmy Phillips. Moved to London to join Freddy Randall in 1956. Left Randall in February 1957 to join Betty Smith's Quintet. Worked mainly with Betty Smith until spring 1961. Did various CSE overseas tours (including several with Tony Hancock). With Fairweather-Brown All Stars from May 1961 until early 1963, then led own trio at the Establishment Club, London. Began long musical associations with Danny Moss, Dave Shepherd, George Chisholm, and led own trio. Played residency at Annie's Room, London (early 1966). Briefly in Bruce Turner's Jump Band (to accompany Ray Nance) June 1966, worked with Danny Moss, Sandy Brown, Dave Shepherd, Spike Heatley Trio and singer Salena Jones during the late 1960s. With Freddy Randall-Dave Shepherd band in the early 1970s, spent three years with Alex Welsh from September 1975. Led own trio, octet, etc., and played occasionally in Ron Russell's band. From the 1960s through the 1990s accompanied many American musicians including Benny Goodman, Milt Jackson, Ray Brown, etc. Founder-member of the Pizza Express All Stars from May 1980, led own line-ups for regular radio work, including string orchestras. Toured Australia with Danny Moss and Jeanie Lambe in 1984. Regularly with Val Wiseman's *Lady Sings the Blues* show from July 1987, took part in Alex Welsh Reunion Band during the 1980s and 1990s, also worked in the World's Greatest Jazz Band in Europe. International touring in Charlie Watts' Quintet in the early 1990s, also regularly featured in the *Best of British Jazz* package into the 1990s. Continues to accompany many visiting musical stars, and maintains extensive freelance work through the 1990s, including work in the Great British Jazz Band and leading own line-ups.

LE SAGE, 'Bill' William A.
piano/vibes/arranger/composer

Born: London, 20 January 1927

His father William (1899–1951) was a drummer, two uncles (George, trumpet and sax, and Ernie, guitar) were musicians. Ukulele at eight, returned to London after evacuation in Sussex during World War II and began playing drums at fifteen. Self-taught pianist. Began playing gigs as a teenager with Johnny Flannigan, Bernie Izen and John Dankworth. Formed own band at eighteen, then did National Service in Royal Signals, played in various service groups. After demobilization played brief summer season in Ilfracombe, then led own quintet for a month's booking in Workington. Returned to London and joined Johnny Dennis and his Ranchers (late 1948). Co-led band (with bassist Peter Huggett) for season at Great Yarmouth (1949), then joined Frank Abbott's Band on the *Queen Mary* liner until becoming a founder-member of the Johnny Dankworth Seven (from March 1950). Began doubling on vibes. Worked with Dankworth line-ups (small and large) until April 1954 (except for brief absence for Z-Men Army re-training in spring 1952). With Tony Kinsey from April 1954 until September 1961 (during this period also played regularly in Kenny Baker's Dozen). Began writing for television and for films. Joined Ronnie Ross Quartet in September 1961, worked regularly with Ross until 1966 (again worked with Ross in the 1970s, including the Tentet). With Jack Parnell's ATV Orchestra and freelancing extensively, including Mediterannean cruise with Chris Barber's Band (spring 1964). Worked again with John Dankworth from 1966. Took own group to Germany, active in composing extended works. Led own Directions in Jazz during the 1960s. Regularly led own Trio from the 1960s through the 1990s, often accompanying visiting American musicians, including annual tours with Tal Farlow. Formed Bebop Preservation Society in 1969 and continued to work occasionally with this ensemble into the 1990s. Again worked with John Dankworth and Cleo Laine during the 1980s and 1990s (including international touring). During the 1970s part of Barbara Thompson's Jubiaba, also worked with Charlie Watts' Big Band (1985–6). Continues to lead own trio, quartet, sextet and Echoes of Brazil through the 1990s, successfully combining this with composing, arranging, and guesting with various line-ups, including Tony Lee's Trio (1996).

LEVIN, Tony
drums/percussion

Born: Much Wenlock, Shropshire, 30 January 1940

Lived in Birmingham from age of five. Played in Hedley Ward's Big Band as a teenager and gained valuable experience in Johnny Collins' Quartet, then worked as accompanist for visiting musicians. Worked regularly with Tubby Hayes from 1965 until 1968. Began long musical association with Alan Skidmore in the late 1960s. Briefly with Mike Westbrook (1968) also worked with Mick Pyne's Trio, John Taylor, Humphrey Lyttelton and in Lionel Grigson-Pete Burden Quintet. Again worked with Tubby Hayes in the early 1970s, with Stan Sulzmann's Quartet, with Gordon Beck's Gyroscope from 1973. During the 1970s also worked with Ian Carr's Nucleus, with Michael Garrick, Norma Winstone, Malcolm Griffiths, John Surman, Mick Pyne, etc. From 1979 was part of German group the Third Eye, again worked with Alan Skidmore (including gigs with Tenor Tonic). Led own Trio in the early 1980s (with Paul Dunmall and Tony Moore) and worked in Holland with Dutch pianist Rob Van Den Broeck. With Keith Tippett line-ups, also ran own Jazz Club Friday in Birmingham from 1986 to 1990. During the 1990s often worked with guitarist Philip Catherine, and with Mujician (with Paul Dunmall, Paul Rogers and Keith Tippett). During autumn 1994 did wide-ranging tour of the Middle East with Trio (Sophia Domaneich on piano and Paul Rogers on bass), subsequently worked in Europe with Tony Oxley's Celebrations, then further freelance work throughout Europe. Worked with the European Jazz Quartet (1996).

LEWIS, Mickey
alto sax/soprano sax/clarinet/flute

Born: London, c.1907
Died: Australia, 19 August 1983

Played flute as a teenager then took up soprano sax before specializing on alto sax. Left Britain and toured Australia with Bert Ralton (1923), then joined American bandleader Frank Ellis in Melbourne. Worked with Cyril Nelson's band before returning to England in April 1926. Worked briefly in Switzerland, then joined Al Tabor in London. Worked in Birmingham, and in Belgium and Holland with van't Hoff's band (1927–8), then joined Con Talson's band (summer 1928). Led own quartet at Century Club, London (early 1931), then worked in Germany and Italy before leading at the Gargoyle Club, London (1931–2). Led at Fischer's, London, with Howard Jacobs (1933), then worked with Sydney Lipton from January 1934 until December 1935. With Cecil Black and Bill Airey-Smith (1937). Joe Loss (1940), John Borelli (1941), Mantovani (1941), then mainly with Al Collins from 1942 until 1946. Left full time playing to work in music instrument production (for Lew Davis) from 1946 to 1948, then joined Billy Munn in November 1948. Thereafter resumed full schedule of freelance playing. Moved to Australia and opened a musical instrument business in Melbourne.

LEWIS, 'Vic' Victor Joseph
guitar/trombone

Born: North West London, 29 July 1919

Began on banjo, soon swopped to guitar and formed own Swing String Quartet (1935), winning talent contest which led to radio work. Gigged with Carlo Krahmer. Visited USA for six weeks in autumn 1938 and recorded there with various American jazz musicians. Worked briefly in Antwerp, then returned to England and joined the RAF in 1939. Played in service bands, including one led by Buddy Featherstonhaugh (1943), then co-led Jazzmen with fellow-serviceman Jack Parnell (both musicians being part of Leslie Douglas' Bomber Command Orchestra). Learnt to play trombone while in the RAF. Discharged from RAF, continued to lead with Jack Parnell, then formed own Jazzmen in summer of 1945. Worked briefly in Stephane Grappelli's Quintet. Led own sextet in Britain and Scandinavia (1946), then formed own big band which made radio debut in November 1946. Led big band at Paris Jazz Festival (May 1949). Toured with own nineteen-piece Music For Moderns, but temporarily reduced line-up to an octet in 1951. Re-formed big band in 1952, which later made four tours of the USA before disbanding in 1960. Vic Lewis subsequently became a booking agent and manager, he did however re-form a big band to back Shorty Rogers and Bud Shank in 1984. He played piano on one track of a quintet recording with these two Americans, issued on Lewis's own label, Concept. His autobiography *Music and Maiden Overs* was first published in 1987.

LEY, 'Eggy' Derek William
soprano sax/alto sax/vocals

Born: Streatham, London, 4 November 1928
Died: Delta, British Columbia, Canada, 20 December 1995

Drums (and boogie-woogie piano) during early teens. Served in RAF, took up soprano sax. Gigged with Mick Mulligan, Ron Simpson's Commodores, etc. With Mick Collier's Chicago Rhythm Kings (1952), briefly with Eric Silk (1953) and with Stan Sowden's Band (1955). Took own band to Germany in August 1955 for residency at New Orleans Bierbar in Hamburg. This booking proved to be the first of many long successful residencies in Germany (lasting until 1962). Ley's band also worked in Scandinavia and made brief return visits to London clubs. In late 1962 Ley became a Radio Luxembourg producer, but continued to play gigs, including residency at London's Tatty Bogle Club throughout the 1960s. Worked on the staff of the British Forces Broadcasting Service from 1969 until 1983. During the 1970s co-led with Hugh Rainey, gigged with George Webb, and led own Layabouts. Co-led quintet with Cy Laurie in the 1970s and 1980s, took up alto sax in the early 1980s. Formed own Hot Shots in 1982, continued to play regularly, led at Chesters Club, Southend. Emigrated to Canada in the late 1980s, where a stroke ended his playing career.

LIGHTFOOT, 'Paddy' Patrick Anthony
banjo/guitar/vocals

Born: Potters Bar, Middlesex, 10 July 1937

Brother of Terry Lightfoot. Began playing banjo in 1951, gigged with the Wood Green Stompers, then toured Switzerland with the Saints Jazzband (from Manchester) during summer of 1953. With Jeremy French (late 1953), Cy Laurie and Vic Roberts' Phoenix Jazz Band, then did National Service in the RAF (1955–7). While serving in Germany did local gigs with German band in Münster and played in station skiffle group. After demobilization joined Terry Lightfoot's band from 1957 until early 1961, then worked with Kenny Ball from March 1961 until 1970. Played for nine months in Alan Elsdon's band in 1971, then again worked with Terry Lightfoot until 1976. Left music to run a pub in Essex from 1976 until 1982, then settled in East Anglia.

LIGHTFOOT, Terry
clarinet/saxes/vocals

Born: Potters Bar, Middlesex, 21 May 1935

Elder brother of banjoist Paddy Lightfoot. First played clarinet while at Enfield Grammar School. Led Wood Green Stompers from age of seventeen, also in Albermarle Jazz Band before serving in RAF 1953–5; played clarinet and piano in service jam sessions. Formed own band in 1955, which turned professional a year later and enjoyed widespread success (including a tour of Britain alongside Kid Ory's band). Led for ten years, then temporarily quit full time music to run a pub. Returned to professional music and joined Kenny Ball from February until November 1967. Re-formed own band in late 1967 which continued through the 1970s. Lightfoot again left full time music to run a pub in Harpenden, Hertfordshire (from 1978 until 1983) but then resumed full time music schedule and continued to lead own band through the 1990s.

LISTER, Eric
vocals/clarinet

Born: Manchester, Lancashire, 20 March 1926
Died: London, 24 April 1988

Left school in Manchester and joined the Merchant Navy at sixteen, war service in the Atlantic and Middle East, played clarinet in Dave Wilson's Band during home leave. Led own Easyriders in Liverpool (1947), then played in Smoky City Stompers (1948), whose off-shoot group the Tasle Alley Washboard Creepers was a precursor of skiffle groups (they played concerts in Manchester and Liverpool in 1948). Eric worked in his father's business, then moved to London in 1955, where he subsequently ran a motor car business, an art gallery and a health food shop, all the while continuing to lead his own band. He also sang with Brian Leake's Kaycee Jazz Band (1962). During the last part of his life his band played a long residency at Langan's Brasserie in London.

LITER, Monia
piano/piano accordion/arranger/composer

Born: Odessa, Russia, 27 January 1905
Died: England, 5 October 1988

Attended Imperial School of Music in Russia at the age of seven, then moved with his father to Harbin in North China. Played piano for silent films in Shanghai and freelanced as a multi-instrumentalist; worked briefly in the Shanghai Symphony Orchestra. Joined Jimmy Lequime's Band in 1922 and moved with them to Calcutta, India, in 1925 and to Singapore in 1926, where Liter took over the leadership and remained until 1933 when he moved to London (he held a British passport). Worked with John Borelli at Oddenino's then wrote music for SS Sunshine revue and accompanied Al Bowlly on variety dates (September 1933), before joining Lew Stone in December 1933. Left briefly in July 1934, then deputized for Stanley Black in late 1934. Rejoined Lew Stone in January 1935 (playing in duo piano presentations with Stanley Black). Regularly with Lew Stone until 1939, also worked with Jack Hylton in spring of 1937 and with Debroy Somers. With Harry Roy (1939–40), then served for six months in the Royal Army Service Corps before doing solo radio work (spring 1941). Worked with Billy Ternent's BBC Radio Orchestra during World War II, also did wartime tours with Larry Adler entertaining troops. Led own 20th Century Orchestra and did solo broadcasts throughout the 1940s. Toured with Sophie Tucker (summer 1948), then joined Maurice Winnick. Again with Harry Roy (1949) and again worked as accompanist for harmonica player Larry Adler. With Harry Robbins' Quartet (early 1951), then joined staff at the Boosey and Hawkes publishing company and quit full time playing. Became Head of Light Music at Boosey and Hawkes, retired in 1977.

LITTLEJOHNS, 'Alan' Albert John Alan
trumpet/flugelhorn/vocals

Born: Highgate, London, 4 January 1928
Died: Barnet, Hertfordshire, 12 November 1995

Bought first trumpet in 1946. Gigged in North London with the Blue Note Swingtet before playing in the Galleon Jazz Band, then joined Cy Laurie (spring 1952). Joined Eric Silk in October 1953. Moved to Manchester for eight months in 1954 and worked in Ron Simpson's band, and in the Saints Jazzband (deputizing for Mike McNamara). Returned to London in late 1954 and rejoined Eric Silk. Led own band from 1955, which played long residency at Putney Jazz Club. Worked with Lionel Kerrien (1958), Len Doughty (1959), Dave Shepherd (1959), then formed own band for Chelsea residency (October 1960). Continued to lead own band but also worked with Wally Fawkes (1962). Co-led band with Tony Milliner from summer of 1963 which accompanied various visiting American jazzmen, including Peanuts Hucko and Earle Warren. Played regularly in the Tally Ho Band (in London) during the 1960s and 1970s. Often worked with Dick Charlesworth in the 1970s and 1980s, two years with Sonny Dee in the early 1970s, also regularly in the Georgia Jazz Band. Played gigs in Spain and did five summer seasons in Munich, Germany (most of them with reed-player Neil Buckley). Led own band for long residency at the 100 Club, London, during the 1970s and 1980s which accompanied many visiting American musicians including Alan's mentor, trumpeter Billy Butterfield. Made guest appearances with the Merseysippi Jazz Band over a long period, and occasionally deputized in its two trumpet line-up. Featured with Laurie Chescoe's Good Time Jazz from August 1990 through to a month before his death.

LITTON, Martin Nicholas
Born: Grays, Essex, 14 May 1957
piano/arranger

Began playing piano at twelve. Studied in Colchester (1975–9) and gained music degree (doubled on flute for a while). During this period led own quartet (featuring Martin Wheatley and Paul Lacey), then joined Steve Lane on piano for two years. With Harry Gold from 1980, left in October 1983 to join Kenny Ball. Spent just over a year with Kenny Ball (including tour of Russia) then left to freelance. During the early 1980s worked with various bands, including the London Vintage Orchestra and Five-a-Slide, also with vocalist Johnny M. Subsequently began long association with Harry Strutters Hot Rhythm Orchestra (which has lasted through the 1990s). Deputized with Humphrey Lyttelton, Ken Colyer, George Melly, etc, and accompanied various visiting American musicians. Toured and recorded with John Petters. Was featured soloist at a Jelly Roll Morton tribute concert at Queen Elizabeth Hall, London, and this led to formation of own Red Hot Peppers (which has continued into the 1990s). Regularly with Bob Hunt's Duke Ellington Orchestra, also often with the Colville Collection, Keith Smith, Digby Fairweather, etc. Featured on annual Fats Waller tributes at the South Bank, London, through the 1990s, also active freelance; continues to accompany visiting American musicians. Uses his home in Hay-on-Wye as a base for widespread freelancing but also plays locally in a trio with Alan Cooper and cellist Stanley Adler (1996).

LLEWELLYN, Jack
Born: Blackpool, Lancashire, 23 August 1914
guitar
Died: 1988

Worked with Bertini's Orchestra in Blackpool (1934), then did a series of hotel residencies with the Orlando Orchestra before moving to London in 1935. Joined Sydney Lipton in summer of 1935, also did radio and recordings with Val Rosing (1935–6). With Harry Saville, George Elrick (1938), then joined Arthur Young's Band (1939), also worked in Eric Winstone's Quintet. With Dennis Moonan's Band (1940), left to join the Royal Marines (January 1941). After demobilization worked with Stephane Grappelli (late 1945–6), recorded with Django Reinhardt in London (1946). Extensive freelance session work, also worked with Eddie Carroll in 1949.

LOCKETT, Mornington
tenor sax/alto sax/clarinet

Born: Stepney, London, 19 November 1961

Raised on the Isle of Wight. Played clarinet at fourteen. Two years later began gigging with the Goose Island Syncopators and the Unity Stompers. Studied for three years at Dartington College, Devon. Remained in Devon, took up tenor sax in 1980, lessons from Bobby Wellins. Gigged with local bands, then moved to London in 1984 and studied at Guildhall School of Music. Played in Bullet Trains (1985–6), worked with Sarah Jane Morris, Jim Mullen's Quartet, led own group and freelanced. Regularly in Ronnie Scott's Sextet from late 1990s until 1993. Often with Sax Appeal from the late 1980s through the 1990s. Guested with Officer Dibble (1995), with vocalist Ian Shaw (1995–6) etc. and worked regularly in John Critchinson's Quartet (1995–6), with Martin Drew and in Andrea Vicari's Jazz Quintet (1996). His brother, Dorian, is a bassist.

LOCKYER, Malcolm Neville
piano/arranger

Born: Greenwich, London, 5 October 1923
Died: 28 June 1976

Attended East Ham Grammar School, then studied at the Royal Academy of Music. As a teenager played semi-professionally prior to joining RAF in 1942. Played with Sid Phillips' service band, then became part of Buddy Featherstonhaugh's Sextet (1944–5). After demobilization joined Ambrose (1946–7) then successfully freelanced as pianist and conductor (occasionally played in Kenny Baker's Dozen during the 1950s). Joined BBC staff and led various ensembles before directing the BBC Radio Big Band into the 1970s.

LODDER, Steve
keyboards/composer/arranger/organ

Born: St Helier, Jersey, 10 April 1951

After organ scholarship at Cambridge (Gonville and Caius College) became a music teacher in a comprehensive school. Organ teacher was Martin Neary. Freelanced in differing areas of music-making, including writing and performing for theatre, television and films. Established jazz reputation, working with Maggie Nicols, Very Varied, Jan Ponsford, John Etheridge, Henry Thomas, Harry Beckett, Deirdre Cartwright, Elephant, etc., and in duos with Paul Nieman. During the late 1980s did three tours with George Russell's Living Time Orchestra. Music director for Sarah Jane Morris (1989); toured Europe supporting Simply Red (May to June 1989). Toured and recorded with Carol Grimes. With Brian Abraham's District Six (including German tours). Began long musical association with Andy Sheppard in the late 1980s, which has involved duo work, in Co-Motion Quintet, the Big Band, then ten piece Big Co-Motion and, during the 1990s, trio work with Andy Sheppard and the Brazilian percussionist Nana Vasconcelos. Also with Sheppard (and John Harle) in Twentieth Century Saxophones. Provided music for dance project *Modern Living*. Formed own quartet in autumn 1992 (with Paul Javasinha, Dudley Phillips and Mike Bradley); with Phillips and Bradley accompanied American singer Ernestine Anderson (1994). Continues to lead own group through the 1990s, and to work in varied musical contexts with Andy Sheppard as well as participating in a wide range of ensembles including Nois, a Brazilian band featuring Monica Vasconcelos on vocals. Again worked with singer Carol Grimes, and in a saxophone and church organ duo with altoist Mark Ramsden. Took part in premiere of Andy Sheppard's *Harmattan* (with the Bergen Big Band from Norway) at the 1996 Cheltenham Jazz Festival.

LOFTS, 'Geoff' Geoffrey Brown
drums

Born: Lincoln, 31 March 1921

Played violin as a child but switched to drums and played them in the school orchestra. Gigged with local bands, then joined Len Marshall in Lincoln. First professional work with Ivor Kirchin, then joined RAF as part of Steve Race's Quintet (1941). With Steve Race through most of World War II, but also featured with Leslie Douglas' RAF Bomber Command Band (1945). After demobilization worked with Howard Lucraft (1946), made trip to Iceland with Buddy Featherstonhaugh (1946), with Frank Weir (1946–7). Regularly with Woolf Phillips' Big Band during the early 1950s, then ten year residency at the Milroy Club, London, with Paul Adam, combining this with increasingly busy freelance schedule. Many sessions with Steve Race for Rediffusion, etc., and many engagements with vocalists, including six week tour with Judy Garland. Active as a session man through the 1990s, regularly featured in Jack Emblow line-ups, and participating in work for film, television, radio and recordings.

LOSS, 'Joe' Joshua Alexander
violin

Born: East London, 22 June 1909
Died: London, 6 June 1990

Studied violin at Trinity College of Music and at London College of Music. Played local gigs, then worked in cinema orchestras before playing summer season in a band at the Chinese Cafe, Blackpool. Played in saxophonist Al Lever's Band at Wimbledon Palais, London (1929), and did broadcasts with Oscar Rabin's Band before leading own Harlem Band for residency at the Astoria Ballroom, London, from September 1930. Played at the Kit-Cat Club (1931–4) then returned to the Astoria from 1934 until March 1941. Thereafter played many ballroom dates, did one-night stands and played variety shows, subsequently achieving widespread popularity on many television shows. His band played in Europe in 1944, and thereafter did many overseas tours including a visit to China. He was awarded the OBE in 1978. He continued to front his band into the late 1980s.

LOVE, Geoff
trombone/arranger/vocals

Born: Todmorden, Yorkshire, 4 September 1918
Died: Middlesex, 8 July 1991

Father was an American professional dancer who settled in Britain. Played violin at school, left at fourteen to work as a motor mechanic. Took up trombone, played in Freddie Platt's Band at Carlton Ballroom, Rochdale (1935). Moved to London, worked with Jan Ralfini's Band, then did summer season at Hastings with Alan Green. Briefly with Sid Millward and with Ivor Kirchin before serving in the King's Royal Rifles from 1941 until 1946. After demobilization worked briefly with Leslie 'Jiver' Hutchinson, led own band, then joined Harry Gold from summer of 1946 to late 1949. Became freelance musician and musical director. Led own orchestra regularly for television, radio and recordings and acted as conductor for Marlene Dietrich, Paul Robeson, Judy Garland, etc. Enjoyed popular success as Manuel of the Mountains, and with own Billy's Banjo Band.

LOWTHER, 'Henry' Thomas Henry
trumpet/flugelhorn/violin/arranger/composer

Born: Leicester, 11 July 1941

Taught cornet by his father. Played in local Salvation Army Band, subsequently switched to trumpet. At eighteen studied violin at the Royal Academy of Music, resumed regular trumpet playing in 1960. Played in (and arranged for) the Keith Sansome-Austin Clarke Quintet in Leicester (1962). Moved to London and began long musical association with Mike Westbrook. Gigged with pianist Mike Taylor, and with drummer Jon Hiseman, then joined drummer Don Brown's Group Sounds Five (1965). Worked regularly with Manfred Mann from late 1965 until October 1966, then joined Fat John Cox. With John Dankworth from 1967, also with Graham Collier (1967), John Mayall (1968), John Warren (1968), New Jazz Orchestra (1968), Keef Hartley (1969); including tour of the USA). Own band 1969–70. During the 1970s worked with John Dankworth, again briefly with Manfred Mann. With Mike Gibbs, Kenny Wheeler, Bobby Lamb-Ray Premru, Michael Garrick, Barbara Thompson's Jubiaba, John Taylor, Kurt Edelhagen, Stan Tracey, Gordon Beck and own long-lasting Quarternity. Active in jazz education, regular teaching at summer schools, etc. Extensive freelance work through the 1980s and 1990s, with Graham Collier (including 1980 tour of India), with John Surman, Pete King, Stan Tracey, Mike Westbrook, Gil Evans, Alan Stuart, Kenny Wheeler Big Band, Charlie Watts, John Harle, the London Jazz Orchestra, touring with Mike Gibbs and the Creative Jazz Orchestra (1996) etc., also leading own Still Waters.

LUSHER, Don
trombone/euphonium

Born: Peterborough, Northamptonshire, 6 November 1923

Trombone from the age of six. Played in Deacon's School Orchestra in Peterborough and alongside father in a Salvation Army Band. Served in the 49th Infantry Division during World War II and played in divisional concert party band the Polar Stars. After demobilization briefly co-led band with Stan Butcher at Pembroke Dock, then joined Joe Daniels in summer 1947. With Lou Preager (1948), Maurice Winnick for a month (1948) then worked in the Squadronaires from December 1948 until April 1951. With Jack Parnell (1951), Eric Delaney (1951), Woolf Phillips (1951) and Geraldo from December 1951 until March 1953, also worked with Wally Rockett in 1952. With Ted Heath from 1953 until 1973, during this period also played on innumerable freelance sessions and led own groups, also worked in Jack Parnell's ATV Orchestra. Led own big band regularly from 1974, and did international touring for various musical directors including Robert Farnon, Nelson Riddle and Henry Mancini, accompanied many international stars including Frank Sinatra. Visited Australia and the USA to give master classes; in 1991 became a Fellow of the Royal Academy of Music. Musical director and leader of the Ted Heath Tribute Orchestra throughout the 1980s and 1990s, also regularly featured in *The Best of British Jazz* during this period. Guested in Kenny Baker's New Dozen and also continues to lead own line-ups. *The Don Lusher Book* was first published in 1985.

LYTTELTON, Humphrey Richard Adeane
trumpet/clarinet/tenor horn/composer

Born: Eton, Buckinghamshire, 23 May 1921

Began playing trumpet while at Eton. Joined the Grenadier Guards (1941). After demobilization (1946), studied at Camberwell School of Art, London, and sat-in with various bands at the Nut

House, the Orange Tree, etc. Played in Carlo Krahmer's band. Briefly led own pick-up band (March 1947), before joining George Webb's Dixielanders later that month. Formed own band in January 1948 and has continued to lead through the 1990s. Appeared with Derek Neville's Band at the Nice Festival in February 1948, also briefly co-led big band with visiting Australian pianist-leader Graeme Bell (1951) and co-led Paseo Band (with Freddy Grant) in 1952. Own band accompanied Sidney Bechet in London (1949) and later accompanied many visiting musicians and singers including Buck Clayton, Buddy Tate, Henry Allen, Jimmy Rushing and Joe Turner. Humph also worked as a cartoonist for the *Daily Mail* from 1949 until 1953, as well as writing the script for Wally Fawkes' 'Flook' strip. From 1948 onwards did regular international touring with own band: throughout Europe, to the USA and the Middle East. Formed own big band in 1958, which often performed in the 1960s. In 1977 toured as a soloist with the *Salute to Satchmo* package, and guested with Alex Welsh's Band when the show toured Australia in 1978. For over thirty years Humph has regularly guested with various British bands including Mike Pembroke's Hot Seven, Mart Rodger's Hot Seven, Dave Morgan's Band, the Red River Jazzmen, Zenith Hot Stompers, George Huxley's Band, the Zenith Six, etc., also made guest appearances in Canada during the 1980s. Prolific composer and successful author and broadcaster. His many books include: *I Play As I Please* (1954), *Second Chorus* (1958), *Take It from the Top* (1975), *The Best of Jazz 1* (1978), *The Best of Jazz 2* (1981), *Why No Beethoven* (1984). Own Calligraph record label from 1984. Own band continues through the 1990s, also concert tours and recordings with singer Helen Shapiro and in group co-led with Acker Bilk.

M

MACAFFER, Don
trombone

Born: Glasgow, Scotland, 14 February 1911
Died: London, 1979

Brother of trumpeter Jimmy Macaffer. Originally a printer, played in Glasgow Boys' Brigade Band and in CWS Band before working with Louis Freeman's Orchestra and with Chalmers Wood (1928). Originally doubled on trumpet. Moved to London, joined Al Collins (late 1930), then worked with Savoy Hotel Orpheans (jointly directed by Howard Jacobs and Carroll Gibbons) before moving back to Scotland to work in brother Jimmy's band (1932–3). Returned to London and in autumn 1933 worked with Jack Harris, Dave Frost and Maurice Winnick. Joined Teddy Joyce (summer 1934), then worked with Lew Stone for a year from late 1934 before rejoining Teddy Joyce. With Ambrose (1936), Roy Fox (1937). Briefly with Cecil Black (spring 1939), then joined Sid Millward. With Joe Loss then joined RAF. Played in Buddy Featherstonhaugh's RAF Sextet, but also managed freelance engagements with various bands, mostly in London (including work with Joe Loss). After demobilization joined the Skyrockets from March 1946, and stayed for ten years; during this period played various freelance sessions including a film appearance with Joe Daniels. Did summer season with Harry Gold in Scarborough in 1958, then worked freelance in London. Having joined the Territorial Army he played in the Middlesex Yeomanry Band in the 1970s and guested with Len Arthur's Big Band during the last years of his life.

MACAFFER, 'Jimmy' James Swan
trumpet/arranger

Born: Glasgow, Scotland, 14 September 1913

Brother of trombonist Don Macaffer. Played in Glasgow Boys' Brigade Band before working with Louis Freeman and Chalmers Wood in Glasgow during the late 1920s. Moved to London, joined Al Collins (late 1930), with Billy Mason Band (autumn 1931), freelanced with Spike Hughes, then moved back to Glasgow to lead own band at Green's Playhouse (1932 and again in 1933). With Bert Firman (late 1932), Jack Harris, Dave Frost, Dick de Pauw (1933), Teddy Joyce (1934), Lew Stone (1935). With Mrs Jack Hylton (October 1935 to April 1936). Rejoined Teddy Joyce (1936). With Eddie Carroll (late 1937). With Lou Preager (1938), brief tour of Scandinavia with Joe Daniels (autumn 1938). With Sid Millward (1939). Served in Army 1941–3. Formed own band (1944), then worked with Edmundo Ros and with Jack Payne. With Harry Leader (1946), then joined Billy Munn, but took leave to do a month's tour with Sophie Tucker (summer 1948). Left Munn to lead own band at Locarno Ballroom, Dundee (1948–9), subsequently mainly active as a freelance.

MACAULEY, Eddie
piano

Born: Oldham, Lancashire, c.1908

Worked at Ferranti's factory in Lancashire and played local gigs. Visited USA, then returned to Lancashire and formed own band which won a contest (organized by *Rhythm* magazine) at Bolton Palais in 1931. Later that year the band won a *Melody Maker* contest and then gained a place in the All-England finals (1932). Turned professional, worked with Billy Woodward at Ashton Palais, then joined Jack Hylton (1935). Settled in London, left Jack Hylton and briefly joined Dare Lea's Band before working regularly in Oscar Grasso's Band in London from 1936 until July 1939. Also played on many Victor Sylvester dates in the 1930s, and accompanied Benny Carter in London (January 1937). Temporarily moved back to Oldham at outbreak of World War II. Worked for local manufacturing company, then returned to London and briefly resumed working with Oscar Grasso (late 1939–40) before joining Ambrose (1940). Left to work in aircraft construction but returned to full time music in 1945 and joined Ben Edwards' Quintet, subsequently freelanced. Lived in West London through the 1950s then moved to Sussex.

MACINTOSH, Adrian Lynn
drums

Born: Tadcaster, Yorkshire, 7 March 1942

Began playing drums in his late teens. Gigged with bands in York, then moved to London in 1966 as part of guitarist Mick McNeill's Band. Worked with John Taylor's Trio at the Lilliput Club, regularly accompanied Bobby Breen, Norma Winstone, etc. (1966–8). Worked with Alan Elsdon, Ray Crane-Maurice Jennings Quintet, and quintet led by tuba-player Ken McCarthy in the late 1960s and early 1970s. Co-led band with pianist Ted Beament which accompanied visiting jazzmen, Sonny Stitt, Teddy Edwards, Red Holloway, Jimmy Witherspoon, etc. Worked at Playboy Club in Lennie Felix's Trio, and in Eddie Thompson's Trio. Together with Paul Bridge accompanied Harold Ashby and Nat Pierce. From the late 1970s through the 1980s regularly in Brian Leake's Sweet and Sour, and in Brian Leake's Trio. Regularly with Humphrey Lyttelton from May 1982 through the 1990s, during this period also leads own trio, quartet and sextet, and guested with the Eastern All Stars, etc. From the early 1980s through the 1990s active on Musicians' Union Committees, and serving as Chairperson of British Association of Jazz Musicians.

MACKENZIE, Henry   Born: Edinburgh, Scotland, 15 February 1923
clarinet/saxes/flute

Was originally taught by Mev Taylor. Worked in Edinburgh in band led by violinist George Adam, then served in Royal Army Service Corps and played in Army band. With Tommy Sampson (1947–8), with Dennis Hale's Band in Southsea (1949), then again worked with Tommy Sampson (1949) before touring with Paul Fenoulhet (1949). Joined Ted Heath in September 1949 and worked with him for almost twenty years, except for brief recall to the Army in 1951. Extensive freelance activities from the 1960s onwards, with Henry Mancini, Billy May, Nelson Riddle, etc. Played residency at the Georgian Club, London, during the 1960s. Worked with Eric Winstone, Stan Reynolds, Billy Ternent, Max Harris, etc., often in George Chisholm's small groups. Continued to freelance successfully through the 1990s, leading own quintet, playing in Don Lusher's Ted Heath Band, etc.

MACKINTOSH, 'Andy' Andrew Kenneth   Born: London, 20 May 1953
saxes/clarinet/flute/arranger/composer

Son of Ken Mackintosh. Began on soprano sax at age of four, also played piano and drums as a child, then specialized on alto sax. Played in the St Joseph College Band in South London. With London Youth Jazz Orchestra in 1967. Played in Ken Mackintosh's Band during the late 1960s, also worked in John Mayer's Indo-Jazz Fusion and with the group Smile. With Maynard Ferguson from 1971 until 1974, settled in Los Angeles. Worked in the USA with Louis Bellson, Les Brown, Lionel Hampton, Quincy Jones, Buddy Rich, Toshiko Akiyoshi-Lew Tabackin, etc. and did prolific freelance work in the studios. Co-led quintet with trombonist Bill Reichenbach in Los Angeles (1980). Returned to London in 1980 and began freelancing in a variety of groups, led own quintet and was musical director of Jack Sharpe's Big Band from 1986 to 1994. Continues to lead own band in the 1990s, but also works regularly with Madelaine Bell, John Dankworth, etc. Worked in Gail Thompson's Big Band in 1994. Continues with extensive freelance work, leading own band and playing sessions (1996).

MACKINTOSH, 'Ken' Kenneth Victor   Born: Cleckheaton, Yorkshire, 4 August 1919
alto sax/clarinet

Father of Andy, uncle of pianist-arranger Robert Hartley (born 1939). Ken's father played violin and trombone. Saxophone from age of fourteen, gigged in Leeds and Bradford area. Professional at nineteen, worked mainly in Leeds and in the West Riding of Yorkshire, often in bands led by Roland Powell. Joined Army at twenty and spent four years in the RASC (including service in France). Later worked with George Elrick and Johnny Claes before joining Oscar Rabin in late summer of 1944. Left Rabin in spring of 1947 to join Frank Weir. Formed own big band, which began long residency at Astoria Ballroom, Nottingham, in March 1948. The band moved to London and gained a national reputation, later playing numerous ballroom residencies throughout Britain, including many seasons in Blackpool and on the Isle of Man. Continues to lead a smaller line-up through the 1990s.

MacRAE, 'Dave' David Scott
keyboards/composer

Born: Auckland, New Zealand, 2 April 1940

Began playing piano at seventeen, worked in local rock groups, then spent six years freelancing in Australia, working mainly in Sydney and Melbourne. Moved to Los Angeles in 1969, joined Buddy Rich. Later toured Europe with Rich. During the early 1970s worked in Britain with Annie Ross, Mike Gibbs, Mike Westbrook, Back Door, Karl Jenkins, Frank Reed's Powerhouse and Ian Carr's Nucleus. Led Pacific Eardrum during the 1970s. Moved back to New Zealand; musically active there and in Australia.

MAIRANTS, Ivor
guitar/banjo

Born: Rypin, Poland, 18 July 1908

Moved to London in summer of 1914. Bought banjo at age of fifteen. Gigged with the Valencians and with the Florentines, then joined Fred Anderson's Cabaret Band from April 1927 to July 1928. Began doubling on guitar. Played for silent films, then joined Percival Mackey (1929). With Emile Grimshaw's Banjo Quartet, Simms Waller's Sons of Guns Orchestra, Marius B. Winter and in house band at the Spider's Web roadhouse (1932), before joining Jack Padbury. Left Padbury to work with Roy Fox from October 1932 until August 1937, playing and singing in the Cubs, (made many freelance recordings during this period). By now specializing on guitar. With Lou Levy's Orchestra briefly in 1937, then freelance sessions for recordings, radio and films, also teaching regularly. With Ambrose from June 1938 until autumn 1939. With Bert Firman (October 1939), remained with the band under George Melachrino's leadership (November 1939). With Lew Stone (1940). Seriously ill in autumn 1940 but by the end of that year had recovered and began long musical association with Geraldo, also worked with Ambrose (1941). Regularly with Geraldo until July 1952, but freelanced on records, and did occasional 'outside' work including some with pianist-vocalist Hamish Menzies (October 1946). Opened Central School of Dance Music in 1950 (ten years later handed over the School to Eric Gilder), during the 1950s directed own Jazz Youth Orchestra. Extensive freelance work after 1952, many overseas tours (and a trip to Russia in summer 1957). Opened own music shop in 1962 but continued to play regularly into the 1980s and to teach. Wrote guitar tutors and teaching manuals. His autobiography *My Fifty Fretting Years* was published in 1980 and his book *The Great Jazz Guitarists* was published in 1995.

MANN, 'Tony' (Anthony PRITCHARD)
drums

Born: Frome, Somerset, 31 January 1942

Lived in Mitcham, Surrey, during childhood, took up drums at seven. Lived in Cheltenham as a teenager and played local gigs. During his late teens played in Peter King's Quintet, then worked with Denny Boyce and in Tubby Hayes' Quartet (1960). Appeared in the play *The Connection* during early months of 1961, and worked in the Vic Ash-Harry Klein Jazz Five. With Bobby Wellins (1961), then freelanced with many jazz groups and worked in Miff Smith's Band at the

Celebrite, London (1963). With Humphrey Lyttelton from 1970 until 1978, during this period also worked in Kathy Stobart's Quintet, and in Tony Lee's Trio. Did several tours of Europe with Barney Kessel. With Werner Müller's Radio Big Band in Cologne, Germany (1980). In 1981 moved to Stockport, near Manchester, and ran own drum shop there until 1993. Continued to lead own trio during this period and freelanced with various line-ups. Toured Italy with Barney Kessel in 1987, then worked often in Italy through the 1990s with Tal Farlow, Art Farmer, etc. Continues to freelance through the 1990s, regularly with pianist Joe Palin and teaching two days a week at Leeds College of Music.

MARKS, Johnny	Born: London, 4 April 1908
drums	Died: London, 25 September 1955

First professional playing took place during a brief sojourn in Ireland. Returned to London and worked in the house band at Salon de Bal in Haringey. With Eddie Gross-Bart and with Bert Firman in 1933. First worked with Lou Preager in the 1920s but joined him on a regular basis in the summer of 1933 and stayed for several years. Recorded with Fats Waller in London (April 1939). With Sid Millward before joining Nat Gonella from late 1940 until summer 1941. Led band at the Nut House, London from late 1941. With Maurice Winnick (1943), Phil Green (1944–5), then left full time music but resumed regular playing in the early 1950s.

MARKS, 'Jon' Jonathan	Born: Slough, Buckinghamshire, 11 July 1947
piano	

Raised in Portsmouth. Piano at seven, joined the San Jacinto Jazzmen (led by Frank Hurlock) at fourteen. Turned professional at seventeen by joining Keith Smith. Left in late 1967, joined Barry Martyn and played first New Orleans Jazz Festival (1968). Returned to England, briefly rejoined Keith Smith, then worked again with Barry Martyn. With Sammy Rimington's Quartet and the Gothic Jazz Band (1968), then regularly with Barry Martyn through to 1974, playing often in the USA. Again with Sammy Rimington (1974), then became road manager of the Legends of Jazz (based in America) and did widespread international touring. Featured in various tours: *Night in New Orleans, Thousand Years of Jazz*, etc. With Legends of Jazz through to 1979. By this time had moved to live in Berlin, Germany. Joined the White Eagle Band and toured Germany with them. Played several seasons on the Italian liner *Eugenio*, leading own band on voyages to South America, USA, Russia, the Far East, etc. Again worked with Sammy Rimington often from 1984 through the 1990s. Played at various international festivals, also did several tours with the Maryland Jazz Band, accompanying visiting American musicians. During the 1990s played drums with the White Eagle Band in Berlin, as a hobby, but continued with busy and varied piano-playing schedule, which included tours with American gospel singer Jan Harrington (in duos and as part of the Gospel Train). Throughout career has made many recordings with various famous New Orleans musicians, including Kid Thomas, Louis Nelson, Alvin Alcorn, Willie and Percy Humphrey, Sam Lee, Wallace Davenport, etc. Toured USA with Sammy Rimington (1996).

MARSH, Roy
vibes/piano/drums

Born: Ealing, London, 6 July 1917

Father played drums. Roy's son Roger 'Tex' Marsh is also a drummer. Began on drums at twelve, also played piano as a teenager. Worked with Billy Wiltshire and Cliff Townshend at the Hotel de Paris, Maidenhead (1935), and began doubling on vibes. Worked with Billy Wiltshire until 1940, but also with Phil Watts for freelance dates in 1939. Often in Harry Parry's Sextet from 1940 until 1942, including *Radio Rhythm Club* broadcasts and touring. Played in duo with Eric Winstone at the Master Robert, in West London (summer 1940), and with organist Robin Richmond's Quartet (late 1940). Briefly co-led sextet with trumpeter Jack Hamilton (summer 1941). Doubled by working with both Harry Parry and with Eric Winstone (early 1942), then from spring 1942 was featured exclusively with Eric Winstone through to the early 1970s (originally on drums and vibes but exclusively on vibes from 1949). Led own small groups in the 1970s and 1980s, made many television appearances and provided background music for television productions. Also played regularly in Henry Mackenzie's Sextet. Moved to Bognor Regis in the late 1980s, continued to play locally through the 1990s.

MARSHALL, John Stanley
drums

Born: Isleworth, Middlesex, 28 August 1941

Began playing drums at school. After studying psychology at Reading University worked at the Club Octave, then joined Alexis Korner's Blues Incorporated in 1963. Did summer season at Filey, Yorkshire. Worked often with Graham Collier from 1966–70. During the late 1960s also worked with Mike Gibbs, with Harold Beckett's Quartet, with Bob Stuckey, Keith Tippett, Joe Harriott and John Mayer's Indo-Jazz Fusions, etc. Founder member of Ian Carr's Nucleus from September 1969, worked with Nucleus until 1971, then toured with Jack Bruce, also worked in Tony Coe-Kenny Wheeler Quintet in 1970. With John McLaughlin, again with Mike Gibbs, and accompanying various visiting American musicians. Regularly with Soft Machine from early 1972 through to 1981 (including period as co-leader with Karl Jenkins). During this period also worked with Chris McGregor, Mick Pyne's Quartet, in Pork Pie, Matrix, and from 1977 in bassist Eberhard Weber's Colours (through to 1981). International freelance work from the 1970s, working in Europe with Gil Evans, Charlie Mariano, Albert Mangelsdorff, Manfred Schoof, Philip Catherine, John Surman, etc. From the early 1980s organized many drum clinics, and took part in jazz education projects. Part of Nucleus reunion (including tour of South America), and also part of Soft Machine reunion in 1984. Appeared with the Hamburg Radio Orchestra. With Elaine Delmar and with Norma Winstone. During the 1990s with many ensembles including Gordon Beck's Trio, John Surman's Brass Project and Quartet, Uli Beckerhoff's Quartet, Theo Travis Quintet, Kenny Wheeler line-ups and freelancing internationally.

MARTIN, Claire
vocals

Born: Wimbledon, Surrey, 6 September 1967

Left stage school and sang professionally in Bournemouth before working on various cruise liners including the *QE2*. Studied in New York with Marilyn J. Johnson then returned to London in 1991 and formed own band which played club residencies and toured. Worked in Washington, DC, in

Hong Kong and Paris. Was featured at festivals and guested with various line-ups including Mick Hutton's Straight Face, the BBC Radio Big Band, Bobby Wellins' Quartet, Ray Gelato's Giants, Martin Taylor's groups, John Stevens, etc. Worked with own successful trio (1995) and did featured solo appearances (accompanied by pianist Gareth Williams) in Germany, Austria and Switzerland. In duos with Jim Mullen, Ian Shaw, Dave Newton, etc. Touring and playing international dates (1966). Own group featured at Ronnie Scott's Club, London (1996).

MARTYN, Barry (Barry Martin GODFREY)
drums

Born: London, 23 February 1941

Father of drummer Emile Martyn. Began playing drums at fourteen. Led own band from 1956. Went to Canada in 1960, played gigs there, then moved on to New Orleans in December 1960, was coached by drummer Joseph 'Cie' Frazier. Returned to Britain in March 1961. Led own Camellia Jazz Orchestra, then returned to New Orleans in early 1962. Returned to Britain in spring 1962 and became part of the Kid Martyn Ragtime Band (which had been led in Barry's absence by pianist Graham Patterson). Returned to New Orleans, gigged with various bands, and received further coaching, recorded with Kid 'Sheik' Colar (1963). Back in Britain he organized tours of Europe for American musicians, and accompanied George Lewis, Albert Nicholas, Louis Nelson, etc. Moved back to USA in 1966, recorded in New Orleans with Captain John Handy, Percy Humphrey, etc. Worked with Sammy Rimington's Band and co-led with Keith Smith briefly before re-forming own band in late summer of 1967. Led with success throughout Europe often accompanying visiting musicians, then moved to USA in 1972. Based in Los Angeles from November 1972. Organized Legends Of Jazz which did international concert tours from 1973, also toured in Barney Bigard's Pelican Trio (1978). During the 1980s toured with the Young Men of New Orleans. Settled in New Orleans in 1984, continued to play regularly with own band, with Chris Burke's Trio, with Rudy Balliu's Society Serenaders, but also active as a jazz historian. Edited Barney Bigard's 1985 autobiography *With Louis and the Duke*. Returns to Europe for occasional tours.

MASEKELA, Hugh Ramopolo
trumpet/flugelhorn/vocals

Born: Witbank, South Africa, 4 April 1939

As a teenager played trumpet in the Johannesburg Native Band. Lessons in playing jazz from saxophonist Kippie Moeketsi. Formed the Merry Makers of Spring with trombonist Jonas Gwanga. Played in Alfred Herbert's *Africa Jazz Revue* (1957) and for the *King Kong* musical. Formed the Jazz Epistles, with Jonas Gwanga and pianist Abdullah Ibrahim (Dollar Brand). Moved to London to study briefly at the Guildhall School of Music, then went to New York to study at the Manhattan School of Music (1960). Toured with his wife, singer Miriam Makeba, and with Harry Belafonte. Made California his base for several years. Playing visits to Europe through to the 1990s, including tours of Britain with All South African Band in 1993. Toured Africa during the 1970s, then moved to Zimbabwe and to Botswana before settling in South Africa in the 1990s.

MASON, Billy
piano/arranger

Born: Scotland, 1897
Died: Scotland, 21 October 1960

His sister Kathleen was a vocalist. Billy qualified as a marine engineer before serving as a pilot in

World War I. First professional work with the Southern Syncopated Orchestra (then on tour in Scotland). Played in Glasgow University Band before joining Manhattan Five in Edinburgh. Led own band and worked as a house pianist at Glasgow Plaza, then joined Alfredo and his Orchestra in London. Brief return to Glasgow, then joined Fred Elizalde in London. Left to lead at Claridges's Hotel, then took own band into Café de Paris from summer 1930 until late 1931. Led own band at Carlton Hotel, Amsterdam (late 1931). Recorded with Spike Hughes. Led band that accompanied Louis Armstrong in Britain 1932, then joined Ennis Hylton's Band for a few months in 1933. Led own band at Florida Club, London (1934), and did extensive freelance recordings, including some with American Valaida Snow. Led own band again in Scotland (1938–9) and on tour, again led in London (1938). Engaged on war work from 1940 until 1943 but continued to broadcast, usually as a solo pianist. Ill health ended war work in 1943, later did service tours with own band for ENSA and for USO, then retired from full time music to help run family hotel near Loch Lomond. Again led band occasionally during the late 1940s and 1950s.

MASON, Pat
piano

Born: c.1932
Died: January 1993

Originally played trumpet, switched to piano in 1953. Gigged with bands in Essex and the East London area. Played in Kenny Ball's Band during the mid-1950s, then gigged with Mick Mulligan, Freddy Randall, Dave Jones, Alan Littlejohns, Dick Williams, etc. Regularly with Charlie Galbraith from 1960 until working briefly with Mickey Ashman in summer of 1963. Deputized for Ron Weatherburn in Kenny Ball's Band (early 1964). Led own band in the 1960s and again worked with Charlie Galbraith and with Freddy Randall. During the 1970s and 1980s continued to lead own groups, played long residency in Buckhurst Hill, Essex, but also worked with Alan Littlejohns, Digby Fairweather, Rod Hamer, etc.

MASON, 'Phil' Philip Anthony
trumpet

Born: Kentish Town, London, 10 April 1940

Father a professional oboist. Phil studied at Dublin University and gained degree in English. While in Ireland played in the Trinity Jazz Band. Returned to London and joined the New Sedalia Jazz Band, then worked with Eric Silk from 1967 until joining Max Collie in 1970. Remained with Max Collie until 1983, then worked for almost two years with Pete Allen before rejoining Collie in 1985. Moved to the Isle of Bute, guested with the Louisiana Jazz Band in Edinburgh during the 1980s and continued to work with Max Collie into the 1990s but from 1992 onwards mainly occupied with leading own New Orleans All Stars (featuring singer Christine Tyrrell).

MASON, Rod
cornet/valve trombone/clarinet/tuba

Born: Plymouth, Devon, 28 September 1940

Played violin during childhood. Took up valve trombone while at Kelly College in Tavistock. With the Apex Jazz Band, then joined the Tamar Valley Jazz Band (in which his father played drums); switched to cornet. Became co-leader with Alan Collinge. Moved to London in 1960, worked with Cy Laurie in summer of 1960, formed own band late in 1960. With Monty Sunshine from February 1961 to January 1965 (except for leave of absence through illness). Worked briefly on bass guitar with a Hertfordshire group, then moved back to Devon to lead Tamar Valley Jazz Band for residencies in Plymouth. Handed over leadership to clarinettist Roy Pellett and joined Acker Bilk in August 1971. Left Acker Bilk in 1973, worked in drummer Colin Symon's Band, then co-led with Ian Wheeler from October 1973 to spring 1976. Season in Guernsey (summer 1976), then again led own band in the West Country, and on tours, until joining the Dutch Swing College Band in early 1981. Left in early 1985 and led own Hot Five throughout Europe, long residencies in Germany, touring and playing festivals through the 1990s.

MATHEWSON, 'Ron' Rognuald Andrew   Born: Lerwick, Shetland Isles, 19 February 1944
double bass/bass guitar

Brother of pianist Matt. Piano from early childhood, double bass from age of fifteen, played in local dance band. Left Shetland Isles at seventeen to work in Germany for five months with trombonist Ken Ramage's Dixielanders. Joined Clyde Valley Stompers in late 1962, which regrouped as Pete Kerr's Scottish All Stars. Brief spell in London, then moved back to Scotland with Kerr's Band until they disbanded in January 1964. Did local gigs, then moved to London to join Alex Welsh's Band in spring 1964, left Welsh a year later. Worked for three months in Fat John Cox's band, then rejoined Alex Welsh for eight months. Worked at Georgian Club, London, then joined John Stevens Septet (late 1965). Again briefly with Alex Welsh in 1966, then began long musical association with Tubby Hayes in 1966, also worked in Ray Russell's Quartet (1968), with Stan Tracey, Philly Joe Jones, and in Ronnie Scott's Octet (1968), Big Band (1969) and Sextet (1970). Often with Clarke-Boland Big Band from 1969. Accompanied many visiting jazz stars in the 1960s, 1970s and 1980s. With Tony Coe-Kenny Wheeler Quintet (1970), with Phil Woods (in European Rhythm Machine and on tour in the USA, 1971). With many line-ups in the 1970s, including Mick Pyne's Trio, Gordon Beck's Gyroscope, Pat Smythe's Trio, Michael Garrick's Sextet, Tony Kinsey's Quintet, Ian Hamer's Sextet, Stan Sulzmann's Quartet, Ronnie Ross's Sextet, John Taylor, Paz, etc. Regularly with Ronnie Scott from 1977 until early 1992. During this period freelanced with various groups and worked in Charlie Watts' Big Band (1985 and 1986). After leaving Scott in early 1992 continued to play regularly, working with many various groups including own line-ups.

MAXWELL, Clinton   Born: Jamaica, West Indies
drums/bongoes

Studied music at Alpha Cottage School in Kingston, Jamaica. Worked in Bertie King's Band in Jamaica. Moved to Britain and joined Ken Johnson. With Al Jennings (1939), Rudolph Dunbar (1940), Don Marino Barreto (1941), Cyril Blake (1941) and Clarie Wears (1941–2). With Jack Hamilton (1942), Jimmy Cummins' Rhumba Band (1942), again with Don Marino Barreto, then rejoined Jimmy Cummins (1943). Radio work with Carl Barriteau. With Leslie 'Jiver' Hutchinson (1944–6), again with Clarie Wears (1946). Led own band (1947), then again worked with Cyril Blake (1947). In Elizabeth Balk's group Beseba and her Jamaicans (1948), again with Cyril Blake (1948). Toured Germany with American cornetist Rex Stewart (1948). With Don Carlos' Rhumba Band (1949). Again with Jimmy Cummins (1951–3), with pianist Kenny Powell, then rejoined Jimmy Cummins (1954–6).

MAY, Tina
vocals
Born: Gloucester, 30 March 1961

Married to drummer Clark Tracey. First vocal training as a teenager. Did first jazz singing while studying for degree in Cardiff. Combined this with work as an actress. Further studies in Paris, sat in with various jazz groups. Returned to Britain, became part of the Back Door Theatre Company. Made many appearances at Edinburgh Festival Fringe theatres both as a singer and actress. Worked in cabaret and with trio (alongside Dylan Fowler on guitar and Thad Kelly on bass), and as part of Frevo (with Dylan Fowler). Formed own quartet in 1989 but continued to make freelance appearances with the BBC Radio Big Band, with Stan Tracey's Orchestra, etc. Extensive and successful recordings. Regular club work, touring and concerts, mostly with own line-ups, including an occasional String Quartet. Guested with the *Ladies of Jazz* (alongside Maxine Daniels and Barbara Jay) in spring 1996. Also active in jazz education, tutoring at weekend jazz courses.

MAYES, 'Chick' Charles
trumpet
Born: Stratford, London, 25 October 1921

Father was a trombonist. Trumpet from age of six. At fourteen did an eight month season at the London Palladium with Bob Busby's Band. Worked with Leon Cortez before joining Sonny Farrar (1938). With George Shearing, Harry Parry, and Jack Hargreaves at the St Regis Club (1940). With Oscar Rabin (1941), briefly with Billy Cotton, then joined Harry Roy. Left Harry Roy in March 1942, worked with Maurice Winnick, then rejoined Harry Roy in August 1942. Led own sextet at Merry Go Round Club, London (late 1942–3), then joined the Army in June 1943. Became director of the Middle East Land Forces' Service Band. Left Army in 1947, immediately joined Joe Loss. Left Joe Loss in May 1948. Freelance session work, then did summer season with Maurice Smart (1949). Worked with Nat Temple until autumn 1952, worked with Charlie Galbraith's Jazz Band (1952). With Carl Barriteau from March to August 1953, briefly with Johnnie Gray then rejoined Nat Temple in October 1953. Toured with Frankie Vaughan's Show, then worked regularly with Confrey Phillips and did extensive freelance work. Ceased playing in the early 1990s.

McDEVITT, 'Andy' Andrew
saxes/clarinet
Born: Scotland, 13 January 1914
Died: England, 15 March 1980

Worked for Louis Freeman in Scotland (and on liner *California*), then did summer season with Slim Grossman in Bournemouth (1934). Worked with Billy Mason, then again with Louis Freeman's Orchestra in Glasgow until joining Teddy Joyce in June 1935. Left Carl Tauber to join Ambrose briefly in spring of 1936. With Sydney Kyte and Gerry Moore (1936). Recorded with Lew Stone. Worked with Benny Carter in London (January 1937). With Roy Fox (1938), then joined Dennis Van Thal's Orchestra (summer 1938). With Oscar Grasso's Band (late 1938), then joined Geraldo (January 1939), also did regular radio work with Phil Watts (1938–9). With Jack Nathan's Quintet (late 1939). Joined RAF in 1940 and became founder-member of the Squadronaires. Also guested with various bands during the early 1940s, including work with Johnny Claes. Remained with the Squadronaires through World War II, and stayed until early

1952. Then became highly successful freelance musician, often with the BBC Variety Orchestra. Studio work through the 1960s and 1970s, regularly with the BBC Radio Orchestra. Continued to play freelance gigs including taking part in Dave Hancock's Big Band during the 1970s.

McFARLANE, Howard Osmond
trumpet

Born: London, 13 November 1894
Died: London, 6 March 1983

Served as a band boy with the British Army in India during his mid-teens, was later with the British infantry in Flanders in World War I. After demobilization played around the Brighton area, then joined Alex Hyde and his Band in London (January 1924). Worked in Germany with Alex Hyde for several months, then joined band led by Bernard Ette. Later worked with other bands in Germany including Marek Weber's and Dajos Béla's, and led own recording bands. Also worked in Switzerland and Holland before returning to London in early 1933. Worked with Jack Jackson in London (1933–4), then spent two years again working with Dajos Béla in Holland and South America. Returned to London, freelanced, then worked for Maurice Winnick in Italy and Norway before settling in London in summer of 1939. Worked with Billy Ternent's BBC Dance Orchestra (1940), then joined BBC Revue Orchestra until 1957. Continued to play regularly until 1972.

McGREGOR, Chris
piano/composer/arranger

Born: Umtata, Somerset West, South Africa,
24 December 1936
Died: Agen, France, 26 May 1990

Raised in the Transkei district from age of two. Piano from six, moved to Cape Town and while attending the College of Music gigged in student jazz groups (1956). Occasionally played in various cities in South Africa during the late 1950s, then formed Blue Notes from participants in the 1962 Johannesburg Jazz Festival (also briefly led own band in 1963). The Blue Notes remained in Europe after playing at the 1964 Antibes Jazz Festival. They busked around the Côte d'Azur and then played engagements in Switzerland before moving to Britain in April 1965. McGregor played at Ronnie Scott's and then settled in London, but fulfilled engagements in Copenhagen, Denmark, in 1966. Worked in drummer Norman Caldas' Quintet (1967). The Blue Notes disbanded (but temporarily re-formed in 1975). McGregor formed Brotherhood of Breath for London debut on 19 June 1970. Moved to Aquitaine, France, in 1974, but continued to lead Brotherhood of Breath for specific engagements during the 1980s, including a tour of Mozambique. McGregor played many solo engagements in the 1980s and worked with saxophonist George Lee, he also toured with Harold Beckett's Quartet 1988–9. Despite suffering from terminal lung cancer he continued to play as often as possible during the last year of his life.

McGUFFIE, 'Bill' William
piano/composer

Born: Carmyle, nr Glasgow, Scotland, 11 December 1927
Died: Middlesex, 22 March 1987

Piano at five, but at eight lost the third finger of his right hand. Soon recommended studies in Glasgow and won the Victoria College Medal at the age of twelve, also studied trombone, sax and violin. Performed on radio and with the Scottish Variety Orchestra during his early teens. Temporarily gave up music, then resumed playing with local dance bands. Briefly with Harry Leader, then worked around Glasgow with Lester Penman, Jack Chapman and Jimmy Gilchrist

(1944–5). With Miff Hobson's Band in Ayr, left to join Teddy Foster (1946). Moved to London, worked with Joe Loss for almost four years from July 1946. Joined Frank Weir in spring of 1950, then spent two years with Sydney Lipton. Freelance recordings. With the BBC Show Band from October 1952 until July 1955. During the 1950s also worked with Phil Green, Maurice Winnick, Ambrose, Robert Farnon, Nat Temple, Mantovani, etc. Played in Kenny Baker's Dozen on many occasions. Led own band at the May Fair Hotel in 1959. Prolific freelance work in the 1960s, 1970s and 1980s, including tours of Europe with Benny Goodman. Achieved considerable success playing and composing for films and television, both in the UK and the USA. Led own quintet and big band. In 1975 formed the Niner Club which raised large sums of money for autistic children.

McGURK, Peter
double bass

Born: Worthing, Sussex, 1927
Died: Putney, London, 17 June 1968

After RAF service worked with pianist Ted Taylor in Manchester through the early 1950s. Left Taylor to join Oscar Rabin in May 1955. With Basil Kirchin's Sextet (1957), then joined Cyril Stapleton (September 1957). Worked in Ray Ellington's Quartet and occasionally in John Dankworth line-ups. Regularly accompanied singer Matt Monro in cabaret. Featured in Dudley Moore's Trio for eight years, from 1960–8. He committed suicide by taking an overdose of drugs.

McHARG, Jim
double bass

Born: Glasgow, Scotland, 1927

Began on drums then played banjo before specializing on double bass. First gigs with Pine City Stompers in Bournemouth, then returned to Scotland in the early 1950s. Led Clyde Valley Stompers (at the Astoria Ballroom, Glasgow, etc.) from 1952 to 1953. Moved to Canada in the late 1950s for nearly four years, then returned to Britain in early 1960. Worked with Dick Charlesworth for a few months in 1961 then formed own band (1961). Toured for a year then played regularly in Scotland before emigrating to Canada. Lived and played in Vancouver, then settled in Toronto in the late 1960s and began leading own band, which achieved long lasting success. During the early 1980s returned to Britain to tour with the Clyde Valley Stompers' Reunion Band.

McINTYRE, Joe
trumpet

Born: Ireland, 1935
Died: Ireland, 1980

Professional musician from the age of fifteen. Worked in band led by his cousin, saxophonist Gay McIntyre (1953), then joined Harry Gold and moved to England. With Harry Gold from March 1954 until 1955, with Laurie Gold (1956). Briefly returned to Ireland, then moved back to Britain to work with Des Williams in Bristol (August 1956). Again with Laurie Gold (1957–8), with Vic Lewis (spring 1958), gigged with Teddy Foster, then joined Sid Phillips. Left Sid Phillips in spring 1962 to work in the Clyde Valley Stompers. With Terry Lightfoot from December 1962 until 1963, then settled in Dublin. Worked in quintet co-led with tenor saxist Jim Farley and freelanced with various bands. During the 1990s, *Portrait of Joe*, dedicated to McIntyre, was performed by the All Ireland Big Band at the Cork Jazz Festival.

McKAY, 'Ron' Charles Ronald   Born: Bootle, Lancashire, 7 February 1929
drums/vocals

Worked for the High Commission for Germany (1946–7), then served in the Royal Navy from 1947 until 1949. Worked for the Air Ministry in London before becoming a professional musician. Gigged in London before joining Bob Dawbarn's Barnstormers (1951), then worked regularly with Cy Laurie from late 1951 until 1955. Worked with Kid Ericson's Band in Copenhagen, also accompanied Albert Nicholas, Peanuts Holland, etc. in Europe. Brief spell as drummer-vocalist with Dave Keir's Band (spring 1956), then returned to Liverpool (1956) to work in Ralph 'Bags' Watmough's Band, also played residency at the Cavern Club, compering and leading skiffle group (1957). Joined Acker Bilk in October 1957 and remained until October 1969. With Max Collie from November 1969 until May 1984. Freelanced in London, then moved back to the North in January 1985 and worked with bands in and around Manchester. Featured at various festivals. During various tours of the USA played with the Onward Brass Band, with Louis Cottrell, Pete Fountain, Roy Eldridge, etc. Regularly with the French Quarter in Manchester during the 1990s, also plays in various parade bands and frequently guests with Phil Mason's Band.

McKENZIE, 'Mike' Oscar Grenville   Born: British Guiana (now Guyana),
piano/vocals/arranger   17 September 1922

Was taught piano by his mother from the age of seven, and violin by his father at sixteen, also played cello. Played regularly in Georgetown, then moved to London in 1949. Freelanced, then worked with Joe Appleton (1950). Toured and recorded with Humphrey Lyttelton (1952), worked in Fela Sowande's BBC Ebony Club Band (1953). Guested with Chris Barber, and appeared in *Jazz Wagon* (with Jack Parnell). Guested with Lonnie Donegan and played as solo act on Moss Empire circuit. Played solo piano (and led own quartet at various London clubs including the Orchid Room, the Milroy, the Hungaria Restaurant, the Caprice, and four years at the Elephant On The River). Did seven-year solo residency at the Dorchester Hotel, London, then moved to the Savoy Hotel in the mid-1980s and began a nine year stay there.

McLAUGHLIN, John   Born: Kirk Sandall, Yorkshire, 4 January 1942
guitar/piano/vocals/synthesizer/composer

Mother a violinist. Piano and violin from age of nine, then took up guitar at eleven. Worked briefly in traditional band led by Pete Deuchar (1960) and with the EmCee Five (and Mike Carr) in Newcastle, then moved to London. Worked with Georgie Fame, in the Tony Meehan Combo and accompanied visiting American 'pop' stars. Joined the newly formed Graham Bond Quartet in 1963, then worked briefly with Brian Auger, and with Alexis Korner. Occasionally with John Surman, also accompanied poet/vocalist/trumpeter Pete Brown. During the 1960s also worked in Herbie Goins' Nightimers, in Mike Carr's Trio, Gordon Beck's Quartet, Danny Thompson's Trio, duos with Howard Riley and with Ronnie Scott, etc. Spent nine months in Germany playing in group led by German vibes player Gunter Hampel. To New York in February 1969, recorded with Miles Davis, joined Tony Williams' Lifetime for a year. By this time was deeply involved in eastern religion and philosophy; adopted the name Mahavishnu in 1970 and formed first of own groups bearing that name in summer of 1971, this disbanded in late 1973. A new Mahavishnu group flourished in 1974–5, other McLaughlin led groups, Shakti and One Truth Band functioned in the 1970s (until 1978). By then McLaughlin had settled in France. He organized another version of Mahavishnu, made further recordings with Miles Davis, and composed a concerto for guitar (1985). Appeared in Bertrand Tavernier's film *Round Midnight* (1986). He guested with various groups, played in guitar duos and trios, and worked with Wayne Shorter, Larry Coryell, pianist Katia Labeque, etc. During the late 1980s and 1990s led various trios for international tours and appearances at festivals. With own Free Spirits Trio in Europe (1995).

McLEVY, John H.
trumpet/flugelhorn

Born: Dundee, Scotland, 2 January 1927

Father was a semi-pro drummer who led his own band. Took up trumpet as a teenager. Played local engagements with Jack Watmore, then joined George Elrick before joining the Black Watch Regiment. After demobilization joined Les Ayling at the Lyceum, London, in spring of 1948. Returned to Dundee in January 1949 and worked with bassist Joe Gibson's Band at the Locarno. Later with Bernie Stanton at the same venue (1950), then joined Bert Tobias at Glasgow Casino (1950), before returning to London. Spent over two years in Cyril Stapleton's BBC Show Band until late 1954, also worked with Barry Morgan (1954). Spent almost ten years with Francisco Cavez at the Savoy Hotel, London, then active freelance, playing on many sessions. With Bobby Lamb-Ray Premru Big Band, the Squadronaires, etc., and was featured on several of Benny Goodman's European tours. Regularly in small group led by accordionist Jack Emblow, from the mid-1970s through the 1990s. Regular duos with Tommy McQuater through the 1980s, also worked alongside Kenny Baker, and Tommy Whittle and played in Bob Wilber's Big Band.

McNAIR, Harold
saxes/flute/clarinet

Born: Kingston, Jamaica, 5 November 1931
Died: Maida Vale, London, 7 March 1971

Played in the Jamaican All Stars in the late 1940s, then moved to the Bahamas and studied music there and played in local bands, mostly on tenor sax. Worked in Cuba, and in Florida, then left the Bahamas in January 1960 to record in New York. Moved on to Sweden before gigging in London (mostly on alto sax) in April 1960. Worked in Paris with pianist Martial Solal and with Kenny Clarke's Quintet, then toured Europe in Quincy Jones' band on tenor sax. Reverted to alto sax for work with Stan Tracey in London (summer 1960). Played residency at Ronnie Scott's Club, London, then returned to the Bahamas. Worked in the USA with Quincy Jones, then returned to London for May 1961 club bookings and work with Charles Mingus in film *All Night Long*. Led own band in Britain during the early 1960s, also freelanced with various leaders and made brief working visits to the USA. Worked in Phil Seamen's Quartet (1966), Mike Carr's Trio (1967), toured with folk singer Donovan and played in Ginger Baker's Airforce (1969–70). With Les Condon and with Jack Sharpe in 1970, until the onset of lung cancer.

McQUATER, 'Tommy' Thomas Mossie
trumpet/flugelhorn

Born: Maybole, Ayrshire, Scotland,
4 September 1914

Both his sons are musicians: Tom Jr plays bass guitar and David plays guitar. Tom Sr began playing cornet at eleven in the Maybole Brass Band. He also played for school dances, then, while still a teenager, began working for pianist Louis Freeman at Green's Playhouse, Glasgow, and on the liner *California* (which visited the USA and South America). While aboard this ship, Tommy 'doubled' by taking the place of ailing American trumpeter Ed Wade in Rudy Vallee's Band. Returned to Scotland, then travelled to London with Louis Freeman's Band for successful audition to play at Murray's and Romano's (December 1933), but left immediately after audition to join Danny McCormick's Band in Dundee. Again worked with Louis Freeman on board cruise ships (summer 1934), then while working with Freeman's Band in Glasgow was spotted by Jack Payne and joined Payne in Newcastle upon Tyne in October 1934. Worked in London and Paris with Jack Payne, then joined Lew Stone (March 1935). Also worked in London and Paris with Lew Stone until March 1936. With Bill Woodward's Orchestra at the Cocoanut Grove, London (spring 1936), doubled by playing with Claude Bampton's Band for stage drama *The Frog* (1936). Joined Ambrose in September 1936 and worked mainly with Ambrose for over two years, except for brief period out of action (in Scotland) with a septic throat. Among the many freelance recordings he made in the 1930s were sessions with Benny Carter in 1936 and 1937. Founder-member of the Heralds of Swing (February 1939). After they disbanded, rejoined Ambrose in late 1939, also worked briefly with Billy Ternent at BBC studios in the West Country (late 1939). Joined RAF in March 1940 and became founder-member of the Squadronaires (1940). Remained with Squadronaires after World War II ended, touring and playing summer seasons at Clacton, Filey, etc. Left and worked with the Skyrockets at the London Palladium for fifteen months. With the BBC Show Band (directed by Cyril Stapleton) from late 1952, also regularly with Kenny Baker's Dozen and playing on innumerable freelance sessions for films, television, radio and recordings. Regularly with Jack Parnell's ATV Orchestra through the 1960s, but continued to be featured on many freelance sessions, both as lead trumpeter and as jazz soloist. During his career accompanied many stars including Frank Sinatra, Lena Horne, Jimmy Durante, Barbra Streisand, Nat 'King' Cole, Benny Goodman, etc. Overcame injuries sustained in an August 1988 accident and continued to play jazz club dates, including continuance of small group musical partnership with trumpeter Johnny McLevy, which had begun in the 1970s. Played at the Ealing Jazz Festival in the mid-1990s.

MELLING, 'Steve' Stephen
piano/composer

Born: Accrington, Lancashire, 12 July 1959

At the age of nine began seven years' study with Jessie Lawton in Preston. Became interested in jazz piano at twelve. Played first gigs with the Lancashire Schools' Big Band, then spent three years in NYJO. First professional work was touring with Harry Beckett and Elton Dean. Worked in quintet with saxist Dave Bitelli and trombonist Ric Taylor. Played on liner *QE2*, moved to New York for a year. Returned to London, played for West End shows. With Barbara Thompson's Paraphernalia (1985). Was first recipient of the Pat Smythe award (March 1986). With Clark Tracey's Quintet (from September 1986). Regularly with Tracey's Sextet through the 1990s, also work with Tim Whitehead, Alan Skidmore, Valery Ponomarev, Charles McPherson, Red Holloway, Bryan Spring, James Moody and singers Claire Martin and Deborah Brown. Leads own successful trio and works regularly with Pete King, Clark Tracey besides freelancing.

MELLY, 'George' Alan George Heywood   Born: Liverpool, Lancashire, 17 August 1926
vocals

Gave first public singing performance in 1946 while serving in the Royal Navy. After demobilization worked in an art gallery and sat in with Cy Laurie and with Humphrey Lyttelton. Sang in a band on Eel Pie Island (autumn 1948) and together with pianist Norman Day, and (then) banjoist John R.T. Davies left that band to join Mick Mulligan. Became part of Mick Mulligan's Magnolia Jazz Band and sang professionally with Mulligan until early 1963, then concentrated on his writing career as a film and television critic. He also wrote film scripts, and captioned Wally Fawkes' *Daily Mail* cartoon strip 'Flook', as well as writing extensively on surrealism. He resumed part time gigging in the mid-1960s, occasionally guesting with bands led by Brian Green, Alex Welsh, Brian White, etc. Continued to guest with these bands in the early 1970s, and with Roy Pellet's Band, the Red River Jazzmen, the Black Bottom Stompers, Chris Watford's Elite Syncopators, Jazz Spectrum, etc., but appeared regularly with Wally Fawkes-John Chilton Feetwarmers from 1970. Continued to work as a writer and journalist until late 1973, then, from January 1974, resumed singing professionally, accompanied by John Chilton's Feetwarmers. Worked and toured (including USA, Canada, Australia, New Zealand, China, Hong Kong, throughout Europe, etc.) with John Chilton's Feetwarmers through the 1990s. Has written many books on art and artists and also three volumes of autobiography: *Owning Up* (1965), *Rum Bum and Concertina* (1977) and *Scouse Mouse* (1984).

MERSEYSIPPI JAZZ BAND

The embryo of this band came into being at the Wallasey Rhythm Club in 1948. After the club's record recital concluded, a trio (consisting of Dick Goodwin on double bass, Frank Robinson on piano and Kent Metcalfe on drums), formed the mainstay of a weekly jam session. The group developed into the Wallasey Rhythm Kings (with Ken 'Nob' Baldwin on banjo and guitar) and played at the Grosvenor Ballroom, Wallasey. In April 1949 it adopted the Merseysippi name (with Pat Evans on clarinet, Wally Fisher on trumpet and Dennis Gracey on trombone). This front line was soon replaced by Don Lydiatt, clarinet (in late 1949), cornetist John Lawrence (1950) and trombonist Frank Parr. In 1950 the band began one of its various Liverpool residencies at the Temple Restaurant. In 1952 it adopted a two trumpet line-up with the addition of Pete Daniels (1927–88). In 1996 Robinson, Baldwin, Lawrence and Lydiatt were still regular members. Dick Goodwin retired from playing in 1964. Trumpeter John Higham took over from Pete Daniels in 1970, and remained through the 1990s. The band played regularly at The Cavern in Liverpool from 1957 until 1959, then had a five year stay at the Mardi Gras Club. In 1984 they began their residency at Hartley's Wine Bar, Liverpool, but frequently play dates in various other cities, including London, and are featured at many festivals (they have appeared at ten Sacramento Festivals in the USA). Over the years, the band has backed various visiting American jazz musicians. Clinton Ford sang regularly with the band in the 1950s, and has guested with them on many occasions since then, including their US tours. Other singers include Edna Gallagher, Pam Peters, Val Barlow, Jill Martin, Jan Sutherland and Julie Dennis. In 1956 trombonist John Howarth replaced Frank Parr, then John 'Archie' Parkes played with the band from 1957 until 1980, when his place was taken by long-serving Pete Fryer. Trombonists who worked with the band occasionally were Alf Jones, Ian Ashworth, John Rubin, Ken Horton and Harry Price. Derek

Vaux played double bass from 1964 until 1977, Bob Rose from 1977 until 1982, and Robin Tankard (doubling tuba) from 1982 through the 1990s. The band's original drummer, Ken Metcalfe, left after a year. George Bennett took over until 1954, then Trevor Carlisle remained from 1954 to 1964. A succession of drummers (at least twenty) passed through the band, then Mike McCombe joined on a regular basis from 1967 until 1982. His place was taken by Pete Darwin, who remained with the band through the 1990s.

METCALFE, Alan
guitar

Born: 5 December 1926
Died: 30 July 1993

Was signed by Joe Loss while working in Morecambe, Lancashire (September 1942). Left Joe Loss in 1943, freelanced in London and played gigs with Buddy Featherstonhaugh. With Ambrose at Ciro's Club, London (1946), radio work with Oscar Rabin, Nat Temple, Billy Amstell, etc. With Harry Gold (late 1947), briefly with the Skyrockets (March 1948), with Sidney Simone (1948). Staff musician with the Decca recording company. With Ian Stewart (1950 and 1952), Ralph Sharon (1951). Prolific freelance work during the late 1940s and early 1950s then moved to the USA in May 1952. Worked with Joe Mooney, Bob Alexander, Vaughn Monroe, etc., then returned to Britain in September 1953. With Tim Clayton at Quaglino's, London (late 1953 to June 1954), with Frank Cava at Savoy Hotel (1954). Long musical association with Bill McGuffie from 1955, also worked with Johnnie Gray (1958) and with Ken Sykora (1959). Prolific freelance work during the 1960s, then moved back to Morecambe in the 1970s and played local gigs, but also continued to play sessions with Bill McGuffie and others.

METCALFE, 'Lennie' Leonard George
piano/vocals/arranger

Born: Tottenham, London,
23 February 1927

Piano lessons from age of ten. Played boogie-woogie and won amateur talent contest, then at eighteen joined band organized by Leon Roy (with Arthur Golding on guitar). Played residency with Leon Roy at the Bebop Shop in Tottenham, did day work but also worked in Leon Roy's Big Band. Gigged with Ronnie Scott, Denis Rose, Dizzy Reece, etc., and co-led Jazz Inc (with Johnny Rogers). Turned professional at 25, worked with Jimmy Skidmore, Terry Brown, Bill Eydon, etc., and late-night residencies with Leon Roy. With Kenny Graham's Afro-Cubists. Did summer season in Jersey (1953). Toured briefly with Ambrose (1954) and accompanied Adelaide Hall for variety tours. Worked in Germany with Harry Robbins for three months, then joined Laurie Morgan's Sextet before working with Chico Arnez (Jackie Davis) from 1955 to 1956. Did season in Scunthorpe with Dave Wilkins (1957), then summer in Scarborough with Maurice Little's Band. With Dizzy Reece Quintet (1957) and with Denny Wright at Don Juan Club, London. In late 1957 began leading own sextet on liner *Mauretania* on Atlantic and Caribbean routes. Continued until summer 1960, worked during stop-overs in England, including spell in Pete King's Quartet (1959). Emigrated to USA in August 1960, soon gained solo residencies in New York but continued to work in various jazz groups. Mainly featured as a solo pianist-singer through the 1990s.

MICKLEBURGH, 'Bobby' Robert
trumpet/trombone/sousaphone

Born: Norwich, Norfolk, 26 September 1920

Bobby's father was a cornet player: his son, Simon, is a pianist. Began on cornet during boyhood and played in Salvation Army Band. Served for six years in the RAF during World War II. After demobilization worked briefly with Sid Roy's Lyricals, then joined Duncan Whyte briefly in spring of 1946. Summer season at Hastings with Remo Cavalotti's Band (1946). With Eddie Carroll and Lou Preager (1947) and Carlo Krahmer (1947–8). To Nice Festival with Derek Neville's Band (February 1948), also with Freddy Randall (early 1948), then summer season with Hector Davies at Hastings (1948). With Sydney Lipton from May 1949 until June 1951, also in Freddy Clayton's Jazz Group during this period. Ran own music shop and taught, also worked with the Skyrockets (August 1951) and occasionally with Ambrose (1951). Led own group and worked with Joe Daniels and with Geraldo. Season with Hector Davies in Scunthorpe (winter 1952), then led own Bobcats from 1952 to 1956, also worked in Jazz Today Unit (1953). With Sid Phillips (1957), briefly with Bruce Turner's Jump Band (early 1958), then led own band in Newquay (summer 1958). Led own band (1959) and toured Ireland with Harry Gold (spring 1959). Worked with Doctor Crock (Harry Hines) and with Sid Millward, then again led own band. With Nat Gonella (1960). Led own Confederates (1961), handed over leadership to Alan Wickham (summer 1962) to work with Frank Weir for six month season in Jersey (1962). Joined the Temperance Seven (October 1962) on sousaphone for seven years, then played trumpet with them for ten years, trombone for eight and doubled for a further three years. Worked occasionally with the band through the 1990s. Occasionally with Freddy Randall in 1966 and 1968, also with Keith Smith's Hefty Jazz in Denmark and Holland (1978). Lived in Bath from the late 1960s (specializing on trumpet). Led own Pit Orchestra in the West Country, re-formed own Bob Cats in the early 1990s. Also regularly with the Titanic Tea Room Quartet and occasionally in Henry's Bootblacks (led by pianist Henry Davies).

MIDGLEY, 'Bobby' 'Robb' Robert
drums/vibes/percussion

Born: Blackpool, Lancashire, November 1923

Drums from age of six. First professional work with Feldman's Minstrels on Isle of Man, toured with Teddy Joyce (early 1941), then to London. Worked with George Evans before joining Freddie Bretherton's London Palladium Orchestra (late 1941-2). Doubled by also playing with Frank Weir's Band in London. Briefly with Geraldo, then joined Tito Burns (July 1942). Service in Army from early 1943. Continued to guest with various bands whenever possible including dates with Ted Heath. Worked again with Frank Weir from January to May 1946, then joined Cyril Stapleton from 1946-8. With Russ Allen Band (1949), with Eddie Carroll Quintet, Ambrose (1950), then active as highly successful session freelance with many various ensembles including Jack Parnell's Orchestra and Peter Knight's Orchestra. Subsequently moved to Scotland and worked with BBC radio orchestras and played numerous freelance engagements into the 1990s from home base in Largs, Ayrshire.

MILLER, 'Harry' Harold Simon
double bass/bass guitar/cello/composer

Born: Cape Town, South Africa, 25 April 1941
Died: Holland, 16 December 1983

Worked with Manfred Mann and with the Vikings in Johannesburg before moving to England in 1961. Gigged in London, then played in ships' bands before joining drummer Don Brown's Sounds Five. During the 1960s and 1970s worked with Mike Westbrook, Mike Osborne, Elton Dean, John Surman, Alan Skidmore, the Brotherhood of Breath, John Warren, Bob Downes, Keith Tippett, Dudu Pukwana, Louis Moholo, Stan Tracey, Ovary Lodge, the London Contemporary Dance Theatre, etc. Led own Isipingo. Studied at the London College of Music from 1966. During the late 1970s made his home in Holland, worked with Leo Cuypers, Van Manen, etc. His death was caused by a road accident.

MILLINER, 'Tony' Anthony George
trombone/valve trombone/
bass trumpet/arranger

Born: Paddington, London, 28 December 1929

Mother was a pianist. Tony played piano by ear as a youngster; he didn't take up trombone until he was 25. Played in the High Curley Stompers before joining Dave Carey, then worked regularly with Sandy Brown and Al Fairweather from 1957 until 1963. Played in Tubby Hayes' Rehearsal Band (1963). Co-led band with Alan Littlejohns which played long residency at the Tally Ho pub in London, and backed various visiting jazzmen including Earle Warren, Peanuts Hucko and Bill Coleman. Was founder-member of the London Jazz Big Band from February 1975 into the 1980s, during this period also worked in Alan Stuart's Octet. Led own Mingus Music and broadcast with Brian Lemon's Octet. Took part in Fairweather-Brown Reunion Band (1975). During the 1980s and 1990s often in Alvin Roy's Band, also continued to lead own line-ups, including one that features compositions by the late Sandy Brown.

MILLWARD, Sid
saxes/clarinet/oboe/sarrusophone

Born: London, 9 December 1909
Died: Puerto Rico, 22 February 1972

Studied at Royal College of Music. Worked with Derek Turner's Dixieland Band, and with Harry Roy before joining Bert Firman in late 1932. With Howard Jacobs (1933), with Jack Payne from autumn 1933 until 1936 and with Jack Hylton. Led own Nitwits from 1938 to 1940, also worked with Lew Stone (1938) and Freddy Bretherton (1940). Joined Royal Artillery in 1941. Led own Army Band, and toured France with it soon after D-Day (June 1944). Appeared in *Stars in Battledress* shows. After demobilization did BBC radio work from late summer of 1945, then re-formed Nitwits and enjoyed widespread international success, including Las Vegas residencies through the 1950s and 1960s. Died while appearing at the Americana Hotel, Puerto Rico.

MILNE, 'Chic' Charles
saxes/clarinet/trumpet/vocals

Born: 17 April 1914
Died: 1972

Worked mainly in club bands during the 1930s, briefly with Nat Gonella. Only white member of Al Jennings' Band at Kit-Cat Club (1939). With Joe Lucas (early 1940), then again worked with Al Jennings before joining the RAF in April 1940. Played in various service groups and took Billy

Amstell's place in the RAF Quintet (then led by Arthur Mouncey). After demobilization (1946), returned to club circuit, then toured South Africa with Billy Farrell's Band from late 1946. Returned to Britain and joined Dave Frost in summer of 1949. Worked with Freddy Clayton and Bobby Mickleburgh (1951), subsequently moved to Brighton and freelanced locally, combining this with work as a piano tuner.

MINSHULL, 'Mac' Ramsay MacDonald
trombone

Born: Manchester, Lancashire, c.1927

Played piano and trumpet before taking up trombone. Worked in Scandinavia with the Royal Kiltie Juniors (spring to summer 1947) alongside Bert Courtley and Eddie Taylor. Left the group in Copenhagen and worked in the Harlem Kiddies before returning to Manchester (1947). Played in local jazz clubs and gigged with Morris Mack, then worked in Manchester and Rhyl with drummer Roy Tomkins (1948). Played at Astoria Ballroom, Manchester, with Tony Stuart's Band, then joined Teddy Foster (late 1948). Moved to London and played in Leon Roy's Orchestra (late 1949). Briefly with John Dankworth, then joined Ken Mackintosh (1950). Left to work briefly in Glasgow with Bert Tobias (August 1950). Returned to Manchester and joined Rae Allan's Band (late 1950), also deputized in Sid Phillips' Band. With Sid Dean, Oscar Rabin and Vic Lewis briefly in the 1950s. With Jack Parnell (1952–4), then worked for a month with Ronnie Scott (August to September 1954). Freelanced, then again worked with Ronnie Scott in August 1955. Left Britain and temporarily left full time music to work in Alaska on an early-warning defence system. Led own quintet in Montreal, Canada (1957 and 1961) and worked with Vic Vogel and with Maury Kaye's Band in the late 1950s. Served briefly in the Canadian Army and played in service band. Moved into the USA and played with various line-ups, accompanying Johnny Mathis, Vic Damone, etc. Returned to England, worked with Phil Moss's Orchestra at the Ritz, Manchester, then again worked with Jack Parnell, John Dankworth, etc., before playing in a Guards' Regimental Band in the early 1960s. Subsequently moved to Australia where he became part of a religous sect. It is thought by various of his friends that he died some years ago.

MIRANDA, Jack
saxes/clarinet

Born: c.1905

Worked in quartet at Jade's Club, London (1926). With Ambrose (1927–8), played in Fred Elizalde's recording band (1927). Joined Fred Elizalde at Savoy Hotel, London, from July 1928 until March 1929. Worked with Al Collins for many years from 1929 through the 1930s, during this period played on many freelance recordings. With Maurice Winnick in 1940, then served in the Army until being invalided out in spring 1943. Briefly led own band, then rejoined Maurice Winnick in late 1943. Quit playing at the beginning of 1945. Moved to South Africa and later that year opened own club near Johannesburg.

MIRFIELD, Freddie
drums

Born: Essex, c.1908
Deceased

Led own band, the Garbage Men, around the Chingford area during the late 1930s. After entering contests organised by the *Melody Maker* they began working further afield and became fully professional. Toured variety halls during the 1940s and recorded in 1944 (Freddy Randall on trumpet, John Dankworth on clarinet and Denny Croker on trombone). Played a season in Portugal (1947), then again worked in variety halls. Featured in the *Old Town Hall* touring show throughout 1948. Continued to lead the Garbage Men until forming quintet for work on *Caronia* liner (1951). Later led own Orchestra for summer residencies at Parkin's Holiday Camp in Jersey from 1955 through to the early 1960s, also led own band in France during the late 1950s. Left full time music and during the early 1970s worked as a site adminstrator for Kenny Ball Caravans in the Chelmsford area.

MITCHELL, Malcolm
guitar/composer/arranger/vocals

Born: Shoreditch, London, 9 November 1926

First gigs with Felix Mendelssohn, then worked with Jack Simpson. With Don Barrigo's Band (1945) Johnny Franks (1946), Reggie Dare (1946), then joined George Evans in June 1946. Left Evans to join Dick Katz's Caribbean Trio (May 1947). Worked in Sweden for several weeks with Django Reinhardt and Stephane Grappelli (spring 1948), then toured Europe (as part of Jack Fallon's Trio) with Duke Ellington during summer of 1948. Formed own trio (October 1948) to play season in Nice, France. Returned to England, led trio successfully, then formed big band in January 1955. Disbanded big band in late 1956, brief period of ill health, then re-formed trio in summer of 1957, which continued for many years. Accompanied various visiting artistes then did solo act in cabaret. Own television shows on BBC and on Southern Television, then formed jingle company which led to him producing shows for Conference Productions.

MOHOLO, Louis T.
drums/cello/vocals

Born: Cape Town, South Africa, 10 March 1940

Father played piano, mother and sisters sang. Worked with Mr Early Mabuza, then co-founded the Cordettes. Worked with saxophonist Ronnie Beer's Swinging City Six before joining Chris McGregor's Blue Notes. To Antibes with McGregor (1964), then eventually to London in 1965. Worked with American saxophonist Steve Lacy in South America, visited USA, then returned to London in 1967. Integral part of the Brotherhood of Breath during 1970s, also worked with Mike Osborne, Stan Tracey, Elton Dean, Harry Miller's Isipingo, Dudu Pakwana, Keith Tippett, etc. From the late 1970s worked extensively in Europe, with Misha Mengelberg, Irène Schweizer, Peter Brötzmann, Archie Shepp, John Tchicai, Roswell Rudd, etc. International touring included playing visits to Africa and the USA. From the 1980s worked with guitarist Russell Bermin, conga player Thebe Lipere, with Keith Tippett in various line-ups and guested with Cecil Taylor in Berlin. From the 1970s through the 1990s has also regularly led own line-ups: Spirits Rejoice, African Drum Ensemble, Culture Shock and Viva Le Black.

MONDESIR, Mark
drums

Born: Stepney, London, 12 December 1964

Brother of bassist Michael Mondesir. Originally a pupil of Trevor Tomkins. Attended Interchange course in London, directed by Ian Carr. Formed Emjiem trio with brother Michael and guitarist Hawi Gondwe. Worked mainly with Courtney Pine from 1985 until 1989. During the 1990s accompanied many visiting musicians including Art Farmer, Larry Coryell, John Scofield, Hermeto Pascoal, Joanne Brackeen, etc. Recorded with Kevin Eubanks in 1991. Guested with Andy Sheppard's Big Co-Motion Band (1993). Part of American tenor saxophonist Pee Wee Ellis' Assembly (early 1996), but during the mid-1990s worked regularly in various of Julian Joseph's line-ups, including the Big Band.

MONDESIR, Michael
bass guitar/composer

Born: London, 6 February 1966

Brother of drummer Mark Mondesir. Originally played drums then switched to bass guitar at sixteen. Formed own Emjiem trio (with Mark and guitarist Hawi Gondwe) in 1983. Attended Interchange jazz course in London, directed by Ian Carr (1984–6) and subsequently worked with Courtney Pine, Jason Rebello, Steve Williamson, Django Bates, Billy Jenkins, Billy Cobham, Nikki Yeoh, Annette Peacock, Trilok Gurtu, etc.

MONK, 'Laurie' Lawrence
trombone

Born: 21 November 1924
Died: Surrey, 1 May 1986

Worked in the Birmingham area with Billy Walker, Arthur Rowberry and Sidney Beere before moving to London to join Oscar Rabin in summer of 1952. With Vic Lewis (June to July 1953), then again worked in the Midlands with Les Williams, Sidney Beere and with own band (1953). With Jimmy Walker (early 1954), then led own group before working with John Dankworth from September 1955. With Donald Purchese (1960), Ronnie Heasman (1962), Freddy Staff (1965), combining work with these bands with varied freelance activities. Left full time playing to become a successful BBC radio producer.

MOORE, Dudley Stuart John
piano/composer

Born: England, 19 April 1935

Spent early years in Dagenham, Essex, later studied at Guildhall School of Music and subsequently gained music degree at Magdalen College, Oxford. Gigged with fellow students, regularly with trumpeter Bob Robinson's Jazzmen (1958). Became professional musician, joined Vic Lewis. Played in USA with Vic Lewis (1959) and also worked briefly at the Duplex Club, New York. With John Dankworth Quintet and Big Band (1960), also composed music for Royal Court Theatre productions. Led own trio in summer of 1960, then began appearing in successful revue *Beyond the Fringe*, which later played in America. Continued to lead own trio (at the Establishment Club, the Marquee Club and on Southern Television, etc.) during the early and middle 1960s. Enjoyed considerable success as a comedian and actor on British television, then starred in a number of Hollywood films during the 1970s, 1980s, and 1990s. Occasionally led own trio (including tours of Britain) in the 1990s.

MOORE, 'Gerry' Gerald Asher
piano

Born: Highbury, London, 8 October 1903
Died: Twickenham, Middlesex, 29 January 1993

Piano as a child, later studied at Brighton Grammar School. Did first paid gigs at nineteen, then (in 1925) made professional debut at Sherry's in Brighton. Moved to London and co-led band with

Philip Buchel. Solo residencies at the Bull Frogs' Club and Café de Madrid, London, then worked in duo with drummer R.B. Saxe at Trident Club, London (1928), and accompanied professional dancer Josephine Bradley. Recorded with Spike Hughes. Worked with Leslie Thompson and Ellis Jackson at Sovrani's Club, London. Took over leadership of the band in summer of 1931. Solo piano at Jack's Club (late 1931), then long residency at the Bag O'Nails Club, London, from 1932 until 1936. During this period also worked at the Ambassadors Theatre (1932), with Dave Zafer's Band (1933), guitarist Jimmy Brown's Trio (1933), and led at the 43 Club (1934–5). Summer season with Jimmy Brown on Isle of Wight (1936). In Victor Sylvester's Ballroom Orchestra from August 1935, also led own quartet at Palm Beach Club from 1937. Worked at Merrie's Club (1939), led band at Adelaide Hall's Florida Club, London (1940), then worked as regular accompanist for Adelaide Hall (1941), combining this with night club work. With Jimmy Macaffer's Band in Glasgow (summer 1944), then joined Carlo Krahmer's Band (1944). With Frank King's Band (1945–6). Again worked at Merrie's Club, London, played on-off residency there for several years, also toured Germany with harmonica player Max Geldray (1947), played at Paris Jazz Festival with Carlo Krahmer (1949), and worked in Dublin with Adelaide Hall (1949). Led own band in Cannes in the late 1940s. With Freddy Clayton's Jazz Group (1951) and briefly with Sid Millward (1953). With trumpeter Dennis Walton's Band (early 1954), then worked with Harry Gold (1954–5) and did summer season in Rhyl with Laurie Gold's Band. During the 1950s and 1960s often worked aboard various liners including the *Caronia* and *Queen Mary*. Freelanced in London, but also played summer season at Newquay with Rick Kennedy (1966). Played entr'acte music in theatres during the late 1960s and 1970s. Worked in clubs and hotels as a solo pianist, playing at Kettner's and at the Royal Lancaster until shortly before his death.

MORGAN, 'Laurie' Laurence
drums/vibes/piano

Born: Stoke Newington, London, 4 September 1926

Drums from age of ten, during early teens played in Rhythm Racketeers, a quartet (with Don Rendell, Denny Termer and Stan Watson). At fifteen worked in a Hal Moss show as part of the Gay Caballeros. In 1943 and 1944 did USO tours of American bases, as part of pianiste Hetty Booth's group. Worked at the Orchid Room, London, in Don Lorusso's Trio (1946), often sat in at the Fullado Club in Soho. Worked at Churchill's with Jack Jackson (early 1947), then visited America with Ronnie Scott, and Tony Crombie. Morgan remained in America for some months investigating the music scene in New York and Los Angeles. Returned to Britain then again visited the USA as part of Ivor Noone's Band on the *Queen Mary* liner, then remained in London and became founder-member of the Club Eleven (December 1948), playing regularly in club quartet (with John Dankworth, Bernie Fenton and Joe Muddel). Worked in Leon Roy's Big Band (1949). Formed own Elevated Music in 1950, and visited France and Belgium with the group. Worked with Harry Hayes (1952), Ambrose (1953), trumpeter Dennis Walton (1954), Dizzy Reece Sextet (1954) and played in Luton with Vic Abbott's Big Band (1955). During the 1950s also worked with Reggie Goff, Harry Robbins, Dennis Rose, Cecil 'Flash' Winston, and Bob White, besides various other freelance dates. Led own Contemporary Jazz Unit (1959). Jammed at Café des Artistes and became part of the inauguration of the Live New Departures projects (with Pete Brown, Mike Horovitz, etc). Worked with Dick Heckstall-Smith and Tommy Whittle in the early 1960s. Active in improvised theatre and music groups, ran *Such Goings On* at the

Mercury Theatre. Long-time resident percussionist and assistant musical director at the National Theatre, also featured in Great Jazz Solos Revisited in the late 1970s. Continues to play regularly in the 1990s, is part of The Jazz (with pianist Iggy Quayle, and bassist Coleridge Goode), also teaches music in schools and runs jazz workshop. His son Paul plays drums.

MORRIS, 'Sonny' Leo
trumpet

Born: Hillingdon, Middlesex, 16 November 1928

Violin at seven, then drums and bugle in Boys' Brigade. Joined Household Cavalry at eighteen, bought first trumpet at nineteen. Demobilized on 1 March 1949, by then was part of a rehearsal band with banjoist Ben Marshall, drummer Ron Bowden and pianist Ralph Dollimore. Ken Colyer joined Morris, Marshall and Bowden on the 12 March 1949 to create the embryo of the Crane River Jazz Band. Sonny Morris took over leadership of the band after Ken Colyer joined the Christie Brothers' Stompers in the summer of 1951. Sonny left in October 1952 to play briefly (as second trumpeter to Pat Halcox's lead) in the Albemarle Jazz Band. Soon resumed leading a second version of the Crane River Jazz Band until joining Cy Laurie in spring of 1956. Left in September 1956 to work with Terry Lightfoot for thirteen months. Co-led band with banjoist Martin Boorman in the late 1950s, then worked with Mickey Ashman from late 1960 until forming new version of the Crane River Jazz Band in August 1961. Led through the 1960s, including a spell in 1968 when the band was billed as the Norman Turner-Rowles Jazzmen. Played in Ken Colyer's Omega Brass Band. Led the Crane River Jazz Band in the 1970s but also played in Len Baldwin's Dauphin Street Six and briefly in Mac Duncan's Band. In early 1972 the original members of the Crane River Jazz Band enjoyed a successful reunion and this led to a series of bookings (some in Germany). The reunion continued to take place intermittently through the 1970s. Sonny Morris co-led a quintet with pianist Ray Smith in 1980 but continued to lead his own bands through the 1980s, and as Sonny Morris' Delta Jazzmen through the 1990s.

MORRISEY, 'Dick' Richard Edwin
tenor sax/soprano sax/clarinet/flute

Born: Horley, Surrey, 9 May 1940

Played clarinet at Sutton High School from age of sixteen. Joined Original Climax Jazz Band, then worked in trumpeter Gus Galbraith's Septet. Began specializing on tenor in early 1960. Worked in jewellery trade, but soon turned professional after leading own quartet at the Marquee Club (from August 1960). Later that year led own band at the Flamingo Club. From summer of 1961 did nine month season in India as part of Ashley Kozak's Quartet (featuring Harry South). Returned to Britain and resumed leading own quartet, also worked with Michael Garrick (late 1963), with Harry South's Big Band and with the Freddie Mack Sound (1967). Accompanied visiting American musicians. Worked with J.J. Jackson (spring 1969). Formed own band in spring of 1968 which developed into the group If (co-led with guitarist Terry Smith). Lived in Sweden (as did Terry Smith) and made this the base for If's widespread international touring during the early 1970s. If disbanded in November 1974, but Morrissey and Smith worked together occasionally in 1976 and 1977. Morrissey worked regularly in Mike Carr's Trio during the summer of 1975, then together with the guitarist Jim Mullen worked in the USA with the Average White Band. During an eight month visit also worked with Herbie Mann and led own group (1977). Returned to

Britain, and regularly co-led with Jim Mullen until 1985 (their first regular work as a group having taken place in 1976). Led own quartet (1986) and worked occasionally in John Burch's Quartet (1987). Mainly active as a leader in the late 1980s and early 1990s, but guested with various groups and took part in tours of Germany where he was featured in drummer Peter York's Band. Working schedule interrupted by long periods of ill health in the mid-1990s.

MORTIMER, John
trombone/harmonica

Born: Stratford, London, 1937

Played violin, drums and piano before taking up trombone. Served in RAF then co-led Storyville Jazz Band (with Hugh Rainey). Left to work briefly with Mike Peters (September 1957) then joined Acker Bilk in October 1957. Left Acker Bilk in September 1980, temporarily ceased regular playing, then freelanced with various bands before working with Keith Smith (1987). With Pete Allen's Band during the late 1980s and early 1990s, then joined Rod Mason's Band in Germany (spring 1994).

MOSS, 'Danny' Dennis
tenor sax/clarinet

Born: Redhill, Surrey, 16 August 1927

Married singer Jeanie Lambe in January 1964. Took up clarinet at thirteen. At sixteen worked on sax and clarinet with Wal Roger's Quintet at Sherry's, Brighton. Served in RAF Band (1945–8), then worked with Vic Lewis (1948), before brief spells with Dennis Hale's Band in Brighton and Southsea (early 1949). With Tommy Sampson (1949), then with Oscar Rabin (1950–1). Again briefly with Vic Lewis (October 1951), then with the Squadronaires from October 1951 until joining Ted Heath from May 1952 until August 1955. With Geraldo (September 1955–6), then joined John Dankworth from March 1957 until December 1961. With Humphrey Lyttelton (January 1962 until November 1963). Often guested with Alex Welsh's Band during the 1960s, and with Sandy Brown's Band, also with the Fourteen Foot Band (in the 1960s and 1970s). Regularly led own quartet, but occasionally returned to big band work, with John Dankworth, Maynard Ferguson, Stan Reynolds, etc. In band co-led by Freddy Randall and Dave Shepherd (1972–3), then successful freelance work: recordings, radio, television, etc. Recorded with many famous singers including Tony Bennett, Bing Crosby, Ella Fitzgerald, etc. and did widespread touring with own quartet and guested with various bands. Active in jazz education. Founder-member of Pizza Express All Stars (May 1980), also part of *Jazz Journal* All Stars at Nice Festival. Toured Australia alongside Digby Fairweather (1983). Worked in USA with Bobby Rosengarden's Band (1984). With Charlie Watts' Big Band (1985 and 1986). Often in Bob Wilber's Big Band. Moved to Perth, Australia, in 1989, making this his base for international touring, often returning to play in Europe in the 1990s. Awarded the MBE in 1990.

MOULE, 'Ken' Kenneth John
piano/arranger/composer

Born: Barking, Essex, 26 June 1925
Died: Marbella, Spain, 27 January 1986

Left John Dankworth Quartette to join Oscar Rabin (October 1945). Did summer season in Scarborough with Remo Cavalotti (1946), then worked with Joe Daniels (1947) before joining Bobby Kevin's Band on *Queen Mary* liner (late 1947). With Nat Allen, Jimmy Macaffer, Duncan

Whyte and Jiver Hutchinson (1948), then joined Frank Weir briefly in early 1949. With Ken Mackintosh (April to December 1949), then rejoined Nat Allen (1950) and again worked with Frank Weir. With Raymonde's Orchestra (1952), then rejoined Frank Weir (1953) before working with Ambrose (1953), further work with Frank Weir until forming own septet in January 1954. Resigned from this septet in March 1955 (they continued to work as the Ken Moule Seven). Formed own trio in May 1955, then worked with Harry Hayes (summer 1955). Again with Ambrose from September 1955 into 1956, then long period mainly active as staff arranger for Ted Heath, and composing extended works. Continued to play freelance dates, including work with Don Rendell and in the Jazz Today Unit. During this period wrote jazz suite *Jazz at Toad Hall*. Worked in Sweden from late summer of 1959 and toured Europe with Kurt Weill's Band until March 1960. Returned to England and worked as musical director for Lionel Bart's show *Fings Ain't What They Used To Be* from May 1960 until February 1962, and for Bart's show *Twang* (1965–6). In 1970 his *Adam's Rib Suite* was recorded by the London Jazz Chamber Group. He continued to write for the theatre and in 1974 arranged several of Cole Porter's number for the show *Cole!* He also wrote for John Dankworth. Worked as a composer/arranger in Germany during the late 1970s until ill health made him choose a warmer climate. He spent the last part of his life semi-active in Spain.

MOUNCEY, Arthur G.
trumpet

Born: Stockwell, London, 5 April 1909
Died: Ealing, London, 21 March 1992

Began on cornet in Norwood School Band. Left school at fourteen, did various day jobs, then gigged around the Brixton area with banjoist Eddie O'Shea and in band led by pianist Hal Griffiths (1930). Worked with Archie Alexander in Aberdeen and then led own band at Aberdeen Palais for three years before moving back to London. Worked with Maurice Winnick, Charlie Kunz, Ambrose and Eddie Carroll (1935). With Lou Preager, Billy Bissett (1936), then again worked with Eddie Carroll (1937–8) before rejoining Billy Bissett (1938–9). With Jack Harris (1939), then briefly with Jack Nathan's Quintet. With Oscar Rabin, Ambrose and Jack Harris (1940). Joined RAF in August 1940, played in Billy Amstell's RAF Quintet (during long posting at RAF Wittering). Became leader of the Quintet when Amstell left the RAF and led this group in India (1945). Returned to Britain for demobilization in September 1945. Again worked with Ambrose (October 1945 to August 1946), then ill in hospital for several months before working with Lew Stone's Orchestra for show *Annie Get Your Gun* (from June 1947). Continued with Lew Stone until June 1950. With pianist Ronnie Taylor (autumn 1950) and Arnold Bailey before joining Eric Jupp (1951). Again worked with Ambrose (at Ciro's, London), before playing in Switzerland with Eddie Carroll's Sextet (September 1951). Again with Lew Stone from October 1953 until March 1954 then decided to quit full time playing and worked for the Civil Service until his retirement. Occasionally resumed playing including work with Eric Delaney's Theatre Orchestra in Brighton (1960).

MUDDEL, 'Joe' Joseph C.
double bass

Born: London, 30 September 1920

Took up double bass at seventeen. First professional work with Ken Grieff's Band. Served in the RAF from 1939 until 1944. Worked with Carl Barriteau (1947) and with Tito Burns (1947–8).

With Jimmy Macaffer's Band (summer 1948), then toured with Hoagy Carmichael before joining Malcolm Mitchell briefly in October 1948. Founder-member of Club Eleven (December 1948). With Ambrose, Ralph Sharon (1949), Paul Adam (1949–50). Founder-member of John Dankworth Seven (March 1950). With Jack Nathan (1951–2), also with Norman Burns' Quintet (1951) and in Kenny Baker's Octet (1951). Led own band (1952–3), then worked for several months with Winston Lee (1953). Long stay in Tommy Whittle's Quintet from 1954, subsequently worked in Tony Kinsey Quartet and played innumerable sessions in London clubs. Prolific freelance work in radio, television and recordings.

MULLEN, 'Jim' James   Born: Glasgow, Scotland, 2 November 1945
guitar/composer

Guitar at ten, took up double bass at fourteen and played in Andy Parks' ten-piece band; accompanied American singer Billy Daniels. Reverted to guitar in 1963, led own trio. Gigged with many bands in Glasgow. Quit job on Glasgow newspaper and moved to London in 1969. Worked with Pete Brown's Piblokto then joined Brian Auger from summer of 1970 until 1973. Worked with Vinegar Joe, Kokomo, Brian Miller, Jim Richardson, etc. Began working with Dick Morrissey in 1976, together they worked in the USA with the Average White Band, and with Herbie Mann. Returned to Britain and co-led group with Morrissey through to 1985. Formed new band in 1986, but did occasional Morrissey-Mullen reunion engagements into the late 1980s. During the late 1980s worked in Geoff Castle's Band, in Dick Crouch's Paz, with Bobby Wellins, etc. During the 1990s continued to work in various line-ups and to lead own band. With trombonist Fayyaz Virgi, with singer Claire Martin, in Martin Drew's Quartet, in Gail Thompson's Gail Force, etc. Duos with John Etheridge in Italy, with Gene Harris (1994), featured at Cuba's Havana Jazz Festival, etc. Active in jazz education, running workshops and master classes. Further touring with Gene Harris (May to June 1996).

MULLIGAN, 'Mick' Peter Sidney   Born: Harrow, Middlesex, 24 January 1928
trumpet/vocals

After leaving Old Merchant Taylor's School served as an officer in the Rifle Brigade until 1948. Formed own Magnolia Jazz Band soon after demobilization which featured singer George Melly. The unit soon turned professional and achieved national success until disbanding in early 1962. The band re-formed for occasional dates in 1963, then Mick left full time music and moved to Sussex. Guested with the Stane Street Jazzmen, with the Fourteen Foot Band and with Brian Green's Band during the 1960s and early 1970s, then gave up playing to concentrate on running his own business in Sussex. Several of Mick Mulligan's sidemen have individual entries. Others who worked with the band regularly include:

Pete Appleby (drums), Ted Bateman (drums), Stan Belwood (drums), Vernon Bown (double bass), Brian Burn (piano), Ian Christie (clarinet), Bill Cotton (banjo), Jimmy Currie (guitar), Bob Dawbarn (trombone), Norman Day (piano), Norman Dodsworth (drums), Alan Duddington (double bass), Ronnie 'Bix' Duff (piano), Terry Forster (double bass), Pete Hull (clarinet), Colin Kingwell (tuba), Johnny Lavender (banjo), James Livesey (clarinet), Barry Longford (double bass), Pat Malloy (double bass), Owen Maddock (sousaphone), Tom Page (double bass), Ian

Pearce (trombone and piano), Jack Richardson (banjo), John 'Chuck' Smith (drums), Frank Thompson (double bass), Cliff Wren (double bass).

MULRANEY, 'Bill' William
trombone

Born: Liverpool, Lancashire c.1905
Deceased

With Jay Whidden from the mid-1920s, then worked in Germany and Italy with Abriani and his Band before settling in London in late 1930. With Percival Mackey (early 1931), then joined Reg Batten (spring 1931). With Henry Hall from October 1932 until October 1935. With Lew Stone from November 1935 until 1937 (also accompanied Benny Carter in London, January 1937). With Bert Firman (1937), Jay Wilbur (1939), Maurice Winnick (1940), Billy Cotton (1941), Chappie D'Amato (1941). Extensive freelance work, also in Harry Parry's Big Band (1944), Jimmy Macaffer's Band (1948), and with Sid Millward and Doctor Crock (Harry Hines). From the 1950s onwards worked mainly in various theatre orchestras in London and the provinces. Also did summer seasons (with Jack Leon in the Isle of Man, 1953) etc. Freelanced through the 1960s, taught trombone and trumpet in the Bromley, Kent, area. Also active as a faith healer.

MUMFORD, John
trombone/bass guitar/double bass/vocals

Born: London, 22 September 1935

Joined the Phoenix Jazz Band in March 1955 for eighteen months, spent six months in Colin Smith's Band. With Trevor Williams, then joined Teddy Layton in 1957. Played in Denmark with Diz Disley (early 1958), then joined Bruce Turner's Jump Band until early 1961. With Dick Williams (1961) and freelancing. With Brian Leake (1962), New Departures and Pete Comton's Big Band. With John Burch's Octet (1962–3) and in Fat John Cox's Band (1962–3). With Neil Ardley's New Jazz Orchestra (1964–8). Began doubling on bass guitar. On trombone with Bob Wallis (1968–75), also with Graham Collier (1967–9), John Williams' Octet (1970), Ashton, Gardner, Dyke and Co. (1971). During the 1970s and 1980s played bass guitar with many groups: McGuinness Flint, Alan Price, etc., including work in the USA. Also played trombone with Sounds of Seventeen, and with Val Wiseman's *Lady Sings the Blues* show in the late 1980s. Settled in Switzerland, playing trombone, bass guitar and double bass through the 1990s.

MUNN, 'Billy' William
piano/piano accordion/trumpet/vocals/
composer/arranger

Born: Glasgow, 12 May 1911

His brother George was a saxophonist, a younger brother Robert plays piano, sister Mae sang in Jack Hylton's Three Rhythm Girls. Played piano in local cinema at age of eleven, and did gigs with local bands at fourteen. Worked with Louis Freeman and with Chalmers Wood in Glasgow, then moved to London and joined Jack Marrin at the Café de Paris, (also 'doubled' by playing in the Blue Lyres), subsequently worked with Godere at the Hotel Cecil before joining Jack Hylton in December 1929. Freelance work included recordings with Spike Hughes and Benny Carter, also accompanied Coleman Hawkins and Louis Armstrong. Left Jack Hylton to join Sydney Lipton in May 1936. Save for a brief illness and residency at Hatchett's, remained with Lipton until 1941. Did war-work but also played for Al Collins (1942–3) and toured with Stephane Grappelli (1943),

233

then joined Chappie D'Amato (also recorded with Victor Sylvester's Jive Band). Led own band at Orchid Room, London, from autumn 1945 until late 1948, during this period regularly organized bands for BBC jazz broadcasts and played summer season in the Isle of Wight in 1946 and 1947. Formed band for Maurice Winnick at Ciro's, London, then became musical director at the Imperial Hotel, Torquay, in November 1949 and remained in this post for 30 years, subsequently played solo piano. Continues to play for theatre shows (1996).

MURPHY, 'Malc' Malcolm
drums/vocals

Born: Norton, Stockton-on-Tees, 21 May 1939

Played drums from age of twelve. Left school at fifteen and soon turned professional, playing in the North East. Worked with San Jacinto Jazz Band, the Climax Band and with the Crescent City Stompers before joining Ken Colyer in late 1966. Remained with Colyer until 1971, then worked with John Bastable's Chosen Six from summer 1971 for a year, before forming own Storyville Stompers which have toured throughout Europe. Malcolm has also guested with bands in Canada and the USA and made playing visits to New Orleans. Worked with Alton Purnell, Louis Cottrell, Jim Robinson, Alvin Alcorn, etc., and took lessons from Zutty Singleton in 1971. Continues to lead own Storyville Stompers, also makes guest appearances with Brian Carrick's Heritage Hall Stompers, the Louisiana Joymakers, Colin Kingwell's Jazz Bandits and has been featured with the Ken Colyer Trust Band through the 1990s.

MURRAY, 'Bert' Robert William Turnbull
piano/trombone

Born: Kirkcaldy, Scotland, 13 June 1930
Died: London, 24 January 1988

Worked with Dave Keir's Band in Scotland and in Germany (1956). To Poland with John Stainer's Band (spring 1957). With Lennie Hastings in Germany (1957). With Al Fairweather (1958) and Cy Laurie, Alan Elsdon, and Freddy Randall in the late 1950s. With Wally Fawkes (early 1960), then with Nat Gonella from May 1960 until joining Charlie Gall in March 1961. With Ken Sims from August 1961 until joining the Clyde Valley Stompers in February 1962. With Alex Welsh from late 1962 until April 1964. With Freddy Randall (1964–5), then joined Monty Sunshine (1966). Again with Alan Elsdon until March 1969. In 1969 began long stay in the Temperance Seven but also gigged with drummer Ian Bell's Band, with trumpeter Brian Jones and worked in Bahrain with Alan Elsdon, Alan Cooper and drummer David Mills during the early 1980s. Played solo residencies on piano during the 1980s.

N

NAPPER, 'Kenny' Kenneth
double bass/composer/arranger

Born: London, 14 July 1933

Piano during childhood, began specializing on double bass while studying at the Guildhall School of Music, London (tutored by James Merret, Sr). Served in the Army (1952), played piano and double bass in Royal Corps of Signals Band, during leave recorded with Mary Lou Williams (1953). After demobilization worked with Jack Parnell from 1953 until autumn 1954. With Malcolm Mitchell (February to July 1955), then toured with Vic Ash (accompanying Cab Calloway) in August 1955. Extensive freelancing, including work with Alan Clare (late 1956). With Basil and Ivor Kirchin (late 1956–7). With Ronnie Scott (including work in USA) and with Don Rendell (1957). Again with Alan Clare (1958) and with Stan Tracey, freelance sessions with various line-ups, With Tubby Hayes, and with Tony Kinsey (1959), then joined Tony Crombie from October 1959 until early 1960, then, together with Tony Crombie, joined Ronnie Scott-Jimmy Deuchar Quintet (March 1960 to January 1962). With John Danksworth (1962) also in Pat Smythe's Trio. Accompanied many visiting American musicians. Joined Ted Heath (April 1965), worked in Tony Coe-John Picard Quintet (1965). Again in Stan Tracey's Trio (1966) and with John Dankworth (1967). Through the 1960s also worked successfully as an arranger and composer, writing for films, television and radio. Worked on double bass with Kurt Edelhagen in Germany during the early 1970s, then moved to Holland and worked there as a composer and arranger.

NATHAN, Jack
piano/arranger

Born: London, 23 August 1910
Died: London, 23 March 1990

Piano from age of five. Joined Edgar Jackson's Band at the Spider's Web Club in 1932. Worked with Jack Padbury, then spent six years with Roy Fox from 1933 until 1939. Briefly with Billy Bissett (1939), then led own Quintet at the 400 Club, London (1940). After demobilization worked with Harry Hayes (1946), briefly rejoined Roy Fox, then again worked with Harry Hayes (late 1946). In 1947 took own band into Churchill's Club, London, and thereafter enjoyed continued success leading own bands, mainly in London night clubs.

NEVILLE, Derek (Derek Neville TREVARTHEN)
saxes/clarinet

Born: Handsworth, Birmingham, Warwickshire, 4 March 1911
Died: New Zealand, 1986

Descended from an old Cornish family. His mother was a pianist and singer. Raised in London. Self-taught saxophonist. Began gigging in his late teens with the Melodians (around the Wimbledon area). Worked with bands around North London and won individual prize at Kingston Band Contest in late 1932. Played in resident band at London's Nest Club and at the Shim-Sham Club and at the Nut House. Joined Johnny Pillitz's Band in Holland (1937) and worked with them in Holland and Switzerland, accompanying American Valaida Snow. Returned to Holland and played briefly in band led by Coleman Hawkins (1937), before working in Holland and France in Eddie Meenk's Band (1937). Moved back to London, again played in various clubs, and worked with George Bright's Band (1939). Played in Nut House Band featuring George Shearing (1939), then joined RAF in late 1939. Continued to play gigs in London whenever possible, then led RAF Band in County Durham until receiving medical discharge from RAF in December 1942. Briefly with Franz Conn's Band, then joined Harry Parry from January 1943 until 1944, also guested with Johnny Claes. Worked in Carlisle (1945), then joined Tony Wayne's Band (late 1945). Briefly with Johnny Franks, then worked with Ken Grieff's Band in Cornwall and London (1946–7). Left Grieff in July 1947 and freelanced before working with Freddy Randall (early 1948). Took band to Nice Jazz Festival in February 1948. With Duncan Whyte (summer 1948), then led own Boptet (October 1948). Continued to play freelance gigs while gaining the knowledge to be a London taxi driver. Gained his licence but soon afterwards emigrated to New Zealand. Worked as a taxi driver in Auckland and played occasional gigs. Became full time musician again in 1961, mainly active on baritone sax, also worked as an accordion repairer. Married a blind Maori pianist and worked in her band, Lottie Neville's Sophisticates, around the Auckland area. Visited England (and the Nice Jazz Festival) in 1980.

NEWMAN, Al
saxes/clarinet/flute

Born: Palestine, 5 March 1929

Took up clarinet at fifteen. Joined Israeli Airforce Band at eighteen, also had own broadcasting quartet. Moved to England in 1953 to study with Sid Fell at the Royal College of Music; gigged with many bands. Joined *Cranks* show in 1955 (which featured Annie Ross and Anthony Newley). Featured on clarinet and sax with Denny Boyce (1958), Oscar Rabin, Paul Adam, Cyril Ornadel, Jack Nathan and Tony Crombie (1959–60). Led own group on BBC radio (1960–78), also broadcast and recorded with John Scott, Tubby Hayes' Big Band, Ronnie Ross' Big Band, Bill Russo's London Jazz Orchestra, Tony Kinsey, etc. Many sessions with Ted Heath, John Dankworth, Geraldo, Johnny Patrick, Dave Lindup, Kenny Baker, Bob Farnon, John Barry, George Martin, the Beatles, etc. Also worked with visiting musicians including Dizzy Gillespie, Stan Getz, Johnny Mandel, Peter Herbolzheimer, etc., and with singers, Ella Fitzgerald, Judy Garland, Lena Horne, etc. Moved to Los Angeles in 1978 and worked regularly in various studio bands, playing for television and films. Moved back to England in 1986, worked with Bob Wilber, Sonny Dee, Harry Gold, Randy Colville's Collection, etc., as well as with the revived Geraldo Band and the re-established Bert Kaempfert Orchestra. Full working schedule through the 1990s.

NEWTON, 'Dave' David
piano/arranger/composer

Born: Glasgow, Scotland, 2 February 1958

Played clarinet, bassoon and piano before specializing on piano at the Leeds School of Music. Led own trio in Bradford (1978), then worked at playwright Alan Ayckbourn's theatre in Scarborough. Returned to Scotland in the early 1980s and worked often with Carol Kidd, and in Bobby Wishart's Quartet, also accompanied various American visiting musicians including Benny Carter, Herb Ellis and Art Farmer (made recording debut with Buddy De Franco in 1986). Moved to London in late 1987, worked with Alan Barnes, then toured with Martin Taylor's Quartet (including trip to India) from 1989 to 1991. During the 1990s worked as musical director for Carol Kidd and accompanied various other singers including Claire Martin, Annie Ross, Stacey Kent, Marian Montgomery, Tina May, etc. With Kathy Stobart, Andy Cleyndert, Gerard Presencer, etc. Part of Don Weller's Big Band. Worked with Alan Barnes-Bruce Adams, and in Alan Barnes' Sextet. Did solo concert tour (1995) and toured with American saxophonist Bud Shank. Leads own line-ups including tentet. Freelance work included duos with Clark Terry (May 1996).

NICHOLS, Keith Charles   Born: Ilford, Essex, 13 February 1945
piano/trombone/reeds/tuba/vibes/
vocals/arranger

Brother Mike is a drummer. Piano from age of five, became junior piano-accordion champion. Trombone from fourteen. Studied at Guildhall School of Music from 1964 until 1967. Led the New Sedalia Jazz Band before working with Mike Daniels from July 1964 until January 1966 (on trombone). Briefly with Phil Franklin's Swing Sextet, then joined Dick Sudhalter's Anglo-American All Stars. Regularly with the Levity Lancers from 1967 until 1973 (including work in the Far East and Germany). With Dick Sudhalter's Commodore Band (1974). Arranged for the Pasadena Roof Orchestra and played and recorded with the New Paul Whiteman Orchestra (from 1976). Recorded with Bing Crosby (1976). Led own Ragtime Orchestra. Became co-leader (with Alan Cohen) of the Midnite Follies Orchestra (from November 1977). Worked regularly with this ensemble through the 1980s, but also played solo dates on piano and accompanied various singers including Rusty Taylor and Johnny M. Deputized on tours with Harry Gold (on trombone and on piano). Did solo tours of the USA. During the 1980s and 1990s organized long-running series of tribute concerts, including *Jazz Classics Revisited, Fats Waller Tribute, Bix Beiderbecke Tribute* (featuring Guy Barker), *The Story of Ragtime*, etc. Continues to lead own Ragtime Trio, Quartet and Orchestra. Played piano for Bob Wilber's *Portraits in Jazz*, and for film on Bix Beiderbecke. Lectures on jazz at the Royal Academy of Music. Music director of the Cotton Club Orchestra.

NICHOLS, 'Nick' John Michael   Born: Barking, Essex, 26 February 1929
drums

Played local gigs from age of eighteen, did glazing apprenticeship from 1944 to 1949 then served in RAF (1949–51). Played in service band with Keith Christie. Turned professional in early 1952, joined Christie Brothers' Stompers briefly, then played summer season at Eastbourne with Harry Roy (1952). With Howard Baker's Big Band, then summer seasons with Frank King's Quartet (1953), and Johnny O'Rourke (1954). Trio work in London, regularly with Geoff Taylor's Sextet (1955). Gigs with Freddy Randall, Denny Boyce, Harry Hayes, Harry Leader, Harry Gold, Ambrose, Ken Moule, Nat Allen, etc. With Johnnie Gray (late 1955 to March 1956) including work in Holland and Switzerland. Released from summer season at Ramsgate with Billy Wells to join Lonnie Donegan (1956). With Donegan from August 1956 to February 1961, including world tours. With Monty Sunshine from February 1961 to May 1962, Freddy Randall (June to November 1962). With Frank King and John Sands in Bermuda (November 1962 to April 1963). With Mark Michele Band on liner sailing South Africa to South America (April 1963 to April 1964). Settled in East Anglia. Played summer seasons with Johnny Love Trio, Allan Robson Trio, then toured with singer Des O'Connor (1966–7). Theatre work in Great Yarmouth, then again worked briefly with Monty Sunshine (1973). With singer Frank Ifield (1974), then emigrated to South Africa in November 1974. Temporarily left music until 1977, then freelanced in Cape Town area with Tommy Allan Trio, Dave Holmes Trio, Johnny Cooper Big Band, Riverboat Jazz Band, etc., and with various theatre companies through the 1990s.

NICOLS, Maggie
vocals/composer/keyboards

Born: Edinburgh, Scotland, 24 February 1948

Worked as a professional dancer, toured North Africa, Italy and Greece before becoming a full time singer. Sang with pianist Denis Rose, and with Peter Nu, Les Condon, the London Jazz Four and the Bird-Curtis Quintet. During the late 1960s and early 1970s with John Stevens and Trevor Watts at the Little Theatre in London and with Alan Wakeman, Paul Lytton, Mick Hamer, the John Williams Octet, etc. Led own various groups from the 1970s through the 1990s, and co-led Voice (with Julie Tippett, Phil Minton and Brian Eley). Also worked with Ken Hyder's Talisker, Tony Richards' Band, Trevor Watts, Keith Tippett's Centipede and with various European musicians including Swiss pianist Irene Schweizer and German saxophonist Alfred Harth. With Cat's Cradle (1995). Co-founder of the Feminist Improvising Group. Active as vocal tutor from the early 1970s (Barry Summer School, etc). Continues to undertake widespread international engagements, Australia, South America, etc. through the 1990s. In her 1996 band, Maggie played piano and keyboards as well as singing and tap-dancing.

NIGHTINGALE, Mark
trombone/arranger

Born: Evesham, Worcestershire, May 1967

Spent formative years in Redditch. Piano at eight, trombone at nine (lessons from Fred Mercer). At eleven played in Mike Beaumont's Midland Youth Jazz Orchestra, later with Trevor Emeny's Worcestershire Youth Dance Orchestra and Peter Cater's Big Band in Walsall. Joined National Youth Jazz Orchestra at fifteen (for six-and-a-half years). Studied at Trinity College, London, from 1985. Played in Bobby Lamb's Jazz Orchestra (including visit to USA). Formed Bone Structure. Turned professional in 1988. Guested with the WDR Big Band in Hamburg, Germany. During the 1990s worked with John Dankworth, Kenny Wheeler, Bob Wilber, Don Lusher, Val Wiseman, Dankworth Generation Band, Barbara Thompson's Moving Parts, Colin Towns' Orchestra, Clark Tracey Sextet and Geoff Castle as well as leading own recording band. Guested with Tony Coe & Co (1996).

NOAKES, 'Alfie' Alfred S.
trumpet

Born: Toronto, Canada, c.1902
Died: Hampshire, 1982

Worked in Toronto with Gilbert Watson's Band before moving to Britain with Hal Swain's Toronto Band (1924), took over leadership and renamed the group the New Princes Toronto Band but then rejoined band led by Hal Swain in summer of 1926. Worked with Alfredo, then joined Billy Mason (1929–30). With Sidney Kyte (1931), then worked with Lew Stone from October 1932 until spring 1936 (except for brief season in Holland with Ray Noble, August 1933). With Jack Harris from 1936 to 1939, during this period also worked with Ambrose, with Bert Firman, and briefly with Lew Stone. Visited Canada in 1939, then returned to London and worked with Maurice Winnick, Jay Wilbur, Ambrose (1939). With Jack Harris, Lew Stone (1940). With Geraldo from 1941 to 1951, then joined George Melachrino and played for various West End shows before again working with Lew Stone (1953). Left the London Casino Orchestra to run own shop in Bournemouth, quit full time playing.

NOBES, Roger Michael
vibes/drums/piano

Born: Holt, Norfolk, 26 December 1939

Father played the violin. Moved to Watford at ten, took up piano at sixteen, drums two years later. During the late 1950s and early 1960s played at holiday camps in bands led by Al Freed and Alex Miller, and worked in ships' bands on the Shaw-Savill line, sailing to and from Australia. Played in Roy Stevens' Jazzmen in the Watford area (1962) and did further summer seasons. Took up vibes in 1966. In Stan Greig's Quartet (1969). Began long musical association with Dave Shepherd which continues through the 1990s. Led own quartet in the early 1970s, also with Lennie Hastings' Band (1970), with Sonny Dee's Band, then regularly with Alex Welsh from 1974 until 1982 (on drums and on vibes). During the 1980s played for various West End shows including *West Side Story*, *Chorus Line*, *Fiddler on the Roof*, etc. Toured with Teddy Wilson, and with Peanuts Hucko, accompanied many other visiting American jazzmen including Ruby Braff. With John Petters in the late 1980s and 1990s, during this period often worked in Bob Wilber's line-ups. Led own quartet at various festivals during the 1990s. Worked in Ronnie Verrell's Quartet (1995). During the 1990s, musical director (and leader of backing group) for singer Pauline Pearce in her Bessie Smith tribute show.

NOBLE, 'Ray' Raymond Stanley
piano/composer/arranger

Born: Brighton, Sussex, 17 December 1903
Died: London, 3 April 1978

Father was a London neurologist. Piano from the age of ten, subsequently studied for five years with Professor Brigain Dale at the Royal Academy of Music; LRAM at sixteen. Worked as a bank clerk in Streatham but led own small local band. Won *Melody Maker* competition for arrangers (1926) and disbanded own group to concentrate on arranging, subsequently wrote for Debroy Somers and Jack Payne. Became staff arranger for Lawrence Wright publishing house in 1927. Appointed staff arranger for BBC Dance Orchestra in March 1928. Became Director of Light Music at HMV in July 1928, shared this post for a while with Carroll Gibbons (until October 1929), then fulfilled the post alone from October 1929 until August 1934, directing many recordings by the New Mayfair Dance Orchestra, which later became Ray Noble and his Orchestra. Noble featured many jazz soloists including Max Goldberg, Sylvester Ahola, Lew Davis, Nat Gonella, etc., and vocalist Al Bowlly. Took all-star band to Holland for August 1933 season, then returned to the HMV studios until moving to the USA in September 1934 (taking with him drummer Bill Harty and singer Al Bowlly). Formed own highly successful band in New York (which included Glenn Miller, Bud Freeman, etc.). Returned to Britain on holiday in 1935 and 1936, later fronted band led by Canadian trumpeter Jimmy 'Trump' Davidson for European tour in summer of 1938. Returned to the USA and formed new American aggregation in autumn 1938, which achieved considerable success on various American radio shows (most of them emanating from the West Coast). Noble was the Musical Director on shows hosted by Jack Benny, Fred Allen and Edgar Bergen (with whom he worked for fourteen years). Resumed vacation visits to England in 1951, thereafter returning regularly to Britain. He lived mainly in the Channel Isles (on Jersey) from 1958–68, then moved back to Santa Barbara, California. He died in University College Hospital, London, during a visit to England. His many compositions include: 'Cherokee', 'The Very Thought of You', 'The Touch of Your Lips', and 'Goodnight Sweetheart'.

NORMAN, Cecil
piano/arranger

Born: Lancashire, 29 September 1897
Died: Bexhill-on-Sea, Sussex, 1988

Brother of saxophonist Leslie Norman. Together they led a band at the Berkeley Hotel, London (January 1922). Later that year Cecil played in Bert Firman's Band at the Metropole Hotel. This began a long musical association, with Cecil fixing musicians for many of Firman's Zonophone recordings and doing arrangements throughout the 1920s. He also worked often for Firman in the 1930s. After working with Jack Hylton, Cecil again co-led with his brother Leslie for a residency at the Carlton Hotel, London (1927). The brothers moved to the USA and directed a band at the Edgewater Inn, Greenwich, Connecticut, in 1928. When they returned to Britain, the brothers secured a recording contract with the Worldecho company, and one of their pseudonyms was the Connecticut Collegians. Worked with Fred Elizalde (1930), with Jerry Hoey (early 1931), with Melville Gideon and with Bert Firman (1931). With Sidney Kyte (1932), then again with Bert Firman (1932–3), but also worked for a month with Ray Noble in Holland (August 1933). With Howard Jacobs and Ord Hamilton (1934), then joined Jack Jackson in May 1935. With Buddy Featherstonhaugh (1935). To Australia with Howard Jacobs in 1936, worked as Orchestrator-in-Chief for Australian Broadcasting Commission. Returned to London and joined Reg Leopold from May to September 1937, then again worked with Bert Firman autumn 1937 to January 1939. With George Melechrino (late 1939), then worked with Billy Ternent's BBC Dance Orchestra until early 1942. With Freddie Ballerini's Sextet (1942), subsequently led own Rhythm Players and freelanced as a pianist and arranger.

O

OAKLEY, 'Ben' Henry Percival Benjamin
trombone/composer

Born: c.1895
Deceased

Served as an Army musician for nine years, then joined Jack Hylton. Subsequently worked in Germany with the Palais Mascotte in Berlin for six months. Moved back to London and played in house band at the Manhattan Club. Joined Bert Ralton and his Havana Band (1925) and worked in South Africa with Ralton (1926). Returned to London when Bert Ralton died and worked with the Savoy Havana Band (September to December 1927). With Reg Batten's New Savoy Orpheans (January to August 1928), briefly with Fred Elizalde (1928). With Howard Jacobs and with Percival Mackey (doubling trumpet) in 1929–30. With Arthur Lally (December 1930 to early 1931). Toured Europe with Jack Hylton (March to April 1931), then joined Jack Payne from spring 1931 until July 1933. Led own Barnstormers for Barnet residency (1933–4) and (1934–6). Led own band at San Marco Restaurant, London, from October 1936, then again led at Barnet (1937–9) as well as playing at the Savoy Hotel, London, and again at the San Marco. Conducted the Concert Orchestra of the Pioneer Corps (based in Ealing) 1941–2. Later led septet at Stage Door Canteen, London. Led own orchestra for summer residencies in Southend (1946–57). Oakley did extensive freelance recordings in the 1920s and 1930s, with Bert Firman, Harry Hudson, Picadilly Players, etc.

O'DONNELL, 'Ed' Dominic Edward
trombone

Born: Leeds, Yorkshire, 13 February 1927

Took up trombone in 1946. Played in Vernon Street Ramblers while studying at Leeds College of Art, then joined Yorkshire Jazz Band in early 1949. Left after two years and formed Paramount Jazz Band, also led White Eagles Band. Joined Ken Colyer in London in June 1954. Toured with Colyer for six months, then returned to Leeds and led White Eagles Marching Band before forming own New Orleans Jazzmen which (together with the White Eagles) continue to flourish through the 1990s.

O'HIGGINS, 'Dave' David
tenor sax/flute/composer

Born: Birmingham, West Midlands, 1 September 1964

Lived in Derby from the early 1970s. Trumpet from age of seven, then switched to drums at nine and played in school band. Piano lessons from fourteen. Did local gigs on drums at fourteen, took up alto sax at sixteen and played locally on sax and on drums. Played in Harold Kyte's Stapleford Big Band (1982) and in the Derbyshire Youth Jazz Orchestra. Led own quintet in Spondon, Derbyshire; switched to tenor sax. Played in National Youth Jazz Orchestra (1983–6). Moved to London in 1983, studied music at City University and at Wavendon Summer School. Led own quartet and quintet from 1983. With Cleo Laine and John Dankworth from 1986, also with Roadside Picnic (with bassist Mario Castronari) from 1986 until 1990. Led own Gang of Three (1987–9) and made tours of Europe with Icelandic group Mezzoforte from 1986 to 1990, also with Derek Nash's Sax Appeal from 1987. Led own Dave Higgins and the Oblivion Brothers (1989–91). Toured Europe and Japan with various pop groups in the late 1980s and early 1990s (occasionally doubling keyboards). Toured Europe with Sarah Jane Morris, worked in France and Tunisia with Argentinian pianist Santos Chillemi, and in Japan with Matt Bianco. With Pizza Express Modern Jazz Sextet from 1989. Toured Europe and Japan with Salif Keita's Band, and toured with Jason Rebello from 1990. With Jim Mullen's Quartet from 1992 (including Havana Jazz Festival 1993). With Itchy Fingers from 1993, Clark Tracey's Sextet from 1994. Worked and recorded in New York (1994). During the 1990s made solo tours of South Africa, playing in Cape Town, Johannesburg and Durban. From 1994 widespead touring with Martin Taylor's Spirit of Django group (including engagements in Sri Lanka and Bangladesh). Continues to lead own quartet and quintet and to make many freelance recordings.

O'LOCHLAINN, Ruan Colm
sax/clarinet/guitar/piano

Born: Ireland, 11 October 1942
Died: London, 8 May 1988

Brother of drummer and vocalist Dara (1939–92). Led Southsiders Dixieland Band and the Dixieland Rhythm Kings in Dublin during the early 1960s, then moved to London and worked with Freddy Randall (1964), Bruce Turner (1965), Eric Lister, Bill Greenow, etc.

ORR, 'Bobby' Robert
drums/trumpet

Born: Canbuslang, Lanarkshire,
Scotland, 15 August 1928

Drums from the age of three, in local pipe band at nine (his father was the drum major). Took up trumpet at sixteen, worked with local Beavers, later joined Bert Tobias at Glasgow Locarno. With

Harry Bentley in Paisley. Left Henry Morrison's Band to work with Basil Kirchin from January 1953 until March 1954. Suffered lip problems and left Basil Kirchin at Belfast Plaza and moved to Ayr, Scotland, where he played drums in Andy Currie's Band. From this point he specialized on drums. With Malcolm Mitchell from June 1955, until joining Jack Parnell in April 1956 for several months. Freelanced, then went to USA with Johnnie Gray for two week tour, remained in the USA to tour with Vic Lewis for three weeks (1958). With Joe Harriott from summer 1958 to spring 1960, then worked with Ronnie Scott (1960–1), also played dates with Tubby Hayes, Sandy Brown, Pete Pitterson, etc., during the late 1950s and 1960s. With Johnny Cooper at Hammersmith Palais (1962), doubling by working with Johnnie Gray at the Stork Club, London. Often worked with Joe Harriott from spring 1962 (through the 1960s). Accompanied many visiting American musicians, and played freelance dates with many groups (with Maynard Ferguson, Colin Purbook, etc.). Toured Japan with Stanley Black (1965). Active freelance from 1970 onwards, did three tours with Benny Goodman, toured with Billy Eckstine, Michel Legrand, Sammy Davis. Recorded with Bing Crosby. Gigged with Bill McGuffie, Dave Shepherd, Harry Pitch, Tommy Whittle, Don Lusher, etc. Often with Bob Wilber's Big Band in the 1980s and 1990s, with Joe Harriott Memorial Quintet (1989). Occasionally sits in on trumpet with various groups. In Johnny Watson's Glenn Miller Tribute Band in the 1990s (including overseas tours) and often with Ray McVea's Band (including tour of Japan, 1994). With Bruce Adams-Alan Barnes Quintet through the mid-1990s.

OSBORNE, 'Mike' Michael Evans
alto sax/clarinet/piano/composer

Born: Hereford, 28 September 1941

Violin as a child. Moved to London to study clarinet and piano at the Guildhall School of Music during the early 1960s. Began working in Mike Westbrook line-ups from 1963, also in drummer Norman Caldas' Quintet (1967). Occasional work with Humphrey Lyttelton in late 1960s. Regularly with John Surman in the late 1960s, often in co-led quartet. With Chris McGregor's Brotherhood of Breath from June 1970, also with Mike Gibbs, John Warren, Harold Beckett, etc. Duos with Stan Tracey during the 1970s, and in Harry Miller's Isipingo. Part of SOS (with John Surman and Alan Skidmore) which did widespread international touring from 1973. Co-led quintet with Ian Bird (1975). Led own trio during the late 1960s and 1970s, and own Septet in the late 1970s until ill health forced his retirement in 1980.

OWEN, Reg
sax/piano/arranger/composer

Born: Bury, Lancashire, 1916
Deceased

Took up saxophone at fifteen. Played in Teddy Joyce's Juveniles and in Royal Kiltie Juniors before forming own band for residency at Montague Ballroom, Ealing, London (1938–40). Studied sax with Benny Glassman and later completed studies at Royal College of Music. With Johnny Claes (1941), Miff Ferrie's Sextet (1941), then worked with Harry Roy from October 1941 until February 1943 (led Roy's Tiger-Ragamuffins in 1942). With Keith Bird's Band in Ealing and with Art Thompson, then served in the RAF during World War II, played in Leslie Douglas' RAF Bomber Command Band. With Ted Heath from 1945 until September 1950, then worked with Heath as a staff arranger. Seriously injured in a car accident (October 1954), resumed work as a freelance arranger six months later and wrote for many leaders including Peter Yorke, Cyril Stapleton, etc., also led own recording bands. *The Reg Owen Arranging Method* was first published in 1956.

OWEN, Rex
saxes/clarinet/flute/vocals

Born: East Ham, London, 11 March 1905
Died: 11 February 1985

Led own band as a teenager, then worked as a song-plugger. With Cambridge Night Watchmen, then joined Fred Elizalde from December 1927 until April 1929. With Arthur Lally (summer 1929), then led own band at Chez Uncle, London (1930), then again worked in Cambridge Night Watchmen. With Ray Starita (1930), Billy Mason (February to March 1931) before rejoining Ray Starita. Led own Nephews (late 1931), then rejoined Billy Mason (early 1932). With Sydney Kyte (summer 1932), Roy Fox from October 1932 until August 1937. With Bert Firman (late 1937–8), Cecil Black, Joe Kaye, Jack Payne, Jack Nathan (1939). With Maurice Winnick, Peter Mendoza, Sid Phillips, Jack Jackson, Norman Cole (1940), George Scott-Wood, Geraldo (1941), Carroll Gibbons (1942–6). Led own quintet at Florida Club (1946). Left London and led own quintet in the Brighton area from the late 1940s, later played freelance gigs with various groups in Sussex including Ken Lyon's Band.

OXLEY, Tony
drums/percussion/piano/composer

Born: Sheffield, Yorkshire, 15 June 1938

Played piano during childhood, took up drums at seventeen. At nineteen joined the Black Watch Regimental Band (and toured North America). After three years' service returned home and worked with Winston Lee in Sheffield before forming own jazz quintet. Began long musical association with Derek Bailey and Gavin Bryars. Did variety of work including playing on cruise liners and residency at Buckingham's Club in Manchester. Led own trio. Moved to London in 1966. Worked as house musician at Ronnie Scott's Club, accompanying many visiting musicians, also worked in Ronnie Scott's Octet and Big Band during the late 1960s and 1970s. Led own line-ups from the late 1960s, including Trio (with Tony Coe and Chris Laurence). Was part of the London Jazz Composers' Orchestra through the 1970s. Worked with Gordon Beck, Mick Pyne, Howard Riley and Alan Skidmore, etc. Toured with various jazz musicians including Bill Evans (1972), Didier Levalle (1986), Anthony Braxton (1989), etc. A central figure in the Barry Summer School in Wales for many years. Worked regularly throughout Europe from the late 1970s. Worked occasionally with pianist Cecil Taylor from the late 1980s. Continued to lead own line-ups through the 1980s and 1990s, including Quintet and his Celebration Orchestra. Worked (and recorded) with quartet led by Polish trumpeter Tomasz Stanko (1993–4), also worked in USA with Derek Bailey (autumn 1995).

P

PALIN, Joe
piano

Born: Lancashire, 1937

Piano from the age of twelve. At sixteen played gigs with local dance bands, then joined the Zenith Six at seventeen. Did two years' National Service in the Army (where he learned to play the French horn). Led own quintet (1957), gigged with bands in Manchester, Macclesfield, etc. Briefly with John Dankworth (late 1959). In Ken Wray's Quintet (1960), also accompanied many visiting Americans from the 1960s onwards. With Gary Cox's Quartet (1964–5), freelanced with many groups, then worked in Maynard Ferguson's Band (1968) and with Syd Lawrence (1969). Played regularly at the Band on the Wall in Manchester. Worked with Randy Colville, in Alan Hare's Octet, guested with the Red River Jazzmen and toured with Bobby Wellins. With Mart Rodger's Band in the early 1990s, then resumed successful freelancing, by this time regularly teaching at the Leeds College of Music.

PALMER, Ian
drums

Born: West Midlands, 3 March 1976

Nephew of drummers Steve and Carl Palmer. Originally taught by Malcolm Garrett. Gigged at twelve. Joined Midland Youth Orchestra and appeared with them at Montreux Jazz Festival at age of thirteen, also toured Russia. Took lessons from Joe Morello. Turned professional immediately after leaving school in 1992. Extensive freelance dates with various groups during the 1990s, also leading own Connection quartet.

PANAYI, Andy
tenor sax/alto sax/flute/composer/arranger

Born: London, 18 January 1964

Son of Greek Cypriot parents, his father was a professional musician, specializing on bouzouki. Began on flute, then played baritone sax in gig bands before changing to alto sax then to tenor sax. Played tenor sax in a wide variety of bands, also played flute in the London Schools' Symphony Orchestra. Studied at Trinity College of Music. Played tenor sax with SuperJazz Big Band. Toured with National Youth Jazz Orchestra. Worked in Duncan Lamont's Big Band, in West End theatre orchestras and with the Blow Monkeys group as well as freelancing. With Alec Dankworth's Quartet in the 1990s, and regularly with the Dankworth Generation Band. Deputized in Pizza Express Modern Jazz Sextet and led own band. Guested with Tommy Smith's Sextet (1996) and worked in Stan Tracey's seven-piece, also led own quartet (1996).

PARAMOR, 'Norrie' Norman William
piano/piano accordion/arranger

Born: London, 15 May 1914
Died: 9 September 1979

Played in various stage bands before working with Freddy Ballerini for summer season in the Isle of Wight (1934). Accompanied drummer Len Berman in stage act (1935). Worked on piano and piano accordion with various bands during the 1930s, then joined Maurice Winnick (1940). With Harry Leader before serving in RAF during World War II. After demobilization in April 1946 worked with Harry Gold until late 1949. Was recording manager for EMI from 1950 until 1967, then worked with great success as freelance musical director.

PARKER, Eddie
flute/composer

Born: Liverpool, Lancashire, 28 May 1959

Father played piano. Gigged around the Liverpool area. While studying at York University began long musical association with Django Bates (which has continued into 1996). Moved to London, played in John Stevens' Freebop and joined Loose Tubes. Worked with Bheki Mseleku in the early 1990s. Formed own Sextet which has gained wide recognition (1996), also in Akasae (1996) and in Django Bates' Delightful Precipice (1996). Is active in jazz education, running workshops at Morley College, London, and classes at the Guildhall School of Music. Composes for own sextet and various other line-ups.

PARKER, Evan Shaw
tenor sax/soprano sax

Born: Bristol, 5 April 1944

Mother played piano. Moved to London at age of nine. Began on alto sax at fourteen, tutored by James Knott (1958–62). Studied botany at Birmingham University from 1962, played in University group (1963), gigged with Howard Riley and led own quartet (1966). Moved back to London in summer of 1966, worked with Spontaneous Music Ensemble, with Trevor Watts and in duos with John Stevens. Began long musical association with Derek Bailey. Toured Europe for two months with Pierre Favre in the late 1960s. During the years 1968 to 1972 co-led Music Improvisation Company with Derek Bailey. With Chris McGregor's Brotherhood of Breath from 1969, with Paul Lovens and in Tony Oxley's Sextet. During the 1970s with Paul Lytton, Alexander Von Schlippenbach, Paul Lovens, Eddie Prévost, Peter Brötzmann, Kenny Wheeler, Barry Guy, Steve Lacy, etc. Intermittent international touring in Globe Unity Orchestra. Solo performances from 1974. Many freelance recordings including work with Basil Kirchin. During the 1980s and 1990s continued to work with Derek Bailey (his co-partner in the Incus record label), with Eddie Prévost, Barry Guy, Paul Lytton, George Lewis, Paul Rutherford, Kenny Wheeler, in Charlie Watts' Big Band and in Ian Carr's Orchestra UK (1989). Toured Romania, Greece and Yugoslavia with own trio (1985). Worked with the Michael Nyman Ensemble, and taught at Leicester University. Own trio and quartet through the 1990s, with cellist Tritan Honsinger and percussionist Alex Maguire. With Argüelles-Purnell Band (1993). Trio with Paul Rogers and Mark Sanders (1994), with Gavin Bryars, with Jon Lloyd's Anacrusis, duos with Louis Moholo and with drummer Eddie Prévost, also did 1996 gigs with bassist Barry Guy and percussionist Paul Lytton, as well as playing in the Freedom Jazz Quintet (with Louis Moholo).

PARKER, 'Johnny' John Robert
piano

Born: Beckenham, Kent, 6 November 1929

Married to African singer-actress Peggy Phango. Took piano lessons during early childhood; became interested in jazz while evacuated to Wiltshire during World War II. Returned to London, played at Catford Rhythm Club, then served in the Royal Army Ordnance Corps from 1948–50, during this period gigged with Harry Brown's Inebriated Seven, with Beryl Bryden's Backroom Boys and with Mike Daniels. After demobilization worked with Mick Mulligan from May 1950 for a year. With Humphrey Lyttelton from May 1951 until forming own band in September 1957. With Graham Stewart from July 1958 for a year, then did day work in a Cricklewood factory, occasionally leading own band and gigging in Danny Haggerty's Band (1960). With Monty Sunshine from February 1961 until August 1962, then worked with Alexis Korner's Blues Incorporated from August 1962 until August 1963. Toured Far East (for Forces' Entertainment) with Diz Disley and Beryl Bryden (late 1963), then worked with Cyril Davies. After death of Davies worked with Long John Baldry's Hoochie Coochie Men (1964). Again did factory work (1965–8), during this period again led own band, played a Southend residency with Will Hastie and David Mills and did widespread touring (1967) with Kenny Ball's Band (deputizing for injured Ron Weatherburn). Led own band and worked with Bill Greenow's Strong Jazz (1968–9), then joined Kenny Ball in March 1969. Absent from Kenny Ball's Band through ill health from late 1969 to early 1970, then rejoined Ball from summer 1970 until 1978. Played for a few months in Sammy Rimington's band (1979). Led own trio, quartet and band in the 1970s and 1980s, also played various solo residencies in London and in Switzerland and Germany, featured regularly at Cork Festival. Worked in Pat Halcox's Summer All Stars, and in Keith Smith's Hefty Jazz (1979–80). Accompanied visiting American jazz musicians, including Eddie Miller, Wild Bill Davison, Doc Cheatham, etc. Guested with Chez Chesterman (1982) and often worked with Sammy Rimington during the period 1983–6, also worked in Denmark and Germany with the Harlem Blues and Jazz Band. Work schedule curtailed by persistent ill health in the 1990s, but continues to play solo dates and to lead own trio for work in London.

PARNELL, 'Jack' John Russell
Born: London, 6 August 1923
drums/vocals/composer

Son of variety artiste Russ Carr, nephew of impresario Val Parnell. Jack's son Marc plays drums. Piano as a child, then drums. Lessons from Max Abrams. Did summer season at Scarborough in Headley's Quartet then, at seventeen, worked with Sammy Ash's Band in Cambridge. Joined RAF and played in Buddy Featherstonhaugh's Sextet. While at Bomber Command played in small band co-led with Vic Lewis and in Leslie Douglas' Big Band. Continued working in Lewis-Parnell Jazzmen until summer 1945, by then Jack had begun his long musical association with Ted Heath. Also with Frank Weir from summer 1945 until January 1946. Became a mainstay of Ted Heath's Music, playing, singing and leading own small band-within-a-band until the spring of 1951. Took own band into the *Fancy Free* show in spring 1951, then formed big touring band which made its debut in January 1952. Played drums with Louis Armstrong at Royal Festival Hall, London (December 1956). Studied conducting and became Musical Director at ATV. Led own Orchestra there for over twenty years from 1956. Resumed regular drumming and worked with Tommy Whittle's Quartet from 1976. Freelanced with many line-ups and played in Ted Heath Tribute Band and in Bob Wilber line-ups. Accompanied many visiting American musicians, regularly worked with Ruby Braff. Featured with *The Best of British Jazz* (with Kenny Baker, Don Lusher, etc.) through the 1990s, also worked with Keith Smith's shows, and accompanied Annie Ross for London residencies in 1995 and 1996.

PARR, 'Frank' Francis David
trombone

Born: Liverpool, Lancashire, 1 June 1928

Was wicket-keeper for Lancashire County Cricket Club during the early 1950s (also represented the MCC in 1953). Took up trombone in 1950 and soon joined the Merseysippi Jazz Band (replacing Dennis Gracey) for four years until joining Mick Mulligan in spring 1956. Remained with Mulligan until 1961. During the early 1960s deputized in various bands, with Mike Cotton, Monty Sunshine, etc., then gave up playing trombone in 1964. Subsequently worked in band management, and advertising.

PARRY, 'Harry' Owen
clarinet/alto sax/vocals/composer

Born: Bangor, N. Wales, 22 January 1912
Died: London, 18 October 1956

Played cornet, tenor horn and flugelhorn in Municipal Brass Band during childhood. Switched to drums and violin at twelve. At fifteen bought alto sax, gigged locally on violin and alto sax with the Marina Dance Band. First professional work at twenty playing alto sax and singing with Eddie Shaw's Band in Llandudno. Moved with this band to Croydon, then on to Brighton. Joined George Colborn's Orchestra in Brighton and remained with them for Streatham residency. Freelanced in London, began specializing on clarinet. Briefly in Neville Bishop's Orchestra, then played baritone sax with Percival Mackey (including films and radio work). With Oscar Grasso's Grasshoppers (1938–9), then worked with Miff Ferrie's Band in London and in Holland (1939). Briefly led own small band and worked with Bert Firman (1939). Brief spells with Paul Lombard and Phil Watt (early 1940), again with Oscar Grasso, then short stay in Jack Hargreaves' Quintet. Led own quintet at St Regis Hotel, London, from May 1940. Own trio at Paradise Club, London, which broadcast on Radio Rhythm Club in September 1940. The group was soon enlarged and became the BBC Radio Rhythm Club Sextet from October 1940 until 1943. Did war work in factory, then toured with Sextet (1942). Again led, at Paradise Club and Cocoanut Grove. Temporarily led big bands (1943, 1944, 1945), then reverted to sextet for long residency at Potomac Club, London (1945–7), also played on one-night stands. Mainly occupied in leading touring band (1947–8), brief illness in late 1947. Led in Holland and Egypt (1949), tour of Middle East entertaining servicemen (1950). Leading Sextet at Washington Hotel, London (1951). Solo tour (mid-1952), and Sextet work. Led quintet for overseas tour (1952), then took Sextet to India (October 1952 to October 1953). Again led at Washington Hotel (November 1953 to January 1954), then did one-nighters before summer season at Weymouth (1954). Did solo work and led at Butlin's Holiday Camp, Filey, Yorkshire, for summer seasons in 1955 and 1956. Shortly after the 1956 season ended, Parry returned to his London home and suffered a fatal heart attack. *A Harry Parry Bio-discography*, by Tony Middleton, was first published in 1995.

PATRICK, John Charles
piano/arranger/composer

Born: Smethwick, nr Birmingham
29 October 1931

Father was pianist John 'Jack' Patrick (died 1993). Began playing piano at age of nine. Turned professional at nineteen, worked with Ray Price's Band and with Arthur Rowberry during the early 1950s (winning *Melody Maker* and *New Musical Express* contests). With the Kirchin Band from late 1954 until summer 1956. Returned to Birmingham and worked with Sonny Rose

(1956–9), during this period also played many jazz gigs with Tommy Webster, etc. Active in Musicians' Union affairs from 1957, eventually becoming Chairman of National Executive Committee, a position he has held for many years (also served as a local magistrate). During the late 1950s and early 1960s worked with Jerry Allen at ATV, then led own group on many television shows throughout the 1960s and 1970s. Formed own big band in the 1960s, which continues to thrive as an occasional band through the 1990s, accompanying various visiting singers including Anita O'Day, Dakota Staton, Ernestine Anderson, Mark Murphy, Jimmy Witherspoon, etc. As accompanist, and as leader of own trio, has backed many top jazz musicians including Ben Webster, James Moody, Nat Adderley, Eddie 'Lockjaw' Davis, Sonny Stitt, Bill Watrous, Phil Wilson, Mundell Lowe, Louis Stewart, Kenny Clarke, Zoot Sims, Tubby Hayes, Guy Barker, Mark Nightingale, etc. Guested with various musicians in Los Angeles and Las Vegas during working visits to USA. During the 1980s and 1990s continued to lead own line-ups, and to accompany visiting musicians, was also featured with Gerry Mulligan in Ireland. Worked as part of drummer Tony Richards' Quartet, and freelanced with various line-ups. Regular participation in Musicians' Union Big Band Workshops during the 1980s and 1990s.

PATTERSON, Ottilie Anna
vocals/piano/composer

Born: Comber, Co. Down,
Northern Ireland, 31 January 1932

Mother was from Latvia. Piano lessons from age of nine. Studied at Belfast College of Art. Sang with local band led by trombonist Jimmy Compton, occasionally with the Muskrat Ramblers and with Ken Smiley. Guest appearances with Chris Barber's Band in summer of 1954 (during holidays from her job as a teacher), then joined Chris Barber on 1 January 1955. Sang with Chris Barber's Band regularly until illness in 1965, thereafter worked on many occasions with Chris through to the early 1970s. The couple were married from 1959 until 1983. Sang occasionally with Chris Barber during the 1980s, and toured with him in 1991. Composes and plays piano at home, but no longer performs in public.

PAWSON, Dan
trumpet/vocals

Born: Birmingham, Warwickshire, 29 August 1936

Played violin from age of eight, later led school orchestra (1952–4). Took up bugle in Army Cadet Band (1953) and switched to trumpet a year later. Gigged with Dutch Swiss Cottage Band in London (1955), subsequently returned to Birmingham and formed Artesian Hall Stompers for February 1960 debut. The band has continued to function successfully through the 1990s. In 1961 formed the Tulane Brass Band (later renamed the Jolly Bunch Brass Band), and in 1965 formed the Silver Leaf Serenaders. Worked with Barry Martyn in London (1966–7), recorded with Harold Dejan and Louis Nelson. Musical career interrupted by University studies (1970–6), subsequently made regular visits to New Orleans (1978–81). In 1982 became musical director of the Mardi Gras Brass Band which played festivals throughout Britain and Europe. Returned to full time playing in 1986, worked in the Oriole Brass Band and led own bands, including own All Star unit for work in Switzerland (1986): Pete Dyer, Ray Smith, Alyn Shipton, Dave Evans and Zoltan Sagi. Returned the following year with a new line-up which included Annie Hawkins, Zoltan Sagi and Paul Munnery. In 1988 toured Switzerland and Germany with Louis Nelson and his New

Orleans All-Stars (Chester Zardis, Danny Barker, Pud Brown, Butch Thompson and Stanley Stephens). Louis Nelson (through illness) didn't play on the entire tour and his place was taken by the Belgian trombonist Philippe de Smet. After this tour Dan temporarily settled in New Orleans, and worked there with Pud Brown, and with the Original Camellia Jazz Band, etc. (1989–90). During the 1990s continues to lead own various ensembles and to freelance throughout Europe.

PAYNE, Jack
piano/vocals

Born: Leamington Spa, Warwickshire, 22 August 1899
Died: Tonbridge, Kent, 4 December 1969

Piano lessons from age of nine. Served in Royal Flying Corps during World War I. After demobilization formed quartet. Worked with Mitchell's Rag-a-Jazz Orchestra in Birmingham (summer 1922) and also in Birmingham with Rector's Ambassador Five (autumn 1922). Moved to London and led sextet at Hotel Cecil from August 1925, began broadcasting in same year and enlarged band to ten pieces. Became conductor-director of his own BBC Dance Orchestra (1928). Appeared at the London Palladium in April 1930 and thereafter played countless stage shows in Britain and abroad. Payne left the BBC in March 1932 and fronted a highly successful stage show, using a big all-star band. He disbanded briefly in May 1937 to work as an agent, but re-formed his twenty-piece band in January 1938, which resumed its successful routine. The band did many troop concerts during World War II, but Payne rarely led after 1945. He again became a theatrical agent but took occasional conducting engagements until 1947 – by then he was a well-established radio compere. He later enjoyed success as a disc-jockey. His second wife was the singer-pianist Peggy Cochrane. After being declared bankrupt in 1965, Payne managed a wine store. His autobiography, *Signature Tune*, was published in 1947.

PAYNE, Laurie
saxes/clarinet

Born: London, 1908
Deceased

Brother of trumpeter/cornetist Norman Payne. Played in amateur band with violinist George Hurley when they were teenagers. With Max Goldberg's Band at Moody's Club, London (late 1925), and at Criterion Restaurant, London (1926). Between summer 1926 and spring 1927 worked with Alfredo in London. With New Sylvians (directed by Howard Jacobs) at Savoy Hotel, London, from April until October 1927. With Howard Jacobs and his Orchestra at Berkeley Hotel January 1928 to December 1929. With Percival Mackey's Orchestra at Savoy Hotel (January to October 1930), then rejoined Howard Jacobs at the Berkeley in October 1930. Joined newly formed Savoy Hotel Orpheans (October 1931), remained with Carroll Gibbons and the Savoy Hotel Orpheans until 1941.

PAYNE, Norman
trumpet/mellophone

Born: Hampstead, London, 29 July 1911
Died: London, 11 February 1992

Younger brother of saxophonist Laurie Payne. Took up cornet, studied briefly in Germany, then returned to London and was tutored by John Sullivan. Played gigs in the East End of London, then turned professional to accompany a dancing act. Played at Florida Club, London, in trio with Lionel Clapper and Ginger Conn (1927), then played residency at Southport Palais with Sydney

Lipton before returning to London to join Fred Elizalde (December 1927). With Arthur Lally at Berkeley Hotel (April to September 1930) then joined Howard Jacobs in October 1930. Extensive freelance recordings from late 1920s through 1930s (with Spike Hughes, Carroll Gibbons, Ray Noble, Bert Firman, John Firman, Jay Whidden, Van Phillips, etc). Often employed by violinist Al Collins during the 1930s and early 1940s, prior to joining RAF (until 1943). With Savoy Hotel Orpheans 1943–4, briefly with Ted Heath and his Music, then retired from playing in 1944 to run a booking agency (J.P. Productions) with drummer Jock Jacobsen. The business was later sold to MGM for whom Payne worked for some years as a booker.

PEARCE, 'Dick' Richard
Born: Forest Gate, London, 19 April 1951
trumpet/flugelhorn

Father was a singer. Dick's cousin is pianist and arranger John Pearce. Trumpet from thirteen, played in Boys' Brigade Band. Served as a musician in the Horse Guards from 1968 until 1971. Was often in National Youth Jazz Orchestra during the 1970s (including visit to USA). With Graham Collier from early 1972 intermittently through to 1978. During the 1970s worked with Mike Westbrooke, Red Brass, Dudu Pukwana, Ken Hyder, Frank Roberts, Julian Marshall, Ken McCarthy, Chris Biscoe, John Williams, Keith Tippett, etc. Often in Jack Sharpe's Big Band during the 1980s, and worked with Gil Evans in Britain. Regularly with Ronnie Scott from 1980, but also worked with Don Rendell, John Williams, in Pete King's Quintet, etc. Injured in motor-cycle accident in September 1990. Resumed full schedule and rejoined Ronnie Scott from 1991 until 1993. Again worked with Mike Westbrook in the early 1900s. Led own quartet through the 1990s, and freelanced with various line-ups including Ron Mathewson's Sextet, Matt Wates' Sextet, Eric Eley, etc.

PEARSON, Dave
Born: c.1935
drums
Died: Wales, 1971

Worked with saxist Bill Findlay's Band before joining Bobby Breen's Band in autumn 1956. With Freddy Randall, then worked with Bernie Stanton (1958) With Vic Ash (1958–9), gigged with Wally Fawkes, then worked in Alan Clarke's Sextet (1960). Freelanced in the 1960s until becoming regular accompanist to singer Dickie Valentine. He died (as did Valentine and pianist Sid Boatman) in a car crash in Wales.

PELLETT, Roy
Born: New Malden, Surrey, 20 March 1935
clarinet

Learnt clarinet at Surbiton County Grammar School and played in school orchestra. Played in various RAF Military Bands (1954–7), led own Dixieland Band during service in Germany. Joined Dave Nelson's Marlborough Jazz Band (autumn 1957), also deputized for Cy Laurie (spring 1960). Left Dave Nelson in late 1960 and joined the Leathertown Jazzmen, an Anglo-German band in Offenbach near Frankfurt in Germany. Toured with Albert Nicholas, and backed T-Bone Walker, Peanuts Holland and Nelson Williams. Left the Leathertown Jazzmen and led re-formed version of the Clyde Valley Stompers from April 1963. Returned to England, gigged with Gerry Brown's Band then worked as Assistant Entertainments Manager at Butlin's, Bognor Regis. Returned to full time music and joined the London City Jazzmen (which included Max Collie). In

February 1966 became founder-member of Max Collie's Rhythm Aces. Joined Bob Wallis in autumn 1968, also played gigs with Charlie Galbraith. In April 1969 joined Rod Mason in Plymouth, took over leadership of the band when Mason joined Acker Bilk in August 1970. Played Mediterranean cruises on *SS Australia* in September 1970 and September 1971. Backed George Melly on brief tours in the early 1970s. Re-formed band in early 1972 which was based in Switzerland. The group toured East Germany (1977) and the Far East (February 1978). Retired from full time music at the end of 1978 and returned to Plymouth to play in local bands. Formed own Hot Four in late 1986, which plays mainly in Devon and Somerset but also features at various jazz festivals and tours Germany and Switzerland (through the 1990s). In December 1979 conceived the idea for BBC radio's long-running *Jazz Score* programme (which has continued through the 1990s). Roy Pellett's compilation of the best anecdotes and one-liners from the first 150 programmes *The Best of Jazz Score* was first published in 1992.

PENDLEBURY, Keith D.
piano/vocals

Born: Stockport, Cheshire, 22 January 1934

Husband of singer Marcia, brother of trombonist Alan Pendlebury (1932–92) and uncle of drummer Chris Pendlebury. Keith was formerly a professional footballer with Stockport County. Piano from childhood. First paid gigs with Eric Batty's Jazz Aces (1951). Worked in brother Alan's All Stars then led own Jazzmen and trio for various residencies. Worked with Alan in the Zenith Six during the 1960s (alongside Marcia), remained after Alan left. Again worked in Alan's band also led own trio and quartet. During the 1980s and 1990s, Keith and Marcia played at many festivals throughout Europe, touring Holland, Sweden, Czechoslovakia and Austria (with Herbie's Swing Unit and with Rolf Ericson). From the mid-1990s they often toured with own Bessie Smith celebration show *The Empress of the Blues*.

PENDLEBURY, Marcia
(née Marcia Carol MACCONNELL)
vocals

Born: Hyde, Cheshire, 14 February 1942

Married to pianist Keith Pendlebury. As Marcia MacConnell she sang with the Climax Jazz Band (1959), subsequently joined the Phoenix Jazz Band and guested with Ken Colyer. Sang with the Jazz Aces (alongside Keith) then both worked in Alan Pendlebury's Jazz Band, and with the Zenith Six (during the 1960s). Thereafter permanently with Keith Pendlebury's Jazz Band, Trio and Quartet, touring Austria, Czechoslovakia, Holland, Sweden, etc. through the 1980s and 1990s. Touring with own Bessie Smith celebration revue *The Empress of the Blues* during the 1990s.

PENROSE, 'Billy' William
piano/vocals/trumpet

Born: 1925
Died: Brighton, Sussex, 1962

Led own Boogie Woogie Quartet for several years, also worked with Lou Preager, Eric Winstone, Joe Daniels, Sid Phillips, Sydney Lipton, Dave Shand, etc., before playing in Calcutta, India, with Harry Bence's Band (1957–8). Contracted tropical illness which ended his playing career. After spending some time in Paddington General Hospital, he moved to Sussex and died in a Brighton hospital.

PERRY, 'Fred' Frederick James   Born: Kensington, London, 15 October 1925
saxes/flute/clarinet

Played at West London Rhythm Club from 1944 onwards. First regular work with the Arcadians in Greenford area, then joined band led by trumpeter Sid Gold. After service in the Royal Navy (during which time he led a Navy dance band in Chatham) worked with Nat Gonella, Eric Winstone, the Squadronaires, etc., and played alongside Jimmy Skidmore at the Music Makers' Club, London, during the early 1950s. With Ralph Sharon from late 1950 until early 1952, Carl Barriteau (spring 1952), Derek Sinclair for Prestatyn summer season (1953). Briefly with Tito Burns in late 1953, left to play for five months in Monte Carlo with Bernard Hilda. With Ginger Johnson's Afro-Jazz (1954), Tony Crombie (1955), Ronnie Scott (spring 1956), then again with Ginger Johnson intermittently from 1956 to 1958. During this period (and later) played many gigs with Nat Temple. With Andre Rico (1959), Revell Terry (1959). During the 1960s played American bases in France, Germany and Spain and various night clubs in London, also did an eight month season in Israel with Tony Crombie (1963). Moved to Bournemouth in 1969 and worked with local bands and played summer residencies until 1985, then retired from full time music but continued to do occasional jazz gigs during the 1990s.

PETERS, 'Mike' Michael   Born: Cornwall, 30 December 1933
trumpet

Took up trumpet shortly before joining the Royal Army Pay Corps in late 1952 (served in Japan). After demobilization (in 1954) played gigs in London and worked briefly in Brian White's Band. Formed own band in 1956 and worked in Germany (1957). With Terry Lightfoot (1958–9), left to join Graham Stewart's Band in April 1959. A year later Stewart left to join Ken Colyer and Peters was appointed leader. He led until moving to the Canary Islands in 1962, where he only played fiesta dates with a local brass band. He returned to London in 1969 and resumed leading a band. Since the early 1980s (through the 1990s) his group has been billed as Mike Peters' World Famous Jazz Band.

PHILLIPS, 'Sid' Isador Simon   Born: London, 14 June 1907
clarinet/baritone sax/piano/arranger/composer   Died: Chertsey, Surrey 25 May 1973

Father of percussionist and musical director Simon Phillips, uncle of saxophonist, composer and bandleader John Altman (born 1949). Sid's younger brother, Woolf, was a successful trombonist, arranger and musical director, who worked for various bandleaders including Teddy Joyce, Ambrose, Joe Loss, Jack Hylton, Ted Heath, etc., before moving to California in 1967. Sid originally played piano and violin, then took up clarinet and sax in his teens. His early schooling in Italy was halted by World War I. At sixteen he played sax in a band at the People's Palace, London. In 1925 he formed the Melodians with brothers Ralph (banjo/guitar/double bass) and Harry (trumpet/violin). This band toured Europe that year, recording in Italy (as the Riviera Five). In 1927 Sid won two *Melody Maker* arranging contests. Late in 1927 the band toured Germany. In 1928 and 1929 they played residencies at the Café de Paris in London. Sid also did freelance arranging and musical direction (for the Edison Bell recording company, etc.). He joined the publishers, Lawrence Wright, as staff arranger in 1930 and began writing for Ambrose.

Sid then led own band before becoming staff arranger (and baritone saxophonist and clarinettist) with Ambrose from September 1933. He wrote compositions such as 'Cotton Pickers' Congregation', 'Night Ride', 'Streamline Strut', etc., especially for Ambrose's Band. He also led own recording bands and made playing trips to the USA in 1934 and 1938 (during the latter visit he led an all-star band for recordings). He left Ambrose in summer of 1937, joined Jack Hylton briefly, then rejoined Ambrose until 1939, also arranged for Jack Harris's Band. With Jay Wilbur (late 1939), then formed own trio (1940). Briefly led Dixieland Band at Le Suivi Club, London, then served for five years in the RAF (as an Intelligence Officer). After being demobilized in January 1946, he formed own successful small Dixieland band and continued to lead this into the early 1970s, also recorded own compositions with a big band in 1958. With Louis Armstrong at Royal Festival Hall, London (December 1956). As Simon Phillips he composed a number of extended works that were performed by various symphony orchestras. His last gig was in Nottingham on 14 April 1973, where he guested with Jazz Spectrum.

PICARD, John Francis
Born: Tottenham, London, 17 May 1934
trombone/piano

Father of saxophonist Simon Picard. Attended Enfield Grammar School, with Terry Lightfoot, and played in Wood Green Stompers (with Lightfoot), first on piano then on trombone. Served in RAF, played weekend dates with Cy Laurie, then worked regularly with Cy Laurie for four months before joining Humphrey Lyttelton from November 1954 until September 1960. With Mike Daniels from October 1960 until working with Bruce Turner from February to July 1961. Left full time music to become a successful estate agent, but continued to play regularly. Led own band from September 1961, briefly with Wally Fawkes (early 1962), then worked with Tony Coe from 1962 through to the early 1970s sharing leadership with Coe. Also co-led quintet with Kathy Stobart in the late 1960s. With Stan Greig's London Jazz Big Band (from February 1975 debut), remained for eight years. Led own band at New Merlin's Cave, London, for long residency, and gigged with Ian Stewart and Rocket 88 during the early 1980s. With Charlie Watts' Big Band 1985, 1986. Continued to play gigs and lead own band throughout the 1980s and early 1990s.

PINE, Courtney
Born: Paddington, London, 18 March 1964
tenor sax/'C' melody sax/soprano sax/
bass clarinet/composer

Both parents from Jamaica. Began on clarinet then specialized on tenor and soprano saxes. Worked with reggae band, Eastwood and Saint, etc., and dance groups such as Hi Tension, then formed own Dwarf Steps. In John Stevens' Freebop (1984–5), playing alongside Evan Parker, Harry Beckett, Paul Rogers, etc. With Charlie Watts' Big Band (1985–6). With Gail Thompson formed Jazz Warriors for January 1986 debut, also led Oasis and played in Mano Ventura Quintet. Toured with George Russell's Orchestra (1986), sat in with Art Blakey (1986) and worked briefly with Elvin Jones, then guested with Art Blakey at the Apollo, New York (1986). Part of World's First Saxophone Posse. Toured USA and Japan with own group. Concert tour with Ellis Marsalis (1991), worked with Marvin 'Smitty' Smith (1991). Toured Britain leading own American Band during the early 1990s. Featured with Gary Crosby's Jazz Jamaica in the 1990s. Continues to lead own line-ups through the 1990s, featuring blends of reggae, hip-hop and jazz, as well as being featured as a soloist at international festivals.

PITT, 'Tony' Anthony Russell
guitar/banjo

Born: Wolverhampton, Warwickshire, 1 March 1940

Brother of bassist Vic Pitt, their mother played piano, their father banjo. Family moved to London in 1947, then to mid-Kent, and then to Chatham where Tony spent his teenage years. Played violin at school, then took up guitar and banjo. Gigged in local Crescent City Stompers and led own skiffle group. Deputized in Kenny Ball's Band (1960) and in Cy Laurie's Band (early 1961), also worked briefly with Nat Gonella. Regularly with Alex Welsh from 1961 to end of 1963, then spent six months with the Mike Cotton Sound before joining Acker Bilk from May 1964 until spring 1974. Freelanced before joining Kenny Ball from 1978 to 1980. Returned to gigging, then again worked with Kenny Ball from 1984 to 1987. Freelanced, often working with Alan Elsdon. Played in Fad's Army with Laurie Chescoe, then became founder-member of Laurie Chescoe's Good Time Jazz from August 1990 through the 1990s.

PITT, 'Vic' Rodney Victor James
double bass

Born: Wolverhampton, Warwickshire, 26 September 1941

Brother of Tony Pitt, their father played banjo, their mother piano. Family moved to Chatham in the late 1940s. Played concerts on mandolin in family trio, then gigged on banjo with the local Crescent City Stompers. Took up double bass and played this in the Deep Bayou Jazz Band (1956). Played in brother Tony's trio at the Skiffle Cellar in Greek Street, London (1958), and while there accepted an offer to join Russell Quaye's City Ramblers on double bass. Extensive work with this group before joining Kenny Ball in 1959. Left Kenny Ball in summer of 1977 and joined Chris Barber, remained with Chris Barber through the 1990s.

PITTERSON, 'Pete' Egbert George
trumpet

Born: Kingston, Jamaica, West Indies, 8 March 1921
Died: England, 2 November 1994

Began on trumpet during childhood, played in St Albans Church School Band and did local gigs, before joining pianist Milton MacPherson's Big Band. Visited USA. Moved to Britain in 1946, played at London's Fullado Club and broadcast with Jack Fallon's Band. Played in Swindon and with Roy Dexter's Orchestra. Worked at Lyceum, London, in Ivor Kirchin's Band, toured with Vic Lewis (summer 1948). With Dennis Hale before joining Tommy Sampson (1949). Toured Scandinavia with Leslie 'Jiver' Hutchinson (summer 1949), again worked with Tommy Sampson. With Leon Roy's Big Band in London (1950), led own band, then worked for nine months in Joe Appleton's Band. With Edmundo Ros, then led own Ebony Six in England and Scotland before working in Birmingham with Cliff Deeley, Andy Hamilton and Sonny Rose (early 1953). With Ambrose from spring 1953, then briefly in Johnnie Gray's Band (spring 1954). With Harry Hayes (1955), played for *The Jazz Train* show, worked with Harry Leader and led own quartet. With Ginger Johnson (1956) and in Harry Green's Sextet in London (late 1956). Led own quartet at Sunset Club, London (1958), also with Chico Arnez (1958). Worked for three months in Turkey with Frank King's Sextet (1960). Played for *King Kong* show (1961) and worked with Frank

Holder. Played for various shows in the early 1960s and freelanced in jazz groups and calypso bands. Led own septet in Italy (1965), toured with Georgie Fame (1966), gigged with Long John Baldry and Jimmy Witherspoon, also deputized in BBC Radio Orchestra. Returned to Jamaica from 1969 until 1973, then moved back to England and freelanced, often gigging with Russ Henderson, until illness ended his playing career.

PITTS, Terry
trombone

Born: London, 1936

Played in RAF bands, then joined Bill Brunskill in late 1955. Left to join Cy Laurie in summer of 1956. Led band while Cy Laurie was absent (late 1960), then took over in July 1961. Led own band during the 1960s, then freelanced. Often with George Webb during the 1970s, but was regularly in singer Judith Durham's Band (including tour of Australia). Played with various bands in the 1980s, and made four trips to Vancouver with Hugh Rainey, also did Mediterranean cruises with Pat Halcox, and worked often in Pete Corrigan's Band during the 1980s and early 1990s. Was part of Cy Laurie Reunion Band, then emigrated to Canada in the early 1990s. Returned temporarily to England to guest with Pete Corrigan's Band (1996).

POGSON, 'Poggy' Edward O.
saxes/all reeds including bassoon/
violin/vocals

Born: Acton, London, 20 October 1904
Died: Crewkerne, Somerset, 31 January 1980

First professional playing at Wimbledon Palais, then joined Herman Darewski's Stage Band. With Bert Firman, Al Starita's Kit-Cat Band, before joining Jack Hylton in the mid-1920s. Worked mainly with Hylton until joining Jack Payne in autumn 1931. Regularly with Jack Jackson's Orchestra from spring 1933 until spring 1939, but did freelance work including summer season in Holland with Ray Noble (August 1933) and various engagements with Victor Sylvester. With Hugo Rignold, George Melachrino, Debroy Somers (1939). With Billy Ternent and Geraldo (1940), then rejoined Jack Jackson in autumn 1940. With Chappie D'Amato (late 1941), then rejoined Jack Payne (1942–3). Briefly with George Evans. Prolific freelance work in the 1940s, often with Victor Sylvester and in quintet led by drummer Ben Edwards. Extensive freelance work in the 1950s and 1960s, regularly in Kenny Baker's Dozen, also played on most of the BBC radio's *Goon Show*. After being taken ill in 1967, he moved to Somerset, where he continued to teach until shortly before his death. He was married to pianist Gwen Austin.

POINTON, 'Mike' Michael
trombone

Born: London, 25 April 1941

Took up trombone after efforts on piano and trumpet. Gigged with youthful Blue Crow Jazzmen in Croydon area, then joined the Perdido Street Six (c.1958). Formed own Jazzmen in 1959, also played in Salutation Brass Band. Helped form Kid Martyn's Ragtime Band (1959), then joined San Jacinto Jazzmen, also played in the New Teao Brass Band and deputized in Ken Colyer's Band. With Uncle John Renshaw's Jazzband in 1960, then joined Keith Smith's Climax Jazzband (1960). With Barry Martyn's Camellia Jazz Orchestra (1961), gigged with Dave Mills' Jazzband. Deputized again with Ken Colyer, and worked with Kid Martyn Band (accompanying Kid Thomas,

Emmanuel Paul, etc.). Guested with Cotton City Jazzband in Belgium (thus accompanied Mezz Mezzrow). Toured with Martyn Band accompanying George Lewis and Alton Purnell (1965) and John Handy (1966). Played in Lounge Lizards, and guested with Brian Green's Band. Worked at Your Father's Mustache clubs, then with Bill Brunskill for a year, before playing for a year in Belgium. Led own quartet there, worked with Albert Nicholas, recorded with Paul Closset's Dixieland Gamblers. Returned to Britain, then played with Les Haricots Rouges in Paris. Rejoined Bill Brunskill in 1984, also gigged with Lord Arsenal (Allan Bradley). Throughout the 1980s was part of British All Stars (organized by Dave Mills and Alan Cooper) making regular tours of the Gulf States. Worked with Jump Jive and Wail and with the European Classic Jazzband. Left Bill Brunskill in 1988. Often guested with Apex Jazzband in Belfast. Toured Cyprus with guitarist/bassist Ken Ames (1992). With Hot Stuff (led by Chez Chesterman) from 1992, also regularly with Dick Laurie's Elastic Band from 1986 through the 1990s. Combines music making with writing documentaries for radio and television.

POLLARD, Tommy
piano/piano accordion/vibes

Born: 1923
Died: 8 October 1960

Worked with Johnny Claes, Jack Hamilton-Roy Marsh Sextet, Derek Neville and Tito Burns, before joining Harry Parry in early 1942. Served in Armed Forces from late 1942 and became part of Ralph Reader's *Gang Show* in India and North Africa. After demobilization joined Ray Ellington (1946). With Buddy Featherstonhaugh (1947), with Bobby Kevin's Band aboard liner *Queen Mary* (1947). Again with Tito Burns (1948), became founder-member of Club Eleven (December 1948). With Cab Kaye (1949), also worked with Ronnie Scott and with Victor Feldman. Played in Holland, then returned to England and worked in duo with Tony Crombie (summer 1951). Again with Ronnie Scott, also in Joe Muddel's Group (1952–3). With Frank Weir (1954), then suffered long illness which only allowed him to work occasionally during the late 1950s.

POTTER, Gary
guitar/banjo

Born: Walton, Liverpool, 15 November 1965

Took up guitar at age of ten, some tuition from his father Keith Potter (who plays and sings country music) but mostly self-taught. By twelve was playing gigs with various country bands in and around Liverpool, then worked further afield (including Wembley Stadium) with Tommy Cline, West Virginia and Kevin Daniels. Heard Django Reinhardt recordings and switched to jazz and soon gained national reputation. Featured at various festivals during the 1990s, and leading own successful quartet.

POVEY, 'Bill' William Frederick
saxes/clarinet/flute

Born: Kennington, London, 15 December 1915

Two brothers were saxophonist: Fred and Joe (1930–49). Bill's two sons, Vincent (born 1950) and Gavin (born 1955) are both keyboard players. After playing in Les Ayling's Band as a semi-pro, worked with Harry Roy before serving in the RAF during World War II. Played in various service quintets. After demobilization again worked with Harry Roy (1946), then joined Harry

Field's Band on the *Queen Mary* (1947), also did radio work with Duncan Whyte. Lived in Canada from late 1947 until late 1950, played club and hotel dates with Mart Kenny, Norman Harris, etc. Returned to Britain, with Sydney Lipton (December 1950 until late 1952), during this period also worked with Harry Gold and with Freddy Clayton in small jazz groups. With Stanley Black from 1953, and Cyril Ornadel from 1954, long working association with Eric Jupp. Prolific freelance work from 1960 to 1990, regularly with Peter Knight and on innumerable sessions. Retired to Blackpool in June 1990.

PRATT, 'Bobby' Robert Stuart
trumpet

Born: Aberdeen, Scotland, 24 January 1927
Died: Alperton, Middlesex, 5 June 1968

Professional musician from the age of sixteen. Worked with pianist Archie Alexander in Aberdeen (1945), then served in Royal Corps of Signals and played in Skyliners' Army Band at Catterick Camp in Yorkshire. With Ken Mackintosh (March 1948 to April 1949). With Ted Heath from April 1949 until November 1960, during this period also worked in Humphrey Lyttelton's Big Band, in Eddie Harvey's Big Band, with Bob Miller, etc. Freelance from 1960, worked with Johnny Keating, Tubby Hayes' Big Band, Downbeat Big Band, Tommy Watt, Jack Parnell's ATV Orchestra, Bob Barter, etc. Took his own life.

PRESENCER, Gerard
trumpet/piano

Born: London, 12 September 1972

Parents are Canadian. Trumpet from the age of ten, four years of lessons from Paul Eshelby. First played with the National Youth Jazz Orchestra at eleven. Later with Roadside Picnic, Clark Tracey, Richard Busiakiewicz's Quartet, etc. With Pizza Express Modern Jazz Sextet from late 1989 through the 1990s. International touring in Charlie Watts' Quintet in 1991 and 1992. With Bob Wilber's Big Band (1991), with John Dankworth and with the Dankworth Generation Band (1992–3). Quintet with Pete King (1994), tour with Gail Thompson's Gail Force (1994), work with Lawrence Cottle's Quintet (1994), etc. During 1995 worked with Geoff Castle, Dave Newton, Colin Towns' Orchestra, Stan Tracey, Don Weller's Big Band, Pete King, and guested with the BBC Radio Big Band as well as doing extensive freelance work. Led own quartet, and worked in Clark Tracey's Quintet in 1996. Continued to play in a variety of line-ups, often in Stan Tracey's Quartet and in duo with Stan Tracey.

PRESTON, Cyril
trombone

Born: Sheffield, Yorkshire, 30 May 1934
Died: 1976

Played piano as a schoolboy, took up trombone in 1955 while qualifying as an analytical chemist. Played in Sheffield's Gloryland Jazzmen before joining Stoke's Ceramic City Stompers in autumn 1957. With Dick Charlesworth from 1959 until 1961. Created Cyril Preston's Excelsior Jazz Band by taking over the leadership of Charlie Gall's Jazzmen (spring 1961). Subsequently moved back to the North and joined the Zenith Six in Manchester (1967). Co-led Old Fashioned Love Band with trumpeter Mel Hill from autumn 1967. Died in a car crash.

PRICE, 'Ernie' Ernest Ivon
double bass

Born: 10 December 1926
Died: Hull, Humberside, 16 August 1988

Was a qualified solicitor. With Bill Brunskill and Mike Peters before working with Acker Bilk from late 1957 until spring 1964. Moved to the North and temporarily gave up music. Began gigging again in 1972 and joined Dave Brennan's Jubilee Jazz Band, subsequently formed own band, the Price Gang, which operated out of Hull.

PRICE, 'Red' Reginald
saxes/piano/organ

Born: Wirral, Merseyside, c.1926
Died: Hong Kong, February 1984

Was a boy champion piano-accordion player before taking up tenor sax. Worked with the Mariners' Dance Orchestra and with Bill Gregson's Band in Liverpool (1948). Doubled on tenor sax and trombone with Hal Graham's Band at the Rialto, Liverpool (1951). With the Squadronaires from May 1952 until September 1955, then joined Jack Parnell. With Ted Heath from March 1956 until August 1958. Featured with Lord Rockingham's XI from August 1958. Combined this with studio work (1959–60). Briefly in hospital (1959), toured with New Orleans Rockers from autumn 1960, then formed own Red Price Combo in early 1961. Led own group in the 1960s, also acted as musical director for various touring recording stars. Occasionally gigged with Fairweather-Brown All Stars on tenor sax and organ. Guested at various jazz clubs, again out of action through ill health (1966). Freelanced on tenor sax in the early 1970s, then further ill health. Occasionally guested with the John Rotherham Trio (1975–6), then did season on the Isle of Man on piano and organ (occasionally playing tenor sax) in 1977. Moved to Hong Kong, freelanced there, then worked for a year in Harry Bence's Band at the Cabaret Club (1979). Briefly returned to England, then returned to Hong Kong and worked with the Jamestown Five (led by Australian Dennis Wilson) until shortly before his death.

PRIESTLEY, Brian
piano/arranger

Born: Manchester, Lancashire, 10 July 1940

Piano from early childhood. Played local gigs while studying modern languages at Leeds University. Led quartet for Inter-University Competition (early 1963) and led quartet for residency at Peel Hotel, Leeds. Played gigs in Manchester with Roy Bower's Sextet (1964). After gaining BA degree in French, he moved to Oxford to work in a bookshop; gigged with local bands and began arranging for the National Youth Jazz Orchestra. Moved to London in autumn 1969. Played gigs with (and did big band arrangements for) Tony Faulkner and Alan Cohen, and for the New York Repertory Company, etc., during the 1970s and 1980s. From 1971 to 1988 hosted BBC Radio London's *All That Jazz* programme, later presented programmes on London's Jazz FM. Led own trio from the early 1970s, also worked often with saxophonist Dave Gelly throughout the 1970s and was part of the Dave Gelly-Jeff Scott Quintet in the mid-1970s. Collaborated with Alan Cohen on television specials during the 1980s. Led own quartet in late 1970s and early 1980s, subsequently led own Ellington Tribute Band before forming own Sextet which has continued through the 1990s, combining this with solo piano work (notably at Kettner's, London) and freelance gigs, with Don Rendell (1996) etc. Active in jazz education since the late 1970s. Taught piano and jazz history at Goldsmiths College, London, from 1977 until 1993 (and organized workshops). Has written biographies of Charles Mingus, Charlie Parker and John Coltrane, and *Jazz On Record – A History* (first published in 1988). His transcriptions of various jazz pianists' work (including Thelonious Monk's) have also been published. Together with Ian Carr and Digby Fairweather co-authored *Jazz, The Rough Guide* (published 1995).

PROCTER, Judd
guitar/mandolin/vocals

Born: Doncaster, Yorkshire, 2 January 1933

Originally played plectrum banjo, switched to acoustic guitar at fourteen. Played gigs with local bands and won regional *Melody Maker* contest with the Zetland Players. Did National Service in the RAF and while stationed at Maidstone played in Les Evans' Rehearsal Band and took lessons from Ike Isaacs. After demobilization did first professional work with Peter Fielding at Nottingham Palais. Played summer seasons with various bands, then moved to London to join Norman Burns from February until July 1955. Member of Ray Ellington's Quartet for six years from July 1955, many radio dates including regular *Goon Show* broadcasts. Left Ray Ellington to concentrate on session work, played for television, recordings, radio, etc. Took time out to tour Japan with Stanley Black (1965) and to work with Benny Goodman on record, and on various concerts in England (1971). Often in Don Lusher's Big Band during the late 1970s and 1980s, but mainly occupied with session work in the 1990s.

PUKWANA, Du Du Mtutuzell
saxes/piano/vocals/composer

Born: Walmer, Port Elizabeth, South Africa, 18 July 1938
Died: Paddington, London, 28 June 1990

Father a pianist, mother a singer. Began on piano during childhood, took up alto sax at eighteen. Gigged in Port Elizabeth with the Broadway Yanks and the Four Yanks. Won award while leading own Jazz Giants at 1962 Johannesburg Jazz Festival and soon joined newly-formed Chris McGregor's Blue Notes. To Europe with this group to play at 1964 Antibes Jazz Festival and remained with them in Europe. Worked with organist Bob Stuckey's Quartet and Band in 1967, subsequently in Keith Tippett's Centipede, Harry Miller's Isipingo, with John Martyn, the Incredible String Band, etc. Also continued to work with Chris McGregor (as part of the Brotherhood of Breath) during the 1970s. Temporarily returned to South Africa in 1969 and toured with own kwela band Spear, then toured USA with trombonist Jonas Gwangwa and trumpeter Hugh Masekela in African Explosion (1969). Returned to Britain and formed own band Assagai, also worked with various reggae bands and with John Surman, Mike Osborne, Misha Mengelberg, etc. Again toured Africa with Spear (1977–8) then returned to Britain and formed new band Zila in 1978 which worked internationally through the 1980s.

PURBROOK, Colin Thomas
piano/double bass/arranger/composer

Born: Seaford, Sussex, 26 February 1936

Piano from the age of six. Father was a professional pianist. Left Fitzwilliam College, Cambridge, in summer of 1957. Joined Sandy Brown on double bass in early 1958, then worked on piano in the Fairweather-Brown All Stars from July 1958. Briefly on double bass, piano and trumpet with Kenny Ball (September 1958). Worked with Allan Ganley-Ronnie Ross Jazzmakers. Played on liner *Queen Mary*. With trumpeter Alan Clarke's Sextet at Jack Of Clubs, London (early 1960). In

Ronnie Scott-Jimmy Deuchar Quintet from August to December 1960 then rejoined Jazzmakers. Gigged with Wally Fawkes (1961). Worked in Germany with Bert Courtley's Sextet (1961), then rejoined Jazzmakers from October 1961 to March 1962. Appeared in film *All Night Long* (1961). Toured with Kenny Baker (March 1962) and worked with Tubby Hayes. Co-led quintet with Tony Coe during the early 1960s, which played Black Sea and Mediterranean cruises (summer 1962). With Tony Coe (1963), also led trio for *Beyond the Fringe* show, and briefly worked on double bass in Dudley Moore's Trio (1963). Accompanied many visiting American jazzmen (including Benny Goodman in 1964). Own groups, including octet in the 1960s and 1970s. Worked in Don Rendell's Quintet (1964) and in Don Rendell-Ian Carr Quintet (1964). With Tony Coe-John Picard Quintet (1965–6). With Sandy Brown again in 1966. Own quartet (1967–8). With Phil Seamen's Quartet (1968). Briefly on double bass in Brian Lemon's Trio (1969). Played residencies in Spain in the late 1960s. Continued to work in Britain with visiting American musicians, including Benny Carter, Chet Baker, Buddy Tate, etc. Often accompanied singer Annie Ross. With Humphrey Lyttelton in 1972 (having previously worked occasionally with Lyttelton in 1968). During the mid-1970s freelanced with many bands, including group led by Gene Cottrell. Accompanied American musicians and was musical director for various shows including *Bubbling Brown Sugar* (1977), *One Mo' Time* (1981), *Lady Day* (1987) and *Rent Party* (1989). Active freelance during the 1990s and leading own trio, which backed Annie Ross for Pizza on the Park, London, residency (March 1996). Although Colin Purbrook has specialized on piano for most of his career, he has worked on double bass on many occasions and was also adept on cornet, trombone and clarinet.

PURCELL, Simon
piano/composer

Born: London, 20 November 1958

Both parents were professional classical musicians. Studied piano and French horn at Trinity College of Music with John Burden and Anthony Lindsay. Later studied at Barry Summer School with John Taylor and Gordon Beck, and was coached by Lionel Grigson. First gigs with Martin Speake and Mick Hutton (1980). Led Jazz Train, and own quartet (with Julian Argüelles) from 1985–90. Accompanied Red Rodney, Eddie Henderson, Kenny Wheeler, Bobby Shew, Valery Ponomarev, Jean Toussaint, Pete King, John Stubblefield, etc. Professor of Jazz Improvisation at the Guildhall School of Music (since 1988), also teaches at Wavendon Summer School and co-directs the Treforrest Jazz Summer School. Founder of Jazz Umbrella (a London-based organization of jazz musicians, which began in 1992). During the 1990s continues to lead quintet (with Stan Sulzmann) and quartet (with saxist Mike Williams, drummer Dave Wickens and bassist Steve Watts).

PYNE, 'Chris' Norman Christopher
trombone

Born: Bridlington, Yorkshire, 14 February 1939
Died: London, 12 April 1995

Brother of pianist Mick Pyne, their father was an amateur pianist. Piano during childhood, trombone as a teenager. Served in RAF, then moved to London, played in Fat John Cox's Band (1963) and with Alexis Korner (from summer 1963 until 1965). With John Stevens' Septet, and Spontaneous Music Ensemble (1965–6), also in London Jazz Orchestra. With Humphrey Lyttelton from summer of 1966 until 1970, during this period also played in the house band at the

Pigalle (1966), led own sextet, worked with John Dankworth, Tubby Hayes, Ronnie Scott (octet and big band) etc. During the 1970s worked in Mick Pyne's Sextet, in John Taylor's Sextet, with John Surman, Philly Joe Jones, Maynard Ferguson, Mike Gibbs, Tony Coe, Kenny Wheeler, Bobby Lamb-Ray Premru, Ronnie Ross, in Barbara Thompson's Jubiaba and in Ian Hamer's Sextet, as well as playing on many freelance sessions. Played in bands accompanying Ella Fitzgerald, Sarah Vaughan, Frank Sinatra, etc. In the 1980s and 1990s worked in John Surman's Brass Project, Charlie Watts' Big Band, with Kenny Wheeler, Mike Gibbs, Gordon Beck, Stan Tracey, and freelanced in theatre orchestras and on sessions.

PYNE 'Mick' Michael John
piano/cornet/arranger

Born: Thornton Dale, Yorkshire, 2 September 1940
Died: Wimbledon, Surrey, 24 May 1995

Younger brother of Chris Pyne, their father was an amateur pianist. Began playing piano during early childhood, later played violin then took up cornet in his early teens. He began specializing on piano and played in bands with his brother around East Yorkshire. Moved to London in 1959 and freelanced for a few months, then again played in Yorkshire before returning to London. Played solo piano at the Down Beat Club, London. Joined Tony Kinsey's Quintet in May 1962. Spent a year playing American bases in France, mainly on tenor sax (working with Ray Warleigh, etc.), also played tenor sax in Alexis Korner's Blues Incorporated. Returned to Bridlington for eight months of intensive practice on piano, then moved permanently to London (late 1963). With John Stevens' Septet (January 1964), with Kenny Wheeler, Les Condon, etc. Toured Europe with Stan Getz, Hank Mobley, Joe Williams, Lee Konitz, Roland Kirk, etc. Regularly with Tubby Hayes from 1966, also led own line-ups from the late 1960s. Worked in Ronnie Scott's Sextet (1970), later with Scott's Quintet (1978). With Phil Seamen's Quartet (1966). With Amalgam and Spontaneous Music Ensemble in 1970, with John Stevens' Dance Orchestra (1974). With Humphrey Lyttelton from autumn 1972 until summer of 1985, worked in other line-ups during this period and also accompanied visiting American musicians. With Georgie Fame and in Charlie Watts' Orchestra, also freelanced on many recordings including Alison Moyet's *That Ole Devil Called Love*. During the 1980s and 1990s often toured with Keith Smith (including dates in the USA in 1985). Was working with Keith Smith and Elaine Delmar for a Great Yarmouth concert on the night before he died unexpectedly from an internal haemorrhage. Encouraged by Humphrey Lyttelton, he resumed playing cornet semi-regularly in the 1970s and made recordings duetting with himself, and playing cornet in Lyttelton's Band.

R

RABIN, Oscar (Oscar RABINOWITZ)
saxes/violin

Born: Riga, Latvia, 16 April 1899
Died: Putney, London, 20 June 1958

Father of clarinettist Ivor, agent David and band-manager Bernard. Oscar's grandson Michael plays sax and clarinet. Family moved to England when Oscar was four weeks old. Studied violin at the Guildhall School of Music. Directed a band at Palace Hotel, Southend (1925–6). Formed musical partnership with Harry Davis, who became Oscar's front-man and conductor for 25 years. Led the Romany Band at Wimbledon Palais 1926–8, which subsequently played various London residencies including Royal Palace Hotel, Kensington (1928–30), Astoria, Charing Cross Road (1930–5) and Hammersmith Palais (1935–40). Oscar eventually specialized on bass sax, and led his own big band for a long residency at the Lyceum Ballroom, London. His big band did a tour of Europe for ENSA (Entertainments National Service Organization) in 1945. After Harry Davis moved to the USA (where his daughter Beryl went to further her singing career), Don Smith briefly became conductor before the position was taken in 1951 by David Ede (born 1926), who lost his life by drowning in 1965.

RACE, 'Steve' Stephen Russell
piano/arranger/composer

Born: Lincoln, 1 April 1921

Piano from early childhood, played in the Vita Dance Band with school friends, subsequently gigged with the Arcadia Dance Band, then moved to London at sixteen to study piano, organ and composition at the Royal Academy of Music. Worked with Harry Leader in late 1939, and with Billy Smith, Ivor Kirchin and Oscar Grasso (1940), before joining RAF early in 1941. Directed various station bands and led own RAF Swing Stars. Played and arranged for RAF Bomber Command Dance Orchestra (led by Leslie Douglas) and continued to lead own RAF Swing Stars. With Howard Lucraft's group. Prolific arranging for Phil Green, the Squadronaires, Ted Heath, the Skyrockets, etc. Demobilized in early 1946, further work with Howard Lucraft Septet, then with Nat Temple, before joining Cyril Stapleton in June 1946. Briefly with Buddy Featherstonhaugh (late 1946). Briefly with Harry Hayes (1947) and with Lew Stone (1949), but by this time was doing prolific freelance work, composing and arranging for films, and working as an accompanist for many singers on radio and television. Wrote for *Musical Express* and *Melody Maker*. Continued to lead own various line-ups: Trio, Quartet, Quintet, Sextet and Orchestra. Became Director of Light Music at a television company in the 1950s, but continued to play piano regularly. Became a highly successful compere on radio and television, and continued to be so into the mid-1990s. Was awarded the OBE in 1992. His autobiography *Musician at Large* was published in 1979.

RAE, 'Ronnie' Ronald
double bass

Born: Edinburgh, Scotland, 24 February 1938

Sons: Ronnie Jr (piano) and John (drums). Played in brass bands from age of eleven. Took up double bass at twenty and joined band led by arranger Edwin Holland. Played professionally at Butlin's holiday camp, and aboard ocean liners, as well as palais work in Scotland. First regular jazz work with pianist Alex Shaw. Spent almost three years with Alex Welsh during two periods in the late 1960s. Returned to Scotland and did prolific freelance work with many visiting musicians including Johnny Griffin, Scott Hamilton, Earl Hines, Doc Cheatham, Barney Kessel, etc., and recorded with Ben Webster, Ruby Braff, Buddy De Franco, Louis Stewart, etc. Continued to freelance in the 1990s, working often in Fionna Duncan's Quartet, and with pianist Dave Newton, as well as in quartet led by pianist Bob Stephenson.

RAINE, 'Jack' John A.
trumpet/violin

Born: Rotherham, Yorkshire, 1891
Died: Sussex, 1952

After Army service in World War I played in the Rag Pickers at Hammersmith Palais, London, then worked on violin with the Albany Five at Birmingham Palais (c.1921). With Jack Hylton on trumpet from 1922 to 1936, then worked with Debroy Somers, John Borelli's Orchestra and Princes Theatre Orchestra before serving in ENSA (Entertainments National Service Organization) during World War II, also worked in Scotland with Ronnie Munro (1942) and Joe Gibson, and toured with Jerry Hoey. Worked mainly on violin in various theatre orchestras during the late 1940s, but reverted to trumpet for 1950 Royal Command Performance reunion of Jack Hylton's Band.

RAINEY, Hugh Colin
banjo/trumpet

Born: Plaistow, London, 6 July 1936

First gigs were as a student with jazz band at Queen Mary College, London. Joined Steve Lane's Southern Stompers in 1956. Left to form own Storyville Jazzmen in 1957, joined Terry Lightfoot briefly in summer of 1957, until called up for Army service. Rejoined Storyville Jazzmen (1958), by then the band was led by trumpeter Bob Wallis. Remained with Bob Wallis until spring of 1964, then joined Monty Sunshine's Band (1964–5). Worked as a teacher but led own band mainly around the Essex area in the late 1960s (and began doubling on trumpet), often gigged with Cy Laurie (from summer of 1968) and with George Webb. Joined Australian singer Judith Durham's Hottest Band in Town (1974) and toured Australia with the group during the following year. Led own Hotter Than That Band regularly from 1977, which played regular annual bookings in Vancouver, Canada. During the 1980s played on Mediterranean cruises with Pat Halcox, Alan Elsdon, etc., was also featured as guest at the 1989 Australian Jazz Convention. Retired from teaching in 1991, played at various festivals. Continued to lead own band through the 1990s but also freelanced with various leaders including Cy Laurie, George Webb, Neville Dickie, Pete Corrigan, Kenny Ball, Dennis Field, George Tiddiman, etc.

RANDALL, Alan
vibes/piano/ukulele/guitar

Born: Bedworth, Leicestershire, 10 June 1935

Piano at six, vibes at eighteen. Worked as an aircraft engineer and gigged with bands in the Midlands before joining Sonny Rose in 1957. Worked with Basil Kirchin (1958), including tour of USA then left in October 1958 to form own group. Worked as a solo act and played Windmill Theatre, London, in 1959. Toured internationally from the 1960s onwards, working in Australia, USA, Africa, etc. Noted for his successful recreations of George Formby's songs, but continues to guest with various jazz groups (mainly on vibes) through the 1990s, occasionally leads own jazz group.

RANDALL, 'Freddy' Frederick James
trumpet-cornet/vocals

Born: Clapton, East London, 6 May 1921

Became interested in music while at Daubeney Road School in East London. Took up trumpet at sixteen and soon joined Albert Bale's Darktown Strutters. Played in Will De Barr's Band before forming own quartet the Saint Louis Four (1939). Served in the Rifle Brigade from 1940 until being invalided out in 1943. Formed own band, then joined Freddy Mirfield's Garbage Men (1944) and won Individual Award in *Melody Maker* concert (September 1944). With Freddy Mirfield (1945–6), then formed own small band in late 1946 (later occasionally led a big band for bookings at Green's Playhouse in Glasgow during the 1950s). Continued to lead own small band through the 1950s, including brief playing visit to USA in 1956, but disbanded in 1958 due to lung strain. Ran own hotel in Brighton (1958–61), then ran nursing home in Berkshire from 1961. Reformed own band in May 1963, again left full time music, but returned to co-lead band with Dave Shepherd from summer 1972 until late 1973, then led own All Stars through the 1970s, backing various visiting American musicians including Bud Freeman. The band co-led with Dave Shepherd was featured at the Montreux Festival. Retired from touring in the late 1970s but continued to play gigs around the Essex area through the 1980s, mainly with own quintet; also recorded with Benny Waters (1982). Gave up playing and retired to Teignmouth, Devon, in early 1993.

RANGLIN, Ernest
guitar/arranger

Born: Manchester, Jamaica, West Indies, 1933

Guitar from age of fourteen, self-taught. At sixteen played at Colony Club, in Kingston, Jamaica. Worked in Haiti, then did engagements in Nassau, Bahamas, before temporarily moving to Florida, USA. With pianist Lance Haywood at Half Moon Hotel, Montego Bay, then led own groups. Worked often in London, England, during the 1960s, including residency at Ronnie Scott's Club and doing session work. Settled in Brooklyn, New York, worked with Monty Alexander, and with Tommy McCook and the Skatalites. Moved back to Jamaica. Active as a bandleader but also featured on innumerable reggae sessions. Worked in London with Monty Alexander (June 1996).

RAPHAELLO, Neva
vocals

Born: Sintra, Portugal, 1915
Died: England, 1975

Moved with family to Evesham, Worcestershire, as a child. Played piano and sang in church choir. Sang with various bands around the Birmingham area during the late 1930s and early 1940s, including one led by drummer Nat Roness, who later became her manager. Guested (and recorded) with Humphrey Lyttelton in the late 1940s. Worked with Christie Brothers' Stompers and toured with Graeme Bell in Europe (1951). Guested with Ken Rattenbury on radio programmes (1951), then left Midlands to move to London in 1952. Again guested with Humphrey Lyttelton in spring 1953, and from 1953 worked often in Holland (and in Europe) with the Dutch Swing College Band. Guested with Freddy Randall, Sandy Brown, and Graham Stewart and briefly led own band, also worked with the Clyde Valley Stompers in 1961. Moved back to the Midlands and guested with pianist Johnny Hocken's Trio. Occasionally worked with Birmingham bands, but mainly occupied during the last years of her life running a restaurant.

RATTENBURY, Ken
Born: Spilsby, Lincolnshire, 10 September 1920
trumpet/piano/composer/arranger

Grandfather was a professional cornet soloist. Played piano from childhood, did first local gigs on piano in July 1933. Took up trumpet in the late 1930s, then did six years Army service (1940–6). Played in Army Big Band, and did local gigs on trumpet, also played piano with violinist George Adams in Edinburgh. Later served overseas and led own service quintet. After demobilization gigged with bands around the Midlands and worked regularly with (and arranged for) Vernon Adcock, (including season at Weston-super-Mare, 1951). Own quartet resident at Midland Jazz Club from 1949, later led own sextet, which did first television work in late 1952, and broadcast on radio regularly. Led various line-ups thereafter, including an octet, and composed various, often-performed extended works for all-star line-ups. Dental problems caused an eight year lay-off on trumpet (1978–86), but then resumed blowing regularly. Gained Master of Arts degree in 1984, subsequently published *Duke Ellington, Jazz Composer* in 1990. Continues to play trumpet and piano into the mid-1990s; his biographical *Jazz Journey 1925–1994* was published in 1995. Regular contributor to *Crescendo* magazine.

READ, 'Bert' Albert T.
Born: Tottenham, London, 26 June 1909
piano/arranger
Died: Malta, 28 January 1985

Piano from age of six, formed own band at school. Played first gigs in 1924 and turned professional by joining Victor Vorzanger's Band in East London (May 1925). Left in June 1926 to join Joe Daniels, then worked with Jack Payne (1926), Jim Easton (1927), Jay Whidden (1927), before joining Ambrose in September 1928. Remained with Ambrose until joining Henry Hall from 1934 until 1937. With Jack Harris (summer 1937), worked with Maurice Loban, then rejoined Ambrose in summer 1938. Gigged with Victor Sylvester until joining Army in August 1939. Served in Royal Fusiliers until October 1945 (occasionally playing in service bands, including spell in Nat Gonella's Army Band in summer of 1942). Became arranger-editor for music publishers Peter Maurice in November 1945, then left Britain in January 1947 to work for Radio Malaya in Singapore, retired as Director General in June 1960. Moved to Australia where he became Deputy Head of Radio, until again retiring in June 1974. Gained OBE in 1971. Moved to New Zealand then settled in Malta, but performed at Alan Dell's BBC *Dance Band Days* concert at the Royal Festival Hall, London, in June 1982.

REBELLO, Jason
Born: Surrey, 29 March 1969
piano/keyboards

Of English, Portuguese and Indian ancestry. Studied piano from age of nine. Was part of Four on Four Quartet at sixteen. At seventeen began studies at Guildhall School of Music. Attended Interchange jazz course in London (1985–6). Won Pat Smythe Award in 1987. Worked with Jean Toussaint's Quartet, Steve Williamson, vocalist Cleveland Watkiss, etc. Played in Holland and Germany. During the late 1980s often worked with Tommy Smith, and in Alan Skidmore's Quartet, and Dave O'Higgins' Quartet. Accompanied various singers, and worked with Courtney Pine, Branford Marsalis, Gary Burton, etc. Worked in USA and Japan with saxophonist Wayne Shorter (December 1900 to January 1991), guested with Andy Hamilton (early 1992). Freelanced with various musicians and played festival dates with Alan Skidmore (summer 1993). Formed own band (and ran own record label). Entered Buddhist monastery in summer of 1995 for period of intense meditation.

REECE, 'Dizzy' Alphonso Son
trumpet/composer

Born: Kingston, Jamaica, West Indies, 5 January 1931

Father was a pianist. Began on baritone horn, played in local brass band, switched to trumpet. Worked with Jack Brown's Swing Stars (1947), then moved to England in 1948. Worked in Europe often with American expatriates Don Byas and Walter Bishop, then returned to London in 1952. Worked with Cab Kaye (1952–3), gigs with Kenny Graham, then again worked in Europe before forming own quintet (1954). Regularly with Kenny Graham (doubling conga drum) during 1954 and 1955, also worked with Tony Crombie (late 1954), with Kathy Stobart and with Jack Fallon. Again led own quintet and worked with Laurie Morgan's Sextet (summer 1955) and with Victor Feldman (1955). Worked in Paris with pianist Martial Solal and again with Don Byas, also played season in Portugal (summer 1956) with Harry Robbins. Led own quartet and quintet in England (1957–8) also briefly in Russia with Geoff Ellison's Band. Wrote music and played on soundtrack for 1958 British film *Nowhere to Go*. Worked in France with Jacques Hélian's Big Band (1958), returned to London and re-formed own quintet. Season in Switzerland with Freddy Ballerini. Played in Downbeat Big Band (1959). Moved to New York in October 1959, led own groups, using American musicians. Toured Europe in Dizzy Gillespie's Big Band (1968), played dates in England as guest star (1969) and again in 1985. Returned to USA and freelanced with various bands and played regularly in Clifford Jordan's Big Band during the early 1990s.

REMY, Tony
guitar/composer

Born: London, 13 August 1962

During the mid-1980s worked with Phillip Bent's Band and with Desperately Seeking Fusion (alongside bassist Nick Cohen), then formed own Lateral Thinking. Played in Jason Rebello's Quartet in the early 1990s and led own band. Worked with Steve Williamson, Cleveland Watkiss, Roger Beaujolais, etc. Toured Australia in 1995. Regularly in various Julian Joseph line-ups, including the Big Band, also worked with Jean Toussaint. Busy freelance schedule included accompanying various visiting musicians: Pee Wee Ellis, Freddie Hubbard, Lonnie Liston Smith and Jessica Lauren in 1996.

RENDELL, 'Don' Donald Percy
tenor sax/soprano sax/clarinet/flute

Born: Plymouth, Devon, 4 March 1926

Both parents were musicians. Piano from the age of five. Raised in London, attended City of London School. Evacuated to Marlborough, Wiltshire, during World War II, took up alto sax in 1942, lessons from Sonny Knight. Returned to London, played in the Rhythm Racketeers (with Laurie Morgan). Worked briefly in a bank at Southgate, then became professional musician, touring with Hal Moss's Mayfair Swingtet (1943). Specialized on tenor sax. Played in London palais bands (including work with Harold Gale at Royal Tottenham) and played in USO groups at various American bases in England. Joined Duncan Whyte in London for a year (1944–5) and guested at London's Fullado Club. With George Evans prior to joining Frank Weir in summer of 1946. With Oscar Rabin from early 1947 until 1949. Co-led small band with trumpeter Derry Gascoigne and worked briefly in Leon Roy's Big Band (late 1949). Again with Frank Weir (early 1950). With John Dankworth Seven from March 1950 for three years. Often worked in Jazz Today Unit during the 1950s. Formed own sextet early in 1954 (which accompanied Billie Holiday on her British visit). With Tony Crombie (spring 1955) then joined Ted Heath from August 1955 until March 1956. Toured Europe for five weeks with Stan Kenton in spring 1956, then worked in Tony Kinsey's Quartet from summer 1956 until January 1957 (including trip to Cyprus). Led own sextet from January 1957 until June 1958. With Cyril Stapleton's BBC Show Band (1958–9) left to co-lead small band with Bert Courtley (March 1959). Toured Britain with Woody Herman (spring 1959), then again worked with Bert Courtley until late 1959. Own quartet until November 1962, then co-led quintet with Ian Carr from 1963 to 1969, during this period occasionally worked with Long John Baldry and in Johnny Hawksworth's Sextet (1964). With Michael Garrick (1970), then formed new quartet in summer 1970. Toured with John Dankworth during the early 1970s. Continued to lead own groups through the 1980s and 1990s. Guested with Barbara Thompson, Neil Ardley, Brian Priestley. Vile Bodies, Willie Garnett, etc. Taught at summer schools from the early 1970s, and at Royal Academy of Music (1974–7) and Guildhall School of Music from 1984 through the 1990s; combining this with regular playing. Tony Middleton's *Bio-discography of Don Rendell* was published in 1993.

REVELL, 'Alex' Alexander William James   Born: Highgate, London, 21 November 1929
clarinet

Began playing clarinet at seventeen. Played in pick-up bands with banjoist-pianist Fred 'Ferdie' Favager, then joined Reg Rigden's Original Dixielanders (late 1949 to early 1950), subsequently worked with Chris Barber from early 1950 until 1953. With George Webb, then briefly with Graham Stewart (1957), before forming own band (1958). With Steve Lane from late 1958 to late 1960. Deputized in Chris Barber's Band in 1961 and in 1962. Led own band 1961–4, then worked regularly in Brian Green's New Orleans Stompers for several years from 1964 before becoming part of London Rhythm Kings. Temporarily retired from music for several years until playing briefly with Rod Mason's Band in 1979. Resumed regular playing, gigged with many bands, with Colin Kingwell, with Ray Foxley's Trio, etc. Took part in Chris Barber Reunion Band in 1991, touring Britain, Holland and Germany. Guested with various groups including the Frog Island Jazz Band (1992) and Brian Green's Band (1994), but from August 1993 has been a regular member of Ben Cohen's Hot Five and Hot Seven. Is a noted author, specializing in aviation history. His books include *The Vivid Air, Brief Glory, High in the Empty Blue*, etc.

REYNOLDS, 'Stan' Stanley Brian   Born: Lincoln, 16 January 1926
trumpet

With father's band at age of twelve, then played in Dot Stevens' Juvenile Band before joining Bertini. Subsequently with Herman Darewski, then led own band in Hull. Led own band in Zurich (early 1947), then worked with Tommy Sampson from February 1947 to July 1948. With Ted Heath from August 1948 until joining Vic Lewis in September 1950. Left Lewis to work with

Dutch bandleader Ernst van't Hoff in Holland and Spain (May to August 1951), then rejoined Ted Heath from August 1951 to August 1954. With Jack Parnell, Geraldo, Alyn Ainsworth, etc., in the 1950s and 1960s, then worked as a highly successful freelance player and bandleader. Worked again with Ted Heath, with John Dankworth, Bobby Lamb-Ray Premru Big Band, etc. Own band accompanied many visiting stars including Tony Bennett, Sarah Vaughan, Billy Eckstine, etc., also briefly led own band on *Queen Mary* liner (1967). From the 1970 through the 1990s continues to lead own successful big band, also takes part in various Ted Heath Band reunions, plays in the Greatest Swing Band, and plays sessions.

RHODES, 'Phil' Philip Stanford
Born: Stoke-on-Trent, Staffordshire, 12 May 1934
trombone/organ

Piano lessons as a child, played clarinet as a teenager, then took up trombone at nineteen. Played in Ceramic City Stompers, then moved to London. Worked with Mike Peters (1957), then briefly with Sonny Morris before working with Terry Lightfoot from late 1958 until joining Alan Elsdon's newly organized band in May 1961. Remained with Elsdon until 1967, during the latter stages of his stay he doubled on organ. Left full time music temporarily to run driving school, then bought Hammond organ and specialized on this during the early 1970s, playing two year residency at the Latin Quarter, London (1971–3). Rejoined Terry Lightfoot (on trombone) in 1975 and remained with him through the 1990s. During this period also gigged with various bands including quintet co-led with Dick Charlesworth, with John Rodber's Band and (playing an electric trombone) with various groups in Germany and Switzerland.

RICHARDS, Trevor Hamilton Edward
Born: Bexhill-on-Sea, Sussex, 29 August 1945
drums

Began playing drums while at school. In 1963 went to Hamburg, Germany, as part of a pupil exchange and played in local bands. To University of East Anglia, Norwich, in 1964, played gigs with own trio. Moved to Germany in 1965, worked in Frankfurt, and in Hamburg with Abbi Hübner's Band. To USA in 1966, informal studies with Zutty Singleton in New York, then moved to New Orleans where he worked with celebrated veterans and began leading own groups (1967). Lessons from Cie Frazier, Louis Barbarin, Alex Bigard and Freddie Kohlman. Returned to UK to finish degree, gigged with Sammy Rimington, New Iberia Stompers and others and toured Europe (and recorded) with Harold Dejan's Olympia Brass Band (summer 1968). Led own bands, then formed trio in March 1973. Successful international touring temporarily curtailed by automobile crash injuries in January 1977. Began working again (in Germany), continued to lead trio and also toured Europe in Bill Greenow's Trio. Moved back to New Orleans in 1982, worked with many bands, regularly (as co-leader) with Clive Wilson in the Original Camellia band, often with Jeanette Kimball; also with Jacques Gauthés Band in the late 1980s. Regular return visits to Europe. Took Camellia Band on several widespread tours of Asia (1985–9). Toured Europe with Art Hodes and with Ralph Sutton. During the 1990s worked for six months each year in New Orleans and six months in Europe.

RICHARDSON, 'Jimbo' 'Jim' James Anthony
double bass/bass guitar

Born: Tottenham, North London, 16 February 1941

Took up double bass in 1958. Played local gigs, then joined pianist Adrian Paton's Quintet (with John 'Chick' Webb on drums) from 1961–3. This group worked with various saxophonists including Don Rendell, Dick Heckstall-Smith, Alan Skidmore, Art Themen and Eric Robinson. Joined Nat Temple's Band for summer season on the Isle of Man (1963). With Alec Coomb's Trio in Plymouth, then worked for eighteen months on the Canadian Pacific liner *Empress of Britain*. Again with Alec Coomb's Trio for Darlington Cabaret Club residency, first worked with Ernestine Anderson there. Two years with saxophonist Dennis Mann's Band in Bristol, then returned to London. Worked with John Dankworth and Cleo Laine, and with Scott Walker and Lulu (1969). With Keith Tippett's Sextet (1970), also worked with American pianist Mal Waldron in Dublin (1970). With If (Dick Morrissey and Terry Smith) from 1970–2. Played residency at the Talk of the Town, London, with Vic Ash Quartet for three years. Began long musical association with Georgie Fame which lasted for fifteen years. Often in BBC Radio Orchestra during period 1979 to 1982. From 1977 often worked with Dexter Gordon, worked and recorded with Chet Baker, and through the 1980s accompanied Benny Carter, Herb Ellis, Art Farmer, Al Haig, Sonny Stitt, Mose Allison etc. Worked with various singers including Mark Murphy, Dakota Staton, Annie Ross, etc. With Barney Kessel often over a ten year period from the 1980s. Spent a year in the Morrissey-Mullen group (1978–9). Deputized in orchestras playing for West End shows in the 1980s, and played for *Guys and Dolls*. With Colin Purbrook for Alan Plater's *Rent Party* (1989). Did various concerts with violinist Nigel Kennedy during the mid-1980s. Led own group Pogo from 1986 with records for Spotlite. Extensive freelance work through the 1990s, continues to lead own Pogo, and to work regularly with visiting American musicians, including engagements with Charlie Byrd (May 1996).

RICHARDSON, John Otto
drums

Born: Kilburn, London, 8 August 1932

His son Gary is a drummer. Took drum lessons as a teenager from Jack Greenwood and Freddy Leeding. Served apprenticeship in jewellery trade, then did National Service in RAF (1953–5). Played in station jam sessions with Terry Lightfoot and after demobilization joined Terry Lightfoot's Band (1956–7). Further drum tuition from Phil Seamen. Left Terry Lightfoot to join Alex Welsh in August 1957. Left Welsh in June 1960 to rejoin Terry Lightfoot (including work in the USA) until spring 1964. Briefly with Bob Wallis, then again with Terry Lightfoot until 1968. Worked in Dave Shepherd's Quintet (1968), led own band and was part of Brian Lemon's Trio (1969). With Acker Bilk from October 1969 until June 1972. With Freddy Randall-Dave Shepherd Band (1972–3). Worked as manager of Drum City shop in London. During the 1970s led own band (at the Tally Ho, London, etc.) played in Stan Greig's Trio, with Ron Russell's Band, with John Picard's Sextet, with Bob Bryan, etc. Accompanied visiting Americans including Wild Bill Davison, Billy Butterfield, and (with Dave Shepherd) toured with Teddy Wilson. In Five-a-Slide from September 1980 through to the 1990s, active freelance with many line-ups: Roger Nobes' Quartet, Alan Elsdon, to Canada with Neville Dickie's Rhythmakers (1994), etc.

RICHFORD, Doug
clarinet/saxes

Born: 1920
Deceased

Piano from age of seven, clarinet at thirteen. During Army service during World War II played in the Lion Swing Stars. With the River City Jazzmen in the early 1950s, then worked with Sonny Morris and with Nat Gonella, before joining Bob Wallis in late 1959. Left Bob Wallis in spring 1961 to form own band. Led own band until 1964, then cut down to a trio for summer season in Jersey. Left full time music but resumed regular playing by working with Steve Mason's Dixielanders in Germany (1978).

RICOTTI, Frank
vibes/percussion/alto sax/clarinet/composer

Born: London, 31 January 1949

Father played drums. Studied at Trinity College in the mid-1960s, also played in National Youth Orchestra and London Schools Symphony Orchestra. Became founder-member of the National Youth Jazz Orchestra. With Graham Collier Septet and Big Band (1967), also led own quartet and played in saxophonist Pat Evans' Big Band (1967). During the late 1960s continued to work with Graham Collier and with the New Jazz Orchestra, Dave Gelly's Quartet, etc. From the 1970s worked with Mike Gibbs, Maynard Ferguson, Stan Tracey, Gordon Beck, Brian Miller's Impulse, Ian Hamer, John Harle, John Taylor, etc., also played for the show *Hair*. Became a highly successful freelance and did a great deal of writing for films and television.

RIDDICK, 'Billy' William
trumpet

Born: London, 7 October 1921
Died: London, August 1993

Brother Charlie a trumpeter. Worked with Derek Hawkins in South London and with George Evans, then became member of Vic Lewis-Jack Parnell Jazzmen during RAF service, also played in Leslie Douglas' RAF Bomber Command Band (late 1945). With Vic Lewis Jazzmen after demobilization, then joined Harry Roy (spring 1946). Summer season with Billy Munn, then worked with the Skyrockets from autumn 1946 until early 1948. Joined Vic Lewis' Big Band, then worked with Joe Daniels (1949), Roy Bradley (late 1949). With Billy Cotton (1951), Harry Gold (1954), Tim Clayton (1954). Led own band (1955), played on summer season with Harry Parry (1956). Played mainly in night club bands from the 1960s, recovered from serious illness in mid-1960s and worked with Tommy Wolfe (1966). Mainly active as a freelance thereafter but played regularly in Terry Seymour's Band in the 1970s.

RIDGE, Pete
drums

Born: 1931
Died: 2 July 1970

Father was a drummer. Worked with Ed O'Donnell's Band in Leeds, prior to moving to London in 1956. Worked with Mike Peters (1957), later with John 'Kid' Shillito, Dave Reynolds and Sonny Morris, also deputized in Acker Bilk's Band for six weeks. Formed own band in 1959, which was taken over by Mike Cotton in early 1961. Pete Ridge then joined Charlie Gall's Band (which was taken over by Cyril Preston in 1961). With Ken Colyer for four years from June 1961, then played in band led by Pat Hawes (1966).

RILEY, 'Howard' John Howard
piano/composer

Born: Huddersfield, Yorkshire, 16 February 1943

Father a semi-professional pianist. Piano from age of six. Led own trio at Le Grenier Blanc in Huddersfield (1960), then worked with tenor saxophonist Mike Oddy at Dyers' Club, Huddersfield (1961), before commencing studies at Bangor University (where he gained BA and MA). Led own trio at Bangor, later in Riley-Clark duo (1965). Played at holiday camps and on liners. Occasionally with Evan Parker's Quartet in Birmingham, before studying with David Baker at Indiana University (obtained MMus degree). Returned to England, led own trio in London from 1967. Studied for MPhil at York University in the late 1960s. Worked with Barbara Thompson, Art Themen, Evan Parker, John McLaughlin (1968–9). Continued to lead own trio through the 1970s, also taught at Guildhall School of Music and worked in Tony Oxley's Sextet, with John Stevens, etc. Worked in Canada and USA while in North America on a year's Arts Fellowship (1976–7). Returned to Britain for spring 1977 tour, then returned to USA prior to moving back to London in October 1977. With Trevor Watts, Barry Guy, John Stevens, etc. Founder member of Musicians' Co-operative from 1970, participated in London Jazz Composers' Orchestra from 1970 through the 1990s. Taught regularly at summer schools. Continued to lead own trios through the 1980s and 1990s, also duos with Jaki Byard, Keith Tippett, Eddie Prévost, and Elton Dean. Taught jazz and held piano workshops at Goldsmiths College, London in the 1980s and 1990s. During the 1990s also co-led quartets with Elton Dean and with Evan Parker, worked with Art Themen, led own trio and played solo engagements (1996).

RIMINGTON, 'Sammy' Samuel
clarinet/saxes/flute/guitar/mandolin

Born: Paddock Wood, Kent, 29 April 1942

Son, Sammy Jr, is also a musician. Studied guitar for four years, did local gigs then took up clarinet and played in London area with Jim Manning's Climax Band and the Paragon Jazz Band (1958). Joined Dave Reynolds (late 1958), then worked in Pete Dyer's Band prior to joining John 'Kid' Shillito (early 1959). During this period also played in the New Teao Band. Joined Barry Martyn in late 1959, then worked with Ken Colyer from May 1960 until spring 1961. Visited the USA and played in New Orleans, returned to Britain in summer of 1962 and rejoined Ken Colyer. Played clarinet in Colyer's Band and mandolin and guitar in Ken Colyer's Skiffle Group until 1965, then again went to the USA. Led own band there and worked in the Hall Brothers' Band, returned to Britain in 1967, briefly with Keith Smith, then rejoined Barry Martyn (September 1967). Accompanied many visiting American jazzmen in the 1960s and 1970s, playing alto sax and clarinet. Led own quartet and worked with Barry Martyn then formed own band in August 1968. Made Denmark his home during the late 1960s and early 1970s, led own band and also worked with the Cardinal Jazz Band in Arhus. Toured Europe with own band then formed Armada (which blended jazz, rhythm and blues, and rock). Continued working in Britain and played in Mike Casimir's Paragon Brass Band. Returned to London, worked with George Webb (1973) and with Judith Durham's Band (1974), including tour of Australia. Lived in USA from August 1974, widespread work with own group, with Duke Burrell's Louisiana Shakers and the Legends of Jazz. Led own band in Britain and guested with Guy Fenton's Band (1975). Toured Europe with Jabbo Smith (summer 1977). With Chris Barber from late 1977 until spring 1979. Played in Kid

Thomas' Band for British tours. Continues to lead own groups through the 1980s and 1990s, also toured with Waso in the 1980s, and worked with various bands throughout Europe, including regularly guesting with the Ginger Pig Jazzband in the 1990s. Throughout his career has made innumerable recordings with famous American jazz musicians, many of whom he brought to Europe including Thomas Jefferson, Alton Purnell, Sammy Lee, etc. During the 1990s has continued to live for part of each year in Sweden, part in England.

RITTE, Ernest (Ernest RITTIE)
saxes/clarinet

Born: 1904
Died: Australia, 12 January 1958

Joined the Piccadilly Players (directed by Al Starita) in September 1929, but soon became part of the Green Park Hotel Orchestra (managed by Jack Hylton but led by Jean Pougnet). With Billy Mason (summer 1930). With Joe Kaye's Orchestra at the Berkeley Hotel from January 1931, later that year joined Roy Fox at the Monseigneur Restaurant, London, and remained with the band when Lew Stone assumed leadership in 1932. Worked and recorded with Nat Gonella (1935-7), also did extensive freelance work including recordings with Ray Noble (1930-4). Emigrated to Australia in late summer of 1939. Served in Australian Army Medical Corps (1940-1). Led own band in Brisbane before moving to Sydney at the end of World War II. Led own band in Sydney and worked in bands led by Leo White and Eric Tann. As Ernest Rittez led own Orquesta Cubana in the late 1940s and 1950s, also worked with Paul Lombard and with Alan Wood in Sydney. Within weeks of becoming the Professional Manager of a music publisher's he suffered a fatal heart attack.

ROBINSON, Damian
piano

Born: c.1928
Died: 1994

Worked with Ted Astley's Band in Manchester (1949-50), then moved to London and worked with Terry Brown (late 1951). With Bernie Stanton, then joined Ivor Kirchin briefly before working with Teddy Foster from May 1952. With Jimmy Walker's Quintet, then went to India with Harry Parry (and Victor Feldman) 1953-4. With Don Rendell for two months (spring 1954) then worked as solo pianist at the Spanish Gardens, London, before rejoining Don Rendell. With Tony Crombie from spring 1955, with Harry Roy (1956-9), also worked with Dave Shepherd and with Harry Hayes before joining Ray Ellington from spring 1959 until June 1961. Freelanced in London, then again worked with Ray Ellington (1965). Also toured Japan with Stanley Black (1965). Again worked with Ray Ellington and did prolific freelance work during the 1970s and 1980s.

ROBINSON, 'Dougie' Douglas
alto sax/clarinet/flute

Born: Birmingham, Warwickshire, 24 October 1921

At fourteen toured with Teddy Joyce's Juveniles, returned to Birmingham and gigged with various bands including one led by Frank Honeymoon. Served briefly in the RAF, then joined Don Marino Barretto in London. Worked with Ambrose and with Tito Burns during summer of 1942, then spent six months with Johnny Claes. Deputized for Nat Temple in Geraldo's Orchestra in late 1942, then joined Geraldo regularly from early 1943 through to summer of 1955. Worked with

Ronnie Scott's Big Band, then freelanced extensively on sessions before working with Jack Parnell through the 1960s and early 1970s. Thereafter enjoyed widespread success as a freelance through to the 1990s, but now spends part of each year in Portugal. Was married to the late singer-actress Jill Day.

ROBINSON, Orphy Everton
Born: Stoke Newington, London, 13 October 1960
vibes/marimba/composer/sax/guitar

Played alto sax as a teenager and was part of the Hackney and Islington Youth Band, studied law for a while at Stoke Newington College, played tuned percussion. On trumpet briefly, then specialized on vibes and marimba. Led own quartet and played with Savannah. Was part of Jazz Warriors from 1986, later worked often in Courtney Pine's groups (including 1987 USA tour), also in Steve Williamson's Band and with Andy Sheppard's Quartet and Big Band. Own Annavas (co-led with keyboard-player Joe Bashorun) made debut at London's Camden Festival in 1990 and subsequently played international festivals (Berlin, North Sea, etc.). Worked with classical Balinescu Quartet and with Shiva Nova Indian Music Ensemble. Toured Morocco for British Council in 1993, and played there with Mustafa Bakbe. Led new group which played at Montreal, Canada, Festival (July 1993), and at Montreux and Israel's Red Sea Festival. Composed for television and wrote for (and played with) the Leeds-based Phoenix Dance Company. Toured with American saxophonist David Murray in May 1994. Own Vibes Summit premiered his *World Percussion Suite Number One* in 1995. Again guested with Shiva Nova (1995), worked with American saxophonist Pee Wee Ellis (1996) and continued to lead own successful group.

ROBINSON, 'Stan' Stanley
Born: Salford, Manchester, 13 April 1936
tenor sax/soprano sax/clarinet/flute

Took up tenor sax at sixteen, did local gigs and played in house band at Manchester's Club 43, accompanying various visiting musicians. Soon after moving to London in 1959 left to work in Bombay, India, for six months with vibes-player Margaret Mason. Returned to London and joined newly formed Allan Ganley-Keith Christie Jazz Makers (summer 1960). Did brief season in Germany (Cologne and Munich) with Bert Courtley (summer 1961), then briefly rejoined Jazzmakers. With Phil Seamen Quintet (1962), Tubby Hayes' Big Band, John Burch's Octet, also worked with Long John Baldry, with Jimmy Nichol and the Shubdubs, toured with the Animals and played London residency with Don Lang. With Sandy Brown, Humphrey Lyttelton and the BBC Radio Orchestra. With Don Rendell from late 1969 to 1970, then two years with Maynard Ferguson (including tour of USA). Regularly with Ronnie Ross Sextet in the 1970s, also worked at National Theatre with Laurie Morgan, and leading own quartet (occasionally quintet). Toured with King Curtis and Aretha Franklin, worked and recorded with Francy Boland Big Band. Accompanied various visiting musicians including Dizzy Gillespie. Again led own quartet in the 1980s, also worked in Ian Henry's Quartet, with Don Rendell, with Martin Drew, etc, and made two tours of USA With Charlie Watts' Orchestra. Toured Norway with singer Magni Wentzel, then led own quartet based in London, also playing wide range of freelance work through the 1990s.

ROBSON, 'Phil' Philip James
guitar/composer

Born: Grantham, Lincolnshire, 28 February 1970

Grew up in Derby. First gigs were with his father (clarinettist Trevor Robson) in Sonus Four (1985). Later played professionally in house band at Brown's Club in Derby. Moved to London attended Guildhall School of Music, studied with Simon Purcell. First gigs in London were with David 'Dill' Katz at the 606 Club, later worked with Big John Patton, Charles Earland, Julian Argüelles, Martin Speake, Christine Tobin, Andrea Vicari, Jean Toussaint, Stan Sulzmann, Simon Purcell and the National Youth Jazz Orchestra. The music he composed for *At the Rose Garden* and *Titus Andronicus* was performed at the Edinburgh Festival. Co-leading quartet with saxophonist Julian Siegel through the 1990s, and freelancing in various line-ups. Temporarily out of action through injuries in late 1995, then resumed working and touring in quartet with Julian Siegel (1996), also worked in Andrea Vicari Jazz Quintet (1996) and with Christine Tobin (1996).

ROCHE, 'Harry' Harold T.
trombone

Born: Cork City, Ireland, 18 February 1918
Died: Cheam, Surrey, 4 November 1987

Served for five years as a musician in the Royal Artillery Band before joining Henry Hall in spring of 1939. With Henry Hall (1940), then worked in Miff Ferrie's Band (1941), before joining the RAF. Played in RAF Fighter Command Band from 1942, also part of Vic Lewis-Jack Parnell Jazzmen (1945). After demobilization worked with Ted Heath (1945), also with Billy Munn in autumn 1945. Left Ted Heath in September 1948, rejoined Billy Munn briefly in autumn 1948. With Ambrose (late 1948–9), guested with the Skyrockets when they accompanied Benny Goodman at the London Palladium (July 1949). With Eric Winstone, then again worked with the Skyrockets before joining Jack Parnell in spring 1951. Part of newly formed BBC Show Band (led by Cyril Stapleton) from October 1952. With Geraldo from late 1953, thereafter concentrated on freelance session work, also led own ten trombone unit, the Harry Roche Constellation.

RODERICK, Stan
trumpet

Born: Barrow-in-Furness, Cumbria, 6 April 1919
Died: Kent, 26 March 1994

Two of his brothers played in brass band, he was the uncle of trumpeter Leslie Wilson. Worked with bassist Reggie Beard in Aberdeen, then moved to London to join Bram Martin (1935). With Jack Harris at Café de Paris (January 1936), with Joe Appleton's Band at Shim-Sham Club (autumn 1937), then worked with Jack Harris at Ciro's (1938–9), also did radio work with Ben Frankel (1939). With Jack Hylton (March to August 1939), briefly with Ambrose (October 1939), then joined Army and served at Dunkirk (1940). Invalided out of the Army, worked with Harry Roy, Teddy Joyce, then joined Billy Ternent's BBC Orchestra (1941). Briefly with Geraldo, then again with Billy Ternent (1943). With Harry Parry from November 1943 until July 1944. Spent summer of 1944 in Scotland, worked with Jack Watmore's Band in Dundee (late 1944–5) before rejoining Harry Roy (in Edinburgh) during spring 1945. With Harry Hayes (1945), Ted Heath (1945–6), regularly with Ted Heath from 1947 until joining the Skyrockets in summer of 1951. With Skyrockets until September 1952, during the early 1950s also worked with Woolf Phillips, Maurice Winnick, Ambrose, Wally Rockett, etc. With Cyril Stapleton's BBC Show Band from October 1952 until July 1957, during this period also worked with Steve Race, Jack Nathan,

Tommy Watt, etc. With Burt Rhodes' Orchestra (1958), Colin Beaton's Orchestra (1959). Mainly worked as a freelance from 1960 onwards, played in London Pigalle Orchestra and accompanied Peggy Lee, Dizzy Gillespie, Frank Sinatra, Nat Cole, Lena Horne, etc., as well as playing innumerable sessions for Robert Farnon, Johnny Spence, etc.

ROGERS, 'Johnny' John Harry O'Dell
alto sax/clarinet

Born: Southgate, London, 14 August 1926

Began playing clarinet as a teenager, then took sax lessons from Les Evans. Did local gigs with guitarist Johnny Wiltshire, pianist Denny Termer, and drummer Laurie Morgan, then worked with Gerry Hoey, Billy Kaye, Nat Gonella, Sid Millward and Carole Fenton during early stages of his professional career. With drummer Arthur Amey's Quartet at the Fullado Club in New Compton Street, London (1946). In Brighton with Johnny Kerrison (1947), with trumpeter Eric Siddons (1947), Harry Java's Band (1948), then became founder-member of the Club Eleven (December 1948). Suffered serious illness in 1949, but resumed playing and co-led Jazz Incorporated (with Lennie Metcalfe) during the early 1950s and worked in Freddy Randall's Big Band in Glasgow (1953). Occasionally with Joe Loss (1954), then did summer season with Freddie Courtenay's Band in Yarmouth (1954), again with Joe Loss (1955). Settled in Redcar, Yorkshire and worked in band led by his father-in-law Danny Mitchell. (Johnny's wife Irene was a professional sax player.) Worked for several years with Danny Mitchell, led own band, worked in the Teesside area with Bob Peacock's Quartet and gigged with alto saxophonist Ronnie Asprey. Freelanced until 1973, then ceased playing in order to run own farm near Whitby, Yorkshire.

ROGERS, Paul
double bass/composer

Born: Chester, Cheshire, 27 April 1956

Moved to London in 1974. Worked with John Etheridge, Howard Riley, John Stevens, Keith Tippett, Elton Dean, Stan Tracey, Kenny Wheeler, etc., and led own sextet. Did widespread international touring: with Harold Beckett's Trio to the Middle East (1984), with Evan Parker to Europe (1985), with Red House to South America (1986), etc. Lived and worked in the USA from 1986 to 1988, then returned to Europe, but toured the USA with the Dennis Gonzales Band in 1990. Based in France during the 1990s but works regularly in Mujician (with Paul Dunmall, Tony Levin and Keith Tippett) and freelances with Derek Bailey, Lol Coxhill, John Zorn, Alex von Schlippenbach, as well as playing in duo with Paul Dunmall.

ROLLINS, Dennis
trombone

Born: Birmingham, Warwickshire, 11 November 1964

Brother of trombonist Winston Rollins (born in Wednesbury, 12 February 1966). Left Birmingham at the age of three and spent childhood in Doncaster. Played recorder and guitar at school, then took up trombone at fourteen. Played in Doncaster Youth Jazz Association (coached by John Ellis MBE). Did local gigs and worked in Michael Mackinder's Big Band, also played on *QE2* liner in the Mike James Sound. Played in the National Youth Jazz Orchestra. Moved to London in 1987. Regularly with NYJO in the late 1980s, also with Robin Jones and with various line-ups before becoming part of the Jazz Warriors (1990). Played in various 'pop' ensembles including three years with Brand New Heavies. With Ivory and Steel on Monty Alexander's 1992 tour. During the 1990s worked with Steve Williamson's Band, with Courtney Pine, with Julian Joseph, as well as leading own successful band Dee Roe.

ROOT, Alan
piano

Born: Croydon, Surrey, 20 March 1929
Died: Caterham, Surrey, 27 April 1993

Worked with Graham Stewart's Band in the early 1950s, left in August 1953. Briefly with Alex Welsh (summer 1954). In George Hopkinson's Band (1955), Jack Hutton's Band (1956), Stan Bellwood's Band (1956), then again worked with Graham Stewart (1957–8). During the early 1960s began long musical association with Brian White's Magna Jazz Band, and was later part of the Muggsy Remembered Band (co-led by Brian White and Alan Gresty). Over a period of some years co-led the Alan Godfrey Quartet (with Godfrey 'Goff' Dubber). Freelanced with many bands, including Mick Mulligan's and worked often with guitarist Jim Forey and drummer Dave Gadd. Continued to work with Brian White until cancer precluded regular schedule; was also part of Gentle Jazz (with John R.T. Davies) during his latter years.

ROSE, Denis David
piano/trumpet/tenor horn/arranger

Born: Clerkenwell, London, 31 May 1922
Died: London, 22 November 1984

Self-taught musician. Began on piano, then took up trumpet. Played club and pub gigs and worked briefly in Happy Blake's Band. Led own band at Jamboree and at Panama Club, London, before being called up for Army service in June 1943. Deserted from Royal Army Medical Corps a year later and after a period of non-musical activity in London worked in Johnny Claes' Band from about September 1944 to March 1945. Led own band briefly at the Gliderdrome in Boston, Lincolnshire (December 1945). Worked briefly in Johnny Brown's Band at the Astoria Ballroom, London, then spent several months playing tenor horn in Johnny Swinfen's Band at Hammersmith Palais (December 1946 to May 1947), during this period also played tenor horn on BBC Jazz Club broadcasts. Briefly with Jack Amlot's Band in London, then worked with Tito Burns' Big Band for summer season 1947, subsequently played piano and trumpet in Tito Burns' Sextet (occasionally deputizing on drums). Left Tito Burns in April 1948 (also worked briefly in Sidney Gross's Swing Shop Package in early 1948). Led own sextet in London, then worked in Cab Kaye's Ministers of Swing (October to November 1948). Became founder-member (and mentor) at Club Eleven from late 1948 until 1950 (also played in Leon Roy's Orchestra in late 1949). Arrested at Club Eleven in April 1950 and charged with Army desertion. Briefly with Sid Millward's Big Band in Glasgow (November 1950), then returned to London to freelance. Led own band (1951), again with Cab Kaye (September 1952 to March 1953). USO tour of Germany with Bernie Stanton's Band (1953), then again with Cab Kaye. Worked as solo pianist and in trios, but occasionally played trumpet with various bands including Norman Burns (early 1955) and Sid Wright (late 1958), then again worked mainly on piano in clubs and in North London pubs. Accompanied singer Maggie Nichols, and played residency at the Maestro Club, London, in the early 1970s, later worked as solo pianist again, mainly in the Archway area of London.

ROSE, Pat (Robert Henry PATERSON)
clarinet/tenor sax/baritone and bass saxes

Born: East London, July 1916

Mother a dancer, father a stage manager. Was given clarinet lessons at Military School, then enlisted as a musician in the Irish Guards at the age of fifteen. Served for four years (including playing at Canadian Exposition), then bought himself out and became a professional musician. Adopted the surname of his step-father, Frank Rose. With George Newmarch's Band in London and Margate and worked in Mendoza's fifteen-piece El Cabaros. Rejoined Army in World War II, served in the Rifle Brigade and played in the Depot Band (service engagements in France, Belgium, Holland, Germany and Denmark in immediate post-war period). After demobilization worked with Tommy Rogan and Eric Siddons before joining Miff Ferrie (early 1948). Gigged with Freddy Randall, again with Miff Ferrie, then worked in Glasgow with Jack Simpson (June to July 1949). Regularly with Freddy Randall from summer 1949 until June 1950. With Nat Allen (1950), Stan Foster (1951), Phil Tate (1951) and again with Nat Allen (1951). Own quartet (1952), with Phil Tate again (1953), and own band in Sunderland (May 1953 to October 1954). With Harry Gold and Laurie Gold from October 1954 until emigrating to Australia in 1957. Played in Sydney area with Merv Atchinson, and in duo with pianist Keith Holt, then freelanced before working regularly (including touring) with banjoist-guitarist Ray Price's Quartet and Band for almost six years during the 1960s. Played for *Funny Girl* show and toured with *Fiddler on the Roof*, played for stage shows in Sydney, then led own band and freelanced until retiring.

ROSEBERY, Arthur
piano

Born: Fulham, London, December 1904
Died: Ealing, London, 26 September 1986

Father wrote and produced stage shows. Began playing piano at eight. Led band at a Chiswick college, at sixteen, became a music copyist and arranger, then worked for two years as a song plugger. Started band co-led with Laurie Johnson and Billy Cotton, played residency at Ealing and at Wembley Exhibition (1924). Joined the Buffalo Band in London in 1925, then formed own band which played for a year at Majestic Dance Hall in Leeds, and later in Brighton. Returned to London in 1927, after period of inactivity formed new band which played various London residencies including Café de Paris and the Kit-Cat Club. His band made many recordings for Parlophone in the years 1928–30. Led at the Savoy Theatre and Romano's (1930). Led own band in Iceland for two years (1934–5), returned to London, led octet at Chez Henri, and did Radio Luxemburg shows. Led at Paradise Club from 1937 until 1939, doubling at Dolphin Square. Led show band *Paradise on Parade* for troop concerts during World War II. Played for many years at American bases in Germany (using the name Al Shine) and again led various bands, then moved back to London and played long solo residency at Flanagan's Restaurant from 1968.

ROSS, Annie (Annabelle SHORT)
vocals/composer/lyricist

Born: Mitcham, Surrey, 25 July 1930

From a large and successful show-business family, whose members include singer Ella Logan, comedian Jimmy Logan, singer Buddy Logan and actor Dominic Allen. Annie's mother, a vaudevillian from Glasgow, was on tour in Surrey when Annie was born. To Los Angeles at the age of four (with aunt, Ella Logan). As a child appeared in films *Our Gang* and *Presenting Lily*

Mars, and won song-writing contest. Moved back to Britain in 1947 and joined Reg Arnold's Band at the Orchid Room Club (autumn 1947). Appeared in West End musical *Burlesque* in 1948. Did double act with song-writer Hugh Martin, then worked as a single in Paris. Returned to USA in 1950 and subsequently achieved great success by writing lyrics to jazz solos, notably Wardell Gray's 'Twisted' (1952). Moved back to Europe and worked at the Mars Club, Paris (early 1953), then toured Europe with Lionel Hampton's Band (1953). At various times worked in France with Jacques Dieval, Emile Stern, Bernard Hilda, etc. Club dates in London (early 1954), then worked with Jack Parnell before joining Tony Crombie in summer 1954. Worked at Florida Club, London (1955), then appeared in *Cranks* show, which transferred to USA in late 1956. Again worked in France (1958), then became part of celebrated vocal trio, Lambert, Hendricks and Ross (with Dave Lambert and Jon Hendricks) from 1958–62. Did widespread international touring. Left this trio in spring 1962 (replaced by Yolande Bevan). Featured in West End review *Three at Nine* (1963) then figureheaded the London club Annie's Room in 1964 and 1965. Sang at international festivals and played club residencies in USA and Britain, also toured with Jon Hendricks in 1970. Gradually became more involved in acting and singing on television and films, and in various theatrical productions including *The Threepenny Opera, The Seven Deadly Sins*, her own one-woman shows, etc. During the 1990s combined singing in cabaret, with acting. Played residencies in London, 1995–96 (at Pizza on the Park, etc.) and throughout the 1990s appeared in films including *Short Cuts* and *The Player*. Widow of actor Sean Lynch.

ROSS, 'Matt' Matthew
piano/organ

Born: South Shields, Co. Durham, 21 December 1924

Moved to London in 1937, later studied at the Royal Normal College for the Blind (then situated in Shropshire). First professional work was playing the cinema organ at the Regal, Uxbridge for three years. Played Novachord in guitarist Wally Chapman's Band at the Dorchester Hotel. Seriously ill from late 1947 until 1950, then played and arranged for Toni Anton's Progressive Orchestra during the early 1950s. Worked in Bobby Mickleburgh's Band throughout the mid-1950s, then joined Freddy Randall (summer 1956). Gigs with Paul Simpson's Band (1957), then worked mainly as a solo pianist, including playing for over seven years at the Studio Club, London. During the 1960s worked regularly with Ken Holman at the Hopbine, Wembley, also did long residencies on Hammond organ at various clubs and restaurants through the 1970s and 1980s. Solo work in the 1990s included playing at Kettner's, at Pizza on the Park, etc.

ROSS, 'Ronnie' Albert Ronald
baritone sax/saxes/flute/clarinet

Born: Calcutta, India, 2 October 1933
Died: London, 12 December 1991

Both parents were Scottish. Returned to London in 1946. Worked as an architectural assistant, took up alto sax. Played gigs (on tenor sax) with Fred Hedley's Band in London (1953), then joined Grenadier Guards and played in military band. Joined Don Rendell on tenor sax (early 1954), but soon began specializing on baritone sax. With Tony Crombie (from spring 1955), with Tony Kinsey (from August 1955 until early 1957). Again with Don Rendell (1957), also worked with big bands led by Tommy Watt, Ted Heath, Johnny Keating, etc. To USA to be featured with the International Youth Band at Newport Jazz Festival (July 1958), returned to England and together with Allan Ganley formed the Jazzmakers (autumn 1958). Played in USA with Ronnie Scott and Jimmy Deuchar (1959), toured Britain with Woody Herman's Anglo-American Herd (1959). Worked in Europe with the Modern Jazz Quartet (1959). After the Jazzmakers disbanded in spring 1960, toured USA with Vic Lewis, then returned to London and formed Jazztet (co-led with Bert Courtley) from May 1960 until March 1961. Led own quartet (featuring Bill Le Sage) during the early 1960s, also led own quintet and tentette. Worked with John Dankworth and in the Kenny Clarke-Francy Boland Big Band, briefly in Alex Welsh Big Band (1963). Worked with Ronnie Scott and Jimmy Deuchar at the Half Note Club, New York, (June 1963). Toured with Maynard Ferguson in the 1960s and worked in Stan Tracey's Big Band as well as playing on innumerable sessions. Recorded with Friedrich Gulda in 1966. Continued to lead own quartet, own sextet and own '8 to 1' during the 1970s and 1980s, and in quintet co-led with Ray Wordsworth. Worked in Stan Tracey's Big Band and with Bob Leaper and (as part of John Altman's Band) accompanied singer Alison Moyet. Took part in John Dankworth Reunion Band. Though stricken with cancer, he continued to freelance successfully through the late 1980s.

ROULLIER, 'Ron' Ronald George
Born: Stoke Newington, London, 9 November 1927
piano/composer/arranger

Piano from age of thirteen. Short career as apprentice research chemist after high school. First professional work with Hughie Waite in Cambridge (1947–8), then played summer season in Jersey with Frank Pritchard's Band (1948). Ill in hospital for nine months until May 1949, then worked with Leon Roy, Victor Feldman and Harry Klein (1949). Again with Leon Roy and with Nat Gonella before working with Ivor Kirchin at the Royal Ballroom, Tottenham (August to November 1950). With Laurie Morgan (early 1951), then joined Teddy Foster from January 1951 to April 1952. Regular freelance arranging, briefly in John Dankworth Seven (while Bill Le Sage was absent in spring 1952). With Jimmy Walker (July 1952). Staff arranger for Ambrose (1953), also worked for Roy Fox (summer 1953), with Nat Temple, Kenny Graham, Basil Kirchin. With Joe Nussbaum's Theatre Orchestra (November 1953 to October 1954). With Eric Lawe at Wimbledon Palais (October 1954 to April 1955). With Jack Parnell as staff arranger from August 1955 until March 1957. Also arranged for Tommy Watt, Matt Monro, the BBC Show Band, etc. With Ted Heath as staff arranger from 1957 until 1959, then emigrated to the USA in October 1959. Composed music for jingles and television, also directed the New York Repertory Orchestra for many years. Widespread success as a orchestrator: for Radio City Music Hall, Boston Pops Orchestra, NBC Tonight Show, and for Broadway shows, for example *Pal Joey*, *Marilyn*, *Lena Horne—The Lady and her Music*. Played piano for Dick Haymes, Brook Benton, Cleo Laine, Frank Sinatra Jr, etc. Toured Germany with singer Paul Wayne in 1968, became US citizen that year. Has worked mainly out of New York since 1959, but in 1973 spent a year in Los Angeles. Ran arranging business with pianist Johnny Weed. Continues to enjoy success as composer and arranger with Mohamed Khashoggi (1995).

ROY, Harry
Clarinet/saxes/vocals/composer
Born: Stamford Hill, London, 12 January 1900
Died: London, 1 February 1971

Younger brother of pianist Sid Roy. Played piano, violin and banjoline before studying clarinet and soprano sax. Worked with Sid's band the Darnswells in 1920, then became part of Sid Roy's

Lyricals, playing residencies in London and Paris during the early 1920s. Harry also briefly led own band at Moody's Club in London. After a 1928 tour of British variety halls Sid Roy's Lyricals played a season in South Africa, then worked in Australia (including Tasmania) in 1929. The band worked briefly in Germany in 1930, thereafter Harry Roy became the leader of the New Lyricals for residency at the Bat Club, London, in 1930. Led larger band, the RKO-leans (which featured the piano duo of Ivor Moreton and Dave Kaye) at the Leicester Square Theatre, London (1930). Subsequently led own band at the London Pavilion and in variety before playing long residency at the Café Anglais, London, until summer 1933. Harry's band played a long booking at the May Fair Hotel, London, and also worked at the London Palladium (and in variety halls) before touring South America (from April until August 1938). He featured a band-within-a-band, the Ragamuffins. Continued to lead own band throughout World War II, often undertaking tours for ENSA. He formed a new band in spring 1946, then disbanded while he visited the USA (September to December 1948). Returned to London and resumed residency at the Café Anglais (1949). Residency at the Lyceum Ballroom, London (1950). Mainly led small groups during the 1950s and 1960s, playing residencies at various London clubs including the Empress, Gargoyle, Femina and Café de Paris, led bigger line-ups for ballroom tours and specific bookings. Briefly ran own drinking club in Bond Street in 1966. Provided music for Robertson Hare play *Oh Clarence* (1968–9), then led own Dixieland Band at Sherry's in Brighton during summer of 1969. A booklet, *Harry Roy* by Keith Fairbridge, was published in 1991.

ROY, Leon (Leon Roy WALLIS)
drums

Born: London, c.1927
Died: 1993

Brother of actress Shani Wallis. At fifteen joined a touring show, later worked in circus band then joined the RAF. Led own band in the service. After demobilization worked in family food-supply business and led own quintet at the Enfield Rhythm Club (1948). Led band (with Lennie Metcalfe on piano) at Bebop Shop in Tottenham, London, then formed own big band in late 1949 which played various London venues including the Paramount Dance Hall in Tottenham Court Road. Disbanded in summer of 1950. Worked briefly with Edmundo Ros, then co-led quintet (with Roland De Casse) on liner *Queen Mary* (1951). With Ralph Sharon (early 1952), then worked for seven months with Carl Barriteau (until September 1952). Played in house band at American Club, London. Lived in Canada (1953), then moved into the USA in 1954. Returned to Britain late in 1954, but paid frequent visits to the USA. Gigged in East Anglia during the mid-1960s then settled in the USA.

RUBIN, 'Ron' Ronald
piano/double bass

Born: Liverpool, Lancashire, 8 July 1933

Brother John plays vibes, piano and valve-trombone. Began on violin, then played piano. Army service in Germany, played in Rhine River Jazz Band. After demobilization took up double bass. Played in and around Liverpool with Ralph 'Bags' Watmough Band, and with Les Harris Six, Wall City Jazzmen and Darryl Dugdale's Trio. Moved to London in 1961, played piano with Glyn Morgan Band, Dick Williams Band, Brian Leake, Fairweather-Brown All Stars (1962–4), on bass intermittently with Mike Taylor small groups during period 1962–8. On bass with Tony Milliner-

Alan Littlejohns Band (1964), with Ronnie Selby Trio (1965), New Departures (1966–7). On bass and on piano with Bruce Turner (accompanying visiting Americans Bill Coleman, Henry Allen, Ray Nance) and with Fat John Cox. With Lennie Felix Trio, including Mediterranean Cruise (1966), also played on world cruise in 1966. With Lennie Best Quartet on bass during the late 1960s, and again in 1970s. Sandy Brown-Kenny Wheeler Band (1967). Toured on bass with Billy Eckstine (1967). During the late 1960s with Milliner-Littlejohns on piano, and with Howard Riley, Michael Garrick and Manfred Mann on bass. With Lionel Grigson-Pete Burden Band (1969), briefly with Humphrey Lyttelton (accompanying Buck Clayton in Germany) 1969, and with Barbara Thompson-Art Themen Band (1969). Played solo piano in Palma, Majorca, from 1969–72. Bass with Colin Purbrook Trio (1972–3), piano or bass with John Picard Band (1973–6), duo bass gigs with Ron Mathewson (1975), own band (1975–6), solo piano work in Malta and cruise with Nina Barry Trio (on bass). During the late 1970s with Keith Ingham Trio, Fred Hunt Trio and solo piano work in Oslo and London. On bass with Alex Welsh 1979–81. In Vienna with Fatty George's Band, in Zurich with Geoff Simkins (1981), in Zurich with Keith Smith (1982), and again in Zurich with Oscar Klein (1982), solo piano work in Germany. Duo work with Earl Okin (1983), toured with Wild Bill Davison (1983). With George Howden Band during the 1980s and touring in Donald Swann-Digby Fairweather shows *Swann in Jazz*, solo work in Europe, and duo work with Brian Leake. On bass with George Melly-John Chilton (1987–8), with Bruce Turner Quartet (1989), solo piano work. With Campbell Burnap at Edinburgh Festival (1990), then piano with George Melly-John Chilton (1990–3), with Phil Franklin in Switzerland (1993–4). Continues to freelance on piano during the 1990s.

RUNSWICK, Daryl
Born: Leicester, 12 October 1946
composer/arranger/double bass/bass guitar/piano

Piano from five, cello from ten, double bass at twelve. Played double bass in local trad band at thirteen. Did three year course in music at Cambridge, gained BA. Was secretary of Cambridge Jazz Club and led trio backing visiting musicians. To Edinburgh as musical director and pianist for university revue, then moved to London. Worked in John Curtis-Ian Bird Quintet (1968–9), also with Reg Powell's Trio at Pickwick Club, London. With Bobby Wellins, the London Jazz Four, Barbara Thompson, Lionel Grigson-Pete Burden Quintet (1969), also worked on bass guitar from 1969. From 1970 worked with John Dankworth and Cleo Laine. (Cleo recorded fifteen of Runswick's songs.) During this period also worked with Ray Russell, Coe Wheeler and Co, Tubby Hayes, Ian Hamer's Sextet and led own quartet. Played bass guitar with Count Basie and Frank Sinatra for London Festival Hall concert (1970). Worked with John Dankworth and Cleo Laine on double bass and bass guitar until 1981, and on keyboards from 1981 until 1983, then became increasingly involved in composing and arranging and gave up playing double bass in 1984. He is the author of *Rock, Pop and Jazz Arranging*.

RUSSELL, 'Rags' 'Tony' Keith Antony
Born: London, 24 May 1929
trombone/baritone horn/piano/vocals/arranger/composer
Died: July 1970

First band was the London-based Washington and Lee Swing (1944), then joined Ken Wallbank's Dixielanders which formed the basis of a band that Tony co-led with trumpeter Alan Wickham: the

Russell-Wickham Hot Six (1946). Briefly with George Webb. Worked with Vic Lewis (1949–50), then did summer season with Paul Fenoulhet in the Isle of Man (1950). With Harry Margolis in London (1951), with Ralph Sharon (September 1951 to April 1952), again with Vic Lewis (April to June 1952). With Cyril Stapleton, then briefly with Bill Collins (October 1952), before joining Oscar Rabin at the Lyceum Ballroom, London, from October 1952 until October 1954. With Jack Parnell from October 1954 until September 1955, then joined Tony Crombie. With Courtley-Seymour Band (1956). Led own band, then worked regularly with John Dankworth from 1956 to 1962, thereafter freelanced successfully as composer and arranger, writing for stage (*Match Girls*, etc.), television and radio, also directed London Jazz Orchestra in the 1960s.

RUSSELL, 'Ray' Raymond　　　　　　　　　　Born: Islington, London, 4 April 1947
guitar/composer/arranger

Guitar from the age of twelve. Played various gigs before working regularly with Georgie Fame and the Blue Flames. With Graham Bond's Organization in the late 1960s, then formed own group. Mainly active as leader of own quartet, quintet and sextet (and as composer and arranger) through the 1970s and 1980s, but also worked and recorded with Harold Beckett, Bob Downes and Mike Gibbs (including touring). Was briefly part of Rock Workshop in the early 1970s, worked with the Four Tops, Butterfield Blues Band, recorded with Tina Turner, Phil Collins, etc. Worked and recorded with Gil Evans in Europe during the 1980s, including appearances at Montreux Jazz Festival. Freelanced on many recording sessions, often as musical director. Achieved success as a composer for television series, beginning with BBC series *Bergerac*, later commissions included *Survival, September Song, The Alleyn Files, Bit of a Do*, etc. During the 1990s wrote for various films including *Dangerous Lady*. Continues to record jazz solo albums, and to record in company with Simon Phillips and Anthony Jackson.

RUTHERFORD, Paul William　　　　　　　Born: Greenwich, London, 29 February 1940
trombone/euphonium

Started on alto sax at fourteen, trombone at sixteen. Gigged with traditional bands. Worked in city (1957–8) prior to spending five years in the RAF as musician. Studied at Royal Air Force School of Music, service in Germany with John Stevens and Trevor Watts. Left RAF in 1963. Studied at Guildhall School of Music from 1964–8. Became a founder-member of Spontaneous Music Ensemble (with Stevens and Watts). Was in Neil Ardley's New Jazz Orchestra briefly, often with Mike Westbrook's line-ups from 1967, also in Tony Oxley's Quintet. Formed Iskra 1903 in 1970 (with Derek Bailey and Barry Guy), also in Harry Miller's Isipingo (1971). During the 1970s worked in Globe Unity Orchestra, in the London Jazz Composers' Orchestra, in duos with Evan Parker, with Mike Westbrook, Peter Kowald, Alan Cohen, John Stevens, Trevor Watts, Tony Oxley. From 1973 onwards often worked as an unaccompanied trombonist. Re-formed Iskra 1903 in 1980, which developed into Oskrastra in the later 1980s and 1990s. In 1985 played in USA as part of International Trombone Workshop. Worked in Charlie Watts' Big Band (1985–6). Continued long association with Spontaneous Music Ensemble, with Spirits Rejoice, and in Kenny Wheeler's Big Band, etc.

S

SABERTON, Peter
piano/composer/arranger

Born: Sheffield, Yorkshire, 9 July 1950

Self-taught pianist, and alto sax player, doubled on these for first professional work in Manchester Stage Band, Nexus. Played in National Youth Jazz Orchestra, subsequently worked with Don Rendell, John Williams, in John Taylor's Foil, with Harold Beckett and in Tim Whitehead's group. Continues to work with various jazz ensembles, notably Pete Hurt's Quartet, Eddie Parker's group, Pete Fairclough's group, Tim Wells' Quartet and composing and arranging for the London Jazz Orchestra.

SAINTS JAZZ BAND

Alan Radcliffe (clarinet, born 1929), Michael McNamara (trumpet, born 1929, died 1996) and John Edward Fish (piano, born 1927), all from Ashton-under-Lyne, played together in the Storyville Jazz Band before becoming founder-members of the Saints in 1949. The band originally worked around the Ashton-under-Lyne and Manchester areas (playing residencies at the Thatched House and at the Grosvenor Hotel). They also enjoyed considerable success on their visits to other cities, playing a celebrated Royal Festival Hall, London, concert in 1951. They also worked in Switzerland. Ron 'Slim' Simpson, the band's early trombonist, was replaced by trombonist-vocalist Fred Fydler in 1952. The band's long-serving drummer John Mills died in 1960, his place was first taken by Merton Kaufmann, then by Denis Grundy (from 1963 until 1980), thereafter the drummer was Mike Carnie. The band's original banjoist, Jim Lolley, was replaced by Jim Ashe who played banjo and guitar with the band through the 1960s and 1970s. Michael McNamara left and was replaced first by Bob Connell then by Barry Dixon. Desmond 'Dizzy' Burton took over on trumpet from 1962 until 1975. Rod Hopton joined in 1962 replacing Fred Fydler on trombone, and Reg Kenworthy on double bass took the place of the long-serving Tom Gregory. By 1970 only two original members, Alan Radcliffe and Ed 'John' Fish remained. In 1974 Radcliffe left and was replaced first by Randolph Colville, then by Joe Silmon. Trumpeters in the 1970s included Denis Gilmore and Doug Whaley. The band's personnel fluctuated during its latter stages and it played its last engagements in 1982.

SALISBURY, 'Gerry' Gerald William Anthony
cornet/double bass/valve trombone/vibes

Born: London, 7 August 1929

Father, William 'Jock' Salisbury, played trumpet, drums, piano and vibes. Worked as a page-boy at the London Palladium after leaving school. Army service in Middle East, took up trumpet. After demobilization gigged with Johnny Parker, Paul Simpson, Jim Bray and Bob Dawbarn, then joined Mike Collier's Chicago Rhythm Kings (1952). With Charlie Galbraith (1953), Norman Cave (1954), Bobby Mickleburgh (1954–5) and worked briefly in Europe with Joe Daniels (1955). Began playing double bass but continued to double on trumpet. Played bass with pianist Mickey

Bryant's Band for six months at USAF bases in France (1956), returned to England and played for three weeks in Teddy Foster's Band. With Freddy Randall for a year, then gigged (on valve trombone) with Teddy Layton (late 1958). With Mick Mulligan (playing bass – occasionally on trumpet) from early 1959 to early 1961. Year with Monty Sunshine (1961–2), then on double bass with Johnny Wiltshire and the Trebletones for a year. Throughout the 1960s and early 1970s worked with Alex Welsh, Sandy Brown, Diz Disley, Charlie Galbraith and Dick Sudhalter, etc. Often with John Richardson at the Tally Ho, London, over a five year period. Led own small band in London, then moved to Norfolk in 1972. Joined drummer Dennis Buck's Trio (1972), later led own quintet in Norwich and worked with pianist Arthur Lee. Moved back to London in 1975, worked during day at a recording studio but played many gigs including being part of Stan Greig's Trio, Digby Fairweather's Friends, leading own trio, and working with Tony Lee's Trio. Suffered heart attack in 1979. After recuperation moved back to Norfolk in 1981. Plays regularly during the late 1980s and 1990s, mostly on trumpet, gigging with Jack Parnell in East Anglia, being part of the Vintage Hot Orchestra and working often with clarinettist and alto saxophonist Pete Oxborough.

SALMINS, Ralph
drums

Born: Farnborough, Kent, 4 June 1964

From a musical family. Started on violin at five, piano at seven, drums at twelve. Began playing in rehearsal bands and youth orchestras from age of fourteen, at sixteen joined Ken Mackintosh. From sixteen to eighteen played in Young Jazz and NYJO; studied classical percussion at Guildhall School of Music and Drama from 1982 until 1986, won the Philip Jones Percussion Prize. Played in Guildhall Big Band, and John Etheridge's Quartet, and did classical work with London Symphony Orchestra, Royal Philharmonic Orchestra, etc. With Tim Whitehead, Loose Tubes, Annie Whitehead, Jim Mullen, Pete Saberton, Salena Jones, Bertice Reading (1987–8). Own trio at Bass Clef Club for eighteen months, taught at Wavendon (1988–91), masterclasses at Royal College of Music (1991–2). Extensive freelance work during the 1990s, with Duncan Lamont, Bobby Wellins, Iain Ballamy, Ian Carr, Martin Taylor, Brian Lemon, Bob Wilber, Annie Ross, Herb Ellis, James Moody, Warren Vaché, Oliver Jones, etc., as well as playing for many West End shows and on a number of film soundtracks, television shows, recordings, etc. From the mid-1990s worked with Guy Barker's Quintet, Stan Tracey, Gerard Presencer-Tim Garland Quintet, Dankworth Generation Band, Laurie Johnson's London Big Band, Kenny Baker's Dozen and Brian Dee's Trio.

SAMPSON, Tommy
trumpet/vocals/arranger

Born: Scotland, 1918

Began playing cornet in Salvation Army Band during early childhood. Joined Army in 1939 and played in RAOC Band in Scotland before gaining commission. Taken prisoner by the Italians at Tobruk, remained a prisoner-of-war until 1945. Led prison camp band. Repatriated to Scotland, led Scottish Command Dance Orchestra until being demobilized in June 1946. Formed own big band which made its debut in Leith, Scotland, on 23 January 1947. The band subsequently toured Britain (and Italy and Germany) and played various ballroom residencies until December 1949, when Sampson's ill health caused him to disband. He worked for various London-based music publishers during the early 1950s, as an arranger and song-plugger, he also sang with the George Mitchell Choir and was part of the Sapphires vocal group until spring 1954. From this time onwards he devoted as much time as he could to Salvation Army activities. He moved back to Scotland and later formed his own band which continued to work mainly in the Glasgow area into the 1990s. During the 1940s Sampson's principal arranger was Edwin Holland (1923–92). Tony Middleton's *Bio-discography of Tommy Sampson's Orchestra* was published in 1992.

SARTELL, 'French' William
trumpet

Born: Canada, 9 April 1914
Died: London, January 1974

Travelled to Ireland from Toronto as part of Dean Dolsen's Band (1933). Moved on to London and worked with Howard Jacobs at the Café Anglais. Joined Stanley Barnett (early 1935). Freelanced successfully, then worked mainly with Carroll Gibbons from 1936 until 1939. Toured briefly with Ambrose (autumn 1939), then rejoined Carroll Gibbons in November 1939. Remained with Gibbons for a further ten years, also did freelance broadcasts and recordings during this period. In spring of 1950 took over leadership of Carroll Gibbons' Orchestra. Worked with Teddy Foster in 1953, then long period of playing for West End shows.

SAYE, Joe (Joseph Joel SHULMAN)
piano/piano accordion/vocals

Born: Glasgow, Scotland, 25 February 1923
Deceased

Blind from early childhood. Toured with Roy Fox in the late 1930s, then toured as a featured accordionist in variety shows, also accompanied Kitty Masters on piano. Formed own band, playing club bookings and summer season including residency in Penzance, Cornwall (1948). Toured Germany with Freddy Barratt in early 1949, then formed own trio in spring 1949. Did summer season in Llandudno, Wales (1949), then played residency in Manchester before working in Howard Lucraft's Sextet (on accordion) in spring 1950. Again led own trio in the early 1950s, playing in Britain and Holland. Led own sextet for residency at Ciro's, London, in summer 1953. Emigrated to USA in December 1955 and enjoyed success throughout North America leading own trio and accompanying various singers including Dakota Staton. Moved from New York to Toronto, Canada, in the early 1970s to run own booking agency.

SCHWEITZER, Freddy
saxes/clarinet

Born: Saarland, Germany, 20 May 1907
Died: Edgware, Middlesex, 16 November 1950

Originally a pianist, led own band, then took up reeds. Worked with Louis De Vries, Stanley Barnett, Tommy Marshal and Marek Weber before being discovered by Jack Hylton in Berlin during spring of 1933. Featured with Hylton from 1933 until 1938, thereafter did successful music hall act, occasionally playing dates with various bands including work with Freddy Bretherton's Orchestra (1940). During the 1940s (and up to the week of his death) was part of a popular variety act with Paul King.

SCOTT, 'Johnny' Patrick John O'Hara
flute/saxes/clarinet/harp/vibes/arranger/composer

Born: Bristol, 1 November 1930

Father played sax, clarinet and viola. Began on clarinet. Became an Army musician at fourteen, joined the Royal Artillery Band. Left Army in 1952. Worked in Denmark, then joined Roy Fox in Britain (suffered temporarily from facial paralysis which meant he had to work on vibes). Played vibes with Norman Burns, then, after making full recovery, resumed reed work and joined Nat Allen. Took up flute. During the late 1950s worked with Vic Ash's Sextet, with Kenny Baker, in group co-led with Art Ellefson, and freelanced in many line-ups. Led own group, and was featured with Woody Herman's Anglo-American Herd (1959), but was increasingly occupied with arranging and composing: for Ted Heath, for films and television, etc. During the early 1960s again led own quintet. Worked briefly in Michael Garrick's Quartet, and on various sessions, but from this period onwards through the 1990s, specialized in composing and arranging, living for part of each year in California, USA.

SCOTT, 'Ronnie' Ronald (Ronald SCHATT)
tenor sax/soprano sax

Born: East London, 28 January 1927
Died: London, 23 December 1996

Father, Joseph 'Jock' Scott (1903–58), was a saxophonist and bandleader; Ronnie's uncle was violinist Dave Scott. Tenor sax lessons at fifteen from Jack Lewis and Harry Gold, first gig with Felix Mendelssohn's Band. Played casual dates in London clubs from the age of sixteen (with various leaders including Clarie Wears and Carlo Krahmer). Left Cab Kaye's Band at Orchard Club, London, to join Johnny Claes (October 1944). Left Claes in late summer of 1945, freelanced, then worked briefly with Dennis Rose's Band at Gliderdrome, Boston, Lincolnshire (late 1945). Short stints in Sid Millward's Swing Circus (early 1946) and with Johnny Brown's Band at the Astoria Ballroom, London, also did ENSA work with saxophonist Sid Raymond's Band and Workers' Concerts with pianist Pat Kaye and Jimmy Skidmore. With Ted Heath from February 1946 until February 1947. Month with Jack Jackson's Band, then played in Bobby Kevin's Band aboard liner *Queen Mary*. Briefly with Woolf Phillips, then again worked on *Queen Mary*. With Tito Burns from October 1947 until August 1948. With Ambrose (late 1948), also founder-member of Club Eleven Band from late 1948 until 1950. Briefly with father's band on *SS Caronia* (late 1949), one further trip on *Queen Mary* (January 1950), later that year joined Jack Nathan for a few months, then worked briefly in Vic Lewis's Orchestra. With Jack Parnell from spring 1951 until organizing own band in late 1952. Augmented line-up made its debut in September 1955. Worked with various line-ups including Tony Crombie's Quintet (1956), then took own sextet to USA (1957). Co-led Jazz Couriers (with Tubby Hayes) from April 1957 until August 1959. Opened own club (with partner Pete King) in Gerrard Street, London (October 1959). Organized new Quintet, featuring Jimmy Deuchar (spring 1960-1). Mainly with own quartet (1962-4) but also worked at the Half Note Club, New York, with Jimmy Deuchar, Ronnie Ross and an American rhythm section. Led own bands (of various sizes from 1965 onwards) including big band tours with Scott Walker (1968), Ella Fitzgerald (1969), Jack Jones (1972), Nancy Wilson (1973). Was also featured in the Kenny Clarke-Francy Boland Big Band from 1962 until 1972. Featured as a soloist at many international festivals and in brief season in Portugal with Mike Carr (1970). Opened new club (with partner Pete King) in Frith Street, London, in

December 1965. Ronnie Scott's Club in Birmingham opened in October 1991. Scott continued to lead own small bands through the 1990s, often playing residencies at his London club and doing widespread touring (including many trips to Australia). Underwent extensive dental surgery in 1995 and 1996. *Some of My Best Friends Are Blues* by Ronnie Scott (with Mike Hennessey) was first published in 1979. *Jazz at Ronnie Scott's* by Kitty Grime (with photographs by Valerie Wilmer) first published in 1979. *Jazz Man–The Amazing Story of Ronnie Scott and his Club* by John Fordham, first published in 1995. Ronnie Scott was awarded the OBE in 1981.

SCOTT-WOOD, George
piano/accordion/vibes/vocals/
composer/arranger

Born: Glasgow, Scotland, 17 May 1903
Died: Eastbourne, Sussex, 28 October 1978

Studied piano and violin as a child. Worked as an accordionist from age of fourteen, and gave piano recitals in North America before joining band led by his brother, Chalmers Wood, in Glasgow, then worked in the Omega Collegians (in Glasgow, Manchester, Liverpool, Brighton, London, etc.) until 1928. With Jay Whidden from 1929–31, then joined Jerry Hoey's Band (late 1931). From the early 1930s led own recording bands, including the Six Swingers. Fronted various Parlophone studio groups and eventually (in 1935) was appointed as chief adviser on light music to EMI. Took augmented orchestra to Opera House, Brussels, for brief visit in spring 1933, also worked in Jack Jackson's Band (1933). Mainly occupied with studio work throughout the 1930s, but took Six Swingers on a tour of Scotland in late 1936. Ran London Piano Accordion Band in the late 1930s. Led own big band on radio during the early 1940s, subsequently did broadcasts with a new version of the Six Swingers (1950). Led Piano Accordion Band in the 1950s and led own orchestra into the early 1970s.

SEALEY, Paul
guitar/banjo/bass guitar

Born: Watford, Hertfordshire, 9 March 1943

With Fron-zi-Me Jazzband, Barry Martyn's Camellia Orchestra and Preacher Hood's Jazz Missionaries before working in Germany with Mac Duncan's Band (March 1961). Returned to Britain and joined Bobby Mickleburgh's Confederates, then worked in Germany with Keith Smith (early 1962). Active freelance during the 1960s and 1970s, worked with Doug Richford, Nat Gonella, Mike Daniels, Bill Greenow, etc. Accompanied many visiting American musicians during the 1980s and 1990s, also worked with Eggy Ley, Bob Taylor's Full Frontal Rhythm Kings, Cy Laurie, Alan Elsdon, Humphrey Lyttelton, Trevor Whiting, Ray Wordsworth-Terry Seymour Band, in various Keith Nichols line-ups and led own trio. Joined Chris Barber in summer of 1994.

SEAMEN, 'Phil' Phillip William
drums

Born: Burton-on-Trent, Staffordshire, 28 August 1926
Died: Lambeth, London, 13 October 1972

Drums from age of fourteen, lessons from Tommy Webster. With Len Reynolds (1944), with Nat Gonella (late 1945). Worked with Ken Turner in Derby and for season in Scunthorpe (1947). Did cabaret work, then rejoined Nat Gonella (1948). With Johnny Smith's Band in Derby, left to join Tommy Sampson. With Paul Fenoulhet (early 1950), then joined Joe Loss from April 1950 to April 1951. With Jack Parnell from April 1951 until joining Jimmy Walker Quintet in January

1953. Briefly with Ambrose in spring 1953, then rejoined Jack Parnell in June 1953, left to work with Ronnie Scott from August 1954 until early 1957. Led own group, worked with Dizzy Reece's Quartet (1957) and with Kenny Baker. With Don Rendell from summer 1957 until early 1958, then again with Dizzy Reece (1958). With Jazz Couriers (1959), Downbeat Big Band (1959), and with Tubby Hayes' Quartet (1959–60). With Joe Harriott from late 1960 until March 1962, worked in pit orchestra for *West Side Story* and in Billy Ternent's Theatre Orchestra. With Georgie Fame from 1962, with Alexis Korner's Blues Incorporated from February to August 1963. House musician at Ronnie Scott's Club, accompanied many visiting musicians, also freelance studio work. Regularly with Dick Morrissey's Quartet (1965–6), also in Harry South's Big Band (1965), in Burt Rhodes' Orchestra (1966) and led own trio and quartet (1966). In Tony Lee's Trio (1967–8), also occasionally with Joe Harriott. Led own trio for Royal Oak pub residency from 1969, occasionally led own big band, and guested with Ginger Baker's Air Force. Freelanced in early 1970s, occasional gigs with John Stevens, and tour with Freddie Hubbard, but mainly active with own trio for London pub residencies at the Hope and Anchor in Islington, the Jolly Cockney in Lambeth and the Plough in Stockwell.

SECOND CITY JAZZMEN

A band that enjoyed success throughout the Midlands from its inception in November 1956 through to its final gig in 1972. Its principal organizer was guitarist-banjoist Stan Keely, who remained with the band throughout its existence. Various other members included:

Len Coton, Basil Wainwright (drums)
Alan Hewitt, Gordon Whitworth, Ken Rattenbury, Mike Taylor (trumpet)
Dave Lee (clarinet)
Jim Hyde (soprano sax/clarinet)
Pete Vicary, Ken Freeman (piano)
Len Bunch, Ray Arnold, Brian Porter, Ken Jones, Dave Smith, Don Gray (double bass)
Barry Phillips, Brian Casson (trombone)
Val Wiseman (vocals)

The band played reunion dates in 1976 and 1977. Its surviving members played a concert at the Grand Hotel, Birmingham, in 1990, and re-assembled again for a Jazz Reunion in May 1996, which also featured two other pioneering Birmingham bands, Ken Ingram's Eagle Jazz Band and the West Side Jazz Band.

SEMPLE, 'Archie' Archibald Stuart Nisbet

clarinet

Born: Edinburgh, Scotland, 31 March 1928
Died: London, 26 January 1974

Brother John was a trumpeter. Archie doubled on trumpet during his teens. Served in the Royal Navy (1946–8). Led own Escom Jazz Band in Edinburgh (autumn 1949), which became the Capitol Stompers. Continued to lead band (which became the Capitol Jazzmen) until moving to London to join Mick Mulligan in spring 1952. With Freddy Randall from January 1953 until August 1954. With Norman Cave's band (late 1954). With Alex Welsh from February 1955 until March 1963 (absent through illness January to July 1959). Led own quartet briefly until again being taken ill in July 1963. Led own band briefly in early 1964, then ill health caused him to retire from playing.

SENN, 'Mike' Michael
saxes/clarinet

Born: London, 25 February 1929

With Les Ayling (late 1945) and Harry Hayes. Summer season with trumpeter Harry Owen in Aberdeen (1946). With Henry Hall (1946–7), then worked with Carl Barriteau at Embassy Club, London (1947). With Tommy Sampson (summer 1948 to October 1948) including tour of Italy and Germany. Year with trumpeter Ken Grieff's Band aboard *Queen Mary* liner (1949), then worked with Paul Fenoulhet before joining Frank Weir in April 1950. With Kathy Stobart (November 1950 to March 1951), Johnny Swinfen (May to July 1951), Basil Tait on *Queen Mary* (August to October 1951). With Basil Kirchin (1952). Temporarily left full time music to run own tobacconist's (1952–4), then again worked with Basil Kirchin (May to August 1954). With Tubby Hayes' Octet (April 1955 to September 1956), then rejoined Basil Kirchin (1957). Co-led Downbeaters (with Jack Sharpe) from 1957, which became basis for Downbeat Big Band, also partnered Jack Sharpe in the running of the Downbeat Club, London (from 1958). Played in Kenny Baker's Dozen (1959–60). Quit full time playing to concentrate on copying and arranging, which he continues to do through the 1990s.

SEYMOUR, Jack
double bass

Born: 1924
Died: 1993

Left-handed bassist. With Les Smith and his Rhythm Aces in Rugby during the late 1930s, then joined the RAF and played in drummer Ralph Green's RAF Band. After demobilization worked with Buddy Featherstonhaugh (1946), then joined Frank Weir. With Woolf Phillips before rejoining Frank Weir in summer of 1947. With Ken Mackintosh (1948–9), then briefly with Paul Adam before working with Ted Heath from June to September 1949. Rejoined Ken Mackintosh in September 1949. Co-led band with Bert Courtley in 1956, then joined Eric Delaney. Subsequently worked in the North of England before joining Bert Courtley's Sextet in 1961. Freelanced successfully from the 1960s onwards.

SHAKESPEARE, John Lloyd
trumpet/vocals

Born: Leytonstone, Essex, 24 May 1923

Son of trumpeter Lloyd Shakespeare; nephew of trumpeter and flugelhorn player Bill Shakespeare (who worked with Carroll Gibbons, Sydney Lipton, Maurice Winnick, etc.). Trumpet at seven, at sixteen led own semi-pro band in the Romford area. With Melville Christie in 1941, then served for four-and-a-half years in the RAF. Worked with George Elrick, Frank Weir, Howard Lucraft, and Leslie Douglas, then joined Vic Lewis in March 1947. Remained with Vic Lewis until spring 1949 (except for two months' absence through scarlet fever). Left Lewis and joined Paul Fenoulhet in spring 1949. Toured, then played London Palladium residency with Fenoulhet, while there doubled by playing also at Churchill's night club. Joined Sydney Lipton in late 1949 and remained for over six years before concentrating on freelance session work, playing regularly in Peter Knight's Orchestra. Began singing regularly in the Sonnets vocal group and formed successful jingle company in 1957. After he gave up playing trumpet in 1962, his company developed and subsequently provided music for many films and documentaries.

SHAND, 'Dave' David G.
saxes/clarinet

Born: Dundee, Scotland, 17 May 1909
Died: Florida, USA, May 1983

Obtained university degree, then led own band at Beach Dance Hall in Aberdeen. Moved to London, worked with Marius B. Winter, Jack Harris, Vic Filmer and Freddie Bretherton, then mainly with Jack Hylton from 1931 until early 1936. During this period also recorded with Spike Hughes, Billy Mason, etc., and played in show *Stop Press* (1935). With Sydney Lipton (1936), then joined Jack Payne (July 1936). With Jack Harris, Maurice Winnick, Ambrose and Carroll Gibbons before joining the Heralds of Swing (February 1939), also worked with Teddy Joyce (1939). Joined Army in August 1939 and became a Captain in the Royal Artillery. After demobilization joined Billy Munn (autumn 1945). Featured on baritone sax with Ted Heath (1946–8), worked with Maurice Winnick (September 1948), then rejoined Ted Heath from January 1949 until November 1950. With Jack Parnell (1951), then joined London Casino Orchestra (summer 1952). Again with Sydney Lipton from late 1952, then formed own band in 1953 and continued to lead at various venues until the late 1960s (including the Savoy Hotel, London, and the Trocadero, London). Retired to Florida.

SHANNON, 'Terry' Terrence
piano

Born: Westminster, London, 5 November 1929

Brother is pianist John Shannon. Played piano from early childhood, self-taught. Did local gigs, including some with Les Condon, but worked in Marine Department of Esso for eight years. Became professional musician, worked with Jimmy Deuchar, Victor Feldman, Dizzy Reece, Vic Ash and Wilton 'Bogey' Gaynair before joining newly-formed Jazz Couriers (with Ronnie Scott and Tubby Hayes) from April 1957 until August 1959. Also worked in Allan Ganley-Ronnie Ross group the Jazz Makers (spring 1959) and in Downbeat Big Band. Regularly with Tubby Hayes from August 1959. Visited USA with Vic Lewis Orchestra (spring 1960) then rejoined Tubby Hayes. Led own trio and worked in Keith Christie-Jimmy Deuchar Five (1965) but mainly with Tubby Hayes in various line-ups (large and small) during the mid-1960s. Also recorded in London with Donald Byrd, Ray Nance and Paul Gonsalves. With Phil Seamen Trio in the late 1960s and again led trio, but career interrupted by illness in the 1970s. Temporarily quit playing but resumed in the 1980s playing occasional gigs including deputizing in the Pizza Express All Stars, etc. Moved to South Humberside in 1988, played local gigs. Returned to London five years later and again played various gigs before settling in Wragby, Lincolnshire. Resumed regular playing, in Sheffield, Manchester, etc., in various line-ups including group led by tenor saxophonist Rick Woolgar.

SHARON, Ralph
piano/arranger

Born: London, 17 September 1923

Brother Denny also a pianist. Played with the Embassy Aces while working in a factory in Slough. Won individual award in contest organized by the *Melody Maker*. Played at Number One Rhythm Club with Carlo Krahmer (1942). In trio led by Harry Lewis (1943), with Victor Feldman (1944), guested with Johnny Claes (1945), but mainly active on war work. Returned to London and joined Frank Weir in late 1945. Briefly with Ted Heath (early 1946), then gigged with Sid Gross before rejoining Frank Weir in summer 1946 (as part of a two pianist set-up alongside George Shearing).

Remained with Frank Weir until summer of 1948, during this period also worked with Norman Burns and in Victor Feldman's Quartet. Accompanied Frank Marlowe and Dutch vocalist Leo Fuld in variety (1949), then formed own sextet in early 1950. Led own sextet until early 1953, including work in Switzerland, touring and a season at Weymouth. Emigrated to USA in May 1953. Played various club residencies in New York, Los Angeles, and Chicago, then, in early 1957, became musical director for singer Tony Bennett, a position he continues to hold through the 1990s. During this period has also made many freelance recordings with various ensembles and singers.

SHARPE, Jack
tenor sax/baritone sax

Born: East London, 19 August 1930
Died: London, 4 November 1994

Took up tenor sax at eighteen, lessons from Jack Lewis and Ronnie Scott. Worked with Vic Lewis and Teddy Foster, then did first of several stints as a London taxi driver (1953). Resumed regular playing, working with Dizzy Reece (late 1954) and with Tubby Hayes from February 1955 until September 1956. Freelanced and led own sextet (1958), worked in Tubby Hayes' Big Band. Together with saxophonist Mike Senn co-led Downbeaters from 1957, which became the basis of the Downbeat Big Band. Sharpe and Senn ran the Downbeat Club in Old Compton Street, London, from 1958. Played gigs with various line-ups during 1980s and 1990s, co-led quintet with Alan Branscombe in 1985. Led own big band from 1986, and occasionally his own septet, until suffering a stroke from which he died soon afterwards.

SHAW, 'Hank' (Henry SHALOFSKY)
trumpet

Born: London, 23 June 1926

Self-taught, played in a Salvation Army Band while evacuated in World War II. First paid engagement was a six week booking with Jack Jackson at the May Fair Hotel, London. Worked with Matt Moors at Streatham Locarno (1943), with Teddy Foster (1943–4). With Oscar Rabin 1945, including tour of France, with Sid Millward, Frank Weir (1946), George Evans (October 1946). Briefly with Woolf Phillips, then joined Carl Barriteau in May 1947. Toured with Tommy Sampson (August to December 1947), then paid extended visit to USA and Canada from late 1947. Returned to Britain, joined Basil Kirchin Sextet (November 1948). Founder-member of Club Eleven (December 1948). With Vic Lewis (early 1949), Jack Nathan (July to September 1949), Leon Roy's Band (late 1949), Ronnie Munro (early 1950), Sid Millward (October 1950). Worked with Roy Bradley and with Laurie Morgan before touring Europe with Cab Kaye from December 1950 until May 1951. With Roy Fox (January to March 1952), Harry Roy (March 1952). With Johnny Rogers-Lennie Metcalfe's Jazz Incorporated, and with Freddy Randall's Big Band in Glasgow (June 1953), also many solo dates at clubs throughout the mid-1950s. With Jack Parnell (June 1953 to July 1954), with Ronnie Scott (September 1954 to 1956) and Tony Crombie's Band. Also played at the Milroy Club, London. With Don Rendell (spring 1957). With Joe Harriott's Quintet (spring 1958 to February 1960). Worked in Redcar, Yorkshire, in Danny Mitchell's Band (1960) and with Johnny Rogers, then returned to London and worked briefly with Tony Kinsey (November 1961) and with Dennis Mann in Bristol (late 1961). From the 1960s onwards active as successful freelance, led own quartet (which played residency at the 400 Club,

London), also from 1971 until 1983 worked regularly in the Bebop Preservation Society. Often in John Burch's Octet from the 1970s through the 1990s. During this period also worked with Harry South's Big Band, Tubby Hayes, Colin Purbrook's Sextet, John Dankworth, Tony Kinsey, Jack Dorsey, Stan Tracey's Big Band, Kenny Wheeler, etc.

SHAW, Ian
vocals/piano

Born: St Asaph, North Wales, 2 June 1962

Studied at Flint High School. Gained ARCM for piano, then went on to receive BMus at University of London (1983). Played in piano bars (and at various festivals) throughout Europe (1984–7), did one man show in Rome and sang in chorus of various West End shows. Worked mainly in London (1987–8), formed Brave New World group. Played Ronnie Scott's Club in London and Birmingham, and toured Europe with Carol Grimes. Featured as vocalist and pianist on television and radio shows during the late 1980s and 1990s. Widespread concert and club work. Guested on Italian tour with Kenny Wheeler and John Taylor. Regular tours with own band (led by Adrian York) through the mid-1990s. Guested with Jan Ponsford's Vocal Chorus, worked in duo with Sarah Jane Morris, and in duo with Claire Martin, accompanied Rebecca Wheatley and continued to follow own successful solo career, also toured with own Very Big Band (1996).

SHAW, Martin Lee
trumpet/flugelhorn/piano

Born: Walsall, Staffordshire, 7 November 1966

Father (Hal) and brother (Dave) both professional pianists. Piano from age of nine, then trumpet a year later. During early teens played in the Walsall Youth Orchestra (directed by John Hughes). Moved to London in 1985, three years' study at Royal Academy of Music, then summer course at Berklee School of Music in USA. Spent a year on jazz course at the Guildhall School of Music and played in the Guildhall Jazz Orchestra. Regularly with the National Youth Jazz Orchestra throughout the early 1990s. Played in various London shows including *Grand Hotel* and *Hot Shoe Shuffle* (1994). World tours with Jamiroquay in the mid-1990s, also leads own group, and works alongside tenor saxist Adrian Revell. Featured with Paz (early 1996), London Jazz Orchestra (1996), etc.

SHEARING, George Albert
piano/composer

Born: Battersea, London, 13 August 1919

Piano from early childhood, doubled on piano-accordion. Attended Linden Lodge School for the Blind during the early 1930s. First paid work was at a South London pub, the Mason's Arms, then played in Claude Bampton's National Institute for the Blind Band (1937). Did first solo broadcast in February 1939. Resident at the Nut House, London, from summer of 1939. Briefly in South Wales, then gigged with Stephane Grappelli before playing solo residency at the Starlight Club, London (spring 1940). Joined St Regis Hotel Quintet which was subsequently led by Harry Parry (1940), also worked at Hatchett's Club, London, with Stephane Grappelli and Dennis Moonan. With George Evans, Harry Parry then joined Ambrose's Octette from July 1941 until April 1942. Toured with Stephane Grappelli Swingtette (1943) and played night clubs, then joined Frank Weir (1944), later (1946) becoming part of Weir's two piano set-up (alongside Ralph Sharon).

Joined Harry Hayes from July to November 1946, then visited the USA for four months. Returned to Britain, again toured with Stephane Grappelli (April 1947). On piano-accordion and piano with Frank Weir (summer 1947), then emigrated to the USA in November 1947. Led own enormously successful quintet in America until 1967, thereafter worked with own trio and in duos with various double bassists as well as being featured with large orchestras. From 1948 onwards made many return visits to Britain. Played Pizza on the Park, London, in 1995. Played concert in London (May 1996).

SHEPHERD, 'Dave' David
clarinet

Born: London, 7 February 1929

Clarinet from the age of fifteen, originally studied with Bernie Izen. Played in Kenny Wallbank's Jazz Band (1946), which formed basis of the Russell-Wickham Hot Six, also gigged in band co-led with trumpeter Johnny Rowden (1947). Served in the Army and was posted to Germany, where he studied clarinet with a member of the Hamburg Symphony Orchestra. After demobilization played in Reg Rigden's Original Dixielanders, then led own quintet (1950). Joined Joe Daniels in summer of 1951. With Bobby Mickleburgh's Bobcats (1952), briefly in Norman Cave's Band (late 1953) and again with Joe Daniels. With Freddy Randall from September 1954 until January 1955. Worked with Reg Wale (1955), led own quintet and worked briefly in Geoff Sowden's Band. To USA on business in 1956, gigged with Billy Maxted and played regularly with bands in Farmingdale, Long Island. Returned to Britain, worked with Jazz Today Unit (late 1956–7). Own quartet, and own band (which played briefly in Milan, Italy, 1956), together with the Dill Jones Trio was featured on Jazz at the Philharmonic tour (1957). Led own group in the late 1950s, occasionally guested with Allan Leat's Band (1959). Formed new band in 1961, then again worked with Freddy Randall (1963). Led own quintet through the 1960s, also worked in Stan Greig's Quartet. Co-led band with Freddy Randall from summer of 1972 until 1973 (featured at Montreux Jazz Festival). Led own All Stars throughout the 1970s, also worked with various visiting American musicians, regularly with pianist Teddy Wilson (including two tours of Africa). During the late 1970s guested with various leaders including Lennie Hastings, Bob Bryan and Nat Gonella, etc. Became a founder-member of the Pizza Express All Stars in May 1980, continued to work with this group through the 1990s, but also continues to lead own successful small bands. Toured Europe with Benny Goodman alumni in 1989 (Barney Kessel, Bobby Rosengarden, Peter Appleyard, etc). Part of the Great British Jazz Band (1995–6).

SHEPHERD, 'Jim' Jeremy
trombone/bass sax

Born: Dulwich, London, 29 March 1936

Played clarinet with Mitzy Mitten's Band in Hanwell at sixteen. Took up trombone during late teens. Played in Dave Burman's Dominant Seven then spent eighteen months in Steve Lane's Southern Stompers before joining Brian White's Magna Jazz Band. With trumpeter Brian Taylor, then long spell with Ian Bell, also worked with Dave Keir (1962). Freelanced with many groups, deputized in Alex Welsh's Band, with the Temperance Seven (in Britain and Sweden) and in Mick Mulligan's Band. Worked regularly, for four years, in trumpeter Brian Jones' Band. Joined Harry Walton's Band in 1968. During the late 1960s spent almost two years in the Anglo-American

Alliance (with Dick Sudhalter, Henry Francis, John R.T. Davies, etc.). Played in Tony Raine's All Stars and in London Vintage Jazz Orchestra, with trumpeter Bob Kerr, with violinist Dick Powell, etc. Accompanied many visiting American musicians including Wild Bill Davison, Ruby Braff, Franc Williams, Yank Lawson, Tom Pletcher, etc. Began doubling on bass sax in the early 1970s. Played in trombone and guitar duo with Laurie Deniz for two years, also regularly with guitarist Allan Leat and in trio with Alan Cooper. Often deputized in the Temperance Seven (on trombone and bass sax) during the 1970s and 1980s. Played trombone in Five-a-Slide from September 1980 through the 1980s and early 1990s. With Richard Williams' Dix Six for two years during the early 1990s, also in trio with Barney Bates and Diz Disley. Mainly active on bass sax during the mid-1990s.

SHEPPARD, Andy
Born: Warminster, Wiltshire, 20 January 1957
tenor sax/soprano sax/composer

Early efforts on guitar and flute, then began playing tenor sax at nineteen (soprano sax two years later). Soon played local gigs around the Salisbury area. Worked in Bristol group Sphere (with pianist Geoff Williams) and in Klaunstance (with Jerry Underwood) during the early 1980s, occasionally in Spirit Level. Lived briefly in London, then moved to France and played in Urban Sax and in Laurent Cugny's Lumière Big Band. Returned to England in 1986 and again made Bristol his base. Led own quintet, then formed quartet which were runners-up in the Jazz Services-Schlitz Young Band of the Year (1986). Sheppard received the Best Soloist award: a recording contract followed. He did various European tours playing in big bands led by George Russell, Gil Evans and Carla Bley during the late 1980s and worked again briefly with Laurent Cugny (1987). Own group did widespread overseas tours including trip to Canada. Worked often with Keith Tippett from the late 1980s. Own acoustic quartet with Ernst Rjeiseger, Nana Vasconcelos and Orphy Robinson (1990), and own big band. Played in the USA. Formed new group In Co-Motion for early 1991 debut, continues to lead this, and big band Big Co-Motion (and Small Co-Motion). Duos with pianist Steve Lodder, and trio with Lodder and Brazilian percussionist Nana Vasconcelos, as well as 20th Century Saxophones with John Harle and Steve Lodder. Composes for his own line-ups and for television, radio, films and dance. In collaboration with the Bergen Big Band from Norway premiered own composition *Harmattan* at 1996 Cheltenham Jazz Festival.

SHILLITO, 'Kid' John Norman
Born: Sheffield, Yorkshire, 3 September 1938
trumpet/vocals

Played cornet as a teenager. Led own band (with Carl Hemmingsfield on clarinet) and gigged with local bands. Left own Gloryland Jazzmen to move to London (1957). Studied at London School of Economics, but played weekend gigs in the Potteries with Ceramic City Stompers, and with Dave Brennan in Rotherham, etc. Gigged with various London groups, then took over leadership of Dave Reynolds' Jubilee Jazzmen (early 1959). Left own band in summer of 1959 and spent a year with Mickey Ashman. With Uncle John Renshaw's Band (autumn 1960), then moved to Southend and gigged with various line-ups, and in quartet with David Mills on drums, Will Hastie on clarinet and Johnny Parker on piano. Did year's National Service in RASC, then did two seasons in

Southend playing for seaside shows before touring with *The Amazing Gas Medicine Show*. With John Bastable's Chosen Six (1971), left Bastable in autumn 1972. Moved to North Devon and worked with Soloheim Mungaash Band from spring 1973 until 1976. Visited New Orleans in 1977 and in following year took own Mardi Gras Band there for Festival dates. Led this group until moving to Plymouth in 1986. Led own Rhythm Aces for several years, playing many festivals, then in the mid-1990s began leading own Dixie Ramblers.

SHORT, 'Charlie' Charles Edward   Born: Merthyr Tydfil, South Wales, 22 January 1921
double bass

Took up double bass at eighteen. Moved to London in 1941, worked with Johnny Claes (1941), Carlo Krahmer, Jack Hamilton-Roy Marsh Sextet (1941), then again with Johnny Claes, until working briefly with Derek Neville (October 1941) and Tito Burns (November 1941). With Harry Parry (late 1941–2) until joining the RAF in September 1942. Worked in various service units including Buddy Featherstonhaugh's Sextet (1943–4) and Vic Lewis-Jack Parnell Jazzmen; while stationed at Uxbridge, Middlesex, guested with various civilian bands in London. After demobilization worked with Ted Heath from 1945 until July 1949. Briefly with Frank Weir, then accompanied Benny Goodman at the London Palladium (July 1949). With Ralph Sharon (July 1949 to October 1949), then briefly with Nat Temple (including radio shows) and with Stanley Black, Norman Burns. Again with Frank Weir (early 1950), Felix King (spring 1950), then toured Europe with Benny Goodman (April to May 1950). Gigged with Kenny Graham, then toured with Lena Horne (July 1950). Rejoined Frank Weir (late 1950), briefly with Eric Delaney, then worked in Clacton with Billy Ternent's Orchestra (1951). Led own quartet and band at the Ritz Ballroom, Manchester (1951–2), briefly with Bert Eckersall at Newton Heath Palais, before returning to London in summer of 1952. Gigged with Carole Fenton, Alan Clare, Norman Burns, etc., then worked with Ian Stewart (November 1952 to February 1953). Absent from music (1953), then gigged with Jimmy Currie, Vic Ash and Norman Cave before working with Jack Parnell from October 1954 to March 1955. Forced to quit regular playing because of arthritis but resumed full schedule from 1959 until leaving profession in 1962. Worked outside of music for many years, moved to South Coast in 1968. Resumed occasional gigging in the early 1990s.

SIDAY, Eric   Born: 1904
violin/alto sax/composer/arranger   Died: New York, USA, 25 March 1976

Violin lessons from the age of six. Studied at Royal Academy of Music. Played in cinema orchestra before joining Kit-Cat Band (1926). With the Piccadilly Revels Band (directed by Ray Starita) for a year from late 1926. With house band at Sovrani's (1929), Al Collins (1929–30). With Howard Jacobs from October 1930, then month with Arthur Lally (March 1931). With Jack Payne from April 1931 until summer 1933, then played in the Barnstormers. Freelance sessions with various bands including those led by Ambrose, Jack Hylton, Ray Noble and Bob Busby. Left music profession temporarily in the 1930s and lived on an island in the South Pacific. Returned to London and worked with Carroll Gibbons and the Savoy Hotel Orpheans from September 1936 until May 1939, then emigrated to the USA, where he was featured with Fred Waring's Pennsylvanians from June 1939. Remained with Fred Waring for six years, then freelanced as a violinist and arranger. Was later mainly active as a composer and arranger, specializing in electronic music during the 1970s.

SIDWELL, Roy
Born: Nelson, Lancashire, 15 March 1927

tenor sax/baritone sax/clarinet

Father of trumpeter Stephen (born 1961), trombonist Neil (born 1962) and trumpeter Richard (born 1966). First professional work was a summer season on the Isle of Man with Joe Kirkham, then briefly toured Moss Empire theatre circuit with Henry Hall. Season in Folkestone with Phil Tate's Band, then returned home to Blackpool and worked for two years with Art Gregory's Band at the Palace Ballroom (1950). Moved to London, worked with Basil Kirchin (1952), Vic Lewis (1952–3). Gigged in France, Belgium and Germany with Canadian trombonist Buddy Hill (summer 1953). Again with Basil Kirchin (1954). With Ken Moule (1955), Carl Barriteau and gigs with Buddy Featherstonhaugh (1956). With Oscar Rabin at the Lyceum Ballroom, London (1956–8), then joined Gracie Cole's Band at Royal, Tottenham (1958–9). Worked in Freddy Staff's Band at American servicemen's club in London during the early 1960s, but from this period onwards played mainly for West End shows: *Fings Ain't What They Used to Be, Hello Dolly*, etc. Continued to do this until the early 1990s, combining playing with copying and with teaching, but continued to play freelance dates, including two tours of USA with Charlie Watts' Big Band (1985–6), in which he played baritone sax.

SIEGEL, Julian
Born: Nottingham, May 1966

sax/double bass

Studied sax with Stephen Cottrell while at the University of East Anglia, Norwich (1984–7). Moved to London, worked with National Youth Jazz Orchestra, London Jazz Orchestra, Django Bates' Delightful Precipice, etc., on sax. Also works on double bass with the Julian Argüelles Quartet, Stan Sulzmann's Band, Iain Ballamy, Simon Purcell's Quintet, Don Weller, Bobby Wellins, etc. Extensive work on sax and double bass in the mid-1990s, leading quartet with guitarist Phil Robson (1995–6). Active in jazz education, running jazz workshops in Forest Gate (and for the Hackney Community College) at the Vortex, Stoke Newington.

SIMKINS, 'Geoff' Geoffrey David
Born: Greenford, Middlesex, 13 October 1948

saxes/clarinet/drums

Father was saxophonist and bandleader Benny Simkins (1911–82), brother is pianist Pete Simkins (born 1939). Family moved to Brighton in 1960. Geoff gigged on drums around the Brighton area from 1961 until 1965, then took up alto sax. Worked with brother and with father, also with Ted Ambrose, Terry Whitney, Roy Bower, etc., and joined Harry Strutters Hot Rhythm Orchestra in the late 1960s. Was based mainly in London during the early 1970s. Gigged with various bands and often worked with the Temperance Seven during the 1970s (and 1980s) on reeds and drums. Moved back to Brighton in 1973. Often with Harry Strutters in the 1970s, but also freelanced extensively. Regularly with Campbell Burnap in the late 1970s and 1980s (including work overseas). Guested with bands in Switzerland. During the 1980s and 1990s worked with Danny Moss, with drummer Dave Wickens, with Bobby Wellins, etc., and accompanied various visiting American musicians. Formed short-lived group with Chas Burchell in 1985. Regularly with Campbell Burnap in the 1990s, also co-led quartet with Dave Cliff as well as playing guest spots with various bands. Occasionally does gigs on drums.

SIMMONDS, 'Ron' Ronald Alan
trumpet/arranger/lyricist

Born: Winnipeg, Canada, 16 October 1928

Moved with English parents to Brentwood, Essex, in 1936 and then to Coventry in 1939. Studied at Coventry Technical College. Trumpet from 1946. Served in the RAF, but played occasionally in Tommy Sampson's Band at weekends before being posted to Germany. After demobilization joined Tommy Sampson from February until October 1949. With Leon Roy's Big Band in London (1949), then worked with Oscar Rabin (1949–50), before joining Vic Lewis from October 1950 to June 1951. With the Skyrockets (summer 1951), then worked with the Squadronaires from October 1951 until January 1953. In January 1953 began long musical association with Jack Parnell, briefly with Ambrose (May to June 1953), then rejoined Jack Parnell. Season in Monte Carlo with Geraldo (1955). With Ronnie Scott (July to August 1956), again with Jack Parnell until 1960. During this period played for three years for show *West Side Story* in London, was part of Bill Russo's London Jazz Orchestra and was also on retainer from Cyril Stapleton for radio and television work as part of the BBC Show Band. Extensive freelance work including playing for Kenny Baker's Dozen, the BBC *Goon Shows, Sunday Night at the London Palladium*, etc. With Ted Heath (1960–2), John Dankworth (1962–3). Moved to Munich, Germany in early 1963, worked with Max Gregor's Television Orchestra and the Bavarian Radio Orchestra. Regularly in Berlin from 1965 until 1974 with studio bands and guesting with visiting American bands led by Lionel Hampton, Stan Kenton, Oliver Nelson, Don Ellis, etc., also with Peter Herbolzheimer in Hamburg and on tour (1970 to 1985). Ran own small group for Saarbrucken Radio Station (1974–94), also regularly active as a journalist, playwright and lyricist during his stay in Germany. Settled in Spain in 1995. Has regularly contributed articles to *Crescendo* magazine since 1963.

SIMPSON, Jack
drums/xylophone/tympani/guitar

Born: London, 6 September 1905
Died: Salinas, California, USA, 7 May 1970

Was a boy entrant in the Army, became a musician at fifteen. Taught percussion at Eton for four years, later worked with Percival Mackey. Featured with Jack Payne from summer 1933 until summer 1935. With Sydney Kyte (1935), then worked with Ambrose from summer 1936 until 1939. With Sydney Lipton in 1940, then formed own highly successful sextet which toured extensively during the 1940s and 1950s.

SIMPSON, Paul
clarinet/piano/saxes/trumpet

Born: Poole, Dorset, 1925
Died: Sydney, Australia, 23 December 1993

With Mike Daniels' Quartet (1947), then joined John Haim's Jelly Roll Kings in spring 1948. Worked with Alan Kirby and again with Mike Daniels, then joined Joe Daniels (1951). With Mike Daniels again in autumn 1951, then with Mick Mulligan (early 1952). Toured with Carl Barriteau (May 1952), then rejoined Mick Mulligan (1953–5). Gigged with Kenny Ball, Stan Sowden and Freddy Randall, then worked with Bobby Mickleburgh for a year from summer of 1955. Formed own band in August 1956, led this until April 1957, then worked in Spain and Africa with a High Life Band (1957). Worked in Germany with Pete Deuchar (1958). With Geoff Sowden (1959), then freelanced before working in Germany with Terry Pitts (spring 1962). During the 1960s and early 1970s freelanced on various instruments (including the contra-bass sax) and played various solo piano residencies. Emigrated to Australia and played with various groups including Geoff Gilbert's Band and Ray Price's Quintet. Left full time music to work as a tally clerk in the Sydney docks. Visited Britain in autumn of 1991 and guested with bands in London before returning to Sydney, New South Wales.

SIMS, Ken
trumpet

Born: Wallasey, Cheshire, 31 October 1935

Blew the bugle in a Boys' Brigade band, then took up trumpet and played in band led by his pianist father. Played cornet (and occasionally trombone) in the 22nd Cheshire Military Band and in the St Vincent Silver Band. Gigged in North Wales with Fred Rae's Band and played jazz gigs around the Liverpool area with the Muskrat Jazz Band and Panama Jazz Band. Deputized on trombone in the Merseysippi Jazz Band. Moved to London, joined Cy Laurie for a year from late 1956. With Alex Revell (1958), gigged with various bands, then joined Acker Bilk from spring 1958 until spring 1960. Co-led band with Ian Wheeler from May 1960, became sole leader when Wheeler left in early 1961. Worked with own band in Germany (1962), then freelanced in Munich, Germany, with Occam Street Footwarmers and with the Munich Hot Dogs during two separate visists. Returned to Britain in 1963, worked with Terry Lightfoot (1964–5). Moved back to Liverpool in late 1960s, led Blue Magnolia Jazz Orchestra for several years, and played various gigs, then returned to live in London. With Colin Symons (1973) and freelanced with various bands. With John Petters New Dixie Syncopators from the mid-1970s, also led own quintet and played many dates with the Eastside Stompers into the 1980s. Formed own Dixie Kings in 1981, for a time in the 1980s the band featured Ken's two daughters Jo and Jacky singing as the Rhythm Girls. Ken has continued to lead the Dixie Kings through the 1990s.

SINGER, Harry
drums

Born: Norwich, Norfolk, 12 June 1919

Played in the Norwich Municipal Orchestra from 1937 to 1940, then moved to London. Worked with Miff Ferrie at the Panama Club and played at various American air bases, then joined Vic Lewis. Was part of Reggie Dare's Sextet, then played in Switzerland with Stan Reynolds in 1947. Worked with Gordon Homer during the late 1940s and with Andre Messeder's Cubans before freelancing in many varied musical aggregations.

SKEAT, Bill
saxes/clarinet/flute

Born: Stratford, London, 25 July 1928

His son Bob is a bass guitarist, his daughter Debbie plays the piano. Bill's brother is bassist Len Skeat. Bill started on clarinet, did local gigs as a teenager, then joined the Army for two years and played clarinet in a military band but also did 'civilian' gigs on sax. Joined Blue Rockets (on tenor sax) in June 1948, then worked briefly with Carl Barriteau before joining Joe Daniels on clarinet for several months from summer of 1948. On alto sax with Tommy Sampson in spring 1949, played summer season, then moved back to London and joined Nat Allen, worked again briefly with Joe Daniels in autumn 1949. Two years with Billy Ternent, left in early 1952 and worked with Felix King (1952–3). Was ill with tuberculosis for two years, then resumed full working schedule, returned briefly to Billy Ternent (summer 1955), then worked with Arnold Bailey's Band and with Arthur Coppersmith (1957) before spending two years in the London Palladium Orchestra. Worked at the Mermaid Theatre, then began extensive freelance work, television, radio, recordings and touring with various stars; accompanying Tony Bennett, Peggy Lee, Bing Crosby, Fred Astaire, etc. Worked in Frank Willoughby's Band (1964). Continued to freelance through the 1970s, 1980s and 1990s, but increasingly active in jazz line-ups, deputized for Bob Wilber at Newport Jazz Festival in July 1978, and later often worked in Bob Wilber's Big Band. With Digby Fairweather for part of *Swann in Jazz* tours during the late 1980s. Toured Belgium and Germany with the Chas-Tet (1988). Guest appearances with bands in Japan and Australia and made many playing visits to Russia during the 1980s and 1990s.

SKEAT, 'Len' Leonard
double bass

Born: East London, 9 February 1937

Brother of Bill Skeat. Began on clarinet, took up double bass in late teens and had lessons from Bernie Woods. Did local gigs in the Poplar area, then played summer season in Yarmouth for Weller's Circus. Subsequently did summer season at Skegness with guitarist Bill Shearer's Quartet (1958). Worked in Gracie Cole's Band, and with Phil Tate and Nat Temple. In Maurice Allen's Trio (1962), also did jazz club work with Tommy Whittle and in Eddie Thompson's Trio. In Ted Heath's Band, left to work in the BBC Radio Big Band. Played for West End show *Cowardy Custard*. Worked in Derek Linter's Trio in the mid-1960s and in Terry Seymour's Big Band. Played in Ralph Dollimore's Ted Heath tribute band. During the 1970s and 1980s worked in Tommy Whittle's Quartet, Danny Moss' Quartet, Eddie Thompson's Trio, also widespread freelance work which included accompanying many visiting Americans including Peggy Lee, Ruby Braff, Joe Newman, Scott Hamilton, Helen Merrill, Harry Edison, etc. Regularly with Stephane Grappelli (including USA and Australia) from 1974 to 1977, also part of Velvet (with Digby Fairweather, Ike Isaacs and Denny Wright) from 1977 into the 1980s. Regular member of Pizza Express All Stars from May 1980 through the 1990s. Played for various shows including *Bubbling Brown Sugar*, also toured with Billy Eckstine, Lionel Hampton, etc. Worked in New York in Bobby Rosengarden's Band, and was featured with *Jazz Journal* All Stars at Nice Jazz Festival (1981). Toured Europe with Charlie Antolini. During the 1980s and 1990s continued widespread freelance playing, often in Bob Wilber's groups, with Dave Shepherd's Quintet, in Val Wiseman's *Lady Sings the Blues*, with Bruce Adams-Alan Barnes Quintet, Kenny Baker's New Dozen, with Dig's Half Dozen and also in the Great British Jazz Band.

SKIDMORE, Alan Richard James
tenor sax/soprano sax/flute

Born: London, 21 April 1942

Son of Jimmy Skidmore. Received tenor sax in the 1950s as a birthday gift from his father but didn't begin playing seriously until a year or so later. Was taught by his father and by Les Evans.

Left school at fifteen, did day job but gigged in North London bands and with father in duo (1960). First professional work with Frank Weir, brief spells with Red Price, Johnny Spence and Brian Auger, then joined Eric Delaney in summer of 1963, often worked with Delaney during following three years but was regularly with Alexis Korner's Blues Incorporated in 1964 and recorded with Eric Clapton and with John Mayall. Occasionally co-led group with Bob Cornford. With Ronnie Scott in 1965, also played for German television and radio programmes. With John Stevens' Septet (1966), worked briefly with John Dankworth and played in Tubby Hayes' Big Band. Played long residency at London's Talk of the Town night club with Phil Phillips' Band (1966–9), toured with Maynard Ferguson (1969). During the late 1960s also recorded film music with Herbie Hancock and worked with Mike Westbrook, in Humphrey Lyttelton's Big Band, in Ray Russell's Sextet, in John Surman's Octet, etc. Led own quintet during the late 1960s and 1970s. With Georgie Fame, including work in USA (1970). With John Warren's Big Band in the 1970s, also with Chris McGregor's Brotherhood of Breath, Elton Dean's Ninesense, toured Italy with Ian Carr's Nucleus, worked with Mike Gibbs, with Elton Dean, with Mike Osborne line-ups, with Harold Beckett, in Ian Hamer's Sextet, Rolf Kühn, Keith Tippett, etc. Was temporarily out of action through car crash injuries in late 1972. Formed SOS (Surman, Osborne and Skidmore) in October 1973, widespread touring and performing for ballet in Paris, also led trio (with Tony Oxley and Chris Laurence/Ali Haurand) and own quartet. With George Gruntz Concert Band (1976–82), also accompanied many visiting Americans. From 1978–84 was featured with West German Radio Orchestra, again worked with Georgie Fame (1978). During the 1980s continued to lead own quartet, also with Charlie Watts' Big Band (1985–6), with Stan Tracey, with Elvin Jones' Jazz Machine, again with Mike Osborne, with Ian Carr's Orchestra UK (1989), etc. Continued to lead own line-ups through the 1990s, played in Hong Kong with Clark Tracey, guested with bands in South Africa, etc.

SKIDMORE, 'Jimmy' James Richard   Born: Manor Park, London, 8 February 1916
tenor sax

Father of Alan Skidmore. Played guitar at eighteen, did local gigs around the Willesden area, also sang and played in talent contests with a local trio. Took up tenor sax at twenty, played regularly in band led by pianist Len Young in and around North West London. Joined band led by a Mexican trumpeter, Jack Hamilton, in 1940, also guested at West London Rhythm Club, and played alongside George Shearing on various occasions. Worked in Harry Roy's Ragamuffins (then led by Reg Owen). Toured with Harry Parry in summer of 1942, then worked with Carlo Krahmer (1943), in Frank Deniz's Spirits of Rhythm (1944) and then joined Eric Winstone's Octet in late 1944. With Vic Lewis-Jack Parnell Jazzmen (1945), also did occasional workers' concerts with pianist Pat Kaye. With Vic Lewis (1946), briefly with Ray Ellington, then rejoined Vic Lewis until December 1947. With Derek Neville's Band to Nice Jazz Festival (February 1948). With Victor Feldman's Quartet, Art Thompson's Band and Basil Kirchin's Sextet (1948), with Nat Temple (1949). Toured Germany with Dill Jones, then worked for a year with Ralph Sharon's Sextet (1950). Briefly with Grischa Farfel (1951), then with Kenny Baker's Sextet from March until September 1951, before brief spell with Eddie Calvert (1951). With Terry Brown's Sextet (early 1952) then joined pianist Denny Termer's Quartet (spring 1952). Worked again with Kenny Baker in the mid-1950s, also with Jazz Today Unit during this period, and with Jazz at the Prom.

Regularly with Eric Delaney from summer 1954 until October 1956. Joined Humphrey Lyttelton in April 1957 (absent through illness in late 1957). Left Lyttelton in September 1960. Active freelance throughout the 1960s and 1970s, often working in small groups with son Alan, with Kathy Stobart, Willie Garnett, etc., also regularly featured with pianist Colin Peters' Quartet in the 1960s. Temporarily became a publican in 1966, later worked for a supermarket. During the 1980s and 1990s continued to play gigs with own Friends (including pianist Ian Pearce), also with Bob Graham's Experience (1995). Celebrated 80th birthday playing alongside his son Alan.

SKIVINGTON, 'Pete' Peter Percy
bass guitar
Born: Edmonton, London, 3 June 1938

Played guitar as a teenager, mostly in Country and Western groups. Did National Service in the Army (1957–9), mostly in Cyprus, then resumed gigging. Joined Capital Five led by tenor saxophonist Frank Cross for tour of American air bases in France and Germany (1963) and began playing bass guitar, on which he specialized thereafter. Co-led the Autumns (with guitarist Jimmy Burridge), then became leader of that group. Joined Stan Greig's Trio in 1970s, then worked for a year with Terry Lightfoot before freelancing with Lenny Hastings, Dave Jones, John Picard, Dave Shepherd, etc. Regularly with Alex Welsh from 1973 until 1982 (during this period he left Welsh's band for a year and freelanced with various line-ups, regularly with Digby Fairweather's Friends). During the 1980s often worked with Stan Greig, Al Gay, Jim Douglas, Johnny Richardson's Trio, etc., also regularly with Five-a-Slide from September 1980 through into the 1990s. Joined Laurie Chescoe's Good Time Jazz in August 1990, was temporarily indisposed through illness, but rejoined the band in January 1994 and resumed full schedule, also worked briefly in Germany with Jim Douglas and the Alex Welsh Legacy (1994).

SKRIMSHIRE, 'Skrim' Nevil Wadham
guitar
Born: Beckenham, Kent, 11 April 1923

Made tentative efforts on the double bass while at Dulwich College with Bruce Turner, later played drums before taking up guitar. Served in RAF from 1942 until 1946; while stationed in Malta took guitar lessons from Bill Bramwell. After September 1946 demobilization began gigging with John Haim, Johnny Speight, etc., and sat in at Orange Tree, Friern Barnet, jam sessions. Joined Humphrey Lyttelton from early 1948 until September 1949. Sat in with Freddy Randall and broadcast with that band, gigged with Bill Thompson, then joined Reg Rigden's Original Dixielanders (1950). With Joe Daniels (1951), then joined Christie Brothers' Stompers (spring 1952–3). Freelanced but also worked regularly with Diz Disley from 1956, also often with Alex Welsh from 1957, briefly with Wally Fawkes in 1957. Guested with Bob Cort's Skiffle Group (including trip to Denmark) and with Mick Mulligan and George Melly. Often with Freddy Randall and part of clarinettist Johnny Toogood's All Stars (1964), with guitarist Allan Leat, trombonist Mike Collier, etc. Regularly with Dick Sudhalter and Henry Francis in the Anglo-American Alliance during the late 1960s and early 1970s. On promotion staff at EMI from 1955 until 1968. During this period appeared on many recordings (and on radio) as Nigel Sinclair: with the Saints Jazz Band, Alex Welsh, the Merseysippi Jazz Band, etc. Busy freelance throughout the 1970s and 1980s, with Digby Fairweather, Cy Laurie, John Petters, Bruce Turner, Dick Williams, etc. Also co-led Swinging Strings with guitarist Ray Catling. Playing regularly through the 1990s with Neville Dickie, Brian White, Cy Laurie, Digby Fairweather, Swinging Strings, etc. Is married to jazz writer Sally-Ann Worsfold.

SLATER, Ashley W.
trombone/bass trombone/tuba/vocals

Born: Quebec, Canada, 20 April 1961

Moved with family to California at the age of one. Took up trombone at twelve. Played in Junior High School Band, in Crescent City, California. Was taught by Gene Petrik. Left High School Stage and Concert Bands and joined the British Army as a musician at the age of sixteen. Studied at Royal Military School of Music (Kneller Hall) and gained AFCM (1979–80). Served as a musician in Northern Ireland, while there played and sang with Otis and the Elevators. Left the Army in 1983, studied at Goldsmiths College, London, and gained diploma. Joined Loose Tubes at its inception in 1984 and remained with the group for over six years until its demise (began doubling on tuba in 1986). From the 1980s also worked with Django Bates' Delightful Precipice, with George Russell's Living Time Orchestra, the London Jazz Orchestra, Carla Bley, Andy Sheppard, etc. By the late 1980s was also leading own band Microgroove which later developed into the widely successful Freak Power, whose use of creative distortion and electronic effects combined with jazz techniques has gained big record sales and a following throughout Europe.

SLAVIN, 'Archie' Aaron
guitar/composer

Born: London, 9 June 1914
Died: Bexhill-on-Sea, Sussex, 1992

Brother of Martin Slavin; another brother, Nathaniel, played double bass. Worked with Stan Atkins as a semi-pro, then, on Al Bowlly's recommendation, joined Lew Stone in 1935. Stayed with Lew Stone until 1936, then worked in Al Bowlly's short-lived band (early 1937). With Eddie Carroll (late 1937), Ambrose (1938), then rejoined Eddie Carroll (1939). Served in RAF (1940–1), played at RAF Bridgnorth in service band led by Stanley Black, and became member of the Skyrockets until being invalided out of the RAF. Rejoined Lew Stone in 1941, also worked at Hatchett's, London, with Stephane Grappelli and George Shearing and played one-night stands with Harry Parry (1942). In Freddie Ballerini's Sextet (1942), also played in London Fire Fighters' Orchestra during World War II. With Carroll Gibbons (1943), also arranged music for vocal group the Debonaires. With Harry Hayes (1945), then worked with Ambrose before again rejoining Lew Stone (1946). Thereafter mainly active as a freelance. Regularly in Lou Levy's *Music from the Movies* radio shows and on Mantovani's recordings, as well as playing for various West End shows including *The Pajama Game*. Featured on many Billy Cotton radio shows and in numerous Anglia Television programmes. From 1975 until 1984 mainly active running own hotel in Bexhill-on-Sea, playing for local charity shows, etc.

SLAVIN, Martin Mordecai
piano/vibes/composer

Born: London, 26 February 1922
Died: London, 25 May 1988

Younger brother of Archie Slavin; another brother, Nathaniel, played double bass. Served in the Army as a Band Sergeant and acted as musical director for *Stars in Battledress* shows. After demobilization accompanied singer Aki Yanai (1946), then formed own seven piece band (1947).

With Johnny Van Derrick Quartet (1947), Duncan Whyte (1948). Played piano, piano-accordion and vibes with Robin Richmond group (1949). With Eddie Calvert (1950–1), own band at Selby's, London (1952). On vibes with Kenny Baker's Dozen (1954) and with Geoff Taylor's Sextet (1955), subsequently became a Musical Director for television shows. Wrote musical *Nancy Wake* in the 1960s. Did prolific session work and arranging before moving to Vancouver, Canada, in 1966. Later settled in Hollywood, where he composed, arranged and played film music. Became Musical Director of *The Pacific Princess* cruise ship, continued with these duties until being involved in a shipboard accident. Moved back to London in the mid-1980s and played occasional freelance dates with organist Ken Penney, etc., until being fatally injured in a road accident in Hampstead, London.

SMILEY, 'Ken' Joseph Kennedy
Born: Londonderry, Ireland, 2 April 1920
trumpet/guitar/piano

Mother played cello. Began on violin at seven, then took up guitar. Played guitar in the Satellites at the Tonic Ballroom in Bangor in 1939. Started on trumpet in 1939 and become part of the Original Carlton Five at Queen's University, Belfast. This band later played at the Paradise and at the Embassy Club. Subsequently Smiley played trumpet and guitar in Eddie Freeman's Band (Freeman also doubled on guitar and trumpet) at the Embassy. Worked with Peter Leslie, then led own Delta Four, which did its first broadcast in June 1943. Ken Smiley's Jazz Band subsequently did many broadcasts in the 1940s (featuring Stan Cox on piano, Norman Watson on guitar and Bryan McCluney on clarinet) establishing a reputation as being one of the first non-American bands in the jazz 'revival'. Smiley moved to London in 1952 to work for the *Daily Mirror* and played in the Fleet Street Jazz Band in the 1950s. During the late 1960s and early 1970s worked in television and radio in Africa, but continued to play club dates in Accra, Sierra Leone, etc. Returned to Britain and settled in Sussex, sat in with various bands on the South Coast, then began to specialize on piano in the 1990s.

SMITH, Betty
Born: Sileby, Leicestershire, 6 July 1929
tenor sax/vocals

Piano from six, sax at nine. Joined Archie's Juveniles on alto sax, then worked with Blanche Coleman on tenor sax, and from then on specialized on tenor sax. With Billy Penrose (1947), then toured with Rudy Starita's Girls' Band before joining Ivy Benson. With Freddy Randall from June to November 1950. Married bassist-trumpeter Jack Peberdy in August 1950. Worked mainly in and around Leicester (with Johnny Smith and Johnny Hearth) until rejoining Randall in 1963. Left Randall in February 1957 to form own quintet (which originally featured pianist Brian Lemon). Led own group through the 1960s and 1970s, playing summer seasons in Guernsey, Cliftonville, etc., and on liner *Franconia*. Also toured Australia and New Zealand, and worked in the USA. Featured as a guest artiste in many shows and played many club dates and concerts alongside Kenny Baker. Was featured in the *Best of British Jazz* during the 1970s and 1980s, also gigged with Eggy Ley's Hotshots in the 1980s and appeared at various festivals. Illness curtailed full working schedule in the late 1980s.

SMITH, Brian
tenor sax/soprano sax/flute/composer/percussion

Born: Mount Egmont District,
New Zealand, 3 January 1939

Studied piano for four years, virtually self-taught on sax and clarinet. Played in all sorts of line-ups in New Zealand and Australia before moving to Britain in 1964. Worked with Alexis Korner's Blues Incorporated and with Fat John Cox's Band. With Mike Westbrook, Graham Collier, Tubby Hayes and Maynard Ferguson, before becoming founder-member of Ian Carr's Nucleus in autumn 1969. Worked often with Nucleus into the early 1980s, and took part in tours of USA, Scandinavia, Italy, Germany, etc., with the group. During this period also worked with Mike Gibbs, Gordon Beck, Keith Tippett, Tony Kinsey, Alan Price, etc. Toured the USA with Maynard Ferguson in 1972 and 1974 and was part of Pacific Eardrum (alongside Dave MacRae) in 1975–6, also in Dick Crouch's Paz. Was regularly in Geoff Castle's Band during the late 1970s and early 1980s. Moved back to New Zealand in 1982. Led own quartet and worked with drummer Frank Gibson. Continues to lead own group, to play freelance dates and teach. Based in Auckland. Not to be confused with the Lancastrian tenor saxophonist of the same name.

SMITH 'Chick'
trumpet

Born: Perth, Scotland, 1909
Died: July 1983

Uncle of Jimmy Deuchar. Began on piano and played semi-pro gigs before specializing on trumpet. Worked in local cinema band in Dundee. Moved to Glasgow to join Louis Freeman. Worked with Maurice Winnick, then spent fourteen months in Germany with Oscar Joost's Band. Returned to Britain to join band led by Mrs Jack Hylton, remained with this group until January 1936, then worked with Tommy Finnigan and briefly with Buddy Featherstonhaugh. Radio work with Val Rosing (1936), then worked mainly as a freelance session player. With Sid Millward (late 1939), then in 1940 worked with Jack Nathan, Peter Mendoza, Lew Stone, Harry Hayes and Sid Phillips. Joined RAF and played in Number One Dance Band from 1941, also worked with Geraldo in 1944–5. Regularly with the Skyrockets until 1951, but also played many freelance dates including some with Joe Daniels. Moved to Bray in Ireland (1951) and opened tobacconist shop, but continued to play regularly. With saxophonist Johnny Devlin's Downbeaters in Dublin (1952), then formed own band (1953). Continued to play gigs and also taught music. Chick's brother Bill (died 1992) was also a trumpeter, who worked in Billy Mason's Band (accompanying Louis Armstrong in Britain, 1932). He also worked with Henry Hall, Sydney Lipton, Teddy Joyce, etc.

SMITH, Colin Ranger
trumpet

Born: London, 20 November 1934

Played clarinet for two years, then took up banjo before becoming a trumpeter at the age of nineteen. Worked as an electrical engineer, but played semi-professionally with Terry Lightfoot (1956). Left to form own band in early 1957, then turned professional and rejoined Terry Lightfoot in late 1957. Left Lightfoot to work with Cy Laurie from spring 1958 until joining Acker Bilk in May 1960 (having previously deputized with Bilk's Band in summer of 1959). Left Acker Bilk in June 1966, worked at the Georgian Club, London, but took time out from music to sail the Atlantic in a 45-foot ketch. Rejoined Acker Bilk in May 1968, then left to freelance in 1971.

Worked with Tony Coe-John Picard Band, in Stan Greig's Quintet, and in Greig's London Jazz Big Band (from February 1975), in Johnny Parker's Quartet, in John Picard's Band, etc. During the 1980s continued to play in the London Jazz Big Band, and regularly with the Pizza Express All Stars (from 1983), also in Brian Leake's Sweet and Sour, the Midnite Follies, Ian Stewart's Rocket 88, Stan Greig's Boogie Band, Bob Wilber's Big Band and Charlie Watts' Big Band. Rejoined Acker Bilk in 1992, but continued to work in the Pizza Express All Stars, with Bob Wilber, Tommy Whittle, etc. Recovered from serious illness and resumed full schedule including tour of Germany with Acker Bilk (April 1996).

SMITH, Derek Geoffrey   Born: Stratford, London, 17 August 1931
piano/arranger

Played piano from age of seven, did local gigs as a teenager and led own band. Worked for an insurance company but played at many jazz clubs and won individual award at contest organized by the *Melody Maker*. Led own trio before turning professional and joining John Dankworth in spring 1954. Left Dankworth in September 1955 to become part of New Jazz Quartet (with Allan Ganley, Harry Klein and Sammy Stokes). Led own trio in 1956 and also played regularly in Kenny Baker's Dozen before emigrating to USA in April 1957. Toured briefly with Art Mooney, then freelanced successfully in New York, for recordings, television and live appearances. Worked in USA with the British Jazz Trio. Played briefly again with John Dankworth during 1959 vacation to Britain. Did overseas touring with Benny Goodman in the 1960s and 1970s, worked in Japan with Benny Carter (1983) and was featured at innumerable jazz festivals with Dizzy Gillespie, Arnett Cobb, Eddie Miller, etc., besides leading own successful trio. Worked regularly in television on the *Johnny Carson Show* (1967–74), on *Tonight*, with Doc Severinsen's Orchestra, from 1968 to 1975. Played on many film soundtracks, and has accompanied many great singers, including Frank Sinatra and Pavarotti. Has done an enormous amount of freelance recordings, including fifteen albums with his own trio.

SMITH, 'Eddie' Edward   Born: London, *c.*1930
banjo/guitar   Died: Balearic Islands, October 1992

Worked as a printer before playing in Lea Valley Stompers (1952). Was in Bob Dawbarn's Barnstormers (1954) which formed the basis of Ian Bell's Band. Left Ian Bell to join Mike Daniels in spring 1955. Remained with Daniels until joining Chris Barber in November 1956. Left Chris Barber in late 1964, replaced by Stewart 'Stu' Morrison (born Brighton, 1938), who played in Portsmouth's Vieux Carré Jazz Band, with Pete Ridge and with Mike Cotton before joining Barber. After leaving Barber, Eddie Smith played occasionally with bands around the London area, then moved abroad.

SMITH, 'Harry' Harold Thomas   Born: Military Hospital, Cologne,
piano   Germany, 24 February 1921

Born while father was serving as a regular soldier in Germany. Learnt piano during teens, served in the RAF (1946–8), played in station bands, etc., and often sat in with Syd Lawrence's Band in Chester. After demobilization worked in drummer Vic Richards Trio at the Colony Club, London, then joined Norman Burns. Left Norman Burns in late 1953 to work with Freddy Randall from late 1953 to late 1955 (with Randall in Cinemascope film *Parade of the Bands*). With Sandy Brown's Quintet (1956–7), then joined Harry Hayes' Quintet (1958). Occasionally worked (and recorded with) Kenny Baker in the late 1950s. During the 1960s worked for long periods with Grischa Farfel's Sextet and in drummer Derek Linter's Trio. Mainly worked as a solo pianist in the 1970s and 1980s, including fifteen year residency at the Holiday Inn, Swiss Cottage, London, but also accompanied visiting Americans and played occasional engagements with Freddy Randall. Active into the 1990s, deputizing in the Pizza Express All Stars, and accompanying Ruby Braff, Scott Hamilton, etc.

SMITH, Keith John
trumpet/vocals

Born: Isleworth, Middlesex, 19 March 1940

Took up trumpet at seventeen. Played in the Powder Mill Lane Stompers, then joined the San Jacinto Jazz Band (led by Norrie Cox) in 1957 and helped organize the New Teao Brass Band. With the Fron-Zi-Me Jazz Band from 1959 until joining Mickey Ashman in the summer of 1960. Later that year co-led Climax Jazzmen (with banjoist Don Cook). With Mac Duncan's Band in Germany (spring 1961), then joined Bobby Mickleburgh's Confederates (1961). Made first visit to New Orleans in 1962, returned to Britain and formed own Climax Jazzmen, continued to play occasional dates with the New Teao. Did month's solo work in USA (spring 1965), again led own band in Britain, then spent eight months working in the USA and Canada (1966), subsequently made many playing visits to the USA. Toured Europe leading the New Orleans All Stars (1966). Led own band, then worked in Denmark's Papa Bue Viking Jazz Band from January 1972 until late 1974. Did solo tours of Europe and Japan (1975), also worked in Africa (1975–6). Ran own successful record business. Settled temporarily in the West Country and co-led band with Ian Wheeler (from spring 1976). After Wheeler's departure in 1979, this group (known as Hefty Jazz) was led solely by Keith Smith and did widespread touring, including dates at Eddie Condon's in New York (June 1985). Smith also fronted a band consisting of ex-members of Louis Armstrong's All Stars and toured Europe in 1983 and 1984. By then Hefty Jazz was being regularly featured in touring shows devised by Smith, these included *Stardust Road* (a tribute to Hoagy Carmichael, which featured Georgie Fame), *A Hundred Years of Dixieland Jazz* (with George Chisholm), etc. Further productions followed in the 1990s for which Smith provided the music, including tribute tours to Cole Porter (with Elaine Delmar and Paul Jones) and a celebration of George Gershwin's music.

SMITH, Malcolm Earle
trombone/composer/vocals

Born: North London, 20 July 1967

Trombone from age of nine. Taught by Dave Chandler, both at primary school and at William Ellis School, London. Studied at Exeter College (1985–8), obtained degree in Ancient History and Archaeology, gigged with local bands including the Storyville Jazz Band (based in Exmouth) and played in Exeter College Big Band. Returned to London and studied with Chris Pyne at the Guildhall School of Music (1988–9). With NYJO from December 1989 until December 1994. During this period deputized regularly in Richard Williams' Dix Six, and gigged with Jack Sharpe's

Big Band, Duncan Lamont's Big Band, Andrea Vicari, Suburban Gorillas, etc. Often worked with Enrico Tomasso, including long stint in the Fortis Green Jazz Band. Toured with Martha Reeves and the Vandellas in 1994. Teaches for Hertfordshire County Council and runs big band for Borough of Waltham Forest. During the mid-1990s often worked with Digby Fairweather, and led own quartet as well as freelancing in various big bands, including Vile Bodies. Continues to teach regularly, including summer courses at Wavendon and running jazz workshops.

SMITH, 'Miff'
trombone

Born: Pendleton, Lancashire, 1903

Gigged around Leeds during the early 1920s, then joined the Coney Island Band. Moved to London, worked with Hal Swain, Rag Batten, Alfredo and Jack Padbury before joining Lou Preager. Left Lou Preager to join Howard Jacobs (summer 1935). With Sydney Kyte (1937), then formed own band. Joined Henry Hall from 1938 to 1942, then did solo act on the music halls, which developed into a double act with Billy Shaw. Miff later worked in a duo with his wife (Marjorie Pointer), then quit music to run own camera shop.

SMITH, 'Ray' Raymond Leslie
piano/arranger

Born: Harrow, Middlesex, 19 February 1941

Younger brother of bassist Dick Smith (born Paddington, London, 2 September 1931), who worked with Ken Colyer, Chris Barber, etc. Lessons from Ray Foxley (1957–60). Joined Jimmy Lougher's Cannonball Jazz Band in 1958. With Steve Lane from 1962 until 1968. Worked with Mike Daniels, Colin Kingwell, the New Era Jazzband, Ken Sims, George Dawson, etc. With Brian Green's Band and subsequently with the London Rhythm Kings. Worked again with Steve Lane before joining Ken Colyer in 1974 (having guested with Colyer since 1968). With Dick Cook from 1977; founder-member of London Ragtime Orchestra (1978), also with Crane River Jazz Band in late 1970s. With Bill Brunskill (1980) and co-leading quintet with Sonny Morris (1980). Took lessons from American pianist Don Ewell in Florida (1981). Co-leader and arranger London Ragtime Orchestra from 1982. In the European Classic Jazzband from 1983 onwards, then (still working with Tomas Ornberg and Bent Persson) became part of the Swedish Jazz Kings in 1985. Continued to work occasionally with Ken Colyer in the early 1980s. With Rod Mason (1986–7). During the 1980s also guested with the Dave Mills-Alan Cooper British All Stars for work in the Middle East. Featured at Ascona Festival in Switzerland in 1988 and 1989, with Bob Wilber, Freddy Kohlman, Alyn Shipton, etc. Based in Holland during the 1990s, he continues to freelance with various jazz bands and to play solo dates.

SMITH, 'Terry' Terrence
guitar

Born: West Norwood, London, 20 May 1943

Guitar from the age of sixteen, played local gigs, then left London to work for six months in Doncaster with band led by trombonist Reg Brooks. Returned to London and played gigs at the Bull's Head, Barnes, then worked with Roy Budd, Trevor Tomkins and Tony Archer.Worked in Ronnie Scott's Big Band (1967) and toured with the Walker Brothers, then led band backing Walker Brothers, and Scott Walker, toured Japan, etc. Began long musical association with Mike

Carr during the late 1960s. Worked alongside Dick Morrissey in J.J. Jackson's Soul Band, and then formed quintet If with Morrissey, which lasted until 1973 (completing many tours of the USA). Worked in ZZebra until 1975, then moved to Sweden (as did Dick Morrissey) in 1975. Returned to London and co-led band with New Zealand tenor saxophonist Brian Smith during the late 1970s. During the 1960s, 1970s and 1980s accompanied many visiting American musicians and led own groups. Worked regularly with singer Jo Ann Kelly for several years in the 1980s. During the 1990s continues to freelance successfully, working often with Mike Carr, Tony Archer, Tony Lee, David Quincy, Don Weller, Pete King, etc.

SMITH, 'Tommy' Thomas
saxes/flute/arranger/composer

Born: Luton, Bedfordshire, 27 April 1967

Father played drums. Raised in Edinburgh: school in Wester Hailes. Did first gig at twelve, led own band at fourteen. Coached by Bobby Wishart. At fifteen toured in the European Community Jazz Orchestra. Featured on television at fifteen. Led own trio for German festival (1983), then toured Britain with the New York Jazz Quintet (summer 1983). Gained scholarship to Berklee School of Music in USA, began studying there in early 1984. While in America led International Quartet, played in Herb Pomeroy's Student Band. Formed own Forward Motion and worked in Gary Burton's Quintet. Settled back in Britain, led own groups and worked with John Taylor, Ian Froman, Chris Laurence, etc., and with Hue and Cry (1990). Studied composition in Paris. Soloist in saxophone concerto written for him by William Sweeny. Featured at many international festivals during the 1990s. Leading own touring sextet (1995–6), also appointed Director of Music at Scottish National Jazz Institute (in January 1996). Enjoying continued success with his own extended compositions.

SMUTS, 'Pat' Patrick
saxes/clarinet/flute

Born: Johannesburg, South Africa, 1913

His brother, saxophonist and violinist Martin Smuts, died in 1994. Played in various bands in South Africa, then came to England in band led by British comedian Charles Heslop. Did a season in Yorkshire with Heslop (1931), then moved to London. Toured with Billy Mason's Band accompanying Louis Armstrong in Britain (1932). Worked with drummer Sid Heiger's Trio at the Bag O'Nails (1933). With Ord Hamilton's Band (1934) and with Howard Jacobs at the Café Anglais, London, before working regularly with Nat Gonella from April 1935 until September 1939. With Harry Roy prior to joining the RAF. Played RAF Band during World War II, then joined the Skyrockets from late 1945 until late 1955. Thereafter freelanced in theatres, night clubs and hotels for many years.

SMYTHE, 'Pat' Patrick
piano/arranger/composer

Born: Edinburgh, Scotland, 2 May 1923
Died: London, 6 May 1983

Served in the RAF as a pilot, then took up law. Temporarily moved to London and worked in Dizzy Reece's Quartet (early 1958), then returned to Scotland to complete law studies and to become a practising solicitor. Soon moved back to London and became a professional musician, working with Joe Harriott (spring 1960), also played occasionally in Tubby Hayes' Quartet.

Worked often with Joe Harriott (including Indo-Fusion group) during period 1960 to 1966, but during these years also led own group at the Establishment Club, London (1961–2). Worked with Bobby Wellins and Annie Ross, acted as musical director for the revue *Looking for the Action* (1963), led own trio at Annie's Room, London (1965–6) and also led own radio bands. Worked in Peter King's Quartet (1968) and directed London Jazz Ensemble, also arranged for BBC Radio Big Band and for Danish Radio Big Band. Accompanied many American musicians including Stan Getz, Ben Webster, Sonny Stitt, Paul Gonsalves, Zoot Sims, etc., and singers Anita O'Day, Tony Bennett, Mark Murphy, etc. During the 1970s often worked with Kenny Wheeler, including being part of Coe, Wheeler and Co (Tony Coe and Kenny Wheeler) from April 1970, and being in Kenny Wheeler's Big Band. Worked with Ronnie Ross, Ronnie Scott, John Stevens, Tony Kinsey, John Dankworth, the Holdsworth-Warleigh Quintet, etc. Often worked as accompanist for Elaine Delmar during the 1970s and early 1980s, also worked with singer Sandra King during the last part of his life. In memory of Pat Smythe, an annual award scheme for the most promising young jazz musician was inaugurated in 1986; the scheme continued for ten years. In 1996, the Trust awarded the remaining funds to pianist Richard Fairhurst to help support his studies in New York.

SOUTH, 'Harry' Henry Percy
piano/composer/arranger

Born: Fulham, London, 7 September 1929
Died: London, 12 March 1990

Played piano from early teens, studied arranging and composing while spending a year in hospital. Worked in alto saxophonist Les Simons' Sextet and with Terry Brown's Band, then joined Basil Kirchin from September 1952 until January 1953. Led own trio and worked with Carole Fenton, Harry Klein and Johnny Rogers (1953), before rejoining Basil Kirchin from September 1953 until October 1954. Regularly arranged for Ronnie Scott's Band during this period. With Tubby Hayes from April 1955 until September 1956. With Bobby Breen, Vic Ash, Sandy Brown, Cab Kaye and Jack Sharpe, also toured with Maria Pavlou (early 1957) and did season in Lugano with Freddy Ballerini. Mainly with Joe Harriott from 1958 to 1960 (including residency in Germany). With Ronnie Ross-Bert Courtley Jazztet (April 1960 to February 1961), then played for West End show. Briefly with John Dankworth (late 1959 to early 1960s). Led own big band from 1960. To India (with Ashley Kozack and Dick Morrissey) in September 1961 for a year's residency in Calcutta. Returned to Britain, worked with Dick Morrissey from October 1962 until 1966. Continued to lead own big band, also worked occasionally with Joe Harriott in the late 1960s. Long-time musical director for Georgie Fame (from the mid-1960s), also composed and arranged for many artistes and various ensembles. Was Annie Ross's musical director for many years. Achieved considerable success writing for television and for films. Wrote *Portraits* suite (and many arrangements) for the National Youth Jazz Orchestra.

SOWANDE, Fela (Oluaw Fe Ola OSOWAMIDE)
piano/organ/composer

Born: Lagos, Nigeria, 1905

Attended Church School in Lagos, subsequently taught there. Was organist and choirmaster at Church of Christ in Lagos. Temporarily became a multi-instrumentalist and played local dance gigs, before moving to England in 1934. Played piano at the Florida Club, London (1934), then worked in John Hendricks' Hot Chocolates (1935). Studied with pianist Gerry Moore. Toured with visiting show from America (Lew Leslie's *Blackbirds*). Worked in Blue Caribbean Band (1937). Led own band to accompany Adelaide Hall at Florida Club (1938–9). Featured on many radio programmes as swing organist (1941–2). Joined RAF (1943), but was soon transferred to become musical adviser to the Colonial Film Unit. After World War II resumed work on BBC radio (including being musical director of the *Club Ebony* programmes, 1953), before being appointed musical director of the Nigerian Broadcasting Service. Moved to USA in 1957. Taught at Howard University, but was mainly active as a composer (conducted the New York Philharmonic in a concert of his compositions in 1962).

SOWDEN, 'Geoff' John Edwin Geoffrey   Born: Leeds, Yorkshire, 30 June 1924
trombone/vocals

First band was the Delta Dixielanders, then (while in the Army) guested with Frank Wilson's Band in Southport. After demobilization worked with Smoky City Stompers in Manchester and with Mick Gill in Nottingham. With the Yorkshire Jazz Band before leading own Happytime Jazz Band in Leeds (1949). With Freddy Randall from October 1949 until June 1951. With Joe Daniels from June 1951 until 1952. Gigged with Doctor Crock (Harry Hines). Formed own band in summer 1952 and continued to lead various line-ups through the 1950s. With Monty Sunshine (1961), Bobby Mickleburgh (1962). Briefly with Bob Wallis (1964) and Terry Lightfoot (1965). Thereafter ran own successful insurance business, but continued to play, and to organize student bands in the Essex area before moving to France. Played dates in France and in Spain during the mid-1990s. Not related to trumpeter Stan Sowden, who worked with Bobby Mickleburgh, Dave Keir, Mickey Ashman, Joe Daniels, Graham Stewart, Dave Mawson and Monty Sunshine, before emigrating to Australia.

SPEAKE, Martin John   Born: Barnet, Hertfordshire, 3 April 1958
alto sax

Started playing alto sax at sixteen. Studied music at Southgate Techical College, then became pupil of Chris Gradwell at Trinity College of Music (1977–81). Attended various jazz summer schools. First gigs with Simon Purcell (during the early 1980s). Left college and played briefly for Royal Shakespeare Company's *Troilus and Cressida*, then became part of saxophone quartet Itchy Fingers which did extensive international touring. Participated in Loose Tubes, the Sabri Ensemble, the Style Council, etc., and worked with Django Bates, Jim Mullen, John Williams, Clark Tracey, Tim Wells, Ann Pigalle, Don Weller, etc. Led own group (John Parricelli, Steve Watts and Steve Argüelles) which did extensive touring in the 1990s, also led own seven piece Fever Pitch as well as being part of a duo with guitarist Phil Lee. In addition, also performs in trio with North Indian musicians Dharambir Singh and Sukhvinder Singh. Teaches at Royal Academy of Music and at Middlesex University. During the 1990s studied at the Banff Centre in Canada with Steve Coleman.

SPRING, Bryan   Born: London, 24 August 1945
drums

Played drums from age of six. Worked with various Stan Tracey line-ups from 1965 until 1977.

During this period also worked with Frank Ricotti (1967–9), John Williams' Octet (1969), Joe Harriott (1969), Tubby Hayes, etc. Was in Bebop Preservation Society 1971 to autumn 1972. With Klaus Dollinger's Passport. Worked in Germany (1972), with Ian Carr's Nucleus (1974), Keith Tippett's Centipede, Dick Heckstall-Smith's Quartet (1976), etc. Accompanied various American musicians including Charlie Shavers, George Coleman, Charlie Rouse, etc. Led own bands and taught regularly from the mid-1970s. Occasionally with Dick Morrissey-Terry Smith (1975) and with Bobby Wellins (1979), but from the mid-1970s worked regularly in quartet co-led with Don Weller, which continued into the early 1990s. With Alan Skidmore's Quartet from 1992. Leading own quartet and own trio in the mid-1990s.

STANTON, 'Bernie' Bernard
Born: Clapton, East London, 13 July 1923
clarinet/alto sax

His son Scott is a tenor saxophonist. Violin and piano during childhood, then took up clarinet as a teenager. Served in Army from 1942 to 1945, played violin and clarinet in service bands. After demobilization began playing alto sax. First professional work with Peggy Poulton's Band on Brighton Pier (1949). Led own band at Locarno Ballroom, Dundee, for nine months in 1950. With Freddy Randall (January to August 1951). Led own band, then worked with Nat Gonella (October to November 1951). Briefly with Harry Hayes, Neville Bishop, Arthur Coppersmith (1952), then played aboard liner *Mauretania* (January to April 1953). With Joe Daniels (May 1953), then did USO tour of Germany with own band (1953). Worked in Paris and Rome with Bernard Hilda (1954). Led own band at Don Juan Club, London, from 1954 until 1960. Led at Columbia Club, London, then formed own Jazz Professors for September 1961 debut. Disbanded after six months and resumed leading at various London night clubs: Milroy's, Les Ambassadeurs, Rheingold, etc. Also wrote words and music for the show *I'm No Millionaire*. Quit full time music and was then forced by ill health temporarily to give up playing, but resumed freelancing schedule in the late 1980s.

STAUNTON, 'Chris' Christopher
Born: Wood Green, London, 7 November 1928
double bass

Played regularly on Cunard liners in Desmond Jack's Quartet (1952–4), then spent three months with Norman Burns (1954). Worked on P&O liners, then joined Alex Welsh (1955). To Australia with Donald Purchese Quartet, then rejoined Alex Welsh (1956). Summer season in Monte Carlo with Donald Purchese then again rejoined Alex Welsh until late summer 1958. Worked in Tommy Whittle's Big Band (1959) and in Arnold Bailey's Band (1959–60). With Art Ellefson-Johnny Scott group (1960), duos with Eddie Thompson, and in Ronnie Ross' Quartet (1961–2). Three months with John Dankworth in 1963. Regularly in London Studio Players for five years in the 1960s. Moved to Birmingham, worked in Midland Light Orchestra, then joined City of Birmingham Symphony Orchestra from 1973 until 1994. During this period also did freelance jazz work, including working in Val Wiseman's Quintet and accompanying visiting musicians. Continues to play regularly.

STENFALT, Norman Vivian
piano/arranger

Born: Ilford, Essex, 20 February 1922
Died: 24 November 1991

First professional work was with Alan Green's Band in 1938, later worked with Teddy Foster and in house band at the Palais Ritz in Manchester before joining Nat Gonella (1940–1). Briefly with Johnny Claes, and Frank Weir (late 1941), then called up for service in the RAF. Played in RAF Northolt Band, was featured in service show *This Is the Gen*, arranged for this production and began arranging for Geraldo. Guested with Harry Hayes' Band. Left the RAF in summer of 1945, guested with Ted Heath's Band and worked regularly with Harry Hayes (1945–6), then joined Ted Heath from spring of 1946 until November 1948, wrote many arrangements for the band. With Ambrose from late 1948, worked intermittently with this leader until summer of 1951, also worked in duo with Kenny Baker for a London production of *A Streetcar Named Desire*. Again with Frank Weir (late 1951–2). With Ronnie Scott for a year from January 1953. With Frank King's Quintet and Dave Shand's Band (1954), then spent a year with Jack Parnell before rejoining Ronnie Scott (summer 1955–6). Often with Kenny Baker's Dozen in the 1950s. Spent many years with Jack Parnell from early 1957. During his latter years he arranged for many bands, and also played in Ted Heath recreation bands organized by Don Lusher.

STEPHENSON, Louis George Alexander
saxes/double bass/vocals

Born: St Ann's Parish, Jamaica, West Indies,
2 June 1907
Died: London, 3 February 1994

To Britain in 1924 as a clarinettist with the West Indies Regiment. Played at British Empire Exhibition at Wembley, then returned to Kingston, Jamaica, to play local gigs. Worked as a steward on cruise liners, then moved to London (arriving 19 November 1935). Briefly with Happy Blake and with Leslie Thompson before working in Ken Johnson's Orchestra (1936). Played in Europe with Benny Carter and Eddie South (1937). Returned to England, worked with Fela Sowande and Don Marino Barretto during the 1930s. Service in the RAF during World War II then joined Cyril Blake's Knights of Rhythm (late 1945). Doubling double bass and sax by this time. Worked with Leslie 'Jiver' Hutchinson (1946), Clinton Maxwell (1947) and again with Cyril Blake (1948), before touring Europe with American cornetist Rex Stewart (1948). Returned to Britain, did freelance work with Robert Farnon, Sid Phillips, etc., also was part of a vocal trio with Lauderic Caton until retiring from full time music in 1952.

STEPHENSON, Ronnie
drums

Born: Sunderland, Co. Durham, 26 January 1937

Elder brother, Billy, a pianist and bandleader; another brother, Bob, is also a pianist. Began playing drums in early teens and gigged in brother Billy's band. Worked professionally in Sunderland with Ray Chester's Sextet, in Pat Rose's Band and (in Edgbaston) with Cliff Deeley, then toured for ten months with singer Lita Roza. Served in Army (Royal Signals Band) from 1955 to 1957. After demobilization worked in Aberdeen with Les Thorpe. Gigged in London clubs, then joined Don Smith in Luton (January 1958). Worked in Newcastle upon Tyne with Don Smith for two years (during this period also played in the Em Cee Five). With John Dankworth from September 1960 until February 1963, then worked in Stan Tracey's Trio and accompanied many visiting musicians at Ronnie Scott's Club. Worked in Jack Parnell's TV Orchestra. During the 1960s also worked with Ronnie Scott, Tubby Hayes, John Dankworth (again) and did a widespread variety of freelance work. After touring Germany with singer Tom Jones, decided to move there and worked with Kurt Edelhagen, Paul John, Rolf Kühn, Francy Boland, etc., and taught at the University of Berlin. Occasionally returns to Britain, played dates in England with Mike Carr's Quartet during one trip in the early 1990s.

STEVENS, 'Dave' David Spenser
piano

Born: Leicester, 26 July 1925

First gigs with John Haim's Jelly Roll Kings (1948–9), then worked in Beryl Bryden's Backroom Boys (1949–50). With Dick Hawdon's Band, then joined Mick Mulligan (1951), gigged with many bands during the 1950s, and worked regularly with Sandy Brown's Band in 1956. With Alexis Korner's Blues Incorporated during the early 1960s, and with singer-clarinettist Eric Lister before emigrating to Australia in 1964. Continues to play regularly with many bands of various styles and toured Britain and the USA with Australian band, the New Wolverines, in 1993.

STEVENS, John William
drums/percussion/trumpet/composer

Born: Brentford, Middlesex, 10 June 1940
Died: Ealing, London, 13 September 1994

Father was a tap dancer. John's son Richard (born 1962) is a drummer. Began on brushes and biscuit tin. Took up drums at fifteen. Worked in an engineering factory but sat in at pubs around the Brentford area. Joined RAF as a musician and served for five years. Studied at RAF School of Music, Uxbridge, Middlesex, was stationed for a while at Weston-super-Mare, but spent most of his service playing in the RAF Regional Band based in Cologne, Germany. During his time in the RAF he played alongside Paul Rutherford, Trevor Watts and Chris Pyne. After demobilization played and sang in the Don Riddell Four, and worked in Pete Lemer's Trio (1965–6), also worked with Brian Dee, Tubby Hayes, Harry Klein, Ian Carr, etc, and as a house musician at Ronnie Scott's Club, London. Led own septet from late 1965. From January 1966 devoted a great deal of time to organizing the Spontaneous Music Ensemble (with Trevor Watts) at London's Little Theatre Club. He continued to be the driving force for this enterprise for over two decades. Played in Denmark and Holland in autumn 1966, then returned to London and resumed SME activities in early 1967. Began long musical association with Stan Tracey in the late 1960s, subsequently worked in various of Tracey's line-ups including Tentacles and Open Circle. In duos with Trevor Watts, and trios with Watts and bassist Mbizo 'Johnny' Dyani in the late 1960s and 1970s, also part of Trevor Watts' Amalgam from 1970. Worked with Evan Parker, and with Bob Downes. Co-led (with Phil Seamen) Splinters group (from 1971). Own Spontaneous Music Orchestra (from 1970), own Dance Orchestra (from 1974), own Away (from 1975). Also led own Freebop and Folkus groups into the late 1980s. Began playing trumpet in the mid-1970s. During the 1970s toured with various visiting American musicians including trumpeter Bobby Bradford, saxophonists John Tchicai and Steve Lacy, etc. With Frode Gjerstad in Detail, with bassist Nick Stephens. With Charlie Watts' Big Band (1985–6). Featured at various international festivals in the late 1980s and early 1990s, increasingly active as a composer (one of his latter works was *Celebration with Voices*). Was musical director of the Jazz Centre Society's Outreach Community

Music Project until 1983, then organized the Therapeutic Community Music Limited. Was consistently successful as a teacher of percussion. Active in jazz education over a number of years, he ran Ealing College workshops from the early 1970s. Died suddenly from a heart attack.

STEVENSON, 'Nick' Nicholas Andrew　　　　　　　Born: Bushey, Hertfordshire, 5 May 1946
trumpet

Began on bugle in School CCF Band, then took up trumpet. Led own band and played in the New Jungle Orchestra before taking over leadership (from Don Cummings) of the New State Jazzband in 1966. During the late 1960s worked with Dave Jones' Band, with Monty Sunshine, and with Ian Armit at the Georgian Club, London. With Ken Mackintosh in 1970, then briefly with Bill Niles. Worked on cruise liners for six months with Lennie Felix (1972) and with Freddy Ballerini at the Embassy Club, London. Regularly in Brian White's Magna Band, also spent a year at the Theatre Royal Stratford East in Ian Armit's Trio. Period of freelancing in the mid-1970s, regular gigs with Charlie Galbraith. Founder-member of the Midnite Follies Orchestra from their January 1978 debut, continued with them through the 1980s and into the early 1990s. During the 1980s and 1990s often in Keith Nichols' Ragtime Orchestra and regularly with Harry Gold from August 1987 into the 1990s. Worked with the Colville Collection during the mid-1990s.

STEWART, 'Graham' Ian Graham　　　　　　　　　　　Born: 1933
trombone

First became interested in jazz while at Whitgift School, Croydon. Took up trombone. Served in the RAF, then formed own band (1952). With Eric Silk from September 1953 until April 1955, with Cy Laurie from April 1955 until June 1956. To Poland with Dave Burman's Band in summer of 1956. Formed own band again in 1957, which played in Poland, Hungary and Germany during the late 1950s and toured Britain. With Ken Colyer from 1961 until 1965. Freelanced in London, then emigrated to the USA in the late 1960s. Worked in pharmaceutical publishing but also led own band in New York from the 1970s, playing club residencies and working with Tony Parenti, Max Kaminsky, Bob Greene, Tommy Sancton, etc. Sat in with various bands during his occasional returns to Britain, including February 1996 visit to London.

STEWART, Louis　　　　　　　　　　Born: Waterford, Ireland, 5 January 1944
guitar/composer

Raised in Dublin. Piano as a child, guitar from fifteen. Played in various show bands, then worked regularly with reed-player Jim Doherty's group including 1961 tour of USA. Gained individual award at Montreux Jazz Festival. Worked with pianist Noel Kelahan's Trio and in trio with organist Dick Keating and Irish-American saxist Jim O'Reilly (1967). Moved to London in 1968, worked in Tubby Hayes' Quartet and Big Band (1968–9), also briefly in London Palladium Orchestra (1968). Did three tours of Europe with Benny Goodman, beginning in 1969. Made Dublin his base during the early 1970s, freelanced and did extensive composing. Returned to London to work regularly with Ronnie Scott from July 1975 through to 1979, also active in duo with Peter Ind from mid-1978. Occasionally played in Harry South's Big Band. During the late 1970s began long musical association with George Shearing and did widespread touring with him including trip to South America. Toured Australia with Blossom Dearie and Don Burrows (1979). Worked with Scandinavian pianist Per Husby. Worked with various line-ups in the USA (1981). Often with Stephane Grappelli in the mid-1980s, but mainly active as a successful international freelance, using Dublin as his base. Guested with the Norwegian All Stars (1988), led own trio and own quartet in Britain and at many international festivals during the 1980s and 1990s. Guested with George Shearing (1995); continues to play regularly.

STOBART, 'Kathy' Florence Kathleen   Born: South Shields, Co. Durham, 1 April 1925
tenor, baritone, soprano saxes/clarinet/flute

Her sons Paul (bass guitar) and Peter (saxes/keyboards) are semi-professional musicians; her eldest son David is not a musician. Mother a pianist, two brothers played sax. Took up alto sax at twelve, joined Don Rico's Ladies' Swing Band (on tenor) at fourteen, did national touring in various shows, then returned home and worked with Peter Fielding's Band in Newcastle for eight months. Moved to London in late 1942, took Keith Bird's place in quartet in Ealing and doubled engagements by also working with Denis Rose's Band at the Jamboree Club in central London. Joined Canadian pianist Art Thompson's Band at Embassy Club, London (February 1943); subsequently married Thompson. Did broadcasts with Eric Robinson's AEF Orchestra in World War II. Regularly with Art Thompson's Band until joining Vic Lewis in spring 1947, soon rejoined Art Thompson and journeyed with him to Canada and the USA (summer 1947). Sat in at Eddie Condon's Club. With Thompson played brief season in Palm Springs, California, before returning to Britain in May 1948. Worked with Thompson in London, then worked as a soloist in Sweden (September 1948). With Vic Lewis again from spring 1949 (including Paris Jazz Festival) then guested in Holland (with Ken Thorne on piano) in early 1950. During the 1940s and 1950s occasionally deputized with Geraldo and Lou Preager, was featured on Ted Heath's Sunday Palladium concerts, and appeared in Sid Gross' jazz concerts. Disbanded own group in spring 1951 and again worked with Vic Lewis. Having divorced Art Thompson, married trumpeter Bert Courtley (24 October 1951). Gigged with Johnny Rogers (summer 1953), then curtailed working schedule to raise family, but continued to play gigs including spell with Jack Fallon (1954–5). Deputized for Jimmy Skidmore in Humphrey Lyttelton's Band from late 1957 until 1958, worked with Tony Kinsey (1959) and in Eddie Thompson's Quintet (1960). Occasionally deputized in various bands (including Blanche Coleman's), and briefly fronted Gracie Cole's Band. Worked at Orchid Ballroom, Purley (spring 1961), then became part of newly formed Bert Courtley Sextet (from April 1961). Worked with this sextet until Bert joined Ted Heath. Formed own group, and also co-led with Bert until his final illness. Studied clarinet at Guildhall School of Music, worked in quintet with John Picard in the late 1960s and early 1970s. Led own quintet and worked regularly with Humphrey Lyttelton from late 1969 until 1978. Taught at the City Literary Institute for nineteen years during the 1960s and 1970s. Occasionally played on Mediterranean cruises and continued to guest with Humphrey Lyttelton in the 1980s, also led own quintet (featuring Fiachra Trench on keyboards) and own sextet. Worked in group co-led with vibraphonist Lennie Best for several years from 1979. Led own student band in Exeter. Own group through the 1980s, guested with Gail Thompson's Gail Force (1986). Co-led quintet with saxophonist Joan Cunningham in the late 1980s and early 1990s. Rejoined Humphrey Lyttelton in spring 1991, and continued to work regularly with him through the 1990s.

STOCK, 'Tiny' Harold Walter Richard
double bass/tuba

Born: *c.*1900
Died: 1935

Served as an Army musician, playing tuba and cello. Tuba with George Bass' Stage Band, then switched to double bass to join Arthur Hetherington in Edinburgh. Played in house band at Wimbledon Palais, then joined Fred Elizalde. With Carroll Gibbons, then rejoined Elizalde in 1929. With Arthur Lally (1930), Maurice Winnick (1932) and the Blue Lyres (1933), before working with Jack Jackson from August 1933 until being taken ill in early 1935. Rejoined Jackson in April 1935 but was forced to leave, suffering from what proved to be a fatal illness.

STOKES, 'Sammy' Albert George William Henry
double bass/guitar/vocals

Born: Gosport, Hampshire, 14 July 1917

Played clarinet in Royal Scots Band and studied at Kneller Hall. Served in World War II and was taken prisoner-of-war. Played clarinet and tenor sax in Stalag VIII B Band, then lost embouchure and became the band's singer. Was repatriated in late 1943, sang on broadcasts with the band, then rejoined his regiment in Edinburgh and took up the double bass. Played under Tommy Sampson in the Scottish Command Band (1945). After demobilization became part of Sampson's newly formed civilian band (1947). Worked with Dennis Hale in Brighton (1948–9) and did a few jobs with Tommy Sampson early in 1949 (mainly on the South Coast). Worked with Paul Fenoulhet (1949), then joined Ted Heath from September 1949 to spring 1951. With Jack Parnell (1951–3). With Tony Kinsey's Trio (1953–5), in New Jazz Quartet (1955), then joined Allan Ganley's Trio (1957). With Oscar Rabin at Wimbledon Palais (1958–60). Freelanced in the 1960s, played Hilton Hotel, London, residency with Judd Solo and then worked in Maurice Smart's Band. Moved back to Gosport in 1980, gave up playing double bass but continued to teach classical guitar through the 1990s.

STONE, 'Lew' Lewis
piano/arranger/composer

Born: Stepney, London, 28 May 1898
Died: London, 12 February 1969

Uncle of trumpeter Leslie Stone. Piano from age of thirteen, played local gigs but did various day jobs (including working in father's timber yard) until turning professional by joining the London Aeolian Band (in Newcastle) during the summer of 1925. Played in London and Margate, then took own band to Holland and Hungary. With Bert Ralton and his Havana Band; began regular arranging from 1927. With Jean Pougnet's Green Park Hotel Orchestra (1928). Joined Ambrose as staff arranger and relief pianist (1928–31), also brief return to Jean Pougnet (1930). From 1931 to 1934 was musical director of British and Dominion Films, conducted, composed and arranged film scores; also did prolific freelance arranging for Ray Starita, Jack Payne, Jay Whidden, etc. Led own recording band. Played with (and arranged for) Roy Fox and his Monseigneur Band (1931) and fronted during Fox's illness. Fox returned briefly, but from October 1932 Stone was appointed leader of the band (which achieved great success on the radio). Left this residency in 1934, toured, did film work, and led for various night club residencies: Hollywood Restaurant (1934); Café de Paris (1936–7, and 1938); El Morocco (1939), as well as acting as musical director for several West End shows. Led own band at Dorchester Hotel (mainly on Novachord) from summer of 1940 until summer of 1942. Played many concerts for troops (1942–5) and also toured variety halls (1943–4). With Novatones at Embassy Club (1945–7), but also led big band for radio work and specific bookings from 1948 until the end of the 1950s. Musical director for *Annie Get Your Gun* (1947–9). Musical director of Pigalle Restaurant (1951–5), Oddenino's (1953–5) and La Romanza (1955). Led at various Mecca venues in Glasgow, Leeds and Manchester (1956–8). Opened own theatrical agency in 1959. Led own sextet (mainly for radio work) from 1959 until 1967, despite suffering severe illness in 1964. Occasional freelance engagements in late 1950s and early 1960s. Wrote *Harmony and Orchestration for the Modern Dance Band* (first published in 1935, revised edition 1944). *Lew Stone–A Career in Music* by Kenith Trodd was published in 1971.

STRANGE, 'Pete' Peter Charles
trombone/arranger/composer

Born: Plaistow, London, 19 December 1938

Played violin as a child, then took up trombone. Gigged in local jazz bands in the East London area, then worked briefly in band led by Tony Ramm (Tony Raine) in 1955. With Eric Silk (1956) and Teddy Layton (1957–8). Two years in the Army (1958–60), served in Cyprus, played in military band. Demobilized in June 1960, joined Sonny Morris. With Charlie Gall (early 1961), then joined Ken Sims' Vintage Jazz Band from February to July 1961. With Bruce Turner's Jump Band from August 1961 to 1964. Gigged with Johnny Armatage's Band. Occasionally deputized in Mick Mulligan's Band and also accompanied visiting American musicians. Left full time music temporarily but continued to play regularly for various leaders including Freddy Randall, Joe Daniels, and Ron Russell, also worked with Nick Stevenson in the New State Jazz Band. During the 1970s worked with Bruce Turner Reunion Band, in Swingtet co-led with trumpeter Clive Peerless, with Lennie Hastings, Digby Fairweather and again with Ron Russell (including trip to Czechoslovakia). Resumed full time playing and worked with Alan Elsdon from the mid-1970s, also founder member of the Midnite Follies Orchestra (from January 1978). Founder of Five-a-Slide in September 1980. Began long musical association with Humphrey Lyttelton in March 1983, but continued to play freelance gigs and occasional to co-lead with Clive Peerless, and be part of Slide by Slide (with Ray Wordsworth). Together with Digby Fairweather formed the Great British Jazz Band in 1994. Continues to work regularly (and arrange) for Humphrey Lyttelton (1996), also does freelance arranging including scoring for Val Wiseman's *Lady Sings the Blues* show.

STRETTON, Gordon (William MASTERS)
drums/vocals

Born: Liverpool, Lancashire, 5 June 1887
Deceased

Was part of the Eight Lancashire Lads (a clog-dancing act) from 1896 until 1904, then toured Britain with the Jamaican Choral Union from 1906 until 1908. Toured variety halls as a vocalist from 1911 until 1915. Worked in various shows before playing drums in W.H. 'Billy' Dorsey's Band *c*.1917. Became leader in 1919 when Dorsey fell ill. Led band at Rector's Club, London, and at Grafton Galleries, then worked in Brussels and Paris (where his Syncopated Six recorded in 1923) before settling in Argentina.

STRINGLE, Julian Marc
clarinet/saxes/flute/piano/composer/arranger

Born: Marlow, Buckinghamshire,
13 June 1967

Educated Latymer Music School and at London College of Music, where he studied clarinet with Wilf Keeley, and composition with William Lloyd Webber. At twelve formed teenage Dixieland Band 'Young Jazz', made television debut at fourteen duetting with Acker Bilk. Turned professional after graduation from college. Toured Europe with own quintet. Returned to Britain, did freelance session work, playing on various albums with Boy George, Marc Almond, Rupert Parker, etc. Wrote scores for television and films and composed many successful advertising jingles. Accompanied various visiting American musicians. From the mid-1990s worked often with Digby Fairweather, and occasionally in Muggsy Revisited. Led own successful small group and toured with a Latin Jazz Quintet featuring pianist Gareth Williams, guitarist Dominic Ashworth, bassist Rufus Philpot and drummer Ian Thomas. Secured own recording contract (1996).

SULZMANN, 'Stan' Stanley
saxes/clarinet/flute/arranger/composer

Born: London, 30 November 1948

Worked with Chessmen at Wimbledon Palais, then joined National Youth Jazz Orchestra in 1964. Worked on liner *Queen Mary* before studying at Royal Academy of Music. Worked with Graham Collier from 1968. With Jack Walker's Opera House Orchestra in Manchester, accompanying Frankie Vaughan (early 1969). During the late 1960s and 1970s worked with many groups including John Warren's Big Band, various John Taylor line-ups, with Alan Cohen, Kenny Wheeler, Mike Gibbs, Brian Cooper, Gordon Beck, John Dankworth, Henry Lowther, the London Jazz Orchestra, the Kenny Clarke-Francy Boland Big Band, own quartet, etc. During the 1980s and 1990s continued widespread freelancing including touring with Gil Evans, playing in duos with John Taylor, working in Kenny Wheeler's Big Band, with the London Jazz Orchestra. During the mid-1990s with Simon Purcell's Quintet, with Geoff Castle, with pianist Steve Plews, Allan Botschinsky's Quintet in Denmark, in flautist Eddie Parker's Sextet and leading own groups, etc.

SUNSHINE, Monty
clarinet

Born: Stepney, London, 8 April 1928

Father was a violinist (and tailor). Played flute as a child. Was evacuated with his school to Northampton, returned to London and studied at the Camberwell School of Art. Served in the RAF (1946–50). During this period took up clarinet and while stationed at RAF Wroughton played in the Eager Beavers (led by trumpeter Les Condon). After demobilization rehearsed with Ken Colyer and Sonny Morris in Cranford and became part of the Crane River Jazz Band. Played in quintet with Chris Barber in late 1952 and early 1953, then became part of the newly formed Ken Colyer Band (spring 1953). Remained with this group after Ken Colyer departed in 1954 and thus became part of the new Chris Barber Band. Left Chris Barber in December 1960, formed own band which made debut in March 1961. Has continued to lead own successful band ever since, through the 1990s. Many guest star appearances overseas with various bands, including stint in Australia with Graeme Bell's Band. Widespread international touring, also featured in Chris Barber Band reunions from the 1970s through the 1990s, and in Crane River Jazz Band reunions.

SURMAN, John Douglas

Born: Tavistock, Devon, 30 August 1944

baritone sax/soprano sax/bass clarinet/
synthesizer/composer

Grew up in Plymouth. Clarinet from age of fourteen, took up baritone sax while at Devonport High School. Joined band organized by Mike Westbrook at Plymouth College of Art (1961). Left Plymouth and studied at London College of Music (1962–5), and at University of London Institute of Education (1965–6). Continued to work in various Mike Westbrook line-ups until 1968, also gigged in Pete Lemer's Quintet (1966) and with Humphrey Lyttelton and Eddie Harvey. Regularly with Humphrey Lyttelton (including Big Band) in 1968, briefly with Russ Henderson's Calypso Band (1968), with Ronnie Scott's Octet (1968). Own octet debut in late 1968. With Maynard Ferguson (early 1969), during the late 1960s also worked with Graham Collier, Dave Holland, Mike Gibbs, John McLaughlin, etc. Lived in Belgium from September 1969, moved back to Britain in 1970. Toured with Francy Boland Big Band (1970) and worked in Brotherhood of Breath. With The Trio (bassist Barre Phillips and drummer Stu Martin) from 1969–72, also worked with Mick Pyne (1971). With SOS (Surman, Mike Osborne and Alan Skidmore) from October 1973 for two years (UK debut in April 1974). Worked with Carolyn Carlson Dance Company in Europe. Formed Mumps (with Phillips, Martin and German trombonist Albert Mangelsdorff). During the late 1970s began long association with Norwegian vocaliste Karin Krog, also did solo gigs and worked with Miroslav Vitous, Albert Mangelsdorff, John Taylor, Tony Oxley, Jack DeJohnette, and in quartets with Paul Bley, Bill Frisell and Paul Motian. Worked on several occasions with Gil Evans during the 1980s, also with Mike Osborne Septet (1981), Barry Altschul Quartet (1983), Graham Collier, Paul Bley, etc. Led own quartet (John Taylor, Chris Laurence and John Marshall) during the 1980s and 1990s, also own Brass Project (co-led with John Warren) through to the mid-1990s. With Ian Carr's Orchestra UK (1989) and duo with Jack DeJohnette, duos with Karin Krog and John Taylor into the mid-1990s. Continues to compose for contemporary dance field, including writing for Sadler's Wells Royal Ballet. Writes for film and television and for Norwegian and German radio orchestras. Continues to tour internationally as a soloist and with own line-ups (quartet, Brass Project, band) through the 1990s. Guested with Inclassificable in London (May 1996).

SUTCLIFFE, 'Bill' William J.

Born: c.1930

double bass/piano/trombone/vocals/
arranger/composer

With Leslie Thorpe's Band at Beach Ballroom, Aberdeen (1950–1), then joined Johnny Swinfen in Norwich (summer 1951). Left Swinfen to work aboard liner *Caronia*, then joined Hector Davies in Scunthorpe (December 1951). With Arthur Rowberry on tour (December 1951 to February 1952). Moved to London and freelanced, toured with Mary Lou Williams (March 1953). After summer season in Yarmouth with Freddy Courtenay (1953), worked briefly with Kenny Graham, Roy Fox, and Maurice Smart (1953). With Vic Ash, Maurice Smart and Sid Wright (1954), then regularly with John Dankworth from December 1954 until July 1956, during this period also did freelance recordings and worked on television with Dave Lee. With Basil Kirchin (1957), then led own group. With Vic Ash (1959), with Dill Jones (1960–1), and Don Rendell (1961). Freelanced successfully during the 1960s. Left Britain in 1967. Worked in Miami, Florida, and in the Bahamas, then toured USA with Billy Maxted and other jazz groups. Worked in Japan, then as 'Billy Anthony' led own group in the USA (doubling trombone), before moving to Spain where he specializes on piano during the 1990s.

SWIFT, Duncan
piano/trombone

Born: Rotherham, Yorkshire, 21 February 1943
Died: Bewdley, Worcestershire, 8 August 1997

Piano from early childhood. Played local gigs from age of fourteen, subsequently with the Jazz Hounds in Rotherham and with Mike Taylor's Jazz Band, then took up trombone. Moved with family to the Midlands in 1960, played trombone in Blue Blood Jazzmen (1961) and with Jim Simpson's Band (1961–2), then worked on piano in Bill Nile's Jazz Band. Gained degree at Birmingham School of Music (and Royal Academy of Music diplomas). Taught music in schools from 1968 until spring 1978. During this period played trombone in Alan King's Orchestra (1972) and in Perdido Street Jazzmen. Formed New Delta Jazzmen in summer of 1974 and worked regularly in this band until late 1977. Often worked with Kenny Ball (on piano) from end of 1977 until spring 1978, then joined that band full time from April 1979 until October 1983. Ran public house at Bewdley, Worcestershire, from November 1983 until April 1987, then resumed full time playing. Worked with Pete Allen from early 1988 until September 1989, left to follow solo piano career. Occasionally played trombone in the early 1990s (including appearances with King Pleasure), but enjoyed considerable success as a solo pianist, playing at many festivals. Also appeared with Paul Munnery's Harlem and with Harlem Hot Five in 1993, then from December 1993 was featured with John Petters in various touring shows but continued to fulfil solo engagements despite health problems.

T

TALBOT, 'Jamie' James Robert
saxes/clarinet

Born: South East London, 23 April 1960

Started playing music at the age of ten while a pupil of Kingsdale Comprehensive School. As a schoolboy played in the London Schools Symphony Orchestra and the National Youth Jazz Orchestra. After leaving school studied briefly at the Royal College of Music. Turned professional at nineteen. Did first solo album in 1985, by that time had worked with John Dankworth and Cleo Laine. With Clark Tracey's Band from September 1986, also with Stan Tracey, Jack Sharpe, Geoff Castle, etc., and with visiting Americans Shorty Rogers, Bud Shank, Mel Tormé and Gil Evans. Concerts and tours with Frank Sinatra, Natalie Cole, Aretha Franklin, Ella Fitzgerald, etc. Guest soloist with the Metropole Orchestra, in Hilversum, Netherlands. Prolific freelance work throughout the 1990s, including leading own quartet.

TANN, Eric
trombone/arranger

Born: East Ham, London, 15 November 1911
Died: Queensland, Australia, 1988

Brother of tenor saxophonist Ernie Tann. Did first professional work at Birmingham Palais, then moved back to London and joined Hal Swain (1928). Worked with Savoy Hotel Orpheans, Bennie Loban, Sydney Kyte and Arthur Rosebery. With Roy Fox (1932–4). Briefly with Alfred Myerscough's Band before joining Henry Hall in November 1934. Played regularly in Louis Levy's Orchestra for film work from the mid-1930s. With Jack Jackson (1934–5), Ambrose (1935) and with Jack Harris and Eddie Carroll's Band (autumn 1938), before working with Lew Stone (1939–40). Joined Royal Army Ordnance Corps (1940) and played in regimental band before becoming leader of its dance band the Blue Rockets in 1941. Injured in 1942 and discharged from Army in spring 1943. With Geraldo (autumn 1943 to January 1945). With Mantovani, then formed own band (March 1945). With Harry Roy (spring 1946), then worked as musical director for an Australian radio station and led own band before returning to Britain in summer 1949. Freelanced on sessions and worked with George Melachrino and Cyril Ornadel in the 1950s but gave up regular playing in 1960 to work as a conductor and arranger. Became musical director for the Moss Empires theatre chain. Left Britain in 1976 and settled in Australia, where he taught brass players until failing health caused retirement.

TAYLOR, 'Eddie' Edmund
drums

Born: Oldham, Lancashire, 12 February 1929

Toured Scandinavia with the Royal Kiltie Juniors (spring 1947). Did two years' service in the RAF (1947–9), then immediately on demobilization joined Leslie Douglas in Birmingham. With Vincent Ladbrooke's Band for Isle of Man season (summer 1950), then worked with Leslie Douglas in Brighton (winter 1950–1). With Rae Allen at New State Ballroom, Blackley (1951), then joined John Dankworth Seven from July 1951 to July 1953. With H. Jefferson Jones aboard liner *Queen Mary* on transatlantic run (from August 1953), also did gigs with Bert Courtley in London (December 1953). With Tommy Whittle from spring 1954 until September 1956, also gigged with Dill Jones Trio in summer 1956. Worked regularly with Humphrey Lyttelton from October 1956 until autumn 1964. Worked with Long John Baldry, with Ray Ellington and freelanced. Did Mediterranean cruise with Lennie Felix (1966). Worked at Mandrake Club, London, with Joe Burns and Ronnie Selby. During the 1950s and 1960s did many freelance recordings, with Cyril Stapleton, Ivor Mairants, Dill Jones, Kenny Baker, etc., also did many freelance radio dates. With Harry Roy Quartet for *Oh Clarence* show (early 1969), other theatre work including playing for *I Do, I Do* featuring Ian Carmichael. Played for London production of *Oh Calcutta!* from 1970 until 1980. During this period doubled by working with Olav Vass at Tiberio's, London. During the 1980s did several summer seasons in Munich, Germany (with Denny Ilett, Alan Littlejohns, Neil Millett and Dick Charlesworth). During the late 1980s worked in Bruce Turner's Quartet and in Val Wiseman's *Lady Sings the Blues* show (until 1990). Gigged with the Georgia Jazz Band through the 1980s. Joined John Chilton's Feetwarmers (accompanying George Melly) in March 1990 and remained through the 1990s.

TAYLOR, 'Geoff' Geoffrey Harold
alto sax/clarinet

Born: Stratford, London, 6 May 1929

Clarinet at thirteen, alto sax at sixteen. Gigged around the Seven Kings area and sat in at various jazz clubs. Won *Melody Maker* individual award at contest and turned professional, joining Roy Fox in June 1952. Later worked with Basil and Ivor Kirchin, and with Oscar Rabin and Denny Boyce. Led own successful Earl Bostic-styled group in the 1950s and 1960s. Left full time music, but continued to freelance (mainly around the Romford area) in the 1970s, then quit playing. Resumed regular playing in the 1990s and freelanced throughout the London area.

TAYLOR, John
keyboards/composer

Born: Manchester, Lancashire, 25 September 1942

Self-taught, from a musical family. Worked in Civil Service in Hastings and gigged with local bands. Was transferred to London in late 1964, played in trio in Bermondsey and worked with Dave Quincy, Terry Smith and Tommy Whittle. During the late 1960s worked with John Surman (in Quartet and Octet), with Graham Collier, Alan Skidmore, Harold Beckett, etc. During the 1970s with Norma Winstone (Taylor married Winstone in 1972), Frank Ricotti's Quartet, John Warren's Big Band, John Dankworth, Cleo Laine, Mike Gibbs, Marion Montgomery, Stan Sulzmann, Kenny Wheeler, Harold Beckett, Ronnie Scott's Quintet, and led own groups. Featured regularly with Azimuth (with Norma Winstone and Kenny Wheeler) from 1977. Played international engagements with Jan Garbarek, Miroslav Vitous, Arild Andersen. Taught regularly at summer school from the 1970s onwards. Backed various visiting musicians in the 1970s and 1980s, including Jon Eardley (1977) and Victor Feldman (1980). Continued to lead own line-ups, also played in Kenny Wheeler groups. Toured Australia with John Surman (1983), worked with Gil Evans, did duos with Stan Sulzmann and played at many international festivals. With Tommy Smith (1988), Ian Carr's Orchestra UK (1989). Own groups in the 1990s, also duos with Michael Garrick, and duos with Kenny Wheeler, as well as working in various Wheeler line-ups. With Mike Gibbs' Band, and in March 1996 guested with the Danish guitarist Karsten Houmark. During the 1990s also taught at the Cologne Academy of Music.

TAYLOR, Mark Anthony
drums

Born: Hampstead, London, 7 November 1962

Began playing drums at five, is entirely self-taught. Professional from the age of sixteen. Varied experience included working on a cruise liner and widespread gigging, including work with Dixieland bands. At sixteen deputized for Jim Hall in Eddie Thompson's Trio, then toured with Al Cohn at seventeen. Subsequently accompanied many visiting musicians including Johnny Griffin, George Coleman, Pharoah Sanders, Kenny Barron, Bobby Watson, etc. During the late 1980s and in the 1990s worked with Geoff Castle, John Dankworth, John Taylor, Gordon Beck, Dick Morrissey, Alan Barnes, Alec Dankworth, Mike Carr and in the Pizza Express Modern Jazz Sextet, etc. Worked in the USA and in Britain during the mid-1990s.

TAYLOR, Martin
guitar/banjo

Born: Harlow, Essex, 20 October 1956

Father, Will 'Buck' Taylor, was a guitarist and double bassist. Played guitar from age of four. Gigged in his father's dance band in early teens. At fifteen played in Sonny Dee's All Stars for six months, then joined Lennie Hastings (late 1972). Gigged with Alex Welsh, etc., and played summer season at Pontin's Holiday Camp with Harry Bence. Played on various liners, including Carribbean cruises on the *Cunard Adventurer* before returning to Britain in April 1975. During the early 1970s occasionally doubled on flute. With Alan Elsdon from September 1975 into 1976. Freelanced with Dave Shepherd, Bob Bryan, etc., and guested with various bands. Led own quartet (1977) and guested with Roy Williams-John Barnes (1978). In 1979 began long musical association with Stephane Grappelli, which lasted into the early 1990s and involved many worldwide tours, also guested with many bands and toured with various musicians including Buddy De Franco (1982). From the late 1970s through into the 1990s did successful duo work with Ike Isaacs, Louis Stewart, Peter Ind, Dave Newton, American mandolinist David Grisman. Solo tours of the USA from 1983 through the 1990s, also regularly tours Australia and plays in India, Israel, Germany, Spain, Hong Kong, etc. Led own trio and quartet (based in Scotland) during the 1990s, made solo recordings in California and Nashville (1995). Led the Spirit of Django group during the mid-1990s, which did widespread touring including a visit to Asia in 1995.

TEMPERANCE SEVEN

The embryo version of this band was formed in London on 24 December 1955; the group made its first public appearance as Paul McDowell's Jazzmen in February 1956. Their early days were intertwined with the Alberts (Dougie Gray and Tony Gray) and it was Dougie Gray who gave the band its name. The original members were: Paul McDowell (trombone/vocals), Philip Harrison (banjo), Martin Fry (tuba), Cephas Howard (cornet), Joey Clark (clarinet), Colin Bowles (piano) and Brian Innes (percussion). Harrison began playing alto sax in 1958 (and baritone sax in 1959), he relinquished his place as banjoist and this was taken (in September 1959) by John Gieves-Watson. In April 1959, John R. T. Davies joined on trombone allowing Paul McDowell to specialize on vocals. Canadian trumpeter Dick Williams played briefly with the band. Cliff Bevan played tuba for a while, then Martin Fry rejoined (working under the name of Franklyn B. Paverty). When Joey Clark died, his place as clarinettist was taken by Alan Cooper (who had deputized in the band previously). John R. T. Davies doubled on alto sax. Beginning in 1961, the band's recordings achieved high ratings in the British Hit Parade. In early 1963 they appeared in Spike Milligan's show *The Bed Sitting Room* (at the Mermaid Theatre, London). By 1963, Clifford Bevan had rejoined the band (playing piano), Bobby Mickleburgh was on sousaphone (he later also played trombone and trumpet in the band), Ray Whittam was on tenor and bass saxes, Malcolm 'Mac' White was on clarinet and tenor sax, Allan 'Moody' Mitchell was the singer. Brian Innes, John Gieves-Watson, Cephas Howard and John R. T. Davies retained their positions (the latter playing alto sax/trombone/trumpet/tenor sax and clarinet). Further personnel changes occurred in the mid-1960s, with Brian Innes leaving in December 1965. During the years 1965–96 the band has continued to function successfully. Some of the illustrious names who have played in the band during these years include: Will Hastie (clarinet/saxes), Christopher Buckley (sousaphone), John Tucker (cornet), Ian Howarth (drums), David Mills (drums), Robert 'Bert'

Murray (piano), Graham Lyons (reeds), Malcolm Everson (reeds), Geoff Simkins (reeds), Michael Deighan (banjo), Gerry Deeble (tuba), Graham Collicott (drums), Alexander Hitchcock-Galloway (vocals).

TEMPERLEY, 'Joe' Joseph
baritone sax/saxes/clarinet

Born: Cowdenbeath, Scotland, 20 September 1929

Brother Bob played trumpet. Joe began on cornet in the Cowdenbeath Brass Band at twelve, then switched to alto sax and gigged in his brother's band. Worked in Eddie Finney's Band and began playing tenor sax. Left Fife to work at the Piccadilly Club in Glasgow with Harold Gale's Band (September 1946). Left Harold Gale in late 1947 and worked with Tommy Sampson until late 1948. Moved to London, joined the Blue Rockets (early 1949), worked in Brighton with Dennis Hale, then joined Harry Parry in summer 1949. Toured Middle East with Harry Parry, left Parry to work with Joe Loss from spring 1950 until joining Jack Parnell in autumn 1952. Left Jack Parnell in March 1954. Worked in Dizzy Reece's Quintet (1954), briefly co-led quintet with Sammy Walker, and worked with Winston Lee at Café de Paris (August to September 1954). With Tony Crombie from October 1954 until March 1955. Joined Carl Barriteau (spring 1955), then worked, on baritone sax, with Tommy Whittle (autumn 1955). With Oscar Rabin (1956), then joined Phil Seamen Quintet (1957). Sang in the Polka Dots group, also played briefly in Russia with Geoff Ellison's Band (July to August 1957). Deputized in Humphrey Lyttelton's Band on tenor sax (late 1957), then joined Lyttelton's Band on baritone sax (early 1958). Remained with Lyttelton until emigrating to the USA in December 1965. Specializing on baritone sax, he worked with many famous bandleaders including: Woody Herman, Buddy Rich, Thad Jones-Mel Lewis, Buck Clayton and Mercer Ellington. Has made many playing visits to Britain through the 1990s. Served on the board of the Manhattan School of Music in the 1990s, and, since 1990, has been part of the Lincoln Center Band with which (under the direction of Wynton Marsalis) he toured Europe in 1995. Continues to play regularly, worked with Junior Mance (1995–6).

TEMPLE, Nat
clarinet/saxes

Born: London, 18 July 1913

Younger brother Harry played sax and clarinet. Began playing alto sax at fourteen. With Sam Costa's Band (1929), then worked with Gaby Robins before spending nine years with Harry Roy. Left Harry Roy in spring 1940 to join the Grenadier Guards. Played in service bands throughout World War II (including tour of North Africa) but also managed to fulfil some engagements with Geraldo and Ambrose. Demobilized in 1946, formed own band in 1947, which played residencies, summer seasons and accompanied visiting American artistes (including Hoagy Carmichael). Did many radio series with British comedy stars. Continued to lead own line-ups through the 1980s and 1990s, often playing in own quintet.

TEMPLETON, Alec
piano/composer

Born: Cardiff, Glamorgan, South Wales, 4 July 1910
Died: Greenwich, Connecticut, USA, 28 March 1963

Blind from birth, educated at Worcester College of Music. Subsequently studied in London at the Royal Academy of Music and at the Royal College of Music (he became an ARCM at seventeen).

Played residency at Pavilion Cinema in Clapham, London, then toured Gaumont-British cinema circuit as a featured act, also appeared with various symphony orchestras in the early 1930s. Joined Jack Hylton in 1933 and went with him to the USA in 1935. Settled in the USA and became an American citizen in 1941. He wrote many successful compositions including *Bach Goes to Town*.

TERNENT, 'Billy' William
violin/saxes/multi-instrumentalist/arranger

Born: Whitley Bay, Northumberland, 10 October 1899
Died: Wembley, Middlesex, 23 March 1977

Played violin from age of eight, at thirteen played at the Empire, Whitley Bay; at sixteen was musical director at Comedy Theatre, North Shields, held similar post in Whitley Bay, then led (on sax) at Tilley's, Newcastle upon Tyne. Took up trumpet, and as multi-instrumentalist was featured with the Selma Four in Newcastle. Was discovered by Jack Hylton and moved to London in April 1927. Briefly in Jack Hylton's Kit-Cat Band, then that same month (April 1927), joined Jack Hylton's main band as principal arranger, a position he held for several years. He also played sax with the band and was its utility musician (occasionally playing clarinet, violin, trumpet, trombone, piano and double bass). Illness in 1933 virtually ended his blowing career, thereafter he worked on piano. Visited USA with Jack Hylton in 1935. Recovered from serious illness (1938) and during World War II led BBC Orchestra before forming own band which did extensive touring. Was musical director of various BBC radio shows, and conducted the musical *Can Can* (1946). Acted as musical director for other Jack Hylton shows (using his own band as the nucleus of the 31-piece orchestra). Later became musical director of the London Palladium (1962), a post he held for five years until illness forced his retirement.

TERRY, Revell
piano/arranger/composer

Born: Stockton-on-Tees, Co. Durham, 24 March 1913
Died: Sussex, 10 January 1995

Piano from the age of seven, played in school band at fourteen. Did first professional work in Redcar, Yorkshire. Toured as accompanist for various variety acts (including Cyril Fletcher), with Fol-de-Rols concert party (1937). Worked in Scotland with the Alan Holmes Sextet. Served in the Army during World War II and was part of *Stars in Battledress*. After demobilization led own quartet at the Silvershoe Club (1946–7), and at the Stork Club, London (1948). With Jimmy Cummins in late 1948. With Bob Mumford-Taylor (September 1950 to February 1951). Led at Milroy Club, London (1951), then co-led band in India with trumpeter Hughie Radcliffe (late 1951 to early 1952). Led own trio and quintet at various clubs (mainly in London) throughout the 1950s and 1960s, but also worked in Andre Rico's Band and in Pete Pitterson's Quintet. Worked on transatlantic liners at at South Coast holiday camps with Jackie Sprague's Band. Settled in Sussex in 1977, where he continued to freelance until shortly before his death.

THEMEN, 'Art' Arthur Edward George
tenor sax/soprano sax/sopranino sax

Born: Lancashire, 26 November 1939

Has managed to combine, with considerable success, being an orthopaedic surgeon and an eminent jazz musician. Played clarinet at school. Did a palais season at Fleetwood, Lancashire, before going to Cambridge to study medicine in 1958. Played in Cambridge University Jazz Group until 1961, then moved to London to study at St Mary's Hospital Medical School. Played in Dave Gelly's Quintet, with Jack Bruce and in Blues by Six (with Charlie Watts) in 1962. With Alexis Korner from March 1963. Occasionally with Long John Baldry, Graham Bond, Rod Stewart and Joe Cocker in the mid-1960s, also played in Pete Comton's Big Band. In the New Jazz Quintet (1966) and in quintets he co-led with Dick Heckstall-Smith, Dave Gelly and Barbara Thompson during the late 1960s. Was featured in the Peter Stuyvesant International Orchestra in Zurich (1965). Worked with Michael Garrick and Graham Collier in the late 1960s. Began long musical association with Stan Tracey in 1974, working in various Tracey line-ups until late 1995. During this period also worked in Michael Garrick's Sextet, with Don Weller, in Henry Lowther's Quarternity, Alan Jackson's Kincade, Alan Cohen's Orchestra, etc. Accompanied many visiting American musicians including Al Haig, Red Rodney, Billy Mitchell, etc. Led own quintet from 1996.

THOMAS, Bert
banjo/guitar

Born: Swansea, Glamorgan, South Wales, 12 January 1907

Son of Dave Thomas (died 1930), banjoist with the Savoy Havana Band. Was in the Boston Orchestra (directed by Howard Jacobs) in early 1925, before joining the Sylvians (led by Carroll Gibbons) in October 1926. Then became part of the Savoy Orpheans in January 1927. With Howard Jacobs (October 1928 to January 1930), with Percival Mackey from January 1930; films and recordings with Carroll Gibbons. Rejoined Howard Jacobs in October 1930. Joined Savoy Hotel Orpheans (directed by Carroll Gibbons and Howard Jacobs) in October 1931, left in June 1932; worked with Howard Jacobs, then rejoined Savoy Hotel Orpheans (Carroll Gibbons) in January 1935 and remained with them into the early 1940s. Regular freelance recordings during the late 1920s and 1930s including many with Ray Noble.

THOMPSON, Barbara (née GRACEY)
saxes/clarinet/flute/composer

Born: Oxford, 27 July 1944

Married to drummer Jon Hiseman. Played recorder and clarinet at school, later took sax lessons from Charles Chapman. Educated at Queen's College. Four month summer season with Ivy Benson on the Isle of Man, then did secretarial work before commencing studies at the Royal College of Music in September 1964 (clarinet, flute, piano and composition). Joined Neil Ardley's New Jazz Orchestra (1965), worked in She Trinity from October 1966 until April 1967, also co-led quintet with Dave Gelly. In the Kit-Kat Band for musical *Cabaret* (1968), continued to play in the New Jazz Orchestra and worked in various line-ups including Don Lusher's Big Band, Mike Daniels Big Band, and with Manfred Mann, Keef Hartley, Keith Emerson, etc. Co-led quintet with Art Themen (1969). During the 1970s established own Paraphernalia, and during that decade also worked with John Dankworth, Cleo Laine, Mike Gibbs, Don Weller, Don Rendell, Derek Wadsworth, Wolfgang Dauner, etc. Played briefly in Belgium with the Charles Loos Trio (April 1975), later appeared as a soloist throughout Europe during the 1980s and 1990s. Active with own Jubiaba from the mid-1970s, was also part of the United Jazz and Rock Ensemble. Led own big band, Moving Parts, from the late 1980s, appeared in Sans Frontiers during the 1990s. Extensive tour of Europe with Paraphernalia in spring 1994. Continues to lead own various line-ups through the 1990s. Her numerous composing successes include a Saxophone Concerto and setting Philip Larkin's poems to music (1995). Awarded MBE in 1995.

THOMPSON, 'Danny' Daniel Henry Edward
(Muslim name: **Hamzah**)
double bass/trombone/composer

Born: Teignmouth, Devon, 4 April 1939

Lived in London from age of five. Made early efforts on tenor sax, drums, trumpet and mandolin, then played tea-chest bass in a skiffle group. Bought double bass and began gigging with New Orleans style bands in the South London area. At sixteen did first professional work at Spider's Web Club, Soho, backing the many visiting jazz musicians who sat in there. At seventeen played at Streatham Locarno with Nat Allen, then did two years in the Army, served in Malaya and played trombone in Army bands. After demobilization played in Tubby Hayes' Student Orchestra (1963), gigged with John Burch's Octet, with Fat John Cox and led own trio (featuring John McLaughlin and Tony Roberts). Regularly with Alexis Korner for three years during the mid-1960s. Freelanced with Tubby Hayes, Phil Seamen, Harold McNair and accompanied visiting American musicians. With Pentangle from early 1968 until early 1973. During this period also played gigs with Stan Robinson, Stan Tracey, Ronnie Scott, Tubby Hayes, etc., and recorded with various folk and rock artistes. During the 1970s worked often in Stan Tracey's Open Circle, and (from 1974) with John Martyn. Led own line-ups, gigged with John Stevens and occasionally played trombone in the Ipswich Fire Service Band and in a Suffolk military band. Continued to play on many freelance sessions and again led own trio (with Bernie Holland and Tony Roberts). Increasingly active as a freelance in the 1980s and 1990s, made recordings with Kate Bush, Talk Talk, Rod Stewart, etc., and took part in brief Pentangle reunion. During the late 1980s and 1990s achieved success with own Whatever group, touring and recording, also did duo work with Richard Thompson (1995). Started own Jazz Label in 1992.

THOMPSON, 'Eddie' Edgar Charles
piano

Born: Shoreditch, London, 31 May 1925
Died: Essex, 6 November 1986

Piano from the age of five. Studied at Linden Lodge School for the Blind in Wandsworth, London, (as did George Shearing), until he was seventeen. Played gigs on piano-accordion and for a time worked as a piano tuner. Joined Freddy Randall in 1947, then toured with a rhumba band and played club dates. To Paris with Carlo Krahmer's Band (1949), worked with Victor Feldman's Sextet (late 1949). Own quintet and trio during the early 1950s, also worked with Tony Crombie, Ronnie Scott, etc., and briefly did double piano-accordion act with Jack Emblow. With Vic Ash (1954), Bobby Mickleburgh (summer 1955), part of Jazz Today Unit (1955), then rejoined Freddy Randall (from December 1955 until July 1956). With Tommy Whittle's Quartet, including trip to USA (1957–8). Own quintet and trio again in the late 1950s, played residency at Ronnie Scott's Club, then did solo work at the Downbeat Club, London (1960). Moved to the USA in March 1962, worked mainly in New York City (including long residency at the Hickory House). Returned to Britain for working vacations during the 1960s, then moved back to London area in May 1972. Led own group for residency at the Jazz Cellar, Stockport, during the mid-1970s, worked with Dave Shepherd, and made occasional return trips to USA. Led own successful trio and also played duos with pianist Roger Kellaway (including engagements in America in 1985). Played regularly at the Pizza Express, London, in the 1980s, often accompanying visiting American jazz musicians, but was virtually inactive through illness during the last year of his life.

THOMPSON, Gail
saxes/clarinet/flute/bass guitar/composer

Born: Herne Hill, London, 15 June 1958

Of Trinidadian parentage. Began on clarinet, switched to sax at Kingdale School, Dulwich. Played baritone sax in National Youth Jazz Orchestra. Worked in Bubbling Brown Sugar Quintet (1984), led own trio, then formed Gail Force. Worked in Charlie Watts' Big Band (1985–6). Founder-member of Jazz Warriors (1986). Left and did widespread travelling which included a stay in Africa (1987). Founded Women in Music organization, and conducted world-wide seminars. Led Gail Force Big Band from February 1994, recorded in Germany and ran own Jazz Africa Project (1995). Visited Australia in 1995, returned to Britain and formed own Didgattack (late 1995).

THOMPSON, Leslie Anthony Joseph
trumpet/double bass/trombone/cello

Born: Kingston, Jamaica, West Indies,
17 October 1901
Died: London, 20 December 1987

Began playing music while a pupil at the Alpha Cottage School in Kingston, Jamaica, later joined the West Indies Regiment (in October 1917) and travelled to Britain (in May 1919) for further studies at Kneller Hall. Returned to Jamaica in December 1920, continued to play in service band (including return trip to Britain in 1924 to play at the British Empire Exhibition, Wembley), also toured Canada. Played engagements in Jamaican cinemas, then moved to Britain in July 1929. Gigged with pianist George Clapham, then worked semi-regularly with Norman 'Cod' Hill and made recordings with Spike Hughes. Played in Percival Mackey's Orchestra for C. B. Cochran revue (1931) and then freelanced in various theatre orchestras. Toured Europe with Louis Armstrong from October 1934 until early 1935 (also worked in Leon Abbey's Band in Europe during this period). Returned to England and toured in the *Blackbirds* show (March to May 1935). Worked with Billy Merrin's Commanders (1935), gigged with Harry Francis and played in various C. B. Cochran revue orchestras. Led own band, which formed the basis of Ken Johnson's Jamaican Emperors (1936) (also known as the Emperors of Jazz). Recorded with Benny Carter (1937). Worked in Ben Frankel's Orchestra (1938). With Edmundo Ros from 1939, then served in the Royal Artillery throughout World War II, became part of the *Stars in Battledress* travelling show from 1944 until demobilization in 1946. Further studies at the Guildhall School of Music (1947–8), played various London club residencies (Embassy, Ciro's, etc), until retiring from full time music in 1954. Taught music in his spare time, but mainly occupied with working as a warden of a hostel. He became a probation offier from 1963 until 1971, and a prison officer from 1971 until 1976. *Leslie Thompson—An Autobiography* (as told to Jeffrey P. Green) was published in 1985.

THORBURN, 'Billy' William Arthur Belmont
piano/organ/composer

Born: North Kensington, London,
12 May 1900
Died: Barnet, Hertfordshire, 4 April 1971

Musical tuition from Harry Beck. Was organist and choirmaster at Holy Trinity Church, London

(1918–19). Played at Harrods' tea dances and on society gigs (1919–20). With Murray Pilcer's Band in London (early 1920s) and played in band for a season in Stockholm, Sweden (1922). With Jack Hylton's Band at Queen's Hall (1922–4), then joined Savoy Orpheans in June 1924. Played in the Sylvians (then directed by Ramon Newton) in early 1927. With Howard Jacobs (1928). Left Savoy Orpheans in early 1930 and spent two years with Sydney Kyte (during this period was briefly with Jerry Hoey in early 1931). Extensive freelance recordings in the late 1920s and 1930s. With Jack Payne from March 1932 until March 1936. Left to lead own band (Billy Thorburn and his Music) which toured extensively. From 1938 enjoyed widespread success with his show *The Organ, the Dance Band and Me*. Later led own groups for touring shows and revues, and for summer seasons at holiday camps. Was featured at the 1951 Royal Command performance. Retired from full time music in 1954 and ran a pub in Barnet.

THORPE, 'Tony' Anthony Reuben
trombone/trumpet

Born: Nottingham, 30 August 1900
Died: 12 December 1972

Served in Royal Flying Corps during World War I, then emigrated to Canada and became a Canadian citizen. Worked in Toronto with Gilbert Watson's Band. Returned to England in 1926 as part of Bill Shenkman's Buffaloes. With Reg Batten's Savoy Havana Band (1927). To Germany with the Original Savoy Orpheans (spring 1928). With Van Phillips' Orchestra for London show *Good News* (late 1928), then worked in the Blue Lyres at the Café de Paris, London, before joining Arthur Lally's Orchestra from spring 1930 to December 1930. Joined Howard Jacobs (December 1930). During the 1930s frequently worked in ensembles at the Savoy Hotel, also did freelance recordings, including sides with Ray Noble. With Peter Rush's Blue Lyres (1933–4), Jack Jackson (1933 and 1935). With Ambrose from summer 1935, then joined Henry Hall from February 1936 until August 1938. Freelanced extensively, then worked with Percival Mackey (1940), with George Scott-Wood, and Mantovani (1941). Active in studios during 1940s and 1950s. During the 1960s played bass trombone in the Royal Opera House Orchestra.

TIPPETT, Keith Graham
piano/composer

Born: Bristol, 25 August 1947

Piano from early childhood, also played cornet and tenor horn in local Youth Band. Gigged in Bristol. Attended Barry Summer School in 1967, then moved to London and formed own sextet in 1968. Recorded with King Crimson. Organized the fifty-piece ensemble Centipede in 1970 and led Ovary Lodge from 1972. Married singer Julie Driscoll. Led big band Ark from 1978. Was part of Just Us (with Elton Dean) from 1974. Duos with Stan Tracey from the 1970s through the 1980s, during this period also worked in Trevor Watts' Amalgam, appeared in 1974 revival of play *The Connection*, with Elton Dean's Ninesense, Marc Charig, Harry Miller, Louis Moholo, Isipingo, and did duos with Julie Driscoll, Howard Riley, etc. Led Mujician from the 1980s through the 1990s, also worked as a soloist, and with the Kreutzer String Quartet. In duos with Andy Sheppard, led own septet and was part of the Anglo-Soviet Project, Dreamtime, etc.

TIPPING, Bernard
trombone

Born: London, *c.*1894
Deceased

Tipping and Stanley Jones were two pioneering British jazz trombonists. Tipping began playing trombone in 1913. He moved to Leeds to work with the Queen's Hotel Orchestra, then returned to London in 1920. During the early 1920s worked with the Syncopated Six in Manchester, with the Albany Five in Birmingham and on tour with the Louisiana Jazz Band. With Jack Hylton (1922 to April 1923). With the Savoy Havana Band from October 1923 until September 1926 (first under the leadership of Cyril Ramon Newton, latterly with Reg Batten as leader, from April 1926). With xylophonist Teddy Brown (1928), then played in Kennedy Russell's Orchestra for *Lucky Girl* show (late 1928). With Percival Mackey (1929), Pierre De Caillaux's Orchestra (1930) then left full time music to work as a film camera man, before moving into advertising.

TOBIN, Christine
vocals/composer/lyricist/piano

Born: Dublin, Ireland, 6 January 1963

Began doing gigs in Dublin during the early 1980s with pianist Noel Kelahan and with Louis Stewart. Sang in various festivals in the North and the South, then moved to London in 1987. Began working with Simon Purcell, and also studied with Purcell as part of the Guildhall School of Music Jazz Course (1988–9). Worked with Jean Toussaint's Band in London, and led own groups (Simon Purcell, piano; Steve Watts, bass; and Roy Dodds, drums). Ceased regular singing and studied anthropology for two years at Goldsmiths College, London (1991–3), then again led own group (with Huw Warren on piano in place of Purcell), which played in Azerbaijan in 1993, and in Austria in 1995. Christine is also a regular member of Lammas (with Tim Garland) and has done work in Italy, Denmark, Holland and Norway with Django Bates' Delightful Precipice. She is featured on the title track of Nick Weldon's *Lavender's Blue* and has worked and recorded with drummer Pete Fairclough's Shepherd's Wheel. Continues to lead own successful group (1996), to work with guitarist Phil Robson, and to freelance with various line-ups including the London Contemporary Jazz Ensemble.

TOMASSO, 'Ernie' Ernest
clarinet/saxes/vocals

Born: Leeds, Yorkshire, 18 September 1912
Died: Great Yarmouth, Norfolk, 1991

Father of Enrico (trumpet) and Peter (piano); brother of trumpeter Freddie. Played piano as a child, then specialized on clarinet. Worked with Sid Seymour and his Mad Hatters (1935–7), then joined house-band at Nest Club in London (1937–8). Served alongside Freddie in RAF during World War II, leading RAF Rhythm Kings, first in Scotland and then in Gibraltar for two years. After demobilization led own band at Middleton Towers, Morecambe (1946–7), then joined Harry Gold (late 1948), worked mainly with Harry Gold until 1953. With Barry Morgan (1954), with Freddy Randall (1955), also with Reg Moore on liner *Mauretania* (1955). From summer of 1955 co-led Tomasso Brothers' Band (with Freddie). Led own band in Channel Islands during summer of 1956, then worked with wife, Jeanne (vocalist and accordionist) in highly successful variety act. During the 1970s led own family band which did widespread international touring.

TOMASSO, 'Freddie' Frederick
trumpet

Born: Leeds, Yorkshire, 24 May 1916

Brother of clarinettist Ernie. Began on violin, then took up trumpet. Worked with Eric Pearson in Huddersfield, replaced Duncan Whyte in house band at the Nest Club in London. Joined RAF and played in RAF Rhythm Kings (alongside Ernie) in Scotland and Gibraltar. After demobilization worked in Ernie's Band in Morecambe (1946–7), then played at Locarno, Leeds, with Teddy Fawcett's Band prior to joining Harry Gold (January 1949). Left Harry Gold in November 1952, with Harry Roy (November 1952 to July 1953). With Barry Morgan at Churchill's Club, London (1954), then rejoined Harry Roy (May to June 1954). With Bob Miller (July to August 1954), Sid Phillips (September to October 1954), then rejoined Barry Morgan. Led own Dixieland Band, then co-led with Ernie from summer of 1955. Retired from full time playing in 1957, continues to play in entertainments unit which visits various hospitals (1995).

TOMKINS, Trevor Ramsey
drums/percussion

Born: London, 12 May 1941

His cousin was the pianist Roy Budd. Early efforts on trombone, then drums from the age of eighteen. Studied at Guildhall School of Music. Left Ian Bird's Quintet to join Don Rendell in late 1962, subsequently worked in Don Rendell-Ian Carr Quintet from 1963 until 1969. During this period also worked on the liner *Queen Elizabeth*, played in the New Jazz Orchestra, worked in Roy Budd's Trio and in Johnny Fourie's Quartet. Joined Frank Ricotti in late 1969. Again worked with Don Rendell from 1970. Often with Michael Garrick in the 1970s, and worked, during the 1970s and 1980s, with Barbara Thompson. With Mike Westbrook, Dick Morrissey, Henry Lowther, John Picard, Ray Wordsworth, Kenny Wheeler, Tony Coe, etc. Active as a teacher from the 1970s, also co-director (with Jeff Clyne) of the Wavendon Summer Jazz Courses. Accompanied many visiting musicians, including Sonny Stitt, Pepper Adams, Phil Woods, etc. Toured Britain in Lee Konitz's Quartet (1985). Continues to freelance and to be a force in jazz education, at Bude Jazz Summer School, etc., runs workshops at the Guildhall, etc. With Brian Priestley's Sextet from the late 1980s, working with Marion Montgomery, Phil Bates' Trio, own groups, etc. (1996).

TOWNSHEND, 'Cliff' Clifford Blandford
alto sax/baritone sax/clarinet

Born: West London, 28 January 1916
Died: Central Middlesex Hospital, 29 June 1986

Married to singer Betty Dennis, all three sons, Peter (of the Who), Paul and Simon, are musicians. Semi-professional work around the Ealing area, then worked with Billy Wiltshire at the Hotel de Paris, Maidenhead (1935). With drummer Phil Watts (1938), then to Scandinavia with Joe Daniels (autumn 1938). Remained with Daniels in 1939, but also did radio work with Phil Watts (1939–41). Joined RAF in World War II, played in station bands, then joined Leslie Douglas' Bomber Command Band and played in Vic Lewis-Jack Parnell Jazzmen (1944). After demobilization worked for ten years with the Squadronaires (1945–55), specializing on clarinet and baritone sax. Often with Kenny Baker (1956) and with Frank Weir, before working regularly with Cyril Stapleton into the 1970s, also freelanced on innumerable sessions.

TRACEY, Clark   Born: London, 5 February 1961
drums

Son of Stan Tracey, husband of singer Tina May. Played piano before taking up drumming at thirteen, played first gigs at fifteen, some tuition from Bryan Spring. Began working in his father's groups at seventeen, soon did widespread touring including India, South America and the Middle East. Worked as accompanist for many visiting American jazzmen. Formed short-lived Quartet in 1983, then formed own Quintet in 1984, which did international touring, including visiting Far East (1987) and playing thoughout Europe (1988). Besides leading the Quintet also worked with Gail Thompson (1985), spent five months with Dee Dee Bridgwater in the *Lady Day* show (1987), worked with Don Weller's Quartet (1988), the Alan Skidmore Quartet (1989–playing in Hong Kong with Skidmore), with Tommy Smith (1989), John Dankworth, Peter King, etc., and continued to freelance with visiting American musicians. Briefly with Val Wiseman in *Lady Sings the Blues* (1991), toured with Guy Barker (1992), worked with NDR Big Band in Hamburg (1992), widespread touring with own quintet, then formed sextet in 1994. Also continues to freelance, including work in Claire Martin's group and accompanying visiting American musicians. Often in Stan Tracey's Quartet (1996).

TRACEY, 'Stan' Stanley William   Born: Tooting, London, 30 December 1926
piano/vibes/composer/arranger

Father of percussionist Clark Tracey. Took up piano accordion at twelve, piano at thirteen. Worked on accordion with Peter Raymond's Band for ENSA tours, first gig on sixteenth birthday. At nineteen joined the RAF and played accordion and piano in *Gang Show* productions (including tour of Middle East). Later led own group (including Vic Ash on clarinet and Victor Graham on trumpet) for USO tour of Germany. After demobilization from RAF played various gigs, with guitarist Tommy Middleton, in duo with singer Barry Martin and at the Paramount Dance Hall, London, in the Malfi Trio. In Eddie Thompson's Quintet (on accordion) 1950–1. With Leon Roy-Roland De Cosse Quartet on liner *Queen Mary*, also worked on liner *Caronia*. In Laurie Morgan's Elevated Music, also toured with Cab Calloway (August 1951). In Kenny Baker's Octet (October 1951 to March 1952) and again from September to December 1952, also worked with Roy Fox (1952). With Vic Ash, Ray Menaldo and Bernard Stetson (on accordion) during 1953. With Kenny Baker's Quartet from August 1953 until November 1954. With Malcolm Mitchell Orchestra (February to August 1955), with Vic Ash's Quartet, before working with Tony Crombie and Bernie Stanton. With Ronnie Scott (early 1956), then briefly with Carl Barriteau and Kenny Graham before working on piano and vibes with the Kirchins (Ivor and Basil) during summer of 1956. To USA with Ronnie Scott in February 1957. Worked in London with Dizzy Reece's Quintet (April 1957), then rejoined the Kirchins from April until June 1957, subsequently worked with Basil Kirchin until joining Ted Heath from September 1957 until September 1959. With Tony Crombie again in late 1959, then (with Crombie) joined Ronnie Scott's Quintet (early 1960). Brief absence from music, then rejoined Ronnie Scott-Jimmy Deuchar Quintet in December 1960, also worked as house pianist at Ronnie Scott's Club, London, accompanying many visiting American musicians. Led own trio at Scott's from 1960 until 1968. During this period also played freelance dates, with New Departures, etc., and leading own quartet; played for stage show *A Thurber Carnival* (1962). Gained increasing recognition after composing *Under Milk Wood* (1964), *Alice in Jazzland* (1966), etc. Led own trio, quartet and band during the 1970s, also duos with Mike Osborne, John Surman, Tony Coe, etc. With Trevor Watts in Amalgam, and in Open Circle (with Danny Thompson, Trevor Watts and John Stevens). Led own Octet (1976–85), extensive touring including engagements in India, Middle East, Greece, etc. From the 1970s also taught at the City Literary Institute, at Goldsmiths College and at the Guildhall School of Music. Led Hexad Sextet. Toured South America (1980), worked with poet Michael Horovitz (1981). Duos with Keith Tippett (1981), also played solo piano dates and continued to lead own big band. With Charlie Watts' Big Band (1985–6), also worked in Fathers and Sons in the late 1980s. During the 1980s and 1990s continued to lead own quartet (new version from 1995), Hexad and Big Band and to arrange, compose and teach. Awarded OBE in 1986.

TURNER, 'Bruce' Malcolm Bruce
alto sax/clarinet/saxes/composer

Born: Saltburn, Yorkshire, 5 July 1922
Died: Buckinghamshire, 28 November 1993

Spent most of his childhood in India, where his father was a teacher. Took up clarinet at fifteen while at Dulwich College. Did war work in Exeter, Devon, and played local gigs with Henry Setters' Band, and with the Watkinson Trio. Joined RAF and took up alto sax. Played in pick-up bands, but worked as a cypher clerk, including service in West Africa. After demobilization worked in Billy Kaye's Band (1947), briefly in Roy Vaughan's Chicagoans, then joined Freddy Randall in June 1948. Left Randall in February 1949 to work aboard *Queen Mary* liner in Ivor Noone's Band. Rejoined Freddy Randall, then worked with Cyril Collins on *Queen Mary* (February 1950), subsequently led own group on this liner (1950) and played briefly in Ronnie Ball's Band. Rejoined Freddy Randall in November 1950s, worked briefly with Joe Daniels (August 1951) but remained with Randall until joining Humphrey Lyttelton in January 1953. Left in March 1957 to form own Jump Band. During the period 1953–7 also did freelance work with Ken Sykora, Kenny Baker, the Jazz Today Unit, etc., and visited Romania with folk singer Ewan McColl (August 1953). Also took own band to Poland in summer 1955. Took own band to Russia in summer 1957. Led own Jump Band from 1957 until 1964. During this period also deputized for Archie Semple in Alex Welsh's Band and guested with various bands throughout Europe. Rejoined Freddy Randall from May 1964 until February 1966, also periodically re-formed Jump Band mainly to accompany visiting American jazz musicians, including Bill Coleman, Ray Nance, Ben Webster, Don Byas, etc. With Acker Bilk from May 1966 until June 1970. During the early 1970s divided his time between playing in reunions of the Jump Band, being part of Wally Fawkes-John Chilton Feetwarmers, working with Peter Ind and with Humphrey Lyttelton. Brief (non-playing) visit to India in January 1973. Regularly with Humphrey Lyttelton from 1974 until 1988. During this time played in Stan Greig's London Jazz Big Band (1975–6), in Peter Ind's Octet, toured (including Australia) with Alex Welsh's Band in *Salute to Satchmo* show, worked in Dave Green's group Fingers, and freelanced. Led own quartet and quintet in the early 1990s, occasionally worked with Dave Green's Fingers, and guested with various bands. Continued to play regularly until a few weeks before dying of a brain tumour. His autobiography *Hot Air, Cool Music* was published in 1984.

TURNHAM, 'Gerry' Gerald Frederick
clarinet/saxes

Born: 11 March 1932
Died: 1979

Gained early playing experience with the Memphis Jazz Band and Tom Collins. Founder-member of Mickey Ashman's Band in summer 1958. Left Ashman in 1961 to join newly re-formed Crane River Jazz Band. Worked with Cyril Preston before joining Len Baldwin's Dauphin Street Six in June 1962. Temporarily led own band (1963), then worked with Dennis Field and Hugh Rainey (in England and in Canada). Freelanced with various bands, including another spell with Len Baldwin in 1968, then joined Ken Colyer in the mid-1970s. Again played in the Crane River Jazz Band in 1978.

TURNOCK, Brian
double bass

Born: Watford, Hertfordshire, 9 June 1943

Played in Bodega Jazzband (led by Derek Winters) in 1961, then worked in Hugh Watts' Ragtime Band (1962). Turned professional in April 1964 and worked in Stockholm, Sweden, with Giles-Fox Hot Four. Joined Keith Smith's Climax Jazzband in September 1964, toured with Alton Purnell and Champion Jack Dupree. Left Keith Smith to join Barry Martyn's Ragtime Band (January 1966), toured USA, played in first New Orleans Jazz Festival in 1968. Recorded and toured with Kid Sheik, Captain John Handy, George Lewis, Don Ewell, etc. Brief return to Keith Smith (late 1966 to summer 1967) but regularly with Barry Martyn until 1970. Left the band and worked briefly in Ireland with Sid Bailey, then rejoined Martyn until moving to North of England. Worked with Dave Brennan's Band and freelanced, made five further visits to New Orleans, recording with Teddy Riley, Jeanette Kimball, etc. Moved to Ghent, Belgium, in December 1983, joined Sammy Rimington's Band, toured with Wendell Brunious, Thomas Jefferson, Sam Lee, Kuumba Williams, etc. Regularly with Lillian Boutté and her Music Friends from September 1987 until January 1989. Joined Butch Thompson's King Oliver Centennial Band in June 1990, and continues to work with this into the mid-1990s, also works throughout Europe in the Superior Dance Band and Rudi Balliu's Society Serenaders.

U

USDEN, Dave
trumpet

Born: Oldham, Lancashire, 1929
Died: Lancashire, 2 June 1975

Played in local bands, then joined Ken Mackintosh (1948). With Vic Lewis in 1950, left Lewis in March 1951. Worked with Frank Weir and in Kenny Graham's Augmented Afro-Cubists, then joined Jack Nathan in early 1952. To New Delhi, India, with Eddie Carroll's Band (May 1952), worked with Victor Feldman's Jazz Group in India (1953). Returned to Britain, joined Ken Moule Seven in March 1954. Left Moule a year later to join Tubby Hayes. Left Tubby Hayes in August 1955 to join Ronnie Scott's Big Band. Toured US bases in Europe with small groups, then began leading own quartet in Nottingham (1957). The onset of multiple sclerosis caused his premature retirement, but he occasionally sat in at Manchester's Club 43 during the last years of his life.

V

VAN DERRICK, 'Johnny' John Arthur
violin/viola

Born: Ealing, London, 11 August 1926
Died: Buckinghamshire, 15 May 1995

Father (trumpeter) from Holland; mother (pianist and cellist) from England. Raised in Ealing, but studied music at Brussels Conservatoire (playing trumpet and violin) as a teenager. Returned to London at outbreak of World War II. Played in London theatre orchestras and toured with Louis Mexano's Accordion Band. Joined Merchant Navy and was on transatlantic voyages and trips to Russia during World War II. Specializing on violin he subsequently toured with ENSA shows, began long musical association with Denny Wright which went through into the 1980s. Played in various London night clubs and worked with Roy Fox and Geraldo. From 1953 led for nine years in Jersey, then led at Churchill's, London, for eleven years. Extensive freelance recordings from the 1960s. Often worked with Diz Disley, in Keith Cooper-Denny Wright group, and regular radio work with Jack Toogood. With Diz Disley's Hot Club Quintet and Soho String Quintette. Recovered from serious illness in 1976 and resumed full playing schedule. Played on several film soundtracks during the 1980s and 1990s and was featured on various television commercials. Toured with Bireli Lagrene (1984), also toured USA and Canada. Underwent heart surgery in 1985, then resumed playing. During the early 1990s worked with Gary Potter (in own Hot Jazz Strings) and in Potter's group. Toured and recorded with guitarist Phil Bond, worked with Capital Swing and played at numerous jazz festivals. Continued to play many freelance sessions, worked with guitarist Howard Alden, and led own quartet. Taught at the Guildhall School of Music and at the Royal Academy of Music. Suffered fatal heart attack.

VASS, Olaf (Olavo Remy Filomeno Felix de VAS)
tenor sax/clarinet/flute/vocals

Born: Nakuru, Kenya, East Africa, 29 January 1935

Played first gigs with own quartet in Nairobi. Moved to Britain in 1956. Worked in Cedric West's Quintet in London and toured with Teddy Foster, freelanced with session bands on television and radio, also played club dates and worked at the National Theatre. Studied at Royal College of Music, majored on clarinet and flute (1961–5). Worked in Alan Clarke's Band, with Jeff Posey Trio. Played long residency with own band at Tiberio's, London. In Alan Cohen's Band during the 1970s, then worked in Midnite Follies Orchestra (from January 1978). Left to play in show *One Mo' Time* (1981). With John Warren, Ian Stewart's Rocket 88, Brian Priestley, Charlie Watts, and Ray Terry. With Nina Barry Quintet (1995) and freelancing with various line-ups. Actively involved in jazz education for many years, at Wavendon, with Ed Harvey, guesting with Fife Youth Orchestra, John Ruddick's Midland Youth Jazz Orchestra, etc.

VAUGHAN, Roy Francis
piano

Born: Mitcham, Surrey, 15 July 1927
Died: Surrey, 16 December 1995

Mother played piano; began piano lessons at ten. Formed own band, Roy Vaughan's Chicagoans, in 1949. Later worked with Dave Carey's Band and gigged with various bands around the London area. With John Chilton's Swing Kings from 1966 to 1967, then led own successful trio for various residencies and played solo piano dates through 1995 until dying suddenly after suffering a stroke.

VERRELL, 'Ronnie' Ronald Thomas
drums

Born: Rochester, Kent, 21 February 1926

One lesson from Max Abrams, thereafter self-taught. Evacuated to Wales during World War II, guested at the Pavilion, Porthcawl, with organist Glan Evans, and with band led by saxophonist Jack Morgan. Returned to Kent and joined Claude Giddins in Gillingham (1943), also played gigs with Johnny Claes. Worked in coal mines as a 'Bevin Boy', then again worked with Claude Giddins (1945–6). With Carl Barriteau (1947–8), then worked briefly in Munich, Germany, with Leslie Holmes and the Londonaires Dance Orchestra (spring 1948). With Cyril Stapleton (1949–51), then worked with Ted Heath from September 1951 until early 1964. Did prolific session work, then worked for ten years with Jack Parnell's Orchestra at ATV (during which time he was featured on *The Muppets* television show doing a drum duet with Buddy Rich). Brief leave from ATV to work in Los Angeles with singer Tom Jones. Continued with session work through the 1980s and 1990s, occasionally with the Pizza Express All Stars. Often featured with Syd Lawrence's Orchestra from 1981. Continues to play regularly, often leads own quintet (1995–6).

VINTEN, Jonathan Jeremy
piano

Born: Maidstone, Kent, 13 June 1963

Began playing ragtime while a pupil at Ashford Grammar School, became interested in jazz and started playing pub gigs. Formed own band while studying psychology at Swansea University. Did post-graduate course at University of Kent, then moved to London in 1986, and began working with Bill Brunskill and Brian White. Subsequently accompanied visiting American jazzmen. Was featured in Brian White and Alan Gresty's Muggsy Remembered Band at Nice Festival, and in USA. With Laurie Chescoe's Good Time Jazzband prior to joining John Chilton's Feetwarmers and George Melly in late 1992.

W

WADSWORTH, Derek
trombone/arranger/composer

Born: Cleckheaton, Yorkshire, 5 February 1939

Trombone from age of eleven. Played in Spenborough Victoria Brass Band and then joined Brighouse and Rastrick Band. Played in Huddersfield with Keith Smith's Jazz Cardinals (1958), with Chris Mercer's Jazz Band and Geoff Lorriman's Band (1958), then worked with Joe Markey before moving to London in 1960. With Teddy Foster (1960), the Squadronaires, and Jack Dorsey (1963), then became musical director for singer Dusty Springfield. Worked with John Burch's Octet, then joined Georgie Fame. Became musical director for musical *Hair* for five years. Toured with Alan Price (including USA). Later did world tour as m.d. for Diana Ross, also worked with Dionne Warwick. Two years with Maynard Ferguson in the early 1970s (including tour of USA). With Barbara Thompson's Jubiaba (1973–5). Worked with John Dankworth, then became Director of Musicians' Union Rock Workshop for intermittent tours. Led own sextet and worked in Geoff Castle's Band, also spent a year at Pinewood Studios composing and arranging for Space 99 (1976). Led own Blind Alley during the 1980s, but was increasingly involved in composing and arranging for films. Continued to play many jazz gigs, with Brian Priestley's Sextet, with Bob Wilber, Harry Gold, etc., through the 1990s. During the early 1990s conducted the Prague Symphony Orchestra for recordings.

WAKEMAN, Alan
tenor and soprano saxes/clarinet/
bass clarinet/flute/piano

Born: Hammersmith, West London,
13 October 1947

Clarinet and sax tuition from Charles Chapman. Attended Drayton Manor Grammar School and there met Mike Westbrook (who was then an art teacher). Further education at London College of Music (1966–9). With London Youth Jazz Orchestra from 1967 (including overseas tours), then became part of the National Youth Jazz Orchestra in the late 1960s. First broadcast with Dave Holdsworth's Quartet (1969). Began long musical association with Mike Westbrook in 1970 (which has continued through 1990s). Led own line-ups from 1970, also active in David Essex's Band from 1974–90. During the 1970s and 1980s worked with Graham Collier, John Dankworth, Harold Beckett, Brian Miller, London Jazz Composers' Orchestra, Don Rendell, Stan Tracey, Michael Garrick, John Warren, duets with Paul Lytton, and was part of Triton (with Paul Bridge and Nigel Morris). Continues to play regularly and is still part of Mike Westbrook's Big Band.

WALKER, 'Chris' Christopher Gordon
clarinet/alto and baritone saxes

Born: London, 28 December 1939

Son of banjoist Geoff Walker (1909–94) who worked with Bob Wallis, Steve Lane, Dave Nelson, Mike Daniels, etc. After playing recorder in a Ruislip school band, Chris took up clarinet in 1956. He joined trumpeter Freddy Shaw's Jazzmen and did his first broadcast with them in 1958. Turned professional in 1960 and worked with the London City Stompers in Britain and Germany. Left full time music in 1962 and gigged with various bands. Briefly led own band, then joined Mike Daniels' Big Band in 1964, he also worked in Mike Daniels' Delta Jazzmen (1966) before joining Colin Kingwell's Jazz Bandits. Moved to Hampshire in 1969, gigged with local bands, including the New Forest Rhythm Kings, then (in 1976) became co-founder (with bassist Stuart Gledhill) of the Real Ale and Thunder Band. Remained with this band until December 1994. Continues to lead own quintet (which was formed in 1987). For sixteen years (from 1980) presented jazz programmes on Radio Solent.

WALKER, 'Jimmy' James Simmers
Born: Edinburgh, Scotland, 22 June 1926
tenor sax/soprano sax/vocals/piano

First professional work at Edinburgh Palais in 1944 with Bertini (Bertram Gutsell). Worked at same venue with John Holton's Band prior to joining Harry Parry (late 1945). With Roy Fox (1946–7), then returned to Edinburgh and played locally before joining Vic Lewis from December 1947 until November 1948. Led own quintet at West End Restaurant, Edinburgh, from late 1948 through 1949. Briefly with Carl Barriteau, then led quintet at Edinburgh Palais (1950–1). Moved to London with own quintet in spring 1952, disbanded a year later. Worked with Ambrose from March to September 1953, then briefly with Frank Weir before becoming part of vocal group the Sapphires, which toured with Jack Parnell's Orchestra in the *Jazz Wagon* show. Played in Jack Parnell's Orchestra (including tour of South Africa) in 1955. Worked with Bernie Stanton, then played tenor and alto sax in Bert Courtley-Jack Seymour Orchestra (1957) and toured with Jazz Today Unit. Returned to singing and became a member of the Polka Dots from 1957 until 1964, before becoming a successful session vocalist (until 1970). Temporarily left full time music, then led own small group aboard the *Spirit of London*, sailing out of Los Angeles (doing cruises to Alaska, Mexico, etc.) in 1973 and 1974. Became a driving instructor, then moved to Portugal and led own group at a hotel in the Algarve (playing piano, tenor sax and singing) from 1982 until moving back to Britain in 1986. Lives near London, continues to play clubs and to freelance through the 1990s.

WALKER, 'Mike' Michael
Born: Salford, Manchester, 1962
guitar

Brother also a guitarist. Began playing guitar at sixteen. Sat in at local jazz clubs during the early 1980s. Joined vibes player Alan Butler in Altrincham for three years, then began working further afield with Some Other Country. With Mike Gibbs' Big Band, then worked in Kenny Wheeler's Band (including touring in Europe). Later worked in trio with Kenny Wheeler and John Taylor. Spent two years with Tommy Smith. Continues to lead own quartet and freelance with various line-ups including national tour as part of Julian Argüelles' Quartet (May 1996).

WALLEN, Byron
Born: London, 17 July 1969
trumpet/composer/keyboards

Piano lessons during childhood, then played euphonium in Boys' Brigade Band before taking up trumpet while in sixth form at school. Studied psychology at Sussex University. With Cleveland Watkiss (1991), then worked in many line-ups including Afro Bloco, Just Friends, Free Speech, John Stevens' Quartet, Gary Crosby's Band, etc., often playing in Europe. His *Tarot Suite* composition was premiered in the early 1990s. Continues to be featured with various bands, touring with Gary Crosby's Nu Troop and working with saxist Ed Jones' Quintet (1995–6). Own Sound Advice (1996).

338

WALLIS, 'Bob' Robert Born: Bridlington, Yorkshire, 3 June 1934
trumpet/vocals Died: Potters Bar, Middlesex, 10 January 1991

His son Jay is a trumpeter and singer. Began on cornet, played in local Salvation Army Band (together with trombonist Keith 'Avo' Avison). Led own band in Bridlington and in Hull (1954), took group to Denmark in summer of 1954, also toured Europe briefly as a singer (May 1956). Moved to London in 1957, played in the Storyville Jazzmen (then led by Hugh Rainey and John Mortimer), and in Ken Colyer's Omega Brass Band. With Acker Bilk from May 1957 to February 1958, then toured Scandinavia with Diz Disley (spring 1958) and worked alongside Sister Rosetta Tharpe. Was taken ill not long after being appointed leader of the Storyville Jazzmen in 1958. After a spell in hospital he resumed leading in early 1959. Despite further health problems he continued to lead with considerable success during the early 1960s (which included a residency at the London Palladium). Wallis disbanded and worked briefly with Monty Sunshine in 1965, but soon re-formed his own band, which worked regularly in Europe throughout the 1970s and 1980s. In 1972, the band began the first of many residencies at the Casa Bar in Zurich, Switzerland. They worked there very often during the following eighteen years (during this period the band also played in Germany, Canada, Scandinavia and Britain). Desperately ill, Bob finally returned to his home in England two months before his death.

WALTON, 'Harry' Henry Charles Born: 9 July 1928
piano Died: 1982

Worked in various dance bands, then played in the Galleon Jazz Band before joining Charlie Galbraith in late 1951. With the Tomasso Brothers' Dixieland Jazzmen in 1955, left to work with Bobby Mickleburgh. Led own band in London from 1956, which played a long residency at the Coleherne Hotel. Worked in Peter Deuchar's Band (1962–3), then freelanced with various bands. With Charlie Galbraith, and deputized in Terry Lightfoot's Band. Re-formed own band in summer of 1968, but played freelance dates including some with Alan Elsdon in 1969. Led own Society Jazz Band in the 1970s, also played in the Elite Jazz Band and organized jazz excursions on riverboats. Played mainly in the Hastings, Sussex, area during the early 1980s, but also led own quartet at the Pizza Express in London. Electrocuted while using a lawn mower.

WARLEIGH, 'Ray' Raymond Kenneth Born: Sydney, Australia, 28 September 1938
saxes/clarinet/flute

Began on flute at ten, then took up clarinet, played in Police Board Boys' Club Band. Alto sax from eighteen, served apprenticeship as an electrician, then became professional musician working with Dave Murray's palais band in Sydney for nine months (1959). Moved to Britain in 1960. Worked with Ken Scott's Band in Aberdeen (1960). Did summer season with drummer Don Robb's Quintet in Guernsey (1961), then season at a Butlin's holiday camp. Worked with Eric Delaney and with Alexis Korner, then played US bases in Europe. With Fat John Cox (early 1964) and in John Burch's Octet (from 1964). With Pete Comton's Big Band (1965), in John Stevens' Septet (early 1966) and later in Spontaneous Music Ensemble. Again with Fat John Cox (1966) and in Chris Pyne's Sextet (1966). Brief return trip to Australia in late 1966. Led own group and worked in Humphrey Lyttelton's Octet and Big Band (1968). With Ronnie Scott's Octet, Big Band

and Sextet (summer 1968 to early 1970). With John Warren's Big Band (1970) and with Tubby Hayes. During the 1970s worked with Mike Gibbs, Mike Westbrook, Mick Pyne's Quartet, Dick Crouch's Paz, Kenny Wheeler, briefly again with Humphrey Lyttelton, and again with John Stevens, etc. Co-led quintet with guitarist Allan Holdsworth. Extensive freelance work through the 1980s and 1990s, including spell with German radio orchestra in Cologne, also worked with Tommy Chase, with Stan Tracey, in Kenny Wheeler's Big Band, in Charlie Watts' Big Band, in Derek Wadsworth's Blind Alley, in the London Jazz Orchestra and leading own groups.

WARNE, Derek John   Born: Lowestoft, Suffolk, 21 August 1932
piano/vibes/percussion

Played semi-professional jobs around Lowestoft, then moved to London. Spent a year in Laurie Gold's Pieces of Eight, then worked in Germany and at US bases in Europe for two years accompanying French West Indian singer Ken Hunter. Began doubling on vibes. Returned to London and became leader of band at the Blue Lagoon Club before joining Ted Heath in September 1959. Spent almost ten years with Ted Heath, then became a successful freelance session musician, playing piano, vibes and Latin American percussion. Moved to East Anglia in the early 1980s, sold his vibes and percussion instruments but continues to play piano and to work as a musical director.

WARREN, 'Huw' Robert Huw   Born: Swansea, Glamorgan, South Wales,
piano/cello/piano accordion/arranger/composer   18 May 1963

Piano studies from the age of ten, also played cello during his early years. Moved to London in 1979. Did classical course at Goldsmiths College for three years, then participated in jazz course at the Guildhall School of Music (studying mainly with Lionel Grigson). Began playing gigs. Deputized for Django Bates in Loose Tubes and this led to work with Mark Lockheart, Julian and Steve Argüelles. Played in various world music ensembles including Somo Somo. During the 1990s has worked and recorded with Perfect Houseplants, with Billy Jenkins and the Fun Horns of Berlin, with Christine Tobin (including overseas tours), with Tim Garland, etc. Works with singer June Tabor, and in trio with clarinettist Pete Whyman and drummer Peter Fairclough. Featured with Steve Argüelles at Le Mans Festival (1996).

WASSER, 'Stan' Stanley Phillip   Born: Hackney, London, 7 May 1928
double bass/guitar   Died: London, 25 April 1961

Originally a guitarist. Worked with Johnny Franks on South Coast (1948), playing guitar, thereafter specialized on double bass. Studied at Guildhall School of Music. Gigged with Kenny Graham and with Harry Klein, then worked with Jimmy Walker in Edinburgh (1950–1). With Teddy Foster, Cab Kaye, Dave Usden, Roy Fox, then joined Oscar Rabin (April to July 1952). With Norman Burns, Harry Klein, Tony Kinsey, then to Iceland with Vic Ash (May to June 1953). With Revell Terry and Don Heywood, then joined Tito Burns (August 1953). With Vic Lewis (1954), then with Johnnie Gray (December 1954 to 1955). With Jackie Fisher and freelancing. With Phil Seamen Quintet (summer 1957), to Russia with Geoff Ellison's Band (July to August 1957). In Dizzy Reece's Quintet (1958), then with Ronnie Ross-Allan Ganley Jazzmakers (from

September 1958 until January 1960), including tour of USA. Freelanced briefly in Bermuda. Worked with Kenny Lack's Band at the Don Juan Club, London, in spring of 1961. Was found dead in a gas-filled room.

WATERMAN, 'Steve' Stephen   Born: near Boston, Lincolnshire, 8 September 1960
trumpet/flugelhorn

Sister is a singer. Began playing trumpet at ten. Moved to London in 1980, studied at Trinity College. Played in Eurojazz, then joined NYJO in the early 1980s. During the 1980s began long musical association with Michael Garrick, which continued through the 1990s; also enjoyed long-lasting participation in Cayenne through the 1990s. With Dave O'Higgins' Quintet in 1987. Played in various John Surman line-ups and in Carla Bley's Band. With Don Rendell's New Five (1992–4). Worked and recorded with guitarist Mark Ongley. Has led own quartet since the late 1980s, with recordings issued. Teaches at Wavendon and at Royal Academy of Music. His book *The Jazz Method for Trumpet* (co-edited by John O'Neill) was published in 1995.

WATKINS, Derek Roy   Born: Reading, Berkshire, 2 March 1945
trumpet/flugelhorn/cornet

His grandfather led a brass band; his father, George Watkins (trumpet and sax), played in brass bands and led a dance band in Reading. Cornet from the age of six. Worked in his father's band at Majestic Ballroom, Reading, as a teenager (occasionally doubling on guitar). Joined Jack Dorsey's Band at Astoria Ballroom, London, in early 1963 for two years, then joined Billy Ternent at the London Palladium. Freelanced in London, then joined Tony Evans prior to working with Ted Heath, John Dankworth, Harry South's Big Band, Tubby Hayes, Maynard Ferguson, Stan Tracey, Mike Gibbs, Bobby Lamb-Ray Premru, Clarke-Boland Big Band, Peter Herbolzeimer, etc. Toured Europe with Benny Goodman in the 1970s, also toured USA with Tom Jones often during the early 1970s (during this period played in various American studio bands, recording with Louis Bellson, Phil Woods, Michel Legrand, etc.). Prolific session work and freelance playing in the 1980s and 1990s, backing Frank Sinatra, Barbra Streisand, Lena Horne, etc., featured with Kenny Wheeler's Big Band, with Julian Joseph Big Band (1995–6) and in Peter Long's Echoes of Ellington.

WATSON, Jimmy   Born: Cowdenbeath, Scotland, 12 October 1922
trumpet/vocals/arranger

Trumpet from age of eleven, played in CWS Brass Band. Professional at seventeen, worked with Herman Darewski, Bennie Loban, Lou Preager and Lew Stone. In drummer Johnny Birks' Band in Glasgow (1944), then joined George Elrick in summer of 1944. With Harry Hayes (1945) and with Teddy Foster, then worked briefly with Ted Heath in 1945 before joining the Squadronaires from late 1945 until April 1951. With Jack Parnell from April 1951 until June 1953 (except for temporary absences through illness). Spent a few months with Ambrose, then temporarily gave up trumpet to sing and arrange for the Sapphires vocal group (1953–4). Recommenced playing trumpet and rejoined Ambrose in summer 1954. With Malcolm Mitchell Big Band from January 1955 until rejoining Jack Parnell in May 1955. Worked in Ronnie Scott's Band (1955), then did studio and session work and played with Denny Boyce's Band at the Lyceum Ballroom, London. Later played in Downbeat Big Band and in Sounds of Seventeen.

WATT, Tommy
piano/arranger/composer

Born: Glasgow, Scotland, 1925

With Carl Barriteau before serving in RAF during World War II. After demobilization worked with Ronnie Munro, Tony Wayne and Kathy Stobart before doing a summer season on the Isle of Man with Paul Fenoulhet (1950). With Ken Mackintosh from November 1950 to February 1951, then worked at the Studio Club, London, and freelanced as a pianist and arranger. Briefly in Harry Roy's Band (1955). Formed own Orchestra (1955) which broadcast regularly, also led own quintet at Quaglino's for two years (1955–7). Freelanced again and wrote music for six Whitehall farces and two Brian Rix films. Became leader of the BBC Northern Dance Orchestra in 1960. Led Centre 42 Band in 1964, then became staff writer for the BBC until leading own band for Dorchester Hotel residency in the early 1970s. Worked again as a freelance musician-arranger, then became successful interior decorator.

WATTS, Arthur Robert
double bass/bass guitar

Born: East Ham, London, 27 May 1928
Died: Enfield, Middlesex, January 1993

Double bass from age of thirteen, played in Enfield School Orchestra. Became a professional musician while still a teenager. With Eric Siddons (1947), Duncan Whyte (October 1947–8), including work in Spain. With Ronnie Odell from late 1948 to early 1950. With Nat Gonella, Carl Barriteau and Jimmy Walker before joining Ambrose in spring 1953. Gigged with Vic Ash, then joined Frank Weir (September 1953 to January 1954). Founder-member of Ken Moule Seven in January 1954, took over leadership of this group in April 1955. Rejoined Ambrose in September 1955, left to join Geraldo from January 1956 until August 1957. Worked with Jazz Today Unit (1957) and with Don Rendell's Quintet and Vic Ash (including trip to USA). Worked with Allan Ganley-Keith Christie Jazzmakers in the early 1960s, also toured USA with Vic Lewis in spring 1960. With Harry Klein-Vic Ash Jazz Five (1961–2), thereafter did extensive freelance work, with Ronnie Aldrich, Geoff Love, Johnnie Gray, etc. From 1952 through to the late 1960s worked often in Ralph Dollimore's Trio. Toured USA with Tony Bennett (in 1972), then did extensive theatre and club work until the late 1980s.

WATTS, Steve
double bass

Born: Sutton, Surrey, 14 September 1961

Took up bass guitar at fourteen, then switched to double bass at seventeen, took lessons at school from Bob Hart. Did eighteen months' study at Guildhall School of Music, then gradually starting gigging with pick-up bands around the London area. Worked with Iain Ballamy and Django Bates during the early 1980s, which was the beginning of a long musical association with these two, and with Julian Argüelles. Did first touring in the mid-1980s with Julian Argüelles and Simon Purcell. Worked with saxophonist Martin Speake and continued to do so occasionally through the 1990s. Has played on many freelance recordings but is regularly with Christine Tobin, Billy Jenkins, Steve Argüelles, Julian Argüelles, Eddie Parker and Iain Ballamy (1996).

WATTS, Trevor Charles
Born: York, 26 February 1939
alto sax/soprano sax/piccolo/flute/composer

Originally played cornet. Took up sax at seventeen. In 1958 signed on for five years as an RAF musician. Studied at Royal Air Force School of Music, then served in Germany. Left RAF in 1963. Moved to London, gigged with Long John Baldry and with the Original All Stars (1964). In New Jazz Orchestra from 1965, founder-member (with ex-RAF colleague John Stevens) of Spontaneous Music Ensemble (1966). Worked in Denmark, then re-formed SME and remained part of it for over a decade. Formed Amalgam in June 1967, which functioned through into the 1980s. During the late 1960s and 1970s toured with own sextet and worked with Harry Miller's Quintet, with Louis Moholo, in Keith Tippett's Ark, in John Stevens' Dance Orchestra, with Pierre Favre, Bob Downes, Bobby Bradford, and in Stan Tracey's Open Circle, etc. Part of London Jazz Composers' Orchestra from 1972. Led own String Ensemble from 1976, and Universal Music Group from 1978. In the 1980s led own Drum Orchestra and Moiré Music which have continued through the 1990s. Composes for his various groups, which are featured at numerous international festivals. Continues to work in varying musical surroundings including duos with drummer Liam Genockes. Has worked alongside many American musicians including Steve Lacy, Don Cherry, Archie Shepp, etc. Did widespread international touring (1995–6) playing in North America, and South America, then worked in Europe with Moiré Music Trio (with Colin McKenzie on bass and Paapa J. Mensah on percussion).

WEATHERBURN, 'Ron' Ronald John
Born: Dagenham, Essex, 31 January 1934
piano/composer
Died: Brampton, Canada, 26 May 1995

Began playing piano at six, took lessons for six years. Worked for several years in Eric Silk's Band before joining Cy Laurie in early 1958. Worked in Germany with Eggy Ley (1959), then co-led band in Germany with Mac White (1960). Joined Kenny Ball in summer of 1960 and remained for over ten years, except for absence through injury in 1967. Played gigs with Monty Sunshine in 1970, then worked mainly as a solo pianist for long periods, also active as a composer. From 1975 until 1980 often worked in trio with Ian Howarth (drums) and Alan Cooper (clarinet). From the 1980s worked regularly in the Original Eastside Stompers, occasionally in Brian White's Magna Band. With Ken Sims' Dixie Kings from the late 1980s through to the mid-1990s. Went to Canada with Ken Sims in May 1995, where both were to appear as guest stars at the Toronto Classic Jazz Society Festival. He died in his sleep on the night of his arrival in Canada.

WEBB, George Horace
Born: Camberwell, London, 8 October 1917
piano

During the early part of World War II, when working in the machine-gun department of the Vickers-Armstrong factory at Crayford, founded the Bexleyheath Rhythm Club. He also helped organize a sixteen-piece band to play in the works canteen, but did not play in that ensemble. He did, however, briefly take lessons from the trombonist Jack May. On Saturday afternoons Webb (on piano) and trumpeter Owen Bryce rehearsed in Webb's front room, and this duo provided the nucleus of the pioneering unit that became known as George Webb's Dixielanders. Webb and Bryce were joined by a Vickers-Armstrong employee, trombonist Eddie Harvey, who recommended the clarinettist Wally Fawkes. Adding Reg Rigden on cornet, they began playing together regularly in the basement of the Red Barn in Barnehurst, Kent. The band went on to make recordings and to play on BBC radio, they also played concerts in various British cities. In latter days the two-trumpet line-up was abandoned and the group's sole trumpeter was Humphrey Lyttelton. The Dixielanders disbanded in early 1948, and later that year Webb joined the band led by his former sideman, Humphrey Lyttelton (from September 1948 until June 1951). Webb also occasionally guested with Mike Daniels at a Deptford residency. He re-formed a new version of the Dixielanders in the spring of 1952 (featuring Ron Abbitt on cornet) but soon disbanded and devoted his time to running a successful jazz club at the Shakespeare Hotel in Woolwich. He rarely played piano during the ten years he worked for Jazzshows promotions (1955–65). Subsequently he became an agent and manager for various rhythm-and-blues artistes and jazz musicians. During the early 1970s he resumed more regular playing, and accompanied singer Jo Starr for work in Czechoslovakia, and was also featured on solo tours of Finland, Hungary, etc. In 1973 he re-formed a new version of his Dixielanders (with Terry Pitts, Dennis Field and Sammy Rimington) and led them until running own public house in Stansted, Essex, for twelve years (from 1974). He often booked bands for the pub, and sat in with them. He moved back to Erith, Kent, and again led own bands and guested with various line-ups (including taking part in reunions of Humphrey Lyttelton's early band). After undergoing a hand operation in the autumn of 1995, he resumed regular playing schedule.

WEBB, 'Ray' Raymond
guitar/double bass/vocals/arranger

Born: c.1916

Worked on guitar with Benny Carter in Scheveningen, Holland, during summer of 1937. Returned to London and played double bass in Don Barrigo's Bandits in 1938. On guitar with Dan Donovan's Music (1938). With drummer Phil Watts (1939). Doubled with Jack Jackson (1939–40), then served in RAF from 1941. After demobilization joined Miff Ferrie in 1946, then worked in Canada (1947). Returned to Britain in 1948 and settled in Thornton Heath, where he freelanced as a musician and writer.

WEED, 'Johnny' John F.
piano/arranger/composer

Born: London, 15 May 1931

Served in the Army before working with Basil Kirchin (1952). Worked briefly in Ireland with Pat Bateson, then joined Dave Kahn's Band on the *Queen Mary* (1952). With Vic Lewis before joining Tito Burns (1953–4). With Denny Wright's Trio at Casanova Club, London (1954–5), then replaced Ken Moule and worked in the 'Ken Moule Seven directed by Arthur Watts' (1955). With Vic Ash (1955), Dizzy Reece, Joe Harriott, Phil Seamen (1956). Emigrated to the USA in 1957. Worked with Buddy Morrow, Charlie Barnet, Woody Herman, Tex Beneke, Ray McKinley, etc., also ran successful arranging business with Ronnie Roullier until 1971. Moved to Florida in 1993, continues to play regularly (1995).

WEEDON, 'Bert' Herbert M.
guitar/composer

Born: London, 10 May 1920

Guitar at fourteen, some lessons from Ivor Mairants. Gigged with night club bands and played in Johnny Shakespeare's Band in Romford (1939). In Laurie Gold's Band (early 1940). Played at Number One Rhythm Club in 1942, joined Hatchett's Swingtette accompanying Stephane Grappelli (1943). In Frank Weir's Quartet (1944), also worked in the Ambulance Service during World War II. With Harry Gerrard's Band (1945), Harry Leader (1945), Howard Baker (1945), Harry Gold (1946–8), during this period also played many sessions and worked with the Squadronaires and with Cyril Stapleton. Period of ill health in the early 1950s, thereafter freelanced successfully and made several best-selling instrumental recordings; featured on television, stage, radio.

WEIR, Frank
clarinet/saxes/bass clarinet

Born: 30 January 1911
Died: 12 May 1981

Served as an Army musician from the mid-1920s, first in the Argyll and Sutherland Highlanders and then in the Dorset Regiment. Joined pianist Ernest Loraine in Brighton (1932). Worked with Howard Jacobs (1934). With Jack Hylton (1936), Val Rosing (1936), Bill Gerhardi (1936), Ben Frankel (1937), also worked with Jack Payne, Van Phillips, Peter Yorke and Fred Hartley in the 1930s. With Geraldo (1938–9), Sydney Lipton (1939), Ambrose (1940), Arthur Young (1940), Dennis Noonan (1941) and again with Ambrose (1941). With Chappie D'Amato (1943), Stephane Grappelli (1943), led own group in 1943, occasionally guested with Johnny Claes. For much of World War II served in the Air Transport Auxiliary as a ferry pilot. Led own band from 1945, played residencies at various London night clubs including the Bagatelle, the Astor, Hatchett's, Fischer's etc. In the mid-1950s led own big touring orchestra but reverted to smaller line-up. As a pilot he took part in the King's Cup Air Races for many years. Freelanced with the London Symphony Orchestra and the London Philharmonic and guested with Roy Fox and Ted Heath. Led own band for summer seasons during the 1960s and 1970s, occasionally playing London club residencies. Occasionally led a twenty-piece orchestra in the early 1970s, and worked as musical director for the Drury Lane Theatre, London. Opened own recording studio in 1973.

WELDON, 'Nick' Nicholas
piano/composer

Born: Cambridge, 19 March 1954

Step-father Ron Weldon played trumpet; Nick's mother is novelist Fay Weldon. Played piano from age of eleven, also made tentative efforts to play the guitar. Gained First Class degree in French and philosophy at University of Keele in the 1970s. Lived in France, specialized on piano and did first gigs with local musicians in Amiens. Worked as a trained chef. Settled in London and became professional pianist in 1979, led own Trio and worked with Joe Jackson. During the 1980s worked with Art Themen, Harold Beckett, Tommy Chase, Jim Mullen, Chris Hodgkins-Max Brittain group, Don Weller-Bryan Spring Quartet, Kathy Stobart, etc. Led own Trio through the 1980s and 1990s which accompanied many visiting musicians including Sonny Stitt, Bobby Watson, Teddy Edwards, Johnny Griffin, Jimmy Witherspoon, etc. Also regularly worked with Peter Ind (in duos and trios) and with Ind accompanied Dewey Redman, Sheila Jordan, Harold Land, etc. Has enjoyed success as a composer, wrote music for a work based on his mother's novel *Puffball*. His radio play *Laura Mae and the Olivardies* was first broadcast in 1994. Continues to lead own Trio (1995), and to work regularly with Pat Crumly, Bobby Wellins, etc., and to freelance. Also active as a teacher, touring schools and colleges with the BP Jazz Workshop and being a long-time member of staff at the Wavendon Jazz Summer Course.

WELLER, Don
Born: Croydon, Surrey, 19 December 1947
tenor sax/soprano sax/clarinet/
composer/arranger

Started on clarinet at twelve, played in Croydon Orchestra and formed own trio for coffee bar gigs. Originally worked as a panel beater, took up tenor sax and played in Kathy Stobart's rehearsal band. Did two summer seasons at Butlin's holiday camps with Eric Winstone. Worked with Harold Beckett in East of Eden, and occasionally with Alex Harvey, Jack Bruce, etc. Formed own Major Surgery in the early 1970s which lasted for almost ten years. During the early 1970s began long musical association with Stan Tracey which continued through the 1990s. Has often co-led quintet with Art Themen. During the 1970s and 1980s also worked with the Bebop Preservation Society, with Bobby Wellins, Alan Price, Georgie Fame, Jimmie Roche, Ian Stewart's Rocket 88, Dave Defries, Charlie Watts' Big Band and worked with Gil Evans on British tour. Has regularly co-led a quartet with Bryan Spring. Has continued to work with Bryan Spring, with Stan Tracey and Alan Stuart through the 1990s. Also leads own touring quartet, and own big band which plays his arrangements and compositions.

WELLINS, 'Bobby' Robert Coull
Born: Glasgow, Scotland, 24 January 1936
tenor sax/composer

Tuition from his father, Max, who was an alto saxophonist (and multi-instrumentalist). Bobby's mother was a singer. Played piano during early childhood, alto sax from twelve, clarinet during teens. Did local gigs, then joined the RAF as a musician and began specializing on tenor sax. After demobilization worked with Bernard Ebbinghouse's Band in Slough, Buckinghamshire. With Buddy Featherstonhaugh's Quintet from autumn 1956 to summer 1957. Worked with Frank Weir, Eric Winstone, John Dankworth and Malcolm Mitchell. Regularly with Vic Lewis in 1958 (including tour of USA). To France in spring 1959, with John Burch and Jeff Clyne. Briefly with Laurie Morgan (1959), then joined Tony Crombie (1959). With Bert Courtley in Jazz Committee (early 1960). With Tony Kinsey (1960), then briefly co-led quintet with Ken Wray, also worked with Tommy Whittle's Orchestra at the Dorchester Hotel, London (1960–1). Formed own quintet (1961), worked in New Departures Quintet in the early 1960s, led own quartet in Annie Ross show. Briefly in Keith Christie-Jimmy Deuchar group (early 1965). During the 1960s began long musical association with Stan Tracey, regularly featured in Tracey's quartet and big band through to the early 1970s, then addiction problems enforced retirement from professional music. Worked outside of music in the early 1970s, but resumed playing around the Brighton area in 1975, then worked in London with Lionel Grigson (1976). Co-led quintet with Don Weller and again worked with Stan Tracey in the late 1970s. Led own groups through the 1980s and 1990s, also active as a teacher (became Honorary Fellow in Music Department of West Sussex Institute of Higher Education). Featured with Charlie Watts' Orchestra (1985–6), during the 1990s worked in big bands led by Kenny Wheeler and Bob Wilber. Continues to play regularly in 1996, occasionally in Tenor Madness (with John Barnes and Spike Robinson) in co-led quintet with trombonist Scott Stroman and as featured soloist with various line-ups.

WELLS, 'Spike' Michael John
Born: Tunbridge Wells, Kent, 16 January 1946
drums

Piano, cello and voice studies at Canterbury Cathedral Choir School. Played in University jazz groups at Oxford. During the late 1960s and early 1970s worked with Tubby Hayes, Ronnie Scott, Humphrey Lyttelton, also led own quartet. Often in Ian Hamer's Sextet (1973–5), also worked in Finland with Dave Horler (1975). Accompanied many visiting American musicians and worked in Europe with Stan Getz, etc. During the late 1970s began long musical association with Bobby Wellins, which lasted into the 1990s. During the late 1970s and 1980s gigged with many line-ups, including the Kelly-Burden Quintet, Pete King's Quartet and Geoff Simkins' Quartet. Combined these activities with his work as a solicitor, then, after intensive religious studies, took holy orders.

WELSH, Alex
Born: Edinburgh, Scotland, 9 July 1929
cornet/vocals
Died: Middlesex, 25 June 1982

Played accordion at Broughton Secondary School, left at eighteen to work as a clerk in the Ministry of Works. Took up cornet, lessons from Bill Taverner. Played in local Silver Band, then joined Archie Semple's Band in 1951. With Nova Scotia Jazz Band (1952), then joined Sandy Brown's Blue Five (1953). Moved to London in May 1954 to work with Dave Keir's Band, but left after three weeks to form own band, which made its debut in June 1954. For over a quarter of a century Alex continued to lead his own band, often accompanying visiting American musicians. His band was featured at the Newport Jazz Festival, USA, in the summer of 1968. In 1963 he temporarily led a big band. His band toured Australia in 1978 as part of the *Salute to Satchmo* show. During the late 1970s and early 1980s his health began to fail and he was forced to disband for several months. He returned to an active schedule in September 1981, and played dates in Switzerland in April 1982. He led his band for the last time at a gig in Nottingham on 10 June 1982, he died two weeks later in Hillingdon Hospital.

WEST, 'Cederick' Herbert Frederick
Born: Rangoon, Burma, 9 December 1918
guitar/trombone

Featured with the Jive Boys in Rangoon (1940), then moved to India in 1942 and later that year joined American bandleader Teddy Weatherford (began doubling on trombone). Moved back to Burma in June 1945 and became musical director of all the NAAFI clubs in Rangoon. Moved to Britain in September 1947. Worked (on trombone and guitar) with Leslie Douglas, then joined Sammy Herman's Windjammers (late 1948). To Scandinavia with Leslie 'Jiver' Hutchinson (1949), then again worked with Leslie Douglas from late 1949 until March 1951. Briefly with Benny Baker's Band at the 21 Room, London, then joined Freddy Grant (June 1951). Left Grant in November 1951 to work in India with Revell Terry's Band. Returned to Britain in spring 1952. Worked with Nat Gonella before joining Alan Kane in late 1952. Briefly with Vic Lewis, then three years in the Tim-Wu-Kee Sextet before leading own band in Brighton (1958). Led own quintet in the early 1960s, then became freelance session player appearing many times in the *That Was the Week That Was* television band. Played in BBC Orchestras through the late 1960s and 1970s. Led own quintet on American liners (1979), and then resumed freelancing. Continues to play regularly in the 1990s, mostly around the Essex area, occasionally co-leading a quartet with Dave Cliff.

WESTBROOK, 'Mike' Michael John David
piano/alto sax/tenor cor/tuba/
composer/arranger

Born: High Wycombe, Buckinghamshire,
21 March 1936

Husband and collaborator of singer and instrumentalist Kate (formerly Katherine Jane Barnard). Originally played trumpet, piano and guitar. Educated at Kelly College, Devon. After National Service spent a year at Cambridge. Organized jazz group at Plymouth College of Art. Formed own band which played mainly in the West Country, combining this with work as a scenic artist for Westward Television. Moved to London in early 1963, taught art at Drayton Manor Grammar School before becoming a professional musician. Led own sextet (which included his star sideman from Plymouth days, John Surman) and was featured at Montreux Jazz Festival in 1968. By then Westbrook was also leading his Concert Band. He co-led (with John Fox) Cosmic Circus and led Solid Gold Cadillac in the early 1970s. Led own Brass Band from 1973, which featured Lol Coxhill, Paul Rutherford and Phil Minton (then on trumpet; he subsequently specialized in singing). Own Orchestra from 1979. Formed own Trio (with Kate singing and playing, and Chris Biscoe on alto sax) in 1982. These various units have done widespread international touring, and Westbrook himself has conducted radio orchestras throughout Europe. His many successful compositions encompass wide areas of music. He continues to play, tour and compose through the 1990s. He was awarded the OBE in 1988.

WESTON, 'Harvey' William Harvey
double bass/bass guitar

Born: Marylebone, London, 2 March 1940

Grew up in the Mill Hill-Hendon area. Took up double bass at sixteen, played with local bands including a skiffle group, the Zephyrs. First professional work was with Lennie Hastings' Band in Germany (1959), then did summer season with drummer Roy Holiday in Jersey (1960). Toured Belgium with a variety troupe (1961), did summer season at Selsey Bill (1962), then worked in Blackpool, and on tour, with singers Nina and Frederik (1963). Freelanced in various jazz clubs, including regular work at the Bull's Head in Barnes, then spent four years in Olav Vass' Band at Tiberio's, London. During the period of this late-night residency also played various evening gigs. Regularly with Alex Welsh from 1968 until 1974, also did gigs with Kathy Stobart-John Picard group, etc. With Stan Greig's London Jazz Big Band from 1976 to 1978, also deputized for Dave Green in Humphrey Lyttelton's Band (including tour of Poland, 1977). With Kathy Stobart's Quintet from 1978 through to the early 1980s, gigged with Ian Stewart's Rocket 88, and accompanied many visiting American musicians including Pepper Adams, Eddie Vincent, Joe Newman, Tal Farlow, Ruby Braff, Warren Vaché, Scott Hamilton, etc. Often worked with pianist Mick Pyne during the 1980s, and also in Pat Halcox's Summer Band. In 1983 began long musical association with Keith Smith which continued through the 1990s, also works with Brian Priestley's Sextet and in Digby Fairweather's Half Dozen. Regularly tours Germany with drummer Peter York's Band, as well as playing many freelance dates. Is an expert repairer of double basses.

WHALEY, 'Doug' Ian Douglas
trumpet

Born: Sale, Manchester, 9 October 1938

Did first gigs with the Cotton City Jazzmen in Bury, Lancashire (1955–7), also played second trumpet (to Dizzy Burton's lead) in Eric Batty's Jazz Aces. Studied at Oxford and played in Oxford University Jazz Band (1957–61). Regularly with Art Taylor's All Stars (1962–5), with Gordon Robinson's Septet (1962–6), gigged in Cheshire and Lancashire with Mike Knowles' Band. In Alan Hare's Big Band (1965–76) as part of Zenith Six (1970 onwards). Also worked in Keith Pendlebury's Quartet, in Randolph Colville's Old Fashioned Love Band, in Eric Brierley's Jazz Cardinals, Ivor Deach's Quintet, and in the Saints Jazz Band (1974–5). With Sounds Eighteen from 1977 to 1986, Blue Notes (1988–93). With Shades Jazz Orchestra from 1983 through the 1990s, also with Fylde Coast Jazzmen from 1992, also featured as soloist at various jazz festivals.

WHEELER, Ian Gordon
clarinet/saxes/harmonica/guitar

Born: Greenwich, London, 13 January 1931

Lived in Blackheath from the age of four. Took up ukulele at fourteen, soon graduated to guitar. Served in Merchant Navy (1949). Played guitar in Charlie Conner's Band, and in Mike Jefferson's Trio. Switched to clarinet and formed own River City Jazzband (with Ted Pryor, Nobby Willett, Ray Knowles and Graham Patterson) in Mottingham, London (1952). With Mike Daniels (1953–4). Joined Ken Colyer in late 1954 and remained until May 1960 (also played in Colyer's Omega Brass Band). Co-led Vintage Jazz Band (with Ken Sims) from May 1960. Joined Chris Barber in January 1961, left in July 1968. Moved to West Country, led own Jazz Band from 1970 until 1973, then co-led with Rod Mason from October 1973 until spring 1976. Co-led Hefty Jazz (with Keith Smith) from 1976 until March 1976, then rejoined Chris Barber in April 1979. Has continued to work with Barber through the 1990s.

WHEELER, 'Kenny' Kenneth Vincent John
trumpet/flugelhorn/composer/arranger

Born: St Catherines, Ontario, Canada, 14 January 1930

From a musical family, father played trombone. Began on cornet at twelve, studied in Toronto at Royal Conservatory (1950–1), then went to Montreal to start a course at McGill University but soon moved to Britain in 1952. Did a day job for four months, then gigged in various bands, including Freddy Courtney's. With Roy Fox (April to May 1953), then worked in Ronnie Rand's Blue Rockets before joining Derek New's Band at the Celebrite Restaurant, London, from November 1953 to January 1954. With Carl Barriteau from January to April 1954, again with Blue Rockets, then joined Tommy Whittle for several months in September 1955. With Buddy Featherstonhaugh from October 1956–7. With Val Merrall (1958), Vic Lewis (summer 1958 to early 1959). Briefly with Laurie Morgan's Band (early 1959), then toured as part of Woody Herman's Anglo-American Herd (1959). With John Dankworth from spring 1959 until 1963 (was to return for brief spells), also in Bill Russo's London Jazz Orchestra and in Maynard Ferguson's Band. Began long musical association with Mike Gibbs in the late 1960s (which was to last over 25 years). Widespread freelance work from the 1960s onwards, also worked with Graham Collier, Tubby Hayes' Big Band, Tony Oxley, the Clarke-Boland Big Band, Ronnie Scott's Sextet and Big Band, Globe Unity Orchestra, with Joe Harriott in Indo-Jazz Fusion, with John Warren, Evan Parker and in John Stevens' Spontaneous Music Ensemble. Occasionally in Bobby Lamb-Ray Premru Band and Alan Cohen's Band. With Alan Skidmore Quintet (1969–70), Coe Wheeler and Co (with Tony Coe) from April 1970. With John Taylor's Sextet and Mick Pyne's Sextet. Toured with own Azimuth (featuring John Taylor and Norma Winstone) from 1976. In small groups with Bobby Wellins, Anthony Braxton, John Surman, John Dankworth, Mike Osborne, Dave Holland, etc. Part of United Jazz and Rock Ensemble. Extensive international touring and innumerable freelance sessions during the 1970s, 1980s and 1990s, continues to lead own groups, and own big band occasionally (as he has done for over twenty years), also in Argüelles-Purnell Band, in duos with John Taylor, etc. With Lee Konitz's Quintet in London (May 1996).

WHITE, Brian Henry   Born: London, 1 December 1934
clarinet/alto sax

Clarinet from age of seventeen. Played in local Epsom youth club band. Served in the RAF from 1953 to 1955, during this time formed Magna Jazz Band in 1954 (during periods of home leave). After demobilization continued to play in the Magna Jazz Band, and later, when the group ceased to be a co-operative unit, took over leadership. Brian White's Magna Jazz Band has thrived ever since, through the 1990s. White also co-leads the Muggsy Spanier tribute band, Muggsy Remembered (with cornetist Alan Gresty, born Manchester, 28 July 1940), a Bob Crosby Bobcats' tribute band, and a salute to Sidney Bechet and Mezz Mezzrow billed as King Jazz. Widespread touring with these groups including appearances at festivals in Brecon, Edinburgh, Cork and the USA (Sacramento, Palm Springs, Los Angeles and San Francisco). Brian White's Magna Jazz Band also played at the New Orleans Jazz Festival in 1986. The band has also accompanied many visiting American musicians including Kenny Davern, George Masso, Howard Alden, Al Casey, Warren Vaché, etc.

WHITE, 'Mac' Malcolm   Born: Send, Surrey, 4 April 1937
clarinet/saxes

Moved with parents to Cirencester. Played trombone and double bass as a teenager, then joined the Royal Armoured Corps Military Band as a clarinettist in 1952. Served for five years in Germany, also led own small groups, before leaving the Army in 1958. Worked with the Delta Jazz Band in Cheltenham (late 1958), then moved to London and joined Eric Silk. Formed own band for residency in Germany, returned to London, worked briefly with Keith Smith (late 1960), then took Cy Laurie's place in band led by trombonist Terry Pitts (December 1960). Left Terry Pitts to join the Temperance Seven in spring of 1962 (replacing Graham Lyons). Left in late 1963, led ship's band briefly and worked in Original Downtown Syncopators, then joined Alan Elsdon from spring 1965 until 1969. Formed Levity Lancers (with Keith Nichols) in 1969 and worked with them in Britain, the Far East, South East Asia and South Africa. With the Pasadena

Roof Orchestra from 1975 to 1981. With Midnite Follies Orchestra from 1982 to 1984, also worked in Eggy Ley's Hot Shots during this period, and played freelance dates. From the mid-1980s through the 1990s freelanced in many bands, working with Harry Gold, Harry Strutters, in many of Keith Nichols' line-ups as well as being featured in duos with guitarist Peter Rampton, etc. Continues to guest with various bands, and from the mid-1990s led own Spirit of Bechet (with reed-player Charlie Conner).

WHITEHEAD, 'Annie' Lena Anne

Born: Oldham, Lancashire, 16 July 1955

trombone/vocals/arranger/composer/
euphonium/tuba

Learnt trombone at school and played with local brass bands. Did first professional work in Ivy Benson's Orchestra (for two years). Moved to Jersey in the 1970s, then settled in London during the late 1970s. Extensive touring (including USA and Canada) with Joe Jackson, Fun Boy Three and Jah Wobble's Invaders of the Heart. With Working Week in the early 1980s, also with the Brotherhood of Breath and Louis Moholo's Spirits Rejoice. Featured with the Guest Stars, and in Lydia D'Ustebyn's Orchestra, also prolific session work with Elvis Costello, Joan Armatrading, etc. With Paul Rogers' 7RPM, District Six and with singers Maggie Nichols, Jan Ponsford and Carol Grimes. Frequent gigs with drummer John Stevens, and work in Europe with the Berlin Experimental Orchestra, the World Trombone Quartet, guitarist James 'Blood' Ulmer, etc. Own band from 1984, widespread international touring throughout the 1980s and 1990s. Worked with Charlie Watts' Orchestra and with Gail Thompson's Gail Force (1986). During the 1990s wrote *The Lonely Heart Suite* for a ten-piece line-up. Work with Penguin Café Orchestra from 1991 through the 1990s, toured with Pili Pili and played in duo with multi-instrumentalist Ian Maidman, (touring and recording). Subsequently with Maidman in Rude ensemble. Continues to be featured in the Annie Whitehead Experience and combines this with freelance work and with teaching a jazz course at the Royal Academy of Music, London.

WHITEHEAD, 'Tim' Timothy George

Born: Liverpool, 12 December 1950

saxes/clarinet/composer

Began on clarinet, worked with local groups in Liverpool while successfully studying for a degree in law. Moved to London in 1976, gave up law, turned professional, specializing on tenor sax. Co-led South of the Border with guitarist Glenn Cartledge (1977), worked with Ian Carr's Nucleus and with Graham Collier during the late 1970s. With Jim Mullen (late 1980 to early 1981), then worked again with Ian Carr. Led own Borderline during the early 1980s, also toured as a soloist and worked in Afro-Caribbean Breakfast Band. Featured with Loose Tubes from 1984 until 1988. Led own band from 1986 until 1990, also worked with Peter Fairclough's Quartet, Martin Drew's Band and with Patrick Wood. Formed own quartet in 1991 which continues through the 1990s, also guests with various bands and runs jazz workshops; is sax teacher at the West London College.

WHITTAM, Ray
tenor sax/bass sax/clarinet

Born: c.1930

Father was a professional pianist. Played gigs in Leeds, including work with the Royal Garden Quartet (alongside Dick Hawdon). Moved to London to work for the *Daily Express* and took the opportunity to organize the Fleet Street Jazz Club in 1954. It flourished for several years and featured many leading jazz musicians. Ray played in Charlie Galbraith's Band, and guested with Alex Welsh, Kenny Ball and with the Electric Light Orchestra. He worked regularly in the Temperance Seven from September 1961 until spring 1964. He emigrated to Canada in June 1968, was very ill but recovered and later led the Gatsby Five in California. During the 1990s freelanced on tenor saxophone in California.

WHITTLE, 'Tommy' Thomas
tenor sax/clarinet/bass clarinet/flute/piccolo

Born: Grangemouth, Scotland,
13 October 1926

Married to singer Barbara Jay (born Cardiff, 1937) who sang with Geoff Love, Ronnie Scott, Harry Hayes, Benny Goodman, etc. Their son Sean is a keyboard player and composer. Tommy took up clarinet at twelve, tenor sax at thirteen (lessons and advice from Alan Davie and Sammy McLean). Moved to live with grandparents in Chatham, Kent, and soon joined band led by pianist Claude Giddins in Gillingham (1943). Worked with Johnny Claes, then joined Lew Stone from August 1944. After Lew Stone temporarily disbanded (through ill health) played for two weeks in Coventry with David Miller's Band, then worked at the Florida Club, London, in Rex Owen's Band. With Carl Barriteau from June 1945, Harry Hayes from spring 1946. With Ted Heath from March 1947 until April 1952. Featured with Cyril Stapleton's BBC Show Band for three-and-a-half years from October 1952. During this period also did jazz club work, notably with Tony Kinsey. Formed own quintet in April 1954, later augmented this to a ten-piece band which toured for fourteen months. Led own quartet and sextet during the mid-1950s; took sextet to USA and to France in exchange for Sidney Bechet visit to Britain, and took quartet to USA in exchange for Gerry Mulligan Quartet. Guested with Stan Kenton during that leader's 1956 tour of Britain. Toured with Cyril Stapleton (summer 1957). Led own quartet and did a good deal of freelance radio and recordings, including work with Frank Cordell. Led own big band at the Dorchester Hotel, London, from August 1958 until February 1961, then again formed own quartet. Worked in Jack Parnell's ATV Orchestra during the 1960s and early 1970s (which accompanied innumerable stars including Bing Crosby, Peggy Lee, Barbra Streisand, etc.) During the 1960s was also featured with Robert Farnon, with Peter Knight's Orchestra, etc. Continued to play regular jazz club dates and for some years ran own jazz club at the Hopbine in Wembley. Widespread freelance playing included many recording sessions. During the 1980s and 1990s often appeared in the Ted Heath Band (directed by Don Lusher). Played in *Jazz Journal* All Stars (summer 1984) at Nice Festival. Worked in Bob Wilber's Big Band. Joined the Pizza Express All Stars in February 1989 and continued to work with them through the 1990s. Visited Australia in early 1993. Continues to freelance, and to lead own groups, also co-leads quintet with Colin Smith (1996). Through the 1990s own quartet has accompanied the successful *Ella Fitzerald Songbook* show, devised by Barbara Jay, and featuring Rosemary Squires, Maxine Daniels and Barbara Jay. The quartet is also featured in another presentation devised by Barbara Jay, *Ladies of Jazz* (with Jacqui Dankworth, Tina May and Barbara Jay).

WHYTE, Duncan
trumpet/vocals

Born: Shawlands, Glasgow, Scotland, 28 March 1910
Died: Ayr, Scotland, 20 December 1988

Played early local gigs with the Black and White Melody Syncopators. At fourteen moved with parents to London. First professional work with the Blue Revels at Clapham Palais. Joined Jay Whidden (late 1929), then worked with Leslie Osborne at Streatham Locarno. With Percival Mackey (1932), Lou Preager (1933), the Masterkeys, Herman Darewski and Norman Impey (1934). With Buddy Featherstonhaugh (April to May 1935), Teddy Joyce (1935), also played in house bands at the Nest, and the Bag O'Nails in London. Worked with Maurice Winnick at Ciro's. With Billy Mason (1938–9). Teddy Joyce (1940), then worked in Glasgow in Benny Loban's Band (1941). Led own sextet for ENSA tours (1943), later led own quintet, and big band at the Astoria Ballroom, London (1944–5). With Phil Green (1945), Harry Gold (1946). Led own octet which played in Spain (1948), also guested with Derek Neville's Band (April 1948). Formed new band which played residencies in Scotland (Dumfries, Dundee, etc.) during the years 1949–54. With George Lappin's Band (1955), then freelanced and played on cruise liners; did summer season with Harry Bence in Dunoon (1959). Freelanced in the 1960s and occasionally led own band. Worked with Benny Litchfield's Orchestra in Cardiff during the late 1960s, then moved to Ayr, Scotland, in 1971. With Mike Deans' Big Band (1971), worked in Ayr with Sammy Pollack's Band, and was also a disc-jockey on Westsound Radio, Ayr. With Jim Cosker's Sunset Sound and gigged in Glasgow and in Ayr during the 1980s. Led own Dixieland Band until shortly before his death.

WICKHAM, Alan
trumpet

Born: High Wycombe, Buckinghamshire, 23 September 1926

Played in Washington and Lee Swing (1944). In Ken Wallbank's Dixielanders (1946), which formed the nucleus of the Wickham-Russell Hot Six (which Alan co-led with trombonist Tony Russell) from 1946. With Beryl Bryden's Back Room Boys (1949), Roy Vaughan's Chicagoans (1950). With Joe Daniels from 1951 until 1956. With Bobby Mickleburgh (1956), Laurie Gold (1957–8), Johnny Parker (1958), Doctor Crock (Harry Hines) (1959), Bernie Stanton (1958 and 1960–1). Gigs with Geoff Sowden, Paul Simpson, etc., during the early 1960s. With Bobby Mickleburgh's Confederates, took over leadership when Mickleburgh left in 1962. With Charlie Galbraith (1964), Monty Sunshine (1968). Co-led with Joe Daniels (1968–9). With Colin Symons (1969), Russell-Wickham Band, with bassist Ron Russell (1970). With Temperance Seven (1975), Harry Walton (1977), Fidgety Feet Jazzband (1977), Ron Russell (1978). During the early 1980s made six trips to Paris (with Charlie Galbraith) to work with various French musicians. Regularly with the Cambridge City Jass band (1987–91). Guested with various bands in the 1990s and continued to freelance.

WIGFIELD, 'Les' Leslie George
tenor sax/clarinet

Born: Nottingham, 5 October 1928

Worked in Nottingham with Dutch pianist Derek D'Hogie and with Al Washbrooke's Band (1950–1). With Edwin 'Ted' Astley's Band at Sale Lido (1951–2), then with Morris Mack (1953) before joining Vic Lewis from September 1953 until March 1954. With Johnnie Gray (1954–5), briefly with Arthur Rowberry (1954), Leslie Douglas (1955), Dave Shand (1955). With Ken Mackintosh

(1956–9), then joined Eric Winstone in 1960, also worked in band-within-a-band, led by Roy Marsh. Did two years at the Savoy Hotel, London, with Freddie Ballerini (backing American cabaret stars), then joined Ray Ellington's Big Band. Did several cruises playing on liners and also toured with Vic Lewis accompanying American singer Johnny Ray. Toured Australia ..nd New Zealand with American singer P. J. Proby. Worked with Joe Loss during the 1970s (including *QE2* cruises), then did extensive freelance work in the 1980s and 1990s. Leads own group in the 1990s, teaches and also plays in Tony Douglas' Big Band.

WILKINS, 'Dave' David Livingstone
trumpet/vocals

Born: Barbados, West Indies, 25 September 1914
Died: London, 26 November 1990

Youngest of ten children. Joined local Salvation Army Band on trumpet at twelve. Worked in St Vincent and in Martinique with pianist Roy Kippings' Quartet. Moved to Trinidad in May 1934, worked in Bert McClean's Jazz Hounds, then joined the Williams Brothers' Blue Rhythm Band, also played in local Police Band. Moved to England in May 1937 to join band led by Ken 'Snakehips' Johnson (made freelance recordings with Fats Waller in London in 1938). Remained with Johnson until that leader lost his life in an air raid (March 1941). Joined Johnny Claes briefly, then worked with Ambrose (1941–2) and with Chappie D'Amato's Orchestra for theatre work, also doubled by playing in various night club bands. With Harry Parry from June 1942 until November 1943, also guested with Johnny Claes. Joined Maurice Winnick in December 1943, then worked in band led by Leslie 'Jiver' Hutchinson (1944). With Eric Winstone (late 1945), then rejoined Hutchinson (1946). With Ted Heath from January 1947 until April 1949, then rejoined Maurice Winnick. Briefly with Cyril Stapleton (late 1949), then with Cab Kaye from February to December 1950. With Jack Nathan (1951), worked with Frank Weir and with Johnnie Gray before joining Frank King (summer 1952). Briefly with Joe Daniels (January 1953), with Joe Muddel's Band, Roberto Inglez, and Joe Saye's Sextet (1953). Summer season with Reg Wale in Jersey (1954), then worked with Denny Wright before joining Don Smith at Wimbledon Palais (1955–6). Led own band for season at Scunthorpe (1957). Thereafter worked mainly as a freelance, with Bruce Turner (late 1959 to April 1960), Danny Hagerty's Band (1960), Wally Fawkes (1960–1), Sandy Brown (1961), Edmundo Ros, etc. Ill health prevented him from playing during the last years of his life.

WILLIAMS, 'Jimmy' James Thomas
saxes/clarinet/violin

Born: St Pancras, London, 13 July 1914
Died: Brighton, 2 September 1988

Led own band at eighteen, then worked with pianist Clive Errard's Band (1934). With Gerry Moore (1935–6), did summer season with Jimmy Brown's Quartet on Isle of Wight (1936). With Joe Appleton and Reginald Foresythe (1937), then worked in Holland with Benny Carter. Recorded in Holland with Benny Carter and Coleman Hawkins (August 1937). With Len Bermon, Eddie Carroll and Maurice Winnick, then worked with tenor saxophonist Johnny Fresco in Holland (early 1939). With Nat Gonella from spring to autumn 1939 (including tour of Scandinavia). With Jack Doyle briefly, then joined Jack Payne (December 1935). With George Hurley in London (1940), then joined Army and did overseas tours with *Stars in Battledress* show until being invalided out of service in autumn 1944. With Harry Parry from January to September

1945, then worked with Harry Hayes. With Carroll Gibbons 1946 to 1949, then rejoined Harry Parry from late 1949 until February 1951. With Benny Perrin, with Frank Weir and worked in Monto Carlo with Bernard Hilda (1953). With Ambrose and Harry Roy (1954), also toured with American singer Al Martino. With Ken Penney (1955), Leslie 'Jiver' Hutchinson (1956), then freelanced in London until moving to Brighton in 1979.

WILLIAMS, Roy
Born: Salford, Manchester, 7 March 1937
trombone

Father of guitarist Andrew Williams. Played piano before taking up trombone at age of eighteen. Lived in Farnworth and joined Eureka Band in Bolton (led by Bill Robinson). Played in Manchester's South Side Stompers (led by drummer Don Bridgeford), then joined Eric Batty's Jazz Aces (1956–7). Gigged around Manchester area before doing two years in the Army, was stationed in Antwerp, Belgium, and sat in with various local bands. After demobilization moved to London to join Mike Peters (late 1960), then worked with Terry Lightfoot from May 1961. Left Lightfoot to join Alex Welsh in April 1965. Left Alex Welsh in February 1978. Freelanced and worked in duo with Johnny Barnes. With Humphrey Lyttelton from May 1978 until May 1983, during 1978 toured Britain and Australia in the *Salute to Satchmo* package (taking the place of an ailing George Chisholm), also made first visit to Dick Gibson's Jazz Party in Colorado, USA (1978). Founder-member of Pizza Express All Stars (May 1980), often with Five-a-Slide in the early 1980s. Widespread freelance work in the 1980s and 1990s, featured at many international jazz festivals. Toured Europe with the Harlem Blues and Jazz Band, and with the World's Greatest Jazz Band, also played in New York with Bobby Rosengarden's Band. Toured Europe with Peanuts Hucko's All Stars, guested with Bob Wilber's Big Band, worked in Europe with Bent Persson and with Tomas Ornberg. Co-led quartet with pianist Stan Barker, worked in Digby Fairweather's All Stars, in *Salute to Satchmo* package, with Val Wiseman's *Lady Sings the Blues* package and with the Great British Jazz Band (co-led by Digby Fairweather and Pete Strange), and with Keith Smith. Annual tours of Germany with Peter York's Band through the 1990s, also trio work with guitarist son Andrew (and bassist Leon Clayton).

WILLIAMSON, Steve
Born: Hackney, London, 28 June 1964
saxes/composer/arranger

Tentative efforts on piano during childhood. Moved with family to West London, played guitar and had clarinet lessons before taking up sax (alto first then tenor). Attended Guildhall School of Music jazz course. Worked with funk groups Parliament and Grover Washington and with reggae bands the Instigators, Winston Reedy, Misty In Roots, etc. With Jazz Warriors and Courtney Pine. Own first album in 1987, later signed for Verve and recorded in America. Led own quintet from the late 1980s, also worked for a week with Art Blakey, recorded with Louis Moholo and played in the Brotherhood of Breath during the early 1990s. Worked throughout Europe. During the 1990s often with Gary Crosby and continued to lead own line-ups. Composed for the Union Dance Company, and wrote and played for the IDJ Dancers, and Jerry Barrie.

WILLOX, Roy
saxes/clarinet/flute/piccolo

Born: Welwyn Garden City, Hertfordshire,
31 August 1929

Pupil of Harry Hayes. Father played sax, mother the piano. Did first gigs in band led by his mother, Maisie Willox. Briefly with Johnny Claes, then played for nine months in Claude Giddins' Band before joining Henry Hall in spring of 1946. Served in RAF for two years, then freelanced in London before joining Ronnie Pleydell in February 1950. Left Pleydell to work with Ted Heath from September 1950 until August 1955. With Geraldo from September 1955, then worked with Bob Miller and with Jack Parnell before joining the BBC Revue Orchestra from 1958–60. Extensive freelance work thereafter, including engagements with Benny Goodman, Frank Sinatra, Henry Mancini, etc. Played regularly in Harry South's Band during the 1960s and 1970s, made many freelance recordings, and did innumerable television and radio shows, also worked in West End show orchestras. Continues to play regularly through the 1990s, with Don Lusher's Ted Heath Band, with Kenny Baker's New Dozen, in Laurie Johnson's Long Big Band, and is featured in *The Best of British Jazz* shows (1996).

WILSON, Frank
trumpet

Born: Rochdale, Lancashire, 15 March 1923

Lived in Southport from the age of two. Began on 'C' melody sax, then switched to trumpet at seventeen. Joined one of Britain's first revivalist jazz bands, Dave Wilson's Dixieland Five, led by clarinettist Dave Wilson (no relation). Dave Wilson's brother, Eddie, played trombone in the band, which played in Southport during the early 1940s and appeared at the Manchester Rhythm Club in the spring of 1943. They disbanded in 1946 and Frank led his own band and played in the Smoky City Stompers before moving to London, where he led his own Dixielanders and worked with Geoff Sowden (1952), Harry Walton, Ian Bell, Doug Murray, etc. as well as freelancing in various jazz groups. Not to be confused with trumpeter Frank Wilson who worked with Jack Payne in the 1930s.

WILTSHIRE, Billy
drums

Born: Chiswick, London, 9 September 1916

Led own professional band at the age of seventeen, then temporarily became a professional cyclist. Served in the RAF from 1939 to 1942, then worked with Harry Roy (1942–3). With Eric Winstone, from June 1943, and featured in Roy Marsh's Swingtette (1943–4). With George Shearing, Frank Weir, Cyril Stapleton and Harry Hayes before joining Lew Stone in late 1946. With Maurice Winnick (late 1947–8), Ronnie Odell (1948–9), Alan Carr (1950), Cyril Grantham (1951), then left Britain to work in Bermuda with trumpeter Jack Wallace. Moved from Bermuda to California, played there briefly, then worked outside music before returning temporarily to Bermuda. Settled in the USA and took holy orders. His son Peter is a drummer.

WINESTONE, Benny (Benjamin WEINSTEIN)
saxes/clarinet/bass clarinet

Born: Glasgow, Scotland, 20 December 1906
Died: Toronto, Canada, 10 June 1974

His brother, Hymie, was a pianist who died in an air raid in 1941. Benny became a professional musician in 1928, working for Louis Freeman in Scotland and on various transatlantic liners. He was based in the USA from January to May 1931. Returned to Britain and did summer season with Gerry Moore (1931). Worked with Jimmy Macaffer (1933), Slim Grossman, Dave Frost (1934), but still did regular trips on liners and led own band on *SS California* (1934). Returned to Britain, worked with Hal Swain prior to joining Teddy Joyce from January to October 1935. With Billy Merson (early 1936), Lou Preager (May 1936 to April 1937). With Reg Leopold, Teddy Foster, Henry Nicholls and on tour with Frank Stewart (1937). With Eddie Carroll (late 1937–8), Phil Cardew and Joe Kaye (1938), then joined the Heralds of Swing from February to May 1939. Briefly with Geraldo, then moved to Montreal, Canada, in July 1939. Worked with Jimmy Namaro, Frank Bogart and Jimmy 'Trump' Davidson in Canada. Played clarinet in Canadian Navy Band (early 1941), invalided out of service in late 1942. Worked briefly in the USA with Jess Stacy's Band (summer 1945), then led own band in Toronto and played in Maynard Ferguson's Band. Worked in Montreal in Louis Metcalf's International Band until arrested in 1950, was sent to prison for six months on drug charges. After release continued to work in Canada with various small groups, also led own band. After injuring his hands in 1963 he played less frequently but continued to freelance until 1969. He left music and worked as a night clerk in a Toronto hotel.

WINSTON, 'Flash' Cecil Jacob
drums/vocals/piano

Born: London, 6 September 1923

Early professional experience included year with Jerry Allen's Trio at the Prince of Wales Theatre, London. With Duncan Whyte (1944–5), then worked with Denis Rose's Band at the Gliderdrome, Boston (also worked in duo with Rose at the Modernaires Club, London). Again with Duncan Whyte (1946–7). With Carl Barriteau (1947), then worked at Astoria Ballroom, London, with Billy Smith. With Duncan Whyte again (1947–8). With Tito Burns (summer 1948), Leslie 'Jiver' Hutchinson (autumn 1948), then further work with Duncan Whyte (1948). With Cab Kaye (1949), also guested with Benny Goodman for London Palladium residency (on drums) in July 1949. Resident compere at Club Eleven from 1949 until 1953. During this period also worked with Sid Millward and did summer season with Frank King in Guernsey (1951). From the 1950s onwards was mainly active as a compere (also playing piano, drums and singing) at various London clubs, including the Sunset, the Mandrake, the Sporting Circle, etc. Occasionally plays jazz gigs in the 1990s.

WINSTONE, Eric
piano accordion/piano/composer

Born: South London, 1 January 1913
Died: Aldwick, nr Bognor Regis, Sussex, 1 May 1974

Played local gigs as a semi-pro on accordion and on piano. Worked in duo with drummer-vibes player Roy Marsh in the late 1930s. Led Novelty Quintette on radio (and Swing Quartet on recordings) in 1940, also led own accordion band. Formed own big band in late 1941, which achieved widespread success: broadcasting, recording and playing ballroom venues, theatres, etc. He served briefly in the RAF, after release led own band which did many ENSA tours entertaining troops during World War II. Winstone also took his band to Czechoslovakia in early 1947. From 1946 until 1969 he regularly played summer seasons at various Butlin's holiday camps, during this period he was also a musical director at Southern Television. His early colleague, Roy Marsh, shared in almost all of these musical achievements, and also led his own band-within-a-band.

Winstone composed many atmospheric pieces including 'Stagecoach', 'Oasis' and 'Slow Train Blues'. He was an active journalist from the 1940s onwards, often writing for the *Melody Maker*; he also wrote children's stories. For the latter part of his career he also ran his own theatrical agency.

WINSTONE, Norma Ann
vocals/composer/lyricist

Born: Bow, London, 23 September 1941

Father was a self-taught pianist. Studied piano and organ at Trinity College; first gigs as a singer were at weddings. Was given vocal tuition at seventeen by Al Dukardo and sang with his band. Worked with Johnny West's Trio. In the early 1960s gigged around Essex and South London in band led by drummer Ted Humphrey (married Humphrey in 1962) and later did five month tour of American bases in Europe with this group (1965). Subsequently gigged with John Stevens, Johnny Fourie, Mike Carr and Neil Ardley's New Jazz Orchestra. Began working at Ronnie Scott's Club (late 1966). Began long musical association with Michael Garrick, but during the late 1960s and 1970s also worked with various other leaders including Mike Westbrook, John Surman, Kenny Wheeler, Ian Carr, Mike Carr, John Dankworth, etc., also with German unit Jazz Track, and notably with pianist John Taylor (married Taylor in 1972). Trio work (with Michael Garrick and Phil Lee) and with the highly successful Azimuth (with John Taylor and Kenny Wheeler) from the late 1970s through to the 1990s. Sang with BBC Radio Big Band, toured with Ian Carr's Orchestra UK (1989) and regularly featured with Kenny Wheeler's Big Band, occasionally with Tony Coe. Appeared at many international festivals. Worked in London Jazz Orchestra (1994), also recorded with American pianist Jimmy Rowles. Dubbed vocals for television play *Doggin' Around* (1994). Part of Jan Ponsford's Vocal Chords (1995), formed new group New Friends in 1995 (Anthony Kerr, vibes, John Parricelli, guitar and Tim Wells, bass). Featured at Jersey Festival (April 1996). Own 1996 quartet featured Canadian pianist (and bassist) Don Thompson.

WINTER, 'Charlie' Charles
double bass

Born: Berwick-upon-Tweed, Northumberland, 10 January 1906

Father played trombone in the King's Own Scottish Borders. Charlie spent his early years abroad at various of his father's postings, but was sent back to Britain in 1915. Played flute, baritone horn and euphonium at school, then joined the 11th Hussars as a musician (at age of fourteen). Served in Egypt, and India playing euphonium, tenor horn and bass trombone, before taking up the double bass. Left the Army in 1928, played trombone in Glasgow Tramways' Band and gigged on double bass. Toured with a revue, then played in Ostend with a jazz band (1930). Returned to London and eventually joined Alan Green's Band before working with Lou Simmons, Terry Morris, Marek Weber, Teddy Foster, Bobby Hinds, Philip Martell, etc. Worked with Noel Gay in musical *Jack o'Diamonds*, then joined Nat Gonella's newly formed band (April 1935). Starred with Gonella until September 1939, then from 1940 until 1945 served in the RAF (for part of this time led the RAF Hebrideans Band). Did Isle of Man season with Joseph Muscant's Band (1946) and summer season with Hector Davies' Orchestra (1947). Toured with Younkman's Czardas Band, and also worked in band led by Leslie 'Jiver' Hutchinson. Was injured in a motor cycle crash in 1951 but resumed gigging with George Crow in 1952. Gave up playing the double bass and worked with the Shell Oil Company until moving to Australia in 1972, subsequently visited Britain for reunions with Nat Gonella.

WINTERS, 'Tiny' Fred (Frederick GITTENS)
double bass/sousaphone/vocals/bass guitar

Born: London, 24 January 1909
Died: London, 7 February 1996

Originally played trumpet, violin and clarinet; taught himself to play double bass. Did local gigs, then worked with a concert party in Bridlington. Returned to London in September 1931 and freelanced, including two week engagement with Ambrose. Joined Roy Fox in January 1932, remained when Lew Stone became leader and worked regularly with Stone until early 1937. During this period also did summer season in Holland with Ray Noble (1933), and played on many freelance recordings (including sessions with Spike Hughes, Coleman Hawkins, etc.). Was part of Nat Gonella's Georgians when Lew Stone featured the group as a band-within-a-band. Left Lew Stone and worked with Ambrose from March 1937 until late 1938. Briefly in Joe Crossman's Orchestra (December 1938), then became founder-member of the short-lived Heralds of Swing (from February 1939). Again worked with Ambrose (late 1939–40), then joined RAF and played in various service bands, regularly with Billy Amstell's Quintet (the RAF Rhythm Five) from 1941; remained with the Quintet when Arthur Mouncey became leader (in 1944). Occasionally played trombone during RAF service. Demobilized in September 1945, again worked with Lew Stone, brief spell with Frank Weir (spring 1947), until rejoining Lew Stone in summer of 1947. From the 1950s onwards did night club and theatre work as well as many freelance sessions. Played in the *Black and White Minstrel Show* (on sousaphone) from 1962 until 1972, for part of this residency was featured on stage with George Chisholm's Jazzers. Continued to freelance in the 1980s, playing on many sessions, leading own Trio and Café Society Orchestra. Toured with Digby Fairweather in a *Nat Gonella Tribute* (1982) and subsequently worked with Fairweather in the Kettners Five. Led own Trio into the early 1990s.

WISEMAN, 'Val' Valerie
vocals

Born: West Bromwich, Staffordshire, 15 August 1942

Sang with local West Side Jazzmen then spent three-and-a-half years with the Second City Jazzmen (during this time made radio debut singing with Alex Welsh's Band). Left Second City Jazzmen to join Monty Sunshine in September 1963, for three years. Left to follow solo career. Lived in the West Country and often guested with Rod Mason's Band in Plymouth during the late 1960s. Moved back to the Midlands and guested with the Midland Youth Jazz Orchestra. Lived in Berkshire for four years and worked occasionally with Pete Allen, Eggy Ley, etc. Sang at Canadian Exposition 1986. Settled again in Birmingham area and (together with Jim Simpson) devised *Lady Sings the Blues*, a highly successful stage tribute to Billie Holiday, which made its debut on 4 July 1987. Continues to tour with own show through the 1990s, also leads own small groups and guests at various international festivals.

WISHART, 'Bobby'
sax/clarinet/flute/piano/vibes/guitar/
arranger/composer

Born: Motherwell, Lanarkshire, 28 July 1939

Sax lessons from Derek Hawkins. Became a professional musician after serving in the band of the Royal Hussars. Studied at Trinity College, London (1965–6), and at Moray House, Edinburgh (1967–8). During the 1970s and 1980s was featured with many line-ups including the Andy Park Tentet, Alex Harvey's Soul Band, the Geraldo Orchestra, John Altman's Orchestra, also musical director for many musical stars and variety artistes. Regularly led own group and composed and arranged for films and television. Accompanied many visiting American jazz musicians. Teacher of woodwind in Ayrshire Schools. Chair person of International Association of Jazz Educators and from 1987 musical director of the Strathclyde Youth Jazz Orchestra. Senior Woodwind Teacher for Renfrewshire Schools, continues to lead own band and to freelance, playing in many radio and television line-ups. He also teaches jazz improvisation at the Royal Scottish Academy of Music and Drama, and is on staff of Scottish National Jazz Institute. The Strathclyde Youth Jazz Orchestra has been featured at several jazz festivals and has accompanied Benny Carter, Bobby Watson, Gerry Mulligan, George Russell, Carla Bley, Arturo Sandoval, John Surman, etc. Its tours include a visit to the USA in 1992. Its members have included pianists Dave Newton, Eddie Richmond and Steve Hamilton, guitarist Kevin MacKenzie, drummer Paddy Flaherty, bassist Andy Hamill, trumpeters Colin Steel, Allan Wylie, Robert Henderson and Kevin Ferris, trombonist Nichol Thomson and saxophonists Russell Cowleson, Jo Fooks and Laura MacDonald.

WOOD, Colin Arthur
piano/flute/arranger

Born: Camberwell, London, 15 June 1943

Played in jazz groups while at University in Durham (1962–5). Returned to London, did jazz gigs on piano and also played organ in various rock groups. Joined Bill Nile's Delta Jazzmen in 1966. Played in rock bands (1967) and toured with Whistling Jack Smith (Billy Moeller). Worked with Monty Sunshine for six months in 1968, then did teaching but also played in Bill Nile's Goodtime Jazz Band in 1969 (including Mediterranean cruise). Taught maths from 1969, but continued to play regular gigs, including work with Mike Cotton, etc. Joined Acker Bilk in September 1977 and has remained through the 1990s.

WOOD, 'Ken' Kenneth
trombone

Born: Norton, nr Stockton-on-Tees,
Co. Durham, 10 March 1927

Took up trombone while in the Army Cadets. Played in local bands, then worked in Stockton and in Hartlepool with bands led by Jack O'Doyle, Benny Nelson and Jimmy Gardner. Left George Nelson's Band to join Harry Gold in 1950. Moved to London and during the 1950s and 1960s worked with Eric Winstone, Ronnie Rand and the Blue Rockets, Sid Phillips, Joe Daniels, Wally Johnstone and tenor saxophonist Jack Massey. Joined Bob Layzell for Penthouse Club, London, residency and thus began long musical association which continues through the 1990s, also worked again with Harry Gold in the late 1970s and freelanced with various line-ups.

WORDSWORTH, 'Ray' Raymond
trombone

Born: Mexborough, Yorkshire, 18 November 1946

Played trombone from early childhood, also learnt piano. Was in a Sheffield brass band at the age of eight. Gigged with various bands in Sheffield and Rotherham, then toured with Jack Ruane's Irish Show Band before working in London (1967) with various line-ups. Briefly with Monty Sunshine, then did summer season with Joe Daniels. Worked with Val Merrall on summer season then joined Ken Mackintosh in 1970. With BBC Radio Orchestra in 1973, then worked for a year with Sid Phillips. Extensive freelance work including studio sessions and tours with Frank Sinatra, Sarah Vaughan, Billy Eckstine, Vic Damone, Thad Jones, Bill Watrous, Bud Freeman, etc., throughout the 1970s and 1980s. Worked with Freddy Randall in 1976 and Alex Welsh in 1978, often deputized in Alan Elsdon's Band (through to the 1990s). Led own quintet (with Ronnie Ross) in the 1980s and occasionally led own big band. Occasionally in Five-a-Slide in the 1980s. Did regular teaching at summer schools and worked for several summers in Norway, touring and playing at jazz festivals. Often in Bob Wilber's Big Band in the 1980s and 1990s. With Randy Colville's Collection in the 1990s and (with Pete Strange) in Slide by Slide, occasionally deputizes for Strange in Humphrey Lyttelton's Band. Played in Argentine and Uruguay with the official Glenn Miller Band during summer of 1995. Continues to play freelance sessions but also regularly co-leads the Ray Terry Band (with drummer Terry Seymour).

WORTH, 'Bobby' Robert
drums

Born: Bermondsey, London, 8 January 1949

Took up drums at the age of eleven after seeing Joe Daniels in action. Early member of the National Youth Jazz Orchestra (from spring 1966). Did summer season in Newquay in quartet led by bassist Rick Kennedy, then joined trumpeter Grischa Farfel for two years (1966–8). Spent four years in Frankie Vaughan's Vee Men (including international touring), during this period also doubled by playing in Jack Walker's Manchester Opera House Orchestra. Quit touring in the early 1970s and spent almost ten years in Burt Rhodes' Orchestra at the Talk of the Town, London, where he accompanied many international artistes including Pearl Bailey, Buddy Greco, etc. Subsequently played in various West End shows, then began working regularly with Brian Dee, Len Skeat, Digby Fairweather, Dave Shepherd, Kathy Stobart, etc., and accompanying visiting American musicians. During the 1990s often worked with Elaine Delmar, also featured with Val Wiseman's *Lady Sings the Blues* show. Worked in Bob Wilber line-ups, with Keith Smith, toured with Buddy Greco, part of Digby Fairweather's Half Dozen, with tenor saxophonist Spike Robinson, in Colin Purbrook's Trio, with Pizza Express Quintet, etc.

WRAY, 'Ken' Kenneth
trombone/valve trombone/bass trumpet

Born: Manchester, 2 February 1925
Died: Manchester, 13 June 1977

Originally a cornetist, played in Besses O'Th' Barn Boys' Band then switched to trombone; studied at Royal Manchester College of Music. With Teddy Foster (1947–8), Joe Loss (1948–9), Oscar Rabin (1949–51). Temporarily left full time music, then again worked with Teddy Foster in early 1952. Occasionally played in Leon Roy's Band during the late 1940s and early 1950s. With Vic Lewis (spring 1952), then joined Jack Parnell in September 1952, left Parnell in January 1953 to join Ronnie Scott's Band. Returned to Jack Parnell in July 1954, then rejoined Ronnie Scott in September 1954. With Tony Crombie, then again worked with Ronnie Scott (August 1955 to spring 1956). Rejoined Oscar Rabin (summer 1956), worked with Jimmy Deuchar. Moved to Germany in March 1957, worked for eighteen months with Kurt Edelhagen, also with Benny Golson, then returned to Britain and joined Tony Kinsey's Quintet in September 1958. Toured with Woody Herman's Anglo-American Herd in April 1959, then worked with John Dankworth (1960). Briefly co-led quintet with Bobby Wellins (late 1960), then freelanced. With Phil Seamen Quintet (1962), Ian Hamer, and Bobby Wellins (1963), John Burch Octet (1964), also regularly in Tubby Hayes' Big Band and Harry South's Big Band. Moved back to Manchester in 1968, worked in television studio band and in Alan Hare's Big Band, also freelanced locally. During the 1970s led own sextet in Salford, played in the Kennedy-Rowland Hot Six and in the Old Fashioned Love Band (then led by Randolph Colville). With Pete Haslam (1976) and with Pete Kennedy (1977).

WRIGHT, 'Denny' Denys Justin Freeth
guitar/piano/vocals/arranger

Born: Bromley, Kent, 6 May 1924
Died: London, 8 February 1992

Started on guitar at age of eight. Gigged in semi-pro band led by his guitarist brother, then joined Happy Blake's Band in Morecambe, returned to London and worked in Cyril Blake's Band (1942). Served in Auxiliary Fire Service during World War II but continued to play regularly. With Jimmy Henney's Quartet (early 1943), before joining Carl Barriteau (1943). Briefly with Stephane Grappelli (1944), with Duncan Whyte, Phil Green (1945), also played piano at the Fullado Club, London (1946), and worked as a house musician at the Decca recording studios. With accordionist Lorna Martin (1947), briefly with Reggie Dare. Joined Francisco Cavez (Frank Cava) in 1948. With Reg Wale (1949), Bobby Leitch (1949–50), Felix King, Bob Navarro (1950). With Martin Mareno, Freddy Randall (1951), Jack Fallon (1952), George Richards (1953). Again worked with Francisco Cavez during period 1951 to 1953, and occasionally led own band. Continued to lead own group in the 1950s, also featured with the BBC Show Band. With Reg Wale again (1955 to June 1956), intermittently with Lonnie Donegan from August 1956 until March 1957. With Bob Clarke's Quintet in Russia (July to August 1957), also worked with Bruce Turner in Russia. Long (often interrupted) employment in Johnny Duncan's Blue Grass Boys beginning in 1957. Again with Reg Wale's Five in 1959 and in the early 1960s. Tour of USA with Lonnie Donegan (autumn 1962). Briefly in new version of Kenny Graham's Afro-Cubists (1967), but mainly occupied with freelance session work in the late 1960s. Often with Diz Disley in the Hot Club of London in the 1970s and 1980s. With Stephane Grappelli from 1973 to 1978, also worked occasionally with violinist Johnny Franks. Regular member of Velvet (with Digby Fairweather, Ike Isaacs and Len Skeat) during the late 1970s and 1980s, also in duo with Digby Fairweather (1981). Co-led quintet with Australian violinist Don Harper in late 1970s and early 1980s, in duo with Johnny Van Derrick through the 1980s, also in new Hot Club of London.

WYNETTE, Al
trumpet

Born: Enfield, Middlesex, 6 June 1921

Father played piano. Trumpet from twelve, toured with Bottle Party show at sixteen, then gigged with Freddy Mirfield and with Mike Silk before joining Jack Riceman at Tottenham Royal

Ballroom. Worked in Nottingham with Leslie Thorpe and Reub Sunshine, then served in RAF (1941–5). During this period also did radio work with Johnny Rosen and gigged with various bands. After demobilization did two weeks with Les Ayling (October 1945), then worked with Teddy Foster (1945–6). With Joe Loss (1946–7), then led own band for three months in Northern Ireland (1947). Spent over three years with Ivor Kirchin, then worked with Matt Moors in Manchester (early 1952). With George Smith, Roberto Inglez (1953), then over two years with Don Carlos. With Jimmy Silver's Band doubling with Philip Martell's London Casino Orchestra (1959). With Ambrose, Harry Gold and Leslie Douglas, also played Caribbean cruises on *Adventurer* liner before working with Sid Phillips from 1965 until 1973. Led own band (as Al Wynn) at the Café de Paris, London, during the 1970s, also led own jazz group and guested with Allan Leat's Band. Toured with singer Tom Jones as part of Ralph Dollimore's Ted Heath Band. Regularly with Harry Gold from 1977 until 1987. Led own quintet from 1988, also did duo gigs with pianist John China and worked with Pete Allen's Band (1989). Joined Sonny Dee's Band and continued to work with this group through the 1990s, also leading own small groups.

Y

YATES, Neil
trumpet/flugelhorn/composer

Born: Stockport, Cheshire, 28 September 1970

Both parents played trumpet. Took up trumpet and played in Northern Lights, a band led by his parents. Studied at Salford College of Technology, gained Foundation Diploma in Performing Arts (1989). Toured Russia in 1987. First class honours BA in Band Musicianship at University College, Salford (1993), before studying at Guildhall School of Music from 1993. Member of National Youth Jazz Orchestra, also works in various London-based groups including Gary Crosby's Nu Troop, London Jazz Orchestra, Pizza Express Modern Jazz Sextet, System X, Gregory Isaacs, Ceri Evans, Simon Bartholomew, Mari Wilson, etc., and co-leading quintet with Jim Hunt through the mid-1990s.

YEOH, Nikki
piano/composer

Born: London, 24 May 1973

Piano from early childhood, studied classical music during teen years. Played in jazz workshops organized by Ian Carr at Interchange, North London. Played in London Fusion Orchestra. During the early 1990s worked with Courtney Pine, Phillip Bent, Dick Heckstall-Smith, Chante Moore, etc., then worked with the Roots, Steve Williamson, etc. Started own Infinitum trio, which has worked regularly through the mid-1990s. In Collaboration (with Gary Crosby, etc.), accompanied American saxophonist Eddie Harris (1996).

YOUNG, Arthur Wilson Colthard
piano/composer

Born: Edinburgh, Scotland, 1904
Died: Sydney, Australia, 15 July 1965

Educated at Strathallan College, then became medical student at Edinburgh University in

1920–3. During this period also studied piano and gained gold medal at Edinburgh Music Festival. Began gigging in Edinburgh cinemas and ballrooms, then moved to London. Signed by Carroll Gibbons for Berkeley House Band. With Geoffrey Goodhart throughout 1925, then worked in Jack Hylton's Kettner's Band from early 1926, joined Jack Hylton's main band in 1927 (later that year suffered injuries in car crash). With Hylton until late 1928, left in Berlin and there teamed up in duo with Birmingham pianist Geoffrey Gaunt. Later worked in duo with Bob Probst. Accompanied Ethel Waters in Britain (spring 1930). Played in Norway with Bert Marshall's Band and led own band in Berlin (1931). After long stay in France, returned to Britain in September 1933. Accompanied June Clyde and Queenie Leonard in films and recorded with Joe Venuti in London (1934). Musical director for Radio Luxembourg (1934), recorded and broadcast with Ambrose, played duos with Reginald Foresythe and accompanied Larry Adler (1935). Again worked in Europe (1936–7), returned to Britain in July 1937, became Musical Director of the International Broadcasting Company until September 1938. Led own Novochordians at Hatchett's (1939–40), led own Swingtette on variety halls (1940). Injured in 1940 air raid. With Jack Payne on piano and novachord (1941), again led own Swingtette (1942). Army service included being featured in *Stars in Battledress*. After demobilization accompanied Elizabeth Welch and wrote extended compositions, including a ballet. Led own sextet on radio, then played in duo with pianist-vocalist Hamish Menzies. Moved to Hobart, Tasmania, and ran own bar, regularly visiting mainland Australia to broadcast, subsequently returned to full time music and became Musical Director in Melbourne for Channel Nine Television (1957–62). Recorded in Sydney and Melbourne during the mid-1950s.

Z

ZENITH HOT STOMPERS

Formed in Birmingham in 1963, the band was originally called the Zenith Hall Stompers. Its original members were Graham Morris (trumpet), Alan Bradley (trombone), Norman Fields (reeds), Ian Dalziel (banjo), Pete Thompson (bass) and Derek Bennett (drums). In 1964 the band was renamed the Zenith Hot Stompers. It has undergone various personnel changes during the past 32 years but founder-member Derek Bennett (drums) is still with the band. Its other current members are Roy Hubbard (clarinet) joined 1969, Brian Mellor (banjo/guitar) joined 1971, Phil Matthews (tuba/bass) joined 1973, Tony Davis (trumpet) joined 1981, and Brian Cotton (trombone) joined 1994. The band has made many tours of Europe, working in France, Switzerland, Holland, Sweden and Finland. They have appeared regularly on television and radio, and made many recordings. Musicians who have played in the band include Tony Pipkin (trumpet/flugelhorn), Terry McGrath (sousaphone), Alan Oliver (banjo), John Read (piano), Brian Lawrence (bass), Terry Fyffe (cornet), Dick Chapman (clarinet), Chez Chesterman (trumpet), Ken Freeman (piano). Norman Field (reeds) again played with the band from 1976–9. The band has accompanied many visiting musicians, including Bill Allred, Humphrey Lyttelton, Wild Bill Davison, Chris Barber, etc.

ZENITH SIX

Began life as bassist Ray Leclerq's New Orleans Jazz Band in September 1952. Within months Leclerq left and the band adopted the name Zenith Six, they played regularly at Manchester Jazz Club sessions. Its original members were Malcolm Gracie (trombone), John Barnes (clarinet), Tony Charlesworth (trumpet), Ron Arnold (drums), Dick Lister (double bass) and Derek Gracie, cousin of Malcolm Gracie, on banjo. The band was a co-operative unit, without a leader. Joe Palin briefly played piano with them but left for Army service and was not replaced. The personnel remained constant until 1955, when John Barnes left to join Mike Daniels. By then the band had played in various other cities and appeared at London's Royal Festival Hall. John Barnes was replaced by Bob Wright, who was in turn replaced by Martin 'Mart' Rodger. Later, Malcolm Gracie was replaced by Alan Roadley on trombone. Tony Charlesworth's place was taken by Alan Dent. Bassist Dick Lister was replaced by Tom Gregory. Drummer Ron Arnold's place was taken first by Dave Berry then by Nick Holdcroft. In 1963 banjoist Derek Gracie left and was replaced by Dennis Tonge, who was in turn replaced by Bob Ascough. Personnel changes became frequent in the later years of the band's existence, players who passed through its ranks include trumpeters: Colin Lounsbach, Colin Tompkins, Dennis Gilmore, Pete Brown, Doug Whaley; clarinettist: Joe Silmon; trombonists: Alan Pendlebury, Keith Brunt, Cyril Preston; pianist: Keith Pendlebury; bassists: Norman Slater, Neville Matthews, Colin Knight, Derek Newton and Geoff Ford. Singer Marcia MacConnell (later Marcia Pendlebury) sang in a later version of the band.

Appendix: A Selected List of Bandleaders Mentioned in the Text

Abbreviations: *b* born
                d died

ADAM, Paul (Carl Tauber)	1914–78
AINSWORTH, Alyn	1924–90
ALLEN, Russ	1917–92
ALTMAN, John	*b*1949
AMBROSE, Ted	1927–82
ANTON, Toni	*b*1925
ARDLEY, Neil	*b*1937
ARTHEY, John (Pasadena Roof Orchestra)	*b*1942
BARCLAY, Bob (Yorkshire Jazz Band)	1911–87
BAKER, Howard	1901–85
BARKER, Stan	*b*1926
BARTON, Ken	*b*1929
BAXTER, 'Fats' Peter	*b*1941
BELL, Ian	*b*1931
BENT, Phillip	*b*1964
BERTINI (Bert Gutsell)	1890–1952
BIELLA, Maurice	*d*1995
BOLAND, Francy	*b*1929
BRENNAN, Dave	*b*1936
BRICKELL, Joe	*b*1927
BRUFORD, Bill	*b*1949
BURTON, 'Dizzy' Desmond	*b*1930
CARLESS, Ray	*b*1956
CASIMIR, Mike	*b*1936
CASTRONARI, Mario	*b*1954
CHACKSFIELD, Frank	1914–95
CLEWS, Dud	1937–64
COLLIER, Mike	*b*1929
COOPER, Lindsay	*b*1951
CORNFORD, 'Bob' Robert Leslie	1940–83
CORTEZ, Leon (Leon Chalklin)	1898–1970

367

COTTRELL, Gene	*b*1928
CROSBY, Gary	*b*1957
CROUCH, 'Dick' Richard (Paz)	*b*1937
CROWE, George	*d*1986
CURTIS, John	*b*1940
DAVIES, Cyril	1931–64
DEAN, Syd	1907–93
DENNIS, Maurice (Harry Strutters Hot Rhythm Orchestra)	*b*1941
DILLON, Barry	1932–92
DORSEY, Jack	*b*1929
DOWNES, 'Bob' Robert George	*b*1937
DYANI, 'Johnny' Mbizo	1945–86
ELLIS, Chris	*b*1928
EMBLOW, Jack	*b*1930
EVANS, Frank	*b*1936
EVARD, Jimmy (James Edwards)	*b*1917
FLANAGAN, Kevin	*b*1958
FISHER, Roy	*b*1930
FOX, Roy Clifton	1901–82
GAINES, Will	*b*1928
GIBBONS, Carroll	1902–54
GILL, Mick	*d*1987
GOFF, Reggie	1915–56
GRASSO, Oscar	1914–82
GRESTY, Alan (Muggsy Remembered)	*b*1940
GRIGSON, Lionel	1942–94
HALL, Adelaide	1901–93
HANCOCK, Dave	*b*1937
HATHAWAY, Martin	*b*1969
HIND, Bobby	1888–1950
HOLDSWORTH, Allan	*b*1946
HOWARD, Johnny	*b*1931
HUTCHINSON, 'Hutch' Leslie Arthur	1900–69
HYDER, Ken	*b*1946
JACKSON, Ellis Thompson	1891–1990
JOHNSON, 'Ginger' Falorunso	*b*1930

JOHNSON, Laurie	*b*1927
JONES, Tommy	*b*1926
KATZ, 'Dill' David	*b*1946
KEATING, Johnny	*b*1927
KERR, Pete	*b*1940
KING PLEASURE (Mark Anthony Skirving)	*b*1966
KINGWELL, Colin (Jazz Bandits)	*b*1931
KINORRA, Phil	*b*1940
LAURIE, Dick (Elastic Band)	*b*1935
LEAT, Allan	*b*1916
LEADER, Harry	1906–87
LEMER, Pete (Peter Naphtali)	*b*1942
LINDUP, David	*d*1992
LIPTON, Sydney	1905–95
LOGAN, Freddie	*b*1932
MACKEY, Percival	1894–50
MACKINTOSH, 'Spike' Ian	1918–96
McPARTLAND, Marian	*b*1920
MANTOVANI	1905–80
MAYALL, John	*b*1933
MENDELSSOHN, Felix	1911–52
MENZIE, Hamish	*b*1920
MENZIES, Ian (Clyde Valley Stompers)	*b*1932
MONEY, 'Zoot' George Bruno	*b*1942
MONK, 'Sonny' Ivan William	*b*1926
MSELEKU, Bheki	*b*1955
MUNNERY, Paul (Harlem)	*b*1942
MUNRO, Ronnie	1897–1989
NASH, Mike	*b*1938
NIEMAN, Paul	*b*1950
PAYNE, Jack	1899–1969
PETTERS, John	*b*1953
PHILLIPS, Van (Alexander Van Cleve)	1904–92
PHILLIPS, Woolf	*b*1918
PLEYDELL, Ronnie	1913–94
POTTS, Mickey	1935–93
POUGNET, Jean	1907–68
POWELL, Dick	1928–77

PREAGER, Lou	1906–78
PREMRU, Ray	b1934
PRÉVOST, Eddie	b1942
PRICE, Alan	b1942
PURCHESE, Donald	b1943
RALTON, Bert	d1927
RICHARDS, Tim (Spirit Level)	b1952
RIGDEN, Reg (Original Dixielanders)	d1992
RIGNOLD, Hugo	1905–76
ROBINSON, 'Spike' Henry Berthold	b1930
RODGER, Martin (Manchester Jazz)	b1936
ROWDEN, Johnny	1928–88
RUSSELL, Ron	b1935
SEYMOUR, Sid	1906–58
SHORT, Tony	1924–88
SILK, Eric	1926–82
SOMERS, Debroy	1890–1952
STAPLETON, Cyril	1913–74
STEWART, Ian	d1989
STEWART, Ian (Rocket 88)	1938–85
STROMAN, Scott	b1958
SUDHALTER, 'Dick' Richard Merrill	b1938
SWIFT, George	1911–85
SYKORA, Ken	b c.1922
TAYLOR, Mike	1938–69
TILBROOK, Adrian (Full Circle)	b1948
TOUSSAINT, Jean	b1960
VICARI, Andrea	b1965
WALTERS, Abe	d1993
WARREN, John	b1938
WATTS, Charlie	b1941
WILBER, 'Bob' Robert Sage	b1928
WILLIAMS, 'Dick' Richard	b1933
WILLIAMS, John	b1941
WINNICK, Maurice	1902–62
WOOD, Mark	b1954